prominent people of the time, legislative politics, relations between Congress and Executive, and administrative problems of anti-poverty programs generally. It also treats each major participant in the life of the agency as a total entity—with a past, a present unique perspective, and a future as well.

The FSA represented an historic attempt to preach hope to the poor of this country, and to exploit the promise, the power, and the possibilities of politics in securing salvation from the human suffering, social injustice, and economic waste of chronic poverty. In many ways, its rise and decline sheds some light on the strengths and weaknesses of the American people, of their political system, and of democracy itself. Its history is a case study in the political problems of governmental efforts to cope with in the problems of poverty; and though the focus is on rural poverty, there are many analogies to the problems of urban poverty today.

This is the only history of the Farm Security Administration that has been written. As an authoritative work on American agricultural history it will be of primary interest to historians, political scientists, and government administrators, but it will also appeal to general readers who lived during the Depression or who are interested in the history of the New Deal and its politics.

Sidney Baldwin is associate professor of political science at California State College in Fullerton.

POVERTY
AND
POLITICS

*THE UNIVERSITY
OF NORTH CAROLINA PRESS
CHAPEL HILL*

POVERTY
AND
POLITICS

THE RISE AND DECLINE
OF THE FARM SECURITY ADMINISTRATION

SIDNEY BALDWIN

COPYRIGHT © 1968 BY
THE UNIVERSITY OF NORTH CAROLINA PRESS
MANUFACTURED IN THE UNITED STATES OF AMERICA
LIBRARY OF CONGRESS CATALOG CARD NUMBER 68–18052
PRINTED BY HERITAGE PRINTERS, INC.

For
DIANA, SUSAN, and JANE,
and my MOTHER

PREFACE

On the eve of Franklin D. Roosevelt's New Deal, Erskine Caldwell introduced Jeeter Lester to the American people. Jeeter was a poor sharecropper, living with his wife and son in a shack on land that had once been part of his grandfather's rich plantation in the west-central area of Georgia. Taxes, delinquent debts, poor management, bondage to cotton culture, and soil erosion had, over the years, pared his inheritance to a portion of land that was too exhausted to produce a crop, and by World War I the remainder of the Lester land was lost through foreclosure.

Jeeter and his family were permitted to occupy one of the old shacks and to work a few acres of land on a share basis, but year after year they sank deeper into hopeless poverty. Family and friends urged the Lesters to leave the land and to seek work in a cotton mill in Augusta, but Jeeter stubbornly refused to abandon his faith in Providence:[1]

> God is a wise old somebody. You can't fool Him! He takes care of little details us humans never stop to think about. That's why I

---

1. Erskine Caldwell, "Tobacco Road," in *Three by Caldwell* (Boston, Mass.: Little, Brown, 1960), pp. 13, 29–30.

ain't leaving the land and going to Augusta to live in a durn cotton mill . . . . Some of these days He'll bust loose with a heap of bounty and all us poor folks will have all we want to eat and clothe us with . . . . He'll put a stop to it some of these days and make the rich give back all they've took from us poor folks.

Never did it occur to Jeeter Lester and his kind that their deliverance might lie not only in the hands of Providence, but also in the State and in themselves.

Later in the decade, after many Jeeter Lesters had languished on many Tobacco Roads, John Steinbeck chronicled the exodus of the Joad family from Oklahoma to the promised land of California. They were cheated by tradesmen along Highway 66, harassed by border guards at state boundaries, and on arrival were burned out of their makeshift camp by police deputies. One dark night the Joads wandered into Weedpatch Camp, a government refuge for migratory farm workers, where they found clean beds, indoor privies, food, friendship, and hope.

"Oh! Praise God," whispered Ma Joad.

"God Almighty, I can't hardly believe it!" pronounced Tom.

Their praises were addressed to Providence, but were intended for Washington. Here, they believed, for the first time in their lives, was hard visible proof that their government, whatever and wherever it was, really cared about them and the hundreds of thousands of people like them—landless, homeless, penniless victims of a fickle climate, an unstable economy, and a pernicious way of life. Between the Lesters of Georgia and the Joads of Oklahoma, a profound change of spirit had come upon the land.[2]

The great revolution of the twentieth century, not only in the United States but also in the emerging nations abroad, is the kindling of an extravagant hope that the human condition of man can and should be improved, through the harnessing of the power, resources, and machinery of government, not in some distant millennium, but during the lifetime of those now living. It is what Adlai Stevenson prophetically described as the "revolution of rising expectations."

The effective response of modern governments to this enormous challenge depends not only on the dreaming of dreams and the preaching of hope, but also on the capacity to convert the pictures in men's heads into the realities in their lives. "Goodness by itself is

2. John Steinbeck, *The Grapes of Wrath* (New York: Viking, 1939), pp. 390, 393.

not enough," wrote Aristotle, and therefore, "There must also be a capacity for being active in doing good."[3]

The Farm Security Administration in the America of the Roosevelt era represented an historic attempt to preach hope to the Lesters and Joads of this country, and to exploit the promise, the power, and the possibilities of politics in securing salvation from the human suffering, social injustice, and economic waste of chronic poverty. In many ways, the rise and decline of the Farm Security Administration sheds some light on the strengths and weaknesses of the American people, of their political system, and of democracy itself.

S.B.

Fullerton, Calif.
December, 1967

---

3. Aristotle, *Politics*, Ernest Barker, trans., *The Politics of Aristotle* (Oxford: Clarendon Press, 1946), p. 1325b.

ACKNOWLEDGMENTS

In large things and small, a great many people have contributed to this study. I owe a special debt of gratitude to the following: to Paul H. Appleby, Roscoe C. Martin, and Alexander Heard for igniting the spark; to Will W. Alexander, C. B. Baldwin, Robert W. Hudgens, and Paul V. Maris for furnishing both the grit and the grain; and to Stephen K. Bailey, Gladys L. Baker, Gordon W. Blackwell, Philip S. Brown, Frederic N. Cleaveland, O. B. Conoway, Charles S. Hyneman, Katharine Jocher, Howard W. Odum, E. E. Schattschneider, Frank Tannenbaum, and York Willbern for their faith and encouragement; and to Aaron Fineberg for providing the opportunity. And, for helping me to carry my burdens during the last stages of this work, I am grateful to my friend and colleague, Ivar L. Richardson.

Finally, without the cooperation of the people listed below, who granted the author interviews, as indicated, this study would have been impossible:

WILL W. ALEXANDER	Nov. 2, 23, 1951; Feb. 2, May 9, 1952.
ALLISON ALLEN	Mar. 27, 1952.
PAUL H. APPLEBY	Jan. 9, 10, Feb. 15, July 18, 1952.
C. B. BALDWIN	Dec. 28, 1951; Apr. 10, 16, 1963; Aug. 16, 1966.

JOHN A. BAKER	Dec. 5, 1951.
LOUIS H. BEAN	Apr. 18, 1952.
EARL F. BELL	Jan. 11, 1952.
HOWARD BERTSCH	Dec. 7, 1951.
PHILIP S. BROWN	Dec. 4, 1951; July 15, 1952; Nov. 22, 1966.
JOHN FISCHER	Nov. 16, 1961.
JONATHAN GARST	Jan. 21, 1952.
JOHN M. GAUS	Apr. 15, 1952.
CHARLES M. HARDIN	Apr. 2, 1955.
BROOKS HAYS	Dec. 13, 1951.
RALPH W. HOLLENBERG	Dec. 5, 1951.
ROBERT W. HUDGENS	Jan. 16, 1952; Mar. 7, 1963; Apr. 19, 1961.
GARDNER JACKSON	Apr. 19, 1952.
MARVIN JONES	Dec. 6, 1951; Apr. 2, 1952.
HERMAN KAHN	Mar. 11, 1952.
DILLARD B. LASSETER	Dec. 4, 1951.
JAMES G. MADDOX	Jan. 16, 17, 1952.
PAUL V. MARIS	Dec. 6, 1951; Jan. 22, Feb. 8, 9, July 17, 1952.
ROBERT E. MARTIN	Apr. 19, 1952.
HELEN HILL MILLER	Dec. 4, 1951.
DILLON S. MYER	May 31, 1960.
REV. JOHN O'GRADY	Dec. 5, 1951.
HOWARD W. ODUM	Feb. 4, 1952.
JAMES G. PATTON	Feb. 11, 1952.
ARTHUR F. RAPER	Apr. 21, 1952.
T. ROY REID	Jan. 21, 1952.
ELEANOR ROOSEVELT	Sept. 24, 1952.
RAYMOND C. SMITH	Dec. 7, 1951.
RAUB SNYDER	Jan. 11, 1961.
BENTON STONG	Feb. 11, Mar. 18, 1952.
FRANK TANNENBAUM	Dec. 18, 1951.
CARL S. TAYLOR	Dec. 7, 1951.
REXFORD G. TUGWELL	July 6, 1967.
RUPERT B. VANCE	June 6, 1952.
PAUL W. WAGER	Nov. 30, 1951.
HENRY A. WALLACE	Jan. 8, 1952.
E. B. WHITTAKER	Dec. 4, 1951.
WALTER WILCOX	Dec. 5, 1951.
M. L. WILSON	Dec. 11, 1961.

ABBREVIATIONS

In order to reduce the number of notes, I have in many cases followed the practice of collecting references that are pertinent to a particular passage in a single note at the end of the appropriate paragraph. Sources cited for the first time are presented in complete form; subsequent citations are simplified, except for the following sources, which are cited in abbreviated form throughout:

FSA, *Annual Report of the Administrator* (Washington, D.C.: GPO), cited as FSA, *Annual Report*, with the appropriate year covered by the issue in parentheses.

Olaf F. Larson, ed., *Ten Years of Rural Rehabilitation in the United States* (Washington, D.C.: BAE, 1937), Processed, cited as Larson, *Ten Years*.

James G. Maddox, "The Farm Security Administration" (doctoral dissertation, Harvard University, 1950), cited as Maddox, "The FSA."

Franklin D. Roosevelt, *Public Papers and Addresses*, Samuel I. Rosenman, comp. (New York: 1938–50), cited as F.D.R., *Public Papers*, followed by the volume number and with the year covered by the volume in parentheses.

U.S., Bureau of the Budget, *The Budget of the United States Government* (Washington, D.C.: GPO), cited as *U.S. Budget*, followed by the fiscal year covered by the volume in parentheses.

U.S., Congress, Joint Committee on Reduction of Nonessential Federal Expenditures, Hearings, 77th Cong., 1st and 2d Sessions, *Reduction of Nonessential Federal Expenditures* (Washington, D.C.: GPO, 1942), cited as *Byrd Committee Hearings*.

U.S., Congress, House, Select Committee to Investigate National Defense Migration, Hearings, 77th Cong., 2d Sess., *National Defense Migration* (Washington, D.C.: GPO, 1942), cited as *Tolan Committee Hearings*.

U.S., Congress, House, Select Committee of the House Committee on Agriculture to Investigate the Activities of the Farm Security Administration, Hearings, 78th Cong., 1st Sess., *Farm Security Administration* (Washington, D.C.: GPO, 1944), cited as *Cooley Committee Hearings*.

U.S., Congress, House, Appropriations Committee, Hearings, *Department of Agriculture Appropriation Bill* (Washington, D.C.: GPO), cited as *House Hearings*, Agr. Approp., with fiscal year indicated in parentheses, followed by the appropriate number of the Congress and Session.

U.S., Congress, Senate, Appropriations Committee, Hearings, *Department of Agriculture Appropriation Bill* (Washington, D.C.: GPO), cited as *Senate Hearings*, Agr. Approp., with fiscal year indicated in parentheses, followed by the appropriate number of the Congress and Session.

U.S., Congress, House, Appropriations Committee, Hearings, 78th Cong., 1st Sess., *Appropriation for the Farm Labor Program, 1943* (Washington, D.C.: GPO, 1943), cited as *House Hearings*, Farm Labor Program.

Following are the manuscript collections cited in the notes, which are abbreviated throughout as indicated:

John A. Baker Papers, in author's possession, cited as JABP.

C. B. Baldwin Papers, in possession of C. B. Baldwin, Greenwich, Conn., cited as CBBP.

Columbia Oral History Collection, Columbia University, cited as COHC. Transcripts of interviews with M. L. Wilson and Robert W. Hudgens made available to author through special permission.

Abbreviations / [xv]

O. B. Conaway Papers, in author's possession, cited as OBCP.
FHA Files, in possession of FHA, USDA, Washington, D.C., cited as FHAF.
Paul V. Maris Papers, in possession of Paul V. Maris, Hemet, California, cited as PVMP.
Frank Tannenbaum Papers, in possession of Columbia University, cited as FTP.
MSS in National Archives, Washington, D.C., cited as NA, followed by RG and number, designating the appropriate record group.
MSS in the Franklin D. Roosevelt Library, Hyde Park, N.Y., cited as FDRL, followed by the appropriate file designation—Official File (OF), President's Personal File (PPF), and President's Secretary's File (PSF).
MSS in USDA, Historical Research Section, Economic Research Service, Washington, D.C., cited as USDAHF.

To all those above who granted me permission to use their personal papers and manuscript collections, I offer my sincere thanks, for without their cooperation, this study would have been impossible.

In addition to the abbreviations noted above, the following have also been used in both the text and the notes:

AAA	Agricultural Adjustment Administration
AFBF	American Farm Bureau Federation
AFL	American Federation of Labor
BAE	Bureau of Agricultural Economics
CCC	Commodity Credit Corporation
CED	Committee for Economic Development
CIO	Congress of Industrial Organizations
FCA	Farm Credit Administration
FDA	Food Distribution Administration
FERA	Federal Emergency Relief Administration
FHA	Farmers Home Administration
FPA	Food Production Administration
FSA	Farm Security Administration
GPO	U.S. Government Printing Office
NAACP	National Association for the Advancement of Colored People
NFU	National Farmers Union
RA	Resettlement Administration
REA	Rural Electrification Administration
RFC	Reconstruction Finance Corporation

SCS   Soil Conservation Service
STFU Southern Tenant Farmers Union
TVA   Tennessee Valley Authority
USDA U.S. Department of Agriculture
WFA   War Food Administration
WPA   Works Progress Administration (until 1939) and thereafter the Work Projects Administration

CONTENTS

PREFACE		vii
ACKNOWLEDGMENTS		xi
ABBREVIATIONS		xiii
I.	THE PAST IS PROLOGUE	3
II.	THE REVELATION: POVERTY ON THE FARM	18
III.	THE RESPONSE: RELIEF, REHABILITATION, AND REFORM	47
IV.	CREATIVE CRISIS: THE RESETTLEMENT ADMINISTRATION	85
V.	TOWARD LEGITIMACY: THE DANCE OF LEGISLATION BEGINS	126
VI.	TOWARD LEGITIMACY: THE BANKHEAD-JONES FARM TENANT ACT	157
VII.	THE FSA IN ACTION: PROGRAMS AND PERFORMANCE	193
VIII.	INSTRUMENTS OF ACHIEVEMENT: POLITICS AND ADMINISTRATION	231
IX.	THE FSA: DISTURBER OF THE PEACE	262
X.	THE QUEST FOR EQUILIBRIUM	295
XI.	THE FSA GOES TO WAR	325
XII.	ARMAGEDDON AND AFTERMATH	365
XIII.	RETROSPECT AND PROSPECT	405
INDEX		421

POVERTY
AND
POLITICS

CHAPTER I

THE PAST IS PROLOGUE

*Each age is a dream that is dying
Or one that is coming to birth.*
                                ARTHUR O'SHAUGHNESSY[1]
                                "Ode"

In the spring of 1935, President Franklin D. Roosevelt signed an executive order which gathered together several administrative bits and pieces and consolidated them as a new federal agency to be known as the Resettlement Administration and dedicated to a campaign against chronic rural poverty in the United States. Twenty months later, he approved the transfer of the Resettlement Administration to the U.S. Department of Agriculture. During the summer of 1937, Congress passed and the President signed the Bankhead-Jones Farm Tenant Act, and in September, the Resettlement Administration was transformed into the Farm Security Administration. Finally, in 1946, President Harry S. Truman signed the Farmers Home Administration Act which abolished the Farm Security Administration and created in its place a new agency called the Farmers Home Administration. Behind this cold chronology lies a significant chapter in institutional evolution. This study is a slice of that experience.

1. Arthur W. E. O'Shaughnessy, "Ode," in Robert Gay, comp., *The Riverside Book of Verse* (New York: Houghton Mifflin, 1927), p. 517.

The Farm Security Administration was many things to many people. To some of its foes, it was a dangerous, radical, and un-American experiment in governmental intervention, paternalism, socialism, or communism; a sop by a reluctant and middle-of-the-road President to political thunder on the left; a plaything created for the diversion of utopian dreamers; an organized conspiracy to undermine the *status quo* in rural America; or an anachronistic effort to turn the clock of agricultural progress backward to the age of the mule and the hand plow. To friends of the Farm Security Administration, on the other hand, it was an heroic institution designed to secure social justice and political power for a neglected class of Americans; a pioneering effort to strike at the causes of chronic rural poverty; a unique and largely successful experiment in creative government; an agency embodying the social conscience of the New Deal; or a model effort in agrarian reform which was destined to serve as a seedbed for future wars on poverty in the United States and in some of the emerging nations of the world.

To humanists, the Farm Security Administration was a courageous effort to fulfill the aspirations for improvement of the human condition, through the harnessing of the power of optimism, knowledge, and man's capacity to direct and control his own evolution. And to militant champions of racial equality, it was little more than a step in the right direction, a disappointing and faint-hearted effort to right ancient wrongs.

To scholars who view politics and government in traditional terms, the Farm Security Administration was simply an instrumentality for the purpose of carrying out the will of Congress and of the President, and its significance lay in formal statutes and administrative rules and regulations. To students of society who see politics and government through a behavioral glass, the Farm Security Administration was a "consciously coordinated system of personal actions, behaviors, and interrelated roles," dedicated officially to achievement of pre-defined public purposes, but compelled to cope with the forces of human ambition, emotion, irrationality, and personality.

The purpose of this study is not to evaluate such judgments, but rather to examine the rise and decline of the agency, in order to understand more clearly the interplay of forces—social, political, economic, ideological, and material—which condition and control the efforts of men and governments to cope with human predicaments. Today the U.S. Office of Economic Opportunity, the Peace Corps, the U.S. Office of Education, the Agency for International Development, and the Farmers Home Administration are some of the agencies of government that are indebted to the experience of the Farm Security Administration and are themselves struggling with similar forces of institutional consolidation and disintegration.

Although this study of the Farm Security Administration is essentially a case history, and consequently suffers from the theoretical limitations of both history and case studies, it is intended neither as history for history's sake, nor simply as an anecdotal increment to the already abundant case study literature. By-passing the ancient quarrels about the utilities and inutilities of history, and the younger debate over the contributions that case studies might make to the building of a political science, it is presumed here that some fruitful insights about institutional evolution can be derived from the experience of this agency over a considerable period of time, unique though that experience may have been.[2]

The experience of the Farm Security Administration offers an opportunity to apply both micro- and macro-institutional analysis. The agency, for instance, was part of a larger institutional world, including the U.S. Department of Agriculture, the executive branch of government, the Roosevelt administration, and a complex network of federal, state, and local institutions of government. At the same time, the Farm Security Administration had an internal institutional life of its own, in which were generated contending forces of change

---

2. For discussion of the uses of historical analysis in the study of politics and public administration, see the following: John M. Gaus and Leon O. Wolcott, *Public Administration and the United States Department of Agriculture* (Chicago: Public Administration Service, 1940), p. 394; Herman Finer, *Theory and Practice of Modern Government* (New York: Holt, 1949), pp. 947–51; Harvey C. Mansfield, "The Uses of History," *Public Administration Review*, Vol. XI (Winter, 1951), pp. 51–57; David Easton, *The Political System* (New York: Knopf, 1953), pp. 42–43; Dwight Waldo, *Perspectives on Administration* (University, Ala.: Univ. of Alabama Press, 1956), Chap. III; C. V. Wedgwood, *Truth and Opinion* (London: Collins, 1960), pp. 35–49, 70–80.

For discussion of the case study approach, see the following: Edwin A. Bock, ed., *Essays on the Case Method in Public Administration* (Syracuse, N.Y.: Inter-University Case Program, 1962); Robert T. Golembiewski, *Behavior and Organization: O&M and the Small Group* (Chicago: Rand, McNally, 1962), pp. 79–85; Herbert Kaufman, "The Next Step in Case Studies," *Public Administration Review*, Vol. XVIII (Winter, 1958), pp. 52–59; Richard McCleery, "Prison Government and Communists; The Use of Case Studies," *Political Research: Organization and Design*, Vol. 1 (Mar., 1958), pp. 21–24; Frederick C. Mosher, "Research in Public Administration: Some Notes and Suggestions," *Public Administration Review*, Vol. XVI (Summer, 1956), p. 171; Harold Stein, "Preparation of Case Studies: The Problem of Abundance," *American Political Science Review*, Vol. LI (June, 1951), 479–87.

[6] / POVERTY and POLITICS

and conservation, consolidation and disintegration, contributing both to its rise and decline.

Efforts have been made in this study, therefore, to apply both the telescope and the microscope. The former, however has been found more readily applicable than the latter. First, the subject dealt with here is not a contemporary and on-going situation in which it might be possible to prepare specimens of living tissue—to supplement the historical record with first-hand observation, with measurement and quantification, with the capture and recording of live data, or with the advantages of what Theodore Reik has called "listening with the third ear." Rather, the focus is on situations and events that have already retreated into the past, precluding the kind of intimate situational familiarity and sensitivity on which micro-institutional analysis depends more greatly. Second, it is easier to read the preserved tracks of bureaucratic institutions than the private minds and hearts of bureaucrats. As far as the data have permitted, however, attempts have been made to focus on the two worlds of the Farm Security Administration.

Although there has been considerable micro-institutional analysis of Congress, the Presidency, the Supreme Court, state legislatures, political parties, and interest groups, there is comparatively little literature on the departments, agencies, bureaus and other administrative institutions that play a vital role in the public policy process.[3]

3. Many studies, with special attention devoted to individual federal departments, agencies, bureaus, and offices, have appeared, but with their focus on the more formal structures, processes, and relationships. Overly committed to the historical approach and to *macro*-analysis, they do not penetrate very deeply into the institutional skin. The following are illustrative: Gaus and Wolcott, *Public Administration and the USDA*; Arthur W. Macmahon, John D. Millett, and Gladys Ogden, *Administration of Federal Work Relief* (Chicago: Public Administration Service, 1941); Victor A. Thompson, *The Regulatory Process in OPA Rationing* (New York: King's Crown Press, 1950); Paul P. Van Riper, *History of the United States Civil Service* (Evanston, Ill., and White Plains, N.Y.: Row, Peterson, 1958).

For some exceptions to the neglect of micro-institutional analysis, see the following: Peter M. Blau, *The Dynamics of Bureaucracy*, rev. ed. (Chicago: Univ. of Chicago Press, 1955); Charles M. Hardin, "The Bureau of Agricultural Economics Under Fire: A Study in Valuation Conflicts," *Journal of Farm Economics*, Vol. 28 (Aug., 1946), pp. 635–68; Herbert Kaufman, *The Forest Ranger* (Baltimore: Johns Hopkins Press, 1960); Arthur A. Maass, *Muddy Waters* (Cambridge, Mass.: Harvard Univ. Press, 1951); Philip Selznick, *TVA and the Grass Roots* (Berkeley and Los Angeles: Univ. of Calif. Press, 1949); Harold Stein, ed., *American Civil-Military Decisions: A Book of Cast Studies* (New York: Twentieth Century Fund, 1963).

Two useful attempts to apply micro-analytical methods to small-scale individual government resettlement projects are the following: Alexander H. Leigh-

It would be a narrative of many pages to adequately explain this neglect, but the clues would probably include scholarly bias against public administration as a focus of research attention and as a source of fruitful insight into politics and government, confusion about the relationships between politics and administration, unfounded fears that micro-institutional analysis inevitably leads to sterile miniaturization of issues and to neglect of public policy impacts, and problems of secrecy and security which discourage research access to the internal lives of administrative agencies of government. Meanwhile, sociologists, social psychologists, small-group analysts, and other "behavioralists" have begun to rush in where students of politics and government have feared to tread.[4]

There are additional theoretical implications in institutional analysis that should be made explicit. First, despite contemporary excitement about such concepts and methods as system-building, decision-making, small-group analysis, quantification, and model-construction, it is presumed here that there is nothing antithetical between the so-called "institutional" and "behavioral" approaches. The study of human behavior in politics and government without reference to the institutional context is no more meaningful than the study of vacant institutional shells without reference to the behavior of human incumbents.[5]

Second, "institutional analysis" implies not only the traditional concern with general description of formal powers and relationships between legally constituted establishments of government—

---

ton, *The Governing of Men* (Princeton, N.J.: Princeton Univ. Press, 1946); and Edward C. Banfield, *Government Project* (Glencoe, Ill.: The Free Press, 1951).

The neglect of micro-institutional analysis of administrative institutions of government is reflected in the virtual absence of such studies among the doctoral dissertations in political science, as listed in recent compilations by the *American Political Science Review*.

4. See the following: John C. Honey, "Research in Public Administration: A Further Note," *Public Administration Review*, Vol. XVII (Autumn, 1957), pp. 238–43; Martin Landau, "The Concept of Decision-Making in the 'Field' of Public Administration," in Sidney Mailick and Edward H. Van Ness, eds., *Concepts and Issues in Administrative Behavior* (Englewood Cliffs, N.J.: Prentice-Hall, 1962), pp. 1–28; Mosher, "Research in Public Administration," pp. 169–78.

5. For discussion of the relationships between the "behavioral" and "institutional" approaches to the study of politics and public administration, see the following: David B. Truman, "The Impact on Political Science of the Revolution in the Behavioral Science," in Stephen K. Bailey, ed., *Research Frontiers in Politics and Government* (Washington, D.C.: The Brookings Institution, 1955), pp. 202–31; John C. Wahlke et al., *The Legislative System* (New York: Wiley, 1962), pp. 3–7.

parliaments, congresses, crowns, presidents, ministries, agencies, and parties—but also such "institutional" characteristics as large organizational size, complex structure, systems of norms, formalized procedures, regularity of expectations, and durability over time. Institutional analysis, therefore, emphasizes the adaptive responses of people in organizations to the internal and external environments, or, in the words of Philip Selznick, the "problems and experiences that are not adequately accounted for within the narrower framework of administrative analysis." For instance, to the extent that we examine the Farm Security Administration in terms of its internal behavioral norms, the ideology with which it justified itself, the pattern of its evolution over time, its adaptive responses to the environment, and its viability as an administrative and political system, we are treating it as an "institution" rather than simply as an "organization."[6]

There is an additional task of definition—clarification of the use of the term "agency." As employed in this study, the term is meant to suggest an administrative organization or institution of government, formally defined by statute or executive action, staffed by public employees, assigned regular governmental tasks, and responsible for serving or regulating a particular clientele. Accordingly, the Farm Security Administration, Soil Conservation Service, Bureau of Agricultural Economics, and Extension Service were "agencies." The term is used generically as a synonym rather than as a special construct implying particular theoretical significance.

One of the major shortcomings in contemporary analysis has been the neglect of the temporal dimension. Despite many years of exhortation, surprisingly little literature in this dimension has been produced. In 1940, John M. Gaus and Leon O. Wolcott, in their ground-breaking study of the U.S. Department of Agriculture, called for greater use of the calendar as well as the clock, in order to capture the changes which only time can tell. Half a generation later, David Easton was moved to declare as follows:

---

6. Philip Selznick, *Leadership in Administration: A Sociological Interpretation* (Evanston, Ill., and White Plains, N.Y.: Row, Peterson, 1957), p. 6. See also the following: Quentin Gibson, *The Logic of Social Inquiry* (London: Routledge and Kegan Paul, 1960), pp. 102–5; Richard T. LaPiere, *A Theory of Social Control* (New York: McGraw-Hill, 1954), pp. 110, 300–1; Wilbert E. Moore, "The Social Framework of Economic Development," in Ralph Braibanti and Joseph J. Spengler, eds., *Tradition, Values, and Socio-Economic Development* (Durham, N.C.: Duke Univ. Press, 1961), p. 63; Selznick, *Leadership in Administration*, pp. 5–22, Chaps. 4, 5.

... in spite of the acceptance as axiomatic, of Heraclitus' well-known propositions about change, over the last seventy-five years political research has confined itself largely to the study of given conditions to the neglect of political change.

If we are to learn from the past—and this we must do—and if the eddy is not to be confused with the tide, then there should be practical and theoretical virtue in a temporal analysis of the rise and decline of a single administrative agency of government.[7]

With the rediscovery of the temporal dimension has come a remarriage of politics and administration. As long as the dichotomous thinking of such students of administration as Frank J. Goodnow and W. F. Willoughby prevailed, the study of public administration was dominated by the spirit of the immaculate conception. The spirit was reinforced by the influence of the scientific management movement, with its devotion to the business model, meticulous attention to the details of work processes, time and motion studies, preoccupation with the organization of authority and supervision, and reverence for science. In 1936, Pendleton Herring launched a major broadside against the neglect of the political content in public administration, and the following year, at the high noon of that orthodox faith, Luther Gulick appended an afterthought to the gospel, suggesting that the dichotomy was not a divorce but a distinction:[8]

The struggle for survival in government thus becomes not so much a fight to the death, a test of destruction, but an endless process of adaptation to changed conditions and ideas . . . . The process of adaptation falls partly in the field of politics and partly in the field of administration.

These trends have led to a rising interest in the linkage of administrative means and political ends—a shift from the separatism of Goodnow and Willoughby, and from the scientific management of Frederick W. Taylor toward the *Realpolitik* of Bismarck and the statecraft of Machiavelli. One of the manifestations of this shift is the growing literature about the conditions, problems, and tasks of institutional survival. Whether conceived in such terms as equilibrium, viability, natural history, life cycle, or adaptive adjustment, and whether insights have been derived from economics, thermodynamics, mechanics, or the biological and psychological sciences,

---

7. Gaus and Wolcott, *Public Administration and the USDA*; Easton, *The Political System*.

8. Pendleton Herring, *Public Administration and the Public Interest* (New York: McGraw-Hill, 1936); Luther Gulick, "Notes on the Theory of Organization," in Luther Gulick and L. Urwick, eds., *Papers on the Science of Administration* (New York: Institute of Public Administration, 1937), p. 44.

there is now a wider realization that public administration takes place on a precarious and shifting ground between the forces of institutional consolidation and disintegration.[9]

In searching for meaningful categories to explain and relate the changes that occur in administrative institutions over time, the natural history approach, with its provocative idea of institutional life cycle, has been applied in recent literature. A seminal textbook, for instance, has distinguished between "pre-natal" and "post-natal" stages in the evolution of governmental agencies. Similarly, other students of institutional life, going beyond the familiar rubrics of public administration to the new language of institutional analysis, have discussed the cyclical pattern of evolution in such terms as growth, balance, equilibrium, decline and decay, and rejuvenation.

Marver H. Bernstein's study of the American independent regulatory commissions, for instance, has suggested that a cyclical pattern of evolution exists, "a rhythm of regulation whose repetition suggests that there is a natural life cycle for an independent commission." Gestation, youth, devitalization, debility and decline—these, according to Bernstein, are the stages of institutional evolution. Marshall E. Dimock has identified four parallel stages in the life cycles of agencies of government, and has concluded that "the same fatigue curve that operates in the individual operates also in institutions and in nations." In institutions, like in all physical organisms, Dimock suggests, there

---

9. For illustrative literature which is based, explicitly or implicitly, on the concepts of equilibrium, institutional viability and survival, and strategic thinking, see the following: Chester I. Barnard, *The Functions of the Executive* (Cambridge: Harvard Univ. Press, 1948), pp. 60–61, 82–83, 251–52, 286, 289; Marver H. Bernstein, *Regulating Business by Independent Commission* (Princeton, N.J.: Princeton Univ. Press, 1955), Chap. 3; Blau, *The Dynamics of Bureaucracy*, and *Bureaucracy in Modern Society* (New York: Random House, 1956), pp. 61–66; Marshall E. Dimock, *Administrative Vitality* (New York: Harper, 1959), Chap. 4; Easton, *The Political System*, pp. 266–306, and "Limits of the Equilibrium Model in Social Research," in Heinz Eulau, Samuel J. Eldersveld, and Morris Janowitz, eds., *Political Behavior* (Glencoe, Ill.: The Free Press, 1956), pp. 397–404, and his book, *A Systems Analysis of Political Life* (New York: Wiley, 1965), pp. 19–21, 271; Norton E. Long, "Power and Administration," *Public Administration Review*, Vol. IX (Autumn, 1949), pp. 257–64; Barrington Moore, Jr., "Sociological Theory and Contemporary Politics," *The American Journal of Sociology*, Vol. LXI (Sept., 1955), pp. 107–15; Charles McKinley, "Federal Administrative Pathology and the Separation of Powers," *Public Administration Review*, Vol. XI (Winter, 1951), pp. 17–25; James G. March and Herbert A. Simon, *Organizations* (New York: Wiley, 1958), pp. 109–10; Herbert A. Simon, Donald W. Smithburg, and Victor A. Thompson, *Public Administration* (New York: Knopf, 1954), Chaps. 18, 19.

is an "aging process," in which the forces of "decay" continually undermine institutional foundations.[10]

Such applications of the organic analogy to institutional evolution very fruitfully consider time and change, the interpenetration of politics and administration, and institutional continuity, but if theories based on this approach are to be researchable and testable, the ambiguities in these concepts must be clarified, for as Abraham Kaplan has felicitously written:[11]

> What makes a concept significant is that the classification it institutes is one into which things fall, as it were, of themselves. It carves at the joints, Plato said.... Concepts, then, mark out the paths by which we may move most freely in logical space. They identify nodes or junctions in the network of relationships, termini at which we can halt while preserving the maximum range of choice as to where to go next. If all roads lead to Rome, then, by the same token, once in Rome we can go anywhere.

Is there in fact a "life cycle" in administrative institutions that endure over time? Is the passage from birth to decay inevitable? Precisely what are the forces that make the difference whether an institution will be rejuvenated and thus complete the cycle? Are internal tensions and external pressures necessarily detrimental to the viability of an institution? Precisely what is "institutional survival" and is it necessarily the overriding objective of rational executives? One of the fruits of this study, it is hoped, will be some light on such questions?

Implicit in this cyclical approach is the notion of equilibrium, which has permeated most of the natural and social sciences. At the risk of over-simplification—any brief discussion of the equilibrium model is probably doomed to this offense—at least it is agreed that the advantages of the idea of equilibrium include its encouragement to focus on time and change, on the functional interdependence of variables, on the coherence of the political process, on the reciprocal effects of the exercise of power, and on the conditions of an "ideal type" of situation toward which institutions may ebb and flow. In

---

10. Simon, Smithburg, Thompson, *Public Administration*, Chap. 2; Bernstein, *Regulating Business*; Dimock, *A Philosophy of Administration* (New York: Harper, 1958), pp. 19–20, and *Administrative Vitality*, pp. 32–58; R. G. Fuller and R. R. Myers, "The Natural History of Social Problems," *American Sociological Review*, Vol. 6 (June, 1940), pp. 320–29; Bertram M. Gross, *The Managing of Organizations*, Vol. II (New York: The Free Press, 1964), Chap. 25.

11. Abraham Kaplan, *The Conduct of Inquiry* (San Francisco: Chandler, 1964), pp. 50, 52.

other words, the idea of equilibrium fruitfully discourages dependence on single-track explanations of institutional evolution, such as economic determinism, the great man theory of history, organizational will to live, and the mechanistic analogy of pressure and counter-pressure.

For instance, the so-called "death" of the Farm Security Administration has often been explained in terms of simple causation, with primary importance ascribed to one of the following: (1) the alleged long-range decline in agrarian democracy; (2) the dissolution of the New Deal and the swing of the country toward the center or the right; (3) the shift from economic depression to prosperity and from peace to war; (4) Franklin Roosevelt's wartime preoccupation; (5) the ideological stubbornness of the leaders of the agency; (6) the lack of "countervailing power" among the agency's clientele; (7) the refusal of the agency's leaders to play the game of "coöptation," or (8) the declaration of war by the American Farm Bureau Federation. Despite the serious theoretical limitations and implications involved in the concept of equilibrium, it does offer an escape from determinism.

David Easton, in his fruitful discussion of the obstacles to proper application of the notion of institutional equilibrium, has suggested that the goal of institutional survival may be considerably more complex than has been presumed by some scholars:[12]

> It is clear that the adoption of equilibrium analysis, however latent it may be, obscures the presence of system goals that cannot be described as a state of equilibrium. It also virtually conceals the existence of varying pathways for attaining these alternative ends. For any social system, including the political, adaptation represents more than simple adjustments to the events in its life.

---

12. Easton, *A Systems Analysis of Political Life*, p. 21. See also his "Limits of the Equilibrium Model in Social Research."

Easton has suggested the following as serious obstacles in the application of the equilibrium model: (1) the difficulty or impossibility, under prevailing conditions in contemporary social and political analysis, of clearly identifying the internal variables and external parameters of institutional change; (2) a necessarily heavy dependence on adequate measurement and quantification, which presumably lie in the future; (3) the fallacious assumption, implicit in many applications of the model, that "the members of a system are seized with only one basic goal as they seek to cope with change or disturbance, namely, to reestablish the old point of equilibrium or, at most, to move on to some new one;" and (4) a system may have goals other than maintaining a close proximity to a condition of equilibrium.

For instance, evidence suggests that there was a Wagnerian strain in the institutional character of the Farm Security Administration, a tendency to ignore or defy what Dimock has called the "rules of survival." Some of the leaders of the agency justified their "suicidal" behavior in terms of ideological integrity, while others viewed this performance as self-immolation.

This interest in the strategy of survival has been reflected in the growth of concern about institutional goal formulation and the nature of and limitations upon rational administrative action. Two decades ago, Dwight Waldo introduced into the literature of public administration the concept of a "hierarchy of purposes" to distinguish among the different kinds of goals pursued by people in organizational situations, and he found a linkage of such a hierarchy to what he called a "pyramid of values," on the basis of which administrative performance might be more objectively judged.[13]

Similarly, in 1953, Robert A. Dahl and Charles E. Lindblom emphasized the multiplicity of goals in organizations, and distinguished between "prime" goals and "instrumental" goals. The organizational task, they suggested, is not merely "goal achievement," but rather "maximization of *net* goal achievement," and they cited the "bitter frustrations" resulting from the limitations that time and other constraints impose on organizational purpose—an administrator cannot and should not attempt to do everything at once.[14]

For our purposes, some insight can be derived from Peter M. Blau's application of Robert K. Merton's concept of "displacement of goals," through which "an instrumental value becomes a terminal value." Orientations toward legalistic, clerical, and other technical values in an organization may lead to a displacement of organizational objectives through what Wallace S. Sayre has called the "triumph of technique over purpose." Blau found, for instance, that in one public agency under his microscope, the initiation of a system of statistical records led to the subversion of organizational purposes by constraining interviewers to avoid activities that would consume their time without helping to improve their records. As we shall see in this study, emphasis on statistical record-keeping, as an instrument of achievement, and anxiety about "making a good showing" tended

---

13. Dwight Waldo, *The Administrative State* (New York: Ronald Press, 1948), pp. 204–5.
14. Robert A. Dahl and Charles E. Lindblom, *Politics, Economics, and Welfare* (New York: Harper, 1953), pp. 26–27.

to displace and subvert the purposes for which the organization was presumably created.[15]

The reverse process, called "succession of goals," has been explained by Blau as follows: "The attainment of organizational objectives generates a strain toward finding new objectives. To provide incentives for its members and to justify its existence, an organization has to adopt new goals as its old ones are realized." The requirements of institutional survival, Blau suggests, may encourage either of these two processes:[16]

An interest in maintaining the organization promotes the *displacement of goals* if the original mission evokes hostility that endangers the organization's existence, but it promotes the *succession of goals* if the original mission has been effectively accomplished, since this too would otherwise endanger the organization's continued existence [italics not in the original].

In a monumental two-volume effort to achieve an "action-theory marriage," Bertram M. Gross has seen a "striking paradox" wherein, "Administrators spend considerable time in trying to achieve, clarify, change, or formulate purposes" for their organizations. Questions addressed to these administrators regarding their organizations' purposes, however, tend to embarrass and discomfit them, and they usually seek escape in glib evasions and glittering generalities. Coining the word "teletics" (from *telos*, the Greek word for "purpose") as a label for his endeavors, Gross has gone on to explore the "principles of teletic inquiry," involving the following complex set of variables: "the time sequence concept of purposeful action, the multiplicity of organizational purpose, the patterns that bring order out of this multiplicity, and the balance between clarity and vagueness in purpose formulation." Accepting the validity of the prevailing principle in modern administrative theory, "that the unifying purposes of an organization are constantly changing in response to new situations," he has emphasized that there is order in disorder: "it is the pattern that provides the unity."[17]

Distinguishing between "action hierarchies" of purpose which reflect the "exigencies of a specific organization in a specific situation," and "analytical hierarchies" of purpose which express "certain stable and all-pervasive relations," Gross has offered the following proposition to explain the equation of organizational input-output:[18]

15. Blau, *The Dynamics of Bureaucracy*, pp. 46, 232–33, 239–41, 247–49, 294; and *Bureaucracy in Modern Society*, pp. 93–96.
16. Blau, *The Dynamics of Bureaucracy*, pp 243–45, 247–49, 262, 264.
17. Gross, *The Managing of Organizations*, Vol. I, p. 244; Vol. II, pp. 467–501.
18. *Ibid.*, Vol. II, p. 480.

The Past is Prologue / [15]

Organizations aim at (1) satisfying human interests, of both members and nonmembers, by (2) producing services or goods with (3) an efficient use of scarce inputs, by (4) investing in their own viability, (5) mobilizing the resources needed as inputs, and doing all these things (6) in conformance with certain codes of behavior, and (7) in a rational manner.

Behind this manipulation of ends and means, which has captured the attention of Gross and other students of politics and administration, lies an enormously complex issue—the nature of rational action and its role in public administration. During the heyday of the scientific management movement, the rationality of an administrative act was measured primarily in technical terms, but with the social science explosion and the rediscovery of man in management following World War II, the earlier simplicities proved inadequate. "To administer a social organization according to purely technical criteria of rationality is irrational," wrote Blau in 1956, "because it ignores the nonrational aspects of social conduct."[19]

A decade earlier, Herbert A. Simon persuasively argued that, "Roughly speaking, rationality is concerned with the selection of preferred behavior alternatives in terms of some system of values whereby the consequences of behavior can be evaluated," and he went on to posit a series of fruitful distinctions:[20]

> ... a decision may be called "objectively" rational if *in fact* it is the correct behavior for maximizing given values in a given situation. It is "subjectively" rational if it maximizes attainment relative to the actual knowledge of the subject. It is "consciously" rational to the degree that the adjustment of means to ends is a conscious process. It is "deliberately" rational to the degree that the adjustment of means to ends has been deliberately brought about (by the individual or by the organization). A decision is "organizationally" rational if it is oriented to the organization's goals; it is "personally" rational if it is oriented to the individual's goals.

Acknowledging the social and psychological environment within which rational calculation must take place and man's cognitive limitations, Simon, in collaboration with James G. March, has gone on to formulate the concept of "bounded rationality" with special attention to the factors that limit human rationality.[21]

Similarly, Dahl and Lindblom have reasoned that, while an "action is rational to the extent that it is 'correctly' designed to maximize goal achievement," the existence of a multiplicity of goals renders

---

19. Blau, *Bureaucracy in Modern Society*, p. 58.
20. Simon, *Administrative Behavior* (New York: Macmillan, 1947), pp. 75–76.
21. March and Simon, *Organizations*, pp. 136–71, 203–4.

the definition of rationality easier than its measurement. They take as given, "Man's limited mental capacity, lack of emotional integration, inhibited foresight, and need for uncalculated actions," but go on to suggest that "the variables are so many, or the relations among them are so subtle and complex, or the communication of information is so dependent on cues which only the unconscious will pick up, that intuitive judgment is more rational than conscious calculation."[22]

Fruitful though this emphasis on the strategy of survival may be, pendulums often swing too far. In the scholar's concern with political and administrative means and methods, there is danger of neglecting substantive ends; and without some attention to such ends, the study of politics and administration may lose its substantive soul. Although considerable attention is devoted in this study to the strategy of survival and to political and administrative means, it is presumed here that the significance of governmental performance lies not so much in the structure and movement of its machinery as in its policy impacts. Politics and government are inconceivable and meaningless on an uninhabited desert island.

For practitioners, the preoccupation with institutional survival may lead to the preservation of the ossified institutional shell, without the living political and programmatic content—a form of diatomic survival. It is a great temptation for the head of an administrative agency of government, faced with what David B. Truman has called the "ordeal of the executive," and compelled to practice the art of compromise, as all executives must in order to survive, to seek the path of least resistance in order to maintain his organization and himself. In the final analysis, it is the organization's purposes and programs that furnish the currency for compromise.[23]

A decade ago, Arnold A. Rogow made the following observation:

> Reflections on the state of the world or nation, the analysis of broad political, economic, and social development, the drafting of policy alternatives and recommendations . . . seem to have given way to an unrelated emphasis on historicism, scholasticism, and methodology.

The major issue or task facing students of politics and government, he asserted, was the discipline's "relationship to the world at large. . .

---

22. Dahl and Lindblom, *Politics, Economics, and Welfare*, pp. 38–64.
23. David B. Truman, *The Governmental Process* (New York: Knopf, 1951), Chap. XIII.

The Past is Prologue / [17]

whether to be relevant or irrelevant to the problems confronting America and the world."[24]

The relevance of the rise and decline of the Farm Security Administration lies not only in the realm of administrative behavior and institutional survival, but also in one of the great issues that strangely has been ignored by both scholars and practitioners—the nexus of poverty and politics. Of all the great social pathologies that have helped to found and confound governments, generate political tensions and aspirations, and shape the form and function of public administration, few have been more resistant to attention, understanding, and remedy than chronic poverty. It is particularly difficult to understand how the social sciences since the depression of the 1930's can have been so thoroughly unconcerned about the social and political implications of chronic poverty in an affluent society. In 1966, for instance, Leonard H. Goodman, a sociologist and member of the Bureau of Social Science Research, pointed to the lack of a viable sociological concept of poverty, and he called for more "sustained interest in the study of organizations and institutions devoted to the amelioration and reduction of poverty." An examination of any recent textbook in political science or public administration suggests that sociologists are not the only ones who have a task before them.[25]

The genesis of the Farm Security Administration, its form and function, its evolution of purpose, its programmatic and administrative performance, and its political viability—all have meaning only in reference to the problem of chronic rural poverty with which the agency was inextricably linked. It is to the discovery, the nature, and the implications of that poverty that we now turn.

24. Arnold A. Rogow, "Comment on Smith and Apter: or, Whatever Happened to the Great Issues?" *American Political Science Review*, Vol. LI (Sept., 1957), pp. 763–75.
25. Leonard H. Goodman, ed., *Economic Progress and Social Welfare* (New York: Columbia Univ. Press, 1966), pp. 15–16.
As recent a textbook as the fifth edition of John M. Pfiffner and Robert Presthus, *Public Administration* (New York: Ronald Press, 1967) sees fit to discuss the implications of poverty for public administration only in terms of the impact of the "Poverty Program" on public personnel administration and cost-benefit analysis, and in merely a few perfunctory remarks at that. Even those students of politics and public administration who have paid attention to the nature of chronic poverty and its impact on politics and governmental institutions have found their data in the so-called emerging nations of the world, and not in their American back yards.

CHAPTER II

THE REVELATION:
POVERTY ON THE FARM

All great idealisms appear to spring from the sail of materialistic defeat.

RALPH T. FLEWELLING[1]
The Survival of Western Culture

In the literature on Franklin D. Roosevelt's tenure in the White House, there has been disagreement about the intellectual ancestry of the New Deal and its instrumentalities. One school of thought, emphasizing the pragmatism, ethical relativism, and practical inconsistencies in the regime's programs and policies, has seen it as a sharp break with historical liberal reform in the United States. Another viewpoint has suggested that the New Deal was many things to many people and that the New Dealers were a mixed flock, but that their flexibility and opportunism should not obscure their intellectual and practical debt to the reform tradition. Whether the New Deal was an authentic link in the progressive tradition or a sharp new departure, there is consensus that a major current in the confluence of thought and practice out of which the New Deal evolved was agrarian poverty and the political dissent which that poverty helped to generate. The genesis of the Farm Security Administration, like

---

1. Ralph T. Flewelling, *The Survival of Western Culture* (New York: Harper, 1943), p. 26.

that of the New Deal itself, was rooted in an idealism in which escape from materialistic defeat was a central motivating force.²

From the dawn of the American Republic to the advent of the Roosevelt era, poverty had been largely submerged in the American mind, inhabiting, in the words of Max Lerner, "the darker side of the crescent moon."³ During the early years, there were brighter hopes and darker fears to preoccupy men—forms of worship and the proper road to personal salvation, gold to dig in the hills and rich soil to work in the valleys and on the plains, the threat of Indian attack, difficulties of transportation and communication, dangers of catastrophic crop failure, fears of extreme winters, and the dread of disease and plague. Farm life was a pioneering existence—ample homesteading land, a prevailing spirit of optimism, and acceptance of material want and hardship as the natural price of personal and national development. For the majority of Americans, at least until the twentieth century, homes were humble, according to modern standards, food was scant, and clothing was spare. Contemporaries, however, did not always recognize this condition as "poverty." A prevailing theme, for instance, in the recollections of men who have risen from humble farm backgrounds has been their rather surprised realization, in later years, that perhaps they had been poor in childhood, although they had not realized it at the time.

A partial explanation of this historical myopia is that poverty is a relative concept—enormously difficult to define and identify precisely. As we shall see, it was not until the first decade of the twentieth century that serious efforts were made to define rural poverty and to develop instruments for its measurement. In 1895, for instance, Alfred Marshall, in the third edition of his influential book, *Principles of Economics*, departed from conventional economic preoccupations to focus some attention on the need for diagnosis of

2. Thomas H. Greer, *American Social Reform Movements* (New York: Prentice-Hall, 1949), pp. 245–48, 275–81; Rexford G. Tugwell, "The Experimental Roosevelt," *Political Quarterly*, Vol. 21 (July, 1950), pp. 239–70, and his book, *The Democratic Roosevelt* (Garden City, N.Y.: Doubleday, 1957); Samuel Lubell, *The Future of American Politics* (New York: Harper, 1951), p. 54; Eric F. Goldman, *Rendezvous With Destiny* (New York: Knopf, 1952), Chaps. XIV, XV; Richard Hofstadter, *The Age of Reform* (New York: Knopf, Vintage ed., 1955), Chap. VII; Louis Hartz, *The Liberal Tradition in America* (New York: Harcourt, Brace and World, 1955), Chap. 10; James MacGregor Burns, *Roosevelt: The Lion and the Fox* (New York: Harcourt, Brace, and World, 1956); Arthur M. Schlesinger, Jr., *The Politics of Upheaval* (Boston: Houghton Mifflin, 1960).

3. Max Lerner, *America as a Civilization* (New York: Simon and Schuster, 1957), p. 334.

chronic poverty in the cities and on the farms. In 1904, Robert Hunter, an American sociologist and social worker, emphasized the need for liberation from a moralistic approach to the subject, and distinguished between poverty, vagrancy, and pauperism. In 1934, with the urgency of this definitional problem punctuated by the great depression, I. M. Rubinow pointed out that as social wealth increased in the country generally and as economic, social, and political contrasts multiplied, the definition of poverty, on the basis of comparative scales and standards of living, became more difficult in a modern society. And a generation later, after the accumulation of much knowledge and sophistication about the causes and cures of poverty, Herman P. Miller reiterated the refrain:[4]

> This word poverty, which is used so loosely, is in reality a very complex concept that can be defined, measured, and analyzed in many different ways. Like a chameleon, it takes on the coloration of the milieu in which it is used. It has one meaning in India and another in the United States. The meaning of poverty in America today is quite different from its meaning at the turn of the century.

As Miller and others have shown, the concept of poverty does not fit easily into the categories of the major intellectual disciplines. Specialists bring to the dialogue their own language and conceptual baggage. Economists tend to analyze poverty—its causes, consequences, and cures—in terms of income and material standards of living. Sociologists and anthropologists approach the subject more broadly, and consider not only income, but "life style" and what Oscar Lewis has called the "culture of poverty." Psychologists have found the essence of poverty to lie in what Warren C. Haggstrom

---

4. Alfred Marshall, *Principles of Economics*, (3rd ed.; New York: Macmillan, 1895), pp. 2–4; Robert Hunter, *Poverty* (New York: Macmillan, 1904), pp. 318–40; I. M. Rubinow, "Poverty," in *Encyclopaedia of the Social Sciences*, Vol. 12 (New York: Macmillan, 1934), pp. 284–92; Herman P. Miller, ed., *Poverty American Style* (Belmont, Calif.: Wadsworth, 1966), p. ix.

During the past decade, the literature on the subject of poverty has grown enormously. For representative works, see the following: Robert L. Heilbronner, "Who Are the American Poor?" *Harper's Magazine*, Vol. 200 (June, 1950), pp. 27–33; John Kenneth Galbraith, *The Affluent Society* (Boston: Houghton Mifflin, 1958); Michael Harrington, *The Other America* (New York: Macmillan, 1962); Warren C. Haggstrom, "The Power of the Poor," in Frank Riessman et al., eds., *Mental Health of the Poor* (Glencoe, Ill.: The Free Press, 1964), pp. 205–21, reprinted in Miller, *Poverty American Style*, pp. 66–81; Wilson C. McWilliams, "Poverty: Public Enemy Number One," *Saturday Review* (Dec. 10, 1966), pp. 48–49, 59; Hanna M. Meissner, *Poverty in the Affluent Society* (New York: Harper and Row, 1966); Oscar Ornati, *Poverty Amid Affluence* (New York: The Twentieth Century Fund, 1966).

has described as the "modal personality of poverty"—the apathy, negativism, pessimism, and sense of fatality of the poor. And, perhaps strangely, students of politics and government have tended to ignore the subject.

For our purposes, one of the more fruitful approaches is that of John Kenneth Galbraith, who, in his provocative book in 1958, *The Affluent Society*, saw no need for a precise definition of poverty. Although adhering to the economist's preoccupation with income and material level of living, Galbraith emphasized an important point— that poverty is a condition in which people fall below the acceptable standard of living in a community:[5]

People are poverty-stricken when their income, even if adequate for survival, falls markedly behind that of the community. Then they cannot have what the larger community regards as the minimum necessary for decency; and they cannot wholly escape, therefore, the judgment of the larger community that they are indecent. They are degraded for, in the literal sense, they live outside the grades or categories which the community regards as acceptable.

For our purposes, there is special relevance in Galbraith's distinction between two types of poverty: (1) "case poverty," which is "commonly and properly related to some characteristic of the individuals so afflicted. . . . [such as] mental deficiency, bad health, inability to adapt to the discipline of modern economic life, excessive procreation, alcohol, insufficient education, or perhaps a combination of several of these handicaps"; and (2) "insular poverty," manifested as an "island" of poverty in which "everyone or nearly everyone is poor," not because of personal handicaps of the people, but rather because of a complex set of circumstances affecting the area or region itself. General enhancement of income, and its more equitable distribution, eliminate neither the personal inadequacies of the poor, nor the "specific frustrations of environment to which the people of these islands are subject."

The chronic rural poverty with which this study is concerned was rooted in both the individual flaws and afflictions of Galbraith's "case poverty" and the environmental circumstances of his "insular poverty." We are concerned not with the poverty of farm families suffering temporary adversity because of weather, blight, or prices, but rather the poverty of those farm tenants, sharecroppers, and migratory farm laborers who lived permanently below the generally accepted standards of living, outside of the general farm economy

---

5. Galbraith, *The Affluent Society*, pp. 323–24.

and the organized rural community, and for whom want had become a normal condition of life.

The Agrarian Myth Unmasked

Another reason why chronic poverty on the farm, however defined, was overlooked by many Americans during the nineteenth century and the first two decades of the twentieth was the "agrarian myth"—a cluster of ideas, beliefs, sentiments, and values presumably representative of the ideal rural way of life—which tended either to deny the existence of poverty altogether, or to explain it away. Drawing particularly on Thomas Jefferson's agrarian ideals, the myth nourished a creed that embraced virtually all aspects of the American farmer's life—his role in society, his farming practices, his political rights and obligations, the role of his government, and the nature of politics. A mystical quality attached to land and its cultivation. The farmer was the elect of God, a priest entrusted with the care of the earth. Agriculture was the only truly moral way to secure wealth and happiness. Rural life was healthier and more righteous than life in the cities. Virtue lay in individualism and self-reliance; wealth and success were the rewards of initiative, hard work, and thrift. Poverty was the wages of sin and sloth.[6]

Conceived as a private matter, rural poverty, the orthodox agrarians believed, was the concern of the individual, the family, or, if necessary, private philanthropy. Governmental efforts to relieve human want and social degradation, and to prevent their recurrence, were undesirable interference in the natural order. Furthermore, needy people should have enough self-respect not to seek or accept public aid. Poverty, in brief, was un-American. "Confess your sorrows, fears, hopes, loves and even your deviltry to men," observed Henry Wheeler Shaw, who amused his fellow Americans in the 1800's as "Uncle Josh," "but don't let them get a smell of your

---

6. Liberty Hyde Bailey, *What is Democracy?* (Ithaca, N.Y.: Comstock, 1918), and *The Holy Earth* (New York: Macmillan, 1923); John Crowe Ransom *et al.*, *I'll Take My Stand* (New York: Harper, 1932); Roger Butterfield, "The Folklore of Politics," *Pennsylvania Magazine of History and Biography*, Vol. LXXIV (Apr., 1950), pp. 165–70; A. Whitney Griswold, *Farming and Democracy* (New York: Harcourt, Brace, 1948), Chap. 2; V. O. Key, *Parties and Pressure Groups* (New York: Crowell, 1952), Chap. 2; Douglas C. Stenerson, "Emerson and the Agrarian Tradition," *Journal of the History of Ideas*, Vol. XIV (Jan., 1953), pp. 95–115.

poverty—poverty has no friends, not even among the paupers."[7]

Admittedly, poverty was more visible in the cities than it was on the farm. Few people could fail to see it in the crowded urban slums; but it could be more easily overlooked behind the beauty of the Appalachian foliage or in the vastness of the Great Plains. Many agrarians who did discover poverty in agriculture were adept in finding simplicities to explain it. They believed that it was caused by natural and inevitable social maladjustments, such as war, reconstruction, and inevitable economic tides; or by drought, blight, and other coercions of catastrophe; by bankers' manipulation of the money or by discrimination of the railroads against the farmers; or by flaws in the personal or moral character of the poor.

A central dogma of agrarian orthodoxy was the belief in land as a symbol of prestige and power. In part, this attitude was inherited from the Old World, where land ownership had long been the mark of social status. Many immigrants may have come to America in search of a place for freedom of religious worship, but an equal number probably came with a worship of land ownership. Rexford G. Tugwell, with whom we shall be concerned in this study, in 1935 described this land hunger and its enduring impact:[8]

> The free lands of the boundless West were a national dream from the dawn of our history on this continent. Men struggled, fought, faced torture, starvation and death to win the right of our people to lands which lay beyond the Alleghenies. Although for forty years this frontier has gone, its memory and its motives still control our national feeling about the land and the people who make their living from the land .... Land is, you see, a fighting question and has been since the dawn of time.

Following the peace at Appomattox, signs began to appear suggesting that the Jeffersonian ideal of the independent small farmer, working his own land, was becoming a hopeless dream for some farm people. In New England, for instance, sons and daughters of farm families were forced to migrate West or to enter occupations in the cities and towns. In the South, the system of plantations worked by slaves gave way to plantations worked by sharecroppers, as the "freed" slaves exchanged one form of bondage for another. Generally throughout rural America in the 1870's, the greatest economic panic in the nation's history, until that time, caused farm foreclosures, credit

---

7. Donald Day, *Uncle Sam's Uncle Josh* (Boston: Little, Brown, 1953), p. 203.

8. Tugwell, in an address in Washington, D.C., Dec. 2, 1935, FDRL, OF 1568.

restrictions, rising railroad rates, and falling farm commodity prices. Many of the victims never recovered.

As a corollary of the traditional worship of land in the United States, land tenure—the customary and legalized rights of a farmer to land—was considered to be a primary factor in determining the wealth and welfare of the farmer. By 1880, a particularly ominous cloud appeared in the sky when the census of that year revealed that 25 per cent of American farm operators either rented their farms as tenants or worked on others' farms and plantations as sharecroppers. When the Census of 1900 indicated that tenancy had climbed to over 35 per cent, alarm grew among the orthodox agrarians who interpreted the trend as a breakdown of the Jeffersonian ideal.

The tenancy system assumed a variety of forms, but in general a farm tenant was a farmer who rented and operated a farm or portion thereof, the use of which he paid for either by a cash rent or by a cash share of his crop, or both. There were four kinds of farm tenancy: (1) *cash tenancy*, in which the tenant rented and operated a farm for a fixed cash or crop rental and furnished all of his own operating needs; (2) *share tenancy*, with the tenant furnishing his own equipment, work animals, and other needs, and receiving the use of land in exchange for a share of his crop; (3) *share-cash tenancy*, in which the tenant provided his own needs, and paid for the use of the land with a combination of cash payment and share of his crop; and (4) *sharecropping*, in which everything—land, implements, work animals, household essentials, food, and farm management—was furnished by the landlord. The first three types of tenants were relatively independent, in that they planned the financing, management, and marketing of their crops, while the sharecropper was in effect little more than a farm laborer, since he had no responsibility in raising or selling the crop and no claim upon its return until everything he had received from the landlord—"furnish"—had been paid out of his share of the crop.[9]

The rental period was usually for one year, without any guarantee of renewal for either party. Often the agreement was not even in writing. In terms of security, the sharecropper was especially vulnerable, since he provided only his labor, while the landlord fur-

---

9. Charles P. Loomis and J. Allan Beegle, *Rural Social Systems* (New York: Prentice-Hall, 1950), pp. 325–26; Edmund de S. Brunner and J. H. Kolb, *Rural Social Trends* (New York: McGraw-Hill, 1933), pp. 38–42, 135–36; Charles S. Mangum, *The Legal Status of the Tenant Farmer in the Southeast* (Chapel Hill: Univ. of North Carolina Press, 1952), pp. 3–85.

nished the rest of what was needed for the year's crop. The sharecropper was very likely to be left helpless if the landlord's support should be withdrawn. Southern tenancy differed from that in other parts of the country by virtue of this combination of land-ownership, capital, and managerial direction in the hands of the landlord or planter.

Tenant farmers and sharecroppers acted as economic shock-absorbers for landowners and planters. Many tenants never made a profit and succeeded only in going deeper into debt from year to year. The landlords usually kept the books and managed the sale of crops. Opportunities for exploitation were increased by the high rate of illiteracy among tenants and sharecroppers, especially in the South where a large proportion of them were Negroes. "A jot's a jot, a figger's a figger," went the old saying, "all for the white man and none for the nigger." It was for such reasons, perhaps, that the southern tenancy system has been described as suggestive of "the economy of the Middle Ages without the cathedrals."[10] A common criticism of the system was that the tenant's and sharecropper's tenure on the land was too insecure, but in view of his bondage to his rented land and his landlord, perhaps he was too firmly tied to his rented acres.

Some agriculturalists, with considerable justification—thinking about the system outside of the South—have viewed tenancy as a normal and even desirable form of land tenure for those farmers who could not afford to own their own farms but who aspired to eventual ownership. Tenancy was considered particularly functional in the case of the young farmer on the first rung of the agricultural ladder. It seemed preferable to invest precious capital in livestock, implements, and other productive means, and to avoid the back-breaking burdens of a mortgage on land, at least until the young farmer had the capacity to carry the load. Under proper safeguards, tenancy could be a natural step in the direction of ultimate farm ownership.[11]

Other agricultural observers, to the contrary, equated farm tenancy with economic insecurity, exploitation of the farmer and his family, and destruction of the land by farmers who had no financial

10. H. C. Nixon, *Forty Acres and Steel Mules* (Chapel Hill: Univ. of North Carolina Press, 1938), p. 19.

11. E. L. Bogart, "The Bright Side of Tenancy Statistics," *Journal of Political Economy*, Vol. XVI (Apr., 1908), p. 201; Alfred Marshall, *Principles of Economics* (8th ed.; New York: Macmillan, 1920), pp. 637–59; Otis D. Duncan, "A Sociological Approach to Farm Tenancy Research," *Rural Sociology*, Vol. 5 (Sept., 1940), pp. 285–91.

stake in the preservation of its fertility. Farm tenancy, ignorance, and unwise exploitation of land and people were links in a vicious circle: "Tenancy breeds ignorance and ignorance breeds more tenancy. . . both keep farmers submerged. . . neither tenancy nor ignorance can be cured without curing the other." The consequences of this vicious circle were believed to affect the welfare of rural people, and the health and security of the nation's communities, land resources, and political institutions.[12]

In areas of one-crop farming, such as the southern cotton and tobacco belts, speculation in cash crops tended toward emphasis on quick profits at the expense of the soil. Landowners and planters seeking speculative profits forced tenants to raise crops which eventually helped to ruin the land. In some areas this led to instability among tenants and to what has been called "suitcase farming." The farmer constantly on the move found it difficult to obtain sufficient credit facilities for successful operations. His family and the rural community generally suffered when he failed to become a member of the community. Furthermore, with farmers losing their lands through mortgage foreclosures, with the ratio of mortgage debt to farm real estate value steadily climbing, and with many of those farmers who managed to hold title to their lands losing equity in it, a permanent class of marginal farmers, tenants, sharecroppers, and migratory farm workers seemed to be developing. Rural youth and farm capital were drifting to the towns and cities. Seemingly invisible to most people in the United States were the growing number of farm families hopelessly in want—without land, credit, farming skill, or a political voice, and living below the contemporarily acceptable standards of housing, food, medical care, and education.

With America mesmerized by the gospel of wealth during the closing years of the nineteenth century, the democrats and social critics of the time were not silent about poverty generally, but the poverty they saw was not that of the farm family permanently trapped in hopeless want. Henry George, for instance, equated poverty with a new form of slavery, but in both his diagnosis and prescription he focused on the problems of people who were participants in the political economy, not those farm families who were incompetent, poorly motivated, and ill-prepared to take advantage of opportunities that might have been offered to them. Similarly, in 1890, Mrs. Mary Elizabeth Lease admonished farmers in Kansas—

---

12. Nixon, *Forty Acres and Steel Mules*, pp. 24–25.

commercial farm owner-operators suffering temporary adversity—"to raise less corn and more hell."[13]

Prior to World War I, economic dislocations in agriculture produced periodic waves of agrarian discontent, and these waves in turn helped to generate occasional tides of political radicalism. From the time of Shays' rebellion against the regime of George Washington, through the pressure for homestead land in Lincoln's day, to the Populism of Bryant's generation and the Progressivism of George Norris and Robert La Follette, agricultural dislocation had been a major spark of political unrest in the United States. The unrest emanated, however, not from the developing "under-class" of chronically impoverished farmers, but rather from those who were part of the agricultural economy, who were reasonably well-motivated, who were suffering temporary economic adversities caused by bad weather, crop failure, or price maladjustments, and who were prepared to take advantage of opportunities for improvement. Not until the cry of "Black Power" and the "long hot summers" in the black ghettos of American cities during the 1960's would there be fully manifest political expression of the discontent felt by those permanently trapped at the bottom of the social and economic pyramid.[14]

For the more fortunate farmers of the country, the first decade of the twentieth century was the "golden age of agriculture," reflected in the customary indicators of prosperity—prices of farm products, real income, the total value of farm exports, and other aggregate statistics. In 1909, for instance, Secretary of Agriculture James F. Wilson jubilantly proclaimed that, "The value of farm products is so incomprehensively large that it has become merely a row of figures."

13. George T. Fairchild, *Rural Wealth and Welfare* (New York: Macmillan, 1900), pp. 178, 304, 338-39, 343, 373-74; Solon J. Buck, *The Agrarian Crusade* (New Haven: Yale Univ. Press, 1920), pp. 33-34, 135-36; John D. Hicks, *The Populist Revolt* (Minneapolis: Univ. of Minnesota Press, 1931); Theodore Saloutos and John D. Hicks, *Agricultural Discontent in the Middle West, 1900-1939* (Madison: Univ. of Wisconsin Press, 1951); Stuart A. Rice, *Farmers and Workers in American Politics* (New York: Green, 1924); Roscoe C. Martin, *The People's Party in Texas* (Austin: Univ. of Texas Press, 1933).

14. Daniel Bell, *The End of Ideology* (Glencoe, Ill.: The Free Press, 1960), p. 30, has made the following important point: "It is not poverty *per se* that leads people to revolt; poverty most often induces fatalism and despair, and a reliance . . . on supernatural help. *Social tensions are an expression of unfulfilled expectations* [italics in the original]. It is only when expectations are aroused that radicalism can take hold."

It is not an accident of history that the poverty of America's urban ghettos did not generate overt radical action until a period of general affluence in the country aroused hope among the chronic have-nots.

From another direction came the boast that, "One American harvest would buy the kingdom of Belgium, king and all; two would buy Italy; three would buy Austria-Hungary; and five, at a spot-cash price, would take Russia from the czar."[15]

Against this background of prosperity and optimism it was easy, perhaps, to miss the fact that by the twentieth century a number of trends had led to the creation of a class of chronically impoverished farmers who could not hope to rise on the agricultural ladder. The disappearance of homesteading land, rising land costs, greater dependence upon credit and costly farm implements and materials, price instability in farm products, insecurity of land tenure for those who could not afford to own their own farms, racial discrimination, and political disfranchisement—these were some of the conditions that challenged the Jeffersonian dream. Reflecting the growing anxiety, President Theodore Roosevelt declared in 1907:[16]

> Nothing is more important to this country than the perpetuation of our system of medium sized farms worked by their own owners. We do not want to see our farmers sink to the condition of the peasants of the old world, barely able to live on their small holdings, nor do we want to see their places taken by wealthy men owning enormous estates which they work purely by tenants and hired servants.

Not content with mere pious expressions of concern, Roosevelt sought to initiate a response to the challenge, and appointed his Country Life Commission, under the chairmanship of Liberty Hyde Bailey, a leading apostle of the orthodox agrarian creed. A disappointment to those who hoped for a thorough-going examination of inequities *within* agriculture, the report of the commissioners offered little in the way of specific policy proposals. A solution to the problems of agriculture, they believed, would depend on observance of the traditional virtues and on education rather than organized political action.[17]

15. USDA, *Yearbook, 1910* (Washington, D.C.: GPO, 1910), pp. 9, 10; Frederick Strauss and Louis H. Bean, *Gross Farm Income and Indices of Farm Production and Prices in the United States, 1869–1937* (Washington, D.C.: USDA Tech. Bull. 703), p. 140; H. N. Casson, *Wallace's Farmer*, Vol. XXXIII (July 10, 1908), p. 871.
16. Carey McWilliams, *Ill Fares the Land* (Boston: Little, Brown, 1942), p. 211; *Wallace's Farmer*, Vol. XXXII (Oct., 1907), p. 1145.
17. U.S., Commission on Country Life, *Report* (Chapel Hill: Univ. of North Carolina Press, 1944), originally published as U.S., Congress, Senate Doc. 705, 60th Cong., 2d Sess., 1909; Liberty Hyde Bailey, *The Country Life Movement* (New York: Macmillan, 1911); Grant McConnell, *The Decline of Agrarian Democracy* (Berkeley: Univ. of California Press, 1953), p. 84.

During the years that followed, the trends continued. By 1910, for instance, the census indicated that 37 per cent of all farmers in the United States were working someone else's land. By 1914, no one could properly deny that there were really two agricultures in the United States—the world of the larger, more efficient, more productive and economically secure farmer who could survive occasional natural disasters and depressions; and the world of the smaller, marginal farmer whose economic position was extremely precarious and whose farm output had little, if any, impact on the aggregate statistics of farm production. The latter world was that of the tenant farmer who could not realistically hope to climb the ladder to farm ownership, and the sharecropper who was completely dependent upon his landlord and credit merchant. Especially in later years, this nether world of agriculture was also peopled by an additional class —migratory farm laborers who followed the crop cycle in search of seasonal day labor and who probably had more in common with low-income industrial workers in the cities than with their more affluent country cousins.

From the administration of Theodore Roosevelt through that of Woodrow Wilson, agricultural policymakers at both ends of Pennsylvania Avenue were concerned primarily with the needs of the more efficient commercial farmers of America. They believed that the structure of American agriculture was basically sound. Farming should be regarded as a business, and therefore the goals of governmental programs should be keyed to business objectives. Farm policies should promote productive efficiency, improve marketing services, stabilize the prices of farm products—the higher the better —and preserve and enlarge the market for the output of American farms.

Historically, the backbone of agrarian orthodoxy had been the "family farm," defined as follows:[18]

. . . a farm on which the operator, devoting substantially full time to farming operations, with the help of other members of his family and without more than a moderate amount of outside labor, can make a satisfactory living and maintain the farm plant.

Those farms above that level have generally been considered large-scale or commercial farms, and those below as residential, part-time, or subsistence farms.

18. USDA, Interbureau Committee on Postwar Agricultural Problems, *Farm Opportunities in the United States* (Washington, D.C.: GPO, 1945), pp. 11, 44–45.

During the 1920's, while the agrarian philosophers continued to hail the family farm as the American ideal, technological progress and commercialization hastened the change from farming as a "way of life" to farming as a business enterprise. Larger farms and concentration of land ownership; greater dependence on banks, industrial and commercial firms, and marketing associations; greater productive efficiency; heavier dependence on hired day labor; and surpluses in certain commodities—these were some of the manifestations of the historic shift in American agriculture. By the middle of the decade, pressures were developing in favor of restricted acreages and against the marginal farmer working with antiquated methods on substandard soil. It was argued that inefficient farmers working on substandard soil contributed to the surpluses and lowered the quality of farm products. Prophetic of things to come, this emphasis on greater efficiency would pass some of the burden of restricted acreages to the small or marginal farmer, without providing him with an alternative course or an escape from agriculture altogether.[19]

Agricultural leaders came to despise the poor and inefficient small-scale farmer. In contradiction to their own argument that his inefficient production contributed to the problem of surpluses and lowered the quality of farm products in the market, they contended that his production was negligible compared to that of commercial producers. He was ignorant and apathetic, and deaf to pleas for improved productive methods. In response to official pleadings by production experts, his typical response was often, "Shucks, I already know better than I do." The poor and ignorant farmer was viewed by some efficiency-minded agriculturalists as a living embarrassment and a potential threat. He challenged the agrarian myth of moral superiority, and served as a reminder that class lines might emerge among American farmers and lead to the very class legislation that the more orthodox agrarians deplored.

Illustrative of the neglect of the low-income farmer's problems was the establishment of the agricultural extension system during the administration of President Woodrow Wilson. Seaman A. Knapp, an influential agricultural scientist, had developed a program of agri-

---

19. Carey McWilliams, *Ill Fares the Land*, and *Factories in the Field* (Boston: Little, Brown, 1939); Paul S. Taylor, "Good-By to the Homestead Farm," *Harper's Magazine*, Vol. 182 (May, 1941), pp. 589–97; Theodore W. Schultz, "Changes in Economic Structure Affecting American Agriculture," *Journal of Farm Economics*, Vol. XXVIII (Feb., 1946), pp. 17–18; C. B. Sherman, "The Farm Labor Problem," *Journal of the American Bankers Association*, Vol. XVII (July, 1925), p. 21.

cultural demonstration and adult education among cotton farmers in the South, based on the idea that more efficient methods of production could be promoted through demonstration projects in rural communities. In 1909, legislative proposals based on Knapp's work were first introduced in Congress, but it required five years for passage of a bill which would create a national agricultural extension system. One issue was whether Negro farmers should be included in the program. When the Smith-Lever Agricultural Extension Act was passed in 1914, the question of the Negro's role was evaded by establishing separate offices for extension work in the U.S. Department of Agriculture (USDA)—one assigned to the North and West, and one to the South. It was provided that national extension policy should halt at state boundaries, where regional and local values and sentiments would prevail.

In effect, the architects of the extension system, like the leaders of agriculture generally, were responsive, not to the needs of the marginal farmer who lived in permanent poverty, but rather to those commercial farmers who were in a position to gain from greater productive efficiency and higher market prices. One critic of the extension system in Texas, for instance, charged in 1915:[20]

The whole tendency of agricultural education is to benefit the man who is already progressive. It does not reach the man who is in most need, the neglected man, who neglects himself, who does not seek knowledge, and to whom the colleges and the department [of agriculture] . . . should go as a missionary.

Normalcy

A century ago John Morley observed that, "Great economic and social forces flow with a tidal sweep over communities that are only half-conscious of that which is befalling them," and that, "Wise statesmen are those who foresee what time is thus bringing, and endeavor to shape institutions and to mould men's thoughts and purpose in accordance with the change that is silently surrounding

20. Orville M. Kile, *The Farm Bureau Movement* (New York: Macmillan, 1921); Gladys L. Baker, *The County Agent* (Chicago: Univ. of Chicago Press, 1939); Russell Lord, *The Agrarian Revival* (New York: American Association for Adult Education, 1939); Joseph C. Bailey, *Seaman A. Knapp, Schoolmaster of American Agriculture* (New York: Columbia Univ. Press, 1945); Association of American Agricultural Colleges and Experiment Stations, *Proceedings*, 1915 Convention, p. 226.

them."[21] Whether the leaders of American agriculture during the 1920's, both within and outside of government, were "wise statesmen," we shall leave to history. However, the record suggests that most of them neither saw nor understood that for an increasing number of American farm families, grinding poverty was becoming the normal way of life.

If the low-income farmer who remained in want both in good times and bad failed to attract official attention and remedial public action during the prosperous and optimistic "golden years" before World War I, he could hardly hope for more during the decade that followed, when the predicament of the *commercial* farmer dominated the public mind. For agriculture as a whole, the Great Depression began not on the fateful day in October, 1929, but in 1920, when farm commodity prices suddenly collapsed and the war-time boom dissolved. During the years that followed, abandoned farm homesteads, dilapidated buildings, equipment in disrepair, longer working hours, especially for farm wives and children, a reduced level of living, lack of ready cash or credit, and a rising wave of political discontent in rural areas nourished agrarian demands for remedial public action.[22]

However, when the leaders of agriculture referred to "the agricultural problem," they were concerned not with the chronically impoverished marginal or subsistence farmer, who was affected by the agricultural depression proportionately less than the commercial farmer who had invested heavily in land, equipment, and consumer comforts during the war. These leaders were thinking not about inequalities *within* agriculture, but rather with what they believed was the "disadvantaged" position of the commercial farmer in his relations with the rest of the economy. Farmers, they believed, were caught in a scissors—the high cost of the things they had to purchase cut against the depressed prices of the products they sold, and thus the farmer in the marketplace was not receiving a "fair share" of the national income.

"Equality" for the farmer was given operational meaning by the invention of the concept of "parity." That is, farmers should receive prices for their products which would provide them with a level of living equivalent at least to that which they had theoretically enjoyed

---

21. John Morley, *The Life of Richard Cobden* (Boston: Roberts Brothers, 1881), p. 636.
22. USDA, *Agricultural Statistics, 1936* (Washington, D.C.: GPO, 1936), Table 460, p. 354; James H. Shideler, *Farm Crisis, 1919–1923* (Berkeley: Univ. of California Press, 1947); M. S. Stedman and S. W. Stedman, *Discontent at the Polls* (New York: Columbia Univ. Press, 1950).

during the "golden years" from 1910 to 1914. Parity prices, it was argued, would eradicate the disparity between agriculture and business, and presumably would confer upon the farmer "economic justice."[23]

To secure this justice, maintenance of parity prices would not be enough, however. Agricultural leaders, especially among the farm organizations, believed that they would have to fight in the political arena for what amounted to a businessman's program for the reform of agriculture—liberalization of farm credit, financing of farm commodities, more sympathetic promotion of cooperative marketing associations, revision of freight rates, tariff legislation to favor agriculture, regulation of the meat-packing industry, highway improvement, and amendments to the federal reserve system and other legislation. Although some low-income farmers, who contributed only a negligible amount to aggregate farm production in the United States, might reap some residual benefits from such a program, this was a businessman's blueprint for solution of the maladjustments in agriculture.[24]

The business conception of agriculture found reinforcement and justification in the work of agricultural economists—the so-called "production economists"—and leaders in the emergent farm management profession. Henry C. Taylor, Richard T. Ely, and Benjamin H. Hibbard at the University of Wisconsin; William J. Spillman in the USDA; Simon N. Patten at the University of Pennsylvania; Thomas Nixon Carver at Harvard University; George F. Warren at Cornell University; and others were preaching the gospel of rationality and efficiency in the use of land and the management of farms.[25]

---

23. Henry C. Taylor, *An Introduction to the Study of Agricultural Economics* (New York: Macmillan, 1905); George F. Warren, *Price of Farm Products in the United States* (Washington, D.C.: USDA Bull. 999, 1921); George N. Peek and Hugh S. Johnson, *Equality for Agriculture* (Moline, Ill.: Moline Plow Company, 1922); John D. Black, *Parity, Parity, Parity* (Cambridge: Harvard Univ. Press, 1942).

24. Arthur Capper, *The Agricultural Bloc* (New York: Harcourt, Brace, 1922); Christiana M. Campbell, *The Farm Bureau and the New Deal* (Urbana: Univ. of Illinois Press, 1962), pp. 30–43; Kile, *The Farm Bureau Movement*, and *The Farm Bureau Through Three Decades* (Baltimore: Waverly Press, 1948), pp. 92–103; Murray R. Benedict, *Farm Policies of the United States, 1790–1950* (New York: The Twentieth Century Fund, 1953), pp. 181–88.

25. The influence of the professors was extended through their disciples— Rexford G. Tugwell, student of Simon N. Patten at Pennsylvania; Henry Morgenthau, Jr., student of George F. Warren at Cornell; John D. Black, who studied under Ely, Taylor, Commons, Ross, and Hibbard at Wisconsin. For Black's work, see the following: John D. Black, *Agricultural Reform in the United States* (New York: McGraw-Hill, 1929); James P. Cavin, ed., *Economics for Agriculture* (Cambridge: Harvard Univ. Press, 1959).

The "agricultural problem," they contended, was caused by a combination of long-term trends and immediate maladjustments—overexpansion of farm production and indebtedness induced by World War I, collapse of foreign demand for American farm products following the war in Europe, changes in American diets from starches to proteins, development of synthetic fibers, price squeeze on the farmer, tightening of farm credit, increase in mechanization and productive efficiency leading to surpluses in farm labor and in farm products, and special maladjustments in man-land relations in such areas as the South and the Great Plains.[26]

They saw many consequences for the American farmer flowing from this commercialization of agriculture—the farmer was compelled to become a businessman with a greater concern about his efficiency; there was a growing interdependence between agriculture and the rest of the economy; the farmer required greater capital; he was forced to specialize his crops; and his dependence on credit and the market increased. Furthermore, commercialization presumably emphasized interdependence among farmers. As rewards and penalties from the swings of the business cycle began to affect the farmer more immediately and profoundly, he became more intimately involved in the larger economy. Now it would be even more difficult for him to preserve the fiction of his traditional self-sufficiency. The self-containment of his family and the division of labor among its members, his awareness of and concern about the larger world around him, and his political behavior and beliefs—all these would be affected by the changes taking place. There would also be a greater inducement for farmers to organize into general farm associations and special commodity groups designed to promote a sense of solidarity and to mobilize for political action.

During the 1920's, pressures from the so-called "farm bloc," reinforced by the arguments of the production economists and professional farm management specialists, led to some ameliorative

---

26. Benedict, *Farm Policies of the United States*, p. 137; Joseph Dorfman, *The Economic Mind in American Civilization*, Vol. 4 (New York: Viking, 1959), Chaps. 8, 9; Edwin G. Nourse, "Agricultural Economics," *Encyclopaedia of the Social Sciences*, Vol. I (New York: Macmillan, 1930), pp. 534–36; Henry C. Taylor and Anne D. Taylor, *The Story of Agricultural Economics in the United States, 1840–1932* (Ames: Iowa State College Press, 1952); M. L. Wilson, COHC, Vol. 10; Henry C. Taylor, "History of Agricultural Economics in the United States," MS, COHC.

One of the influential exponents of the business approach to farming was George F. Warren at Cornell University—the "professor" to many farm organization leaders. For a time, he was influential with Governor Franklin D. Roosevelt at Albany.

programs. However, virtually none of these had immediate or substantial effects on the chronically impoverished farm families whose problems were rooted not only in the economy, but also in society and in themselves.[27]

Meanwhile, the shape of things to come was heralded in a modest experiment in Montana. Taylor persuaded M. L. Wilson, director of the Rural Economics Division at Montana State Agricultural College, and Richard T. Ely to form a commercial company designed to "rehabilitate" marginal or subsistence farms, and to help farm tenants to become owners. With assistance from the Laura Spelman Rockefeller Foundation and a loan of $100,000 from John D. Rockefeller, they established a commercial organization, incorporated in Montana as Fairway Farms. Despite a large measure of productive efficiency and managerial success, Fairway Farms was overcome by depression and drought, and ended in financial failure. Although the experiment was discontinued and the land sold when the mortgage was foreclosed by the Farm Foundation, which had received it from the Rockefeller interests, Fairway Farms provided an opportunity for meaningful innovation. The experience was destined to exert some influence a decade later.[28]

The most intense political battles in agriculture during the second half of the 1920's—over "McNary-Haugenism"—were, like most of the farm policies at the time, largely irrelevant to the hard-core farm poverty with which this study is concerned. The political commotion provoked by the struggle, however, and the loyalties and enmities that resulted, helped to create the climate in which the New Deal and some of its instrumentalities evolved.

Starting in 1924 and continuing until the advent of the New Deal, the "McNary-Haugen Plan," in its various versions, sought a formula for artificial governmental support of certain farm commodity prices. Initially introduced by Senator Charles L. McNary and Representative Gilbert N. Haugen, bills based on the plan were twice passed by Congress and twice vetoed by President Calvin Coolidge.

One of the more articulate advocates of the plan was Henry A. Wallace, son of President Harding's Secretary of Agriculture, a prom-

---

27. Herbert Hoover, *The Memoires of Herbert Hoover: The Cabinet and the Presidency, 1920–1933*, Vol. II (New York: Macmillan, 1952), p. 36; Harris G. Warren, *Herbert Hoover and the Great Depression* (New York: Oxford Univ. Press, 1965), pp. 97–124; Black, *Agricultural Reform*, p. 74.

28. M. L. Wilson, "The Fairway Farms Project," *Journal of Land and Public Utility Economics*, Vol. II (1926), pp. 156–59; Paul K. Conkin, *Tomorrow a New World* (Ithaca, N.Y.: Cornell Univ. Press, 1959), pp. 76–77; Wilson, COHC; Wayne D. Rasmussen to author, Aug. 10, 1967.

ising young Republican leader in midwestern agricultural circles, and, as editor of his family's publication, *Wallace's Farmer,* an influential spokesman for a more rational and efficient commercial agriculture. In 1924, "Young Henry," as the agricultural old hands called him, laid the blame for opposition to the McNary-Haugen plan not at the door of the White House, but rather on an alleged alliance composed of grain exchanges, meatpackers, livestock exchanges, the National City Bank of New York, and the Chase National Bank.

After four years of frustration and failure, in June, 1928, and with presidential nominating conventions about to convene, Wallace sounded a call to arms that fell on deaf ears at the time, but would re-echo to greater effect four years later—"To your tents, O Israel, now see to thine own house, David." The second presidential veto of the McNary-Haugen bill, Wallace declared, "has made it impossible for any farmer with self-respect to vote for Coolidge or for any candidate who, like Hoover, supports the Coolidge policy toward agriculture."[29]

In March, 1929, with one of the leading opponents of the McNary-Haugen bill now Coolidge's successor in the White House, the American Academy of Political and Social Science in Philadelphia issued its *Annals.* The issue was almost completely devoted to the problems of farm prices, production, and marketing, but sandwiched between the conventional business interpretation of agriculture's difficulties was a provocative new voice.

Rexford G. Tugwell, a former student of Patten at the University of Pennsylvania, and in 1929 a professor of economics, at Columbia University, acknowledged that McNary-Haugenism "would undoubtedly make a breach in our careful attitudes of individualism," but that the detour from *laissez faire* would have been only a minor one. Opponents of the bill, Tugwell suggested, were slaves to doctrine, and were actually undermining *laissez faire* itself by their "hysterical fears of allowing the camel's nose to get under the tent." The time was ripe, he contended, to follow the advice of his mentor, who had argued that "what is essential might be preserved by sacrificing what seems important."[30]

Tugwell shared Patten's belief in some form of collectivism,

29. Henry A. Wallace, *Wallace's Farmer,* Vol. 49 (Apr. 11, 1924), p. 587; Vol. 53 (June 1, 1928), p. 844.
30. Rexford G. Tugwell, "Farm Relief and a Permanent Agriculture," *The Annals of the American Academy of Political and Social Science,* Vol. CXLII (Mar., 1929), pp. 271–82.

but disagreed with the conventional idea that it could be achieved through voluntary cooperative action. To the agriculturalists he boldly suggested that, "There are actually those who do not want [*laissez faire*] saved," that agricultural policy makers should go beyond the mystique of production economics, and that governmental planning and control "ought to be examined . . . quite dispassionately and without preconception." His message was addressed specifically to the issue of governmental regulation of prices and production, but in challenging some of the dogmas of agrarian orthodoxy, and in going beyond the doctrines of production economics, he was at least opening the door to a dialogue in which chronic rural poverty—the poverty of the Lesters of Georgia and the Joads of Oklahoma—might no longer inhabit the darker side of the crescent moon.

The New Imperative

Although poverty on the farm was not entirely ignored during the 1920's, and, as will be shown below, attracted the attention and compassion of many scholars, journalists, and philanthropists, it failed to win official recognition and commitment by the federal government until Herbert Hoover became President of the United States. It presumably had been invisible to Warren G. Harding when he promised a return, not to "heroism but healing, not nostrums but normalcy, not revolution but restoration, not agitation but adjustment, not surgery but serenity." And poverty had been seen but misunderstood by Calvin Coolidge who, as Vice President, proclaimed that a man's poverty was his own fault, that governments are "not warranted in furnishing employment for anybody," and that anyone "who is not capable of supporting himself is not fit for self-government."[31]

In sharp contrast, Herbert Hoover, during his presidential campaign in 1928, dedicated himself publicly to fight "undernourishment, cold and ignorance, and fear of old age," and he expressed his conviction that "we shall soon, with the help of God, be within

31. Karl Schriftgiesser, *This Was Normalcy* (Boston: Little, Brown, 1948), pp. 9, 155; Kirk Porter and Donald B. Johnson, comps., *National Party Platforms* (Urbana: Univ. of Illinois Press, 1956), pp. 217–18, 225, 232; John H. Rich, *Journal of the American Bankers Association*, Vol. XVI (Jan., 1924), p. 407; Renzo Bowers, ed., *The Inaugural Addresses of the Presidents* (St. Louis: Thomas, 1929), p. 430.

sight of the day when poverty will be banished from this nation." Before he could properly launch his program for the revival of agriculture, however, the farmer—rich and poor—was submerged in a larger economic disaster. By 1930, more than 25 per cent of the nation's farms, involving approximately 7,700,000 people, were producing less than $600 worth of farm products annually, including the value of those products that the families themselves consumed. Approximately one third of all American farm families were living at a level that was comparable to that of urban slum families.[32]

For a generation, the Hoover administration has been condemned for the nature of its response to this disaster, but in perspective, Hoover's assumption of responsibility for national recovery, especially after 1931, was an innovation whose historic significance has been obscured by the drama of the depression itself and by the radiance of the man who succeeded to the Presidency in 1933. Walter Lippmann, however, perceived Hoover's effort to mobilize the public wisdom in achieving recovery as "something utterly unprecedented in American history." To whom might President Hoover have turned in fathoming this public wisdom?[33]

Not surprisingly, he consulted with Republican party leaders, state governors, and a variety of experts, including especially the production economists and professional farm management specialists. To the extent that the depression in agriculture was a problem of economics and technology, the advice offered would likely have been salutary. However, by 1931, even some of the professional agriculturalists realized that chronic poverty on the farm—the poverty of penniless, landless, helpless, and hopeless rural people at the very bottom of the heap—was more than a matter of economics and engineering. "I am afraid that when economists begin to set up goals and objectives in human affairs," wrote John D. Black in the fall of 1931, "they conceive them in economic terms," and he went

---

32. Herbert Hoover, *The New Day: Campaign Speeches of Herbert Hoover, 1928* (Palo Alto, Calif.: Stanford Univ. Press, 1928), pp. 16, 23, and *The State Papers and Other Writings of Herbert Hoover*, William Starr Myers, ed., Vol. I (Garden City, N.Y.: Doubleday, Doran, 1934), p. 6; Black, *Agricultural Reform*, p. 490, and "Fundamental Elements in the Current Agricultural Situation," *Journal of Farm Economics*, Vol. 23 (Nov., 1941), pp. 712–25; Carl C. Taylor, Helen W. Wheeler, and E. L. Kirkpatrick, *Disadvantaged Classes in American Agriculture* (Washington, D.C.: USDA, 1938), pp. 3–5, 108–21.

33. Walter Lippmann, *The New Imperative* (New York: Macmillan, 1935), pp. 12–13.

on to speculate whether a "mere economist can decide for all society what is 'welfare'."[34]

In his search for understanding of *chronic* rural poverty, or even of farm poverty generally, President Hoover might have turned to the accumulating knowledge about the causes and consequences of increasing farm tenancy and sharecropping, and the problem of land tenure. Long a matter of concern to some of the agricultural economists, the rate of farm tenancy had climbed from 35 per cent of the farmers in 1900 to over 45 per cent in 1930. Affecting virtually every rural area in the United States, the trend was concentrated in the South. In Mississippi, 70 per cent of the farm operators were working someone else's land.

This long-range rise in farm tenancy was viewed by some of the economists with considerable anxiety. In 1920, for instance, Marshall devoted special attention to the problems of land tenure, and declared that the causes of poverty and the human problems among those who were "overworked and undertaught, weary and careworn, without quiet and without leisure," should provide economists with "their chief and highest interest." Similarly, Ely warned that the ownership of land should be preserved, in order "to ward off that dangerous radicalism which in the modern form of Bolshevism always attacks, first of all, the private ownership of land."[35]

For a different point of view, Hoover might have turned to the rural sociologists. Their approach rested on the study of social pathology in rural America, pioneered by the country life movement which followed in the wake of Theodore Roosevelt's Country Life Commission, and on the work in community analysis by Franklin H. Giddings at Columbia University and Charles H. Cooley at the University of Michigan. Rural sociologists focused their attention not on the economic factors of agricultural production but on the farmer

---

34. Black, *Agricultural Reform*, p. 368; his "Agricultural Credit," *Encyclopaedia of the Social Sciences*, Vol. I (New York: Macmillan, 1930), p. 529; and his address at Univ. of Chicago, Sept. (n.d.), 1931, in Cavin, *Economics for Agriculture*, pp. 580–81.

35. E. M. Banks, *Economics of Land Tenure in Georgia* (New York: Columbia Univ. Press, 1905); Thomas J. Edwards, "The Tenant System and Some Changes Since Emancipation," *Annals of the American Academy of Political and Social Science*, Vol. XLIX (Sept., 1931), pp. 38–46; George E. Putnam, "Agricultural Credit Legislation and the Tenancy Problem," *American Economic Review*, Vol. V (Dec., 1915), pp. 805–15; Marshall, *Principles of Economics*, 8th ed., pp. 2–4; Richard T. Ely, "An American Land Policy," in Elisha M. Friedman, ed., *America and the New Era* (New York: Dutton, 1929), p. 149.

himself—his level of living, his physical endowments, his health, his beliefs and values, his marital relations, his freedom and capacity to make rational entrepreneurial decisions, his social and political status in the rural community, and his representation and voice in the political arena. Their interest in chronic poverty centered not on the rising farm tenant who was temporarily in economic straights, due perhaps to the collapse of the economy, but on the landless, penniless, helpless and hopeless tenant or sharecropper who seemed doomed to remain on the bottom rung of the agricultural ladder.[36]

By 1920, sociologists had discovered that this chronic rural poverty had become concentrated in particular areas of the country—forty years before President John F. Kennedy and his poverty-fighters discovered Appalachia. The deforested "cut-over" areas of the Lake States, the Appalachian plateau and its valleys, sections of the southern coastal and Piedmont plateaus, the Ozarks, and the low hill country between the Appalachians and the Mississippi River—here poverty had stagnated.

Appropriately, the University of North Carolina became a center of research and teaching in the social problems of agriculture. Professor Howard W. Odum provided the spark and the drive. A native of Georgia and a graduate of Emory University and the University of Mississippi, he took his Ph.D. degree in psychology under G. Stanley Hall at Clark University in Worcester, Massachusetts. There he enjoyed the benefits from Hall's invitations to Sigmund Freud and other German psychologists. Odum went to Columbia University and secured a second doctoral degree, in sociology, under Franklin H. Giddings. After a variety of academic and other professional positions in the South, he became a professor of sociology and chairman of the department at the University of North Carolina, where he established in 1924 the Institute for Research in Social Science. With his associates, he contributed greatly to the accumulating litera-

---

36. The moralistic orientation of early American rural sociology was reflected in the work of two of its pioneers. Albion W. Small, the son of a New England Protestant minister, and himself trained in the ministry, left the presidency of Colby College in 1892, to join the faculty of the University of Chicago, where he established the first department of sociology. John M. Gillette, often regarded as the "dean of rural sociology," wrote the pioneering textbook in the field, *Constructive Rural Sociology* (New York: Sturgis and Walton, 1913), which reflected his earlier background as an ordained Presbyterian minister and rural Kansas preacher. For a detailed chronicle of the development of rural sociology in the United States see Howard W. Odum, *American Sociology: The Story of Sociology in the United States Through 1950* (New York: Longmans, Green, 1951).

ture on the human costs of certain types of farm tenancy and cotton culture.[37]

How did the sociologists explain this poverty? In 1927, Odum rejected the common explanations—economic maladjustments, the Malthusian population curve, the Spencerian law of Social Darwinism, the religious belief that poverty was Providence's penalty for sin and sloth, and the biological explanation. The diagnosis was given, rather, in terms of multiple causation—the physical environment of the land; varying natural endowments of individuals; hereditary defects, such as physical impairment; overpopulation; maladjustments of production and distribution; and social problems, such as inadequate education, marital conflict, and lack of proper social hygiene.

Similarly, in 1929, Rupert B. Vance, one of Odum's associates at Chapel Hill, examined the problem in the South and detected a form of determinism in the chain that bound the southern tenant and sharecropper to King Cotton:[38]

> There exists a kind of natural harmony about the cotton system. Its parts fit together so perfectly as to suggest the fatalism of design. Nature's harmony of the soil, the rainfall, the frostless season, the beaming sun, and the transplanted tropic plant fit well with a transplanted tropic race, landless white farmers, and the slow but all surviving mule to supply the world's steady demand for a cheap fabric. The spinner, the cotton buyer, the landlord, the supply merchant, and the cotton farmer form an economic harmony that often benefits all except the producer.

---

37. Odum's pre-New Deal works included the following: *Social and Mental Traits of the Negro* (New York: Columbia Univ. Press, 1910); *Sociology and Social Problems* (Chicago: American Library Association, 1925); and *The Negro and His Songs*, with Guy B. Johnson (Chapel Hill: Univ. of North Carolina Press, 1925).
The publications of one of Odum's associates in Chapel Hill, Rupert B. Vance, included the following: *Human Factors in Cotton Culture* (Chapel Hill: Univ. of North Carolina Press, 1929); and *Human Geography of the South* (Chapel Hill: Univ. of North Carolina Press, 1932).
Another influential collaborator in Chapel Hill was Thomas J. Woofter, whose relevant works include the following: *Negro Migration: Changes in Rural Organization and Population of the Cotton Belt* (New York: W. D. Gray, 1920); *Black Yeomanry* (New York: Holt, 1930); and *Seven Lean Years*, with Ellen B. Winston (Chapel Hill: Univ. of North Carolina Press, 1939).
A leading graduate of the Chapel Hill institution, Arthur F. Raper, also made a contribution in the following works: *Preface to Peasantry* (Chapel Hill: Univ. of North Carolina Press, 1936); *Sharecroppers All*, with Ira de A. Reid (Chapel Hill: Univ. of North Carolina Press, 1941); and *Tenants of the Almighty* (New York: Macmillan, 1943).
38. Howard W. Odum, *Man's Quest for Social Guidance* (New York: Holt, 1927), pp. 487-91; Vance, *Human Factors in Cotton Culture*, p. 295.

What Vance gently implied, others openly proclaimed—that there was also a political explanation for rural poverty, especially in the South. Among the earliest to see this were the editors of some of the southern rural journals. Immediately after publication of the data in the Census of 1900, for instance, some of these editors expressed alarm, but from the point of view of the landlord and planter: they saw a need to make tenants and sharecroppers more efficient and responsible in their use of the land, in order to maximize the owners' return. By the early 1920's, however, the editorial policy of these journals had shifted to a concern about the predicament of the tenant and sharecropper, which they saw in political as well as economic terms—his insecurity on the land; his bondage to the landlord and credit-merchant; his helplessness, especially in times of depression, drought, and blight; his political impotence and lethargy; his lack of farming skill; and most seriously, perhaps, his inability to understand the need for reform.[39]

One of the earliest and most candid statements of the politics of rural poverty in the South was drafted by Frank Tannenbaum at the time that President Calvin Coolidge was winning re-election. Tannenbaum, a young journalist and historian who was destined to play a role in events a decade later, also argued that cotton was the tyrant of the South:[40]

> . . . a single crop develops tenancy; it causes migration of the farmer; it reduces the farmer to the status of a city worker; it depletes the soil; it places the producer of the crop at the mercy of the creditor; it affects the literacy and the schooling of the community; it destroys civic interest; it fosters local political bossism; it stimulates agrarian discontent; it affects the social life of the rural community; it destroys the traditional stability of the farmer; it hastens removal of the farmer to the city; it kills, or nearly kills, the local church. . . it seems to industrialize the farming community and to make of the farm an outdoor factory.

Overdependence on cotton, Tannenbaum reasoned, led to concentration of land and monopolization of economic and political power in the hands of the creditor-banker-merchant class whose control over the tenant farmer and sharecropper illuminated Louis XIV's assertion that "credit supports agriculture, as the rope supports the

---

39. George C. Osborn, "The Southern Agricultural Press and Some Significant Rural Problems, 1900–1940," *Agricultural History*, Vol. 29 (July, 1955), pp. 115–22. This article traces the treatment of farm tenancy and related issues in the following southern rural journals: *Progressive Farmer, Southern Planter, Southern Agriculturalist*, and *Southern Ruralist*.

40. Frank Tannenbaum, *Darker Phases of the South* (New York: Putnam, 1924), pp. 144–45.

hanged." Illiteracy accompanied tenancy, and together they correlated directly with the incidence of lynching. In effect, Tannenbaum suggested what might be described as the tenancy syndrome—productive inefficiency, one-crop farming, submarginal land, social maladjustment, economic insecurity, racial injustice, political impotence, and violence. This was one face of the "southern way of life."

There was yet another direction toward which President Hoover might have turned in his effort to fathom the public wisdom—the experience of American philanthropy, best exemplified, perhaps, by the Julius Rosenwald Fund. In 1917, after several years of interest in and support for education of the Negro, as the way to break his chain to poverty, Rosenwald established the Rosenwald Fund. During the next ten years, the Fund contributed more than four million dollars to the building of rural schoolhouses, aid to high schools and colleges, fellowships to enable promising Negroes to advance their careers, assistance to Negro hospitals and health agencies, improvement of library facilities in the South, and to educational experiments at such institutions as Swarthmore College, the Social Science Research Council, the American Council on Education, and the New School for Social Research in New York. Many young Negroes who received assistance from the Fund became prominent leaders in later years. President Hoover might have learned much from the experience of the Rosenwald Fund, but at least there should have been one lesson in particular for him—the refutation of the myth of racial inferiority and the demonstration of the capacity of Negroes to respond to opportunity.[41]

On this note, let us return to President Hoover and the predicament of 1930. The best informed and most literate President since Wilson, he was not entirely unfamiliar with the work of the economists, social scientists, publicists, and "philanthrapoids" of that time. As a matter of fact, in the fall of 1929, only a month before the stock market collapsed, he created his Research Committee on Social Trends. For the committee's staff, Hoover skimmed the cream of academic leadership—Wesley C. Mitchell, professor of economics at Columbia University and "father of business-cycle analysis"; Charles E. Merriam, the prominent chairman of the Department of Political

41. The list of Negro beneficiaries might include the following: Charles R. Drew, scientist and surgeon; Allison Davis, anthropologist; Ira de A. Reid, sociologist; Abram L. Harris, economist; Charles S. Johnson, sociologist, author, and president of Fisk University; Mordecai Johnson, president of Howard University; W. E. B. DuBois, sociologist, author, and political activist; Ralph Bunche, political scientist turned United Nations diplomat; and many others.

Science at the University of Chicago; William F. Ogburn, the prolific professor of sociology at Columbia University and the University of Chicago; Howard W. Odum, the rural sociologist at the University of North Carolina; and others. This was an impressive assembly of experts, and one of the problems on which they would focus was chronic rural poverty.[42]

One sympathetic historian has credited Hoover with having had a "sound estimate" of the situation in the country, but has explained that the President was "unwilling to take the bold coercive steps necessary to remedy the troubles that he saw so clearly." Another historian has defended the "genuineness of Hoover's sympathetic understanding of the farmer's plight," and has concluded that "Hoover's thinking on agricultural matters was more sophisticated and complex than that advanced by the principal agricultural organizations." We shall leave the final judgment to the historians, but it is quite likely that the agricultural distress that Hoover understood was not the poverty of Tobacco Road, the Cotton South, the Okies on Highway 66, or the tomato pickers in the fields of California.[43]

If the President was unwilling to invoke the new imperative in order to stabilize prices, restrict crop production, withdraw submarginal lands from production, and provide adequate drought relief, then who seriously could have expected him to support the more daring reforms that were required to combat chronic poverty among the lower-income farmers of the nation?

The remainder of Hoover's tenure in the White House was punctuated by rising tension and frustration. In 1930, Clarence Poe, editor and publisher of the *Progressive Farmer,* sounded the call from Raleigh, North Carolina. Urgent measures were needed to create a "land of plenty, a land of beauty, a land of rural comradeship," and

---

42. President's Research Committee on Social Trends, *Recent Social Trends in the United States* (New York: McGraw-Hill, 1933). Odum prepared a chapter on public welfare activities (pp. 1224–73); Woofter wrote on the status of racial and ethnic groups (pp. 553–601); Brunner and Kolb prepared a comprehensive chapter on rural life generally (pp. 497–552); Merriam contributed a trenchant chapter on government in society (pp. 1489–1541).

In great contrast to the way Franklin Roosevelt would announce such a document, President Hoover, on January 2, 1933, issued the report of the committee with a perfunctory public announcement. For several weeks, newspapers featured commentary on the findings and their implications. There seems to be no evidence to suggest that Hoover actually read the report or fully comprehended some of its more provocative conclusions. *New York Times,* Jan. 2, 4, 5, 8, 12, 1933.

43. Warren, *Herbert Hoover,* p. 183; Albert U. Romasco, *The Poverty of Abundance* (New York: Oxford Univ. Press, 1965), pp. 101–2.

to provide security against unemployment, sickness and old age. "The reactionaries," Poe declared, "will oppose them as 'socialistic' or 'bolshevistic'," but these measures would be "the smart way to prevent the people from turning to bolshevism."[44]

In the spring of 1932, Milo Reno, the militant leader of the National Farmers Union in Iowa, organized the Farm Holiday Association, largely composed of land owners in temporary distress and oriented to the market problems of commercial farmers. To regain "equality in the marketplace," Reno urged his followers to withhold their products from the market. In May, the marching war veterans of the Bonus Expeditionary Force set out for Washington. In June, gloomy Republicans assembled in Chicago to renominate their national leader, and later in the month the Democrats converged on the city in jubilation. On October 4, President Hoover opened his campaign at Des Moines, Iowa, as angry mobs gathered, carrying placards that proclaimed, "In Hoover we trusted; now we are busted;" and "Hoover, Hyde [the Secretary of Agriculture], Hell and Hard Times. The Republican 4-H Club."[45]

Thus, the stage was set for the great contest of 1932. Chronic rural poverty had been ignored, revealed, rationalized, and explained, and while virtually nothing had been done to strike at its causes or ameliorate its consequences, it could no longer be officially ignored. During the 1920's, there had probably been political virtue in ignoring the predicament of those who were hopelessly and permanently in want; now, with reinforcement from the Great Depression, it would be politically costly to do so. Poverty generally had long been considered a lamentable, although inevitable, deviation in mankind's upward march; now there was an impressive body of knowledge and experience about the "culture of poverty" which suggested that it was not inevitable, that it need not be self-perpetuating, and that it was amenable to amelioration and reform. Whether remedies would also be applied to the chronic poverty with which this study is concerned, only time would tell.

By the summer of 1932, therefore, there was a confluence of thought and experience about the causes and cures of rural poverty; ideas and their authors were waiting to be put to work. Of course, one stream that had already influenced farm policy was the idea of agriculture as business, in which the talisman was productive efficiency in an industrialized society, not some sentimental nostalgia

44. Clarence Poe, *Progressive Farmer*, Jan. 4, 1932, p. 4.
45. *New York Times*, Oct. 5, 1932.

for an idealized past. Farmers who were unable or unwilling to compete as businessmen should become the cheap labor required by large-scale commercial farmers, or they should leave the land. Those who could not remain productive on the land, as farm operators or as laborers, should be recognized for what they were—cases for social welfare assistance or charity, and not a part of the agricultural economy.

Another ideological stream was the idea of agriculture as a way of life, with faith resting on the trinity of agrarian tradition, folk sociology, and Christian love. Here it was believed that the marginal farmer—a victim of the industrial revolution in agriculture—should be spared the fate of his urban cousin. If necessary, traditional agrarian virtues should be preserved against the encroachments of industrialization and urbanization through organized political action and governmental power.

There was also a stream of thought, rooted in the earlier challenge to classical economic doctrine and nourished by the historical liberal reform tradition, which deprecated the classical faith in atomism and *laissez faire* and maintained that deliverance could be found only in some kind of collective state intervention. One interpretation of poverty explained the predicament of the pauper as the consequence of the fault in himself, and not in his stars; another implied that he was what society had made him.

Buried in the 1,541 pages of the report of Hoover's Committee on Social Trends was a pregnant query by Charles E. Merriam:[46]

> How shall we blend the skills of government, industrial and financial management, agriculture, labor and science in a new synthesis of authority, uniting power and responsibility, with a vivid appeal to the vital interest of the day, able to deal effectively with the revolutionary developments of our social, economic and scientific life, yet without stifling liberty, justice and progress?

This was both an admonition to the old order and a challenge to the new, and the squire of Hyde Park presumably had some answers.

46. *Recent Social Trends*, pp. 1540–41.

CHAPTER III

THE RESPONSE:
RELIEF, REHABILITATION,
AND REFORM

The country needs and, unless I mistake its temper, the country demands bold, persistent experimentation... take a method and try it: If it fails, admit it frankly and try another. But above all, try something. The millions who are in want will not stand by silently forever while the things to satisfy their needs are within easy reach.

FRANKLIN D. ROOSEVELT[1]
Campaign Address, 1932

According to purposive theory of organization, new administrative agencies of government come into existence to satisfy felt needs in society, but this complex natal process is neither automatic nor symmetrical. Despite the accumulation of much knowledge about the nature and causes of chronic rural poverty, and despite Franklin D. Roosevelt's experience in the rehabilitation of agriculture, as Governor of New York, the diagnosis was insufficiently clear in 1932 to support a detailed blueprint for federal action. Nevertheless, the election campaign of that year provided an opportunity to seek solutions, frame issues and programs, and win the power to act. Roosevelt did not delineate the New Deal while on the campaign trail,

1. F.D.R., *Public Papers* (1928-32), Vol. 1, p. 646.

but his rhetoric, strategy, and tactics did project the shape of things to come.[2]

From the start of the campaign, it was clear that the squire of Hyde Park intended to make chronic rural poverty one of the issues. As Governor of New York, he had recognized and acted upon the needs of impoverished people in the state, including very low-income farm families, and in 1932 he was prepared to exploit the situation. With Henry Morgenthau, Jr., a former student of George F. Warren at Cornell; Rexford G. Tugwell, the disciple of Simon Patten in Pennsylvania, and now the spokesman for a more comprehensive approach to agricultural reform; and Harry L. Hopkins, the harnessmaker's son from Sioux City, Iowa, and his state relief administrator in New York, generating ideas for him, it was natural to expect, during the summer and fall of 1932, that the marginal farmer would receive some attention.

Even before his nomination, Roosevelt promised, in a radio address in April, 1932, to build from the least to the greatest, "from the bottom up and not from the top down," and that he would remember "the forgotten man at the bottom of the economic pyramid." In his acceptance address to the Democratic National Convention on June 2, however, he recited the litany of the agriculturalists—efficiency in production, higher and more stable prices, improved markets at home and abroad, and avoidance of surpluses. At Topeka, Kansas, he pledged to fight for equality between agriculture and the rest of the economy, to strengthen the established machinery of the Department of Agriculture, and to promote a more rational and efficient use of the land. And at Springfield, Illinois, he promised to give farmers "fair prices" for their products and to reduce the burden of taxation and mortgage indebtedness. His program, he was careful to explain, had been formulated in cooperation with the "wisest leaders of agriculture."

---

2. Herbert A. Simon, Donald W. Smithburg, and Victor A. Thompson, *Public Administration* (New York: Knopf, 1954) pp. 25, 31.

In contemporary textbooks on public administration, the emphasis is on "response to social need," the "achievement of desired ends," and the "particular tasks to be accomplished." Goal theory is therefore central to the theory of modern public administration. See the following: Dwight Waldo, *The Study of Public Administration* (Garden City, N. Y.: Doubleday, 1955), pp. 6, 11; Marshall E. Dimock and Gladys O. Dimock, *Public Administration* (New York: Holt, Rinehart, and Winston, 1964), p. 22; John M. Pfiffner and R. Vance Presthus, *Public Administration* (New York: Ronald, 1953), p. 3; John D. Millett, "Working Concepts of Organization," in Fritz Morstein Marx, ed., *Elements of Public Administration* (New York: Prentice-Hall, 1946), p. 140.

Just as revealing of the future was Roosevelt's political style. J. T. Salter, with admiration for the Democratic candidate's apparent knowledge of people, has described "the Roosevelt smile and spiritual handclasp." Hopelessly impoverished low-income farmers, for instance, who could not possibly have comprehended Herbert Hoover's somber warnings about preserving constitutional government, sound administration, free enterprise, and rugged individualism, could readily have cheered Roosevelt, had they had radios or read newspapers, when he closed his campaign at New York's Madison Square Garden in November with the following declaration:

Our real enemies are hunger, want, insecurity, poverty and fear . . . . There is among you the man who has been brought up to believe that a livelihood could always be wrung from the soil by willing labor. You have broken your back in your efforts to make the soil produce. And when you have gathered your harvest you have found that harvest worthless.

Roosevelt's enemies called him a pied piper who outpromised his opponent and thus snared the hearts and minds of the electorate. Hoover called the Democratic candidate's promises "vote flypaper," and Republican Frederick M. Davenport of up-state New York, running for reelection to Congress, declared:

Democratic psychology in control of the national party this year is agitatory, superficial, demagogic, emotional, impulsive, bent on getting votes. Its success would be the millenium of the hill-billies, and not the sound sense of the . . . American people.

As far as agriculture was concerned, Roosevelt was more than vote hunting. Politically, he tried to touch all bases, or, in the words of James MacGregor Burns, "he knew how to pick up votes, how to capture group support, how to change pace and policy," but he was talking about matters with which he had a great deal of familiarity, and about which he had plans for action.

Democratic victory at the polls in November—control of both the White House and Congress, and electoral rout of the radical left—did not mean that the agrarian dissenters would long remain silent. The most militant of the agrarian groups, the Farm Holiday Association, convened in Des Moines, Iowa, a week after the inauguration and reiterated their demands—higher prices, moratoria on mortgage foreclosures, federal exercise of eminent domain in removing lands from the hands of insurance and mortgage companies and opening land to settlement, and broader control over the nation's monetary system. These demands were addressed, however, not to chronically impoverished farmers at the bottom of the heap, but rather to the credit and marketing needs of commercial farmers. The Holidayers pointedly warned the new regime in Washington that, unless Congress enacted adequate legislation by May 3, they would initiate a marketing strike.

Meanwhile, angry little bonfires of violence erupted in rural communities in the Middle West and the Great Plains. Local and state government relief agencies were beginning to close their doors, for lack of funds. Farmers forcibly attempted to prevent court foreclosures on bankrupt farms. In the towns and cities, banks were failing, hunger marchers were parading in the streets, and tension was mounting.[3]

First Things First: The AAA

High on Roosevelt's agenda for agricultural reform, when he entered the White House, was redemption of a pledge he reputedly had made to Edward A. O'Neal, president of the powerful American Farm Bureau Federation (AFBF), during the campaign. "One of the first things I am going to do," he promised, "is to take steps to restore farm prices. I am going to call farmers' leaders together, lock them in a room, and tell them not to come out until they have agreed on a plan." On March 10, only a few days after the inauguration, the President and his Secretary of Agriculture, Henry A. Wallace, invited about fifty farm organization leaders and rural editors to meet in Wallace's office and to discuss a program for the relief of agriculture.

---

3. For analysis of Franklin D. Roosevelt's record in the field of agricultural policy in New York State, see the following: Frank Freidel, *Franklin D. Roosevelt: The Triumph* (Boston: Little, Brown, 1956), pp. 13–15, 35–41, 62–63, 77–78, 95–97, 224–74, 342–50; and Daniel R. Fusfeld, *The Economic Thought of Franklin D. Roosevelt and the Origins of the New Deal* (New York: Columbia Univ. Press, 1956), Chap. IX.

F.D.R., *Public Papers* (1928–32), Vol. 1, pp. 625, 654–55, 697–705, 813, 862, 864; Rexford G. Tugwell, *The Democratic Roosevelt* (Garden City, N. Y.: Doubleday, 1957), p. 219; J. T. Salter, *The Pattern of Politics* (New York: Macmillan, 1940), p. 199; Thomas H. Reed, ed., *Government in a Depression* (Chicago: Univ. of Chicago Press, 1933), p. 3; William Starr Myers, ed., *The State Papers and Other Writings of Herbert Hoover* (Garden City, N. Y.: Doubleday, Doran, 1934), Vol. II, p. 351; James MacGregor Burns, *Roosevelt: The Lion and the Fox* (New York: Harcourt, Brace & World, 1956), p. 144; Theodore Saloutos and John D. Hicks, *Agricultural Discontent in the Middle West* (Madison: Univ. of Wisconsin Press, 1951), pp. 446–51; *New York Times*, Feb. 6, 12, 13, 1933.

Relief, Rehabilitation, and Reform / [51]

The outcome of these negotiations is now a well-told story, but it merits brief attention here for purposes of contrast with some of the other phases of the administration's response to the challenge of the times.

The lineage of the plan that emerged was many-branched—(1) the proposals of farm organization leaders, designed to raise farm commodity prices, and their disappointments suffered in behalf of the McNary-Haugen bill in the 1920's; (2) the interest in monetary reform and the idea of the "commodity dollar," conceived by Warren at Cornell University; (3) the production control ideas of William J. Spillman in the U.S. Department of Agriculture (USDA); (4) the so-called "domestic allotment plan," conceived and promoted by several agricultural, business, and academic leaders, including especially M. L. Wilson at Montana State College, Beardsley Ruml of the Laura Spelman Rockefeller Foundation, Henry I. Harriman of the U.S. Chamber of Commerce, George N. Peek of the Moline Plow Company, and Henry A. Wallace, then editor of *Wallace's Farmer*; and (5) futile legislative efforts, during the lame duck session of Congress in 1932–33, which had whetted the appetites of agricultural leaders. Through Tugwell's participation in the brain trust in Albany in 1932, Roosevelt was kept informed of the evolving ideas.[4]

Following the November victory, Tugwell, Wallace, Wilson, Morgenthau, Democratic congressional leaders, and the leaders of the farm organizations held a series of meetings in Chicago, Washington, and Warm Springs, Georgia, where the so-called "voluntary domestic allotment plan" was a key item on the agenda. The essence of the plan included provisions for a processing tax, formal contracts between the federal government and the producer, voluntary participa-

---

4. Clifford V. Gregory, "The American Farm Bureau Federation and the A.A.A.," *Annals of the American Academy of Political and Social Science*, Vol. CLXXIX (May, 1935), p. 152; Ernest K. Lindley, *The Roosevelt Revolution* (New York: Viking, 1933), pp. 27–28, 68–69, 96–100; Edward A. O'Neal, radio address, Mar. 30, 1933, quoted in Lawrence Sullivan, "Saving the Farmer," *American Mercury*, Vol. XXXI (Apr., 1934), pp. 457–58; Gilbert C. Fite, *George N. Peek and the Fight for Farm Parity* (Norman: Univ. of Oklahoma Press, 1954); Murray R. Benedict, *Farm Policies of the United States, 1790–1950* (New York: The Twentieth Century Fund, 1953), Chap. IV; Orville M. Kile, *The Farm Bureau Through Three Decades* (Baltimore: Waverly Press, 1948), Chap. XVI; Russell Lord, *The Wallaces of Iowa* (Boston: Houghton Mifflin, 1947), pp. 305–24; Arthur M. Schlesinger, Jr., *The Coming of the New Deal* (Boston: Houghton Mifflin, 1959), pp. 36–45; Tugwell, *The Democratic Roosevelt*, pp. 231–33, 275–77; William J. Spillman, *Balancing the Farm Output* (New York: Orange Judd, 1927); Edward A. O'Neal and M. L. Wilson, COHC; Tugwell to author, Mar. 2, 1967.

tion, and administrative decentralization. By the time of the March 10 meeting in Secretary Wallace's office, the groundwork for action had been completed. The conferees promptly reached agreement on a program, and on the following day a committee headed by Wallace presented the plan to the President.

A sidelight of the meeting of March 10, with portentous meaning for the future, was the attitude displayed by one of the key participants—O'Neal of the AFBF, the wielder of much influence with members of the so-called "farm bloc" in Congress, and himself an owner of a large plantation in Alabama. M. L. Wilson has recalled O'Neal's jubilation during their walk to Wallace's office on the morning of the meeting:[5]

> Edward O'Neal singled off and got alongside of me. His face was beaming, he was feeling good, and he said, "This is great. This is wonderful. You just watch me. We're going to come out all right with this new President. Yes sir!" He went on to say how good it was that Henry Wallace was Secretary [He had proposed Chester C. Davis for Secretary]. Then he said, "How well do you know this fellow Rex Tugwell?"

O'Neal, a consummate politician and not unmindful of the potential power that Tugwell might wield as a confidant of the President, listened to the Columbia University professor's holistic talk about the need for "fundamental reform," "readjustment of man-land relations," and "comprehensive economic and social planning" with some apprehension. It might be prudent, O'Neal believed, to keep an eye on this unconventional economist.

Wallace, working closely with Tugwell, who was now his Assistant Secretary of Agriculture; with Wilson, who had been persuaded to come to Washington to help in the effort, presumably as a prelude to his assignment to an important role in administering the new program; and with Mordecai Ezekiel, his chief economist who held a Ph.D. in economics from The Brookings Institution, and who had started to work in the USDA in 1922 and had served with Hoover's Farm Board from 1930 to 1933; promptly assembled a departmental group to draft a bill. Included in the group was Frederick P. Lee, a veteran agriculturalist who had served for many years as a bill draftsman and legislative counsel for the Senate, and who had assisted in drafting the McNary-Haugen bill.

By mid-March, Roosevelt had a draft in hand, and sent it to Congress with his personal acknowledgment that it represented a "new and untrod path." Despite some lack of enthusiasm among a few

---

5. Author's interview with M. L. Wilson.

members of the Democratic leadership in Congress, and charges from the left and the right that the bill would accomplish too little and too much, the bill won lop-sided victories in the House and Senate. On May 12 the President signed the Agricultural Adjustment Act of 1933 into law.[6]

In essence, the Act sought to secure "economic justice" for agriculture as a whole by promoting "parity prices," based on the idealized period of 1909–1914, through a system of benefit payments to farmers, financed by a tax on the processors of certain farm products. The Secretary of Agriculture was empowered to enter into marketing agreements with processors of food and fiber, with farmers' cooperative associations, and with others who handled farm commodities, in order to regulate trade practices, production quotas, prices, and supply areas. The Secretary would exercise control through a licensing system over processors and distributors. The voluntary nature of the program would presumably moderate its potentially coercive character, but the carrot did not entirely conceal the stick.

Passage of the Act represented a multiple victory—for the established leaders of agriculture, for the Democratic party, and for the nonpartisan agrarian alliance between the South and the Middle West. The measure also marked the consummation of unity among many professional agriculturalists who had long labored in vain to secure governmental assumption of responsibility for solving the problems of farm commodity price instability and surpluses. Their common backgrounds and their past association in battle encouraged among them a sense of group solidarity unlike the collaboration of convenience behind some of the other New Deal programs. These agriculturalists harbored some ideological anxieties about a program that would encourage farm prosperity through scarcity, but there seemed to be no viable alternatives. They also looked askance at some of the new young men who were coming to Washington to manage the New Deal. Consequently, the staffing of the new agency created by the Act became a subject of intense concern.[7]

---

6. Henry A. Wallace to Roosevelt, May 16, 1933, FDRL, PPF 471; Mordecai Ezekiel to O'Neal and Gregory, Mar. 7, 1933, NA, RG 16; author's interview with Paul H. Appleby; Tugwell to author, Mar. 2, 1967; F.D.R., *Public Papers* (1933), Vol. 2, pp. 74, 175–76; *Nation*, Vol. 136, Mar. 29, 1933, p. 329; Pub. Law No. 10, 73rd Cong., 1st Sess., 48 Stat. 31.

7. Christiana M. Campbell, *The Farm Bureau and the New Deal* (Urbana: Univ. of Illinois Press, 1962), p. 65, has reported that on the basis of a careful tally of congressional voting on the measure in 1933, the leaders of the AFBF concluded that passage had been facilitated by the nonpartisan alliance of the South and Midwest—the same axis on which the strength of the AFBF grew during the decade.

In staffing the Agricultural Adjustment Administration (AAA), conservatives and "sound men" won most of the top positions. George N. Peek, energetic businessman of conservative persuasion, protégé of Bernard Baruch, president of the Moline Plow Company, and a militant veteran of the McNary-Haugen wars, secured appointment as head of the agency, despite his well-known reservations about some features of the new Act and about the prospect of having to work with Wallace, Tugwell, and their young disciples in the USDA. Peek's appointment was justified by the Roosevelt administration on the grounds that it would confer upon the AAA greater political acceptance among some farmers, processors, and members of Congress who feared the planning and control provisions of the Act. It was also expected that Peek's aggressive energies and administrative competence would strengthen the new agency in its development.[8]

To be "co-administrator" of the AAA, Roosevelt and Wallace agreed on Charles J. Brand, veteran agriculturalist and expert on clover and alfalfa, cotton handling, and marketing problems, head of the National Fertilizer Association, and author of the first version of the McNary-Haugen bill. Chester C. Davis, executive president of the National Cornstalk Processes Company and the Maizewood Products Corporation, won the position of director of the important Production Division; and Wilson agreed to run the Wheat Division.

The liberals, however, were not entirely forgotten. Jerome N. Frank, a highly successful young corporation lawyer from Chicago and New York, a research scholar at Yale University Law School, and a man with a very perceptive mind and sharp pen, secured the strategic Office of General Counsel, and proceeded to build a staff of energetic young urban liberals whom Peek acidly described as "an entirely new species." There were also Thurman Arnold and Abe Fortas from the Yale University Law School Faculty; Alger Hiss, Lee Pressman, and Nathan Witt who came as young graduates from the Harvard University Law School; and John Abt and Adlai Stevenson came from Chicago.

The Office of Consumers' Counsel in the AAA, created in an effort to protect consumer interests from overzealous administration of the agency's programs, also provided a focus for liberal influence. The man selected to be the chief of the office was Frederic C. Howe, an Ohio attorney who had been a reform member of the Cleveland

8. Henry A. Wallace, *New Frontiers* (New York: Reynal and Hitchcock, 1934), p. 168.

City Council and the Ohio State Senate, Commissioner of Immigration for the Port of New York, a leader in many reform movements, and author of books on municipal reorganization, problems of monopoly, socialism in Germany, and other volumes that would have produced raised eyebrows in the straight-laced bureaucracy of the USDA.

Howe's deputy in the Office of Consumers' Counsel was Gardner "Pat" Jackson, a younger but more militant Quixote who claimed as friends some of the most influential liberals in Washington. "One never knew who to expect at Pat's parties," a friend once remarked. From his wealthy father, a large landholder and railroad tycoon in the West, Jackson had inherited a modest fortune, which he proceeded to invest in a chain of causes—the defense of Sacco and Vanzetti in Massachusetts and Tom Mooney in California during the 1920's, the bonus army during the early depression years, the promotion of interracial harmony in the South, and the organization of southern tenant farmers and sharecroppers. Later he was destined to support the loyalist cause in Spain, and, apocryphally, to fight Hitler by attempting to convert the kitchen help of the German Embassy in Washington against Naziism.

From the very beginning, the Consumers' Counsel was suspect by the more orthodox agriculturalists, and the unit never achieved lasting power or influence in the AAA. Howe and Jackson personally enjoyed rapport with most of the liberal movements and leaders in the country, and they never hesitated to mobilize them on behalf of some issue in the program. Jackson, in particular, claimed personal entree to Wallace and the President, and he would not be constrained by administrative hierarchies or organization charts. In the event of any conflict with their more conservative superiors in the AAA, Howe and Jackson believed they could count on their friends in the Wallace office and perhaps on Wallace personally.[9]

In the Secretary of Agriculture's office there was Paul H. Appleby, the son of a Congregational minister in Iowa. A classmate of Davis at Grinnell College, upon graduation he accepted Davis' invitation

---

9. Author's interview with Gardner Jackson; Harry L. Mitchell, COHC, pp. 76–78; Murray Kempton, *Part of Our Time* (New York: Simon and Schuster, 1955), Chap. 2.
A trail of correspondence from Jackson to the White House, on virtually every issue and problem of the day—not always related to Jackson's official duties at the time—runs through the manuscript files on agriculture and the USDA in the National Archives in Washington, D. C., and in the Roosevelt Library at Hyde Park.

to work with him on a newspaper in Montana. Appleby went on to become an editorial writer for the *Des Moines* (Ia.) *Register and Tribune*, and editor and publisher of his own farm journals in Montana, Iowa, and Virginia. He was an effective administrator and ardent New Dealer, and when Roosevelt selected Wallace as Secretary of Agriculture, some of Wallace's family friends, knowing of "Young Henry's" strengths and weaknesses, urged the new Secretary to take Paul Appleby along as his executive secretary. Appleby accepted the offer, presumably for only a year or two, but he was destined to remain for a decade.

Shortly after his arrival in Washington, Appleby secured a place on the Secretary's staff for a friend from Radford, Virginia—C. B. ("Beanie," for Benham) Baldwin. The son of a flour miller in Radford, Baldwin had been raised in a home in which Woodrow Wilson had been revered as a hero. He had studied at Virginia Polytechnic Institute, had worked in an administrative position for the Norfolk and Western Railroad, and then had gone into the electric supply business at Radford where he was later bankrupted by the depression. The invitation to join Wallace's staff gave him an exciting opportunity, he believed, to work with Appleby, to secure some financial security, and to put his administrative skills and militantly liberal ideas to work. "Beanie" Baldwin was destined to become one of the principal actors in the drama to come.

In the Secretary's office there was also Mordecai Ezekiel, the undoctrinaire economist who had participated in drafting the Agricultural Adjustment Act and who would serve for several years as Wallace's chief economist. There was Louis H. Bean, a Russian-born economist with a graduate degree from Harvard University, who had come to the Bureau of Agricultural Economics (BAE) in 1923, and was at this time Wallace's master statistician. Finally, there was Tugwell, the Assistant Secretary of Agriculture, and who was destined to move up within a year to the post of Under Secretary. Still close to the President, still harboring hopes that the New Deal would work for basic comprehensive reform of American institutions, Tugwell was expected by the liberals in the AAA to be their rock and redeemer.[10]

10. George N. Peek and Samuel Crowther, *Why Quit Our Own* (New York: D. Van Nostrand, 1936); Russell Lord, *The Agrarian Revival* (New York: American Association for Adult Education, 1939), pp. 155–57; Fite, *George N. Peek*, Chap. XV; Schlesinger, *Coming of the New Deal*, pp. 46–52; author's interviews with Wallace, Appleby, and C. B. Baldwin.

Like most large and complex administrative agencies of government, the agency's pattern of purpose embraced a set of diverse and, in some ways, contradictory organizational and personal goals. First of all, the Agricultural Adjustment Act was a double compromise— (1) between those who saw the AAA narrowly as an agency for the raising of farm commodity prices, and those who hoped that it could promote the more ambitious and controversial goal of reforming agriculture and removing the disparities of income among different classes of farmers; and (2) between those who believed in the "domestic allotment plan" idea, with its emphasis on crop restriction combined with provision for disposal of surpluses abroad, and those who basically opposed crop control and stressed the use of marketing agreements that would permit price increases to be passed along to consumers.

There were also personal incompatibilities and competing ambitions. Peek, a prima donna who had little faith in crop restriction and who tended to view the AAA narrowly as simply a device for raising farm crop prices, wanted to run the agency without intervention from Wallace and Tugwell. As a matter of fact, he had hoped to have the AAA created as an autonomous agency, outside of the USDA. Peek was also resentful toward Wallace personally, allegedly because "Young Henry" had won the cabinet post which he himself had coveted and which Bernard Baruch and others had attempted to persuade the President to grant. Toward Tugwell and the energetic young liberals around the iconoclastic professor, Peek and the conservative agriculturalists felt both fear and contempt.

Wallace, on the other hand—Appleby strongly favored this—realized the perils of administrative diffusion within a department so large, complex, and divided by regional, commodity, procedural, personal, and ideological differences, and sought to enhance the Secretary's power over the individual heads of agencies and bureaus. From the very beginning, Peek sought to escape the departmental harness.

Before the year was over, after only seven months, both Peek and Brand had departed. Disagreement with Wallace, Wilson, Ezekiel and others over their emphasis on production control; the persistence of Frank and his legal staff in attempting to use the AAA as an instrument for long-range social and economic reform; resentment over Frank's relations with Wallace and Tugwell, and Tugwell's alleged interest in ridding the agency of Peek—these were the major factors in Peek's decision to resign in December and to accept a face-saving appointment as special adviser to the President on foreign trade.

To replace Peek as administrator, Roosevelt and Wallace agreed upon Chester C. Davis—more pragmatic in his conservatism, more efficient as an administrator, a hard bargainer but one who understood the need for compromise, and a man in whom upward loyalty to the Secretary would be countered by an insistence on strict downward control over his subordinates. According to Gilbert Fite, the definitive historian of Peek's experience in the AAA, Peek offered some last-minute advice to his successor: "Get rid of Jerome Frank and the rest of that crowd as a condition to your acceptance." Davis, however, confidently believed that he would be able "to handle them."[11]

Despite these internal divisions and competing interpretations of institutional purpose, the AAA was successfully launched as a permanent agency of the USDA, and the pattern of its genesis bestowed upon it a large measure of political legitimacy that would buffer it from some of the shocks experienced by other agencies of the New Deal. The devotion of the AAA to the principle of "equality" for agriculture through price enhancement; its passage through the gantlet of extended deliberation, compromise, and concession; its assignment to "sound men" in whom the leaders of agriculture had trust; its devotion to the interests of a broad agricultural clientele, cutting across regional and commodity differences; and its role as the government's major instrument for fulfillment of the President's commitment to relieve agriculture—these were the features which sanctioned the AAA in both law and subjective attitudes.

First Things First: The FERA

"It had not been forgotten," Tugwell wrote in retrospect, "that the most pressing national business—even before recovery—was the relief of the unemployed." In a rapid-fire sequence of actions, Roosevelt and his congressional leaders proceeded to redeem their campaign pledge. On the day following his inauguration, he approved emergency grants of funds to the governors of seven states where the need seemed greatest. The next day he warned a conference of governors at the White House that if the states and localities failed to

---

11. Fite, *George N. Peek*, p. 266.

relieve the unemployed in the cities and on the farms, he would not hesitate to intervene. He also informed the assembled governors that he was formulating a national policy—the first in American history—to save farmers from foreclosure. On March 21, he sent an omnibus message to Congress requesting enactment of legislation providing for an Office of Federal Relief Administrator, a Civilian Conservation Corps to furnish constructive relief work for unemployed youths, and a program of work relief for cities and rural communities. In the Senate, Democrat Robert F. Wagner of New York promptly sponsored a so-called "Hunger Relief Bill," while Democrat David J. Lewis of Maryland introduced a companion measure in the House.[12]

Critical Republicans called the proposed program a violation of states' rights, a dole, a threat to the moral fiber of the American people, and unfair competition with private and local charity, but they could not impede the tide. Within ten days, the bill easily passed the Senate, and three weeks later, the companion measure hurdled the House by a vote of 326 to forty-two. Approved by the President on May 12, at the same time that he signed the Agricultural Adjustment Act, the new statute authorized the creation of the Federal Emergency Relief Administration (FERA) and an increase of half a billion dollars in Reconstruction Finance Corporation (RFC) funds, for direct relief grants to the states. It was provided that, as far as feasible, administration should be carried out through existing state and local agencies of government, and under rules to be formulated and prescribed by the Federal Relief Administrator.

The President then promptly appointed, as Administrator of the FERA, Harry L. Hopkins, a harnessmaker's son from Sioux City, Iowa. Hopkins had been a contemporary of Davis and Appleby at Grinnell College in Iowa. Upon graduation, he decided to go to New York City and launch a career in social welfare work, instead of accepting Davis' invitation to join him in newspaper work in Montana— Appleby went instead. Hopkins began with the Association for Improving Conditions of the Poor, and went on to serve with the Board of Child Welfare in New York, the American Red Cross in New Orleans, and the New York Tuberculosis Association. In 1931, he

---

12. Tugwell, *The Democratic Roosevelt*, p. 277; F.D.R. *Public Papers* (1933), Vol. 2, pp. 80–84.

The chroniclers of the New Deal have seen the AAA as the "characteristic instrumentality in agriculture," or the expression of the "hard side" of the New Deal. If there was a "hard side" and a "soft side" of the New Deal, then the FERA was an expression of the latter.

accepted Governor Roosevelt's offer to direct the New York State Temporary Emergency Relief Administration.[13]

With unprecedented imagination and vigor, Hopkins went to work as Federal Relief Administrator in May, 1933, and began to assemble a group of unorthodox and action-oriented men around him. Meanwhile, newspaper headlines, congressional hearings and debates, governmental and private reports, and a blizzard of letters to the President punctuated the pressure for urgent unemployment relief. During the summer of 1933, the leaders of the FERA conducted a special Unemployment Relief Census which revealed that approximately 15,150,000 persons—about 12 per cent of the entire population of the United States—were dependent to some degree on public relief funds. The number included more than one million farm families.[14]

In the beginning, the leaders of the FERA made no distinction between unemployed farmers and other idle needy people. As calls for help came from rural areas, Hopkins and his staff began to realize the need for greater ingenuity and specialization in their efforts to find meaningful constructive relief work for unemployed farmers. Raking leaves in a park was perhaps acceptable in the cities, but in the small towns and rural areas there must be a more productive way of putting unemployed farmers to work. Hopkins and some of his associates in the FERA may have had rural backgrounds, but they were not agriculturalists. They knew much about public welfare programs, but work relief for farmers called for a different approach. They needed ideas.

---

13. U.S. Congress, House, Committee on Banking and Currency, *Hearings on Unemployment Relief*, 73d Cong., 1st Sess. (Washington, D. C.: GPO, 1933), pp. 84–85; Federal Emergency Relief Act of 1933, Pub. Law 15, 73d Cong., 1st Sess.; F.D.R., *Public Papers* (1933), Vol. 2, pp. 183–85; Harry L. Hopkins, *Spending to Save* (New York: W. W. Norton, 1936); Edward A. Williams, *Federal Aid for Relief* (New York: Columbia Univ. Press, 1939); Frances Perkins, *The Roosevelt I Knew* (New York: Viking, 1946), pp. 182–91; Robert E. Sherwood, *Roosevelt and Hopkins* (New York: Harper, 1948), Chaps. 2, 3.

14. FERA, *Monthly Report of the Federal Emergency Relief Administration*, Sept. 1–30, 1933 (Washington, D. C.: GPO, 1933); FERA, *Unemployment Relief Census of 1933* (Washington, D. C.: GPO, 1934).

From the American Public Welfare Association, Hopkins borrowed, as a temporary consultant, Frank Bane, a Virginian who had once been director of public relief in Knoxville, Tennessee, a professor of sociology at the University of Virginia, and chairman of President Hoover's Emergency Employment Committee. As Bane's permanent successor, Hopkins appointed another southerner—Aubrey W. Williams, a native of Alabama and former executive director of the Wisconsin Conference of Social Work. From the Federal Employment Stability Board, he took Corrington Gill, an economist and statistician who had worked in a variety of capacities as independent researcher and consultant.

One of the precedents from which Hopkins might learn, paradoxically, came from Herbert Hoover himself. In 1927, while serving as President Coolidge's Secretary of Commerce, Hoover had attempted to rehabilitate farm families who had been flooded out along the lower Mississippi River. True to his faith in individualism, he secured one million dollars from the Rockefeller family, matched by an equal contribution from the affected communities, and with the help of the U.S. Chamber of Commerce he created a private non-profit organization to grant low-interest loans to stricken flood victims.[15]

A more relevant experiment, reminiscent of Wilson's Fairway Farms in Montana, was the work of Robert W. "Pete" Hudgens, who was destined to play an important role in our drama. He had grown up in Mountville, South Carolina, located in an impoverished Piedmont community. His stepfather managed a general merchandise store and therefore was familiar with the credit needs of southern tenant farmers and sharecroppers. When Hudgens was fifteen years old he went to study at The Citadel, and after graduation entered the army, where he eventually became an infantry captain. After an almost mortal wound during World War I, followed by three years of hospital convalescence, he married the daughter of a well-established investment broker in Greenville, South Carolina, and became a partner in the firm.

While serving as state Red Cross chairman in 1930, Hudgens found that unemployment was mounting in the cities and destitution was spreading on the farms, and he wondered whether idle land, money, and men might be fruitfully combined in a program for the rehabilitation of impoverished farmers. With a grant of five thousand dollars from the Red Cross, Hudgens assembled forty-two idle farm families in the Greenville area, resettled them individually on separate farms, and furnished them with credit and technical guidance. They were later absorbed by the South Carolina Rural Rehabilitation Corporation, and eventually more than half of them became successful owner-operators.[16]

Following the example of such experimental efforts, and understanding the need for a program that would reform as well as ameliorate, the President, at the urging of Hopkins, issued a press release

---

15. Herbert Hoover, *The Memoires of Herbert Hoover: The Cabinet and the Presidency, 1920–1933,* Vol. II (New York: Macmillan, 1952), p. 126.
16. Russell Lord and Paul H. Johnstone, eds., *A Place on Earth, A Critical Appraisal of Subsistence Homesteads* (Washington, D. C.: BAE, 1942) pp. 13–14; author's interview with Robert W. Hudgens; Hudgens, COHC.

at the end of February, 1934, announcing that the relief program would be specialized, to serve three categories of needy people— (1) distressed families in rural areas; (2) stranded populations, such as those families left helpless in one-industry towns where employers' doors had closed, probably forever; and (3) unemployed urban workers. For the latter, general economic revival and large-scale public works were the probable solutions, but for stranded populations, the method should be physical relocation. For idle farmers on the land, the expenditure of relief funds should be aimed at helping them to achieve self-support—"habilitation" for those who had never earned an adequate living and had always subsisted below the generally acceptable minimum level, and "rehabilitation" for those who had slipped down the agricultural ladder. The distinction between "habilitation" and "rehabilitation" was promptly lost in the rhetoric, however.[17]

Proceeding without delay, Hopkins appointed Colonel Lawrence Westbrook, relief administrator for Texas, to head a new unit in the FERA called the Division of Rural Rehabilitation and Stranded Populations, with responsibility for a program of rural rehabilitation. All direct relief activities and all programs of the Civil Works Administration conducted in rural areas were to be replaced on April 1, 1934, by a national program of rural rehabilitation. "The objective of this program," Hopkins declared, "is to make it possible for destitute persons eligible for relief in such areas to sustain themselves through their own efforts," and he emphasized that, "Our rural rehabilitation program is not predicated upon charity."

Late in June, Hopkins issued a policy statement that was destined to become the charter for all future rural rehabilitation activities. The goal of a particular project or program would be the promotion of self-support among destitute farm families, on a plane consistent with American standards, and preferably on the family's own farm. For those farmers already on productive land, rehabilitation would be administered "in place." For those families uprooted by drought, erosion, crop failure, foreclosure, or government purchase and retirement of submarginal lands, the FERA would provide rehabilitation "on the wing." A variety of specialized programs would be applied—financial credit, technical assistance and supervision, relocation, subsistence gardens, community farmsteads for urban families desiring to return to the land, and community work centers for

17. F.D.R., *Public Papers* (1934), Vol. 3, pp. 108–11.

farmers to supplement agriculture with part-time industrial activities.[18]

Conceived as a federal-state enterprise, this omnibus program was designed to be administered by agencies of the states, in accordance with national policies and standards formulated by the leaders of the FERA in Washington. The FERA would exercise its veto power through control of the purse strings. During the early months of the program, it was administered through the various state relief agencies. However, the temporary status of the state agencies and the limited powers of the FERA to purchase lands and to build houses for client families soon emphasized the need for improved organizational arrangements. Philip M. Glick, one of the young lawyers who had come to the USDA in 1933, suggested that state rural rehabilitation corporations should be created to handle the financial operations of the program. Hopkins readily approved the idea, and between June, 1934, and May, 1935, forty-nine of the corporations were established. They were governed by boards composed of regional directors of the FERA and the Land Policy Section of the AAA, state relief administrators and extension directors, and three private citizens selected by the ex officio members. Each state rehabilitation director served as the executive director of the corporation.

Within the Washington office of the FERA, Westbrook's Division was responsible for the formulation of general policies, promotion of state corporations, and review of state plans and budgets. During most of the first year, there were no more than sixteen staff members of the Division in Washington. For purposes of program administration, five regional FERA field representatives were appointed as liaison officers between Washington and the states. When the leaders of the AAA discovered the close relationships between the rural

18. Harry L. Hopkins, "Rural Program—Statement of Policy," Mar. 22, 1934, NA, RG 96; Hopkins, memorandum, published in *Rural Rehabilitation*, Vol. I, FERA, Processed (Nov. 15, 1934), p. 5; FERA, "Objectives and Suggested Procedure for Rural Rehabilitation," June 27, 1934, USDA Library; Larson, *Ten Years*, pp. 26–29; Paul K. Conkin, *Tomorrow a New World* (Ithaca, N. Y.: Cornell University Press, 1959), pp. 131–33.

The term "rehabilitation" was borrowed from the work of rehabilitating disabled veterans of World War I and other persons during the 1920's, in which the word referred to "the occupational re-establishment, with a view to complete or partial economic independence, of the physically handicapped and covers measures of every kind which tend to bring this about, whether they be therapeutic, psychological, educational, or socio-economic." Oscar M. Sullivan, "Rehabilitation," *Encyclopaedia of the Social Sciences*, Vol. 12 (New York: Macmillan, 1930), pp. 221–24.

rehabilitation program of the FERA and the established programs of the USDA, the state agricultural colleges, and the state extension services, they created a special section in the Program Planning Division of the AAA to help assure coordination. Extension service personnel from the states were given a central role in the coordinating machinery, and at state and county levels, citizen committees were established to advise on the rural rehabilitation program.

Funds for the rural rehabilitation program came from congressional appropriations for emergency relief. The FERA assigned money earmarked for rural rehabilitation to the state corporations, where it was disbursed in accordance with general policies prescribed by the Washington office of the FERA. By June, 1935, Hopkins had disbursed about fifty million dollars to the state corporations, most of which went in the form of loans to about half a million individual farmers. Some federal control over expenditures was secured through the power to withhold grants to the states, through the watchfulness of the Investigation Division in the Washington office, and other arrangements, but the essential characteristic of the system was its operational decentralization and the strategic role played by state officials.[19]

As the FERA evolved, three specialized programs developed. First, was the standard rural rehabilitation program, based on the idea of "supervised credit" for farmers already on productive land. The farmer was granted financial credit, but with strings attached—he was expected to operate in accordance with an approved farm and home budget, and to observe prescribed farm and home methods. Periodic supervision sought to assure compliance. Within a year, the program advanced almost forty-nine million dollars to farm families, nearly half of whom were in the South.[20]

19. Larson, *Ten Years*, pp. 30–33, 62–65; Philip M. Glick, "Memorandum on Federal Government Agencies Involved in Land Acquisition and Planning," NA, RG 68; Emergency Relief Appropriation Act of 1934, Pub. Law 93, 73d Cong., 2d Sess.; Emergency Appropriation Act for Fiscal Year 1935, Pub. Law 412, 73d Cong., 2d Sess.; Emergency Relief Appropriation Act of 1935, Pub. Law 11, 74th Cong., 1st Sess.; Executive Orders of the President 6442, 6603, 6689, 6709, 6735, 6747, 6910–B, 6952, 6983; FERA, *Monthly Report*, Aug. 1–31, 1935, pp. 19–20; FERA, *Final Statistical Report of the FERA* (Washington, D. C.: GPO, 1942), pp. 115–16; minutes of regional directors' conference, Resettlement Administration, Jan. 30, 1936, NA, RG 96; *Cooley Committee Hearings*, Pt. 2, p. 864; Williams, *Federal Aid for Relief*, p. 169.

20. Paul V. Maris, "Policy Interpretations," *Rural Rehabilitation*, Vol. 1 (Feb. 15, 1935), p. 13; FERA, *Monthly Report*, Aug. 1–31, 1935, p. 20; M. L. Wilson, COHC, Vol. 8, pp. 1367–73.

Second, there was the community program of the FERA, consisting of a variety of rural-industrial communities, intended for stranded populations, where part-time industrial employment was combined with subsistence farming. Representing the convergence of three streams of thought and practice—Jeffersonian reverence for the land, renewed interest in the back-to-the-land movement, and the growing interest in national planning—the program was a sharp departure from anything previously attempted by the federal government. Altogether, the community program accounted for less than half of the funds granted to state rural rehabilitation corporations. By June, 1935, the leaders of the FERA had planned or initiated ten communities in the South, eleven in Nebraska, Minnesota, and the Dakotas, one in New Mexico, and one in Arizona, designed to accommodate approximately 2,400 families at a cost of more than twenty-one million dollars.[21]

The third program, in which the FERA was only one of the agencies involved, was part of a larger movement to reform the land itself—the purchase of submarginal land and its retirement from production as a means of improving land use, conserving fertility and resources, raising the social and economic standards of chronically depressed rural areas, and helping to reduce crop surpluses. The program was designed to cope with an estimated 100 million acres of land in the United States believed to be submarginal—incapable of supporting a satisfactory level of living through farming.

Land reform had been one of Roosevelt's special interests during his governorship in Albany, and one of his campaign pledges in 1932. At the White House governors' conference two days after his inauguration, he was gratified to secure a promise of support for a plan to improve the use of land. During the months that followed, the President, assisted by Assistant Secretary of Agriculture Tugwell, Interior Secretary Harold L. Ickes, Agriculture Secretary Wallace, Farm Credit Administrator Morgenthau, Relief Administrator Hopkins, and others, reached agreement on a program. It would be designed by the Land Policy Section of the AAA, under Lewis C. Gray, and administered by the Land Program Section of the FERA, under John S. Lansill. During the brief period of participation by the FERA in the program—from June, 1934, to April, 1935—the Land Program Section operated in all but three states; it proposed for

21. Conkin, *Tomorrow a New World*, Chap. VI.

[66] / POVERTY and POLITICS

purchase more than eighteen million acres, and it granted final approval to eighty-two land improvement projects which involved more than five million acres of land at a total planned cost, for land improvement only, of more than twenty-five million dollars.[22]

Measured in terms of the scope of the land problem in the United States at the time, the program was modest, indeed, but in character it was one of the more truly reformative efforts of the New Deal. Not content with simply feeding the hungry, clothing the naked, and housing the homeless, the planners aimed at what they believed was the basic cause of chronic rural poverty—maladjustments in man-land relationships. Throughout rural America, they argued, the following condition prevailed:

> . . . an unwise use of land resources has led to the creation of "rural slums" where standards of living often parallel those of the urban slums, and where the deleterious effects of poverty, disease, and ignorance impose their handicap upon the surrounding community.

Poor land, they believed, made poor people, and poor people made poor land.[23]

This was risky talk, and in the enthusiasm of the hour the planners and administrators of the land program gave little thought to the challenge which their ambitious and unorthodox objectives presented to traditional values and beliefs in the United States—especially the principle of fee simple ownership of land, and the

---

22. Burton D. Seeley to C. C. Clayton, July 23, 1936; "Special Reports and Items on the Land Utilization Program," Vol. III; records of conferences of regional directors of the Land Utilization Program, BAE, Jan. 23, 1938; National Conference on Land Utilization, *Proceedings*, Chicago, Ill., Nov. 19–20, 1931, p. 126; John S. Lansill to Harold L. Ickes, July 16, 1934; NA, RG 114.

Also the following: Rexford G. Tugwell and Edward C. Banfield, "Governmental Planning at Mid-Century," *Journal of Politics*, Vol. XIII (May, 1951), p. 143; F.D.R., *Public Papers* (1928–32), Vol. 1, pp. 116–17; (1933), Vol. 2, pp. 23–34; (1935), Vol. 4, pp. 145–47, and his book, *Looking Forward* (New York: John Day, 1933); FERA, *Monthly Report*, Aug. 1–31, 1935, pp. 9–13; *New York Times*, Feb. 28, 1934.

The land program owed some of its inspiration to the work of Richard T. Ely, Simon N. Patten, John D. Black, M. L. Wilson, Lewis C. Gray, and others during the previous decade, but the major debt was to Roosevelt's program of retiring land from production during his governorship of New York. Starting with a pilot project in Tompkins County, his Temporary Emergency Relief Administration, by the spring of 1931, had relocated 244 families on improved land. In his last message to the New York State Assembly in 1932, Governor Roosevelt elaborated on his ideas about the need for retirement of submarginal land, relocation of low-income families, and restoration of "sociological balance" in the United States between urban and rural areas.

23. FERA, *Monthly Report*, Apr. 1–30, 1935, p. 10.

fear of large-scale government land ownership. Zoning, building codes, and land-use planning and control generally in the cities required long years of struggle against bitter political resistance before they were recognized as legitimate. Here, by administrative action rather than legislative deliberation, the leaders of the FERA were going far beyond their city cousins and were actually relocating people and even attempting to reform the people themselves. Only time would tell what the political consequences would be for the agency and for its leaders.

Rural rehabilitation, model communities, resettlement of people, and land-use planning—this was the repertory of the attack by the FERA upon chronic rural poverty. Despite the decentralized character of the program and the presumably rational objectives it embraced, the FERA had a more tenuous claim to political legitimacy than did the AAA. Devotion to the relief function, with its stigma of charity; the highly intimate character of the programs' intervention in the private affairs of client families; absence, in the genesis of the programs of the FERA, of the long participative process enjoyed by the AAA; the lack of a clear-cut congressional mandate comparable to that granted to the AAA and other major New Deal agencies; and the wide area of executive discretion enjoyed by the President—these were the features of the FERA which were destined to cause the agency to pay a heavy political price in the future.

The leaders of agriculture, business, industry, and the conservative press may have been absent at the birth of the FERA, but they did not remain disinterested very long. Almost immediately, a thunder of criticism developed. From the AFBF, for instance, came the charge that the FERA represented a "fast developing dole system which is being encouraged and demanded by communistic and socialistic influences," and the leaders of the organization warned that unless the agency were immediately stopped, it would "destroy American ideals and the self-respect of millions of our citizens." Similarly, the National Association of Manufacturers protested that the industrial projects of the FERA communities constituted "an extravagant use of taxpayers' money in further experimentation."

Opposition also came from within the New Deal family itself. Davis of the AAA, for instance, reflecting the anxieties among some agriculturalists who viewed the FERA as an interloper on USDA terrain, complained to Secretary Wallace that the leaders of the FERA were attempting to monopolize the land program and the relocation of displaced farm families. He argued that the FERA should not be permitted to build a large technical staff which would duplicate efforts and compete with the USDA.[24]

Had the FERA been assigned a more permanent function than emergency relief, and had it been established as a constituent agency of one of the major executive departments, its viability would probably have been enhanced. Under the circumstances, however, it had to be a temporary and independent agency—an administrative orphan, compelled to fend for itself.

Adventures in Utopia: Subsistence Homesteads

Franklin Roosevelt and the architects of the New Deal did not leave history as a weapon exclusively to the conservatives. With unemployment increasing in the cities and idleness growing on the farms, they exploited three historical streams of thought and practice —(1) the agrarian reverence for the land; (2) the nineteenth-century back-to-the-land movement; and (3) the line of communist and celibate communities that had played a significant and interesting role in American development, such as those of the Shakers and Rappites in New England and the Middle West, the Amana Villages of Iowa, the Mormon settlements in Utah, and the Greeley Colony in Colorado.[25]

---

24. F.D.R., *Public Papers* (1935), Vol. 4, p. 20; Harry L. Hopkins, "Hope for the Millions," *Today*, Vol. IV (May, 1935), pp. 3–4; resolutions adopted by the AFBF and the National Association of Manufacturers, reported in *New York Times*, Aug. 11, Oct. 8, 1934; Chester C. Davis to Wallace, Sept. 19, 1934, NA, RG 114.

25. Stimulated by fear of the burgeoning cities and by nostalgia for the presumed simplicity and security of rural life, the back-to-the-land movement had been advocated during the pre-New Deal years by such influential "dreamers" as Henry Ford, Bernard Baruch, Bernarr Macfadden, and Ralph Borsodi, and by the leaders of such organizations as the National Catholic Welfare Conference, the Catholic Rural Life Conference, the American Friends Service Committee, the Federal Council of Churches of Christ in America, and the Salvation Army. The movement ripened in 1932 when Republican Senator Charles L. McNary of Oregon and Democratic Representative Loring M. Black of Brooklyn, New York (of all places), united in introducing and promoting measures for the resettlement of stranded families. These measures were popularly known as the "Macfadden bills," after the publisher of *Liberty Magazine* and *New York Graphic*.

Ralph Borsodi, *This Ugly Civilization* (New York: Simon and Schuster, 1929), and *Flight From the City* (New York: Harper, 1933); Frederic C. Howe, *The Land and the Soldier* (New York: Scribner, 1919); Harold L. Ickes, *The Secret Diary of Harold L. Ickes*, Vol. I (New York: Simon and Schuster, 1953), pp.

In 1932, "colonization bills" were introduced in Congress, and there they met their deaths, but during the election campaign, M. L. Wilson took advantage of an opportunity, while discussing the "domestic allotment plan" with Governor Roosevelt in Albany, to raise the subject of what he called "subsistence homesteads." Although Roosevelt made no commitments on the matter during the campaign, he was interested, and after the November victory the President-Elect and his wife discussed Wilson's idea enthusiastically in private.[26]

Meanwhile, the idea of subsistence homesteads, based on individual farming rather than collective communities, found a friend in Democratic Senator John H. Bankhead, of Alabama. At the first session of the "Congress of 100 Days," in March, 1933, he introduced a bill in the Senate to provide $400 million "for the distribution of the overbalance of population in industrial centers by aiding in the purchase of subsistence farms." Committed to conservative Democratic Senator Ellison D. "Cotton Ed" Smith's strategic Senate Committee on Agriculture and Forestry—a "dim dungeon of silence," in the phrase of Woodrow Wilson—the bill was believed by everyone to have gone to its death there. It was never seen again alive.

A few weeks later, Mrs. Edith Lumsden, one of the lobbyists for similar legislation in the preceding Congress, persuaded Bankhead to try again, and she offered him her services in drafting a new proposal. On April 17, Bankhead dropped his second bill into the Senate hopper. It differed from the first in only two respects: it would authorize only $25 million instead of $400 million, and it called for "subsistence homesteads" instead of farms. This revised bill also went to a silent death in the Senate Committee on Banking and Currency.

Roosevelt, of course, followed Bankhead's efforts with interest, but he did not believe in placing all his eggs in one basket. On the same day that the Senator introduced his revised bill, the President wrote to insurgent Republican Senator George W. Norris of Nebraska:[27]

129, 152, 154, 159–60, 205–19, 227–32, 253–54; Lord and Johnstone, *A Place on Earth*, pp. 23–27; Clarence E. Pickett, *For More Than Bread* (Boston: Little, Brown, 1953); Eleanor Roosevelt, *This I Remember* (New York: Harper, 1949), pp. 126–33; Rev. Edgar Schmiedeler, "Rescuing Agriculture," *Commonweal*, Vol. 22 (May 17, 1935), pp. 69–71; M. L. Wilson, "The Place of Subsistence Homesteads in our National Economy," *Journal of Farm Economics*, Vol. XVI (Jan., 1934), pp. 73–87, and in COHC, Vol. 6, pp. 1081–97, and Vol. 7, pp. 1283–85; author's interview with Rev. John O'Grady.
26. Author's interview with Mrs. Eleanor Roosevelt.
27. Roosevelt to George W. Norris, Apr. 17, 1933, FDRL, OF 292.

I really would like to get one more bill which would allow us to spend $25 million this year to put 25,000 families on farms, at an average cost of $1,000 per family. It can be done. Also we would get most of the money back in due time. Will you talk this over with some of our fellow dreamers on the Hill?

In May, while the Senate Finance Committee was conducting hearings on the bill for the National Recovery Administration, Bankhead and Mrs. Lumsden conceived the idea that a foothold for subsistence homesteads might be secured in that measure. The Senator agreed to secure the President's personal intervention, and later he reported to M. L. Wilson his conversation at the White House:[28]

F.D.R. threw back his head, stretched out his hand saying, "I want to shake hands with a man who's got that much foresight and imagination.... That's just one of the most important things that can be done in that recovery program. I've thought about it two or three times, I've talked with Mrs. Roosevelt about it, and I have been intending to talk to somebody to see if we could get a little started at the time of the bill."

The President agreed to call Senator Pat Harrison, of Mississippi, chairman of the Senate Finance Committee, and to urge prompt Senate approval.

With very little discussion, the subsistence homesteads proposal was attached to the bill as Section 208. On July 13, the National Industrial Recovery Act won final congressional approval, and a few days later the President signed it. Section 208 gave him what he had asked for:[29]

To provide for aiding in the redistribution of the overbalance of population in industrial centers $25,000,000 is hereby made available to the President, to be used by him through such agencies as he may establish and under such regulations as he may make, for making loans and for otherwise aiding in the purchase of subsistence homesteads.

Roosevelt now had a free hand: the Act explicitly mentioned the need for rural-industrial balance, one of the President's pet notions at the time, and although it provided only $25 million for a beginning, it made no attempt to define the nature of the projects to be carried out or to specify any of the administrative details.

Dr. Arthur E. Morgan of the Tennessee Valley Authority wanted to administer the program, but in July, according to plan, Roosevelt assigned responsibility to Secretary of the Interior Ickes. At about

---

28. Author's interview with M. L. Wilson.
29. National Industrial Recovery Act, Pub. Law 67, 48 Stat. 195, 73d Cong., 1st Sess.; F.D.R., *Public Papers* (1933), Vol. 2, pp. 202–06.

the same time, the President called Secretary of Agriculture Wallace aside during a cabinet meeting and persuaded him to release M. L. Wilson from his post as head of the Wheat Section in the AAA, in order to direct the new program. Wilson had not been particularly happy in the AAA, and therefore welcomed the challenge and excitement promised by the new post. He held no illusions, however, about the difficulty of working under Ickes.

Late in the summer of 1933, Ickes created the Subsistence Homesteads Division in the Department of Interior and appointed Wilson as director. Wilson, in turn, appointed Clarence E. Pickett, a prominent Quaker social worker, to serve as his deputy. From North Carolina State College, he recruited Carl C. Taylor, a professor of rural sociology. For his public information officer he selected Roy F. Hendrickson, a newspaperman with an Iowa farm background. To fill the important post of regional director for the South, he persuaded Hudgens to take a leave of absence from his investment firm in Greenville, South Carolina, and to join the staff.

Advice for Wilson and Ickes on how to spend the money seemed to come from every direction. A sponsoring group calling itself the National Advisory Committee on Subsistence Homesteads was organized, and in September, on the initiative of Henry I. Harriman, president of the U.S. Chamber of Commerce, it held its first meeting, with Bankhead presiding over an astonishingly diverse group of people. They talked for two days, and then issued a list of recommendations calling for prompt action, a permanent program, more money, local administration, and assurance that technical advice and guidance would be provided for the homesteaders.[30]

30. The National Advisory Committee on Subsistence Homesteads held its first meeting on September 26, 1933. In addition to Wilson, Ickes, Tugwell, Bankhead, and Harriman, the participants were the following: John D. Black, the Harvard University economist; Louis Brownlow, the specialist in municipal administration; P. V. Carden of the Utah Agricultural Experiment Station; Ralph E. Flanders of Vermont, industrialist and future U.S. Senator; Clark Foreman, consultant to the Department of Interior on problems of the Negroes; William Green of the American Federation of Labor; Hayden B. Harris, the head of the Harris Trust and Savings Bank of Chicago; Meyer Jacobstein, labor economist, arbitrator, and political activist; William A. Julian, Treasurer of the United States; Bernarr Macfadden, high priest of the movement; Edward A. O'Neal, president of the AFBF; Rev. John A. Ryan of the National Catholic Welfare Conference; George Soule, editor of the *New Republic*, who had long been interested in opportunities for colonization in the South; Louis J. Taber, master of the National Grange; Bernard G. Waring, Philadelphia industrialist and leader of the American Friends Service Committee; Philip Weltner, chancellor of the Georgia University system.

Advice and intervention also came from the White House. Mrs. Eleanor Roosevelt, for instance, took special proprietary interest in the community planned for Reedsville, West Virginia, where she helped to decide the details of interior decoration for the homes. Louis McHenry Howe, Roosevelt's longtime confidant, also intervened from time to time, to the dismay and impatience of Ickes, and on one occasion the Secretary of the Interior and others reportedly were compelled to conduct a conference on the program around Howe's sickbed in the White House.

As Wilson and his staff struggled to translate the dream into reality, a flood of exotic proposals flowed in—communities for experiments in birth control, eugenics, aesthetic dancing, and revival of medieval craft guilds, and proposals for the use of Greek robes for rustic homesteaders. The author of the subsistence homesteads idea "did a good job if his idea was to create interest and excite imagination," wrote Pickett in retrospect. "Every kind of new idea concerning community life that had been brewing in the minds of people over the country found its way to the office of Dr. Wilson and myself."[31]

In February, 1934, Ickes reported that projects costing a total of $4 billion had been proposed, while Wilson estimated that more than $750 thousand in proposals had sufficient merit to warrant serious study and consideration. The Division finally agreed to concentrate on the following four kinds of communities: (1) for stranded industrial workers, (2) for subsistence farming combined with part-time decentralized industry, (3) garden homes for industrial workers on the boundaries of existing industrial centers, and (4) for stranded farm populations.[32]

In an effort to deflect charges of centralized paternalism, to escape expected bureaucratic delays in the regular departmental system, and to provide for local variations in the administration of the communities, Ickes acceded unhappily to Wilson's determined faith in "grass-roots democracy." Consequently, he set up a parent organization called the Federal Subsistence Homesteads Corporation, and subsidiary corporations—generally one for each project—to serve as the governing bodies of the communities. The Secretary of the In-

31. Ickes, *Diary*, Vol. I, p. 218; Pickett, *For More Than Bread*, pp. 48–49; Eleanor Roosevelt, *This I Remember*, pp. 126–33; author's interview with Mrs. Eleanor Roosevelt.
32. Wilson, "The Place of Subsistence Homesteads," pp. 73–84; Pickett, *For More Than Bread*, pp. 50–51; Lord and Johnstone, *A Place on Earth*, p. 41; Conkin, *Tomorrow a New World*, pp. 99–100, 107–16.

terior held the stock in the parent corporation and the leaders of the Subsistence Homesteads Division served as corporate officers. With considerable independence of the Secretary's Office, the Division acted as a staff agency to the parent corporation and to the subsidiaries.

Despite these formal efforts toward administrative decentralization, there was a gradual trend toward concentration of power in the Office of the Secretary and a restriction of the powers of the local corporations. In January, 1934, the President issued an executive order providing that the accounts of all government corporations, including the Federal Subsistence Homesteads Corporation and its subsidiaries, would be reviewed by the General Accounting Office, in accordance with standards and procedures prescribed by the Comptroller General.

To Wilson, this meant the beginning of the end for his experiment in grass-roots democracy. There followed a series of conflicts with the Secretary's Office over administrative procedures and by March, Ickes had had enough of "grass-roots democracy." He issued an order abolishing the subsidiary corporations and centralizing authority in his own hands. The parent corporation remained as a paper unit of the Subsistence Homesteads Division, while the Division itself was assigned responsibility for direction of the local projects through its field organization. In June, Wilson resigned to become Assistant Secretary of Agriculture when Tugwell became Under Secretary. A few months later, Taylor left to join the staff of the land program in the AAA and his departure was followed by an exodus of the original staff.

In the hands of the business manager, Charles Pynchon, the Subsistence Homesteads Division struggled to carry on under increasing difficulties. Factories failed to materialize in the communities, as private industry refused to locate in or near them. Organized business groups and members of Congress increased their opposition to what they believed was unfair and illegal government promotion of industrial activities in competition with private enterprise. Within the Department of Interior itself, the Solicitor issued an opinion that had the effect of eliminating as an objective the "redistribution of the overbalance of population in industrial centers" and forbidding full-time farming projects.[33]

33. Lord and Johnstone, *A Place on Earth*, pp. 49–51.

During the fall, Wallace, Tugwell, and Wilson discussed the wisdom of reshaping the program and having it transferred to the USDA, where it might be more adequately related to the submarginal land program. Wallace was a professional agriculturalist, with a deep respect for science and planning. Some of the activities of the Subsistence Homesteads Division seemed to violate both sets of principles, and the idea of a return to the land made little sense to him. He believed it was a mistake to combine land purchase and resettlement activities with rural housing and industrial projects for urban families on relief. Echoing Davis' criticism of the FERA in September, Wallace contended that the resettlement of farm families was properly an agricultural function and that it belonged in the USDA. Furthermore, Wallace privately believed that it was a mistake to assign such a creative program to Ickes.

Tugwell favored governmental planning, certain collectivist economic remedies, and community cooperation, but he too believed that many features of the program conflicted with the economic and political facts of life. Abolition of urban poverty would not be achieved through a return to the land by the outcasts of urban industrial society. Massive, well-planned government purchase of land, retirement of submarginal land, and resettlement of farm families seemed to be more desirable, feasible, and permanent solutions to the problem of rural poverty. A year earlier, he had described the subsistence homesteads program as an adventure in escapism. "I am inclined to believe," he declared, "that such settlements will function merely as small eddies of retreat for exceptional persons; and that the greater part of our population will prefer to live and work in the more active and vigorous main stream of a highly complex civilization." In agreement with Wallace, Tugwell believed that some kind of rural resettlement program might have a proper place in the USDA, but Roosevelt's faith in this approach, he believed, was a sentimental and impractical "echo of utopian notions out of the past."[34]

Toward the end of 1934, there was considerable talk at the White House about the inadequacies of the programs designed for chronically low-income farmers, and about the administrative conflicts and confusions involving the related programs of the AAA, the FERA, and the Subsistence Homesteads Division. One proposal was that the subsistence homesteads be transferred to the FERA under Hopkins, and one Sunday morning in November Ickes went to report to

---

34. Rexford G. Tugwell, *The Battle for Democracy* (New York: Columbia Univ. Press, 1935), p. 156, and *The Democratic Roosevelt*, p. 158.

the President on a trip he had just completed. Roosevelt took the occasion to tell Ickes about the idea of transferring the Division to the FERA. "I won't be at all put out if I lose Subsistence Homesteads," Ickes later wrote in his diary, "It has been nothing but a headache from the beginning."[35] Unable to persuade Hopkins to inherit the albatross, Roosevelt would not relieve Ickes of his burden for several more months.

Meanwhile, as the spring of 1935 arrived and it became apparent to the leaders of the Subsistence Homesteads Division that major administrative reorganization was imminent, they began to tally up their score. Altogether, the Division had planned or initiated thirty-four communities intended to accommodate 3,304 families, at an anticipated cost of more than $30 million. Approximately 700 homes had been completed and construction was underway on 1,369 others. Progress on most of the other projects, however, had gone no further than the purchase of land. Of the original $25 million appropriation, only $8 million had been expended.[36]

In two short years, the men of the Division had experienced almost every conceivable difficulty—legal entanglements, political attack, diffusion and confusion of responsibility, loss of leadership and direction, administrative delay, technical miscalculations, and worst of all, growing doubts about the desirability and feasibility of the program. Perhaps it was too early for final judgment, but there was already an impression among some of the program's leaders that what had started out as a millennial dream was turning into a political and administrative nightmare.

The Subsistence Homesteads Division thus approached its crucial spring of 1935 as a particularly unorthodox, politically embarrassing, and administratively unfeasible stepchild of the New Deal. Its purpose—promotion of collective communities—was exceedingly vulnerable to criticism. Despite the sponsorship of the program by Bankhead, an influential member of the "farm bloc" in the Senate, it had not won clear congressional sanction. Its funds had been secured as an afterthought by being grafted to an appropriation bill intended for very different emergency purposes. Most serious of all, the program had been launched without a clear design and with little understanding of the obstacles before it. "Brave new worlds are laid out on paper," it has been written, "with careful regard for the law of gravitation, the movements of the sun, and the prevailing winds, but

---

35. Ickes, *Diary*, Vol. I, p. 227.
36. Conkin, *Tomorrow a New World*, pp. 332–34.

with little regard for the complexities of political, economic, and social forces."[37]

The Shadow Falls: Institutional Conflict

From the very beginning, the AAA was a house divided in which competing interpretations of institutional purpose generated considerable internal tension. A major issue was the interpretation of the rules governing the making of marketing agreements with processors and distributors. The so-called "liberal faction," including Frank and his legal staff in the Office of the General Counsel, Howe and Jackson in the Office of Consumers' Counsel, and, presumably, Tugwell, viewed marketing agreements as devices to promote competition, improve trading practices, regulate processing methods, and distribute costs more fairly rather than pass them on to the consumer. The liberals sought to strengthen the government's power to inspect books and records of processors and distributors, and they resisted pressures upon and within the USDA for exemption of large food canners and meat packers from anti-trust regulations. This issue, it will be recalled, had been a factor in Peek's resignation in December, 1934, and it continued to plague his successor. Davis, with Wallace's acquiescence, vigorously opposed such a reform role for the AAA.

There was a second, and for our purposes more relevant, issue at stake—the distribution of AAA benefits between cotton landlords and their tenants. The liberals feared that crop restriction would encourage landlords either to anchor their tenants in place under onerous tenure terms or to drive unneeded tenants from their land. They were also apprehensive that reduction in acreage would reduce tenants' output more than enough to balance higher prices and benefit payments, and that landlords would divide the reduced acreage among fewer tenants. The liberals were familiar with the juggling methods sometimes employed by landlords and plantation owners in settling accounts with illiterate or inexperienced tenants and sharecroppers at the end of the crop year, and therefore they feared that benefit money would never trickle down. In other words, they wanted to make certain that farm tenants and sharecroppers would receive an equitable share of AAA benefits. They believed that the AAA represented an opportunity to promote land tenure im-

---

37. Herbert A. Simon, Donald W. Smithburg, and Victor A. Thompson, *Public Administration* (New York: Knopf, 1954), p. 438.

provement and to secure some substantial redistribution of income.

The conservatives in the AAA, on the other hand, were sympathetic toward the problems of the tenants and sharecroppers, but they too were fearful. They hoped to avoid discouraging landlords and plantation owners from enrolling in the program and they desperately wanted to escape the political perils involved in any attempt to interfere in the sensitive relations between southern landlords and their tenants and sharecroppers. The paramount goal of the AAA, the conservatives believed, should be crop restriction and price enhancement, not the equalizing of income, the promotion of equality of opportunity for tenants, nor the solving of all the South's ills.

During the first year of the AAA, evidence began to suggest that, at least in the cotton program, conservative goals were paramount. In April, 1929, the price of cotton had stood at eighteen cents per pound, and by April, 1933, immediately prior to passage of the Agricultural Adjustment Act, it had dropped to six cents. By April, 1934, the price rose to over eleven cents. One study at the time reported that as of July, 1934, cotton farmers had actually destroyed a potential crop of over four million bales on approximately ten million acres, but with the plight of cotton tenants and sharecroppers in mind, added a cautionary observation that, "The attainment of these objectives, however, does not mean that this program has been a success from the standpoint of national welfare."[38]

The AAA cotton contracts had included provisions to protect the rights of tenants and sharecroppers by requiring that the landlord or plantation owner should commit himself to reducing his production acreage in a manner that would create a minimum of labor, economic, and social dislocation, and that he would have to maintain on his farm or plantation the normal number of tenants and sharecroppers. The contracts also guaranteed the tenant and sharecropper certain rights, such as use of his house on the farm or plantation rent-free until the end of the 1935 crop year, access to woodlands for fuel, and use of adequate acreage to produce food for his family's subsistence. Adjustment and enforcement of the contract provisions were considered to be the responsibility of local AAA administrators, but in practice the landlords and owners were empowered to handle their own renters' problems.

38. Henry I. Richards, *Cotton Under the Agricultural Adjustment Administration* (Washington, D. C.: The Brookings Institution, 1936), Chaps. 7, 8, 9; David E. Conrad, *The Forgotten Farmers: The Story of Sharecroppers in the New Deal* (Urbana: Univ. of Illinois Press, 1965). The Conrad book is a detailed case study of the struggle within the AAA leading to the so-called "purge" of 1935.

Despite these formal precautions, some of the fears of the liberals in the AAA materialized during the first year. Many of the landlords, for instance, found that the most economical way for them to reduce cotton acreage by 40 per cent was to reduce the number of their tenants and sharecroppers by approximately that percentage. Furthermore, many landlords tried to coerce their renters into agreeing to arrangements that seemed to justify the fears of the liberal faction in the AAA.

In the country generally, tenants who paid their rent in cash were eligible to contract independently with the AAA and receive all of the benefit payments. In the South, however, where most of the renters were either tenants or sharecroppers, who furnished only their labor and received their payment in the form of a share of the crop, landlords contracted with the AAA directly and agreed to pass on a share of the benefits to their renters on the basis of the prevailing rental agreement. In many of the southern states, landlords refused to enroll in the program unless they were guaranteed a larger share of the benefits. The leaders of the AAA either would not or could not design a contract that would effectively guarantee the renters' portion of the federal money. Landlords in wheat, corn, and other crop areas also used this coercive weapon, but in the South, where tenants and sharecroppers were particularly docile and unaccustomed to demanding their rights, opportunities for exploitation were especially prevalent. It was found that acreage reduction payments failed to reach the small tenant farmer or sharecropper in any appreciable number.[39]

During the drought-ridden summer of 1934, protests began to rise throughout the South. One critic, Clarence Poe of the rural publication, *Progressive Farmer*, declared:[40]

The production control policies of the A.A.A. must be so shaped as to safeguard "the right of the little man to live." The small farmer who has only been growing enough cotton or tobacco to provide decent American standards of living for a family should not be required to reduce production of money crops to the same extent as big scale commercialized farms.

---

39. Edwin G. Nourse, Joseph S. Davis, and John D. Black, *Three Years of the Agricultural Adjustment Administration* (Washington, D. C.: The Brookings Institution, 1937), pp. 120, 324–53; Charles S. Johnson, Edwin R. Embree, and Will W. Alexander, *The Collapse of Cotton Tenancy* (Chapel Hill: Univ. of North Carolina Press, 1935); Thomas J. Woofter and Ellen B. Winston, *Seven Lean Years* (Chapel Hill: Univ. of North Carolina Press, 1939), pp. 71, 108.

40. Clarence Poe, *Progressive Farmer*, Aug., 1934, p. 26.

The issue, Poe believed, was more a matter of justice and the sharing of burdens than it was a question of administrative details. The predicament of the southern tenant and sharecropper under the AAA, he contended, was just another chapter in the long struggle between those who conceived of agriculture as a business and those who saw it as a way of life:

> These pathetically short-sighted doctrinaires think of the farm as having no value except to turn out low-priced food for the nation just as a steel mill has no function except to turn out low-priced steel . . . . "Efficiency" is their only god and their only standard of worth.

The Socialist leader, Norman Thomas, went South to see for himself, and later wrote that, "No satirist ever penned such an indictment of a cruel and lunatic order of society as was written by the author of the Agricultural Adjustment Act." He acknowledged that the AAA might be a "pillar under the New Deal," but he saw it as, "No foundation for a new world. It postpones and ultimately intensifies evils it does not solve."[41]

In response to this situation, as well as to strike at deeper causes, a group of tenant farmers and sharecroppers—white and Negro—assembled one night in July, 1934, at Tyronza, Arkansas, and organized the Southern Tenant Farmers Union (STFU). Their leader was Harry L. Mitchell. Inspired by his own father's fall from farm owner to tenant, by his boyhood memories of personal poverty, by his readings of Socialist literature, and by Norman Thomas' campaign speeches in the South in 1932, Mitchell believed that only by organized political action could the disadvantaged southern tenant and sharecropper ever achieve justice.

With the blessings of the liberals in the AAA, and with some of Jackson's money, Mitchell and his organizers worked to extend the union throughout the state of Arkansas, against the bitter resistance of landlords and public officials. Union organizers were threatened, arrested, and flogged in the night in traditional fashion. Some landlords attempted to prevent union meetings by padlocking the churches where they met and filling the schoolhouses with hay. Tenants who were active in union affairs were evicted by their landlords. Denied meeting places, the union convened in the open air and occasionally they were harassed by gunfire aimed over their heads. Unlike the violence of Milo Reno's Farm Holiday Movement

---

41. Norman Thomas, *The Choice Before Us* (New York: Macmillan, 1934), pp. 7, 101.

in the Great Plains, the STFU followed a strategy of passive resistance and resorted to the judicial process. Their defeat in the courts of Arkansas, where they tried to invoke section seven of the AAA cotton contract, to reverse eviction of twenty-seven tenants from a 5,000-acre plantation owned by a Kansas City lawyer, persuaded Mitchell and four of his union leaders to take their grievances to Washington.

Carrying a letter of introduction to Appleby from William R. Amberson, a classmate of Appleby and Davis at Grinnell College, Mitchell and his friends arrived unannounced at the office of the Secretary of Agriculture. Appleby greeted them and listened to their demands for an honest investigation of the problems of tenants and sharecroppers in the South, and then he persuaded Wallace to come out and talk with them for about a half hour. Wallace listened, and then told them: "You just go back and say to your members you saw Henry Wallace, and he told you that something was going to be done; that we are going to look into this matter and take action." Mitchell and his delegation returned disappointed, and called a mass meeting at Marked Tree, Arkansas, to report on their mission. When the union spokesman, Reverend E. B. McKinney, completed his speech, he was arrested for "anarchy, attempting to overthrow and usurp the Government of Arkansas, and blasphemy."[42]

Meanwhile, the AAA crop restriction program, the drought, and other more long-range factors continued to displace tenants and sharecroppers. By the thousands, stranded farm families poured onto the highways of the South where they camped along the roadsides or went on to join the swelling tide of "Okies" and "Arkies" heading for the promised land of California. In February, 1935, Walter White of the National Association for the Advancement of Colored People (NAACP) sent a desperate telegram to the White House, declaring that the AAA crop restriction program had already evicted more than 100,000 sharecroppers and tenants from their land and urging the President to intervene.[43]

Roosevelt, however, remained cautious in becoming personally involved in what amounted to a hot potato. There was no question about his sympathy for the displaced farm families, or about his intention to take positive action to ameliorate their predicament, but he believed he had to tread softly in any attempt to intervene in the

---

42. William R. Amberson, "The New Deal for Sharecroppers," *Nation*, Vol. CXL (Feb. 13, 1935), pp. 185–87; Howard Kester, *Revolt Among the Sharecroppers* (New York: Covici, Friede, 1936), pp. 53–69; Harry L. Mitchell, COHC, Pt. 1, pp. 1–38; author's interviews with Appleby and Wallace.

43. Roosevelt to Davis, Feb. 18, 1935, FDRL, OF 1650.

relationships between renters and their landlords. The fate of his overall program in Congress rested heavily on Senator Joseph T. Robinson of Little Rock, Arkansas, the Democratic majority leader, and on several other southern legislators who would be quick to react to any furor among the southern planters. Roosevelt knew that there was some dissatisfaction in his administration regarding the handling of the relief, rural rehabilitation, and resettlement programs, and that conversations were in progress among Wallace, Tugwell, Hopkins, and others regarding the desirability of some changes in both policy and administration of these programs. Dramatic intervention at this time, such as the rigid requirement that planters keep their tenants and sharecroppers on the land, or official support for the organizational efforts of the STFU would likely prove too costly in political capital.[44]

During the winter of 1934-35, the dissatisfaction of the liberals in the AAA continued to grow. After considerable negotiation between the Cotton Section, the Legal Division, and the Consumers' Counsel, the leaders of the AAA reached a compromise over the issue of renters' rights under the crop restriction program. Landlords contracting with the cotton program had to agree not to reduce the *number* of their tenants or sharecroppers; modification of this stipulation and local enforcement, however, would continue to be the responsibility of AAA field officials. In view of the local orientation of the field officials to southern values and beliefs, this compromise was hardly the ironclad protection that the more ardent liberals in the AAA had demanded.

Finally, a climax to the dispute came in February, 1935. With Davis on a field journey to the Middle West, with Tugwell in Florida, and with Victor Christgau, a former Farmer-Laborite congressman from Minnesota who sympathized with the liberals in the AAA serving as Acting Administrator, Frank seized the bull by the horns. He directed his legal staff to prepare a reinterpretation of the cotton agreement, and with Christgau's consent he issued a telegram to all state AAA offices in the South compelling all landlords and plantation owners to retain their renters, regardless of circumstances. The explosion in the South was immediate, and from the Middle West, Davis hurried back to Washington with an ultimatum for Wallace—the liberals had been conspiring against him and would have to go.

Davis argued that Frank's reinterpretation of the cotton agree-

---

44. Conrad, *The Forgotten Farmers*, Chap. 9; Davis to Thomas, Mar. 19, 1935; author's interviews with Mrs. Eleanor Roosevelt, Wallace, Appleby, and Tugwell.

ment would overturn the basis on which cotton contracts had been administered during the first year. If the contracts were to be construed in accordance with Frank's ruling, and if the USDA were to attempt to enforce such a reinterpretation, "Henry Wallace would have been forced out of the Cabinet within a month. The effects would have been revolutionary." Davis threatened to resign unless Wallace authorized him to request the resignations of Frank, Pressman, Shea, Howe, and Jackson. Had Appleby been working in the AAA instead of the Secretary's office, Davis later recalled, he would also have been proscribed.

What was Wallace to do? He had sympathies with both sides in the dispute, and he had been attempting, in his words, "to keep both teams in harness." With characteristic distaste for such internal conflict, he sought to avoid a disruptive confrontation between the right and the left, especially at this time and over this issue. However, he believed, the departure of the liberals from the AAA would not necessarily represent a victory for the conservatives, despite the clamor, to the contrary, that might be expected to erupt in the press. Frank, Pressman, Howe, Shea, and Jackson may have been the most visible and articulate members of the liberal faction in the Department, but they had not had time to entrench themselves very deeply in the AAA and in the Department, and, Wallace believed, their departure would not represent a serious blow to his effort to maintain balance within the AAA and the USDA.

Wallace therefore acquiesced in Davis' ultimatum. The next day, at a meeting of the Emergency Council at the White House, he reportedly informed President Roosevelt, who presumably had his mind on other matters, of his decision. He then returned to the Department and directed C. B. Baldwin to call in the press, who already had heard of the decision, and he invited Davis to make the announcement.

Sitting at his desk in the outer office, Baldwin was outraged, for he had been discreetly in sympathy with the liberals and their goals. He telephoned Tugwell in Florida, reported the happening, and announced that he was going to resign in protest. "Rex told me that I was young, that I should cool off, that the fight was only beginning, and that I should save myself for another day."[45]

45. Lord, *The Wallaces of Iowa*, pp. 393–409; William H. Riker, *The Firing of Pat Jackson*, case study prepared by the Inter-University Case Program (University, Ala.: Univ. of Alabama Press, 1951); Wilson, COHC, Vol. 9, pp. 1620–59; John B. Hutson, COHC, pp. 180–86; author's interviews with Wallace, Appleby, Jackson, Baldwin, Tugwell.

The fight that was just beginning has invariably been interpreted as an ideological contest between the liberals and conservatives within the AAA and within the USDA generally. To some extent it was such a contest, but the cleavage between the right and left did not explain everything. The AAA was not immune to the conflicts and frustrations that are implicit in large-scale institutional life. To borrow Bertram Gross' phrase, there was a "global matrix of purposes" in which were imbedded competing values, commitments, and organizational objectives. In retrospect, Appleby has suggested that the so-called "purge of 1935," like much of the combat in government generally, can be explained not entirely in ideological terms, not between those who were right and those who were wrong, nor between right and wrong facts, but rather between *different* bodies of fact and information which led naturally to competing conclusions and conflicting behaviors.

For Tugwell, on the other hand, the "purge of 1935" represented a serious defeat for himself and for the liberal cause in the USDA. He may have cautioned "Beanie" Baldwin to keep his powder dry, but he himself returned to Washington in anger, and went to the White House, prepared to tender his resignation to the President. The AAA, he believed, had been captured by the commercial farming interests and the food processors, and Wallace was becoming their pliant tool. Tugwell therefore believed that the time had come for him to leave the USDA and to go to the Department of the Interior where, Secretary Ickes had suggested, he should supervise an ambitious program of land reform and conservation. Roosevelt persuaded Tugwell to remain with Wallace, but as far as Tugwell himself was concerned, there was little hope at this time that his own brand of land reform could be realized within the USDA.[46]

The Logic of Events: A Time for Boldness

By the winter of 1934-35, it had become apparent to Tugwell and others that the establishment of an agency especially devoted to the problems of chronic rural poverty and to substantial land reform would be an exceptionally difficult and complex task requiring extraordinary political and administrative methods. After almost two

---

46. Ickes, *Diary*, pp. 250, 292, 302–3; Rexford G. Tugwell, *The Stricken Land* (Garden City, N. Y.: Doubleday, 1947), p. 24; Bernard Sternsher, *Rexford Tugwell and the New Deal* (New Brunswick, N. J.: Rutgers Univ. Press, 1964), pp. 204–05; author's interview with Tugwell.

years of experimentation, no adequate machinery had been developed to cope with the problems. The AAA had emerged as a reasonably effective instrument for promoting greater equality between agriculture and the rest of the economy—this had been the goal of the agriculturalists and this they were achieving, but at the cost of inequities *within*. The FERA had proven to be an innovative institution, but inadequate for the purpose of combatting rural poverty. And the Subsistence Homesteads Division was little more than an esoteric experiment. One fact was now clear—not one of these agencies offered any real promise of becoming an effective vehicle for a determined campaign against stagnant poverty on the farm.

Many mistakes had been made and inconsistencies had developed during the first eighteen months, but much had been learned about the causes and cures of chronic rural poverty and about the political and administrative resistances that would have to be overcome. Furthermore, of particular importance to Tugwell, at least the crust of custom was now cracked. Old doctrines had been challenged. The doors of the government were now open to men with bold new ideas. Innovative programs were being set in motion toward new horizons. Finally, expectations were rising among the impoverished and hitherto hopeless farm families themselves.

Seeing both peril and opportunity in the coming year, Tugwell believed that the time was ripe to take advantage of the logic of events. He therefore decided to assert bold leadership, and it is to his exercise of that leadership that we now turn.

CHAPTER IV

CREATIVE CRISIS:
THE RESETTLEMENT
ADMINISTRATION

It is precisely the function of the executive to facilitate the synthesis in concrete action of contradictory forces, instincts, conditions, positions, and ideals.
CHESTER I. BARNARD[1]
The Functions of the Executive

If ever there was a time for the leaders of the U.S. Department of Agriculture (USDA) to exercise the function of social consolidation, that time was the spring of 1935. Whether Rexford G. Tugwell and other New Dealers realized it at the time or not, they were faced with the fact that the Roosevelt administration reached a watershed in 1935. The rising hurricane being stirred on the flanks by Senator Huey Long, Father Charles Coughlin, Milo Reno, Dr. Francis Townsend and other demagogues of the right and left made it more difficult for Franklin D. Roosevelt to travel his middle course. Conservative members of Congress were beginning to escape the constraints of the depression's darker days. The congressional election of 1934 had strengthened the Democratic majority on Capitol Hill, giving Congress a more determined leftward cast and height-

---

1. Chester I. Barnard, *The Functions of the Executive* (Cambridge: Harvard Univ. Press, 1948), p. 21.

ening the likelihood of conflict with the conservatives in both parties. Despite the unprecedented experimentation, innovation, and expenditure of funds, the economic depression remained unsolved, and the hard core of farm poverty continued, relatively unassuaged. Especially for marginal farmers, there was the added impact of the drought which began to dispatch its ominous clouds of dust across the nation. Finally, there was transition in the regime in 1935—from the older, more ideological reformers to the new, younger, supposedly more hard-boiled tacticians; from the earlier crusading zeal of the so-called "First New Deal," to the more opportunistic concern with means rather than ends, with strategy and tactics; and from the early exuberance to somewhat more prudent experimentation and consolidation.[2]

Like the Agricultural Adjustment Administration (AAA) and other agricultural agencies, the USDA itself was a house divided by different and competing allegiances, ambitions, and interpretations of the Department's institutional purpose. There were agriculturalists, for instance, who persisted in viewing the USDA as the farmer's department, and the farmer they had in mind was not a chronically impoverished tenant, sharecropper, or migratory worker, but a commercial farmer who made a significant contribution to the nation's agricultural output. If they thought about chronic rural poverty at all, they tended to view it as a problem of productive efficiency and business management. They also tended to see some of the New Deal innovations as dangerous social tinkering.

On the other hand, there were those with a more sociological point of view—Henry A. Wallace, M. L. Wilson, Paul H. Appleby, Tugwell, and others—who saw the problem of chronic rural poverty in more organic terms, and who believed that the USDA should have concern, not only for the farmer's land, crops, machinery, cows, and chickens, but also for the farmer and his family. Yet, even among this latter group, there was no consensus about the alternative roads to farm security—large-scale land purchase and resettlement of people, liberalized credit for small farm operators and promotion of family farming, rural rehabilitation based on a coupling of economic reforms and social welfare services, ambitious reform of the political structure in rural communities, or the encouragement of marginal farmers to leave the land.

2. Arthur M. Schlesinger, Jr., *The Politics of Upheaval* (Boston: Houghton Mifflin, 1960), pp. 385–98; James MacGregor Burns, *Roosevelt: The Lion and the Fox* (New York: Harcourt, Brace & World, 1956), pp. 220–26.

From an institutional point of view, Appleby, in particular, saw the need for a strategy that would protect the USDA from domination by any particular geographical area, commodity interest, unduly narrow definition of clientele, professional point of view, or departmental agency or bureau. The function of the Secretary of Agriculture and his staff, he believed, was "to make a mesh of things," or, in the language of modern administrative theory, to create conditions within which the unifying purposes of the Department might adjust to new environmental circumstances and, at the same time, be made acceptable to the departmental members.

It was out of this contention between clashing doctrines, different and competing bodies of information, opposing institutional rules and ideologies, different interpretations of organizational purpose, and conflicting personalities and ambitions that emerged one of the distinctive agencies of the New Deal—the Resettlement Administration. Conceived in crisis, born without clearcut congressional sanction, nourished by the optimism and humanistic spirit of its leaders, and buffeted by the winds of a hostile climate, the agency and its evolution demonstrated the wisdom of Alfred North Whitehead's assertion that the "clash of doctrines is not a disaster—it is an opportunity."[3]

An Act of the President

Tugwell's critics may have disagreed about his ideological commitments, but on one point, at least, there was agreement—he was basically an iconoclast. Hostile to the traditional business outlook, with its tendency toward anarchy in the marketplace, he saw national salvation lying not simply in productive efficiency, technological innovation, and competition, but also in economic growth guided by public planning and control. Unimpressed by the shibboleths of conservative economics, he challenged some of the most sacred dogmas of the orthodox agrarians. For many farm people, he believed with feeling, rural life was bleak and irrational. The family farm, that pillar of the orthodox faith, may have been a beneficial institution for the more competent farmers with equity in substantial acreages and with able-bodied sons, but for the chronically insecure small farmer, it often became a trap. To Tugwell, there was

---

3. Alfred North Whitehead, *Science and the Modern World* (New York: Macmillan, 1925), p. 266.

no romance in agriculture and rural life, and in 1930 he painted the following picture:[4]

> A farm is an area of vicious, ill-tempered soil with a not very good house, inadequate barns, makeshift machinery, happenstance stock, tired, overworked men and women—and all the pests and bucolic plagues that nature has evolved. . . a place where ugly, brooding monotony, that haunts by day and night, unseats the mind.

The central purpose of agriculture in society, Tugwell believed, was the production of food and fiber. What was needed was a reorganization and reform of agriculture along industrial lines. Exhausted lands should be taken out of production, and fatigued farmers should either be relocated on more productive land or encouraged and helped to enter industry. Efforts to maintain marginal farmers on their submarginal lands was a waste of time and money. America, he believed, was an enormously large and innovative nation. Here was a rare opportunity for almost limitless experimentation in land-use planning, cooperative farming, community planning, massive retirement of land, and the restoration of life to exhausted people.

During the second half of 1934, Tugwell was becoming disillusioned with the New Deal. It was running off in too many irrelevant directions, he believed, and was falling prey to a false faith in the twin panaceas of business recovery and emergency relief. His private hope of reorganizing and shaking up the USDA had not materialized; as the whipping boy of the New Deal, he was being attacked more frequently; and he was becoming fearful that Roosevelt was paying too dear a price to special interests for their support of his overall program.

As Tugwell talked with Wallace, Appleby, Wilson and others, he came to the conclusion that his strategy should be geared to the following situation:

> 1. The congressional elections of 1934 indicated considerable Democratic strength in Congress and the country, but the "old dealers" were beginning to arise from their prostration, and, therefore, haste was necessary in trying to solve the socioeconomic problems before the institutional crusts hardened once again.
> 2. Administrative difficulties and inter-agency rivalries in the submarginal land program—so dear to his heart—suggested the need for some kind of program consolidation, administrative reorganization, and strengthening of leadership.

4. Rexford G. Tugwell, Thomas Munro, and Roy E. Stryker, *American Economic Life and the Means of its Improvement* (New York: Harcourt, Brace, 1930), pp. 85–90.

3. Rural rehabilitation, under proper arrangements, might have some merit, but it was a long-range purpose and should not be confused with Hopkins' emergency relief measures.
4. The Subsistence Homesteads Division did not offer an effective solution, and it was corrupting the idea of rural resettlement with its unfortunate emphasis on a back-to-the-land approach and its lamentable administration.
5. If he were ever going to stamp his brand upon the shape of things to come, he would have to operate from a more effective bureaucratic base than his current position as Under Secretary of Agriculture.

Wallace arrived at a similar interpretation of the situation. He realized the perils involved in any administrative reorganization—it was especially likely that Harry L. Hopkins would not relish losing the funds and personnel that were going toward rural rehabilitation under the FERA—but the arguments favoring consolidation seemed sound. Every day people were reminding the leaders of the USDA that the AAA was penalizing the marginal or low-income farmer, and that the Department had an obligation to serve the meek as well as the mighty. There was increasing talk, especially in the South, of a farmers' march on Washington, and that the USDA had better be prepared. There was also the danger that discontent among low-income farmers might feed the attack on the New Deal from such demagogues on the left flank as Huey Long, who was trying to exploit rural discontent in extending his influence beyond the state of Louisiana.

Wallace realized that the new Congress convening in January, 1935, would be heavily Democratic, but as the legislators began their work, it became apparent that the Roosevelt administration's ambitious plans for social security, holding-company regulation, banking reform, labor legislation, and other key measures were headed for rough seas. Wallace was also aware that the "old dealers" among the Republicans and Democrats were sharpening their knives. "With the old crowd shouting the same cries and whimpering the same old incantations," he warned, "it seems to me that the faster the showdown comes, the more definite the division between the old dealers and the new dealers of both great present parties, the better."

Meanwhile, at the White House, the President was not unmindful of the criticism from planners, economists, and others who decried the New Deal for its improvisation, political expediency, and seeming lack of coherent direction. "Mr. Roosevelt's 'New Deal,' admirable though it is in some respects," charged the economist Sumner Slichter during the congressional campaign of 1934, "has yielded disappointing results precisely because it represents, not an integrated program, but a series of self-defeating attempts to convey favors on too many special groups."5

To Roosevelt, however, the choice was not between integrated institutional reform and acquiescence to special interests. Forever the masterful improviser, he sought to blend principle with practicality. In some program areas, a large measure of consistency might be desirable and possible; in others, a price might have to be paid in deference to special demands. Programs to raise the level of living and security for special groups might violate certain principles of economics, but consistency might also be measured in terms of long-range political strategy. Appleby later echoed this argument when he suggested that "the governmental doing of inconsistent things in balanced responses to inconsistent demands" is a proper governmental function in the search for consent and agreement.

The President was no worshipper of consistency, but he did agree that programs for low-income farmers were becoming too highly dispersed, that greater administrative coherence was necessary if there were going to be significant progress, and that such provocative goals as land-use planning, resettlement, and rural rehabilitation would need a strong bureaucratic base. This was more than simply a concern with administrative efficiency and symmetry. Roosevelt was also responding politically to the crescendo of cries for help from desperate farm families. Some came from educated and articulate people; others were from people who were hardly literate; but they all expressed the hope and the expectation that the government would somehow rescue them.

Roosevelt also knew that some members of Congress, with help and encouragement from a group of southern agrarians, social scientists, and amateur agitators and lobbyists, had been working on special proposals to help impoverished farm tenants and sharecroppers, and that bills were going to be introduced in the current session of Congress. The creation of a separate agency, within which all

---

5. Rexford G. Tugwell, *The Battle for Democracy* (New York: Columbia Univ. Press, 1935), pp. 14, 39–40, 108–10, 156–57, 178, 194–96, 206–07, 239–40, 260, 266–67, 305–06, 309–11, and "National Significance of Recent Trends in Farm Population," *Social Forces*, Vol. 14 (Oct., 1935), pp. 1–7; M. L. Wilson, COHC, Vol. 8, pp. 1406–07, Vol. 9, pp. 1613–17; Will W. Alexander, COHC, pp. 400–01; Henry A. Wallace, address, reported in *New York Times*, Aug. 19, 1934, and published in his book, *Democracy Reborn*, Russell Lord, ed. (New York: Reynal and Hitchcock, 1944), p. 84; Sumner Slichter, *Towards Stability* (New York: Holt, 1934), p. 185.

existing activities concerned with the problems of chronically impoverished farm families would be consolidated, seemed to offer several advantages—it would dramatize the Roosevelt administration's current efforts and the need for permanent legislative authorization; it would strengthen the President's hand in his forthcoming struggle with Congress over other New Deal programs; it would help to improve his posture in preparation for the re-election campaign of 1936; and a separate agency would likely be free to make a more rapid start on new programs.[6]

Tugwell would be a natural leader for such a new agency, since he had the vision and the determination that would be called for, and from a personal point of view, he was ready for a change—he was unhappy in his anomalous position as Under Secretary of Agriculture, and was impatient for an opportunity to apply some of his reform ideas.

There was consensus among all those concerned that the creation of such an agency, outside of the USDA, would probably free the proposed agency from the bureaucratic snares of an old-line executive department, where ossified administrative procedures, preoccupation with the commercial farmer and his problems of price and production, and entrenched conservatism would probably stifle the energy and imagination needed for launching bold new programs. With Tugwell serving in a dual capacity as both Under Secretary of Agriculture and as administrator of his own agency, some measure of coordination with the main stream of agricultural policy might be assured. Meanwhile, the USDA would have time to re-examine its own position, and perhaps find a place in its structure for the new agency at some time in the future.

During the month of March, 1935, Congress was deliberating over the new emergency relief appropriation, when it was proposed that the rural rehabilitation program, as developed by the Federal Emergency Relief Administration (FERA) under Hopkins, was sufficiently advanced and recognized to be specifically financed by Congress through the new appropriation act. At the written request of the chairman of the Senate Appropriations Committee, the acting Comptroller General submitted a list of projects or activities which he believed could lawfully be carried out with funds allotted for "rural rehabilitation and relief in stricken areas." They included the furnishing of subsistence goods and services for both the farm and home; acquisition of land for rehabilitation purposes; technical advice and

---

6. Paul H. Appleby, *Morality and Administration in Democratic Government* (Baton Rouge: Louisiana State Univ. Press, 1952), p. 35.

supervision; construction of homes, barns, and other improvements; rehabilitation and resettlement of stranded populations in rural areas; direct relief to needy rural families; and the purchasing, processing, and distributing of livestock.

Congress was agreeable, and as finally enacted, the Emergency Relief Appropriation Act of 1935 specified "rural rehabilitation and relief in stricken agricultural areas" as among the authorized purposes for which relief funds might be expended. Section 1 of the Act included the following paragraph, which served as the only basis of a definite congressional mandate:[7]

Funds made available by this joint resolution may be used, in the discretion of the President, for the purpose of making loans to finance, in whole or in part, the purchase of farm lands and necessary equipment by farmers, farm tenants, croppers, or farm laborers. Such loans shall be made on such terms as the President shall prescribe and shall be repaid in equal installments, or in such manner as the President may determine.

There were no restrictions regarding the income status of eligible borrowers or the organizational and procedural forms to be employed. To strict constructionists, this was hardly a sound statutory basis for the establishment of a large bureaucratic enterprise, but to Tugwell and his assistants it represented a green light.

By the end of March, the die was cast. Early in April, the President signed the Act, and on the last day of the month he issued Executive Order 7027, establishing an agency to be known as the Resettlement Administration. The order designated Tugwell as Administrator, and specified three basic areas of activity: (1) a land-use program; (2) resettlement of destitute low-income families from rural and urban areas, and the construction of model communities in suburban areas; and (3) a program of rural rehabilitation loans and grants to help small farmers purchase land and necessary equipment and livestock. Roosevelt authorized an initial allocation of $250,000 to launch the new agency, and in subsequent actions he transferred to the Resettlement Administration the rural rehabilitation and land-use programs of the FERA, the programs and projects of the Subsistence Homesteads Division, the land-use planning program of the AAA, and the farm debt adjustment program that had been financed by the FERA and managed by the Farm Credit Administration (FCA).[8]

---

7. Emergency Relief Appropriation Act of 1935, 49 Stat. 115; Monroe Oppenheimer, "The Development of the Rural Rehabilitation Loan Program," *Law and Contemporary Problems*, Vol. IV (Oct., 1937), pp. 478–79.

8. Executive Orders of the President numbers 7027, 7028, 7041, 7143, 7200; F.D.R. *Public Papers* (1935), Vol. 4, pp. 143–56.

The Resettlement Administration / [93]

The Resettlement Administration may have incorporated in its name Tugwell's main concern with land planning and resettlement of people, but the new agency actually inherited an astonishing diversity of projects, programs, and problems:

    Rural and urban resettlement projects
    Suburban community projects
    Migrant labor camps
    Loans and grants to purchase land and to help equip farmers
    Farm debt adjustment
    Soil erosion
    Stream pollution
    Seacoast erosion
    Forestation and reforestation

There were challenges and opportunities in this cluster of assignments, but the overall mission of the new agency—what Bertram M. Gross has called the "pattern of purposes"—did not represent the coherent and rational set of objectives that Tugwell had originally conceived. With some disappointment, he described his new responsibilities as "everybody else's headaches." To compound the difficulties, the agency would also have to fight emergency brush fires resulting from drought and depression. There was an impression around Washington at the time that no one but Tugwell would have had the courage or foolhardiness to assume such a burden. In retrospect, the creation of the Resettlement Administration demonstrated that there is virtue in not knowing that certain things are impossible.

Proceeding on the assumption that the Resettlement Administration was going to be a permanent agency, Tugwell and his assistants created an elaborate structure, consisting eventually of fifteen coordinate divisions: (1) the Division of Land Utilization, to which was assigned responsibility for planning and execution of a program of submarginal land retirement and improvement; (2) the Rural Resettlement Division, with responsibility for both the resettlement program, including the communities initiated by the Subsistence Homesteads Division, and the rural rehabilitation program and projects inherited from the FERA; (3) the Division of Suburban Resettlement, which was assigned responsibility for a special program of model communities on the peripheries of selected cities; and (4) twelve separate divisions for technical and managerial functions.

During the first year, there were many organizational changes in this structure, the most important of which was the creation of a separate Rural Rehabilitation Division in the Washington office and with twelve regional headquarters offices. An important innovation, with prophetic meaning for the future, was the establishment of a separate section in the Rural Rehabilitation Division to administer a special "farm tenant security program," consisting of loans and technical guidance to 1,000 selected farm tenants in ten southern states, who were desirous of becoming farm owners, and helping them to become established on improved and productive family-sized farms.

One of the most important policy decisions was the determination to build a centralized and unified administrative structure running from Washington to the rural communities. In sharp contrast to the FERA and the Subsistence Homesteads Division, the Resettlement Administration was going to be a truly *national* agency. The leaders therefore divided the country into twelve regions, with a regional office in each to which power and responsibility would be delegated. Smaller offices were established in the states, in districts within the states, and in the counties.

The leaders of the agency decided that, at least in the beginning, the rural rehabilitation program would be administered through the state rural rehabilitation corporations, which had been inherited from the FERA. The Comptroller General, however, informally advised Tugwell that the provisions of the Emergency Relief Appropriation Act of 1935 did not empower the Resettlement Administration to grant funds to the state corporations, so it was decided that the states should transfer the assets of the corporations to the Resettlement Administration, where they were to be held in trust and to be expended under separate accounting procedures. Meanwhile, Tugwell hastened to complete the organization and staffing of the agency as soon as possible, and within a year it flowered into a full-fledged institution, comparable in scope, power, resources, and complexity to some of the major federal establishments.[9]

The Prophets Assemble

Paraphrasing Ralph Waldo Emerson, the Resettlement Administration was the shadow of a man cast large. By the spring of 1935, Tugwell, in more than seven books, seventy published articles,

9. RA, Administrative Order 2, Rev. 1, Dec. 9, 1935; RA, *First Annual Report* (Washington, D. C.: GPO, 1936); Tugwell to Lewis C. Gray, Nov. 14, 1935, and to Division Directors and Section Chiefs, RA, June 11, 1935, NA, RG 96.

twenty-six published addresses, and a variety of syndicated columns, letters to editors, lectures, and interviews had proclaimed, like a prophet of old, his vision of the future. He was not only the prime mover in the actual establishment of the agency, but he also breathed into it his prophetic vision and zeal. With great wonderment, for instance, a personnel analyst of the U.S. Civil Service Commission in 1936, presumably unaccustomed to such a performance, described what he had found in a routine personnel audit of the Resettlement Administration:[10]

At its head stands a visionary administrator with a pot of gold at his feet, looking across a mist-darkened valley to a rainbow-crowned mountain ... the rainbow of a new era is clearly apparent now, but will it remain there when the mountain is scaled? The Administrator is not interested in the transmutation of baser materials into gold and silver but in the transformation of gold and silver into material things that will bring supermaterial benefits to underprivileged classes throughout the nation.

The executive order of April 30, 1935, was only the first step in the journey across the mist-darkened valley to the rainbow-crowned mountain. Subsequent orders transferred the functions, paraphernalia, and some of the people with the various programs that were consolidated. Despite the pressure for haste, however, there was no mass transfer of personnel. Since none of the employees enjoyed civil service protection, Tugwell was free to pick and choose. This would be a relatively easy task for appointments to the Washington office, but for key positions in the regional, state, district and county offices he knew that there would be stubborn political constraints.

To serve as Deputy Administrator, Tugwell selected not an agriculturalist to help him run this basically agricultural agency, but rather Will W. Alexander—son of an Ozark farmer in southern Missouri, holder of a divinity degree from Vanderbilt University, former Methodist minister in Tennessee, president of Dillard University in New Orleans and associated with several other Negro educational institutions, and veteran of a quarter of a century as leader of the interracial movement in Atlanta, Georgia. "Dr. Will," as his friends and associates affectionately called him, had become interested in the predicament of the southern tenant farmer and sharecropper, and, as we shall see in chapter five, had been working for several months

10. John A. Overholt, "Report and Recommendations of Key Positions in the Resettlement Administration," MS (Apr. 29, 1936), p. 19, CBBP. For a catalogue of virtually everything that Tugwell has written, see Bernard Sternsher, *Rexford Tugwell and the New Deal* (New Brunswick, N. J.: Rutgers Univ. Press, 1964), pp. 413–24.

in 1934 and 1935 with a group promoting remedial legislation in Congress. Alexander was thoroughly experienced in interracial work at the community level, but as far as national politics and large-scale public administration were concerned, he was an amateur. He had made many friends through the years in educational and public service circles in the South, and his efforts on behalf of racial equality had earned him many enemies as well as friends—the epithet "Nigger Lover" he well knew.

From Secretary Wallace's office, Tugwell recruited C. B. ("Beanie" for Benham) Baldwin to be an Assistant Administrator, with special responsibility for program operations. As we have already seen, Baldwin had been brought to Washington in 1933 by Appleby, who had published a rural journal in Radford, Virginia, and there had befriended the Virginian. In the backwoods environment of Radford, a community of about 5,000 people, Baldwin had been dazzled by Appleby's knowledge. "Paul opened my eyes to a world I never knew existed," he later confessed. Thus, Baldwin became Appleby's friend and admirer.

He was the son of a flour miller in Radford and the grandson of a southern liberal who had privately believed that it was probably a good thing that the North had won the Civil War. Raised in a family that had welcomed Woodrow Wilson's New Freedom, Baldwin was taught to hate the machine politics of Virginia and the caste system he saw imposed on the Negroes of the South. He went off to Virginia Polytechnic Institute to study business administration, but before winning his degree he returned to Radford to marry his childhood sweetheart. For a while he worked unhappily at an administrative job with the Norfolk and Western Railroad, and then went into the electric supply business in Radford, only to be overwhelmed by the depression. The invitation to join Wallace's staff in 1933, as we have seen, represented a welcome escape as well as an opportunity.

By the spring of 1935, Baldwin had accumulated more than two years of experience with Appleby on the Secretary's staff, where he had proven himself to be an exceptionally competent administrator, with considerable political acumen and resourcefulness. On more than one occasion, he had demonstrated his loyalty to Tugwell.

To be a second Assistant Administrator, with special responsibility for the Land Utilization Division, Tugwell appointed Dr. Lewis C. Gray, an *eminence grise* among land planners in the United States— a disciple of Richard T. Ely and Henry C. Taylor, a former chief of the Bureau of Agriculture Economics (BAE), and a pioneer in the land-use planning movement. Gray lamented the neglect of interest in the social costs of unguided land development and unrestricted private exploitation of the nation's natural resources. With Tugwell, he agreed that "either some economic opportunity must be brought to these poverty-stricken rural areas, or the people must be offered the chance of moving to a place where opportunity now exists." When the Land Policy Section of the AAA was transferred to the Resettlement Administration, Gray went along and took with him some of the personnel who had worked with the BAE.

To be a third Assistant Administrator, and to direct the Rural Resettlement Division, Tugwell considered Colonel Lawrence Westbrook, who had headed the Rural Rehabilitation Division of the FERA, but Westbrook insisted on a free hand in running his program, so Tugwell appointed instead Carl C. Taylor, the rural sociologist who had worked with Wilson in the Subsistence Homesteads Division and had then gone to the Land Policy Section of the AAA.

For the fourth Assistant Administrator, with responsibility for managing the completed resettlement communities, Tugwell appointed Eugene E. Agger, a friend and fellow professor of economics at Columbia University. To be still another Assistant Administrator, responsible for the surburban resettlement program, John S. Lansill was appointed. To head the rural rehabilitation program, first as a subdivision of the Rural Resettlement Division, and later as a separate Rural Rehabilitation Division, Tugwell selected Joseph L. Dailey, a lawyer and judge from New Mexico. To direct the Labor Relations Division, Tugwell appointed George S. Mitchell, a Rhodes Scholar from Virginia who had taught economics with Tugwell at Columbia University, and who, with his more militant brother Broadus Mitchell, came from a distinguished old southern family. For General Counsel and head of the Legal Division, Tugwell appointed Lee Pressman, one of the lawyers in the AAA who, with Jerome Frank and others, had been a victim of the so-called "purge of 1935."

To be an assistant to Taylor in the Rural Resettlement Division (and later to become a director of the rural rehabilitation program), Tugwell approved the transfer of Paul V. Maris, one of the very few professional agriculturalists in the top management levels of the Resettlement Administration. Maris was a graduate of agriculture at the University of Missouri, a former county agricultural agent in Oregon, a founder of the first State Farm Bureau Federation in the United States, and a director of the Oregon State Extension Service.

Westbrook had persuaded Maris to join the Rural Rehabilitation Division in the FERA, where he had been the innovator of many rural rehabilitation techniques.

For the managerial positions on his Washington staff, Tugwell collected a very diverse and unorthodox group of people. As his Executive Assistant and confidante, he appointed Miss Grace E. Falke, a young woman in her twenties who had worked as his secretary at Columbia University and who had remained with him in Washington. She was also to become deeply involved in labor problems, research assignments, public information tasks, and administrative procedures. To direct the Information Division, Tugwell brought with him from the Under Secretary's Office John Franklin Carter, the newspaper columnist who wrote under the name of Jay Franklin or "The Unofficial Observer."

Tugwell also surrounded himself with several special assistants drawn from academic and political circles, one of whom was Thomas C. Blaisdell, an economist who had served as Assistant Consumers' Counsel in the AAA and as an economic consultant to the National Emergency Council. Another special assistant was Brooks Hays of Little Rock, Arkansas, a prominent southern liberal, unsuccessful Democratic candidate for governor of his state at the age of twenty-nine, Democratic national committeeman from Arkansas, lay leader of the Southern Baptist Convention, and a man who had ambitions for a seat in Congress. Hays' tasks would include congressional relations and special political assignments in the South.

In his top-level Washington appointments, Tugwell had a free hand in choosing people he believed would be competent, loyal, and compatible. In the selection of more subordinate personnel, especially for field assignments, the task was considerably more difficult. The summer of 1935 was a particularly job-hungry period, and it was clear to most political people that the Resettlement Administration was going to become a major federal establishment and an important dispenser of patronage in many states. State party organizations could be expected to press their demands.

Tugwell was privately contemptuous of practical politicians, but he was realist enough to know that he would have to defer to state party leaders and to members of Congress. For the more subordinate or routine appointments, he voluntarily agreed to conform to a clearance procedure that Baldwin, Appleby, and James A. Farley, chairman of the Democratic National Committee, had worked out and had persuaded Wallace to accept for the USDA in 1933. Wallace therefore appointed Julian N. Friant as special assistant to handle the recruitment of personnel for positions not covered by civil service protection. Friant then established a system of close collaboration with Farley and the staff of the U.S. Civil Service Commission, in which the USDA would defer to patronage considerations *providing* politically endorsed candidates for specific positions could pass the tests of proficiency. In other words, when two qualified candidates sought the same position, the USDA would accept the candidate who enjoyed the Democratic party's blessing. Friant's office proved to be a boon to the harassed administrators of the Resettlement Administration during the first weeks and months.

Since time was precious, Tugwell and his assistants were compelled to transfer many of the staff members from predecessor agencies, especially in the field, but they screened as many as possible. To the surprise of the Civil Service Commission and other agencies in Washington, the leaders of the Resettlement Administration requested the assistance of the Commission in screening candidates and in classifying positions, despite the fact that none of the positions were covered by the civil service laws. In cases of doubt, transferred personnel were accepted on temporary appointments. These precautions proved particularly valuable in the case of the people transferred from the various state corporations, many of whom were basically antagonistic toward some of the new agency's goals and methods. Others were tainted with extremist affiliations, or were simply political hacks. Illustratively, on one occasion, Tugwell secured the help of Wallace's office in checking on the alleged Farm Holiday connections of the director of farm debt adjustment work in Iowa, who was about to be transferred from the FCA.[11]

The leaders of the Resettlement Administration were particularly careful in their appointments of state directors. Although the focus of field operations was going to be in the regional headquarters, presumably buffered from special state partisan pressures, it was expected that state Democratic party organizations would be sensitive

11. C. B. Baldwin to Tugwell, Apr. 26, 1935, CBBP; Wilma Dykeman and James Stokely, *Seeds of Southern Change: The Life of Will Alexander* (Chicago. Univ. of Chicago Press, 1962), pp. 3–17; Gray, "Land Utilization, Explanation of the Program," FDRL, PPF 1820; "Unofficial Observer," *The New Dealers* (New York: Literary Guild, 1934); RA, minutes of regional directors' conference, June 19, 1935, NA, RG 96. Appleby to Julian Friant, May 17, 1935; Appleby to Baldwin, June 20, 1935; Wilson to W. E. Joseph, June 25, 1935; Appleby to Morris Sheppard, Aug. 20, 1935; James D. LeCron to Donald R. Murphy, Oct. 17, 1935; NA, RG 16. Author's interviews with Alexander, Brooks Hays.

to state appointments, irrespective of the particular powers that these state officers might exercise in the agency's programs.

The selection of a state director for Louisiana was illustrative. By 1935, relations between Huey Long's forces and the Roosevelt administration had reached open warfare, and to neutralize the Resettlement Administration in the struggle, Roosevelt and Tugwell sought an appropriate strategy. Actually, Long had no reason to oppose the agency for its own sake. His primary concern at the time was the role that the Resettlement Administration might play, wittingly or otherwise, in his struggle with his own political enemies, especially with the anti-Long members of the Louisiana congressional delegation. He was therefore particularly sensitive to any federal appointments in his state that might tip the scales against him in the struggle. The anti-Long members of Congress, on the other hand, expected that the federal appointment of anyone not a Long man would be a victory for them. Any state director of the Resettlement Administration in Louisiana, therefore, would face a dilemma.

Shortly after Taylor was appointed director of the Rural Resettlement Division, he called Robert W. Hudgens, the Greenville, South Carolina, investment banker and rural rehabilitation innovator whom we have already met, and invited him to Washington to talk with Tugwell and Alexander about whether he would be interested in serving as state director in Louisiana. Hudgens was not enthusiastic about becoming a sacrificial lamb, but Tugwell and Alexander were greatly impressed with his achievements in South Carolina and his sophisticated understanding of the Louisiana situation. Besides, they especially liked the idea of sending a South Carolinian into Louisiana, who could stand up against the Senator, if necessary, without fear of political reprisal, instead of attempting to find someone for the job from Long's own state.

Tugwell and Alexander persuaded Hudgens to accept the appointment, and then invited the anti-Long Congressmen in and introduced Hudgens as the President's man for state director—he would be neither Long's man nor theirs. Tugwell next sent George M. Reynolds, who had prepared a doctoral dissertation in political science at Columbia University on machine politics in New Orleans, to talk with Long and to assure him that Hudgens and the Resettlement Administration would be strictly neutral in Long's personal political struggles.

Long, in turn, promised that the Resettlement Administration would have no trouble with him, just so long as it avoided his enemies. With about 400 jobs to dispense, Hudgens knew that he would be choice prey for both sides, but he was going to take the Senator at his word, and he was determined to remain neutral. He rode off to New Orleans in a mood of cautious optimism.

Almost immediately upon his arrival, the anti-Long forces invited him to a meeting to discuss not only patronage, but, to Hudgens' dismay, their plans to promote the candidacy of an opponent to run against Long for the Senate, and they wanted Hudgens to pledge his support. The gentleman from South Carolina adamantly insisted that he was in Louisiana to run the Resettlement Administration—no more, no less.

"My God!" Hudgens has recalled one congressman having exclaimed, "Here he sits with the most powerful patronage weapon in Louisiana, and he's not going to do a Goddam thing about it."

Long soon heard about the meeting and warned Hudgens that the only thing that he was concerned about was helping the needy farmers of Louisiana, and that as long as Hudgens avoided the anti-Long forces, the Resettlement Administration had nothing to fear from him. "The first time I catch you appointing somebody because one of these sons of bitches tell you to," he warned, "I'll drive you out of Louisiana." That was the last Hudgens ever heard from Long, and a few months later an assassin's bullet removed the stormy Senator from the scene.[12]

Louisiana was not the only state in which the Resettlement Administration had to face the perils of patronage. In Raleigh, North Carolina; Montgomery, Alabama; Little Rock, Arkansas; Amarillo, Texas; Lincoln, Nebraska—wherever the Resettlement Administration established a regional, state, or county office the patronage brokers were active. Sometimes, the motive was explained as merely precautionary, as in the case of Democratic Senator James E. Murray of Montana, who ostensibly wanted only to be certain that merit would prevail in appointments.

There was also the case of Senator Hugo L. Black of Alabama, the future Justice of the U.S. Supreme Court, who took no part in the patronage process, but insisted on being informed of all appointments in his state so that he could send letters of congratulations to

12. George M. Reynolds, *Machine Politics in New Orleans, 1897–1926* (New York: Columbia Univ. Press, 1936); V. O. Key, *Southern Politics in State and Nation* (New York: Knopf, 1949), pp. 156–82; Allan P. Sindler, *Huey Long's Louisiana* (Baltimore: Johns Hopkins Press, 1956), pp. 85–87; Robert W. Hudgens, COHC, pp. 154–71; Alexander, COHC, pp. 518–20; author's interviews with Appleby, Baldwin, Alexander, Hudgens, Carl C. Taylor.

appointees, thereby giving them the impression that he had been responsible for their good fortune.

One of the most difficult states was Tennessee, where Senator Kenneth D. McKellar had an insatiable appetite for patronage. It was satisfactory to him for the Resettlement Administration to furnish relief to Democrats, Republicans, Communists, or members of any other political party or persuasion, he warned Tugwell, "but those engaged in administering relief under a Democratic administration, especially those in key positions, should be Democrats." And in Tennessee that meant the Crump machine.[13]

The Resettlement Administration also became the target of impatient demands for emergency action to cope with the human costs of the depression, the crop restriction program, and natural catastrophe. From newspaper editors, special interest groups, and members of Congress and state governors of both parties came urgent pleas. Laurence I. Hewes, Jr., one of the enthusiastic young assistants in Tugwell's office, whose task it was to help process these demands, later described the situation as follows:[14]

> For months we had no regular life; we ate and slept as we could. Office hours were a bedlam of telephones, visitors, hourly crises; evenings and weekends were devoted to accumulated paper work spewed forth by our infantile field organization. We held fingers in dikes of improvisation against bureaucratic tidal waves; rushed firemanlike from one catastrophic threat to another; frantically recruited unknowns, then flung them unprepared into well-paid positions . . . . Cash grants were poured into the parched northern and southern Great Plains; ill-nourished, apathetic sharecroppers and cotton tenants from the Atlantic seaboard to Texas began to eat regularly; food and medical care went to thousands of wandering families in Arizona and California. But Tugwell took no pride in conducting a first-aid program; our real job was to cure the deeper malady.

Although Appleby was not directly involved in the administration of the Resettlement Administration, which was an independent agency outside of the USDA, his position in Wallace's office, Tug-

---

13. Kenneth D. McKellar to Tugwell, May (n.d.), 1936, FDRL, OF 1568–Misc.; Hugh Peterson to Franklin D. Roosevelt, Aug. 26, 1935, FDRL, OF 1650. Charles M. Martin to Wallace, July 1, 1935; John M. Costello to Appleby, June 28, 1935; Alfonso Valdes, Antonio Reyes, and Rafael R. Zayes to USDA, May 3, 1935; Malcolm C. Tarver to Tugwell, Apr. 26, 1935; James E. Murray to Wilson, Aug. 20, 1935; Alf Landon to Wallace, Sept. 16, 1935; NA, RG 16. Carl Vinson to W. A. Hartman, Sept. 17, 1935; Vinson to R. L. Vansant, July 9, 1935; NA, RG 96.

14. Laurence I. Hewes, Jr., *Boxcar in the Sand* (New York: Knopf, 1957), p. 219.

well's dual role as Under Secretary of Agriculture, and Appleby's personal sympathy with the agency's work inevitably immersed him in some of its problems. As impatience grew in some of the stricken areas with the alleged slowness of the Resettlement Administration in meeting these urgent demands, Appleby worked patiently to placate farm organization leaders, members of Congress, state governors, and visiting delegations of farmers. A heated accusation of "red tape" came from the director of regional planning in Madison, Wisconsin, and provoked Appleby to the following response, which was illustrative of countless others:[15]

> While I resent many things that come under the general description of red tape, it is my observation that 99 percent of the attack on red tape—including that which comes from well informed people experienced in other large administrative fields—is not well-founded. . . . The best functioning parts of the Governmental machine are those that have been slowly built. It takes years to build a large organization in a way that will permit . . . a minimum of friction and something approaching a maximum of production. This administration has seen the establishment of a considerable number of large new agencies. It cannot be expected that these agencies can be assimilated and coordinated with other agencies . . . until time has perfected the set-up. Nevertheless, some of these new agencies have done rather unbelievable jobs.

In spite of these urgencies—perhaps because of them—the leaders of the Resettlement Administration succeeded in establishing the agency and building its staff in an extraordinarily short time. It started out on May 1, 1935, with only twelve employees. By the end of the year it employed 16,386 people—3,524 in the Washington office and 12,862 scattered around the country. Approximately 4,200 of them came from nine different agencies. In seven months they had built a major federal agency which, in terms of size, scope, and cost, was rivaled only by the Veterans' Administration and the Departments of Treasury, War, Post Office, Navy, Interior, and Agriculture. There remained the task of completing the conversion of the organization into a viable institution.

Evolution of Purpose: Resettlement to Rehabilitation

Reflecting the malleable and complex character of the pattern of organizational purpose, as discussed in the introductory chapter of this narrative, the purpose of the Resettlement Administration was

15. Appleby to M. W. Torkelson, Sept. 19, 1935, NA, RG 16.

neither simple, self-revealing, nor static. The Emergency Relief Appropriation Act of 1935 specifically referred to "rural rehabilitation and relief in stricken areas" as authorized purposes, but the President's executive order creating the agency made no mention whatever of these purposes in its delineation of the functions and duties to be performed. The omission of "rural rehabilitation" as a specific purpose was a reflection of impatience to escape from connotations of emergency relief. Wallace and Tugwell in particular believed that the new agency should address more fundamental and long-range causes of rural poverty.

Although Wallace had no official responsibility for the Resettlement Administration at the time, he had participated in negotiations leading to its establishment. Furthermore, as Secretary of Agriculture he had a special interest in its relationship to overall agricultural policy. For some time prior to the spring of 1935, he had fretted about what he believed was a tendency for the rural rehabilitation program of the FERA to serve as little more than a stopgap relief operation. On the evening before the President issued his executive order, Wallace explicitly urged that the rural rehabilitation concept be broadened to include more than emergency relief, and that it be extended to include farmers above the relief level. He prophetically warned that continued emphasis on rehabilitation of the most needy farm families would eventually doom the nascent agency.[16]

Tugwell's approach to the major purpose of the Resettlement Administration was based on what he believed were the overriding facts of rural poverty. In 1930, there had been more than 100 million acres of land in cultivation that were judged by land-use planners as unsuitable for normal farming methods. Living on these lands were more than 650,000 farm families in a condition of permanent poverty. On top of this stark situation, the economic collapse during the early 1930's had impoverished an additional one million farm families. A large proportion of these people in need were victims of the long-range causes of the agricultural depression that had persisted for over a decade. Rural rehabilitation techniques and resettlement projects might ease the immediate burdens of these people and, if applied for a sufficiently long period of time, might help them to become self-sufficient. However, there was no substitute for fundamental reform of the land itself.

Tugwell believed that he who controls the land has leverage over

---

16. Wallace to Ellison D. Smith, Apr. 29, 1935, NA, RG 46.

the lives of the people upon it, and without such control, rehabilitation and resettlement would be unable to achieve basic reforms. He therefore determined that the central purpose of the Resettlement Administration would be land reform. The immediate goal would be the purchase of approximately ten million acres of substandard land, conversion of it to more appropriate uses, and resettlement of approximately 20,000 farm families who were expected to be uprooted. This land program, he believed, would also serve subsidiary purposes, such as classification of land and water resources, greater governmental regulation of private exploitation of land resources, assistance to state and local governments through the payment of delinquent taxes, federal aid in rural public works, and encouragement of state and local land-use planning.[17]

The legacy of powers, programs, money, and people inherited from predecessor agencies imposed limitations, however, on Tugwell's freedom to pursue his vision. This legacy included the land program of the AAA and FERA, involving options on more than six million acres of land and completed purchase of more than 175,000 acres; more than 225,000 rural rehabilitation clients of the FERA, with over four million dollars in funds transferred from the state corporations; approximately half a million rural relief families from the FERA and the Subsistence Homesteads Division, together with an administrative establishment involving 3,000 district and county offices employing more than ten thousand people; and sixty-three approved model communities and other projects from the Subsistence Homesteads Division, together with $18,275,735 in transferred funds.

Irrespective of his earlier intentions, Tugwell was now responsible for the following four distinct programs: (1) *land reform*, involving more than 275 land acquisition projects providing for eventual purchase of approximately twenty million acres of land and the resettlement of more than 20,000 dislocated farm families; (2) *rural resettlement*, providing for a variety of model rural communities, individual farms, small garden home projects for farm laborers, and migratory labor camps; (3) *suburban resettlement*, consisting of model suburban communities for families with "modest" incomes—$1,200 to $2,000 per year—called Greenbelt, near Washington, D.C.;

17. Tugwell, "The Reasons for Resettlement," radio address, Dec. 2, 1935, FDRL, OF 1568; Tugwell to Robert D. Carey, July 14, 1936, and to Fred L. Crawford, Mar. 28, 1936, NA, RG 96; L. J. Peet, "Relocation of Farmers Living in Lands Acquired in Land Use Projects," memorandum, RA, May 5, 1937, and RA memorandum, "Statement Regarding Land Adjustment Program," July 23, 1936, NA, RG 114; RA, *First Annual Report*, pp. 1–2.

Greenhills near Cincinnati, Ohio; Greendale, near Milwaukee, Wisconsin; and Greenbrook, near Bound Brook, New Jersey; and (4) *rural rehabilitation*, embracing five different but closely related types of activity—a standard loan program, based on the coupling of credit and farm and home planning; an emergency grant program for subsistence needs; a feed and seed loan program; a farm debt adjustment program designed to assist the farm debtor and his creditor in reaching an equitable settlement; and a cooperative loan program to assist client families in organizing or participating in various kinds of cooperative enterprises.

By the late summer of 1935, the leaders of the Resettlement Administration discovered that administrative resistances, legal and financial limitations, differences and conflicts among the diverse personnel of the agency, and shifts in the political environment compelled them to re-examine their original intention of giving primary emphasis to land reform and resettlement. Large-scale land acquisition and retirement, for instance, proved to be an exceedingly difficult, costly, and time-consuming process, and the leaders of the program struggled in vain to assemble even enough productive land for the resettlement of dislocated families.

Farm people on submarginal lands may have been imprisoned and victimized by their barren acres, but their subjective attachments to home and community and their terror at the prospect of being uprooted made them reluctant to participate in resettlement. Some of the lands that had been classified as substandard proved capable of supporting productive agriculture, if adequate adjustments were made in farming methods, while many small-scale farm operators were proven to be technically and emotionally unprepared to readily operate larger farms or to adopt different farming methods. Finally, it became apparent that the idea of large-scale land acquisition and resettlement was hopelessly chained to unpopular connotations of governmental regimentation. With the election campaign of 1936 looming on the horizon, charges that the leaders of the Resettlement Administration were conspiring to "socialize" the land in America and "collectivize" the people rose to a crescendo. The Resettlement Administration, Tugwell confessed in retrospect, "was thus faced with a task it could not possibly do well."[18]

18. RA, *First Annual Report*, pp. 21–29, 33–51, 121–57. SCS, "Pertinent Information Concerning the Submarginal Land Program of the Department of Agriculture," memorandum, Feb. 11, 1939; Gray to J. C. McFarland, Dec. 14, 1935; NA, RG 114. Gray to Eleanor Roosevelt, Sept. 5, 1936, NA, RG 96. Rexford G. Tugwell, *The Democratic Roosevelt*, (Garden City, N.Y.: Doubleday, 1957), p. 424.

Peter M. Blau, it will be recalled, has employed the concept of "goal succession" to describe the organizational search for new purposes as its old ones are realized. The experience of the Resettlement Administration suggests that goal succession may also occur where organizational goals are perceived as operationally unfeasible or politically unacceptable.

By the fall of 1935, Tugwell and his assistants heeded the logic of the new situation and decided to shift the emphasis of the agency to rural rehabilitation. To what extent was "rural rehabilitation" a socially meaningful and operationally feasible organizational purpose? At first, program goals were limited to such physical objectives as provision of emergency subsistence and the raising of the client family's material level of living. However, as more was learned about the causes and cures of chronic rural poverty, the concept of rural rehabilitation became synonymous, at least in the minds of some of the agency's leaders, with the notion of the general welfare—relief of human suffering, permanent self-sufficiency, preservation and reinforcement of the family farm, achievement of a more rational man-land relationship, full utilization of manpower among low-income farmers, and wider participation in democracy. As a basis for economic analysis or as a blueprint for public policy, this was an exceedingly ambiguous purpose, but as an expression of social and political aspirations, the idea of rural rehabilitation was deeply humanistic and its goals were the improvement of the human condition. [19]

Eschewing the difficulties of translating such a broadly conceived purpose into measurable achievements, and despite the skepticism of some of the leaders of the agency about whether such objectives were achievable, Tugwell and his assistants exploited the symbolic and ideological potentiality of the concept. Instead of mobilizing the rhetoric and images of economics and political philosophy, they approached the task as existentialists. A wagon, a plow, a tractor, a mule, improved feed and seed, a new farm house, a terraced hillside—these were the symbols offered to the client farmer. And to his wife were held out such meaningful things as screens for the windows, a new cook stove or refrigerator for the kitchen, running water and indoor privies, and fresh milk for the children. Pressure cookers—client wives called them "precious cookers"—with which to preserve

19. Executive Order 7143, Aug. 19, 1935; RA, Administrative Order 40, Rev. 2, and Administrative Order 41, Rev. 1; testimony of Hudgens, *Cooley Committee Hearings*, Pt. I, pp. 158–68; Olaf F. Larson, "The Rural Rehabilitation Program as an Instrument of Social Change," *Proceedings of the Pacific Sociological Society, 1947* (Pullman, Wash.: State College of Washington, 1946), pp. 121–27, and *Ten Years*, pp. 45–57.

fruits and vegetables for the winter table became badges of liberation from the old ways, and colorful glass jars of preserved fruits and vegetables were proudly displayed in the family's parlor as testimony of achievement. Economics-minded men judged the rural rehabilitation program in terms of cold aggregate economic impact, but the leaders of the program emphasized the importance of little things.

By June, 1936, the Resettlement Administration had 536,302 active rural rehabilitation client families on its roster, embracing more than two million farm people—approximately 8 per cent of the total farming population in the United States at the time. The agency had expended approximately ninety-five million dollars on the program, which was 60 per cent of the total budget for the year. The shift from land-use planning and resettlement to rural rehabilitation was thus well underway. During the months that followed, the trend was further reinforced, so that by January, 1937, Wallace was moved to declare that "it would have been better if [the Resettlement Administration] had been given a name more accurately describing it—Farm Security Administration, or the Tenant Security Administration, or something like that."[20]

Crisis and Consolidation

From the very beginning of the Resettlement Administration, Tugwell clearly knew that in attempting to build a viable administrative institution he would be compelled to travel a very rocky road. "If you have any illusions of getting away with anything," he warned at a staff meeting in July, 1935, "I advise you to get that out of your mind right away." He predicted that the agency would be highly vulnerable to attack, that it would be closely watched by its enemies, and that its leaders had better prepare their defenses against internal conflict and external attack. "We are operating in a field in which policy necessarily governs," he cautioned, "and in which we have got to move from the top down."[21]

A manifestation of potential conflict and instability was internal

20. Paul V. Maris, address to conference of regional RA directors, June 18, 1935, NA, RG 96; Wallace, "The Rural Resettlement Administration of the Department of Agriculture," radio address, Jan. 12, 1937, NA, RG 46; Larson, "The Rural Rehabilitation Program as an Instrument of Social Change," and *Ten Years*, pp. 309–31.
21. RA, minutes of staff conference, Washington, D. C., July 26, 1935, NA, RG 96.

tension among the staff. Many of those who had been transferred were resentful about their loss of status, authority, and prestige enjoyed in their more autonomous previous positions. Similarly, many of them had been transferred as a matter of expediency, and they lacked sympathy for the agency's purposes and loyalty to its leaders.

In 1935, Tugwell was forty-four years old—handsome, well educated, intellectually bright, urbane, and exceedingly articulate, and he surrounded himself with a group of younger men, some of whom were in his own image. At his elbow was his executive assistant and confidante, Miss Grace Falke—a sophisticated, intelligent, and ambitious young lady in her early twenties, from the Bronx, New York, who was destined to become his wife. Finally, Baldwin, although very different in personality and background, was a member of this group who came to be known as Tugwell's Clique.

In contrast to this so-called in-group, was Deputy Administrator "Dr. Will" Alexander. He was, to borrow the picture sketched by his biographers, "Modest, lacking personal ambition for high position or backstage power, short and plump and genial." Alexander had come to the Resettlement Administration not because of some grand vision of a new order, but rather because he believed that in an official position in Washington he might help to improve race relations in the South and to ease the hardships of low-income farm families, many of whom were colored.

It was inevitable, perhaps, that "Dr. Will" should eventually come to feel isolated and neglected by Tugwell and his disciples. This was more than a difference in personalities. Alexander found it particularly difficult to support what he believed were the esoteric projects of the Special Skills Division, under the direction of Grace Falke— ceramics, weaving, furniture design, folk singing, and other unorthodox activities promoted among resettlement project families. He also privately doubted the wisdom and practicality of the resettlement projects and some of the more ambitious cooperative enterprises. "The trouble with the Tugwell approach," he confided in retrospect, "was that it attempted a clean sweep rather than trying to build with what we had."

Another odd-man-out at the upper level of the Washington office was Maris, the professional agriculturalist who had been transferred from the FERA to direct the rural rehabilitation program. Raised on an Oregon stock ranch, a graduate in agriculture, and a veteran of twenty years in the extension system, he had the personal qualities of both the Puritan elder and the Methodist missionary. Governed by a strong personal code, skeptical of mass movements, he was a purist in his approach to the idea of rural rehabilitation. Solution of the problem of poverty, he believed, lay in the combination of careful technical planning and supervision, coupled to maximum self-help among the clientele. "Tugwell's preference for idealists in his staffing of the Resettlement Administration," Maris later charged, "led to a loose and sloppy field organization, technical carelessness, and disregard for businesslike requirements."

In the Washington office, there was also Taylor who, as director of the Rural Resettlement Division, had responsibility for the rural rehabilitation program during the first six months. Taylor was a rather orthodox agrarian idealist, and he had little faith in the rural rehabilitation program. During the summer of 1935, for instance, he went to Fayetteville, Arkansas, to address a conference of extension officials, and there he declared that "sooner or later, the Extension Service shall take over entire responsibility" of the rural rehabilitation program. He had agreed to serve as director of the program only on the condition that it "would be liquidated as far and as fast as possible into the hands of the Agricultural Extension Service." He believed that the federal government should not become involved in supervising the personal affairs of low-income farm families, and he saw the future of the Resettlement Administration lying in other directions. According to Hudgens, it required several months of effort to restore the staff's morale after Taylor had made a visit to New Orleans.[22]

The stability of the Resettlement Administration was also threatened by external political attack, although the measure of danger

22. Maddox, "The FSA," p. 29; Dykeman and Stokely, *Seeds of Southern Change*, pp. 216–17; Taylor, address to annual conference of farmers and agricultural extension services, Fayetteville, Ark., Aug. 9, 1935, FHAF; author's interviews with Appleby, Alexander, Maris, Hudgens.

"The kind of tensions experienced by the Resettlement Administration were hardly news," Appleby has commented in retrospect. "Government agencies that do nothing may be monolithic, although I doubt even that, but an agency as creative as the Resettlement Administration—especially at a time as hectic as the mid-1930's—could hardly have been expected to be a brotherhood in fellowship."

Some of the more orthodox people in the USDA, and most of the press, were quick to cultivate the notion of a "Tugwell Clique" in the agency. Although there were differences among the staff, and some tensions developed, the cleavage was greatly exaggerated at the time. Appleby has offered the suggestion that, "Rex was an enormously interesting person, and he had a tendency to surround himself with a wide and varied crowd of people. There were those with whom he spent more time, or with whom he participated in personal give-and-take, but the fact that some of them were his 'disciples' should not suggest that they were simply sponges. Rex could not suffer dull people."

involved in any particular skirmish was not necessarily commensurate with the noise of battle. The hostility assumed various forms and degrees of intensity, and came from many different directions. Some of the foes were simply disappointed claimants for patronage and porkbarrel prizes; some were partisans performing the rites of opposition; some were bureaucratic competitors jealous of their preserves, and welcomed no trespassers. Still others were foes of the Roosevelt administration and the New Deal, and found it more politically expedient to attack Tugwell and the Resettlement Administration. Finally, there was an ideological content in the opposition of those who believed that the agency threatened "the American way of life."

The objects of much of the political hostility to the Resettlement Administration were the resettlement projects and model communities. Senator Harry F. Byrd of Virginia, for instance, condemned what he believed were silly extravagances and costly absurdities, such as electricity, refrigerators, factory-made furniture, and indoor privies for "simple mountain people." Similarly, Senator McKellar of Tennessee rebuked the agency for constructing "wonderfully fine stone houses or mansions" on top of the Cumberland Mountains, and he resented the idea of a relief worker "living in a stone mansion very much handsomer that I ever lived in in my life."[23]

Haste in planning, expensive experimentation in construction methods, and relatively high housing standards for resettlement families tended to push construction costs upward, and thus provided an additional target for attack. Furthermore, critics charged that the projects were built on fallacious economic and financial assumptions. Bernard M. Baruch, for instance, wrote to Mrs. Eleanor Roosevelt in the spring of 1936, criticizing her favorite projects at Reedsville and Arthurdale in West Virginia, and declaring that, "I hate always to be the devil's advocate, but I constantly have before me the picture of those unfortunate people to whom we have made promises [that can never be realized]."[24]

Attack also came from the courts. In December, 1935, a group of local citizens in New Jersey filed an injunction against the Resettlement Administration, in an effort to prevent development of the proposed suburban Greenbrook community, near Bound Brook. They opposed the project on the grounds that it would cause a loss of tax

---

23. Mordecai Ezekiel to Tugwell, May 2, 1935; Harry F. Byrd to Wallace, May 21, 1937, NA, RG 16. Adrian Dornbush to Grace E. Falke, Nov. 27, 1935, NA, RG 96. McKellar, in *Byrd Committee Hearings*, Pt. 3, p. 720.

24. Bernard M. Baruch to Eleanor Roosevelt, Apr. 28, 1936, NA, RG 16.

revenues to the local government, that the contemplated architectural style was inappropriate, and that the project would attract a "low class of people." They claimed in their injunction that the proposed community would not promote the general welfare or the common defense, that the Resettlement Administration was, in effect, usurping the powers of the states, that the President's executive order creating the agency had not been authorized by statute law, and that the Emergency Relief Appropriation Act of 1935 was unconstitutional.

When the court denied their injunction in January, 1936, the group from New Jersey filed a new claim against Tugwell personally in the Court of Appeals for the District of Columbia. On May 18, 1936, the District Court ruled that the entire Emergency Relief Appropriation Act of 1935 was unconstitutional on the grounds that Congress, in failing to specify the programs to be financed by funds under the Act, had unlawfully delegated legislative powers to the President. This was "delegation running riot," declared the Court, and the Resettlement Administration was violating states' rights by regulating housing and resettling people. On the following day, the Attorney General removed some of the sting when he ruled that the decision of the District Court, despite its sweeping language, applied only to the Greenbrook project.

Tugwell's first impulse was to seek a review by the U.S. Supreme Court, but on May 27, the Court struck heavily at the New Deal when it invalidated the National Industrial Recovery Act of 1933, the Frazier-Lemke Farm Mortgage Moratorium Act, and the President's removal of a Federal Trade Commissioner. Realizing that judicial review in the Supreme Court was too dangerous a risk under these circumstances, Tugwell, Alexander, and their assistants decided to sacrifice Greenbrook and to proceed with haste in completing the three remaining suburban "greenbelt" communities. This whole judicial skirmish may not have had any profound impact on the actual operations of the Resettlement Administration, but it did implant some additional doubts in the minds of men, especially among members of the Congress and conservative newspaper editors, about the legitimacy of the agency and its programs.[25]

25. *Schechter Poultry Corp. v. United States*, 295 U. S. 495 (1935), invalidating the National Industrial Recovery Act; *Louisville Joint Stock Land Bank v. Radford*, 295 U.S. 555 (1935), finding the Frazier-Lemke Farm Mortgage Act unconstitutional; *Humphrey's Executor v. United States*, 295 U.S. 602 (1935); Paul K. Conkin, *Tomorrow a New World* (Ithaca, N. Y.: Cornell Univ. Press, 1959), pp. 173–75.

The resettlement projects also provided considerable grist to the conservative press. One of the noisier press attacks occurred on November 17, 1935, when the *New York Times* carried a page-one feature story by Frank L. Kluckhohn, which reported that Tugwell had allegedly hired 12,089 persons to provide relief jobs for only 5,012 workers. Kluckhohn also reported that the Resettlement Administration, sprawled about in eighteen Washington buildings, had spent $1,750,000 monthly on staff salaries, compared with $300,000 monthly to relief workers. Within twenty-four hours, presidential assistant Marvin H. McIntyre received a note from James A. Farley on Democratic National Committee stationery, expressing concern about the charges and suggesting that the White House investigate them.

Meanwhile, newspapers throughout the country carried the *New York Times* story. Tugwell angrily wrote the editor a letter of protest, refuting the charges and explaining that the Resettlement Administration had an administrative force of 12,812 persons who were actually serving 354,000 farm families—approximately 1,500,000 persons in the rural rehabilitation program, and not simply 5,012 relief cases as reported. The *New York Times* printed Tugwell's letter and corrected figures, but most of the other newspapers that had printed the original story did not.

On November 25, Roosevelt wrote to Tugwell from Warm Springs that he "was outraged by that rotten *New York Times* story," and described it as "a case of deliberate misrepresentation." Tugwell replied to the President that the "whole affair is calculated to make me more than ever sure that our enemies do not mean to give us a fair shake, but mean to use any tactics which will serve their purpose." He enclosed a review of press coverage and editorial comment on the story which showed that more than one hundred newspapers had failed to carry his own explanation and correction.[26]

Three months later, a series of four articles by Felix Brunner in the *Washington Post*, entitled "Utopia Unlimited," spread the impression that the Resettlement Administration represented a subversive attempt "to make America over." Brunner went on to charge that, "Occupying all parts of 19 Washington buildings, are the administrators, directors, and staff of one of the most far-flung experiments

---

26. *New York Times*, Nov. 17, 1935; James A. Farley to Marvin H. McIntyre, Nov. 19, 1935, FDRL, OF 1568–Misc.; *New York Times*, Nov. 20, 1935; Roosevelt to Tugwell, Nov. 25, 1935, FDRL, OF 1568; Tugwell to Roosevelt, Nov. 26, 1935, FDRL, PSF-Tugwell.

in paternalistic government ever attempted in the United States." Specifically, Brunner contended that the agency had been created by the President rather than Congress, that it did not have express congressional sanction, that its programs did not require congressional review, that its personnel were not under civil service laws, and that the agency "directly affects, virtually rules, the lives of hundreds of thousands of people, who are told how much they shall spend for food, for clothes, for rent, what crops they shall plant, [and] how they shall conduct. . .their lives."

Carried by other newspapers throughout the country, the impact of the series went far beyond the readership of the *Washington Post*. It also provided convenient ammunition for hostile members of Congress and others in attacking the agency and its leaders. Senator W. Warren Barbour of New Jersey, for instance, took advantage of an opportunity, on March 11, 1936, during the legal battle over the Greenbrook project in his state, to introduce a resolution in the Senate asking for an investigation of the Resettlement Administration. Although his resolution was tabled by a close vote of thirty-two to thirty, he prosecuted the attack further with arguments from the Brunner series in the *Washington Post*, and persuaded the Senate to demand a full report from Tugwell on the operations of his agency.[27]

During the month of May, the Resettlement Administration weathered another storm when an amendment to the deficiency appropriation bill, which would have substituted "loans" for "rural rehabilitation," was defeated in the Senate by a vote of thirty-eight to twenty-eight. Had the amendment been approved, the rural rehabilitation program would have been seriously crippled by limiting expenditures to loans, thereby eliminating the grant program. The deficiency appropriation for 1936 did not extend the right of the Resettlement Administration to purchase land, but this right, which was granted by the President under the 1935 emergency relief act, continued under executive order until 1937.[28]

Although the foes of the Resettlement Administration focused their attention on the alleged administrative faults of the agency, especially in the resettlement program, there was an ideological current in the attack. In the hostile sectors of the press and in some

27. Felix Brunner, "Utopia Unlimited," *Washington* (D.C.) *Post*, Feb. 10, 11, 12, 13, 1936; *Congressional Record*, Vol. 81, pp. 3547, 6194, 6263–67, 7141; U.S., Congress, Sen. Doc. 213 (1936), *Resettlement Administration Program* (Washington, D. C.: GPO, 1936); W. Warren Barbour to James Bamford, Mar. 25, 1936, CBBP.

28. *Congressional Record*, Vol. 81, pp. 8184–85, 8202.

RUSSELL LEE

RUSSELL LEE

MARION POST WOLCOTT

4

RUSSELL LEE

5

RUSSELL LEE

6

RUSSELL LEE

7

ARTHUR ROTHSTEIN

RUSSELL LEE

ARTHUR ROTHSTEIN

of the congressional criticism, there was a subtle insinuation that the Resettlement Administration was "un-American." Early in 1936, for instance, Appleby, who realized the unpopularity and the political liabilities involved in some of the agency's activities and who, from time to time criticized particular administrative faults, observed that "there is widespread sentiment against communities operated on a mutual-sharing basis," and that any program even suggesting such an arrangement "is greeted by a very vociferous public as proving that this Administration is dominated by Russia!"

Two months later, as if to punctuate his words, the Republican National Committee accused the Roosevelt administration of sponsoring farm communities which were "communistic in conception," and went on to charge that, "President Roosevelt's Resettlement Administration is establishing. . .communal farms which follow the Russian pattern." Similarly, from California came charges by local chambers of commerce and organized growers that the migratory farm labor camps were becoming "hotbeds of radical agitation and communism."

Some of the most potentially dangerous opposition came from the so-called "power structure" in agriculture—the Extension Service in the USDA, state extension services, state land-grant colleges of agriculture, the system of county agricultural agents, and including especially the American Farm Bureau Federation (AFBF). As we shall see in greater detail later in this study, these institutions tended to ignore the problems of chronically impoverished farm families. The power of the cliental bloc in agriculture was based on a monopoly of access to farmers at the local level, and they considered the growing field activities of new federal action agencies a threat to their political power base. To many of the leaders of these institutions, the Resettlement Administration was a dangerous competitor.[29]

Even before the creation of the Resettlement Administration, Mordecai Ezekiel, in a report to Tugwell early in May, 1935, raised the question of the relationships that should exist between the planned agency and the state agricultural institutions. Later in the month, the Committee on Extension Organization and Policy, a standing

29. Appleby (addressed to n.n.), Jan. 27, 1936, NA, RG 16; *New York Times*, Mar. 31, Aug. 2, 1936; Gladys L. Baker, *The County Agent* (Chicago: Univ. of Chicago Press, 1939), Orville M. Kile, *The Farm Bureau Through Three Decades* (Baltimore: Waverly Press, 1948), pp. 265–66; Christiana M. Campbell, *The Farm Bureau and the New Deal* (Urbana: Univ. of Illinois Press, 1962), pp. 157, 165, 167–69; see Chap. X.

committee of the American Association of Land-Grant Colleges and State Universities, accompanied by several state extension directors, conferred with Tugwell, and after a series of meetings with Alexander, Taylor, and Maris of the Resettlement Administration, they reached an agreement on provisions for mutual cooperation in the field.

On June 7, Extension Service Director C. W. Warburton and Tugwell signed a "Memorandum of Understanding," in which it was agreed that the leaders of the Resettlement Administration would make every effort to operate in a decentralized manner, similar to that of the FERA. As far as possible, the state rural rehabilitation corporations would be utilized, county farmers committees would be employed in the selection of client families, state rural rehabilitation directors and their staffs would be housed in close proximity to state extension staffs, and in each state a rural rehabilitation director would be appointed by the board of the state corporation, on nomination by the state extension director. In essence, the agreement, if adhered to, would have permitted considerable participation by extension service officials in the administration of the programs of the Resettlement Administration.[30]

Within a year, however, a committee of state extension directors reported that the Resettlement Administration was too highly centralized in Washington, that it was not in harmony with the objectives and ideals of the Extension Service, and that too many of its field employees were not sufficiently trained in agriculture and attuned to "the spirit of the people." Dan T. Gray, director of extension and dean of the College of Agriculture in Arkansas, for instance, charged that, "The Resettlement Administration is doing some things in Arkansas, and teaching some things that the people connected with the College of Agriculture can not endorse." The two organizations, he correctly concluded, "are just moving along side by side, without any serious attempt at fundamental cooperation."[31]

To remedy the situation, the committee of state extension directors

30. Flora Rose to Eleanor Roosevelt, Apr. 26, 1935; Ezekiel to Tugwell, May 2, 1935; Thomas C. Blaisdell to Tugwell, Jan. 17, 1936; "Memorandum of Understanding Between the Extension Service of the [USDA] and the Resettlement Administration," Jun. 7, 1935; C. W. Warburton to Directors of Extension, Jun. 10, 1935; NA, RG 96. Maddox, "The FSA," pp. 27–28; Hudgens, COHC; author's interviews with Appleby, Alexander, Baldwin, T. Roy Reid.

31. Appleby to Milton S. Eisenhower, A. D. Stedman, C. B. Baldwin, C. W. Warburton, Dec. 12, 1935; Raymond A. Pearson to Dan T. Gray, Mar. 31, 1936; Gray to Pearson, Apr. 20, 1936; Alexander to (n.n.) Bartlett, Jun. 1, 1936; NA, RG 96.

The correspondence between Pearson and Gray suggests that both Pearson recommended a series of changes that would have completely emasculated the Resettlement Administration and delivered its programs into the hands of the state institutions and the Extension Service, where some of them promptly would have been extinguished. Their proposals were phrased in such innocuous terms as "coordination, decentralization, government close to the people, elimination of duplication, and practicality," but, as William A. Robson has observed, "There is a real struggle for power underlying words and phrases of apparent innocence." No one knew this better than Tugwell, and so he did not take their proposals seriously. However, for purposes of political protocol, he refrained from a typically sharp "Tugwellian" rejoinder. The tension, however, remained.[32]

When the Resettlement Administration was created in May, 1935, Tugwell and his assistants had expected to face considerable hostility in the country; they therefore had wasted no time in launching an ambitious public information program designed to propagate the faith of the new agency and its prophet. Under the direction of John Franklin Carter, who served in a dual capacity as special assistant to Under Secretary of Agriculture Tugwell, five sections were organized in the Information Division—(1) an editorial section, to handle all news releases, bulletins, circulars, and other material designed to inform the general public and the agency's personnel about the work of the Resettlement Administration; (2) a special publications section to furnish information and articles about the agency to magazines, feature syndicates, yearbooks, and a variety of other periodicals; (3) a photographic section in which photography was employed for purposes of historical record, immediacy and news value, and work of art; (4) a radio section, to help build the historical record, disseminate information, and exploit the dramatic quality of the agency's work; and (5) a documentary film section.

During the first eighteen months, the Information Division proved itself to be enormously creative and energetic. It generated a flood of descriptive materials, about the work of the Resettlement Ad-

---

and Carl C. Taylor were out of joint with the established position of the Resettlement Administration—they were generally in agreement with the conclusions and recommendations of the Ramsower Committee. Furthermore, while the leaders of agency were operating on the assumption that the Resettlement Administration would be permanent, Pearson wrote to Gray that, "The Resettlement Administration is, of course, temporary, and as long as it functions it should be on the best terms and in close cooperation with all other governmental agencies serving in similar lines."

32. William A. Robson, *The Development of Local Government* (London: Allen and Unwin, 1948), p. 9.

ministration and the problems of its clientele, that found their way into newspaper stories, magazine articles, radio scripts, and the speeches of sympathetic public officials and politicians. Representing a revolutionary innovation in the character of governmental information work, the Division harnessed the creative abilities of writers, journalists, and scholars to the purpose of educating the country about impoverished land and people and promoting an acceptance of the agency and its programs.[33]

The most impressive phase was the work of the Photographic Section under the direction of Roy E. Stryker (Tugwell's former pupil and colleague at Columbia University), first under the Resettlement Administration, and then after 1937 under the Farm Security Administration. With a modest budget and without any detailed blueprint as to what they were to do, the Photographic Section opened the door to some of the country's most exciting young photographers—Walker Evans, Arthur Rothstein, Dorothea Lange, Ben Shahn, Margaret Bourke-White, Marion Post Wolcott, John Collier, Carl Mydans, John Vachon, Gordon Parks, Russell Lee, Jack Delano, and others.

Between 1935 and 1943, with no more than six of them working at any one time, these highly creative young men and women captured more than 272,000 photographs of the face of America, with a candid honesty that has moved Edward Steichen, director of photography at the Museum of Modern Art in New York, to describe their work as "the most remarkable human documents that were ever rendered in pictures." Within a few years, many of the photographs found their way into books of great drama and beauty.[34]

33. RA, *First Annual Report*, pp. 97–98; Hartley E. Howe, "You Have Seen Their Faces," *Survey Graphic*, Vol. XXIX (Apr., 1940), pp. 236–41; Beaumont Newhall, *The History of Photography From 1839 to the Present Day* (New York: Museum of Modern Art, 1949), pp. 178–81; Robert J. Doherty, "Farm Security Administration Photographs of the Depression Era," *Camera*, Vol. 14 (Oct., 1942), pp. 9–13; *New York Times*, June 4, 10, 12, Oct. 8, Dec. 30, 1936; John Franklin Carter, address at conference of regional directors of land program, RA, June 20, 1935, NA, RG 96; Carter to regional directors of land protion advisers, RA, Feb. 15, 1936, FDRL, OF 1568; W. R. Alstaetter to Alexander, Sept. 11, 1936, CBBP; author's interview with Alexander; photographic collection, Division of Prints and Photos, U. S. Library of Congress, Washington, D. C.

34. These books include the following: Erskine Caldwell and Margaret Bourke-White, *You Have Seen Their Faces* (1937); Archibald MacLeish, *Land of the Free* (1938); H. C. Nixon, *Forty Acres and Steel Mules* (1938); Dorothea Lange and Paul S. Taylor, *An American Exodus* (1939); Sherwood Anderson, *Home Town* (1940); Richard Wright and Edwin Roskam, *12 Million Black Voices* (1941); James Agee and Walker Evans, *Let Us Now Praise Famous Men* (1941); and Arthur Raper, *Tenants of the Almighty* (1943).

To produce his documentary films, Tugwell selected Pare Lorenz, one of the great pioneers in that medium, and from their collaboration came two films—"The Plow that Broke the Plains" in 1936, and "The River" in 1937, with accompanying music by Virgil Thompson. Greeted at the time by opponents of the Resettlement Administration as costly and unauthorized propaganda for the New Deal, the films were hailed by leading film critics as among the finest documentaries ever produced.

These aesthetic achievements were admittedly propaganda, but their approach was literary and artistic rather than polemical. The published materials, for instance, were addressed not to the people of the small towns, the editors of rural journals, or the political people in rural county courthouses, but rather to the presumably more literate and sophisticated people in the cities and among academic audiences, and to the editors of slick national publications.

Illustratively, the *First Annual Report* of the Resettlement Administration in 1936 pointed with pride to the coverage the agency had received in *Survey Graphic, Time, Fortune,* and the *Literary Digest*—not publications with wide circulations among dirt farmers and rural politicians. Even the *First Annual Report* itself was prepared for highly literate readers. It was a very attractive glossy publication of 173 pages, including some of the agency's dramatic photographs, well-footnoted and with uncharacteristically literate governmental prose, a fifty-three page statistical section, and an impressive multi-colored pictorial map that would have made the editors of *Fortune* magazine proud. The report was received by economy-minded members of Congress and other conservatives, however, with something less than acclaim.

The Information Division tended to focus on the activities of the Washington office rather than on the field, and the unit became what some resentful field officials of the Resettlement Administration called a personal press agency for Tugwell. Insufficient attention, it was asserted, was devoted to programs and people at regional, state, and local levels. During the election campaign in the fall of 1936, one field investigator, following a trip through the South, reported to the Washington office that "85–90 per cent of the people in the small towns did not have the vaguest idea what Resettlement is trying to do."

Despite its achievements—perhaps also because of them—the Resettlement Administration, by the fall of 1936, was highly vulnerable to attack. The most significant reasons, representing a crisis of legitimacy for the agency, were the following: (1) many of the programs, at best, were viewed by critics as necessary but unfortunate relief measures that should be only temporary in nature, and, at worst, dangerous violations of accepted American principles; (2) the agency as a whole presented a challenge—real and imaginary—to the *status quo*, especially in the sensitive rural South; (3) created by executive action rather than through the traditional legislative process, the Resettlement Administration seemed to have sprung into existence, and its rapid growth and expansion took many people by surprise; and (4) many of the agency's officials in policy-making and supervisory positions were not agriculturalists and did not have agrarian orientations.

In addition, there were some subordinate reasons for the agency's vulnerability which were more easily remediable but were exploited by hostile forces as targets of convenience: (1) the agency was headed by Tugwell, probably the most controversial and criticized member of the Roosevelt administration; (2) administrative and construction expenses, although technically justified by the difficult and unprecedented nature of the goals sought, were excessively high, at least by contemporary standards; (3) the promotion of esoteric activities among the agency's clientele, such as folk dancing and basket weaving, were difficult to explain and justify; and (4) despite the elaborate and creative public information program, the Resettlement Administration did not enjoy adequate public exposure among its potential supporters.

For Tugwell personally, the fall of 1936 was also a time of crisis. Over many months there had been speculation about how long he would remain in the government. On November 28, 1935, for instance, Secretary of Interior Ickes had reported in his diary that, "There seems to be pretty general feeling that Rex Tugwell will soon be out of the government," and on January 2, the *New York Times* had echoed the rumors. The general decline of his influence in the Roosevelt administration, the personal attacks on him in the press and in Congress, the decision of Roosevelt and Farley to keep him silent and out of sight during the political campaigning in 1936, plans in Congress to legitimize programs for low-income families through special legislation, and his own growing sense of despair regarding the course of the New Deal were some of the factors which led Tugwell to decide during the summer of 1936, that as soon as the campaign ended he would resign.

Another contributing factor was his personal domestic situation.

In retrospect, Alexander maintained that Tugwell's decision to resign was because of his intentions to divorce his wife and to wed his assistant, Miss Grace Falke. "Better he should be out of the public eye and away from Washington at the time," "Dr. Will" has suggested. According to Bernard Sternsher, the chonicler of Tugwell's role in the New Deal, "'simple withdrawal' became the dominating impulse of this complex man in an unbearably complex situation." The denouement was as expected: he resigned in December; early in 1938 he divorced his wife, after more than twenty years of marriage; and later that year he married his former secretary.[35]

During the fall of 1936, with Tugwell's departure imminent, an important question emerged—what would become of the Resettlement Administration? About the time that he decided to resign, Tugwell proposed to Wallace that his agency be transferred to the USDA, where it presumably would be in reasonably safe hands. For the remainder of 1936, the idea was discreetly discussed in the Department and in the Resettlement Administration.

On the negative side were officials of the Department, including some of those close to Wallace, who opposed the transfer on the grounds that it would open the doors of the USDA to some very unorthodox and controversial people and would complicate the tensions and divisions already present there. The Resettlement Administration, they reasoned, had made many enemies; to bring the agency in would likely expose the USDA to a whole range of new antagonisms, especially among the planters of the South at a time when special efforts were being made to smooth southern acceptance of the AAA.

There were also fears among the people of the Resettlement Administration—fears that the enthusiasm and creative drive of the agency would be throttled, and that the programs for migratory farm laborers and very low-income farmers could not survive in a department which was responsive to higher income commercial farmers and conservative farm organizations. In brief, there was fear that the Resettlement Administration would be butchered.

On the other hand, there were many arguments in defense of the transfer. Although Wallace and his assistants did not rush into a decision, they favored the transfer in principle on the grounds that Tugwell's agency had proven itself to be economically and socially justifiable, and that its integration into the USDA would strengthen

35. Sternsher, *Rexford Tugwell and the New Deal*, p. 327; Alexander, COHC, p. 634; author's interview with Alexander.

the latter's institutional balance. Appleby, in particular, had viewed the Resettlement Administration as the offspring of the USDA, and its transfer would be a natural continuation of the process of "agriculturalization" which had started with the creation of the agency in 1935. He also emphasized the value of the transfer in strengthening the "sociological balance" of the USDA by countering the influences of the Extension Service, the AAA, and other bureaus that were concerned primarily with the problems of commercial farmers.[36]

During the fall of 1936, with Wallace still publicly uncommitted on the issue of the transfer, Tugwell persuaded him to make a tour of Resettlement Administration operations and to see for himself the importance of the programs and the need for their integration in the USDA. On November 17, 1936, he set out, accompanied by Tugwell, Alexander, Baldwin, USDA budget director Jump and others, on a tour of the South which was described as 2,000 miles of Tobacco Road. Wallace was visibly shaken by the impact of what he saw, and he returned to Washington determined to proceed with the transfer and to build the Resettlement Administration into the fabric of his department.

Meanwhile, Tugwell had already submitted his resignation, to become effective at midnight on December 31. Somewhat to the surprise of Alexander, he announced to the press that "Dr. Will" would succeed him as Administrator. On December 21, Wallace announced that the Resettlement Administration would be transferred to the USDA at the end of the year, and on December 31, the President issued an executive order implementing the transfer. Wallace promptly appointed Alexander as Administrator, and Baldwin as deputy, and a week later he addressed the nation by radio to declare that the USDA was setting out to help the small farmer at the bottom of the ladder, to get him started upward.

With Tugwell's departure went some of the evangelical zeal and articulate intellectual justification. There was also an exodus of what Appleby later called "rather wild-eyed persons who acted in an amateurish, overzealous, and half-baked way."[37]

To assist in the task of infusing a more "practical" set of values among the personnel and the constituency of the agency, Alexander promptly appointed John Fischer, a competent young newsman and former Rhodes Scholar from Oklahoma, to direct the Information Division and to carry the story of the Resettlement Administration to

---

36. Appleby to author, Apr. 29, 1952; Louis J. Taber, COHC, Vol. 2, p. 329.
37. Louis H. Bean, COHC, p. 185; Wallace, radio address, Jan. 12, 1937; author's interviews with Bean, Appleby.

Capitol Hill, to the editorial rooms of small rural newspapers, and to the political people in the rural communities of the country.

For many of the leaders of the Resettlement Administration, this passage through crisis, from unsettlement to consolidation, had been a painful personal ordeal. The temptations had been great, particularly among the technical specialists, to flee the conflict and uncertainty of their situation—to conceive their roles narrowly in instrumentalist terms, to focus on immediate tasks, to eschew conflicts of doctrine and principle, to let sleeping dogs lie, to allow the agency's future to take care of itself.

On the other hand, Tugwell, for himself, chose the path of ideological integrity, and in doing so he proved expendable. However, in his readiness to shift from land reform and resettlement to rural rehabilitation, in his determination to find an institutional haven for the Resettlement Administration within the USDA, and in his careful concern about the transition after his departure, he demonstrated that he was not entirely oblivious to the requisites of institutional survival.

Legitimacy: A Requisite of Institutional Survival

The transfer of the Resettlement Administration to the USDA was more than a convenient organizational shift in the wake of Tugwell's resignation. The move was, rather, a stage in the larger process of conferring upon the agency, its programs, and leaders a measure of legitimacy.

The original creation of the Resettlement Administration and the initiation of its provocative programs were accomplished through the power of an embattled President, enjoying a large measure of popular support, struggling in a dark hour of national crisis to cope with a numbing economic and social emergency. In the sense that he was responding to overwhelming popular need and expectations—this he was doing—his exercise of power was legitimate, that is, it largely satisfied cultural preferences and social values regarding the role of the state in society, the uses of governmental powers, and the right or responsibility of the executive branch of government to exercise initiative.

There was also historical precedent to support the President's exercise of this initiative, for as Bertram M. Gross has suggested:[38]

38. Bertram M. Gross, *The Legislative Struggle* (New York: McGraw-Hill, 1953), p. 158.

History is full of cases in which Executive officials, without waiting for legislative authorization, have taken actions never dreamed of under the Constitution or existing statutes. If the occasion is serious enough and if there are enough supporting interests and groups, Executive officials will often go far into uncharted seas.

So long as the occasion remained sufficiently grave, and enough interests and groups supported the regime, Roosevelt's assault on chronic rural poverty enjoyed a measure of acceptance or acquiescence which concealed the fact that in many ways the programs of the Resettlement Administration collided with cultural preferences and social values on which political legitimacy rests.

Legitimacy, however, is a cloak of many colors. Its sources lie in the structure and ideology of institutions, and in the personal qualities of incumbent authorities, and it may attach to a regime as a whole or to its parts. Certain programs and practices pursued by a popular regime may challenge accepted preferences and values more immediately and sharply than others. Distinctions are often made between the whole regime and its parts, and interest groups and strategically situated political people tend to be selective in their responses to administrative action, supporting those programs, practices, and people they approve, and attacking or ignoring those they disapprove. Franklin Roosevelt and the New Deal as a whole, for instance, remained acceptable among many groups and individuals for whom Tugwell was a devil and the Resettlement Administration an abomination.

Of all the generally accepted cultural preferences and values which the Resettlement Administration challenged, the most serious, in terms of political consequences, was the belief that major governmental policies and programs should evolve through a political process in which clear-cut legislative authorization is a major stage of genesis. The leaders of the agency and some of the leaders of the USDA may have believed that the provisions of the emergency relief appropriation acts would constitute an adequate statutory basis, but there was very little conscious congressional sanction behind much of the activity of the Resettlement Administration and its predecessor agencies. In retrospect, Tugwell confessed: "I blame myself for undertaking the conglomerate administration of Resettlement without first having it legitimized by the Congress, but in those days the President had so much prestige that doubts of this sort seemed unimportant."[39]

39. David Easton, *A Systems Analysis of Political Life* (New York: Wiley, 1965), pp. 278–87; Tugwell to author, Mar. 2, 1967.

As long as the land-use, resettlement, and rural rehabilitation programs were relatively modest in scope and were considered emergency in character, and as long as the national climate of crisis continued, the unorthodoxy of these programs and their lack of political acceptance in some quarters was tolerable. However, once these programs expanded in scope and cost, were considered permanent in character, and were administered by a large and powerful bureaucratic establishment, and once the climate of crisis began to cool, then the lack of adequate statutory justification became a serious flaw in the foundations of the agency. With the transfer of the Resettlement Administration to the USDA in the winter of 1936–1937, the need for securing legislative sanction became a major concern. Let us now examine that long and complex process.

CHAPTER V

TOWARD LEGITIMACY: THE DANCE OF LEGISLATION BEGINS

Once begin the dance of legislation, and you must struggle through its mazes as best you can to its breathless end,—if any end there be.
WOODROW WILSON[1]
Congressional Government

The global matrix of purposes, within which the Resettlement Administration was imbedded, also served as a seedbed for the campaign to secure legislative authorization. Although the thrust for special legislation to support the assault on chronic rural poverty was essentially a desire for greater legitimacy, the movement represented an exceedingly complex set of personal and institutional motives. A decisive congressional affirmation of principle; legislative sanction of a modest program to promote small farm ownership among qualified farmers, rather than legitimization of programs already launched; promotion of political education and participation among impoverished and impotent low-income farm families in the South; congressional constraint and delimitation of programs that had evolved primarily through executive discretion; and the winning

---

1. Woodrow Wilson, *Congressional Government* (New York: Meridian Books, 1956), p. 195. Originally published 1885.

of congressional consent while the legislative-executive pendulum was still in a position relatively favorable to the executive branch of government—these were some of the different and contradictory goals sought by those who promoted the campaign.

The unfolding of the campaign, however, was not symmetrical in rationality, timing, or intensity, and the various motives were not always clear or easily distinguishable. To properly examine the long and complex dance of legislation that occurred, it is necessary to stop the clock of our chronology and return to the summer of 1934.

The Agitators and Amateurs Respond: Act One

During the drought-ridden and anxious summer of 1934, Will W. Alexander, who was then serving as director of the Commission on Interracial Cooperation, in Atlanta, Georgia, became convinced that the predicament of the chronically impoverished farmer—especially the colored farmer—had a great deal to do with the structure of power, the play of politics, and the economic facts of life in the South. From his work and travels in the southern interracial movement, and from the mounting body of research and writing, he had learned much about the linkage in the South between productive inefficiency, one-crop farming, submarginal land, social maladjustment, economic insecurity, racial injustice, and political impotence. He believed that, despite the denials of southern apologists, the hard core of poverty was based upon the trinity of cotton culture, farm tenancy, and race.

In the fall, he received a telephone call from Stacy May of the Rockefeller Foundation inviting him to conduct a study of the impact of the federal government's programs on the economy and the people of the South. Viewing this is an opportunity to strike a blow against both poverty and racial injustice, he organized a "committee of three" —Edwin R. Embree of the Rosenwald Fund, which had been supporting the commission in Atlanta; Charles S. Johnson, a sociologist at Fisk University in Nashville, Tennessee, a prominent Negro educator, and a consultant to the Rosenwald Fund; and himself. Publicly calling themselves the Committee on Negroes in the Economic Recovery, and with funds from the Rockefeller Foundation and the Rosenwald Fund, they recruited a small staff to conduct research.

One of the men they recruited was Frank Tannenbaum, a Jewish immigrant and political refugee from Austria in 1905, who had attracted considerable attention in 1924, it will be recalled, with his book, *Darker Phases of the South*. As a newspaper correspondent in Mexico during the 1920's, he had become a confidant of the revolutionaries there. For some years, he had studied agrarian reform problems in Mexico and other Latin American countries, and had developed personal ties with Catholic Church leaders in Latin America and the United States. Tannenbaum's skills would presumably be valuable in their study of the South.

Alexander, Embree, and Johnson promptly sent Tannenbaum out to survey the southern situation and to report on what the social scientists had to offer regarding the causes and cures of chronic rural poverty. After ten days of wandering along Tobacco Road, he reported back that no further investigation was necessary. "This system is over," he declared. "It's gone. It's collapsed. You'll have to do something about it. The New Deal will have to do something about it. This calls for long-time heroic treatment."[2]

During the next few weeks, Alexander and his associates decided that, instead of merely gathering facts, they would exploit the opportunity to attempt to exercise influence upon the federal government in undertaking an ambitious assault on chronic rural poverty in the South. Tannenbaum would go to Washington to write a comprehensive book that might enlighten and dramatize, while Alexander and Embree would attempt to carry the message to whomever in the federal government might listen.

On their arrival in Washington, Alexander and Embree talked first with Senator Bronson Cutting of New Mexico, reputedly a liberal with proper connections, but he proved devoid of useful ideas on how he might help. Their next stop was at the office of Henry A. Wallace at the U.S. Department of Agriculture (USDA). The

---

2. Wilma Dykeman and James Stokely, *Seeds of Southern Change: The Life of Will Alexander* (Chicago: Univ. of Chicago Press, 1962), pp. 199–216; Gordon W. Blackwell, "The Displaced Tenant Farm Family in North Carolina," *Social Forces*, Vol. 13 (Oct., 1934), pp. 65–73; John L. Gillin, *Poverty and Dependency* (New York: Century, 1926); Charles S. Johnson, "Incidence [of the New Deal programs] Upon the Negroes," *American Journal of Sociology*, Vol. XL (May, 1935), pp. 737–45; Claudius T. Murchison, *King Cotton is Sick* (Chapel Hill: Univ. of North Carolina Press, 1930); Will W. Alexander, COHC; Frank Tannenbaum to Alexander, FTP; author's interviews with Alexander, Rupert B. Vance, Howard W. Odum.

From Chapel Hill, North Carolina, Alexander and his fellow lobbyists secured the services of Odum, Vance, and some of their associates at the Institute for Research in Social Science.

Secretary appeared to show no interest during their conversation, but a few hours later, after they had returned to their suite at the Hay-Adams Hotel, Wallace came to see them, and he seemed enthusiastic.

At Wallace's suggestion, they met the following night for dinner with Rexford G. Tugwell, Paul H. Appleby, M. L. Wilson, Lewis C. Gray, and others from the USDA, where they were given an opportunity to present their ideas and where they, in turn, happily learned of the concern which some of the people in the USDA felt about the problems of low-income tenants and sharecroppers in the South. As a follow-up, Tannenbaum met several times late in December with Appleby and with Chester C. Davis of the Agricultural Adjustment Administration (AAA). Appleby requested that Tannenbaum prepare a memorandum for the Department, which might be useful in consideration of proposed legislation.

Delighted with this official indication of interest, Tannenbaum promptly sent a letter to Appleby, in which he emphasized the cluster of long-range interrelated trends in southern agriculture, and offered a number of recommendations which embraced some of the activities already being performed by the Federal Emergency Relief Administration (FERA) and the Subsistence Homesteads Division. The government, it was proposed, should purchase land held by insurance companies and federal land banks, subdivide it into separate farms, sell part of the land to tenants and sharecroppers working upon it, and the remainder to landless farm people who were afloat. The government should create a special public corporation to handle the land transactions, and a supervisory credit and service agency to assist the client families in diversifying their crops and improving their productive efficiency. The government's objective, Tannenbaum suggested, should be "the conversion of tenants and sharecroppers, and those recently set afloat, into independent small landowning agriculturalists as quickly as possible."[3]

Although this proposed program was considerably less ambitious and reformative than Tugwell's larger vision, Tannenbaum and his associates believed that the program would, if properly financed and applied long enough, amount to a major reconstitution of southern rural life. Anchoring tenants and sharecroppers more securely to improved land of their own; encouragement of crop diversification and facilitation of the long-range crop restriction program of the

---

3. Tannenbaum to Alexander, Dec. 29, 1934, FTP; author's interviews with Alexander, Tannenbaum.

AAA; provision of land for approximately ten thousand farm families displaced from areas being flooded by the Tennessee Valley Authority (TVA); promotion of rural education; reduction of racial tension in the South; the creation of a market, in the long run, for cheap electric power being developed in the South by the TVA; and return to native local populations those lands that had fallen into the hands of absentee owners—these were the socially desirable goals that Tannenbaum and his associates believed their proposed program would help to accomplish.

With Tannenbaum's time and energies being pre-empted by his consultations with people in the USDA and in his promotional work with others in Washington, Alexander, Embree, and Johnson decided to prepare a simplified book themselves on the subject of southern tenancy. Drafted by Johnson, it appeared as a concise, eighty-one page "handbook," entitled *The Collapse of Cotton Tenancy*. In their foreword to the book, they explained that it was intended "for general readers who may not care to delve into the intricacies of a complex subject, but who, as citizens, should know the outlines of a significant and tragic situation that is of immediate concern to public policy."

To help publicize the book, they created an "advisory committee" of prominent Americans to endorse it in a preface. Finally, in March, 1935, while Tugwell was preparing for the creation of the Resettlement Administration, Alexander, Embree, and Johnson held a press conference at the Chatham Hotel in New York, and with the help of a publicity specialist, they succeeded in attracting the attention of some of the major newspapers in the United States.[4]

A noteworthy feature of the book—one that did not endear it to the leaders of the USDA—was its candid criticism of the southern

4. Charles S. Johnson, Edwin R. Embree, and Will W. Alexander, *The Collapse of Cotton Tenancy* (Chapel Hill: Univ. of North Carolina Press, 1935), p. vii; *New York Times*, Mar. 21, 1935.
The advisory committee consisted of the following: Samuel McCrea Cavert of the Federal Council of Churches of Christ in America; William Green of the American Federation of Labor; Clark Howell of the *Atlanta* (Ga.) *Constitution*; Benjamin Hubert of the Georgia State Industrial College; former Governor Frank O. Lowden of Illinois; Robert Russa Moton of Tuskegee Institute; Frederick B. Murphy of the *Minneapolis* (Minn.) *Tribune*; Howard W. Odum of the University of North Carolina; Charlton Ogburn of the American Federation of Labor; Clarence Poe of the *Progressive Farmer*; B. Kirk Rankin of the *Southern Agriculturalist*; Rev. John A. Ryan and Rev. Edgar Schmiedeler of the National Catholic Welfare Conference; Edgar B. Stern, cotton merchant and philanthropist of New Orleans, Louisiana; William Allen White of the *Emporia* (Kan.) *Gazette*; Robert E. Wood of Sears, Roebuck and Company, of Chicago; and George Foster Peabody (chairman of the advisory committee).

cotton program of the AAA. The authors made their point with some bitterness:

> It is but the blunt truth to say that under the present system the landowner is more and more protected from risk by government activity, while the tenant is left open to risks on every side. Only after he loses first what property he may possess and then his tenure, does the tenant come to the form of risk insurance designed for him—relief.

In brief, the book supported the contention that the programs of the AAA were of the planters, by the planters, and for the planters.

One of the key members of the advisory committee of sponsors was George Foster Peabody, a supporter of Alexander's Interracial Commission in Atlanta. A native of Columbus, Georgia, who had gone North to accumulate a personal fortune in the banking business, a prominent elder Democrat and long-time friend of Franklin D. Roosevelt, Peabody had persuaded the polio-stricken future President to convalesce at Warm Springs, Georgia. Pleased with the results, Roosevelt built himself a cottage there, and organized the Warm Springs Foundation. To "keep an eye on his friend," Peabody also built a cottage at Warm Springs, and during the following years he maintained close touch with Roosevelt. By 1934, the old gentleman was outside of the center of affairs in the Democratic party, but Alexander and his associates believed that his access to the President would make him a useful patron.

In January, 1935, Peabody sent a telegram to Marvin H. McIntyre at the White House, requesting that Alexander and Embree be granted an appointment with the President. When Roosevelt next visited Warm Springs, he invited Alexander for lunch, and to his dismay, Alexander found his host very well-informed on the subject of southern tenancy—Roosevelt had already read *The Collapse of Cotton Tenancy*, and had a copy of the book with him. The President did most of the talking and showed considerable interest, but to Alexander's disappointment he made no commitments. As "Dr. Will" returned to Atlanta, he was certain that the USDA remained the most responsive target for their future efforts.[5]

5. Johnson, Embree, and Alexander, *The Collapse of Cotton Tenancy*, pp. 49–52; Vance, *The Negro Agricultural Worker Under the Federal Rehabilitation Program*, report prepared for the Committee on Negroes in the Economic Recovery, Sec. 1, Pts. 1–2, USDA Library; Franklin D. Roosevelt, *FDR: His Personal Letters*, Elliot Roosevelt, ed. (New York: Duell, Sloan, and Pearce, 1950), Vol. II, pp. 564, 568, 618; Frank Freidel, *Franklin D. Roosevelt: The Ordeal* (Boston: Little, Brown, 1954), p. 193; *Time*, Vol. 38 (Mar. 14, 1938), p. 70; telegrams exchanged between Peabody and Marvin H. McIntyre, Jan. 10, 11, 14, 1935, FDRL, OF 1650; author's interviews with Paul H. Appleby, Alexander.

John Bankhead and Marvin Jones Respond

Although it may be true that, as Woodrow Wilson long ago observed, legislation "is an aggregate, not a simple, production [and] it is impossible to tell how many persons' opinions and influences have entered into its composition," the essential creative spark in the drive for tenancy legislation was provided not by the agitators and amateurs, but by two veteran members of Congress—John H. Bankhead of the Senate and Marvin Jones of the House.

In many ways, Democratic Senator Bankhead of Alabama was a complex man. His friends called him "Parity John," while some liberal critics saw him as a pompous southern Bourbon, with no deep interest in or commitment to the problem of rural poverty in the South. They charged that his interest in cotton was so great that conversation about anything else simply interrupted his thoughts about the white staple, and they believed that he was not nearly as human or as committed as his brother, William B. Bankhead, father of the actress Tallulah, and Speaker of the House from 1936 to 1940.

In reality, Senator John Bankhead was one of that breed of southern politicians in the 1930's who helped to bridge the gap between the conservative agrarian ideals and racial sensitivities of an age that was dying, and the new needs of a changing South. Born in Lamar County, a cotton region on the far western boundary of the state, in 1872, he was the son of John H. Bankhead, Sr., who had served in the House for twenty years and in the Senate from 1907 to 1920. John II won a degree and a Phi Beta Kappa key from the University of Alabama, and a law degree from Georgetown University Law School. Formerly a successful corporation lawyer for steel interests in Birmingham, and president of the family coal company, he had become an effective spokesman for cotton planters and one of the South's most influential members of the "cotton bloc" in Congress. The Alabama Farm Bureau Federation called him, "America's greatest agricultural statesman." First elected to the Senate in 1930, his power and influence grew when the Democrats captured the Congress and the White House in 1932.

Despite his conservative background, Bankhead was essentially a southern moderate who attempted, with considerable success, to balance his allegiance to a conservative southern constituency while supporting the liberal goals of the New Deal. In 1933, for instance, it was he who authored the unorthodox subsistence homesteads pro-

The Dance of Legislation Begins / [133]

vision, yet, at the same time, he was active in the fight against antilynching legislation. His resultant national image was therefore one of ambivalence, to the disappointment and confusion of those liberals who did not bear the burdens of public office and political responsibility. His record in the Senate confirmed the impression held by those who knew him that he cared very much indeed—albeit paternalistically—about the problems of low-income farm families in the South. His flexibility and political skill as a bargainer had won him considerable respect in the Senate and the country.

Even before Tannenbaum's letter to Appleby had been reviewed in the USDA, Bankhead informed Secretary Wallace that he was going to introduce legislation to help impoverished farm tenants and sharecroppers, and he requested that the Department offer him some suggestions on a bill. After a series of discussions were held with the staff of the Land-Use Planning Section of the AAA, a program began to take shape.

At the direction of Appleby and Davis, Gray of the Land-Use Planning Section assumed the leadership in preparing a draft for Bankhead. Assistant Secretary of Agriculture Wilson arranged a conference with Alexander, Embree, Tannenbaum, and Bankhead, in which they urged the Senator to introduce a bill that would authorize an annual appropriation to the USDA to finance the purchase of farms for resale to farm tenants and other landless people on long-term contracts.

On February 11, Bankhead introduced his original bill (S.1800), entitled, "The Farm Tenant Homes Act," which was a rough proposal that followed the general lines of the recommendations by the USDA. The bill called for the creation of a government corporation, similar to the Home Owners' Loan Corporation, financed by government guaranteed bonds not in excess of $1,000 million, and empowered to make loans to farm tenants, sharecroppers, and farm laborers only. Although the leaders of the USDA would have preferred financing through annual appropriations to the Department, and eligibility not so limited, they were particularly gratified with the bill's declaration of purpose, which read as follows:

> The powers conferred in this Act shall be exercised with a view to checking the rapid increase of tenancy in the United States, reducing unwarranted speculation in farm real estate, lessening the economic instability of tenant operators, and reducing the waste of soil resources which characterize the predominant systems of farm tenancy in the United States, alleviating conflicts between landowners and tenants which tend to develop, providing types of farm homes better adapted to the require-

ments of persons engaged in farming, promoting a more secure occupancy of farms and farm homes, improving farming systems and modes of living, contributing to agricultural adjustment, returning to the control of farm operators lands that have reverted to corporate ownership through foreclosure, and, in accordance with the example of many other civilized countries, providing, in general, a democratic system of land tenure.

It was proposed in the bill that the corporation should be established as an agency of the USDA, administered by the Secretary of Agriculture and a board of directors in accordance with rules and regulations prescribed by the Secretary. The corporation should be empowered to make loans to farm tenants and sharecroppers, to purchase farm homes, supplies, equipment, and livestock; to improve, develop, sell, or lease any lands acquired; and to provide for repayment of loans over a period of thirty to fifty years, at a "rate of interest . . . as low as the Corporation can secure the money plus a reasonable charge for administration."[6]

The bill (S.1800) was assigned to a sympathetic subcommittee of the Senate Committee on Agriculture and Forestry, and on March 5, Secretary Wallace led a parade of friendly witnesses. He defended the proposed bill as a bulwark against the perils of political upheaval, and declared, in part, as follows:[7]

6. Tannenbaum to Alexander, Jan. 11, 1935, FTP; James G. Maddox, "The Bankhead-Jones Farm Tenant Act," *Law and Contemporary Problems*, Vol. IV (Oct., 1937), pp. 434–36, and "The FSA," pp. 42–50; S.1800, 74th Cong., 1st Sess., Feb. 11, 1935, *Congressional Record*, Vol. 79, p. 1782; Vol. 78, p. 10471; author's interviews with Alexander, Maddox.

The first bill dealing directly with farm tenancy was H.R.9841, to provide farm homes for tenants, and was introduced in the House on June 4, 1934, by Reuben T. Wood, Democrat of Missouri. On Jan. 3, 1935, Democrat Andrew J. May of Kentucky introduced a bill authorizing the federal government to purchase productive lands, to subdivide them, and to establish farm homes for rural families in need. Both bills were stillborn.

7. U.S., Congress, Senate, Committee on Agriculture and Forestry, Hearings on S.1800, 74th Cong., 1st Sess., March 5, 1935, *To Create the Farm Tenant Homes Corporation* (Washington, D.C.: GPO, 1935), pp. 5–14.

The subcommittee consisted of Senator John H. Bankhead of Alabama and the following Senators: Farmer-Laborite Henrik Shipstead of Minnesota, Democrat James R. Pope of Idaho, Democrat Louis Murphy of Iowa, and Democrat Theodore G. Bilbo of Mississippi.

The parade of friendly witnesses, on March 5, included the following: Lewis C. Gray of the AAA, J. F. Jackson of the Central of Georgia Railway, B. Kirk Rankin of the *Southern Agriculturalist*, C. H. Hamilton of the Agricultural Experiment Station in Raleigh, North Carolina, Lawrence Westbrook of the FERA, Hugh McRae of the Southeastern Council, and Carl C. Taylor of the AAA. In addition, the subcommittee received a flood of letters, telegrams, and petitions from such people as Clarence Poe of the *Progressive Farmer* and the *Southern Ruralist*, and Elwood Mead of the Bureau of Reclamation in the Department of the Interior.

The present conditions, particularly in the South, provide fertile soil for Communist and Socialist agitators. I do not like the bitterness that is aroused by this sort of agitation, but I realize that the cure is not violence or oppressive legislation to curb these activities but rather to give these dispossessed people a stake in the social system. The American way to preserve the traditional order is to provide these refugees of the economic system with an opportunity to build and develop their own homes and to live on the land which they may call their own and on which they can make a modest living year after year.

Admittedly, Wallace went on, there were some people who might call this approach radicalism, but in his mind it was conservatism. The Russian Revolution, he declared, was caused not by the Bolsheviks, but by the large landowners who had exploited their tenants. And with this, Bankhead was moved to declare his own political faith:

I think there are two types of radicals: one is the soap-box orator who is willing to destroy by force all our institutions. The other is the extreme, old line, stand-pat conservative element that is willing to risk destruction of everything we have in order not to lose anything .... I think the latter element is just as dangerous to the country as the former, and they are both radicals.

Wallace acknowledged that the crop restriction program of the AAA had "probably added to the immediate difficulties," but he maintained that the causes were more deeply rooted. A healthy rural civilization in America would be impossible, he declared, "unless she acts to convert tenants of this sort into owner-farmers." The Bankhead bill, he believed, was squarely based on the traditional American principle of "trying to get the good farm land of America into the hands of owner-operators who live on family-sized farms, but with proper safeguards to prevent [land] ... speculation."

Despite dissatisfactions which he and others in the USDA saw in the bill's narrow emphasis on the problem of farm tenancy, Wallace gave the *objectives* of the bill his unqualified endorsement, as follows:

In short, I am happy to support a measure which has as its aim the creation of a substantial group of farm owners out of our present tenant class. I know of no better means of reconstructing our agriculture on a thoroughly sound and permanently desirable basis than to make as its foundation the family-sized, owner-operated farm. I believe that the provisions of this bill can be put into effective operation in such manner as to bring greater individual opportunity and security to thousands of tenants. At the same time, they should be of substantial aid in our crop-adjusting programs and in our attempts to conserve soil fertility and prevent erosion. Moreover, these provisions will aid materially in bringing about the development of a rural civilization embodying a higher standard of living and a better developed and more stable community life than has been possible under a system characterized by land speculation, absentee landlords, and migratory tenants.

In response to questions about the likely costs and difficulties of administering such a program, the Secretary reported that the USDA had not yet been called upon for a formal critique of the bill, but that his staff would examine the administrative details with great care.

Others appearing before the subcommittee were equally forthright in their recitation of what was becoming a litany on "the evils of farm tenancy." However, there was virtually no serious discussion of political and administrative problems that might be encountered in the proposed program. Eloquently absent were the powerful farm organizations which invariably were represented at congressional hearings on farm legislation by impressive delegations of persuasive spokesmen. The united support expressed by the witnesses who did appear, therefore, was not a true reflection of the reception that the bill would receive in Congress. As a matter of fact, several days of hearings had been planned originally, but due to the inability of some witnesses to testify, and because the subcommittee preferred not to encourage hostile witnesses to appear, further hearings were cancelled. With the help of majority leader Joseph T. Robinson of Arkansas, Bankhead prepared to drive the bill through the Senate. Meanwhile, what of progress in the House?

Bankhead's counterpart, in the House, was Marvin Jones—younger in years, less subject to caricature, and considerably more reticent than the Senator from Alabama, but an equally complex man. Born in 1882 on a small cotton farm near the northern Texas boundary with Oklahoma, he was raised, with his five brothers and five sisters, in a family that struggled against poverty. When Marvin was fifteen years old, his family's farm house burned to the ground, leaving them almost destitute, and it was necessary for the children to be dispersed among hospitable neighbors.

After a rudimentary grammar-school education, he worked for a few years selling stereoscopes, farming as a cotton tenant, riding the range as a cowboy, and teaching in a one-room school. With savings from these pursuits, he put himself through Southwestern University—predecessor of Southern Methodist—in three years, and then went on to complete the three-year law course at the University of Texas in two, graduating at the top of his class with a prize in oratory. One of his friends and classmates in law school was Sam Rayburn, who was destined to become the Speaker of the House. Showing no inclinations toward business, farming, or law practice, he seized his first opportunity to run for Congress, and in 1916 he defeated a veteran member of the House.

The conventional liberal-conservative dichotomy offered few clues to the political philosophy and practices of Marvin Jones in Congress. According to some of those who knew him well, he was "very agrarian" in the sense that he harbored a deep and abiding belief in the value of farming and rural life, and a commitment to the welfare of agriculture in the nation. As did many other Democrats of the South and Southwest of his time, he felt a sense of loyalty both to the conservative agrarian ideals under which he had been raised, and to a set of principles which, for lack of a better term, he called "Christian Charity." From his father, who had had no schooling but who was exceedingly interested in politics and public affairs, he inherited a sense of responsibility for those who were less fortunate than himself—some of his critical admirers called it a form of *noblesse oblige*.

Less prone to quotable verbalizations of his faith than some of the more articulate New Dealers, Jones believed that the rise of farm tenancy and the persistence of rural poverty represented a denial of "the American dream." Owner-operators of submarginal farm lands, farm tenants, sharecroppers, and farm laborers were unable to save enough surplus capital, to secure needed credit, and to develop equity in productive land of their own. Since landless people made poor farmers and irresponsible citizens, he believed, society had a stake in their habilitation or rehabilitation. Government, therefore, should assume major responsibility for remedies. Furthermore, Jones believed, the dangers of social discontent, especially in the South, would lead to political instability, and therefore there was political virtue, as well as economic and moral justification, in the New Deal farm programs designed to help this class of chronically impoverished farm families.

Like Bankhead, Jones was a loyal congressional stalwart of the President, but he succeeded at the same time in balancing the liberal and conservative tendencies in his constituency. He was an extremely able legislative strategist, who had learned much from his friend and mentor, Vice President John Nance Garner. As chairman of the House Committee on Agriculture since 1931, and as a personal friend of Roosevelt and Wallace—the Congressman and the Secretary maintained close communication and mutual admiration—Jones was a major influence in congressional farm policy. His support for a bill was a crucial asset, but such support was not easy to secure, for he studiously avoided promoting a measure which he did not firmly believe could win House passage. Above all else—even above his strong loyalty to the Democratic party—he perceived his role, as chairman of the House Committee on Agriculture, to be that of a great compromiser, balancing the competing interests in agriculture and keeping his committee as bipartisan as possible.[8]

Reflecting a streak of Populism in his character, derived perhaps from an uncle who had become a strong Populist, Jones had had a long history of activity in Congress on behalf of cheap money, and several times he had introduced "bank note legislation." On February 25, 1935, he therefore introduced a bill in the House entitled, "The Agriculture Bank Note Act" (H.R.6151). It proposed a reduction of interest rates on loans made by federal land banks to small farm owners actually engaged in farming, or to persons desirous of purchasing land to be operated as family farms. Annual interest rates were to be limited to 2 per cent, and loans were to be granted only to operators of farms that did not exceed $7,000 in normal value. Two weeks later, he introduced as a separate bill (H.R.6503) that portion of H.R.6151 that proposed the granting of mortgage loans through the Farm Credit Administration (FCA) to owners and purchasers of small farms at 2 per cent interest.

There was, therefore, a significant divergence in approach between Bankhead and Jones. Bankhead's S.1800 was essentially a proposal for a program of land purchase and resale to farm tenants, sharecroppers, and farm laborers, while Jones' H.R. 6503 was simply a proposal to offer lower interest rates on farm mortgage loans to small farm operators. In providing for loans "to buy farm homes and farm supplies and equipment, including livestock," S.1800 could have been construed as an authorization of "rural rehabilitation," even though the phrase was not used, while H.R.6503 was nothing more than a proposal for liberalized farm credit with which to promote farm ownership. Bankhead believed that there was a need for a special agency within the USDA, to be administered by the Secretary, while Jones was content to assign the program to the more conservative FCA.

In a series of conferences between the forces of Bankhead and Jones, assisted by borrowed staff from the USDA, there was a partial reconciliation of opposing approaches. On March 26, Bankhead introduced a compromise bill (S.2367), entitled "The Farmers Home

8. Author's interviews with Marvin Jones, Henry A. Wallace, Appleby; M. L. Wilson, COHC, Vol. 6, pp. 1040–41.

Act," in the Senate, while Jones submitted a companion bill (H.R. 7018) in the House.[9]

Popularly called the "Bankhead-Jones Farm Tenancy Bills," the compromise measures substituted an abbreviated declaration of purpose, in place of the brave paragraph in S.1800, and avoided mention of such goals as reducing land speculation, lessening economic instability, reducing the waste of soil resources, alleviating tenant-landlord conflicts, improving farming methods, reversing the trend toward absentee corporate land ownership, and providing a more democratic system of land tenure. The compromise bills were more flexible, however, in the sense that they were not restricted in application to tenants, sharecroppers, and farm laborers, and "rural rehabilitation" was specified as one of the powers of the proposed corporation.

The most important administrative feature of the bills was provision for the creation of a Farmers Home Corporation *outside* of the USDA, to be governed by a five-man board of directors, consisting of the Secretary of Agriculture, the Governor of the FCA, and three members to be appointed by the President and confirmed by the Senate. The program would be financed by a subscription of $50 million to the capital stock of the corporation from funds provided under the Emergency Relief Appropriation Act of 1935.

Neither as narrow as the original Jones bills, nor as broad as they would have to be in order to authorize the programs already in operation and about to be consolidated in the Resettlement Administration, the compromise bills specified rural rehabilitation as a purpose, but left some doubt as to whether that program was clearly authorized. In a letter to Charlton Ogburn of the American Federation of Labor, for instance, Bankhead declared that, "This bill, as changed, does not contemplate the temporary rural rehabilitation idea such as is now being conducted for relief purposes." Rural rehabilitation was specified in the bill, he explained, "merely ... to get money from that allocation [in the emergency appropriation acts]."[10]

The compromise bills (S.2367 and H.R.7018) were referred to their respective committees, where it was expected that favorable action would be taken promptly. In the Senate Committee on Agriculture and Forestry, the optimism proved well founded, and on April 11, S.2367 was favorably reported. Marvin Jones' Committee on Agriculture, however, became the dim dungeon of silence in this

9. *Congressional Record*, Vol. 79, pp. 4418, 4490.
10. Bankhead to Charlton Ogburn, Apr. 2, 1935, FTP.

case. Meanwhile, the interested leaders of the USDA continued their study of the proposals, while Alexander and his companions in agitation pressed their efforts to mobilize popular support.[11]

The Department of Agriculture Responds

Bankhead's introduction of S.1800 in the Senate on February 11, 1935, marked not the culmination of efforts by the leaders of the USDA to influence the proposed legislation, but the beginning. As the new year opened, their attention was concentrated on other departmental problems, and they were not particularly enthusiastic about a campaign to secure tenancy legislation at this time. It was more prudent, they believed, to permit the Resettlement Administration to be created and become well-established before opening the uncertain door to congressional action. However, with the congressional mill already beginning to grind, the cat was out of the bag. If there had to be congressional action at this time, at least it should be in the right direction.

Bankhead's S.1800, of course, was a disappointment to Wallace, Tugwell, and their staffs. Gray in the AAA immediately studied the bill, line by line, and found much to criticize both in its substantive features and its administrative and legal details—unduly narrow limitation to a simple loan program; absence of provision for "supervised credit" or technical assistance to borrowers; and insufficient dedication to the promotion of the economic and social progress of the family.

A few weeks later, after the leaders in the USDA were still further discomfited by the provisions of Jones' HR.6503, Gray, assisted by James G. Maddox and Howard R. Turner, prepared a report for general departmental distribution. In this document, which attracted considerable attention in the USDA, they emphasized that if there were going to be a program narrowly concerned with tenancy problems, rather than the larger issues of rural poverty in the country generally, then at least the program should have as one of its objectives the stimulation of "a fuller identification of farm laborers and tenants with community life by reducing the number of migratory farm tenants and laborers, and by encouraging group activity among low-income farmers." During the weeks that followed, efforts

---

11. U.S., Congress, Sen. Report 446, Apr. 11, 1935, 74th Cong., 1st Sess. (Washington, D.C.: GPO, 1935).

continued, both within the USDA and among the agitators and amateurs, to influence the final compromise on a bill.

On April 16, the House Committee on Agriculture, under Jones' chairmanship, conducted a one-day hearing on his compromise bill (H.R.7018), with support for its objectives coming from Secretary Wallace, Westbrook of the FERA, Gray of the AAA, and Clarence Poe of the *Progressive Farmer*. The hearing, which was little more than a formality, was marked by an absence of enthusiasm among Jones' fellow members of the committee. From comments made during the hearing, it was obvious that some members of the committee harbored doubts about whether they would support any tenancy legislation whatever. The American Farm Bureau Federation (AFBF), the National Grange, and other influential farm organizations were absent.

The only noteworthy feature of the hearing was Wallace's call for caution. "I would trust," he declared, "that the bill would not pass suddenly," and he urged that "the bill might be made as nearly perfect as can be." His caution, he explained, was due not to disinterest, but rather to his hope "that it will not be possible for some future Congress, 10 or 15 years hence, to say that this law was enacted without sufficient thought as to mechanics."

Some of Alexander's more ardent associates were promptly disappointed with what they believed was Wallace's ambivalence, and they criticized him for "coolness of heart." The Secretary's lack of enthusiasm at the time was partly due, presumably, to some reservations about the mechanics of the bill, but there were other reasons too.

For one thing, he was a midwesterner from Iowa, and while he was very well-informed about agricultural science and economics generally, the special problems of the South probably had not made as forceful an impact upon him as they had upon the liberals around Alexander. In retrospect, Tugwell has suggested that, to the contrary, "Wallace was familiar enough with the South [but] by this time he was under pressure from the agricultural power structure and had been captured by an ambition to become President. His base was in agriculture and tenants did not vote."[12]

Wallace's ambivalence was symptomatic of the posture of the USDA itself; as were Bankhead and Jones, the leaders of the Depart-

---

12. Gray's personal, annotated copy of S.1800; Gray to Wilson, Feb. 18, 1935; Gray, Maddox, Turner, memorandum to Wilson, based on National Resources Board, *Certain Aspects of Land Problems and Governmental Land Policies* (Washington, D.C.: GPO, 1935), Pt. VII, pp. 17–42; FTP.

Record of hearings on H.R.7018 published in U.S., Congress, House, Comment were compelled to cope with the competing interests and groups that composed their constituency. While the amateurs and agitators were free of official constraints, the men in the Department were not. As we shall see later in this study, the USDA was a house divided by a multiplicity of regional, commodity, personal, and bureaucratic tensions and competitions, and if the programs to combat rural poverty were to be administered successfully within the Department, a number of administrative issues would have to be resolved—budgetary questions; staffing problems; relations with the Extension Service, the Soil Conservation Service (SCS), and other departmental agencies and bureaus; and relations with the state agricultural institutions. This would require time and careful planning. Furthermore, the leaders of the USDA believed that they should husband their political capital and not invest it all in one legislative campaign involving programs that were actually peripheral to the main concerns of the USDA. This was particularly true during the spring of 1935, when other USDA-sponsored bills were beginning to meet more stubborn congressional resistance.

Unhappy about the narrowing of the bills' declaration of purpose and the provision for creation of the corporation *outside* of the USDA, Wallace and his assistants were particularly disturbed about the prospect that the proposed programs, if devoted entirely to the problems of southern tenancy, might become too closely identified with temporary relief measures. Inclusion of "rural rehabilitation" as a specified purpose in the compromise bills might enhance this danger. In April, Wallace sent a letter to Senator Ellison D. "Cotton Ed" Smith, chairman of the Senate Committee on Agriculture and Forestry, suggesting that all references to "rural rehabilitation" be stricken from the measure. "The long-time program contemplated in this Bill," he wrote, "can be more effectually administered if connotations of 'relief' are not associated with the Corporation."

The leaders of the USDA were therefore in a dilemma—they were dissatisfied with the pending legislation, but at the same time they were defensive about discrimination against tenants and sharecroppers in the AAA programs. Any suggestion that the USDA was opposed to the Bankhead-Jones bills might feed the impression among

---

mittee on Agriculture, Hearings on H.R.8, *Farm Tenancy*, 75th Cong., 1st Sess. (Washington, D.C.: GPO, 1937), pp. 323–62.

Author's interviews with Alexander, Gardner Jackson, Rev. John O'Grady, John Fischer; Tugwell to author, March 2, 1967.

Wilson was chairman of the Land Policy Committee and Gray was director.

liberals that the Roosevelt administration was not interested in low-income farmers.

A few months earlier, Tugwell had persuaded Wallace and Davis to investigate the impact of the AAA on cotton tenants and sharecroppers in the South, and, at Tugwell's suggestion, Calvin B. Hoover, a professor of economics on leave from Duke University and an economic consultant to the AAA, was sent to the South to survey the situation. In his report, in the spring of 1935, Hoover was carefully circumspect in his criticism of the AAA, but he did report that the cotton program was discriminating against cotton tenants—in impact, if not by design. His report, which was made public, provided further ammunition for the critics of the AAA, the USDA, and the New Deal generally. Wallace was therefore extremely careful to avoid any action that might alienate him and his Department from the liberal coalition behind the tenancy bills.

Tugwell also was uncertain about the proposed legislation. As far as he was concerned, farm tenancy was not the problem, and promotion of small farm ownership was not the solution. As we have already seen, he had no great enthusiasm for the rural rehabilitation program of the FERA, and in the spring of 1935 he was in the full tide of excitement about the launching of the Resettlement Administration. In his opinion, the Bankhead-Jones proposals would merely promote inefficiency and a "contented and scattered peasantry." Tugwell agreed with others in the USDA that if there were going to be legislation, they should attempt to secure the best possible terms, but he knew something else as well—there was little likelihood of White House intervention on behalf of the legislation in the current session of Congress. Therefore, Tugwell reasoned, after the Resettlement Administration was successfully underway, there might be some virtue in securing legislation sufficiently broad to grant the new agency a sound statutory basis. For the present, he preferred to remain on the sidelines.[13]

---

13. Hearings on H.R.7018; Wallace to Ellison D. Smith, Apr. 29, 1935, NA, RG 46; Calvin B. Hoover, "Human Problems in Acreage Reduction in the South," Processed (n.d., 1935), NA, RG 145; exchange of correspondence between Roosevelt and Rexford G. Tugwell, Nov. 21–25, 1935, FDRL, OF 1568; author's interview with Wallace; Wallace address at Atlanta, Ga., Apr. 13, 1935, quoted in *New York Times*, Apr. 22, 1935; John P. Davis, "A Black Inventory of the New Deal," *The Crisis*, Vol. XLII (May, 1935), pp. 141–42; David E. Conrad, *The Forgotten Farmers: The Story of Sharecroppers in the New Deal* (Urbana: Univ. of Illinois Press, 1965), pp. 123–26; Tugwell, "Behind the Farm Problem: Rural Poverty," *New York Times*, June 10, 1937.

The Agitators and Amateurs Respond: Act Two

Before proceeding with our chronology, it seems appropriate here to stop the clock and to acknowledge the differences between *influence* and *attempts* to influence, between the *potentialities* and *actualities* of power. Since 1936, when Harold D. Lasswell defined the "study of politics" as the "study of influence and the influential," the concepts of power and influence have attracted increasing attention from students of politics and government.

In 1961, Edward C. Banfield defined "influence" as the "ability to get others to act, think, or feel as one intends," and, drawing on Chester I. Barnard's concept of rational cooperative action, he equated cooperative activity with the exercise of influence:

> To concert activity for any purpose . . . a more or less elaborate system of influence must be created: the appropriate people must be persuaded, deceived, coerced, inveigled, or otherwise induced to do what is required of them. Any cooperative activity . . . must be viewed as a system of influence.

Writing at the same time, Robert A. Dahl, in what is probably one of the most fruitful attempts to clarify and apply the concepts of power and influence, made explicit what was implicit in Banfield's analysis. "One of the most elementary principles of political life," Dahl wrote, "is that a political resource is only a *potential* source of influence." Focusing on the political outputs as well as the human inputs in the equations of influence and power, Dahl has distinguished between "the rituals of power and the realities of power." The democratic mold of American political life and the requisites of legitimacy lead to the performance of democratic ceremonials in which participants may have no illusions about the *real* political outputs. While attempts to exercise effective political influence may not significantly affect ultimate decisions, such efforts are not entirely meaningless. According to Dahl, such ritualism may help to clothe official decisions with legitimacy, mobilize the allegiance of constituencies, clarify social issues, and enlarge the social basis of democratic participation in political life. With these provisos, let us now return to the dance of legislation in 1935.[14]

14. Harold D. Lasswell, *Politics: Who Gets What, When, How* (New York: Whittlesey House, 1936), p. 223; Edward C. Banfield, *Political Influence* (New York: The Free Press, 1961), pp. 3–12; Robert A. Dahl, *Who Governs?* (New Haven: Yale Univ. Press, 1961), pp. 108–14, 271–73.

For the ardent champions of tenancy legislation, the second act in the campaign was performed in a mood of deepening pessimism. Neither the President, the leaders of Congress, nor the Secretary of Agriculture and his assistants had shown any sense of urgency. In the House, Jones seemed to be in no hurry to report H.R.7018, and in the Senate in April, after only a few days of debate, S.2367 was recommitted to "Cotton Ed" Smith's committee.[15]

Meanwhile, agitated, Alexander and his associates decided to concentrate their efforts on attempting to mobilize a coalition of support among a diverse combination of groups—northern liberals who normally rallied behind New Deal causes; southern liberals and moderates who had long sought remedies for the chronic rural poverty around them; orthodox agrarians who still clung to the Jeffersonian ideal of the family farm; organized labor groups who viewed the campaign for tenancy legislation as an opportunity to promote their own movement in the South; academic people, who for more than a decade had hoped in vain to see their research findings applied to chronic rural poverty; minority and ethnic groups, especially in the Northeast, who felt a sense of moral solidarity with low-income farm people in the South; and social action groups in the churches, whose moral sense was offended by the human costs of poverty.

To provide an instrument, they organized the National Committee on Small Farm Ownership—the name, they believed, would help to exploit the mystique of land ownership and the family farm. With Peabody, the President's friend from Warm Springs, serving as chairman, and with assistance and encouragement from Wilson and Gray in the USDA, they completed their organization by the second week in April, and scheduled a national conference to be held later in the month.

Meanwhile, far more significant developments were unfolding within the government. Early in April, opportunity knocked for Alexander when Tugwell offered him the new post of Assistant Administrator of the Resettlement Administration, which was to be created at the end of the month. Despite his personal belief that ultimate solutions to social problems lay in the local communities rather than in Washington, and his personal distaste for large bureaucratic operations, "Dr. Will" accepted Tugwell's offer, and within a few weeks he was established in an office in Washington. To help

---

15. Exchange of correspondence between Alexander and Tannenbaum, Jan. 11, Feb. 2, 18, Mar. 12, 1935; George E. Haynes to Tannenbaum, Mar. 15, 1935; Tannenbaum to Haynes, Apr. 10, 1935; FTP.

fill the gap in the lobbying campaign which resulted from his departure, he promptly appointed Brooks Hays, the Democratic National Committeeman from Arkansas, as his special assistant in the agency, with responsibility for helping to mobilize southern members of the House of Representatives.

While Alexander was preparing to join the professionals, the National Committee on Small Farm Ownership assembled in Washington in April, and there they listened to Senator Bankhead and Assistant Secretary of Agriculture Wilson explain the purposes and provisions of the pending legislation. The delegates discussed the "evils of farm tenancy," and prepared a statement, which they duplicated and sent to every member of Congress. "No greater problem confronts our rural community than the persistent growth of farm tenancy," the statement declared. The tenancy legislation pending before Congress, it added, was "one of the most important and constructive pieces of legislation" ever presented to the Congress.[16]

A few days after the conference, while the bills remained in the House and Senate committees, welcome support came from an influential group of southerners who called themselves the Southern Policy Committee. Officers of the group were H. C. Nixon, professor of political science at Tulane University, chairman; Hayes, vice chairman; and Francis Pickens Miller, a leader of the anti-machine faction of the Democratic party in Virginia, secretary. Starting about 1935, an informal and open-ended group of Washington-based members of the Southern Policy Committee and others, including people from both Congress and the administration, made a practice of holding informal Thursday night dinner meetings at Hall's Restaurant in Washington, to discuss southern politics and policy. From time

---

16. Tannenbaum to Alexander, Apr. 4, 1935; Statement of the National Committee on Small Farm Ownership, Apr. 19, 1935; Alexander to Tannenbaum, Apr. 6, 1935; Wilson to A. R. Mann, Mar. 27, 1935; FTP. Author's interview with Brooks Hays; Hays to author, Apr. 4, 1955.

In addition to Alexander, Embree, Johnson, and the sponsors of their book, *The Collapse of Cotton Tenancy*, the membership of the National Committee on Small Farm Ownership consisted of the following diverse people: Rev. Howard Bishop of the Catholic Rural Life Conference; Donald Comer of Avondale Mills, in Birmingham, Ala.; Ivan Lee Holt of the Federal Council of Churches of Christ in America; J. F. Jackson of the Central of Georgia Railway; Hugh McRae of the Southeastern Council; John B. Miller of the Farmers Cooperative Council; Frank O'Hara of the Catholic University, Washington, D.C.; Louis J. Taber of the National Grange; and M. W. Thatcher and Cal Ward of the National Farmers Union. All of the members, with the exception of the two most conservative people on the list—Miller and Taber—attended the conference. The only full-time professional agricultural leaders in attendance were Thatcher and Ward of the liberal National Farmers Union.

The Dance of Legislation Begins / [147]

to time, participants included Hays, Miller, John Sparkman, Lister Hill, Maury Maverick, Alexander, Baldwin, Appleby, and others.

For four days, during the last week of April, twenty-seven delegates from the Southern Policy Committee, representing nine southern states, held a policy conference in Atlanta, Georgia, to discuss the Bankhead-Jones bills and the problems of rural poverty in the South generally. The list of participants was a constellation of thoughtful southerners from the fields of education, law, social work, labor, and business. On April 28, they issued a letter to every member of the Senate, in which they declared:

> As members of the Southern Policy Conference representing nine Southern States, we regard Senator Bankhead's Farm Tenant Bill as the most constructive piece of land legislation yet introduced. At our recent meeting in Atlanta . . . we unanimously voted to support prompt and favorable action on the Bankhead Bill as the most promising means of removing the devastating tenant system. We urge you to give this bill your immediate support.

As a follow-up on the conference, Miller wired the membership, warning them that the Bankhead bill might be emasculated or allowed to die in "Cotton Ed" Smith's hands, and urging them to wire the Senator from South Carolina. A few days later, more in spite of these efforts to influence him than because of them, Smith agreed to report the bill to the Senate floor. Miller again wired the membership, claiming credit for the Senator's change of heart and urging them to continue to work on individual Senators. The result was a deluge of telegrams and letters upon the offices of Smith and other members of his committee. However, "This kind of thing fools nobody," Donald R. Matthews has written, for, "It is expected, quickly recognized, and heavily discounted by the senators and their staffs."[17]

---

17. Francis Pickens Miller to membership of Southern Policy Committee, May 7, 10, 1935; Miller to Tannenbaum, May 8, 1935; FTP. H. C. Nixon to Ellison D. Smith, May 7, 1935; Mercer G. Evans to Smith, May 7, 1935; "National Policy Group" (Donald Davidson, Frank L. Owsley, Lyle H. Lanier, Robert Woodruff, Brainerd Cheney, James Waller) to Smith, May 7, 1935; NA, RG 46.

The delegates to the Atlanta conference of the Southern Policy Committee included the following: Brooks Hays of Arkansas; Will W. Alexander, representing the Interracial Commission in Atlanta; Tarleton Collier of *The Georgian*; Mercer G. Evans of Emory University; J. L. Harris and A. M. Snyder of the *Atlanta Constitution*; A. Steve Nance of the American Federation of Labor in Georgia; H. C. Nixon of Tulane University; Clarence Poe of the *Progressive Farmer*; Philip Weltner, chancellor of the Georgia University system; Virginius Dabney of the *Richmond* (Va.) *Times-Dispatch*; Francis Pickens Miller, secretary of the Southern Policy Committee; and others.

One of the telegrams received by Senator Ellison D. Smith, as a result of

One sector of potential support on which Alexander and Tannenbaum personally concentrated was the social action groups in the churches. The Catholic Rural Life Bureau in the Church's Social Action Department, and the Catholic Rural Life Conference, for instance, for more than a decade, had been concerned about the problems of impoverished Catholic farmers. In April, one of the Catholic social action leaders reported, following a tour of poverty areas in the South, that, "As far as Catholics are concerned, the South is a missionary territory," and he urged that the Church mobilize its resources accordingly. With encouragement from Tannenbaum, the National Catholic Welfare Conference circulated a petition among clergy and lay leaders seeking signatures to a statement in support of the Bankhead-Jones bills. "None of the many and sometimes powerfully cogent arguments advanced against government 'interference' in economic problems," the petition read, "can be justly made against the Bankhead bill." In publishing the statement, the Catholic periodical, *Commonweal*, editorialized that the Church's support of the proposed legislation represented a devotion to "the true principles not only of Christian teaching but of traditional Americanism" as well.[18]

---

the agitational efforts of the committee, came from a group in Nashville, Tennessee, called the "Nashville Policy Group," who wired the Senator that if the Bankhead-Jones bills failed, "the South faces a period of increasing poverty and class antagonism which will be capitalized by agitators and demagogues." Four of the signers of the telegram had participated, during the previous decade, with a group of other southern intellectuals, called the "Southern Agrarians," who joined in writing a book which was a nostalgic call for a return to the Jeffersonian agrarian myth. "Twelve Southerners" (John Crowe Ransom, Donald Davidson, Frank L. Owsley, J. G. Fletcher, Lyle H. Lanier, Allen Tate, H. C. Nixon, A. N. Lyttle, Robert Penn Warren, J. D. Wade, H. B. Kline, Stark Young), *I'll Take My Stand* (New York: Harper, 1930).

See also the following: Owsley, "The Pillars of Agrarianism," *American Review*, Vol. IV (March, 1935), pp. 531–47, and his book, *Agrarianism* (Chapel Hill: Univ. of North Carolina Press, 1935). For the role of this kind of inspired communication with members of Congress, see Donald R. Matthews, *U.S. Senators and Their World* (Chapel Hill: Univ. of North Carolina Press, 1960), p. 186.

18. Aaron I. Abell, *American Catholicism and Social Action: A Search for Social Justice, 1865–1950* (New York: Doubleday, 1960), pp. 217–19, 234–63; Rev. John A. Ryan, "The Concept of Social Justice," *Catholic Charities Review*, Vol. 18 (Dec., 1934), pp. 313–15; Paul Kiniery, "Catholics and the New Deal," *Catholic World*, Vol. 140 (Apr., 1935), pp. 10–20; Francis L. Broderick, *Right Reverend New Dealer: John A. Ryan* (New York: Macmillan, 1962); Rev. Edgar Schmiedeler, *Our Rural Proletariat*, National Catholic Welfare Conference, Social Action Department, Social Action Series No. 11 (New York: Paulist Press, 1938); *Commonweal*, Vol. 21 (Apr. 26, 1935), pp. 719–21.

Rev. George M. Nell to Rev. Edgar Schmiedeler, Apr. 9, 1935; Tannenbaum to Alexander, Apr. 24, 1935; FTP. Author's interview with Rev. John O'Grady.

The Protestants were somewhat slower than the Catholics in joining the campaign, but following persuasive pressures by "Dr. Will" on the Federal Council of Churches of Christ in America, the executive committee of the Council adopted a resolution in April which called for prompt congressional action to remedy "the deplorable conditions under which two millions of our fellow-citizens—both Negro and white—live and work." Meanwhile, Alexander urged members of the Protestant churches to "go after" four members of the Senate Committee on Agriculture and Forestry who had voted in favor of the motion to recommit the bill and three members who had failed to vote.[19]

Tenancy legislation may have been primarily an agricultural affair, but Alexander and Tannenbaum were prepared to seek support from any of the interests and groups which formed the political coalition behind the New Deal, whether they came from the farm or the factory, the town or the metropolis. During his interracial work in Atlanta, for instance, Alexander had developed a friendship with George Googe, Southeastern Representative of the American Federation of Labor (AFL), and Steve Nance, President of the Atlanta Federation of Trades. Familiar with the generally unsuccessful efforts of the AFL to organize industrial workers in the South, Alexander suggested to Googe and Nance that one of the reasons for their difficulty was the great reservoir of unskilled labor on southern farms "who were ever ready to step in and take the jobs away from those who are now in the industries." The Bankhead bill, he argued, would help to stabilize marginal farmers and farm laborers on the land, and thus reduce their threat to industrial labor. With the help of Googe, Nance, and Ogburn, William Green was persuaded to depart from AFL policy of restricting its attention to labor problems and to endorse the Bankhead bill.[20]

In all of this lobbying effort—much of it fell on deaf ears—it was frustrating to Alexander in particular that, despite the special relevance of the proposed legislation to impoverished Negro farm families, there was virtually no adequate national machinery through which Negro power might be mobilized. There were, of course, the

---

19. George E. Haynes to Tannenbaum, Mar. 15, 1935; Tannenbaum to Haynes, Apr. 10, 1935; Tannenbaum to Alexander, Apr. 24, 1935; Resolution adopted by executive committee of the Federal Council of Churches of Christ in America, Apr. 26, 1935; Peabody to Samuel McCrea Cavert, Apr. 26, 1935; FTP.

20. Alexander to Tannenbaum, Mar. 12, 1935; Ogburn to Bankhead, Apr. 9, 1935; FTP; author's interview with Alexander; Alexander, COHC, pp. 592–93; *New York Times*, Apr. 15, 1935.

National Association for the Advancement of Colored People (NAACP), and the National Urban League, but they tended to focus on strictly racial issues, education, and litigation over civil rights. Besides, the mobilization of "Black Power" was a task that remained for a future generation.

For lack of a better tactic, Alexander sent urgent night letters to the presidents of Negro colleges and universities requesting them to communicate with their friends in the North and with members of the Senate from New England. He also sent a night letter to his friend, W. E. B. DuBois, the prominent Negro writer, scholar, and educator at Atlanta University, urging that he in turn apply some pressure to Senator Arthur Capper of Kansas, a key midwestern Republican member of the farm bloc.[21]

With these efforts completed, Alexander, Embree, Johnson, and Tannenbaum believed that they had done what they could, and that the stage was now set for a showdown in the Senate.

Stalemate in Congress

The spring of 1935 was not an opportune time to seek passage of tenancy legislation in Congress. The year had opened in a climate of "acute political turbulence," Arthur M. Schlesinger, Jr., has written, as "Squalls were making up in every quarter, while the skipper stalled and vacillated, now beating to windward, now turning and running before the blow." And viewing the relations between the White House and Capitol Hill, Charles S. Johnson observed from Nashville that, "It is just our luck—and that of the chronic underdog—that the Senate should select this precise moment to challenge the divinity and omniscience of the President." Locked in struggle over such other major measures as Robert F. Wagner's labor disputes bill, Joseph F. Guffey's coal bill, the Wagner-Costigan anti-lynching bill, Harry L. Hopkins' emergency relief appropriation bill, Frances Perkins' social security bill, and Marriner Eccles' banking reform bill, it was unlikely that either the Congress or the President would grant a very high priority to legislation for impoverished farm tenants and sharecroppers.

On April 11, the Senate Committee on Agriculture and Forestry

21. Peabody to Tannenbaum, Apr. 23, 1935; Tannenbaum to Alexander, Apr. 25, 1935; Clarence Poe to Ellison D. Smith, May 1, 1935; Alexander to Robert Russa Moton, Arthur Howe, Thomas E. Jones, and others, May 1, 1935; FTP. Alexander, COHC, pp. 596–97.

The Dance of Legislation Begins / [151]

favorably reported S.2367 to a Senate that was immobilized by a determined southern filibuster to prevent consideration of the Wagner-Costigan anti-lynching bill. However, majority leader Robinson of Arkansas persuaded Costigan to forego his previous motion on the anti-lynching measure, to allow debate of the Bankhead bill, and on April 16, S.2367 arrived on the Senate floor.[22]

For more than a week, with Costigan seated at the rear of the chamber watching for every opening to bring up his anti-lynching measure, the Senate debated S.2367. Since every new amendment provided an opportunity to further impede action on the anti-lynching bill, some of the proposed amendments, and debate upon them, were simply exercises in dilatory tactics. Harry F. Byrd of Virginia, for instance, sought to have S.2367 referred to the more hostile Senate Committee on Banking and Currency. Josiah Bailey of North Carolina offered an amendment to eliminate from the bill the authorization for a bond issue—in the opinion of Robinson, it would "take the heart out of the bill." Henry Ashurst of Arizona offered an amendment to subject the bonds provided for in S.2367 to taxation, and in the acrimonious debate that followed, Georgia's Richard B. Russell vigorously opposed the amendment as an attempt "to increase the burden on farm tenants by raising the interest rates on loans." Arthur H. Vandenberg of Michigan attempted to have the bill recommitted to Smith's committee, and provoked Tom Connally of Texas to charge that, "Instead of meeting the enemy at the gate and hitting him on the nose, the Senator from Michigan wants to toll him off down the alley and hit him with a blackjack while he is hidden behind a corner."

All of these and other attempts to kill or emasculate S.2367 were defeated by partisan votes. On April 24, however, Republican William E. Borah of Idaho, unwittingly abetted by a switch of eight liberal Senators who had consistently supported the bill but who were dissatisfied with its narrow concern with farm tenancy and believed that it could be broadened in committee, succeeded in winning recommitment to Smith's committee, with instruction to report back not later than May 12.

In all of these tests on the Senate floor, a voting pattern had emerged, which showed a generally cohesive group of thirty-one Democrats, largely from the South and Middle West, and one lone Republican, George W. Norris of Nebraska, in defense of the bill. In consistent opposition were a hard core of sixteen Republicans and

---

22. U.S., Congress, Sen. Report 446; *Congressional Record*, Vol. 79, p. 5748.

twelve Democrats, largely from the Eastern Seaboard states and the Far West. However, there was no direct relationship in every case between each Senator's voting behavior on S.2367 and his attitudes toward rural poverty and the "evils of farm tenancy." Partisan advantage was certainly a factor, as reflected in the virtual absence of Republicans from the roster of consistent supporters of the bill. There were also personal reasons for the way some Senators voted. Theodore G. Bilbo of Mississippi, for instance, was as interested in fighting his neighbor, Huey Long, as he was in combatting rural poverty, and he looked upon the Bankhead bill as "not only one of the most constructive bills that has been before Congress this session but with it we can drive Huey Long out of the South." It is also probable that the filibuster against the anti-lynching bill partially explained the collaboration of Bailey of North Carolina, Clark of Missouri, and McCarran of Nevada with the opponents of the bill, but who finally voted for its passage.

On May 9, two days short of the deadline, Smith's committee reported S.2367 back to the Senate, with only minor changes. The committee incorporated in the bill all of the amendments adopted by the Senate, but they changed the amendment, which had provided that the property of the proposed Farmers Home Corporation should be subject to taxation, so as to exempt its franchise, capital, reserves, surplus, loans, income, and personal property. Another change was a limitation placed on the speed with which the corporation might issue the $1,000 million in government guaranteed bonds. None of the bonds were to be issued within one year after approval of the Act, nor were more than $300 million to be issued within three years after passage. Capital stock of the corporation, to be used as the working fund during the first year of operation, was reduced from $100 million to $50 million.

The last scene of the act was anti-climactic. On June 21, largely through the efforts of majority leader Robinson, S.2367 was brought up again for reconsideration by a Senate heavily burdened with other particularly urgent New Deal measures. For two days, time was consumed by the delaying tactics of Republican and Democratic conservatives, but all attempts to prevent the inevitable were doomed, and in the late afternoon of June 24—it was 133 days since the introduction of Bankhead's original bill in February—S.2367 passed the Senate by a vote of forty-five to thirty-two. Forty Democrats, assisted by Progressive La Follette and Farm-Laborite Shipstead, thus defeated the bloc of eighteen Democrats and fourteen

Republicans. Of the nineteen members of the Senate Committee on Agriculture and Forestry, only three—Smith of South Carolina, Moore of New Jersey, and Norbeck of South Dakota—voted against the bill. Of the eleven wavering Senators, on whom Tannenbaum and his friends had attempted to exert special pressure, all voted affirmatively. With its work on the measure completed, the Senate referred S.2367 to the House, where Jones' companion bill, H.R.7018, had remained in committee. Finally, at midnight on August 26, 1935, without Jones ever having brought the bill up again before his committee, the first session of the Seventy-fourth Congress adjourned, and with it went the hopes for enactment of the bills in 1935. Thus, the curtain descended on the first act in the dance of legislation, leaving the Congress, the USDA, and the White House in approximately the same postures—one house, so to speak, able to pass the bill in its present form, and one house either unwilling or unable to do so.

In the post-mortem on the stillbirth of the Bankhead-Jones bills in 1935, the liberal lobbyists, whose world was peopled by saints and sinners, sought to assign blame primarily to Jones' alleged failure to mobilize support in the House of Representatives. Actually, there was some justification for the charge—the Texan really had not expended a great deal of energy and political capital on the measure. As we have already seen, he was a shrewd politician and parliamentary strategist who did not believe in lost causes, and in 1935 there was no doubt about it—the Bankhead-Jones bills were a lost cause. Jones knew his Committee on Agriculture—their special commodity interests, their fears, and their flaws—and he had no hope in 1935 of winning their support. His usual strategy was to try to secure a unanimous committee in reporting any bill, because, he believed, passage in the House was difficult enough without having to carry the burden of internal committee differences to the floor. Contrary to some liberals' belief, his behavior was not simply disinterest. He was no less interested than were Roosevelt, Wallace, Tugwell and others in the USDA, none of whom had demonstrated much enthusiasm for the bills in 1935.[23]

---

23. *Congressional Record*, Vol. 79, pp. 6120–37, 6187, 6193, 6195–96, 6204, 6272, 6288–90, 6417, 6493–6501, 9952–60; *Washington* (D.C.) *Post*, Apr. 21, 24, 1935, Theodore G. Bilbo to Joseph T. Robinson and Roosevelt, Aug. 18, 1935, FDRL, OF 1650; U.S., Congress, Sen. Report 603, May 9, 1935, 74th Cong., 1st Sess. (Washington, D.C.: GPO, 1935); author's interview with Marvin Jones.

Some of the disappointed advocates of tenancy legislation, especially among the agitators and amateurs, placed blame also on the leaders of the USDA—Wallace was allegedly "cool of heart," and did not fully understand the needs of the South; Tugwell was immersed in building his Resettlement Administration; and Davis was viewed as a conservative tool of the commercial farming and processing interests. What some of the agitators and amateurs presumably failed to fully understand was that while they themselves were free to follow their zeal, the men in positions of official responsibility were compelled to assume equivocal positions and to remain open to amendments and concessions. The problem of the drought; the Supreme Court's declaration of the Frazier-Lemke Act for the relief of farm mortgagors as unconstitutional; the imprisonment of the amendments to the Agricultural Adjustment Act in Senator "Cotton Ed" Smith's committee; the developing cleavage in the Department between liberals and conservatives, between the interests of the producer and the processor of farm products—these were some of the items that enjoyed higher rank on the agenda of the USDA.

Finally, this post-mortem examination is not complete without an evaluation of the performance of Alexander and his fellow lobbyists. Despite their feverish activity and the letterhead impressiveness of their conferences, committees, and communications, there is no evidence to suggest that they succeeded in persuading, deceiving, coercing, inveigling, or otherwise inducing a significant number of men at either end of Pennsylvania Avenue to act, think, or feel as they intended. With a measure of consensus already existing in the Senate and in the White House before the lobbyists and amateurs commenced their performance in the democratic ritual, and with the effective leadership exercised by Senators Bankhead, Robinson, and a few of their southern colleagues, Senate passage of S.2367 was really never in doubt, and the credit belonged not to Alexander, Tannenbaum, Johnson, and their associates, but to the professional political people.

If anything was accomplished in these amateur efforts to exercise influence it was in the direction suggested by Robert Dahl—they helped to clothe the drive for tenancy legislation with legitimacy, they helped to clarify and dramatize the issue of chronic rural poverty, they mobilized their heterogeneous army of liberal interests and groups behind their cause, and they helped to create opportunities for broader participation in the public policy process.

The Dance of Legislation Begins / [155]

Toward Legitimacy: Success in Failure

As a campaign to achieve a forthright congressional commitment to the assault on chronic rural poverty and to secure unequivocal affirmation of programs already launched by the Resettlement Administration and its predecessors, the drive in 1935 for passage of the Bankhead-Jones bills was a failure. Whether motivated by an interest in productive efficiency, land conservation, political stability, social equity, morality, or sheer sentimentality, an army of politicians, writers, social critics, and commentators had helped to convert the farm tenant and sharecropper into symbols of America's sense of guilt. The amplitude and intensity of the dialogue, and the feverish efforts to exert influence upon the Congress were not necessarily indicative of either an understanding of chronic rural poverty or a readiness to cope adequately with it.

In 1936, James Agee, accompanied by photographer Walker Evans, journeyed to the South to prepare a documentary report on southern rural poverty for *Fortune* magazine. In their chronicle they asserted that the crescendo of concern about this poverty was not necessarily indicative of widespread understanding of it or commitment to its abolition. The use of the term "sharecropper," for instance, they believed covered a host of subjective attitudes and motivations:[24]

... it has very swiftly, and within a very few years, absorbed every corruptive odor of inverted snobbery, marxian, journalistic, jewish, and liberal logomachia, emotional blackmail, negrophilia, belated transference, penis-envy, gynecological flurry and fairly good will ... and is one of the words a careful man will be watchful of, and by whose use and inflection he may take clear measurement of the nature, and the stature, and the causes, and the timbre, of the enemy.

One face of "the enemy" was not his outright opposition to helping the chronically impoverished farm family, but rather his well meaning belief that the times called for business as usual—conventional farm programs would eventually solve the problem.

Despite the failures of 1935, there was some success in creating the preconditions for passage of appropriate legislation. Although no mandate was won, a measure of consensus was reached at each

---

24. James Agee and Walker Evans, *Let Us Now Praise Famous Men* (New York: Ballantine Books, 1966), p. 415. First published in 1941 (Boston: Houghton Mifflin).

end of Pennsylvania Avenue and between them. A dialogue between responsible officials of the government and interested private citizens was begun. Although the bills failed to pass Congress, they provided a symbol and a rallying point for a very diverse set of interests and an opportunity for participation in the public policy process. In brief, advocates of the strategy of gradualness could find grounds for some gratification.

However, the experience of 1935 suggests that, if major innovations are necessary to cope with problems of our culture, issue articulation, popular education, and citizen participation are not enough. Ultimate reliance must be placed upon harnessing the organized power of the government itself to the felt needs of society; otherwise, legitimacy may not be achieved and democratic participation might be nothing more than ritualism.

The harnessing of the organized power of the government was essentially the contribution that the President and his administration were in a position to make. During the campaign for tenancy legislation in the House and Senate, Roosevelt stayed his hand, but in many other policy areas he was conferring organization upon some real drives, interests, and concerns in the nation and was making them more potent than they otherwise would have been. This was precisely one of the roles that the Resettlement Administration was about to play. It is tempting to speculate upon the confusion that probably would have ensued for Tugwell's new agency in 1935 had the tenancy bills been enacted at that time.

With the crystallization of sentiment in Congress already underway, with the President about to assert the leadership that would characterize his administration during the election year of 1936, and with the Resettlement Administration rapidly approaching the time when legislative ratification of its programs would be strategically desirable, the structure of the situation was becoming more hospitable for passage of appropriate legislation.

Although there may be a tendency for "strategic thinking" to lead to intellectual defeatism, and for the value of gradualness to become an argument for doing nothing, the experience of 1935 suggests that in a large and complex democracy, there is political virtue in pursuing issues when the likelihood of success is greatest—when the time is ripe.

CHAPTER VI

*TOWARD LEGITIMACY:
THE BANKHEAD-JONES FARM
TENANT ACT*

> *Every fury on earth has been absorbed in time, as art, or as religion, or as authority in one form or another. The deadliest blow the enemy of the human soul can strike is to do fury honor. Swift, Blake, Beethoven, Christ, Joyce, Kafka, name me a one who has not been thus castrated. Official acceptance is the one unmistakable symptom that salvation is beaten again, and is the one surest sign of fatal misunderstanding, and is the kiss of Judas.*
>
> JAMES AGEE[1]
> *Let Us Now Praise Famous Men*

From Senate passage of S.2367 in June, 1935, until the Seventy-fifth Congress convened in January, 1937, there was an interlude of inaction for the Bankhead-Jones bills, but when the curtain rose on the second act, it revealed a differently structured situation. For the nation as a whole, many of the customary indicators—national income, wholesale prices, unemployment, market value of stocks, production figures—suggested that the atmosphere of economic urgency was dissolving. Through the improvement of farm

---

1. James Agee and Walker Evans, *Let Us Now Praise Famous Men* (New York: Ballantine Books, 1966), p. 14.

commodity prices, the reduction of cotton and grain surpluses, and the programs of the Agricultural Adjustment Administration (AAA), federal land banks, Federal Farm Mortgage Corporation, Farm Credit Administration (FCA), and other agencies, agriculture as a whole had shared in the emergent national recovery.[2]

However, chronic rural poverty remained. Agriculture still possessed its victims—marginal midwestern farmers for whom the drought meant total failure; southern tenants, sharecroppers, and laborers for whom restriction of cash crops meant eviction from their rented lands and homes or complete destitution where they were; subsistence farmers of Appalachia who were actually outside of the farm economy; and migratory farm laborers for whom the filtering-down effects of rising prices was a snare and a delusion. For the chronic underdogs of agriculture, the circumstances in 1937 remained grim.

One of the sources of political dissatisfaction in the South, which had been a factor in the so-called "purge" in the AAA in 1935, it will be recalled, was the situation among evicted tenants, sharecroppers, and laborers in cotton areas of the South—especially in Arkansas. It was this kind of dislocation which had contributed to the drive for tenancy legislation in 1935. The Arkansas situation remained a stark reminder that for some farm people, prosperity was still around a very long corner. During the early months of 1936, for instance, the White House and the U.S. Department of Agriculture (USDA) had received a steady stream of anguished pleas for help from Arkansas. Norman Thomas, still the gadfly to the New Deal and again preparing for another quixotic race for the Presidency, wired Franklin D. Roosevelt in February, appealing for an investigation of the eviction of tenants and sharecroppers who were living in a tent colony and who were being threatened with mob violence. From Harry L. Mitchell of the Southern Tenant Farmers Union (STFU) came a telegram urging White House intervention. In March, Gardner Jackson, one of the victims of the AAA purge of 1935, re-entered the scene as chairman of an organization called the National Committee on Rural Social Planning, and he urged the President to intercede in defense of tenant farmers and sharecroppers

2. Murray R. Benedict, *Farm Policies in the United States, 1790–1950* (New York: The Twentieth Century Fund, 1953), pp. 352–64; USDA, *Agricultural Statistics, 1945* (Washington, D.C.: GPO, 1945), pp. 19, 28, 76, and *1950*, pp. 628, 636, 642, 643.

allegedly being evicted because of their membership in the STFU.[3]

In May, 1936, cotton choppers and others working as day laborers in Arkansas went on strike for $1.50 for a ten-hour day, instead of the seventy-five cents offered by cotton planters. As a result of complaints made to the Office of the Attorney General by the STFU and others, charging that strikers were being fined for vagrancy and then compelled to work out their fines on their employers' cotton plantations, in violation of federal anti-peonage laws, Attorney General Homer Cummings assigned a special investigator to the area. These pressures from the South, together with the impact of the drought, the work of the Resettlement Administration, and the debate during the election campaign of 1936 all converged to dramatize the issue of chronic rural poverty in a way that no group of amateur lobbyists could have done.[4]

Arthur M. Schlesinger, Jr., in discussing Roosevelt's decision-making habits—his "technique of protraction," and his practice of postponing a final commitment in a particular issue until "the opportunity for decision came safely into his orbit"—has offered a key to the difference between the situation of 1935 and that of 1937:[5]

His complex administrative sensibility, infinitely subtle and sensitive, was forever weighing questions of personal force, of political timing, of congressional concern, of partisan benefit, of public interest. Situations had to be permitted to develop, to crystallize, to clarify; the competing forces had to vindicate themselves in the actual pull and tug of conflict; public opinion had to face the question, consider it, pronounce upon it—only then, at the long, frazzled end, would the President's intuitions consolidate and precipitate a result.

This was the kind of political gantlet through which the AAA had been compelled to pass, and it was a route from which the Resettle-

---

3. Norman Thomas to Franklin D. Roosevelt, Feb. 28, 1936; Harry L. Mitchell to Caroline O'Day, Feb. 28, 1936; FDRL, OF 1650. Gardner Jackson to Marvin H. McIntyre, Mar. 12, 1936, FDRL, OF 4207. Jackson to Webster Powell, Henry A. Wallace, and Rexford G. Tugwell, Nov. 12, 1936, CBBP. Author's interview with Jackson.

The list of sponsors of the National Committee on Rural Social Planning included the eccentric Republicans, Representative Vito Marcantonio of New York and Senator Gerald P. Nye of North Dakota, Socialist Norman Thomas, Professor Rupert B. Vance of the University of North Carolina, Walter White of the National Association for the Advancement of Colored People, Harry L. Mitchell, and others.

4. *New York Times*, June 4, 1936.

5. Arthur M. Schlesinger, Jr., *The Coming of the New Deal* (Boston: Houghton Mifflin, 1959), p. 528.

ment Administration had detoured. During the interval, between passage of the Senate bill in June, 1935, and the convening of the new Congress in January, 1937, a number of forces had ripened, as the President and Congress prepared for action.

Setting the Stage for Decision

Following the adjournment of Congress in August, 1935, rural poverty and the "evils of farm tenancy" remained favorite topics among journalists, writers, publicists, and leaders of reform organizations, while the drive for legislation was transformed from a narrow preoccupation with tenancy to the larger issue of conferring upon the Resettlement Administration a measure of permanency and stability. The change was reflected in the transfiguration of Will W. Alexander from a lobbyist interested in legislation which would promote farm ownership among landless farm people, to a strategy-minded public official interested in the viability of his agency. By January, 1936, for instance, he had already begun to sound more like Rexford G. Tugwell than the sentimental agrarians with whom he had worked earlier, when he declared that there was no virtue in mere land ownership. Reflecting the humanism of the Resettlement Administration, he suggested that "if we can break up this idea that it is an achievement to break your back and ruin your family, just to own land, I think you have maybe done something to civilize America a bit."[6]

One of the reasons for the ill-fated career of the Bankhead-Jones bills in 1935, it will be recalled, was the absence of the hand of the President. On January 6, 1936, Roosevelt made his first move when he met with John H. Bankhead, Marvin Jones, Governor William I. Myers of the Farm Credit Administration, and Alexander of the Resettlement Administration, to formulate a battle plan. They agreed that Jones should immediately attempt to persuade his committee to report the bill, that Alexander and Tugwell should harness the resources of their agency, and that the President should throw his weight into the battle where needed.

Jones remained with the President, to discuss other matters, while Alexander returned to his office, and within a few minutes a bombshell struck which exploded their plans. Marvin H. McIntyre entered

6. Will W. Alexander to Frank Tannenbaum, Sept. 21, 1935, FTP; RA, minutes of regional directors' conference, Jan. 28, 1936, NA, RG 96.

The Bankhead-Jones Farm Tenant Act / [161]

the President's study with a typewritten take-off from the teletype machine, reporting that the U.S. Supreme Court had just invalidated the Agricultural Adjustment Act, keystone of the administration's entire farm program. "The President was thunderstruck—his face turned white," Jones has recalled.[7]

Once again, the Bankhead-Jones bills were shoved aside by more urgent pressures. For the next two months, Jones' time was preempted for the task of securing enactment of the Soil Conservation and Domestic Allotment Act, as a substitute for the ill-fated Agricultural Adjustment Act. The new measure won congressional approval within a few weeks, but the attention of the White House and Congress remained preoccupied with other measures enjoying high priority—the Farm Mortgage Amendatory Act, the Cotton-Tobacco-Potato Act, the Tobacco State Compact Act, the Commodity Exchange Act, the general Agricultural Appropriation Act, and the Deficiency Appropriation Act, all of which were approved before congressional adjournment in June.

Despite the low priority assigned to the Bankhead-Jones bills, Alexander, Laurence I. Hewes, Jr., Brooks Hays, and others in the Resettlement Administration continued to act on the assumption that there was going to be House action in the current session. They therefore pressed their efforts to persuade the members of Jones' Agriculture Committee to report the bill. "It looks as though the Committee . . . will vote to bring out the Bill tomorrow morning," Alexander reported on April 22 to Frank Tannenbaum, who had retired from the campaign and had gone to teach history at Columbia University. He confidently predicted that the bill would reach the House floor within a week and be approved.

The following day, Jones' committee met in executive session to vote on whether to report the bill. "Now, finally," Hewes has reported, "the House Agriculture Committee was ready for the Bankhead-Jones Bill." Time was short, with the national party conventions approaching, and with the call of politics ringing in their ears. The bill's friends in the Resettlement Administration had kept a careful tally of committee members' attitudes toward the bill, and they were confident of at least a small majority. "We were stunned, then, when the bill was stopped in committee by one vote." According to Hewes, Democratic Representative Walter M. Pierce of Oregon, who

---

7. *United States v. Butler*, 297 U.S. 1 (1935); Alexander to Tannenbaum (n.d.), FTP; author's interviews with Marvin Jones, Alexander; Jones, COHC, Vol. 5, p. 1116.

switched his vote at the last moment, had allegedly used this opportunity to take revenge against the Resettlement Administration, because the agency had transferred a county office from one Oregon town to another, against the wishes of Pierce. Thus the bill died.

In the early morning hours of June 21, the Seventy-fourth Congress adjourned. Two days later, Alexander went dejectedly to Chapel Hill, North Carolina, to talk as a southerner to southerners about the South's stake in the fight for policies to improve land tenure, economic development, race relations, and public health. Using the occasion to conduct a post-mortem examination on the death of the bill in the House, he placed the major blame for failure not on the general political climate, not on the shoulders of the President, and not on the equivocation of the men in the USDA and the Resettlement Administration, but rather on southern opposition and indifference. While the House Agriculture Committee callously allowed the bill to languish in its pocket, Alexander explained, in the South, "The churches were holding revivals and getting people ready for Heaven, and our colleges were doing research work, and the women's clubs were busy with a lot of dead issues. No one seemed to care about this, and so it died."

What Alexander presumably did not know at the time was that for several weeks previously the President, majority leader Robinson, Bankhead, and Jones had given up hope for House action in the current session, and were already looking ahead to 1937. On June 8, for instance, Roosevelt had sent a memorandum to Robinson and Bankhead, in which he had frankly confessed, "I am assuming that there is little likelihood of action on a Farm Tenant Bill at this session, but I hope that by next January I can have, with your help, a well worked out plan to be taken up early in the next session." With the Congress champing at the bit to escape Washington, in order to attend the party conventions and other election-year chores, the deliberations of the House Agriculture Committee on the tenancy bill, about which Alexander, Hewes, and others had agonized, had been little more than a ritual. Of much greater significance was the fact that the President of the United States had clearly and unequivocally assumed command of the campaign for legislation.[8]

Next in importance to presidential intervention during the interval

8. Alexander to Tannenbaum, Apr. 22, 1936, FTP; Roosevelt to Joe T. Robinson and John H. Bankhead, June 8, 1936, FDRL, OF 1650; *New York Times*, June 24, 1936; Laurence I. Hewes, Jr., *Boxcar in the Sand* (New York: Knopf, 1957), p. 85.

of congressional inaction, was the convergence of the thrust for tenancy legislation with the realization, especially among Tugwell and his assistants, that the time had come for the Congress to sanction the programs of the Resettlement Administration. By the summer of 1936, it will be recalled, the agency had reached a critical situation. Challenges in the courts, attacks in the press, increasing opposition from hostile members of Congress, growing resentment among the more established agricultural agencies, increasing fiscal instability as a result of the dependence upon quarterly or semiannual presidential allocations from emergency funds, the rumored departure of Tugwell, and the anticipated transfer of the agency to the USDA—all these factors reinforced the belief that the survival of the Resettlement Administration depended upon securing permanent legislation in the next Congress.

Hitherto disinclined to go to Congress, Tugwell by late 1936 became a persuasive proponent of the idea, but of one thing he was adamant—the tenancy tail, representing 10 per cent of the needy farmers, should not wag the Resettlement Administration dog whose most important function was to serve the 90 per cent in need. On January 10, 1937, a few days after leaving the agency in the hands of its new Administrator, Alexander, the departing prophet used his valediction to reemphasize the need for a war not against the false enemy—farm tenancy—but rather against farm poverty from whatever cause.[9] He refused to accept the panacea of farm ownership, and went on to defend the essence of the rural rehabilitation idea:

> Farm ownership? Yes, some day for some, under the right conditions, at their own choice and with a clear view of its costs and after they have demonstrated their ability to rise. But now, most importantly for many, treatment of disease, better diet for children, a mule, some seed and fertilizer, clothes to lift the shame of going ragged to town, some hope for the future, a friendly hand to help in every farm and home crisis.

Setting out to abolish farm tenancy in favor of ownership, he argued, merely served as an easy escape from the deeper and thornier issues. With characteristic candor, he charged that some of the emphasis on tenancy legislation provided an opportunity for politicians to reward the "better citizens among rural folk who can be expected to suitably repay political efforts made in their behalf." Many of the clients of the Resettlement Administration, Tugwell pre-

---

9. *New York Times*, Jan. 10, 1937; *Congressional Digest*, Vol. 16 (Feb., 1937), pp. 57–58.

dicted, would remain untouched by a program of promoting farm ownership, and, in the following sentence, he revealed his disenchantment with the New Deal:

> If we have no intention of attacking poverty at its source, if we only intend to make owners out of a few of the better tenants, the administration ought not to have credit for helping really forgotten families; only for doing what democracies have usually done—helped those who needed help less because those who needed it more did not count politically.

Another important difference between 1935 and 1937 was Henry Wallace's change of heart. As we have already seen, in our discussion of the transfer of the Resettlement Administration to the USDA, in the fall of 1936 he agreed to make a tour of the South to see for himself. The exhausted faces of the farmers, diseased children, scrawny cattle, crumbling and overcrowded shacks, and eroded fields made an indelible impact on him. Shortly after his return, he wrote an article for the *New York Times*, in which he declared that, "I have never seen among the peasantry of Europe poverty so abject as that which exists in this favorable cotton year in the great cotton States." A third of the farmers of the United States, he believed, were living "under conditions which are so much worse than the peasantry of Europe that the city people of the United States should be thoroughly ashamed." Before his train returned him to Washington, he had decided not only that the Resettlement Administration should be transferred to the USDA, but that appropriate supporting legislation should be enacted as soon as possible.[10]

Derivative support for legislation in 1937 also came from the presidential election campaign of the previous year. As the Republicans and Democrats prepared to assemble at their conventions in June, newspapers reported that crop losses in the South, due to the drought, had passed the $100 million mark, that Governor Talmadge of Georgia was urging all preachers to conduct Sunday afternoon prayer meetings for rain, that the cotton workers in Arkansas were still on strike, that the skies of the western dustbowl were filling with blown topsoil, and that the highways of Oklahoma and other western states were streaming with uprooted farm families on their exodus to California. Rural poverty would inevitably be a leading campaign issue in 1936.

The closest the Republicans came to the issue in their platform was

---

10. *New York Times*, Nov. 14–26, 1936; Henry A. Wallace, "Wallace Maps a Farm Program," *New York Times*, Jan. 3, 1937; Russell Lord, *The Wallaces of Iowa* (Boston: Houghton Mifflin, 1947), pp. 459–62; author's interviews with Wallace, Appleby.

their promise to promote the family farm, provide emergency benefit payments to needy farmers within the limits of a balanced budget, and provide "ample farm credit at rates as low as those enjoyed by other industries," with preference to loans for acquiring or refinancing farm homes. The platform made no pledge of support for legislation to combat farm tenancy and poverty, but throughout the campaign, the Republican candidate for President, Governor Alf Landon of Kansas, repeatedly attacked the Democrats for the failure of Congress to enact a tenancy bill.[11]

The delegates to the Democratic convention in Philadelphia were not much more enthusiastic about an open endorsement of tenancy legislation than were the Republicans. They rejected a proposal from the resolutions committee, whose membership included some of the most consistent champions of the Bankhead-Jones bills in 1935, that the bills be specifically endorsed, and a recommendation by Gardner Jackson and Harry L. Mitchell, of the STFU and the National Committee on Rural Social Planning, that the party declare unequivocally its support for the defense of the civil rights of farm tenants and sharecroppers, including especially their right to peaceable assembly and to bargain collectively with landlords and planters. Finally, Marvin Jones, the great compromiser, succeeded in winning convention endorsement of the following plank: "We recognize the gravity of the evils of farm tenancy, and we pledge the full cooperation of the Government in the refinancing of farm indebtedness at the lowest possible rates of interest and over a long term of years."

More important than the formality of platform promises was Roosevelt's actual performance in the campaign. Free to exploit the initiative of an incumbent President, he forced his opponent to accept his leadership in coping with the drought emergency. On June 27, he symbolically delayed his departure for the Philadelphia convention to accept the nomination, in order to confer with Wallace about the establishment of a committee to coordinate the government's relief activities in agriculture. Throughout the summer, newspaper headlines linked Roosevelt's name with the efforts to cope with the drought emergency.

Against this background, Roosevelt seized an opportunity, late in August, to further dramatize the situation—and his concern about it—and conducted what he described as a "non-political" tour of the

11. Kirk Porter and Donald B. Johnson, comps., *National Party Platforms* (Urbana: Univ. of Illinois Press, 1956), pp. 367–68; Alf Landon, address at Oklahoma City, Oct. 23, 1936, quoted in *Congressional Record*, Vol. 81, p. 6670; *New York Times*, July 24, 1936.

drought-ridden Great Plains. Accompanied by Secretary Wallace, Works Progress Administrator Hopkins, Robert Fechner of the Civilian Conservation Corps, and Farm Credit Administrator Myers, followed by a large delegation of newsmen, observers, and local and state political people, he set out for Bismarck, North Dakota, on what Tugwell has called "one of President Roosevelt's most elaborate non-political charades." With additional stops in several other states, he sought not only to harvest votes, but also to focus attention on the national scope of rural poverty, and he took the occasion to publicly and unequivocally commit himself to remedial legislation in the next session of Congress.

As the presidential campaign shifted into high gear in September, Roosevelt wrote to Bankhead and Jones, asking them to work together in preparing plans for legislation in the next Congress, and to meet with him early in December—victory at the polls, of course, was taken for granted—to "complete our recommendations to Congress for legislation designed to bring about improvement in the tenancy situation." From Jasper, Alabama, Bankhead immediately responded with a renewal of his commitment to the cause:

> I am ready when Congress meets to do everything in my power to get a farm tenancy bill passed by both Houses of Congress. I whipped the opposition in the Senate when I was asking for a billion dollar fund. I guess we ought not to have any great difficulty in the Senate in getting a bill appropriating much less money.

Roosevelt then went to Omaha, Nebraska, and delivered a major campaign address entitled, "The American Farmer Living on His Own Land Remains Our Ideal of Self-Reliance and of Spiritual Balance." He claimed that a good beginning had already been made by his administration through such agencies as the Resettlement Administration, pledged himself to a continued long-range attack on rural poverty, and announced his intention to submit and promote legislative proposals in the next Congress. "We cannot, as a Nation," he declared, "be content until we have reached the ultimate objective of every farm family owning its own farm." Even the President of the United States—perhaps he especially—appreciated the political appeal in the mystique of land ownership.[12]

Finally, after his November victory, Roosevelt went before the

12. Porter and Johnson, *National Party Platforms*, p. 361; *New York Times*, June 25, 28, front page headlines of July 6, 7, 8, 11, 17, and Aug. 8, 11, 18, 1936; Mitchell, COHC, Pt. 1, p. 72; Roosevelt to Bankhead and Jones, Sept. 21, 1936, and Bankhead to Roosevelt, Sept. 25, 1936, FDRL, OF 1650; Rexford G. Tugwell, *The Democratic Roosevelt* (Garden City, N.Y.: Doubleday, 1957), pp. 424–25; author's interviews with Jones, Jackson.

The Bankhead-Jones Farm Tenant Act / [167]

Seventy-fifth Congress on January 6, 1937, and in his State of the Union Message he reiterated his faith in the Jeffersonian aspiration:[13]

> Another example [of substandard conditions in the United States] is the prevalence of an un-American type of tenant farming. I do not suggest that every farm family has the capacity to earn a satisfactory living on its own farm. But many thousands of tenant farmers—indeed most of them—with some financial assistance and with some advice and training, can be made self-supporting on land which can eventually belong to them. The nation would be wise to offer them the chance instead of permitting them to go along as they do now, year after year, with neither future security as tenants nor hope of ownership of their homes nor expectation of bettering the lot of their children.

The President's Committee on Farm Tenancy

During the summer of 1936, Tugwell, M. L. Wilson, and Paul H. Appleby decided that a special citizens committee should be appointed to do belatedly for the Resettlement Administration what the preparatory committees and conferences had done for the establishment of the AAA—provide a forum for a competition of ideas and an instrument through which some consensus might be reached among organized interests regarding the agency's future form and function. A few days after the landslide victory in November, the President instructed Wallace to organize a presidential committee, with Wallace himself as chairman, and with Lewis C. Gray of the Resettlement Administration as executive secretary and technical director. The committee was charged to report to the President not later than February 1.

Wilson, Appleby, Alexander, Gray, and C. B. Baldwin promptly set to work. Drawing names from government, agriculture, education, the press, the churches, and other institutions, they assembled more than forty people representing very different and often conflicting interests and points of view. For reasons of political strategy—there was no virtue, they believed, in arousing sleeping dogs unnecessarily by loose talk about agrarian reform—they decided to call the group the President's Committee on Farm Tenancy, and they advertised it as a study group on the causes and cures of farm tenancy. Privately, however, they intended that it should serve a variety of purposes— (1) heighten interest and concern about rural poverty generally;

---

13. Roosevelt, campaign address at Omaha, Neb., Oct. 10, 1936, in F.D.R., *Public Papers* (1936), Vol. 5, p. 438; State of the Union Message, *New York Times*, Jan. 7, 1937.

(2) help to provide a cloak of legitimacy for considerably more than the promotion of farm ownership and reduction of tenancy; (3) enlist the support of influential interest groups; (4) provide a forum for competing ideas about the causes and cures of rural poverty; (5) disseminate information about and promote interest in the achievements and plans of the Resettlement Administration; and (6) reinforce the campaign for permanent legislation for the agency.

In conformity with the desire of the President, they created the committee under the auspices of the National Resources Committee, and to conduct public hearings and draft a preliminary report, they designated a working committee, consisting of Gray as chairman, assisted by Alexander, Albert G. Black, Charles S. Johnson, Lowry Nelson, M. W. Thatcher, John D. Black of Harvard University, and Edwin G. Nourse of The Brookings Institution. The full membership of the President's Committee met in Washington on December 16, where they were urged by Wallace to approach the problem of rural poverty comprehensively, rather than to focus narrowly on farm tenancy problems. During the first two weeks of January, 1937, the working subcommittee conducted public hearings in Montgomery, Alabama; Dallas, Texas; Indianapolis, Indiana; Lincoln, Nebraska; and San Francisco, California. About the middle of January, the subcommittee returned to Washington to prepare technical materials, formulate preliminary recommendations, and draft a report for submission to the full membership of the committee.

Within the USDA, a series of departmental discussions, chaired by Alexander, were held, presumably to assure that the proposals might harmonize as far as possible with the thinking of the Department's leaders. Finally, on February 11, after a number of disputes between liberals and conservatives among the membership, the President's Committee completed its work and reported to Roosevelt.

In view of the diversity and incompatibility among some of the participants, it was not surprising that the report included minority expressions of dissent. On February 16, Roosevelt submitted the report to Congress with a hope that any new legislation that might result would be closely integrated with programs already being carried out by his administration. "If action is now called for," editorialized the *New York Times*, "Mr. Roosevelt and Congress have only to say the word."[14]

14. Wallace to Roosevelt, Nov. 13, 1936, and Roosevelt to Wallace, Nov. 16, 1936, FDRL, OF 1650; National Resources Committee, *Farm Tenancy: The Report of the President's Committee on Farm Tenancy* (Washington, D.C.:

In essence, the report of the President's Committee was an endorsement of the Resettlement Administration. Favoring an enlargement of programs already underway, emphasis was placed on the following four kinds of recommended action: (1) a program to assist farm tenant families and other landless farm people who had the necessary ability and experience to become owner-operators, and to prevent present farm owners from slipping down to the status of tenants, sharecroppers, or migrant laborers; (2) a rural rehabilitation program designed to provide modest loans, farm and home supervision, and other services to needy farmers; (3) a submarginal land program in which land unsuitable for farming would be retired, and families living on these lands would be assisted in finding new farm homes on more productive land; and (4) cooperation with state and local governments in improving landlord-tenant lease arrangements, in encouraging states to enact preferential tax policies to promote farm ownership, and in strengthening rural health and

---

GPO, 1937), pp. 25–30; Maddox, "The FSA," pp. 45–46, and "The Bankhead-Jones Farm Tenant Act," *Law and Contemporary Problems*, Vol. IV (Oct., 1937), p. 441; Wallace, quoted in *Congressional Digest*, Vol. 16 (Feb., 1937), p. 4; *New York Times*, Jan. 17, Feb. 17, 1937; M. L. Wilson, COHC, Vol. 10, pp. 1749–50, 1775–76; author's interviews with Wallace, Alexander; Appleby to author, July (n.d.), 1954.

From the government, the members of the President's Committee on Farm Tenancy were Secretary Wallace, Under Secretary Wilson, Tugwell and Alexander of the Resettlement Administration, Lewis C. Gray of the Resettlement Administration, W. I. Myers of the FCA, A. G. Black of the BAE, Lowry Nelson of the Utah Agricultural Experiment Station, W. F. Brokaw of the Nebraska Agricultural Extension Service, Assistant Secretary of Labor Edward F. McGrady, and Governor Carl Bailey of Arkansas.

From agriculture there were Edward A. O'Neal of the AFBF, Louis J. Taber of the National Grange, Henry C. Taylor of the Farm Foundation, M. W. Thatcher of the NFU, Murray D. Lincoln of the Ohio Farm Bureau Federation, and several working dirt farmers.

The universities were represented by Mrs. Mary McLeod Bethune of Bethune-Cookman College, Charles S. Johnson of Fisk University, A. R. Mann of Cornell University, Howard W. Odum of the University of North Carolina, and F. D. Patterson of the Tuskegee Institute.

Members of the press were James Chappell of the *Birmingham* (Ala.) *News-Age-Herald*, Mark Etheridge of the *Louisville* (Ky.) *Courier-Journal*, A.G. Pat Mayse of the *Paris* (Tex.) *News*, Clarence Poe of the *Progressive Farmer and Southern Ruralist*, Clarence Roberts of the *Oklahoma Farmer and Stockman*, Paul C. Smith of the *San Francisco* (Calif.) *Chronicle*, and W. W. Waymack of the *Des Moines* (Ia.) *Register and Tribune*.

The membership also included Louis Brownlow of the Public Administration Clearing House, Edwin R. Embree of the Julius Rosenwald Fund, Mrs. Una Roberts Lawrence of the Southern Baptist Convention, Mrs. W. A. Newell of the Methodist Episcopal Church's Women's Missionary Council, and Rev. John A. Ryan of the National Catholic Welfare Conference.

educational systems. This prescription was virtually a paraphrase of the President's executive order establishing the Resettlement Administration two years earlier.

The underlying objective in the report was the notion of "farm security," that is, protection against the economic, political, social, and personal forces which had conspired to place chronically impoverished farm people in a "disadvantaged" position as compared with the rest of rural society. Without ever defining their terms, the committee agreed that for many farm tenants, sharecroppers, migratory laborers, families on submarginal land and on farms of inadequate size, owner families hopelessly in debt, and young farm people unable to obtain farms, the so-called agricultural ladder had indeed become a fiction. Urgent though they believed remedial action was in assisting these various classes of farm people, the committee warned against too ambitious a beginning, and insisted that a permanent program was needed on a scale commensurate with the government's experience and resources. In time, programs should be expanded and elaborated to a scope proportionate to the problem.

The comprehensiveness of the committee's approach—there had been nothing comparable to it since the report of President Theodore Roosevelt's Country Life Commission in 1909—and especially its escape from the narrow preoccupation with farm tenancy were reflected in the following list of recommended programs and activities: (1) loans and grants to assist approximately 420,000 farm families; (2) similar assistance for approximately 600,000 farm families normally above the subsistence level, but temporarily destitute as a result of such catastrophes as the drought, and therefore in need of capital and credit; (3) loans and grants for a large number of farm families in need of credit and farm and home management services—"supervision" in the language of the Resettlement Administration; (4) debt adjustment services; (5) assistance to tenants in improving their leasing contracts; (6) development of farm and home plans for those families without sufficient experience in planning and cultivating their own crops; (7) encouragement of production and marketing cooperatives among low-income farm families; (8) services for migratory farm laborers, such as transient camps, medical care services, emergency grants and loans for subsistence needs, and other assistance in helping migrants to establish themselves on farms as tenants or owner-operators; and (9) resettlement and rural rehabilitation of submarginal farmers who were tied to substandard soil and therefore doomed to defeat. This was virtually a paraphrase of the list of activities reviewed in the then recently published *First Annual Report* of the Resettlement Administration.

With respect to administrative and organizational details, the report of the President's Committee echoed the dissatisfaction of Wallace and others in the USDA with the stigma of the Resettlement Administration as a temporary agency concerned with emergency relief measures, the relocation of people—there seemed to be something sinister and un-American in "moving people around"—and resettlement projects and model communities that smacked too much of collectivism. The authors of the report agreed that the proposed programs should be assigned to the USDA, but they observed that no agency with adequate powers and status to cope with rural poverty in a comprehensive, unified, and integrated manner existed. They therefore suggested that the Resettlement Administration "may well serve as a nucleus for whatever organizational adjustments the Secretary may find desirable," and went on to propose that, "In order better to describe the activities recommended herein it is suggested that the name of the administrative organization be the 'Farm Security Administration'." For purposes of facilitating legal transactions, there should be an affiliated Farm Security Corporation, governed by a board of directors composed of the Secretary of Agriculture, the Under Secretary, and three additional officials designated by the Secretary.

One of the purposes of the President's Committee on Farm Tenancy, it will be recalled, was to provide a forum for the competition of ideas. It was not surprising, therefore, that on a few of the more sensitive issues there were sharp clashes of opinion. Probably the most heated dispute turned on the provisions in the draft report regarding the civil rights of farm tenants, sharecroppers, and migratory laborers. Acknowledging the existence of violence and intimidation in certain rural areas, the report recommended (1) "that States guarantee to these groups and enforce the rights of peaceful assembly and of organization to achieve their legitimate objectives," and (2) "repeal of State laws which make it a misdemeanor to quit a contract while in debt, since such laws abridge civil liberties of tenants and tend to nullify Federal antipeonage acts." Edward A. O'Neal of the American Farm Bureau Federation (AFBF)—he was himself a cotton planter in Alabama—demanded that the section be deleted from the report to the President, but he was overwhelmingly defeated by the membership, and the section remained.[15]

The civil rights issue was only one of the objections that O'Neal voiced during the discussions of the committee. The recommendation of a program, for instance, for restrictions on the alienation of land by borrowers collided with the AFBF leaders' consistent defense of the principle of fee simple private ownership of land. The heavy emphasis in the report on the use of credit as a means of promoting the security of low-income farm families also clashed with the AFBF belief that a fair price system and parity of income were all that were needed to achieve farm security in an uncertain economy. Furthermore—and this goes to the heart of the matter—the recommendation that the proposed programs be administered by a new and more powerful federal agency in the USDA challenged the monopoly held by the AFBF, in collaboration with the Extension Service in the USDA and the state land grant colleges and extension services, over field contacts with farmers in the nation. Anything that might undermine this symbiotic relationship was anathema to the leaders of the AFBF.

To a considerable degree, O'Neal's position might have been explained by his role as the president of one of the largest and most powerful general farm organizations. An exceedingly effective farm spokesman, a close personal bourbon-and-branch-water friend of the most influential members of the farm bloc in Congress, his greatest accomplishment was the role he had played in the creation and maintenance of an alliance between the farming interests of the South and the Middle West. On the foundation of that alliance, he had built the power of the AFBF. In taking positions on New Deal farm policies, he invariably funneled those policies through the strainer of his organization's self interest. He therefore submitted a

---

15. National Resources Committee, *Farm Tenancy*, pp. 11–20; *New York Times*, Feb. 13, 1937; Clinton Rossiter, "The Political Philosophy of F. D. Roosevelt: A Challenge to Scholarship," *Review of Politics*, Vol. XI (Jan., 1949), p. 90; John Kenneth Galbraith, *The Affluent Society* (Boston: Houghton Mifflin, 1958), pp. 104–05; Sidney Fine, *Laissez Faire and the General-Welfare State* (Ann Arbor: Univ. of Michigan Press, 1956), pp. 397–98; author's interview with Mrs. Eleanor Roosevelt; Francis Pickens Miller to author, Mar. 11, 1955.

The proposal for an agency devoted to the promotion of "farm security" reflected the idea of "security" which underlay much of the New Deal. "Security," suggested Clinton Rossiter, "was the bright word in Franklin Roosevelt's lexicon." A number of people—Wallace, Alexander, Miller, Gray among them—have claimed the credit for suggesting the name of the new agency, but according to Mrs. Eleanor Roosevelt, the President himself was due the credit.

minority statement for inclusion in the final report, in which he carefully pointed out that he could sign the report only if it were clearly understood that he approved nothing which conflicted with or went beyond the policies of the AFBF, as delineated in a statement he had presented earlier to the House Agriculture Committee.[16]

In that statement of policy, O'Neal had declared that any law enacted to alleviate the evils of farm tenancy should be based on the following provisions: (1) the law should be administered by the Secretary of Agriculture through the extension services; (2) local administration should be assigned to appointees of the Secretary from a list of candidates furnished by the state extension director, and the eligibility of borrowers should be determined in each county or region by a committee of three local members similarly appointed; (3) assistance should be restricted to "farm tenants and worthy young men of farm background, ability, and moral worth;" (4) during a probationary period, borrowers should lease farms from the government at reasonable rental rates, during which time a portion of the client's profits should be turned over to the Secretary of Agriculture and the money should accumulate until it equaled 25 percent of the value of the farm, after which the lease should cease; and (5) all loans to clients for production purposes should be limited to two-thirds of the amount needed.[17]

O'Neal's attitude toward the proposals of the President's Committee was also governed by his own values and personal point of view. Born on an Alabama plantation in 1875, a descendant of the family that founded Nashville, Tennessee, a great-grandson of Alex Coffee, close friend and partner of Andrew Jackson in land speculation, and the nephew of a former governor of Alabama, he was a southern aristocrat who would have made a superb politician. He had believed in and had fought strenuously for some substantial reforms of agriculture, and he reputedly harbored a paternalistic interest in improving the position of all farmers, high and low, but the remedies should not upset the established social and political order, and—especially important to him—should not undermine the power and strategic position of the AFBF and its state and local affiliates. As a plantation owner and landlord, his inability or refusal to believe the somber indictments of tenancy in the South may have

16. Christiana M. Campbell, *The Farm Bureau and the New Deal* (Urbana: Univ. of Illinois Press, 1956), pp. 58–59.
17. National Resources Committee, *Farm Tenancy*, pp. 22–24; Hearings on H.R.8, *op. cit.*, p. 316.

been due to simple economic self-interest, but it is just as likely that his antagonism toward the work of the Resettlement Administration and the proposals of the President's Committee was the result of his southern milieu.

Ed O'Neal, as all of his friends knew, was an affable raconteur who enjoyed the effect of his eloquence on his audience, yet he sometimes revealed, more clearly than he realized, his attitudes and values toward poverty and the poor. In retrospect, in 1952, for instance, he casually remarked that on his plantation his tenants were the grandsons of his grandfather's slaves—even the old slave cabins were still there! His tenants and sharecroppers, he insisted, were happy and contented:

> When you talk to one of these niggers, you say, "Robert, are you happy out here?"
> "Why, Mr. Ed, this is your land, your home. I don't pay you any rent for the house. I've got plenty of water, plenty of wood, a nice garden, some pigs, a couple of Jersey cows. I got a nice little pasture. When I make something, you get it, and when I don't make anything, you don't get anything. It's heaven here."

O'Neal invariably opposed anything that might, in his view, jeopardize this "climate of contentment." "The share and tenant system," he believed, "has improved the economic stability of the South."[18]

Another conservative dissenter at the sessions of the President's Committee was Henry C. Taylor of the Farm Foundation, whom we have already met as the University of Wisconsin professor who became the "father of agricultural economics." He submitted a minority statement which expressed the typically conservative view that the government should proceed very slowly, because, "The proposals contain the possibility of doing more harm than good to the farming population of the United States, particularly in reducing thrift by making the entry into land ownership too easy and by increasing competition in agriculture."

Dissatisfaction with the draft report also came from the political left. W. L. Blackstone of the STFU, for instance, contended that the report did not go nearly far enough in protecting the rights of tenants, sharecroppers, and farm tenants. In a minority report he predicted that the programs would be sabotaged if they were assigned to the USDA, which he viewed as an agent of large commercial farming interests. In a similar mood, Charles S. Johnson predicted that unless careful safeguards were enforced in the decen-

18. O'Neal, COHC, pp. 13, 112–13.

tralization of administration, Negro farm tenants and sharecroppers would continue to be discriminated against in the distribution of benefits.[19]

Aside from the more extreme objections, such as those cited above, there were some weaknesses in the report which made it vulnerable to economic criticism. Theodore W. Schultz, at that time an economist at Iowa State College, for instance, granted that the report was a good beginning, "a first approximation of the probable solution . . . a step toward farm security," but he considered it to be overly ambitious, containing "many gaps, vague recommendations, and parts . . . which do not readily fit into a broad, consistent policy." The idea of farm security, on which so much of the report hinged, was exceedingly complex, and, although there were ambiguities and contradictions in the report's use of it, the authors of the report did deserve praise for having made the attempt. Schultz believed that there was too much emphasis on action in the report, and not enough attention to the economic justification of the recommendations. The dependence of commercial farming on non-farm capital, the need for stable prices, the role of land speculation in maintaining economic optimism, and the inevitable dependence of remedial programs on the cyclical swings of the general economy were some of the issues, he believed, with which the committee had failed to cope.[20]

Somewhat more critically—presumably with a little wisdom of hindsight and reflecting more conventional thinking in agricultural economics—Murray R. Benedict, in his authoritative 1953 history of American farm policies, has raised the following criticisms of the report: (1) the "land for tenants" program was "poorly conceived and was unlikely to exert any rapid or significant influence on the tenancy problem;" (2) the low interest rates and special arrangements for tenants to purchase farms were "discriminatory;" (3) despite the committee's expressions of concern about land speculation, the massive government purchase of farm lands, for leasing to landless tenants and marginal farmers, would inevitably have an "inflationary impact on land prices which might well nullify expected advantages;" (4) if the "land for tenants" program were conducted on an experimental basis with small appropriations, the "great mass of farm tenants would be neglected and no significant gains could

---

19. National Resources Committee, *Farm Tenancy*, pp. 20–22, 24.
20. Theodore W. Schultz, "A Comment on the Report of the President's Committee on Farm Tenancy," *The Journal of Land and Public Utility Economics*, Vol. XIII (May, 1937), pp. 207–8.

result;" (5) the problem was not tenancy itself, but legal landlord-tenant relationships; changes in state laws and constitutions to permit revision of these relationships were necessary, but unlikely; in the absence of such legal changes, the committee was, in effect, promoting a perpetuation of the very system it deplored; (6) the committee called for a modest beginning, but with tenant farmers increasing at the rate of about 40,000 each year, at least that many tenants and other landless people would have to be converted into owner-operators before the amount of tenancy could be reduced—this would be impossible in a modest program; and (7) the committee revealed a lack of understanding of the problem of submarginal land in its proposal that two to five million acres of poor land, on which half a million farm families were located, should be removed from production each year; "poor lands are not necessarily unprofitable to operate," but rather they "need to be operated extensively in relatively large units." Such a procedure, Benedict believed, would probably require public ownership and strict governmental controls—radical and unlikely innovations.[21]

In such evaluations of the report, there was a tendency to criticize it for aiming its sights too low, and, at the same time, to charge it with attempting too much. Some of the criticisms were technically justified, of course, but underlying the disagreement was an important difference of approach. The President's Committee tended to think in terms of micro-economic measures to increase the security and happiness of individual farm families, and protecting them from the uncertainties and adversities of the economy and rural life.

Some of the more conventional economists, on the other hand, approached the problem of farm poverty in macro-economic terms, focusing primarily on the larger forces and institutions in the economy and the political system. The *micro*-economist concentrated on the behavior of individual human beings, while the *macro*-economist concentrated on the more or less stable laws of the economic order. Actually, as John Kenneth Galbraith has persuasively contended, "The two efforts," micro-economic and macro-economic, "would be in the highest degree complementary," and not necessarily in conflict.[22]

One of the intended purposes of the President's Committee on Farm Tenancy, as we have seen, was to provide a forum for competing ideas about the causes and cures of rural poverty—this it

---

21. Benedict, *Farm Policies in the United States*, pp. 358–62.
22. Galbraith, *The Affluent Society*, pp. 104–07.

unquestionably accomplished. The work of the committee, at the same time, demonstrated the enormous difficulties that are inherently involved in the translation of sound economic analysis into politically feasible public policy. Furthermore, the work of the committee foreshadowed the struggles that lay in wait for any agency seeking to accomplish such controversial goals. "There is no paved highway connecting 'economic analysis' and 'public policy'," Theodore Schultz has observed, and, "For the most part it is an unmapped, badly maintained, and hazardous stretch to travel." For the next stage in this hazardous journey, let us now return to Marvin Jones in the House of Representatives.[23]

Action in the House of Representatives

Immediately after the Seventy-fifth Congress convened, it was showered with bills to promote farm ownership, combat the "evils of farm tenancy," support the Resettlement Administration, and in other ways to assist needy and drought-stricken farm families. Most of the bills were mere political "grandstanding," with no serious legislative intentions behind them, but two of them were exceptions— H.R.8, entitled, "The Farmers Home Act," introduced by Marvin Jones in the House on January 5; and S.106, a companion bill with the same title, submitted by John Bankhead in the Senate the following day.[24]

The major difference between these two bills was that H.R.8 provided for a Farmers Home Corporation, to be governed by a board of directors consisting of three officers or employees of the federal government designated by the President; under S.106, the board of the corporation would consist of the Secretary of Agriculture, the Under Secretary, and the Assistant Secretary. Both bills were similar to the bill passed by the Senate in 1935, except that the two new bills provided for an *appropriation* of $50 million in the beginning, and an additional *appropriation* of that amount for each of the following ten fiscal years. The 1935 bill had provided for an original capitalization of $50 million, to be allotted by the President

23. Theodore W. Schultz, *Agriculture in an Unstable Economy* (New York: McGraw-Hill, 1945), p. 186.
24. Senate bills included S.103, submitted by Senator Tom Connally of Texas, and S.596, submitted by Senator Kenneth D. McKellar of Tennessee. House bills included H.R.154, submitted by Rep. John A. Martin of Colorado; H.R.8 and H.R.1645, submitted by Rep. Marvin Jones of Texas; and H.R. 3896, submitted by Rep. Carl Vinson of Georgia.

from emergency relief funds, and for subsequent years, *power to issue government guaranteed bonds* to a maximum of $1,000 million. Both H.R.8 and S.106 were dedicated to the following purposes:

> to establish the Farmers Home Corporation, to encourage and promote the ownership of farm homes and to make the possession of such homes more secure, to provide for the general welfare of the United States, to provide additional credit facilities for agricultural development, to create a fiscal agent for the United States, and for other purposes.

The bills were promptly assigned to their respective committees.

In the Senate, Ellison D. "Cotton Ed" Smith's Committee on Agriculture and Forestry decided to wait for action in the House, while Marvin Jones, chairman of the House Committee on Agriculture, decided to commence general hearings, using the draft of the 1935 compromise bill and his H.R.8 as the bases for discussion. Jones' problem, as he saw it, was to secure the unanimous approval of the nineteen Democrats, seven Republicans, and one Progressive who composed his committee's membership. If necessary, he could probably win a floor fight in the House without the Republicans in his committee, but, as we have seen, he habitually sought a bipartisan consensus, and therefore the Republican votes were needed. Jones also knew that all of the key members of his committee were one-interest men whose committee assignments in the House were limited to the Committee on Agriculture, and that they were particularly interested in any bill that might affect their special commodity and regional interests.

There were, for instance, Hampton P. Fulmer, ranking member of the committee and a conservative Democrat from South Carolina who was a cotton planter at home and an author or sponsor of much cotton legislation in Congress; Richard M. Kleberg, Texas Democrat, who was reputedly interested in one thing—his family's King Ranch of some 1,250,000 acres covering five different counties and embracing an area larger than the state of Connecticut; and Harold D. Cooley, a Democrat from North Carolina, and an attorney whose political power was dependent on tobacco. There was Democrat Fred Cummings of Colorado, a sugar beet farmer and sheep raiser, and a former president of the National Beet Growers' Association. There was Democrat Walter M. Pierce of Oregon, a rancher and wheat farmer. And there was Harry B. Coffee, Democrat of Nebraska, president of the Coffee Cattle Company, with extensive holdings in northwest Nebraska, and who was also the owner and operator of several farms, and a real estate and insurance company.

In addition, there were a number of conservative southern Democrats who, although not dirt farmers or plantation owners, were agents or advocates of cotton and tobacco interests—Wall Doxey of Mississippi, John W. Flannagan of Virginia, and Emmett M. Owen of Georgia. The southern members of the committee came from states that enjoyed the highest tenancy rates and the lowest per capita farm incomes in the United States, but they were generally indifferent to the work of the Resettlement Administration and to the growing interest in remedial legislation. Since the bills before the committee members were clearly oriented toward the problems of the South, committee members from the Middle West and the Great Plains also were disinterested. Jones' goal was to convert that indifference to acquiescence, if not active support.

Starting on January 26 and continuing through eleven days of hearings, the House committee listened to a familiar parade of witnesses who generally favored, or at least did not openly oppose, some kind of remedial legislation. Alexander, Gray, and Westbrook of the Resettlement Administration, for instance, recited the now-familiar litany of "the evils of farm tenancy." The peripatetic Gardner "Pat" Jackson inveighed against H.R.8 as "utterly inadequate," and charged that at best the bill would tend to perpetuate an undesirable subsistence mode of farming. Democratic Senator Tom Connally of Texas objected to "merely scraping around like we are doing with this Resettlement Administration." M. L. Wilson reiterated his call for a broad program of land for landless people, complemented by rural rehabilitation for all those in need of it, and again he emphasized the importance of guidance, education, and supervision for the client families. Wilson Gee, an economist from the University of Virginia, warned against assigning the proposed program to the Resettlement Administration, which, he declared, was interested only in the people at the "bottom of the pile," and predicted that, "If this measure is made a broad one for alleviating poverty in the rural areas . . . it can become so cumbersome and idealistic and visionary that it would break of its own weight." Finally, O'Neal of the AFBF presented his organization's prepared statement of policy, and Democratic Representative Scott Lucas of Illinois introduced for the record an address by Earl C. Smith, vice-president of the AFBF and leader of its Illinois affiliate, which warned against panaceas that would obstruct the major goal of farm policy—controlled farm production and maintenance of parity prices.

On February 16, Roosevelt submitted the report of his Tenancy

Committee to Congress, and two days later, Secretary Wallace testified before Jones' committee. He found many provisions in H.R.8 inadequate, but he emphatically warned against too ambitious a beginning. A bill should be passed, he believed, that would provide for an experimental and pragmatic approach, permitting the government to retreat from error, if necessary, and to learn from experience. In conclusion, he reiterated that strife in certain rural areas, especially in the South, was to be deplored, and that programs of assistance to landless farm families in becoming owner-operators was the best way to combat Communist and Socialist agitation.

Throughout the public hearings, and in a number of executive sessions, Jones attempted to placate the fears of some reluctant members of his committee. Ranking Democrat Fulmer of South Carolina and ranking Republican Clifford R. Hope of Kansas, for instance, repeatedly warned that a program to sell farms to tenants, sharecroppers, and farm laborers would mean, in effect, the rewarding of inefficiency. The best way to combat poverty on the farm, they argued, was to promote parity prices for all farmers and to expand the markets for products of American farms. Besides, they believed, the tenancy proposals represented class legislation, and that was both un-American and undesirable.

Calmly but persistently, Jones reminded the hostile members of his committee that stabilization of farm commodity prices, reduced interest rates for farmers, adjusted tax rates on farm land, the promotion of productive efficiency and improved marketing in agriculture, and other general goals had already been addressed in other legislation, but that in all fairness, something special was needed for that class of farm people who were incapable of deriving benefit from general farm prosperity. The government had a responsibility to promote self-help among these impoverished people; to leave them to their own devices and to expect them to secure their share of the benefits of rising farm prosperity was tantamount to ignoring them. To calm the fears that the proposed program would upset established relationships in the affected rural communities, special provisions should be made to assure as much local control as possible.[25]

25. U.S., Congress, House Committee on Agriculture, Hearings in H.R.8, *Farm Tenancy*, 75th Cong., 1st Sess. (Washington, D.C.: GPO, 1937), pp. 19–21, 47–48, 178–81, 215–67, 272–73, 276–78, 316; Maddox, "The Bankhead-Jones Farm Tenant Act," pp. 443–44; author's interviews with Jones.

The most determined objections in the committee centered on the belief that the proposed procedure for large-scale government purchase of land for resale, with trial leasing and delayed transfer of title to borrowers, represented "dangerous socialization of land and regimentation of farmers." Some of the committee members also feared that any large-scale government land-buying would inevitably promote land speculation and contribute to inflated land prices.

The President's Committee on Farm Tenancy, witnesses in the public hearings, and Jones himself defended the procedure against the first charge by pointing out that farm tenants, sharecroppers, and migratory laborers in a low economic and political status with little experience in farm management would be most effectively aided by government purchase, resale, and trial leasing. Through the resources of the USDA, government purchase would be superior, especially in the South, to a program which would allow individual farmers to purchase their own farms. Through the use of supervision —Wallace was particularly anxious to avoid using the unpopular word "control"—the government's investment would be protected and its risks minimized. This procedure, it was argued, would make the difference between the kind of credit needed for chronically impoverished farmers, and the more conventional credit normally obtainable from commercial banks and from the FCA.

In reply to predictions that the proposed procedure would encourage land speculation and raise land prices, it was asserted that in a period when millions of dollars were going to be spent each year for land purchase anyway, with many buyers to be added to the market, land prices would inevitably rise. The government, it was believed, was more capable of resisting exploitation by land speculators than were individual farmers. This was particularly true in areas like the plantation South, where tenants were especially inexperienced and thus would be vulnerable to exploitation. Government land purchasing, it was further argued, was superior in areas like the plantation South, where large tracts of new land were needed for cultivation.[26]

President Roosevelt was anxious to hasten the legislation through the House of Representatives, so on March 30 he called Jones, House Speaker William Bankhead, Secretary Wallace, and Alexander to the

26. National Resources Committee, *Farm Tenancy*, pp. 12–13, 41–43; Maddox, "The Bankhead-Jones Farm Tenant Act," pp. 451–55; author's interviews with Jones, Wallace, Alexander.

White House for a conference on the bill. Jones reported that a majority of his committee believed that a new bill was needed which would conform more closely than H.R.8 to the recommendations of the President's Committee, to the thinking of Wallace and his assistants, and to the views of most of the witnesses before his committee. With pledges of support from the conferees, Jones introduced H.R.6240 on April 8, entitled "The Farm Security Act of 1937," which was designed to incorporate the broader approach.[27]

Except for the provisions governing farm purchase loans, in which large-scale government land purchase and resale were rejected, H.R.6240 represented the most ambitious and comprehensive bill to emerge from the long campaign for permanent legislation. The new bill provided for the following three action programs:

1. Loans to assist tenants, sharecroppers, and farm laborers to become owner-operators, to be financed by annual appropriations of $50 million for each fiscal year ending on July 1, 1942, and in very broad language empowered the Secretary of Agriculture to prescribe rules and procedures for repayment by the borrower and for enforcing supervision of the borrower's operations;
2. A rural rehabilitation loan program, to be financed by annual appropriations of $75 million for each of the two succeeding fiscal years, for the purpose of assisting borrowers in purchasing livestock, farm equipment, supplies and other needs, refinancing indebtedness, and for family subsistence, and empowering the Secretary to determine repayment rules and procedures; and
3. A submarginal land program of conservation and utilization, including land retirement and development, financed by an appropriation of $10 million for the first fiscal year and $20 million for each of three subsequent years.

The bill also empowered the Secretary of Agriculture to exercise powers previously vested in him for the completion and administration of resettlement, land development, and land utilization projects already initiated. To administer the programs, H.R.6240 omitted the provision for a special government corporation, but it called for the creation of an agency within the USDA, to be named the Farm Security Administration.

Within a few days after submission of the new bill, Jones secured the unanimous consent of his committee, and on April 13 he reported H.R.6240 to the House. This time, progress was arrested not by the

---

27. *New York Times,* Mar. 31, 1937; author's interviews with Jones, Alexander.

reluctance of his committee, but by the opposition of some leaders in the House and by officials of the USDA. They objected most strenuously to the power delegated to county farmers committees in the administration of the farm purchase program under Title I of the bill and to features of the mortgage and lease arrangements.

Jones insisted that local farmers committees represented the democratic aspirations of the times and the price that must be paid to secure passage. To some of the leaders of the USDA, the most alarming weakness of H.R.6240 was this delegation of administrative responsibility to such committees. While Wilson welcomed such an arrangement as a "democratization of public administration," Appleby viewed the committees, in anything more than an advisory capacity, as a dangerous diffusion of executive responsibility. Alexander dreaded the committees, and looked upon them as an invitation to amateur incompetence, irresponsible favoritism to friends and kinsmen, and abdication to parochial pride and prejudice.[28]

When the House Rules Committee deferred to some of these objections and to the growing economy tide in Congress, and refused to grant a rule which would permit the bill to be brought up in the House for discussion, Marvin Jones introduced yet another bill, H.R.7562, on June 17, as a substitute for H.R.6240. One of the most important differences in the new measure was the reduction of the amounts authorized for appropriation. For the purchase of farms under Title I, the amount was cut to $10 million for the first fiscal year, $25 million for the second year, and $50 million for the third year. No appropriation was recommended for rural rehabilitation under Title II, although the bill did provide that, "The President is authorized to allow to the Secretary, out of appropriations made for relief or work relief for any fiscal year ending prior to July 1, 1939, such sums as he determines to be necessary to carry out the provisions of this title." The amount authorized for the submarginal

---

28. U.S., Congress, House Report 586, Apr. 13, 1937, 75th Cong., 1st Sess. (Washington, D.C.: GPO, 1937); Gray to E. H. Wiecking, May 1, 17, 1937, NA, RG 114.

The leaders of the USDA were critical of H.R.6240 for a number of reasons—the delegation of certain powers to farmers committees; lack of a provision for loans to cooperatives; lack of provision to prevent lending to borrowers eligible for credit from the FCA; the thirty-year time limit on repayment of farm ownership loans; provision in H.R.6240 for distribution of loans among the states on a basis of "farm population" and "prevalence of tenancy" (considered inadequate because "farm population" was irrelevant and the term "prevalence of tenancy" was not clear); and inadequate authorized appropriations.

land program was cut to $10 million for the first fiscal year, and $25 million for each of the two following years. Except for the reduction of funds, restoration of the provision for a forty-year repayment period on farm ownership loans, and the creation of a Farmers Home Corporation as an agency of the USDA, H.R.7562 was identical to H.R.6240.

On June 18, Jones' committee reported the new bill to the House, and under a special rule of the Rules Committee, H.R.7562 finally reached the House floor on June 28, 1937. Under the terms of the special rule, no amendments were offered during the first day of debate, which was largely devoted to a recitation of the "evils of farm tenancy," the need for permanent legislation, and the modesty of the authorized appropriations. As far as the bill itself was concerned, attention of the House was focused on the provisions of the farm ownership program under Title I of the bill. There was virtually no discussion of the rural rehabilitation and submarginal land programs. Instead of a line-by-line review of H.R.7562, there was a sudden outpouring of sentimentality about the glories of family farming and rural life, punctuated by recitations from Oliver Goldsmith's "Deserted Village," Edwin Markham's "The Man with the Hoe," and other rustic imagery. Perhaps the most eloquent declamation—it would be invoked again and again in future darker days—was that by John Bankhead's brother, Speaker of the House William B. Bankhead of Alabama:

> And there stands a desolate, hopeless, dejected man, working some other man's property, pillaging it, despoiling its rich resources by virtue of the fact that it is not his, but some other man's, and at the end of the year, when they cast up the account, this man who has worked in season and out of season during the whole crop season finds himself with no profit with which to go through the winter, with nothing with which to buy magazines, medicines, or comforts for his family . . . the satisfaction is great to go out on your own acres, on your own land, put your foot down upon it, look up into the sky and say this, thank God, this little bit is mine [Applause].

After two days of anticlimax, "The Farm Security Act of 1937" finally passed the House on June 29 by an overwhelming vote of 309 to twenty-five. Of those who voted against it, seventeen were Republicans, most of whom came from New England, New York, New Jersey, Pennsylvania, and Michigan. Only two southerners were opposed, one of whom was Jones' Democratic colleague from Texas, Richard M. Kleberg, a co-owner of the giant King Ranch. The bill was promptly referred to the Senate. Let us now turn the clock back and trace the course of the Bankhead bill through the Upper House.[29]

Action in the Senate

In April, while Bankhead's S.106 was still in "Cotton Ed" Smith's pocket, President Roosevelt, responding to the economy spirit of the time, extracted a promise from Bankhead to reduce the proposed appropriations in S.106 from $50 million for each fiscal year to $10 million for the first year, $25 million for the second, and $50 million for each year thereafter. This reduction, it will be recalled, had also been made in the appropriations to be authorized by Jones' H.R.7562. On June 15, Smith's committee favorably reported S.106.[30]

Re-written in committee, the bill was virtually unchanged, except for the difference in method of financing, the elimination of the 1935 provision in S.2367 for a $1,000 million bond issue, and the reduction in annual funds. As reported, S.106 was broader than Jones' H.R.7562, in that it still contained the provision for government purchase of land for resale to borrowers, which the House rejected, but it was considerably more limited than H.R.7562 in that it made no provision for rural rehabilitation and submarginal land programs. It also diverged widely from the recommendations of the President's Committee on Farm Tenancy.[31]

When S.106 reached the Senate floor on July 1, Bankhead and majority leader Robinson had an intricate parliamentary strategy prepared. To exploit the consensus that already existed in the Senate, and to secure a compromise between House and Senate in the

29. U.S., Congress, House Report 1065, June 18, 1937, 75th Cong., 1st Sess. (Washington, D.C.: GPO, 1937); U.S., Congress, H. Res. 261, 75th Cong., 1st Sess., June 28, 1937; *Congressional Record*, Vol. 81, pp. 6431–43, 6450–87, 6533–83.

30. F.D.R., *Public Papers* (1937), Vol. 6, pp. 140–44, 156–57, 163–69; John M. Blum, *From the Morgenthau Diaries: Years of Crisis, 1928–1938* (Boston: Houghton Mifflin, 1959), pp. 293–96.

Starting with his Budget Message to Congress in January, and continuing during the following months, the President pressed for economies in his administration, reportedly at the urging of Morgenthau. Finally, on June 4, Roosevelt called Bankhead to the White House and persuaded the Senator to agree to reduce the amounts to be authorized in his bill before the Senate.

31. U.S., Congress, Sen. Doc. No. 732, June 15, 1937, 75th Cong., 1st Sess. (Washington, D.C.: GPO, 1937).

conference committee rather than on the floor of the Senate, they agreed that debate should be carefully restricted to the provisions of S.106. The Senate should then bring up the House bill (H.R. 7562) for consideration, amend it by substituting S.106 in its place, and then have the Senate version of H.R.7562 sent to a conference committee where Bankhead and Jones could arrange a "deal"—the House would accept the Senate bill in place of Title I in its own version of H.R.7562, and the Senate, in turn, would accept Titles II and III of the House bill providing for rural rehabilitation and submarginal land programs.

With the Senators eager to escape the heat of Washington for their Fourth of July holiday, debate was little more than a ritual. After Senator Alben Barkley succeeded in persuading his colleagues to rename the measure "The Bankhead-Jones Farm Tenant Act," the Bankhead-Robinson strategy unfolded as planned. On July 2, the new bill, H.R.7562, was passed by a voice vote and sent to the conference committee, in which the Senate would be represented by Democrats Bankhead of Alabama, Pope of Idaho, and Frazier of North Dakota. The House designated Democrats Jones of Texas and Doxey of Mississippi, and Republican Hope of Kansas.

In the conference that followed, Bankhead attempted to secure his deal with Jones, but the House conferees were determined not to accept the Senate's provision for government land purchase and resale, nor to accede to the criticisms of the officials in the USDA regarding assistance for migratory laborers, discouragement of land speculation, greater clarity in the provision covering the equitable distribution of loans among the states, the promotion of cooperative associations, the need for a trial lease period, and the dangers inherent in the delegation of administrative responsibility to county committees. Bankhead's plan therefore failed, and the conferees finally agreed on a measure which closely conformed to H.R.7562 as passed by the House.

The House conferees, on the other hand, consented to the following changes, most of which were in deference to the Senate: (1) farm purchase loans might be made for a period of up to forty years, rather than thirty years as provided in the House bill; (2) county committees would be empowered to exercise administrative functions in the program for farm purchase loans only, and loan applications were to be filed not with the county committee but with the county agricultural agent or with anyone else designated by the Secretary of Agriculture; (3) loan instruments were to con-

The Bankhead-Jones Farm Tenant Act / [187]

tain a requirement that the borrower must carry out such proper farming practices as the Secretary might prescribe; (4) in so far as practicable, the Secretary was to exercise his powers under the Act to avoid expansion of farm production where such expansion might defeat the parity policy under Section 7 of the Soil Conservation and Domestic Allotment Act; and (5) administrative expenses for carrying out the provisions of Title I (the farm purchase program) were not to exceed in any fiscal year 5 per cent of the amount appropriated for that fiscal year, rather than the Senate provision for a fixed upper limit of $400,000.

On July 13, the House of Representatives, saddened by the news that Senate majority leader Robinson of Arkansas had just died of a heart attack, took up the conference report. There was virtually no further discussion or debate, although conservative Democrat Stephen Pace of Georgia charged that the bill would "put the farmers of this Nation into irons," and he declared that he would never consent to granting any Secretary of Agriculture the power to "tell the farmers in my State how, what, when, and where they may plant and harvest their crops." Before the day was over, the conference report was approved by voice vote. After adjourning for a day in respect to the memory of their fallen majority leader, the Senate met on July 15, approved the conference report, and sent it to the President who signed it on July 22. Thus, the dance of legislation quietly came to an end.[32]

Postscript: Transition and Evaluation

The passage of the Bankhead-Jones Farm Tenant Act embraced many compromises, but in one particular respect there was a flaw that was destined to have serious political consequences—the Act did not unequivocally declare congressional affirmation of the Resettlement Administration and its programs. Tugwell, who was out of the government at this time but who remained concerned about the agency he had founded, urged the President to waste no time in sustaining the hand of the Secretary of Agriculture in the process of transition.

Early in August, Roosevelt therefore wrote to Wallace. He ac-

32. *Congressional Record*, Vol. 81, pp. 6648–49, 6662–67, 6677–82, 6885–87, 6750–60, 7138, 7141, 7162; U.S., Congress, House Report No. 1198, July 12, 1937, 75th Cong., 1st Sess. (Washington, D.C.: GPO, 1937); Pub. Law 210 (1937), 50 U.S. Stat. 522.

knowledged the defects in the Act, directed the Secretary to draft amendatory legislation for the next session of Congress, and called for an orderly transfer of operations under the Resettlement Administration, in conformity with the new statute. On the first of September, Wallace issued a memorandum which simply changed the name of the Resettlement Administration and assigned to it the relevant functions provided for in the Bankhead-Jones Farm Tenant Act. In the following language he unceremoniously created the Farm Security Administration (FSA):[33]

> In view of the fact that the Administration established by me in the Department of Agriculture . . . as the "Resettlement Administration," is now carrying out a program which involves resettlement activities only as a minor part of its functions, the name of said Administration is hereby changed, effective September 1, 1937, to "Farm Security Administration." The Administrator of the Resettlement Administration shall continue to perform the same functions . . . but shall . . . be hereafter known as the "Administrator of the Farm Security Administration."

In order to consolidate all research, planning, service, and administrative functions related to the conservation, retirement, development, and utilization of submarginal land, Wallace issued a second memorandum on September 1, which transferred the land program of the Resettlement Administration to the Bureau of Agricultural Economics (BAE) in the USDA. There it would be responsible for administering the relevant provisions of the new Act, and would continue to be headed by Gray. One of the official reasons offered for this transfer was that it would give the FSA a measure of functional coherence—the FSA would be an agency concerned with *people*. To some of Tugwell's disciples who remained in the agency, including especially Assistant Administrator Baldwin, this reasoning represented a specious attempt to conceal the fact that the loss of the land program "was a burnt offering to those in Congress and in the USDA who feared that the FSA would pursue Tugwell's ambitious land reform goals."

In further compliance with the Bankhead-Jones Farm Tenant Act,

---

33. Roosevelt to Wallace, Aug. 6, 1937, NA, RG 16; Third Deficiency Appropriation Act, fiscal year 1937, Pub. Law 354, 75th Cong., 1st Sess.; Roosevelt to Wallace, July 8, Dec. 20, 1937; William A. Jump to Alexander, Dec. 27, 1937, CBBP; USDA, Secretary's Memorandum No. 732, Sept. 1, 1937.

In view of the cooling of political relationships between Congress and the White House in 1938, few leaders in the administration seriously expected that more could be wrought from the Congress in 1938 than in 1937.

Wallace performed the final rite late in September when he created the Farmers Home Corporation, as an agency of the USDA. He designated Assistant Secretary of Agriculture Harry L. Brown, BAE chief Albert G. Black, and FSA Administrator Alexander as the board of directors. Since the Act empowered the Secretary to employ the corporation in any manner he might judge appropriate, Wallace chose to create it as a strictly advisory body, and in practice it became no more than a paper organization.[34]

What exactly did passage of the Act achieve? For those who had expected much, passage of the Act and the "agriculturalization" of the Resettlement Administration represented, in James Agee's phrase, the "kiss of Judas." The mood was bitterly expressed, for instance, when Representative William Lemke of North Dakota, a Nonpartisan elected on the Republican ticket, an activist in liberal farm organizations, and Union party candidate for President in 1936, declared on the floor of the House that, "I am surprised to hear so much fuss about nothing. If ever a mountain labored and produced a mouse, this bill is it.... [It] is a joke and a camouflage." Under Secretary Wilson believed that the measure was a highly inadequate half a loaf and, to the amusement of some of the realists in the USDA, he expressed the hope that Congress might be persuaded to bring the Act more in line with the recommendations of the President's Committee during the next legislative session. To James G. Maddox, the young economist who had helped to draft the report of the President's Committee and who was destined to play an important role in the administration of the Act, it was "very questionable whether the present law permits inauguration of a program which will aid the ordinary southern sharecopper and laborer," and he suggested that, "If America is to have increased farm security and a greater stability of rural life, Congress has yet to act."[35]

34. USDA, Secretary's Memorandum No. 733, Sept. 1, 1937, No. 738, Sept. 30, 1937; author's interview with Baldwin.
Harry L. Brown and Albert G. Black resigned from the corporation in December, 1939, and were replaced by AAA Administrator R. M. Evans and Milo Perkins, president of the Surplus Commodities Corporation and an Associate Administrator of the AAA. At the same time, Alexander became chairman of the corporation's board. On February 8, 1941, Baldwin replaced Alexander. None of these new members of the board ever attended a meeting, and the last session was held on November 1, 1939.

35. *Congressional Record*, Vol. 81, p. 6438; Wilson to Director of the Budget Bureau, July 10, 1937, NA, RG 16; Maddox, "The Bankhead-Jones Farm Tenant Act," pp. 434, 450–51, and "The FSA," pp. 48–50.

A less pessimistic judgment was offered by Resettlement Administrator Alexander, on the day the bill finally passed the Senate, when he dispatched his final communiqué to Tannenbaum, which read in part as follows:[36]

> The Tenant Bill has finally passed both houses. It is on its way this afternoon to the President for signature. While the Bill is not all that I think we should have, it is much more than you, Johnson, Embree and I thought we should have when we wrote the original memorandum in my house in Atlanta . . . . I consider that in this legislation we have gone a long way.

In view of the neglect of previous years, there was cause for some gratification, if not exultation, but the passage of the Bankhead-Jones Farm Tenant Act did not signal a formidable assault on hard-core rural poverty. Had the Act bestowed clear statutory life upon the FSA, either as a permanent agency in the USDA or as an autonomous agency, had it provided for programs at least as ambitious as those recommended by the President's Committee on Farm Tenancy, had it clearly authorized adequate appropriations for the rural rehabilitation program, and had it evoked a politically conscious and determined constituency comparable to that behind the AAA and other powerful action agencies—if these and other conditions had been met, then there might have been considerably less doubt about the magnitude of the legislative sanction. The most eloquent expression of the limited goals which most members of Congess and most leaders of the USDA perceived for the FSA was the provision for *loans* for rural rehabilitation, rather than outright appropriations. Despite protestations to the contrary, the FSA was created in the image of a banking institution.

As matters stood in the fall of 1937, the FSA was an agency created not by direct congressional action but by executive prerogative. The rural rehabilitation program, which was the heart of the enterprise, enjoyed no more than tacit congressional consent, as a temporary and emergency relief expedient. The chief beneficiary of congressional action was the very modest program for farm purchase loans to selected farm tenants who could satisfy what amounted to banking requirements.

In retrospect, it is clear that the process of legitimization—transfer of the Resettlement Administration to the USDA, passage of the Bankhead-Jones Farm Tenant Act, and creation of the FSA around the nucleus of the predecessor agency—represented the establishment

---

36. Alexander to Tannenbaum, July 15, 1937, FTP.

of a condition of equilibrium within which the new agency might become a viable institution. Congress withheld a forthright benediction, but it did grant sufficient mandate to permit continued exploration, through administrative means, of programs which might eventually have a substantial impact upon chronic rural poverty. In the light of the subsequent fate of the New Deal, it is clear that had the Act not been passed in 1937, considerably less, if anything, would have been wrung from a more reluctant Congress during the years that followed.

With the transfer of the Resettlement Administration to the USDA, the latter, in order to receive the former and to contribute guidance, feasibility, practicality, and acceptance to its programs and people, moved toward it; but the Resettlement Administration was compelled to move a greater distance in this process of mutual accommodation. Consequently, as some of the leaders of the Resettlement Administration had feared in 1936, there was substantial danger that the requisites of institutional survival within the framework of the USDA would force the agency to sacrifice some of its more ambitious and provocative goals. "The price an organization pays for the privilege of remaining in existence in the future," Bertram Gross has written, "is usually continual changes that prevent it from remaining what it was in the past."[37]

Despite their dissatisfactions with the content of the Bankhead-Jones Farm Tenant Act, most of the leaders of the newly-created FSA were optimistic about the capacity of the agency not merely to survive—to avoid liquidation—but to convert the raw materials at hand into a formidable assault on hard core rural poverty. Although disappointed in the ambiguity, procedural restraints, and absence of definite appropriation authorization for the rural rehabilitation program, they were quick to perceive the Act's permissiveness. In large measure, they believed, the FSA would become whatever they might determine it should be. To Robert W. Hudgens, for instance, the Act "was a piece of legislation that would have permitted almost anything," while to Appleby, "it was destined to become meaningful only in the course of its administration."[38]

This long and tortuous genesis of the FSA demonstrates the dif-

---

37. Bertram M. Gross, *The Managing of Organizations*, Vol. II (New York: The Free Press, 1964), p. 666.
38. Author's interviews with Hudgens, Appleby; Paul H. Appleby, *Morality and Administration in Democratic Government* (Baton Rouge: Louisiana State Univ. Press, 1952), pp. 72–82.

ficulties and complexities involved in securing sufficient consensus within the government to respond rationally and coherently to different and competing felt needs. Granted, that in a large democracy consensus cannot and should not become conformity, yet, without a considerable measure of agreement on ends and means, no modern government can govern. In the search for this consensus, the contention among competing interests and groups in society is reflected in a parallel contention within and between the agencies of government, which in turn are themselves actors in the process of reconciliation.

Political legitimacy—acceptance or tacit acquiescence—of an agency, its programs, and its people is not permanently conferred in a single act of investiture. Under altered circumstances, the approval or consent which is implicit in congressional sanction may turn to manifest disapproval or opposition. Political tables may turn, legislators may change their minds, zones of indifference may narrow, and friends may become foes. If the sense of legitimacy is to be preserved, it must be continually reinforced, not only in external relations with the constituency, but also in the myriad of small internal daily decisions, struggles, and supposedly petty management procedures which also comprise the universe of governance.

Whether passage of the Bankhead-Jones Farm Tenant Act was the fatal kiss of Judas or a golden opportunity would likely be determined only in the future, for as Gross has suggested:[39]

> A Federal law is after all only a piece of paper with a number, a great many words, and three names signed at the bottom. Whether or not it has any really compelling force behind it depends on the precision with which it is drawn, the will and ability of those who are supposed to administer it, the extent to which the right people know about it, and the amount of organized or potential support it commands.

For the denouement, we now turn to the substantive programs and the political and administrative means through which the leaders of the FSA demonstrated the possibilities of American political life.

---

39. Bertram M. Gross, *The Legislative Struggle* (New York: McGraw-Hill, 1953), p. 177.

CHAPTER VII

THE FSA IN ACTION:
PROGRAMS AND PERFORMANCE

Once a human interest is recognized as legitimate, a principle of conduct is derived from it.

KARL POLANYI[1]
The Great Transformation

Perceiving a mandate, not for a war on chronic rural poverty, but rather for more orthodox purposes—preservation of the family farm and reduction of certain forms of farm tenancy—the leaders of the Farm Security Administration (FSA) proceeded with caution. As reasonably sophisticated veterans of American political life, they cloaked their ambitious goals in traditional agrarian symbolism, and the family farm became the hallmark of the agency, despite the fact that some of their programs were devoted to a more collective organization of agriculture and rural life. During the years that followed, there were conflicts, defeats, disappointments, and retreats, but the extent to which they achieved their goals, improved the human condition for hundreds of thousands of destitute farm families, conceived and successfully applied unique social innovations, maintained their agency's viability, and explored the parameters of the possible surprised their friends and alarmed their foes.

---

1. Karl Polanyi, *The Great Transformation* (New York: Farrar and Rinehart, 1944), p. 261.

In accordance with conventional management practice, the performance of the FSA was usually measured in terms of immediate program impacts, such as the number of loans approved and repaid, the amount of emergency grant funds disbursed, the degree of improvement in client families' farming operations, the increase in their farm value, the number of cooperative associations established, and similar technical indices of program productivity. These measures were meaningful, manipulable, and quantifiable for men in budgeting and accounting offices, in congressional appropriations committees, and in the field offices of the FSA. But there were tendencies, as we shall see in the present chapter, toward *goal displacement*, in which the instrumental values of loan and grant administration became terminal values, and *goal succession*, through which the leaders of the agency sought to adapt to the changing world around them.

To some of the leaders of the FSA, for instance, the major mission was to demonstrate the value of a limited, high-quality, well-administered experimental program of promoting farm ownership and improved farming methods among carefully selected low-income landless farm families—the number of client families was less important than the technical integrity of the program. To other leaders of the agency, the central purpose was to dispense governmental assistance to as many recipients as possible and to maximize the spread of the net, with technical integrity subordinated to improvement of the human condition. For some leaders, political awareness and participation among the agency's clientele became the terminal values, rather than instruments for achievement of program goals. There were some leaders in the FSA and in the U.S. Department of Agriculture (USDA) who became more concerned with the contribution that the FSA might make to institutional balance in the Department and to the Secretary's leverage. There were also those who resisted the bureaucratic tendencies toward routinism and political safety and who concentrated on the opportunities for innovation—for them the essential purpose of the FSA was to disturb the peace.

In this dissection of the agency's institutional purpose, there is danger, however, in becoming too dichotomous, for as Herbert A. Simon has suggested:[2]

---

2. Herbert A. Simon, "Recent Advances in Organization Theory," in Stephen K. Bailey *et al.*, *Research Frontiers in Politics and Government* (Washington, D.C.: The Brookings Institution, 1955), pp. 30–31.

We are in danger, through our renewed interest in power struggles and human attitudes, of neglecting one central truth that was known to the older administrative theory. Behavior in organizations is neither completely emotive nor completely aimless. Organizations are formed with the intention of accomplishing goals; and the people who work in organizations believe, at least part of the time, that they are striving toward these goals.

Despite changes in command of the FSA over the years and a continual process of goal displacement and succession, the central purpose pattern of the agency—the purposes in terms of which the leaders sought to justify themselves—were those prescribed or authorized by the Bankhead-Jones Farm Tenant Act, by supporting appropriation language, by executive orders of the President, and by the administrative rulings of the Secretary of Agriculture. In seeking subsidiary goals, which sometimes replaced or conflicted with official goals, the leaders of the FSA were, to borrow Simon's phrase, "intendedly rational."

The Tenant Purchase Program

Under Title I and relevant sections of Title IV of the Bankhead-Jones Farm Tenant Act, a Tenant Purchase Division was established in the Washington office of the FSA, under the direction of Paul V. Maris, whom we have already met as the innovator of rural rehabilitation methods under the Federal Emergency Relief Administration (FERA) and the Resettlement Administration. The Tenant Purchase Division was assigned responsibility for the tenant purchase program (in later years called the farm ownership program), which was a careful demonstration program designed to help selected farm tenant families and other *qualified* landless low-income farm people become owner-operators of family-sized farms.

Based on a coupling of credit and technical assistance (called supervision), tenant purchase loans were employed to complement the older rural rehabilitation program. A tenant purchase loan was therefore conceived as a rung up the agricultural ladder. A central dogma of the tenant purchase program was the belief, emphasized by Maris, that the public interest would not be served by helping unqualified farm families to become owner-operators of inadequate farms. Maris was zealously loyal to this principle.[3]

The cautious character of the tenant purchase program was partly

---

3. Paul V. Maris, *"the land is mine"* (Washington, D.C.: GPO, 1950), p. 87; his article, "National Land Tenure Objectives," *Land Policy Review*, Vol. IV

due to congressional intent, as expressed in the provisions of the Act, and partly to Maris' persistence in adhering to his principle of careful experimentation. To implement the general statutory provision, Maris and his assistants prescribed carefully detailed restrictions on the size and quality of farms to be purchased by borrowers, farming methods to be employed, and eligibility for loans. Although administratively distinct from other programs at the national level, the tenant purchase program was designed as a step toward eventual farm ownership, and was held out as an incentive for lower-income client families enrolled in the rural rehabilitation program.

In view of the conservative character of the tenant purchase program and the difficulties that would have been involved in making the necessary adjustments, it was not surprising that there was *de facto* discrimination against Negro tenant farmers. The particularly low economic and social level of Negro farmers automatically rendered most of them ineligible for tenant purchase loans, while the climate of apathy and paternalism that surrounded their relations with landlords and planters made those who were eligible difficult to reach. Furthermore, difficulties in finding adequate farms on which Negro farm families might be allowed to settle; the tendency for acceptance policies of the program to reflect local racial attitudes; the decision of FSA leaders not to earmark funds for tenant purchase loans to Negroes; and the policy of attempting to make loans to Negroes, not on the basis of actual need, but on the basis of the same ratio as applications were received from Negroes and whites, reinforced the tendency toward discrimination.[4]

Despite occasional expressions of concern about the problem, and efforts by Maris, which he believed would correct the inequity, such as subdivision of large tracts into individual family-sized farming units on a segregated basis, and the making of individual loans to Negro borrowers for settlement, discrimination diminished only slightly over the years. The following percentages of total tenant

---

(July, 1941), pp. 34–37; and his address at annual agricultural workers' conference at Tuskegee Institute, Jan. 14, 1952, "Essential Requirements of a Good Farm and How to Acquire Such Farms," PVMP; Maddox, "The FSA," pp. 98–99, 397–98, 415–68; Edward C. Banfield, "Ten Years of the Farm Tenant Purchase Program," *Journal of Farm Economics*, Vol. 31 (Aug., 1949), pp. 469–86; author's interviews with Maris, Will W. Alexander, C. B. Baldwin, Paul H. Appleby.

4. Maris, *"the land is mine,"* pp. 100–06; FSA, *Annual Report* (1939), pp. 15–16; Richard Sterner, *The Negro's Share* (New York: Harper, 1943), pp. 305–07.

purchase borrowers in eight southern states having more than 30,000 Negro tenants, for the years 1938 and 1945, are illustrative:

State	Per cent of Negro Tenants to Total in State	Per cent of Negro Tenant Purchase Borrowers	
		Fiscal Year 1938	Fiscal Year 1945
Mississippi	75	26	35
South Carolina	64	20	30
Louisiana	59	9	27
Alabama	55	29	24
Georgia	48	25	26
North Carolina	44	25	17
Arkansas	44	10	16
Texas	16	15	7
Average for Eight States	51	20	23

Maris' overriding concern was that his program should "make a good showing." Selection of borrowers more likely to succeed; rejection of applicants needing special assistance, training, and supervision; and the program's freedom from an excessive case load helped to assure programmatic success. James G. Maddox, who became Maris' counterpart in the rural rehabilitation program, accused Maris of "skimming the cream off" the clientele. In other words, success was built into the tenant purchase program. For a variety of reasons —personal differences in background and beliefs, zealous concern about managerial details, and deference to what he believed were the political realities—Maris sought and achieved considerable technical, statistical, and ideological separatism for his program. His personal loyalty to the leadership of the FSA was unimpeachable, but he jealously guarded his program's technical integrity and separate identity.

During his tenure as director of the program, he avoided publicly criticizing the alleged "errors" and "excesses" of the Resettlement Administration and the FSA, but later, in his chronicle of the tenant purchase program, he ostentatiously disavowed any personal connection with or authorship for such practices as the encouraging of client families to participate in the social and political life of their communities, counseling and supervision with respect to client families' personal and family affairs, control or supervision over their bank accounts, or intruding into the client farmer's decisions as to what to grow on his farm, where and how to plant, how to spend his money, or where to spend it. All of these practices, which the tenant purchase program easily avoided because of the higher caliber of its borrowers, Maris regarded as "regimentation," and therefore technically undesirable and politically dangerous.[5]

Appropriately, the ideology and rhetoric of the tenant purchase program harmonized with its purposes and methods. While the leaders of the FSA generally employed such value-laden terms as "potential, capacity, opportunity, social justice, security, humanity, equality, and adjustment," Maris preferred other language—"initiative, self-reliance, resourcefulness, efficiency, promptness, sane, sensible, and practical." While the self-conscious New Dealers among the leaders of the FSA called their families "clients," Maris preferred the term "borrowers." Will W. Alexander called them "our people."

The caution and separatism of the tenant purchase program were only partly a reflection of Maris' conservatism and predilection for technical perfection. There was also involved an attempt to practice *Realpolitik*. Alexander, C. B. Baldwin, Maddox, Robert W. Hudgens, and Maris all realized that, at least as far as Congress was concerned, the tenant purchase program was the most legitimate aspect of the overall FSA program. Any attempt to lower eligibility standards or to liberalize the program's repayment requirements and other administrative regulations would jeopardize the repayment record, alienate some key members of Congress, and therefore dilute the agency's political capital. While there was occasional impatience among the leaders of the FSA with Maris' chauvinism, there could be no denying the fact that his program was a source of considerable political strength for the agency as a whole. On more than one occasion, Alexander's sweating hand was sustained during congressional appropriations hearings by opportunities to wave the tenant purchase banner before congressional critics.

Paradoxically, this program, which enjoyed the greatest political

---

5. Although Maris, to the extent that it was within his power, carefully avoided anything that might provoke the Congress, he was not immune to their wrath. In 1941, for instance, in his article, "National Land Tenure Objectives," he included in his recommended national land tenure objectives the following: "Expand cooperative farm leasing and purchasing associations as rapidly as experience justified. See to it that low-income groups not well adapted to operations and management of independent farm units are included among those served by leasing cooperatives." Some members of Congress perceived this as a threat to the principle of fee simple land ownership and as bordering on socialism.

Author's interviews with Marvin Jones, Maris, Appleby, James G. Maddox; minutes of administrative staff meeting, FSA, Washington, D.C., Oct. 8, 1941, CBBP.

appeal, represented the tail on the FSA dog. From its inception in 1937 through the end of June, 1940, 11,939 initial tenant purchase loans averaging $5,500 in amount were granted, representing 13 per cent of the total funds obligated by the FSA during the period. On the basis of the 1940 Census, the 6,678 tenant purchase borrowers in 1940 represented approximately 2 per cent of the total number of tenant farmers in the United States. Throughout the years, only a fraction of the applications for tenant purchase loans could be accepted. During the second year of operation, for instance, 147,972 applications were received for only 7,000 loans, and in 1942, more than 175,000 applicants competed for 8,000 available loans.

With one eye on conservative members of the congressional appropriations committees, Maris carefully watched the barometer of his program's repayment record. By June 30, 1943, a total of $191,487,749 had been loaned, of which $18,807,447 had fallen due, with collections totaling $24,496,036 (including refunds and proceeds from sales of timber and mineral rights). Repayments against maturities represented 98.4 per cent of the total amount billed. The conservatives in Congress were especially gratified.[6]

The tenant purchase program therefore represented the most highly agriculturalized facet of the program of the FSA. In view of Maris' extension background, the caliber and status of tenant purchase borrowers, and the technical integrity of procedures employed, the program enjoyed a closer affinity with the more conventional agencies of the USDA and with the state agricultural colleges and extension services than did the rural rehabilitation program. Not unexpectedly, a good deal of whatever cooperation there was between the FSA and the agricultural establishment was achieved through Maris and his program.

The Rural Rehabilitation Program

Inherited from the Resettlement Administration and further developed and refined by the FSA, the rural rehabilitation program

---

6. Maris, *"the land is mine,"* pp. 319–23, and "The First Year Under the Bankhead-Jones Farm Tenant Act," Processed (n.d., 1938), PVMP; FSA, *Annual Report* (1939), pp. 15–16, and *Annual Report* (1944), pp. 7, 11.

Maris reported, several years later, that by June 30, 1949, a total of $345,625,707 had been loaned to 62,044 borrowers, and that of the principal, 49.9 per cent had been repaid by that date, with 44.2 per cent of the total number of borrowers ahead of schedule on their repayments.

was, in reality, a cluster of inter-related processes variously orchestrated to achieve different but related program objectives. Under Title II and relevant provisions of Title IV of the Bankhead-Jones Farm Tenant Act, a Rural Rehabilitation Division was created in the Washington office of the FSA, under the direction of Philip Maguire. To it was assigned responsibility for the cluster of rural rehabilitation activities inherited from the predecessor agency. As the years passed, the leaders of the FSA responded to their innovative bent, engaged in the process of goal succession, and expanded the overall program to include the following differentiated sub-programs, tools, and activities.[7]

1. *The Standard Rural Rehabilitation Loan.* This combination of credit, farm and home management planning, and technical service or supervision represented the essence of rural rehabilitation. The standard rural rehabilitation loan was governed more by welfare objectives than conventional banking principles and was consciously intended to serve higher-risk client families, thus increasing the government's gamble. This type of loan, sometimes supplemented later by additional credit, averaged $240 in amount in 1937, and $600 in 1940. By 1943, one out of nine farm families in the United States had received such a standard loan; this involved more than 695,000 farm families. Distribution of the loans was concentrated in the South.

In view of the professed goals and values of the rural rehabilitation program, it was paradoxical that it too discriminated against Negro

---

7. Statements of rural rehabilitation goals, as they evolved under the FSA, were not all formalized in authoritative documents. Testimony before congressional appropriations committees, procedural rules and their interpretations, minutes of staff meetings and field conferences, public information issuances, and internal communications are some of the sources that have been drawn upon here. The following are illustrative: Ralph W. Hollenberg, "The Meaning of Rehabilitation," statement at staff meeting, FSA Region 9, Mar. 21, 1940; FSA, "Objectives of the Farm Security Administration," *Induction Training Course*, training manual for new personnel, Oct., 1941, p. 58; statements by Baldwin and Robert W. Hudgens at conference of regional directors, Nov. 25, 1942; FSA, *Rules and Regulations of the Farm Security Administration* (Washington, D.C.: GPO, 1940); Henry A. Wallace to Baldwin, Dec. 21, 1940; minutes of staff meeting, FSA, Washington office, Mar. 4, 1941; Carl N. Gibboney to Baldwin, July 21, 1941; Baldwin to Appleby, July 22, 1941; Baldwin, "The Farmers Job in Strengthening Democracy," address at St. Paul, Minn., Dec. 14, 1940; CBBP.

The two most authoritative histories of the rural rehabilitation program are the following: Larson, *Ten Years*, which was prepared in 1947 by the BAE as a "capture and record" document; and Maddox, "The FSA," whose author was former director of the Rural Rehabilitation Division of the FSA.

low-income farm families. In 1940, for instance, a white low-income farm family had a two-to-one advantage over a Negro family in obtaining a standard loan. The odds against a Negro family ranged from three-to-one in Tennessee to seven-to-one in Mississippi. The leaders of the FSA, who personally deplored the situation, offered a variety of reasons for persistence of discrimination—the particularly low economic status of Negro applicants which disqualified them for eligibility; timidity of Negroes in applying for assistance; paternalistic tenant-landlord relations and the Negro tenant's fear of antagonizing his landlord by applying for outside help; the tendency of many FSA county supervisors to accede to their own racial attitudes in selecting client families, and their tendency to select families who were more likely to make a good showing in improving farm and home operations and in repaying their loans; and the agency's lack of adequate funds and knowledge necessary to penetrate the walls of apathy and fear among the potential clientele.

Despite the especially risky character of rural rehabilitation loans from a banking point of view, the repayment record was surprisingly good. In 1938, for instance, FSA Administrator Alexander predicted that 80 per cent of them would be repaid, and by 1943 his prophecy was on its way to fulfillment—80 per cent of all maturities had been repaid, and enough advance payments had been made to bring the collection rate up to 93.5 per cent of maturities. More than 260,000 low-income farm families had repaid their loans completely.[8]

2. *The Grant Program.* Under the FERA and the Resettlement Administration, grants of money, averaging $20 each and for which there was no obligation for repayment, were provided to meet a variety of natural disasters, such as drought, flood, hail, and grasshoppers, or to sustain needy farm families until they might either become rural rehabilitation clients or be accepted on state and local relief rolls. For the first two years of the FSA, grants were employed primarily for such emergency relief purposes, but in 1940 the leaders

---

8. Larson, *Ten Years,* pp. 7–9, 84–129, 163–71, 354, 387–90; USDA, *Report of the Secretary of Agriculture, 1943* (Washington, D.C.: GPO, 1943), p. 176; FSA, *Annual Report* (1939), p. 3, and *Annual Report* (1941), pp. 29–39; Maddox, "The FSA," pp. 133, 142–212; FSA, Rural Rehabilitation Division, Planning and Analysis Section, *Racial Aspects of Rural Rehabilitation Acceptance,* Program Analysis Report No. 14, Dec. 5, 1940, CBBP; Sterner, *The Negro's Share,* pp. 296–304.

By the end of 1946, of the 893,000 farm families who had received rural rehabilitation loans since the beginning of the program, more than 434,000 had repaid them in full. Of the total of $1,005,392,816 loaned, $688,690,714 had been repaid, and an additional $95,347,194 in interest had been collected.

of the agency decided to liberalize the program and to try to employ it for purposes of rehabilitation as well. They provided grants for such purposes as subsistence needs, medical care and hospitalization and for participation in approved health and medical associations, sanitary facilities, household equipment, supplementary funds to help balance farm and home plans for standard loan borrowers, and work grants to be awarded as incentives and rewards for following recommended farm and home practices under signed "pledges of cooperation."[9]

Altogether, the grant program accounted for approximately 13 per cent of all rural rehabilitation funds obligated by the FSA. By June 30, 1940, approximately $70 million had been expended for the program. Grants were concentrated in the northern Great Plains, where the effects of drought were particularly severe, in troubled southeastern Missouri, in the depressed "black belt" of Alabama, and in the Central Valley of California. By the end of 1943, more than $136.5 million had been dispersed as grants, averaging $20 each, and awarded to close to 500,000 destitute farm families.

The major problem faced in the grant program involved the subjective attitudes of both the recipients and their neighbors—recipients tended to view the grants as "free money" involving no commitment on their part, while neighbors deplored them as rewards to unworthy people for sin and sloth, and tended to deprecate those who received them. Conceived as a relief measure, the grant program was unable to escape its birthmark.

Like tenant purchase and standard rural rehabilitation loans, grants also discriminated against Negroes. In December, 1940, for instance, it was revealed that in most of the South the grant policy was "shot through with gross discrimination against colored clients." The average net worth of white borrowers, before acceptance on the standard rural rehabilitation loan program, was 57 per cent greater than that of Negro clients, yet, white clients received 20 per cent more grant money per family than did Negro client families. The average grant to Negroes was $29 compared with $35 for whites. At

9. Wallace to Daniel W. Bell, Nov. 3, 1937, CBBP; Larson, *Ten Years*, pp. 182–93, 407–12; FSA Instruction 741.1, Rev., Dec. 12, 1940; USDA, Secretary's Memorandum No. 796, Nov. 16, 1938, and Secretary's Memorandum 850, Jan. 29, 1940; FSA, *Rural Rehabilitation*, Monthly Report, Oct. 31, 1941, p. 12; FSA, Rural Rehabilitation Division, Planning and Analysis Section, *Racial Aspects of Rural Rehabilitation Borrowers*, Program Analysis Report No. 15, Dec. 6, 1940, p. 8.

The FSA in Action / [203]

modern inflated prices, a difference of six dollars seems negligible, but for the low-income farm family of the 1930's, the difference probably meant shoes for all the children or many days' food for the family.

3. *Promotion of Group Services.* The expansionist bent of the FSA was particularly manifest in the promotion of group and cooperative activities among the clientele of the agency. Despite the absence of any specific congressional policy supporting such a program—it had been advocated by the President's Committee on Farm Tenancy— group and cooperative activities became one of the most important and controversial instruments of rural rehabilitation.

Initiated by the FERA and further developed by the Resettlement Administration, the policy of dealing with client families on a group or collective basis was exploited by the leaders of the FSA who believed that such an approach was entirely in accord with American rural tradition. Promotion of collective economic and social intercourse among the clientele, they believed, would help to strengthen the economic and political power of client families, encourage improved farming and conservation practices, soften the loneliness and isolation of American rural life, and promote "democratic mass action" among low-income farm families, most of whom hitherto had lived outside of organized community life.

The policy of the FSA was to encourage client families to participate in group or cooperative enterprises that were already in existence in their communities, but where they were lacking, the FSA granted loans to small groups of client families who pooled their funds for the purchase of breeding stock, farm machinery, and other facilities. By the end of June, 1942, more than $8 million had been loaned to over 16,000 cooperative groups then active. Distribution of loans for group services was widely dispersed nationally, but concentrated in the Upper South and in the corn states of the Middle West.

The program encountered serious problems, such as administrative pressures from the agency's field organization to establish groups without adequate reference to their need among client families, lack of sufficient understanding and stability among participants, and community hostility; but according to objective judgments, the groups were substantially successful. By the end of June, 1946, only 16 per cent of the 25,543 cooperative groups which had been established with funds from the FSA were then inoperative or liquidated, and 63 per cent of the loans were completely repaid. The remaining groups were still functioning actively, with their payments being made as due.[10]

4. *Promotion of Cooperative Associations.* The most important form of cooperative activity promoted among the clientele of the FSA was a more elaborate and formal application of the group approach—encouraging client families to participate in existing cooperative associations, or to organize new ones. Some of the associations were established in connection with the resettlement projects and model communities inherited from the Resettlement Administration.

Seeking to exploit the mystique which they believed lay in the cooperative movement generally, and hoping to learn from the experience of predecessor agencies, the leaders of the FSA encouraged the establishment of cooperative associations designed to serve the following purposes: leasing of large tracts of land either for cooperative farming by the association as a whole or for sub-leasing to members for individual farm operation, veterinary services, local purchasing and marketing, the purchasing of insurance, agricultural and processing services, water facilities, and other purposes. The promotion of these associations was justified on economic, educational, and social grounds. One argument offered was that the cooperative association was a useful device in reaching and habilitating or rehabilitating particularly low-income and inexperienced farm families. More discreetly, the leaders of the agency hoped that such associations would significantly promote a sense of social and political solidarity among the clientele, and weld them into a politically more formidable power base for the FSA itself.

The most prevalent type of association that the FSA promoted was for local purchasing and marketing purposes, through which clients in a county might sell their produce and purchase their needs. Neither the leaders of the FSA nor their conservative critics failed to perceive what such collective action, if successful, might do to the traditional dependence of low-income farm tenants and sharecroppers on the

---

10. Larson, *Ten Years*, pp. 200–08, 413; Maddox, "The FSA," pp. 260–74; Hudgens, address to American Institute of Cooperation, Atlanta, Ga., Jan. 13, 1942, NA, RG 96; Joe J. King, "Cooperative Development Among Low-Income Rural Families in the Pacific Northwest," *Social Forces*, Vol. 21 (Dec., 1942), pp. 194–98; Raub Snyder, "Small Farmers Discover Rural Cooperation," *Land Policy Review*, Vol. VI (Fall, 1943), pp. 22–26; FSA Instruction 734.1 (Oct. 25, 1938), and No. 831.1 (July 10, 1941); FSA, *Supervisor's Guide for Community and Cooperative,* 1942; FSA, *Annual Report* (1940), pp. 19–21, and *Annual Report* (1939), pp. 8–9.

"furnish system" provided by landlords and plantation owners.

Another type of association promoted was for the purpose of providing grain elevator services. As a result of depression and drought during the 1930's, many grain elevators in the wheat-growing areas of Kansas, Minnesota, Montana, Nebraska, and the Dakotas were either idle or liquidated. Consequently, a wave of speculation developed, as bargain hunters sought to exploit the situation. Anxious to restore some stability in the area, which coincidentally happened to be a stronghold of the American cooperative movement, the leaders of the FSA, in collaboration with the directors of the Farmers Union Grain Terminal Association, of St. Paul, Minnesota, and the West-Central Cooperative Grain Company of Omaha, Nebraska, provided loans, grants, and technical assistance to groups of clients, to purchase and restore to operation some of the grain elevators. Altogether, 177 such associations were established.[11]

In their promotion of these grain elevator cooperatives, and in granting loans to client families, to help them participate in cooperative associations connected with the National Farmers Union (NFU), the leaders of the FSA were not oblivious to the political advantages that might accrue to both the FSA and the NFU. The Farmers Union Grain Terminal Association, headquartered in St. Paul and led by M. W. Thatcher, chairman of the Legislative Committee of the NFU, was the most powerful and prosperous part of the parent organization. As we shall see in greater detail in chapter ten of this narrative, the resulting constituency relationship between the FSA and the NFU was a source of both political strength and vulnerability for the agency.

One of the most ambitious and controversial types of cooperative association promoted was that devoted to the leasing of large tracts of land, for sub-leasing as family-sized individual farms to clients of the FSA. Aimed at one of the basic causes of agricultural maladjustment—insecure land tenure—the land-leasing cooperatives were most extensively used in cotton plantation areas of the South and the western grazing areas where landlords were unwilling to subdivide their tracts into smaller parcels for piecemeal sale or lease to individual small-scale farm operators. With no congressional policy supporting such enterprises and with no provisions for them in the Bankhead-Jones Farm Tenant Act—they were favorably recom-

11. M. W. Thatcher to Emil A. Syftestad, Nov. 20, 1936; Thatcher to Baldwin, June, 21, 1938; Baldwin, address at St. Paul, Minn., Dec. 14, 1940; CBBP.

mended by the President's Committee on Farm Tenancy—the leaders of the FSA launched the program during the winter of 1938–39. On the basis of proposals made by Regional Director T. Roy Reid of FSA Region 6 in Little Rock, Arkansas, they arranged for 827 families to combine and lease seventeen cotton plantations in Arkansas, Mississippi, and Louisiana. By the time the program reached its peak in 1943, the FSA had helped to establish fifty-two such associations, holding a total of 136,368 acres in eight states, and concentrated in Arkansas and Louisiana.[12]

Finally, there was a particularly unorthodox type of cooperative enterprise—the cooperative farming association. In view of the sharp controversies destined to rage over them, there is some virtue in focusing our microscope briefly on their operations. The association was organized under the statutes of the state in which it was located, and was governed by a board of directors selected from the membership and elected annually at a general membership meeting. The board, in turn, appointed a manager who directed specialized foremen. Members of the association were employed by the association and received cash wages throughout the year on the basis of rates which corresponded to those prevailing for hired farm labor in the local area. Each member was also furnished with a house, small out-buildings, and a garden plot on which he might raise subsistence crops, or keep dairy cows and poultry. At the end of each fiscal year, members of the association were entitled to their share of the association's profits, on the basis of the number of hours worked during the year. Members were free to resign from the association at will, at which time they would receive a cash settlement representing their equity in the enterprise. The association leased the land from the owner, usually for periods of five to ten years, paid fixed rental fees corresponding to the prevailing rent for similar land in the area, and received an operating loan from the FSA at an interest rate of 3 per cent.

Once the cooperative farming association was in operation, it usually re-invested its proceeds in necessary equipment, livestock, seed, feed, fertilizer, and other needs. At virtually every stage of development, the FSA played an active role in providing technical

12. Larson, *Ten Years*, pp. 209–30, 414; Maddox, "The FSA," pp. 224–25, 234–47, 276, 280–81; Hudgens, "The Plantation South Tries a New Way," *Land Policy Review*, Vol. III (Nov., 1940), pp. 26–29; FSA, *Annual Report* (1942), pp. 12–15, and *Annual Report* (1941), p. 52; author's interview with Maris.

assistance and supervision. Only a few of the associations were racially non-segregated. Friends of the FSA hailed these farming associations as "exciting social laboratories," while some critics, as we shall see later, called them "communist collectives" or "American soviets."[13]

In attempting to evaluate the experience of these various types of cooperative associations, Maddox, who was instrumental in their conception and administration, has concluded that, despite the lack of adequate and complete data for an authoritative judgment, there was a high incidence of business failure among the smaller and more informal ones, presumably due to inadequate management, insufficient volume of business, inexperienced membership, and restrictions imposed by Congress starting in 1943. Nevertheless, there were some successes, most of which were later buried under the avalanche of criticism and clamor. Early in 1943, for instance, before congressional restrictions began to have their effect, records in the headquarters office of FSA Region 6, in Little Rock, Arkansas, revealed some impending failures among the smaller associations devoted to marketing, canning, and community services, but predicted success for most of the associations then active. Twenty-two associations, embracing a total of 86,262 acres and serving 1,738 farm families, showed a profit, were current on their loan payments to the FSA, and, in the judgment of regional officials, indicated the prospect of continuing profitable operations. Similarly, a special report on cooperatives associated with resettlement projects, inherited from the Resettlement Administration, revealed in 1940 that there was considerable financial failure among them, although, it was pointed out, the record was no worse than the prevalence of failure and bankruptcy among private manufacturing enterprises.[14]

5. *Promotion of Neighborhood Action Groups.* Another type of cooperative activity, which whetted the sociological and political appetites of the leaders of the FSA, was the promotion of small neighborhood action groups, consisting of from six to eight client families who were encouraged to meet regularly in each others' homes to discuss mutual problems as a prelude to collective action. Following the example of the federal and state extension services,

---

13. Maddox, "The FSA," pp. 234–47; *Cooley Committee Hearings*, Pt. 3, p. 1005.
14. Maddox, "The FSA," pp. 292–302; FSA, "Cooperative Associations in Arkansas," MS, JABP; FSA, *Report of the Administrator's Committee on Cooperatives in Resettlement Communities*, Jan. 2, 1940, Processed (n.d.), PVMP.

which had utilized the group discussion-study approach for many years, the field personnel in FSA Region 7, embracing North and South Dakota, Nebraska, and Kansas, promoted the approach among rural rehabilitation client families. In 1941, discussion groups were introduced in all regions, as cooperative specialists from the Washington office fanned out into the country to train FSA field personnel.

The rationale of the program was based on the lack of adequate social organization among rural rehabilitation client families, the desire of the leaders of the FSA to deepen the community involvement of their client families and thus to enhance the exercise of "their rights as citizens and their role in the democratic process." Difficulties in implementation were plentiful—subjective fears and embarrassments among participating families, lack of training and understanding among supervisory personnel of the FSA, the tendency for supervisors to dominate the discussions, and difficulties in launching and maintaining a regular schedule of meetings. In 1944, there were approximately 4,000 neighborhood groups then active, concentrated in Arkansas, Mississippi, and Louisiana. These groups were viewed by some suspicious critics of the FSA as particularly subversive of the *status quo*. Who could tell what might emerge from such "clandestine" activity?[15]

6. *Medical Care Program.* When the architects of the rural rehabilitation program under the Resettlement Administration discovered the syndrome of ill health, physical defects, and chronic poverty among client families of the program, "one thing led to another," in the words of "Pete" Hudgens, and a medical care program evolved. In 1936, a Public Health Section was organized in the Washington office of the Resettlement Administration, headed by a medical officer on leave from the U.S. Public Health Service. The new section was assigned the task of developing a medical care program which was to be governed by the following principles: freedom of choice for client families in selecting their physicians, voluntary participation, group prepayment with clients' contributions based on means, and all purely medical matters governed by standards prescribed by county and state medical societies. After the program was transferred to the FSA, it was liberalized to include

---

15. Larson, *Ten Years*, pp. 194–200; Joe J. King, "Small Farmers of the Pacific Northwest Organize Neighborhood Discussion Groups," *Rural Sociology*, Vol. 9 (Mar., 1944), pp. 38–44; FSA, *Annual Report* (1941), pp. 13–17, 52–53; Baldwin to all regional directors, Sept. 25, 1941, CBBP; author's interview with Hudgens.

hospital and dental care. The program became an integral part of the overall rural rehabilitation program of the FSA—farm and home plans for client families included provisions for a fixed medical fee, which was paid to a special fund, and participating physicians sent their bills to the trustees of the funds for payment.

By 1942, when the program reached its peak, there were 787 medical and 221 dental groups operating in forty-one states, involving 142,074 client families, and including rural rehabilitation clients, tenant purchase borrowers, and resettlement project families. The disruptive effects of World War II, including especially the movement of FSA client farmers to war industry and the departure of many participating physicians and dentists for military service, made a full evaluation of the program's performance impossible. The program enjoyed an unexpectedly large measure of cooperation from physicians and medical societies, and, in contrast to the Truman years of the 1940's, the cry against "socialization of medicine" was virtually absent, although there were cases of resentment and resistance among local physicians in some rural communities.[16]

7. *Debt adjustment and Tenure Improvement.* As we have already seen, hopeless indebtedness, nagging anxiety about imminent mortgage foreclosure, and insecure and inequitable land tenure relationships and state tenure laws were among the factors contributing to chronic rural poverty. During the decade of the 1920's, agricultural economists and others had recommended a variety of reforms, and during the early New Deal years, some remedies were applied, such as the debt adjustment work of the Farm Credit Administration (FCA) and the so-called "rescue loans" of the federal land banks, but little, if anything, was done to improve the legal and operational relationships between tenants and landlords.

Initiated by the FCA in 1933, further developed by the Resettlement Administration in 1935, and inherited by the FSA in 1937, the debt adjustment program became an important tool of rural rehabilitation. County FSA supervisors, often working with the assis-

---

16. Larson, *Ten Years*, pp. 230–53, 415–19; National Conference of Social Work, *Medical Care Experience of the Farm Security Administration in California* (New York: Columbia Univ. Press, 1941), pp. 495–500; Earl H. Bell, "Culture of a Contemporary Rural Community," BAE, Rural Life Studies II (Sept., 1942), p. 67; RA, *First Annual Report*, (Washington, D.C.: GPO, 1936), pp. 93–94; National Emergency Council, *Report on Economic Conditions of the South* (Washington, D.C.: GPO, 1938), pp. 29–32; FSA, *Annual Report* (1939), pp. 9–11, and *Annual Report* (1940), pp. 23–24; author's interviews with Alexander, Hollenberg, Baldwin.

tance of volunteer committees of local farmers, arranged to bring distressed farm debtors and their creditors to mutual agreement on terms that would make foreclosure and bankruptcy unnecessary, through reduction of interest rates on old mortgage loans, extension of the maturity period, and refinancing of previous commercial loans.

By the end of June, 1940, the FSA had completed over 58,000 debt adjustment cases, involving a total reduction in indebtedness of $43,554,421 and averaging a percentage reduction in indebtedness of 21 per cent. The program reached its peak in 1941, after which time the need was reduced as a result of improved economic conditions in the country. Approximately one-third of the cases involved farm families who were not clients of the FSA. Taxes paid to local governments as a result of the debt adjustments represented an additional benefit from the program. The costs to the government for the program averaged $1,748,000 annually for salaries and expenses of FSA personnel and for state and county committees participating in the work. Although the program had only a negligible impact on the overall national rate of foreclosures and bankruptcies, it did make a difference to the 58,000 farmers who were saved.[17]

While the tenant purchase program was devoted to the promotion of farm ownership, and thus the reduction of farm tenancy, the tenure improvement activities of the rural rehabilitation program represented an effort to make the tenancy system work more effectively. Tentatively initiated during the second year of the Resettlement Administration, tenure improvement became an important rural rehabilitation tool under the FSA. In 1938, the record revealed that one-year tenure agreements, without guarantees of renewal, were reported by three-fifths of the farmers in the corn belt, four-fifths of the southern Negro farmers, and almost four-fifths of the southern white farmers in the cotton and tobacco areas. Assistant FSA Administrator Hudgens declared in 1938 that the most fundamental part of any cure for chronic rural poverty was tenure improvement: "No rehabilitation is possible without land, and land on which the family has some right to remain."

Like debt adjustment, and like so much of the work of the FSA generally, tenure improvement activities represented the general policy of the agency to serve as mediator between the tenant and

17. Larson, *Ten Years*, pp. 253–62; Ernest Feder, "Farm Debt Adjustment During the Depression—The Other Side of the Coin," *Agricultural History*, Vol. 35 (Apr., 1961), pp. 78–81; Rainer Shickele, *Agricultural Policy* (New York: McGraw-Hill, 1954), p. 400; Maddox, "The FSA," p. 216.

his landlord, and for this the FSA was often accused of substituting one kind of paternalism for another. The ostensible goal of the program was stability, under improved tenure conditions, during the period of the client family's rehabilitation. The promotion of written tenure agreements or contracts, in accordance with model leases, and the education of the tenant regarding his legal rights, especially in the South where oral agreements and tenant ignorance were common, did not make the FSA particularly popular among landlords and plantation owners.[18]

8. *Special Rural Rehabilitation Programs.* Finally, the omnibus rural rehabilitation program included a variety of special programs designed for particular geographical areas, special classes of people, special poverty problems, and experimentation in special techniques. The special programs included, for instance, the southern Great Plains program, devoted to farm enlargement, tenure improvement, and soil conservation, in cooperation with a number of other federal agencies; the southeastern Missouri program in the "bootheel" of Missouri, often called the "laboratory for the Cotton South;" the "grubstake program" in Minnesota; a special Negro community program in eleven southern states, designed to promote Negro community leadership, although in a segregated manner; and a housing and sanitation program launched in 1937 in response to the situation described by the *Report on Economic Conditions in the South* by the National Emergency Council.[19]

Having explored this elaborate set of rural rehabilitation subprograms, tools, and techniques, it is proper to ask this central question: what, if any, were the concrete accomplishments of the overall rural rehabilitation program? Precise and meaningful statistical measurement of progress is virtually impossible for several reasons—inadequate *measures* of progress toward certain goals, the lack of "before-and-after" data on client families' situations, incom-

---

18. Larson, *Ten Years*, pp. 262–67; Edgar A. Schuler, "Social Status and Farm Tenure—Attitudes and Social Conditions of Corn Belt and Cotton Belt Farmers," FSA Research Report IV, Processed (Apr., 1938), p. 37; Hudgens, address at Atlanta, Georgia; Maddox, "The FSA," pp. 226–30.

19. Larson, *Ten Years*, pp. 268–308; Rachel R. Swiger and Conrad Taeuber, *Ill Fed, Ill Clothed, Ill Housed—Five Hundred Families in Need of Help*, BAE and FSA, Processed (Apr., 1942); Arthur F. Raper, *Tenants of the Almighty* (New York: Macmillan, 1943); National Emergency Council, *Report on Economic Conditions of the South*, pp. 34–36; FSA, *Annual Report* (1941), pp. 19–20; Roosevelt to Wallace, Jan. 19, 1939, NA, RG 16; author's interviews with Arthur F. Raper, Jonathan Garst, Earl F. Bell, and T. Roy Reid.

plete records, price changes between 1937 and the 1940's, and substantial variations in standards and methods among FSA regions. However, there is sufficient reasonably dependable data to suggest a general *profile* of farm productivity by client families, as follows:[20]

Program Objective	Annually Before Acceptance	1941
Annual net income per client family	$375	$538
Value of home goods produced	$150	$247
Milk produced for family consumption	184 gals.	472 gals.
Home produced fruits and vegetables canned	114 qts.	297 qts.
Meat produced for family consumption	85 lbs.	447 lbs.
Average acreage cultivated	107 acres	142 acres

The overall rural rehabilitation program probably had only a negligible impact on the nation's agriculture, but profound consequences for the human condition of the low-income farm families who were served. Although comprehensive independent evaluations of the program have been strikingly few, Olaf F. Larson of the Bureau of Agricultural Economics (BAE) made an ambitious and systematic attempt to measure overall progress of the program through a series of sample surveys of client families accepted by the Resettlement Administration and the FSA between 1936 and 1939. The study suggested that a number of achievements had been made in the lives of the client families, which were summarized as follows:[21]

1. Suffering and misery have been relieved.
2. Considerable gains have been made in restoration to permanent self-support, provided the general economic conditions are favorable.
3. Considerable gains have been made toward achieving security. . . . [but] prospective technological changes in agriculture give rise to a question concerning the duration of this security.

20. BAE, Progress Reports and Tables on Progress of Rural Rehabilitation Clients in Twelve FSA Regions, CBBP.
21. Larson, *Ten Years*, p. 326. Larson based these conclusions on a BAE study of standard rural rehabilitation borrowers in twelve FSA regions, through statistical analysis of a representative sample of 39,295 borrowers; the findings were published during the years 1941–43 in twenty-three reports and 123 progress tables.

4. Remarkable gains have been made toward obtaining a physically healthful level of living; perhaps the greatest gains have been made toward this goal.
5. Gains have been made toward attaining a socially desirable level of living.
6. Gains have been made toward the acquisition of skills and abilities needed to manage the farm and home successfully and independently.
7. Some gains have been made toward obtaining land resources for an economic unit of the family-farm type; a long distance remains to be covered particularly as the Nation moves increasingly away from the "self-sufficient" type of economy.
8. Spotty gains have been made toward becoming full participants in a democratic way of life.

Larson also suggested that there were what he called beneficial "spilling over effects" on the thousands of rural communities in which client families lived, worked, spent their money, sent their children to school, and—*perhaps*—voted in elections. The rural rehabilitation program was believed to have served the general welfare of the nation in a variety of ways—taxpayers' money was saved, in that client families would probably have had to go on relief rolls if they had not received assistance from the FSA; insecure farm families were stabilized on the land, although in some cases such stability was probably undesirable, and the farms remained the families' prisons; to a modest degree, undirected migration of farm families was retarded; to "some degree," farming as "a way of life" was enhanced; the family-type farm, as an institution, was strengthened; man-land relations were improved, and conservation of resources promoted; progress was achieved in preparing the nation for a fuller utilization of manpower among low-income farm families, and therefore the nation's wartime production goals were served; and democracy was, "to some degree," strengthened by making its opportunities more readily available to a class of people who hitherto had lived outside of the organized political system.

Despite the unorthodoxy of some features of the program—and this should be borne in mind in later chapters—the program represented no revolution. On the other hand, disappointed critics of the program often belittled the importance of small loans and grants as mere "tokenism." In our own time of billion-dollar budgets and astronomical prices, it is easy to miss the profound impact which $20, $100, or a few hundred dollars had upon those who received the money. For some families, the loans and grants represented the difference between hope and despair, between remaining on the farm for at least another year and being cast adrift.[22]

The Resettlement Project Program

When the FSA inherited responsibility from the Resettlement Administration, under Title IV of the Bankhead-Jones Farm Tenant Act, for completion and management of 150 resettlement projects, it received a technically difficult and politically costly legacy. At the time of transition, in the fall of 1937, construction had been completed on only thirty-eight of the projects, and on which only 4,441 families were actually in residence. Virtually all of the agricultural projects were based on the family farm type of operation, with only four cooperative farms that together involved approximately 450 families. Administered by the Resettlement Division in the Washington office of the FSA, under the direction of Major John O. Walker, and in the field through assistant regional directors and local project directors, the program became a lightning arrester which attracted to the FSA some of the most bitter political fire. The purpose here is to briefly sketch the program and its performance, leaving the political struggle to chapter eleven in this narrative.[23]

Individual project families were given trial leases, and some were awarded purchase contracts. In the case of the four cooperative farms, ninety-nine year leases were granted to the governing associations. In those projects where families operated on a family farm basis, it was generally assumed that the farming units would be sold to them as soon as they demonstrated their capacity to become successful owner-operators. In other words, the leaders of the FSA justified resettlement projects as sociological and economic experiments, or testing grounds for future family farmers.

During the struggle for passage of the Bankhead-Jones Farm

---

22. *Ibid.*, pp. 330–31.
23. Wallace to Roosevelt, Nov. 3, 1937, NA, RG 16; Harry A. Moore to Roosevelt, Sept. 8, 1938, FDRL, OF 1568-Misc.; Chester C. Davis to Harold D. Cooley, June 17, 1943, CBBP; *Senate Hearings*, Agr. Approp. (1940), 76th Cong., 1st Sess., pp. 826–30; Russell Lord and Paul H. Johnstone, eds., *A Place on Earth, A Critical Appraisal of Subsistence Homesteads* (Washington, D.C.: BAE, 1942); FSA, *Annual Report* (1940), pp. 13–15; Mordecai Ezekiel, COHC, p. 35; author's interviews with Appleby, Hollenberg, John Fischer, Alexander, Baldwin.

Tenant Act, some members of Congress had expressed fundamental opposition to large-scale government land ownership, and were determined that the government "should get out of the land business." At the time of the passage of the Act, there was a general understanding, not only among the members of Congress, but also among the leaders of the USDA, that the farming units in the resettlement projects would be turned over to the participating families as soon as practicable, although there was no clear consensus regarding a policy of liquidation for the projects. The only specific commitment made was Secretary Henry A. Wallace's pledge that no new resettlement projects would be built.

The resettlement project approach, it will be recalled, had been downgraded during the last year of the Resettlement Administration, while rural rehabilitation emerged as the primary route to a solution of the problem of chronic rural poverty. Under the FSA, the resettlement project program remained a very minor activity, but in 1938, the agency initiated its promotion of land-leasing and land-purchasing associations, as part of the rural rehabilitation program. As farm families began to be displaced by construction of army posts and airfields in the early 1940's, the leaders of the FSA established relocation corporations, which began to purchase large tracts of land, until a ruling by the Comptroller General forced the discontinuation of the practice. Although there were fundamental differences between the old resettlement or community projects inherited from the Resettlement Administration, the land-leasing and land-purchasing associations, and the war relocation corporations, they were all based on a collective approach that collided with deeply felt congressional fears, as we shall see in later chapters.

Altogether, the resettlement project program accounted for less than 10 per cent of total FSA expenditures. Even during the peak period of the program's activity, ending in 1938 and including the costs of retiring submarginal land and resettling dislocated families, funds obligated for the projects did not exceed 20 per cent of total FSA obligations.

Of all the programs of the FSA, the resettlement projects attracted the most uniform verdict of failure. Even had many of them not been liquidated before they had had an opportunity to prove themselves, it is likely that the record of failure as business ventures and social experiments would have remained largely unchanged. The catalogue of reasons for their failure is virtually endless—inadequate planning, lack of understanding and cooperative spirit among project families, faulty administration, inherent technical difficulties in cooperative farming, the dissolution of enthusiasm for the projects among leaders of the government at the national level, unfounded assumptions of human rationality, arbitrary restrictions on the program that made failure inevitable, and a hostile political climate which influenced even the project families themselves. Edward C. Banfield's grim autopsy of the Casa Grande cooperative farming project in the Arizona desert reinforces the impression that that project, like most of the others, was doomed to failure, although failure might have been less complete if planning and management had been more rational.[24]

Was nothing achieved by the program? Paul K. Conkin, whose study of the community planning aspects of the resettlement projects and model communities is one of the fairest and most thoughtful attempts to evaluate the experience, has suggested that, at least from the viewpoint of the historian, the program was not entirely in vain. In providing homes for approximately 10,000 families, in creating jobs for thousands of unemployed workers, in revealing the problems involved in a rapid shift from an individualistic to a more collective society, and in contributing new ideas and methods to the city planning movement, the program made a significant contribution.

Similarly, in a confidential report to War Food Administrator Chester C. Davis in 1943, John D. Black at Harvard University wrote as follows:[25]

> At some future date . . . it will be highly desirable to have a review and analysis made of this whole undertaking to see what was really accomplished and what lessons can be derived from the experiments. By no means will all results be negative. It may easily happen that the balance struck runs considerably in favor of the projects. Furthermore, even though this particular major experiment on the whole proves not to have yielded results hoped for, one need not conclude that the objectives of these projects were wrong nor that an opportunity should not be sought to pursue the same objectives at an early occasion.

Since men are not guinea pigs and society is not a laboratory, students of politics and public administration are generally denied the benefits of controlled experimentation. Yet, the resettlement project

---

24. Edward C. Banfield, *Government Project* (Glencoe, Ill.: The Free Press, 1951), pp. 231–60.

25. Paul K. Conkin, *Tomorrow a New World* (Ithaca, N.Y.: Cornell Univ. Press, 1959), p. 331; John D. Black to Davis, May (n.d.), 1943, p. 38, USDAHF.

program did offer a unique experimental opportunity whose lessons have not yet, a generation later, been fully evaluated, let alone applied.

Goal Displacement: Skimming the Cream Versus Digging Deeper

For the rural rehabilitation program and for the FSA as a whole, two major policy questions emerged: (1) to what extent the leaders of the agency should adhere to conventional credit principles and to political considerations, and emphasize the repayment record of loan borrowers; and (2) whether funds and energies should be allocated intensively among a limited clientele, as in the tenant purchase program, or spread more extensively over a larger number of the hard-core cases of farm poverty. Since there was no statutory direction in the Bankhead-Jones Farm Tenant Act or in the appropriation acts regarding these issues, it was a matter of administrative discretion. How they would be resolved would profoundly affect the political and administrative viability of the FSA.

The leaders of the agency appreciated the political virtue that lay in emphasis upon a good loan collection record, but they also knew that such an emphasis might lead client families to make great sacrifices in order to meet their repayment obligations, and thus subvert rehabilitation goals. Privately they believed that paid loans were not necessarily indicative of rehabilitation goal achievement, but publicly, especially at congressional appropriation time, they talked more like bankers than social workers. With respect to the second issue, they believed that raising eligibility standards for rural rehabilitation loan borrowers would automatically reduce the number of deeply impoverished families who might qualify, and thus blunt the agency's social purpose. Lowering the standards, on the other hand, would strengthen the agency's social welfare character, increase the need for flexibility in lending policies generally and for intensive supervision, and thus compel them to devote a greater proportion of their funds to administrative expenses. And they well knew that for most members of Congress and newspaper editors, high administrative expenses were like a red flag to a bull.

Until 1940, authority to select rural rehabilitation loan borrowers was officially assigned to regional FSA offices. In the beginning, regional directors and their staffs exercised their power of approval, but development of a log-jam during the first year encouraged the leaders of the agency to delegate the power of loan approval, first to district offices and then to county supervisors. After 1940, district supervisors were authorized to approve all but the largest loans, which remained regional responsibilities. The leaders of the FSA justified this delegation of loan approval power to county supervisors not only on grounds of administrative expediency, but also because they believed that these supervisors were in closer proximity to the situation, that they knew the applicants and their problems more intimately, and that administrative discretion might therefore be exercised more effectively in the county than in district and regional offices.

By 1939, after two years of experience under the FSA, it became apparent that the process of goal displacement, as discussed in the introductory chapter of this study, was at work. County supervisors tended to become preoccupied with "making a good showing" in their loan collection records, to seek escape from the local agriculturalists' suggestion that the FSA was wasting its time with the dregs of rural society, and to simplify their tasks. They therefore tended to select loan borrowers from higher social and economic levels—applicants with larger farming units, higher net incomes, greater net worth, fewer dependent children, better health, and more education. In other words, many of the county FSA supervisors were working with the "upper crust" of the low-income farm population.

FSA Administrator Alexander, Assistant Administrators Baldwin and Hudgens, and Rural Rehabilitation Director Maddox deplored the trend on economic and moral grounds. Only by reaching lower in the selection of clients could the potential purchasing power of deeply impoverished people contribute to the economic rehabilitation of their communities, they believed, and the moral commitment of the FSA to deal with hard-core rural poverty be fulfilled. They feared that if the upward trend were allowed to continue, it would subvert the very essence of the agency. In characteristically naïve fashion, Alexander went so far as to predict that, "if we don't do the job, some other agency eventually will be established in our place."

In a letter to the field staff in January, 1940, Alexander reminded them that, "FSA was set up to help the farm people at the very bottom of the heap," and that supervisors should resist the understandable temptations to select safer credit risks, to develop caseloads that would be easier to handle, to avoid acceptance of the most needy and handicapped families, and to try to show a good collection record. He insisted that the field staff should "dig deep enough into the lower economic levels to reach the people who need our help most."[26]

The authors of a report by the Rural Rehabilitation Division, however, avoided laying all of the blame at the door of county supervisors, and suggested that the upward trend in client selection was due to flaws in the rural rehabilitation program itself:[27]

1. Rural rehabilitation techniques were perhaps inapplicable to very low-income farm families;
2. Increasing competition, mechanization, and commercialization of American agriculture were causing farms generally to increase in size and therefore probably encouraged county supervisors to select applicants with larger farming units and greater working capital;
3. County supervisors were perhaps convinced that it was hopeless to work with operators of smaller farming units; and
4. Fewer operators of small farms were applying to the FSA, either because they did not believe that their farms were capable of supporting even the small debt and interest payments on loans, or they believed that the FSA was not interested in assisting them, and therefore it was a waste of time to apply.

Later in 1940, the leaders of the FSA applied what they believed would be at least a partial remedy—liberalization of policies governing grants for rural rehabilitation loan borrowers, in order to facilitate the acceptance of loan applicants who otherwise might not have qualified. This would permit the client family to live on grant funds while using current farm income for payment of operating expenses and for repayment of the loan. In effect, the client family was relieved of responsibility for feeding and clothing itself, while efforts were made to increase its productivity and to raise its standard of living. This was, according to Rural Rehabilitation Director Maddox, "an overt attempt on the part of the national office to lower the eligibility standards being followed by county supervisors." He warned at the time that the liberalized grant policy would be only a temporary palliative in arresting the upward trend in client selection.

The leaders also realized that their new grant policy would likely create internal antagonisms among the agency's personnel, who

26. Alexander to Fellow Workers, Jan. 31, 1940, CBBP.
27. FSA, Rural Rehabilitation Division, Planning and Analysis Section, "Trend in Family Selection for the Rural Rehabilitation Program, 1935–1940," Oct. 20, 1941, CBBP.

believed that, "To combine public relief assistance with credit and banking functions in one office was . . . like mixing oil and water." They also knew that they would be accused by their critics in the country generally of promoting among their clientele "disrespect for their obligations to repay borrowed money."

They therefore faced a dilemma. To ignore hard-core cases, because of technical difficulties, administrative resistance, and cliental ignorance and apathy would result in subversion of purpose. On the other hand, even if more strenuous efforts were made to enforce liberalized eligibility standards and to encourage potential client families to come forward, the very nature of the loan method probably rendered it inappropriate. Loans in themselves presumed that borrowers possessed at least some of the necessary managerial ability, initiative, land and resources, and capacity to repay. In the opinion of Maddox at the time, the only effective solution was probably some kind of public works program similar to that which had been carried out for years by the Works Progress Administration (WPA). In a memorandum to Alexander, he confessed that, "Maybe a 'works program' isn't the answer [but] the point is that we should find the answer, and not fool ourselves by thinking that we have it in our present program."[28]

There was also a dilemma on a still higher policy level. With the trend toward greater commercialization and mechanization of agriculture, perhaps the FSA was being quixotic in attempting to find any productive role for hard-core poverty cases in agriculture. If American agriculture could not sustain them in reasonably profitable farm production, or at least in productive farm wage labor, and thus permit them to secure a satisfactory level of living, then perhaps the FSA should devote its energies not to rural rehabilitation, but to facilitating the escape of very low-income farm families from the land and their re-establishment in non-agricultural enterprise.

Some critics of the FSA charged the agency with seeking to foster reform or revolution on the farm, but in a real sense the FSA represented a conservative or even a reactionary attempt to sustain or restore a very unsatisfactory *status quo.* Frequently voiced was the charge that the FSA, in the name of immediate rural rehabilitation

28. Maddox, address to regional FSA personnel, Denver, Colo., Jan. (n.d.), 1940; FSA, Rural Rehabilitation Division, Planning and Analysis Section, "Distribution of Rural Rehabilitation Activities in Relation to Need," Apr. 29, 1940; Maddox to Alexander (n.d.), presumably written during the summer of 1939; CBBP. Also, Maddox, "The FSA," pp. 153–55, 164–71.

objectives, was delaying necessary long-term "elimination" of inefficient and surplus farm families from agriculture. If the charge was in fact justified, then it can now be said that the FSA sought to retard the mass exodus to the urban ghettos of America.

On the other hand, the champions of the policy of "digging deeper" insisted that by helping deeply impoverished farm families to help themselves, rural rehabilitation would help to eliminate inefficient farming methods and to remove land-use maladjustments, thus making it possible for low-income and marginal farm families to succeed in commercialized and mechanized agriculture.

The leaders of the FSA continued to wrestle with their dilemmas until 1942, when the wartime emphasis on rapid expansion of American farm production swept other depression-based purposes aside, and forced the agency to turn from the problem of goal displacement to the need for goal succession. With the active involvement of the United States in World War II, the FSA placed considerable emphasis on granting loans to applicants who could demonstrate their capacity to increase production rapidly, and thus the contest between skimming the cream and digging deeper came to an end.

Goal Succession: The Migratory Farm Labor Program

Perhaps no other aspect of chronic rural poverty attracted greater public attention than the problems of migratory farm laborers in the 1930's. John Steinbeck wrote about them. FSA photographers snapped their pictures. And western sheriffs guarded communities against them. As a result of the same long-term trends that had dislocated agriculture generally for two decades and had deepened the pool of stagnant rural poverty, literally an army of farm people—the "Okies" and "Arkies" in particular—were uprooted and either flocked to the slums in the cities and towns, or traveled westward to the promised land to find seasonal work in the so-called "factories in the field." Between July 1, 1935, and March 31, 1938, for instance, more than 250,000 unemployed migratory farm workers arrived in California in search of work.

Early measures by the FERA and the Resettlement Administration provided low-cost emergency housing in labor camps, subsistence needs, and free low-cost medical care to needy migrants. In 1937, the President's Committee on Farm Tenancy recognized the problem and recommended expansion of the Resettlement Administration's experimental efforts. Later in the year, a group of officials representing several agencies in the USDA proposed an elaborate program to cope with the social, economic, and political aspects of the migratory labor problem.[29]

With establishment of the FSA in 1937, a Migratory Farm Labor Section was created in the Resettlement Division, with responsibility for administering a labor camp program. Without specific congressional authorization—Congress did not appropriate funds for the program until 1939—the FSA proceeded with funds from emergency relief appropriation acts and earmarked for "rural rehabilitation." While the tenant purchase and rural rehabilitation programs were devoted primarily to assisting needy farm families "in place," and to anchoring them on the land, the migratory farm labor program during the 1930's was designed to provide succor to families "on the wing."

The program promptly expanded to include temporary and permanent camps and shelters, with sanitary facilities, medical care, and recreational facilities, located wherever migrants congregated along the routes of seasonal travel in several states. By the end of 1942, the FSA had built ninety-five camps, with accommodations for approximately 75,000 people. Although the primary purpose of the program was merely to improve the living conditions of the migrants while en route between work and not to alter their status, the leaders of the FSA continued to dream of a program that some day might grant this class of farm families greater permanent economic and social security and stronger bargaining power.

With deepening American involvement in World War II during 1940 and 1941, the leaders of the FSA perceived a triple opportunity:

---

29. Carey McWilliams, *Ill Fares the Land* (Boston: Little, Brown, 1942), pp. 35, 85, 231; David G. Burgess, "The Joads—Still Out of Luck," *New Republic*, Vol. 10 (Jan. 10, 1944), pp. 46–48; John M. Gaus and Leon O. Wolcott, *Public Administration and the USDA* (Chicago: Public Administration Service, 1940), pp. 246–49; William T. Ham, "Farm Labor in an Era of Change," in USDA, *1940 Yearbook of Agriculture* (Washington, D.C.: GPO, 1940), pp. 907–21; FSA, *Annual Report* (1938), pp. 20–21, and *Annual Report* (1941), pp. 21, 38–39; John Steinbeck to Roosevelt, Feb. 29, 1939, FDRL, OF 1568-Misc.; Harry L. Mitchell, COHC, Pt. 2, p. 127; USDA, Committee on Agricultural Labor, memorandum to Secretary of Agriculture, Sept. 3, 1937, CBBP, also reported in Wayne D. Rasmussen, *A History of the Emergency Farm Labor Supply Program, 1943–1947*, BAE Monograph XIII (Sept., 1951), p. 12; author's interviews with Hollenberg, Garst, Eleanor Roosevelt.

(1) to help rationalize and stabilize the farm labor supply, which had turned from a problem of labor surplus to a problem of manpower distribution; (2) to do more than attack the symptoms of the farm labor problem, and to fulfill their dream of an ambitious reform of the system; and (3) to exploit the program as a means of strengthening the agency's justification at a time when the country's concerns had shifted from peace to war, from depression to rising prosperity.[30]

In accordance with rules prescribed by the Secretary of Agriculture, and later by the War Manpower Commission, the FSA eagerly collaborated with the U.S. Employment Service, the BAE, and the Extension Service in an ambitious program to recruit and transport migratory farm laborers to meet wartime production needs on the farms of the United States. One of the potential sources of supply of such labor was importation of foreign workers. Responding to pressures from cotton growers in Arizona, New Mexico, and Texas for easing of restrictions on admission of Mexicans, Raymond C. Smith of the Interbureau Labor Committee in the USDA, conducted a survey of the needs and the methods that might be employed in a program for importing Mexican farm workers.

In May, 1942, the President created a Special Committee on Importation of Mexican Labor, and late in June the Secretary of Agriculture attended an inter-American conference on agriculture in Mexico City where he opened negotiations with the Mexican Government. On June 23, Major Walker of the FSA and David O. Meeker of the Office of Agricultural War Relations in the USDA signed an agreement with Mexican officials for the importation of Mexican farm workers.

Provisions in the agreement, some of which the Mexican Government had insisted upon but all of which the leaders of the FSA were exceedingly happy to enforce, guaranteed the following: (1) Mexican workers would not participate in any kind of military service; (2) they would not be subjected to any kind of discrimination; (3) they would be provided with adequate transportation, housing, and

---

30. Rasmussen, *History of Farm Labor Program*, pp. 13–15; Bela Gold, *Wartime Economic Planning in Agriculture* (New York: Columbia Univ. Press, 1949), p. 182; testimony of Rev. John O'Grady, *Senate Hearings*, Agr. Approp. (1943), 77th Cong., 2d Sess., p. 528, Raymond C. Smith, address to Agricultural Outlook Conference, Washington, D.C., Oct. 21, 1942, and Proceedings of FSA Administrator's Staff Conference, Nov. 25–29, 1942, CBBP. Author's interviews with Rev. O'Grady, Smith, Louis H. Bean.

subsistence, and would be assured repatriation; (4) they would not replace other workers; (5) the FSA would sub-contract with employing farmers to assure observance of all conditions; (6) local prevailing wages would be paid, with a minimum of thirty cents an hour; and (7) all guarantees would be formalized by contracts in Spanish.

With the FSA responsible for the total Mexican operation, the program commenced in the fall. By the end of 1942, more than 4,000 Mexicans had been recruited and transported, primarily to sugar beet ranches in California. By May 1, 1943, the FSA had imported 12,800 Mexicans, and, under similar arrangements, 1,185 farm workers from the Bahama Islands.[31]

With respect to domestic migratory workers, the FSA and the U.S. Employment Service proceeded on the basis of directives issued by the War Manpower Commission in June, 1942. In the fall, acting in response to demands for workers to harvest record-breaking crops, representatives of the FSA negotiated a series of agreements with potential employers, in which the leaders of the agency used the leverage of their transportation function to extract specific guarantees. No farm workers would be transported by the FSA unless standards respecting working conditions, wage rates, the provision of adequate housing, and freedom from discrimination were satisfied. Local prevailing wages were to be paid, with a minimum of thirty cents an hour.

Between September, 1942, and May, 1943, the FSA transported more than 8,000 domestic farm workers under these arrangements. Also, during the same period, more than 5,000 year-round farm workers from submarginal farming areas, especially the Appalachians and the Southeast, were transported to areas where labor shortages existed. The FSA made arrangements for these year-round workers to have two to four weeks of training at special centers in state colleges of agriculture, to prepare them for the new types of farm work they would be expected to perform. During this period, the program was financed with money from the President's Emergency Fund—this was prior to any congressional declaration of policy.[32]

---

31. Rasmussen, *History of Farm Labor Program*, pp. 199–206; Otey M. Scruggs, "Evolution of the Mexican Labor Agreement of 1942," *Agricultural History*, Vol. 34 (July, 1960), pp. 140–49; FSA, *Annual Report* (1943), p. 23.
32. FSA, "Model Cooperative Employment Agreement" (n.d.); Baldwin, draft of article for publication by National Association of Housing Officials, Feb. 6, 1943; CBBP. *House Hearings*, Farm Labor Program, pp. 20–21, 49–51, 113–18; FSA, *Annual Report* (1943), p. 23; Maddox, "The FSA," pp. 107–08.

Until 1943, responsibility for the *domestic* wartime farm labor program was highly diffused. The FSA, for instance, furnished transportation and subsistence for migrants in transit, and built and operated labor camps. The Sugar Section in the USDA established minimum wage rates for sugar beet and sugar cane workers. The BAE conducted research. State land-use planning committees, assisted by the Extension Service and the BAE, planned the use of farm labor. And the U. S. Employment Service, in the Department of Labor, was responsible for the actual recruitment and placement of the workers.

Here was a power vacuum, with an exceedingly important program in search of an institutional home. The leaders of the FSA, as we shall see more clearly in chapter twelve of this study, had no illusions about the political struggle that was developing in the background over who would control this program upon which large-scale commercial farmers depended so heavily for the provision of farm labor. It was no secret that the FSA coveted the total responsibility, nor was there any doubt about the likelihood that whichever agency won control would be enormously strengthened. Let it suffice for now to emphasize that the fate of the FSA as a viable administrative agency hinged heavily on the role it would be allowed to play in this crucial program.

Goal Succession: Programs to Win the War

As we have just seen, in the case of the migratory farm labor program, the coming of World War II presented the leaders of the FSA with both a challenge and an opportunity. As the tempo of war grew during 1940 and 1941, as the agency's depression-related purposes became increasingly more difficult to justify, as key staff members of the FSA and the USDA were attracted to emergency jobs in the military services and in other civilian agencies and departments, as the conservative cry for "reduction of nonessential federal expenditures" grew in amplitude, the leaders of the FSA came to realize that despite the large measure of success they had achieved in many of their purposes, they would have to strengthen their agency's *raison d'être* or face the prospect of liquidation toward which other New Deal agencies were headed. The development of wartime emergencies furnished them the opportunity; the challenge lay in the problems of institutional adjustment. Briefly, the new wartime programs, into most of which the FSA rushed with characteristic enthusiasm, included the following.

1. *Wartime Relocation.* By the end of 1941, the federal government had acquired more than two million acres of land for the construction of army posts, airfields, artillery ranges, and other war-related installations, displacing an estimated 18,000 farm families, of whom more than 6,000 were in urgent need of assistance in relocating. Since most of the displaced families were in a low-income status, President Franklin D. Roosevelt, on the basis of proposals by Chester C. Davis, Director of the National Defense Advisory Commission, assigned to the FSA the task of resettling the displaced families.[33]

Seeing this new responsibility as an opportunity to extend the agency's land purchasing, leasing, and cooperative activities, the leaders of the FSA would have preferred to assist families through the establishment of new cooperative associations. However, time was short and associations required considerable detailed planning, so they resorted to an expedient—defense relocation corporations, to be established under the corporate laws of the states as non-profit enterprises, and governed by boards of directors consisting of officials employed by the USDA. They viewed this arrangement as temporary, until such time as the normal type of cooperative management might be practicable. The program was to be financed with rural rehabilitation funds borrowed from the Reconstruction Finance Corporation (RFC), under authority contained in the Emergency Relief Appropriation Act for fiscal year 1941 and the Agriculture Appropriation Act for the same year.

The manner in which the program unfolded was reflected in the experience in Missouri, where the Missouri Defense Association, Inc., purchased 45,000 acres of the so-called Lord Scully estate at a total cost of $1,019,000, averaging $25 per acre. It was expected that the acquired land would provide adequately-sized farms for 255 families, at an average cost of $4,000 per farm. The leaders of the FSA estimated that improvement of the land, including houses and other

---

33. John O. Walker to Howard H. Gordon, Nov. 5, 1940; Jack H. Bryan to Edward R. Trapnell, Apr. 1, 1941; FSA, memorandum, "Defense Relocation Corporations" (n.d., n.n.); NA, RG 96. Davis to Roosevelt, Nov. 28, 1940, FDRL, OF 1568; USDA, Sub-committee of the Interbureau Coordinating Committee, "The Impact of War and the Defense Program on Agriculture," Report No. II, Pt. 1, to Roosevelt, Feb. 19, 1941, FDRL, OF 227; FSA, "Defense Relocation Program of the Farm Security Administration, Dec., 1940, to May, 1942," MS (n.d., n.n.), OBCP; *Cooley Committee Hearings*, Pt. 3, pp. 1138–40; author's interview with Baldwin.

structures, would average approximately $3,000 per farm. The Rural Rehabilitation Division would grant loans where necessary, and families relocated on the farms would be given opportunities to purchase them in a manner similar to that employed in the tenant purchase program.

Between December 27, 1940, and February 6, 1942, eighteen defense relocation corporations were established in an equal number of states, most of which were located in the South and Middle West. The FSA loaned during that period a total of $9,921,766 to seventeen of the corporations—one remained inactive—for the purchase and development of 256,062 acres of land, which was estimated to be sufficient for 2,500 farms. When a dispute developed between the Attorney General and the Comptroller General over the legality of the expenditure of funds for purchase of land for this purpose, and over the powers of the FSA to create such corporations, Secretary Claude R. Wickard and his advisers decided to order an end to the program, and it ceased in May, 1942.[34]

Under the wartime relocation program, the FSA was compelled, with considerable reluctance, to perform a much more melancholy task. As a result of the forced evacuation of approximately 100,000 Japanese nationals from the West Coast of California, following the attack on Pearl Harbor, over 200,000 acres of land, involving more than 6,000 small farms, were abandoned in the middle of the growing season. In February, 1942, Lt. Gen. John L. De Witt, commander of the Western Defense Command, assigned to the FSA the task of formulating a program to insure continuation of the proper use of agricultural lands vacated by the enemy aliens, and which would provide "fair and equitable arrangements between the evacuees and the operators of their property." Under the powers of the Wartime Civilian Control Authority, Laurence I. Hewes, Jr., FSA Regional Director in California, supervised the recruitment of qualified operators for the abandoned farms, and with $5 million of emergency funds completed the task within two months. With the assistance of FSA personnel in several western states, operators were found for 6,664 farms embracing 232,159 acres, and the FSA granted loans totaling $3,544,639 to assist in resettling the new farm operators and main-

34. FSA, *Annual Report* (1941), pp. 22–27; FSA, "Defense Relocation Corporations," MS; testimony of Baldwin, *Tolan Committee Hearings*, Pt. 28, pp. 10870–79; Francis Biddle to Claude R. Wickard, May 1, 1942, and Lindsay C. Warren to Wickard, Mar. 5, May 18, 1942, NA, RG 96; *Cooley Committee Hearings*, Pt. 3, pp. 1138–40.

taining the farms in operation without interruption. For its zealous concern in protecting the interests of the evacuees, the FSA earned the label of "Jap-Lovers" to pin alongside that of "Nigger-Lovers," which it had long worn.[35]

2. *Defense Housing.* A minor and less painful task was participation in construction of emergency housing. Under the Lanham Housing Act of 1940, the Urgent Deficiency Appropriation Act of 1941, and the Additional Deficiency Appropriation Act of 1941, Congress authorized the President to construct temporary housing for workers in defense areas, and appropriated a total of $150 million for the purpose. Under the general coordination of the Federal Works Administration, three projects were assigned to the FSA, presumably because of its experience in home construction under the resettlement project program. By June 30, 1941, work was in progress on 1,350 family units located near various wartime industrial installations. With intensification of wartime mobilization, following the attack on Pearl Harbor, Congress enacted the First War Powers Act, creating the National Housing Agency, and on February 24, 1942, the President issued an executive order transferring the defense housing activities, including those of the FSA, to the new agency.[36]

3. *Food for Freedom.* Finally, Roosevelt's declaration late in December, 1940, that America would become the "Arsenal of Democracy," and the entry of the United States into active hostilities a year later presented the leaders of the FSA with their greatest challenge and opportunity. With critics of the agency demanding the curtailment of expenditures for helping marginal and inefficient small-scale farmers to increase production, when large-scale commercial farmers were presumably better prepared to satisfy the country's farm production needs, the leaders of the FSA strained toward a larger role in the food production programs of the USDA. To an even greater degree than in the case of the migratory farm labor program, the fate of the FSA hung on the outcome of this issue. The denouement is discussed within a larger context in chapter twelve.

A major objective of the process of goal succession, we have been

---

35. FSA, Rural Rehabilitation Division, memorandum (n.d., n.n.), NA, RG 96, also published in *Cooley Committee Hearings*, Pt. 3, pp. 1170–71; Laurence I. Hewes, Jr., *Boxcar in the Sand* (New York: Knopf, 1957), pp. 155–75, 203–4, Chaps. 14–16; Alexander H. Leighton, *The Governing of Men* (Princeton, N.J.: Princeton Univ. Press, 1946), pp. 37–41.

36. FSA, *Annual Report* (1941), pp. 25–37; Baldwin, draft of article for National Association of Housing Officials; Lanham Act of 1940, 54 Stat. 1125; Urgent Deficiency Appropriation Act of 1941, 55 Stat. 14; Additional Deficiency Appropriation Act of 1941, 55 Stat. 198; Executive Order 9070, Feb. 24, 1942.

told, is organizational maintenance. However, the global social and political matrix within which a strategy of goal succession fails or succeeds is not stable. The situation during the early war years may have called for extension and enlargement of organizational purposes, but the winning of political acceptance for these larger purposes was neither easy nor automatic. Against this background of profound political and administrative change, the FSA went to war—against the Axis abroad and against its own foes at home.

In Transaction: Program Purpose, Administration, and Environment

Whether in conformity to a prior grand design or a pragmatic response to a fluid environment, the unfolding of FSA programs and policies represented a seemingly irresistible drive toward expansion and proliferation which characterized the agency as a whole, from its creation in 1937 to approximately 1942. Tenant Purchase Director Maris, who became increasingly more isolated and alienated from the top leadership of the FSA as the years passed, has offered, in retrospect, his own explanation of this pattern of institutional growth:[37]

> The trouble with the FSA was its refusal to restrict itself to what it could handle effectively as a demonstration program. I was never able to get them to do that. Baldwin and Hudgens wanted to take on everything and everybody in a hit-or-miss fashion. They didn't understand that you can't help the low-income farmer that way. Theirs was a lick-and-a-promise policy, and the tenant purchase program, which avoided their mistakes, was an inherited and unwilling step-child.

Although Maris may have over-stated the case, he was correct in ascribing the growth of the FSA, at least in part, to the choices and decisions made by a few zealous men. Without doubt, the leaders of the agency were eager to extend its reach, build its clientele, deepen its roots in the federal bureaucracy, enhance its power, *and* effectively combat chronic rural poverty. If there was personal ambition, it was not entirely an appetite for power. The essential difference between Maris' position, as expressed above, and that of Alexander, Baldwin, Hudgens, and others lay in competing judgments as to where institutional strength lay. Maris, who was particularly sensitive to the political hostility that surrounded the FSA, saw virtue in what we have called goal displacement—the narrowing of organizational pur-

---

37. Author's interview with Maris.

pose in order to escape that hostility and to conform to technical norms. Alexander, Baldwin, Hudgens, and others, on the other hand, were less concerned about political hostility and technical integrity, and therefore strained for enlargement of organizational purpose.

Although some of the leaders' choices and decisions, as will be shown, led to dysfunctional consequences, there was, in Simon's phrase, "intended rationality" in their refusal to defer more greatly to a minority of strategically placed congressmen, in their efforts "to dig deeper," in their going beyond conventional economic goals to what they believed was the "good life" for client families, in their persistent promotion of cooperative associations and land-buying schemes, and in their refusal to rush into a hasty liquidation of resettlement projects.

The roots of the evolution of the FSA lay not in some organismic will to live and multiply, but rather in the interaction between the agency and its environment—in the political character and involvement of public administration. The FSA, like government itself, was presumably created to satisfy the "felt needs of the time." Pressures to cope with catastrophe; demands from members of Congress, state governors, and local officials for greater shares of largesse from the FSA for their constituencies; and demands by leading reform organizations, labor unions, social service agencies, ethnic groups, civil rights organizations, academic and professional groups—these were some of the manifestations of felt needs to which the leaders of the FSA responded.

According to the folklore of scientific management, there is no Republican or Democratic, liberal or conservative way of organizing an office, classifying personnel, preparing a budget, operating a typewriter, and performing all of the details of public administration. Nevertheless, new administrative agencies of government do not come into this world through some process of politically immaculate conception, nor is institutional survival entirely a matter of substantive programs and performance. Significance lies not only in *what* is done, but also in the *how* of it. It is therefore to the administrative and political instruments of achievement employed by the FSA that we now turn.[38]

38. For early statements of the idea of an inter-penetration of politics and administration, by a participant in the events discussed here, see Appleby, *Big Democracy* (New York: Knopf, 1945), Preface, p. viii, and his book, *Policy and Administration* (University, Ala.: Univ. of Alabama Press, 1949), pp. 26–46.

CHAPTER VIII

INSTRUMENTS OF ACHIEVEMENT: POLITICS AND ADMINISTRATION

> ... *the scene on which public administration takes place is a field on which mighty forces play. Here are great pulls and propulsions: forces of self-interest; forces of idealism and aspiration; forces of habit, convention, and prejudice; forces of personalities at their various vantage points; organizational forces; forces of unorganized sentiment seepage; forces that seem to be expressions of impersonal conditions, time, and place; intragovernmental and extragovernmental forces. Many of these tend to be embodied in the governmental organizations that become representative of them. Where these forces contend is a political battleground, and one part of it is occupied not by partisan politicians but by administrators.*
>
> PAUL H. APPLEBY[1]
> *"Toward Better Public Administration"*

When Henry A. Wallace signed the memorandum on September 1, 1937, changing the name of the Resettlement Administration to the Farm Security Administration and assigning to the new agency the relevant powers in the Bankhead-Jones Farm Tenant Act, most

---

1. Paul H. Appleby, "Toward Better Public Administration," *Public Administration Review*, Vol. 7 (Spring, 1947), pp. 93–99.

of the transitional "house-keeping chores" had been completed six months earlier, in connection with the transfer of the former agency to the U.S. Department of Agriculture (USDA). Working together, C. B. Baldwin, Assistant Administrator of the Resettlement Administration, and Paul H. Appleby, Special Assistant to the Secretary, had arranged for the transfer of some budgeting and accounting functions to William A. Jump's Office of Budget and Finance, certain personnel management functions to Warner W. Stockberger's Office of Personnel, and some of the agency's legal tasks to Mastin G. White's Office of the Solicitor. Standard departmental procedures for budgeting, accounting, personnel management, record-keeping, labor relations, purchasing, and materials handling had been devised and hopefully prescribed. Where it was thought to be advantageous, personnel of the Resettlement Administration had been transferred to appropriate divisions of the USDA. Except for the transfer of the land utilization program (and Lewis C. Gray) to the Bureau of Agricultural Economics (BAE), and the formal establishment of the Farmers Home Corporation later in September, the process of transition seemed to require no other major changes in the mode of operation. The agency's letterhead was redesigned, name plates were changed at office doors, and Will W. Alexander and his associates assumed their new titles.[2]

These were merely the immediate and routine tasks of administrative transition. Far more difficult to resolve, and having profound ramifying political implications for the FSA as a viable institution, were a number of administrative issues involving questions of legislative direction, organizational structure, administrative procedure, personnel management, allocation of funds, delegation of responsibility, and relations with the constituency. In fashioning their administrative instruments and in seeking to resolve these underlying issues, the leaders of the FSA were constrained by contending forces affecting all public agencies—the larger institutional structure within which the agency would be compelled to operate; expectations of the constituency; limitations of time, funds, resources, and political sufferance; internal administrative resistances; and inevitable opportunity costs. Having received their baptism of fire under the Resettlement Administration, the leaders of the FSA were familiar with the

---

2. C. B. Baldwin to Appleby, Dec. 20, 1936; Percy L. Gladmon to Appleby, Dec. 23, 1936; William F. Littlejohn to Baldwin, Dec. 28, 1936; Will W. Alexander to Appleby, Jan. (n.d.), 1937; Burton D. Seeley to Fred P. Bartlett, Apr. 1, 1937; CBBP. Also, Appleby, "Toward Better Public Administration."

terrain of the political battleground on which they would have to contend. And they hoped that the young agency would be granted time and freedom to mature, in order to survive the challenges that would surely come.

Money and Discretion

The factor that probably contributed most to the growth and maturation of the FSA during its formative years was the comparatively large measure of permissiveness in the Bankhead-Jones Farm Tenant Act and in subsequent appropriation acts. For the tenant purchase program, funds during the first year were provided in the Third Deficiency Appropriation Act, passed on August 21, 1937, which simply provided $10 million to carry out the provisions of Title I, with no additional restrictions. For the second year and for each year thereafter, tenant purchase loans and the work of completing and managing resettlement projects were financed with funds contained in the regular appropriation acts for the USDA.

For the rural rehabilitation program generally, funds were provided in emergency relief appropriation acts until fiscal year 1942, when Congress initiated the practice of including funds for "rural relief and rehabilitation" in the USDA appropriations. In the appropriations for both the tenant purchase and rural rehabilitation programs for fiscal year 1941, Congress introduced an additional change, which it continued during the following years—it appropriated funds for administrative expenses only; for the financing of loans in both programs, it authorized the FSA to borrow from the Reconstruction Finance Corporation (RFC) at an interest rate of 3 per cent. Under these arrangements, the FSA borrowed, for fiscal year 1941, $50 million for tenant purchase loans and $100 million for rural rehabilitation loans. An important feature of this appropriation pattern was the sharp distinction that was maintained between funds for the tenant purchase program, and funds for rural rehabilitation.[3]

3. Third Deficiency Appropriation Act, fiscal year 1947, 50 Stat. 757; Emergency Relief Appropriation Act, fiscal year 1938, 50 Stat. 357; Emergency Relief Appropriation Act, fiscal year 1939, 52 Stat. 809; H. J. Res. 83, 53 Stat. 507; Department of Agriculture Appropriation Act, fiscal year 1939, 52 Stat. 711; Emergency Relief Appropriation Act, fiscal year 1940, 53 Stat. 927; Department of Agriculture Appropriation Act, fiscal year 1940, 53 Stat. 939; Department of Agriculture Appropriation Act, fiscal year 1941, 54 Stat. 532; Department of Agriculture Appropriation Act, fiscal year 1942, 55 Stat. 408; Department of Agriculture Appropriation Act, fiscal year 1943, 56 Stat. 664.

The primary source of legislative direction for the rural rehabilitation program, which accounted for 75 to 85 per cent of all FSA funds during these years, were the appropriation acts, but very little congressional direction was provided. For the fiscal year 1939, for instance, in the spare language in the Emergency Relief Appropriation Act of 1938, a sum of $175 million was made available for "administration, loans, relief and rural rehabilitation for needy persons:"[4]

To the Secretary of Agriculture, $175,000,000, together with balances of allocations heretofore made or hereafter to be made to the Farm Security Administration under the Emergency Relief Appropriation Act of 1937 and the joint resolution of March 2, 1938 [House Joint Resolution 83, which prohibited the use of emergency relief funds, including those in this Act, for establishing industrial enterprises on resettlement projects, for compensation of personnel covered by civil service regulations, or in any way to influence elections], which remain unobligated on June 30, 1938, and such sums shall be available for administration, loans, relief and rural rehabilitation for needy persons. . . .

There was no attempt to define or specify the purposes for which funds were to be used, other than for "administration, loans, relief and rural rehabilitation for needy persons," nor was there any suggestion as to the allocation to be made among these purposes.

The Emergency Relief Appropriation Act for fiscal year 1940 was also highly permissive, although it did specify the purposes for which funds were to be expended—general administration, debt adjustment service, loans, relief, and a variety of land development, resettlement, water facilities, and migratory labor camp projects. The closest that the Congress ever came toward granting the FSA clear statutory life was one paragraph in the 1940 Act which read as follows: "The Farm Security Administration within the Department of Agriculture is hereby extended until June 30, 1940, to carry out the purposes of this section."[5]

In retrospect, the absence of specificity in the appropriations for the FSA during its formative years came at a fortuitous time, and had both immediate emancipating effects and ultimate dysfunctional political consequences. At a time when the felt needs for FSA programs were great, when the area of political sufferance was relatively broad, and when the agency needed freedom of action, the absence of detailed congressional direction and surveillance permitted the

4. Emergency Relief Appropriation Act, fiscal year 1939.
5. Emergency Relief Appropriation Act, fiscal year 1940.

leaders of the FSA to explore their discretion, experiment with programs, and improvise with administrative forms. Had the agency been subjected to the kind of congressional specificity that lay in wait for it beyond the horizon, much of its administrative strength and programmatic effectiveness would have been impossible.

This very freedom, however, was a politically costly luxury, for it liberated the leaders of the FSA from having to adhere to a carefully specified path of congressional consent. It also freed them from the requirement of having to defend themselves frequently in Congress and thus building acceptable justifications for practices which challenged conventional ways and which overstepped the bounds. Consequently, the political muscles of the FSA became flabby; a number of influential members of Congress, who were basically sympathetic toward most of the programs, lost touch with the FSA; and a strategic and hostile congressional few, especially in the House, were allowed to cultivate the impression that the FSA was defying congressional will. Later, when the time would come for the leaders of the FSA to explain and justify some of their more controversial practices, they would find ignorance and disinterest where knowledge and support should have been.

The U.S. Department of Agriculture: A House Divided

A particularly forceful influence which shaped the organizational structure and administrative procedure of the FSA and the behavior of its leaders was the institutional character of the USDA itself. Many efforts have been made to convey a sense of its enormous size, complexity, and diversity. John M. Gaus and Leon O. Wolcott, for instance, described the Department in 1940 as "one of the largest agencies of government in the world," and they asserted that it "cannot be understood from a description of it at any time, or as an isolated and self-contained unit of government." Upon his arrival in the USDA in 1933, Appleby reportedly could find "only eight persons who commanded an overview of the entire Department." Alexander, in retrospect, has confessed that upon his arrival in Washington as an assistant to Rexford G. Tugwell in 1935, he was terrified by the Department and that he never lost his feeling of being overwhelmed by it.

Perhaps a horseback impression of this complex bureaucratic institution can be derived from a quick look at its actual expenditures for fiscal year 1938, amounting to approximately $775 million, or 10 per cent of the total federal expenditure of $7.6 billion.[6]

USDA: *Expenditures for Fiscal Year 1938*

Office of the Secretary	$ 617,142.86
Office of the Solicitor	321,871.04
Office of Information	1,191,684.18
Library	103,744.48
Office of Experiment Stations	6,459,961.75
Special Research Fund	1,046,893.29
Extension Service	18,135,682.33
Foreign Agricultural Service	285,715.23
[1] Weather Bureau	4,529,616.74
Bureau of Animal Husbandry	9,635,477.34
Bureau of Dairy Industry	670,787.46
Bureau of Plant Industry	5,043,079.57
[1] Forest Service	34,049,862.17
Bureau of Agricultural Chemistry and Engineering	1,330,736.42
Bureau of Entomology and Plant Quarantine	15,309,501.38
Bureau of Biological Survey	3,911,482.82
[1] Bureau of Public Roads	91,704,465.19
Bureau of Agricultural Economics	1,105,828.78
Agricultural Marketing Service	5,283,921.50
Bureau of Home Economics	1,220,604.77
Enforcement of Grain Futures and Commodity Exchange Acts	497,548.59
Food and Drug Administration	2,178,163.95
Soil Conservation Service	27,772,748.29
Conservation and Use of Agricultural Land Resources	303,852,184.12
Farm Security Administration	180,149,108.66
Farm Tenant Act, Titles I and III	3,051,656.62
Agricultural Adjustment Administration	57,807,125.23
Miscellaneous	1,770,821.99

1. To be precise, the Weather Bureau, Forest Service, and Bureau of Public Roads were in the USDA at this time, but their budgets were treated by Congress as lying outside of the regular budget for agriculture.

The full magnitude of these expenditures becomes more meaningful when it is understood that this was before the revolutionary explosion of governmental budgets that began during World War II. The only other federal department with a greater expenditure for ordinary purposes was the Treasury Department, which exceeded the USDA by 16 per cent.

Behind these figures of USDA expenditures stood an array of semiautonomous agencies, bureaus, and offices reflecting the specialized

6. *U.S. Budget* (1940), pp. 917–18.

character of agriculture itself—staffed at the top by professional career specialists with widely divergent backgrounds, training, and philosophies; with far-flung field organizations throughout the nation; with a diversity of political and administrative linkages to state and local agencies of government and to organized interest groups; and with different and sometimes clashing interpretations of what was best for agriculture and the country. Furthermore, there was a shifting cleavage between those in the USDA who wanted it to remain the "Farmers' Department" and who desired to preserve the political and administrative *status quo* within it, and those, especially in the newer agencies, who harbored broader concepts of the Department's social purpose and who looked upon it as an instrument for more ambitious social, political, and economic reforms.[7]

Some participants, in retrospect, have oversimplified the complicated divisions and contentions within the USDA during the New Deal years into primarily an ideological conflict between liberals and conservatives. There was, of course, an ideological dimension involved, but ideology was as frequently invoked as a weapon of administrative and political tactics as it was an expression of intellectual or philosophical commitment. If there was an identifiable "left wing" in the USDA, then the leaders of the FSA were certainly among its vanguard.[8]

Because of their history, size, scope of operations, and strategic position, four of these agencies in 1937—the Extension Service, the Forest Service, the Agricultural Adjustment Administration (AAA), and the Soil Conservation Service (SCS)—accounting for approximately 30 per cent of the regular annual departmental budget, were the major contenders for power. By virtue of its own size and character, the FSA would join their ranks, followed in 1939 by the Rural Electrification Administration (REA), the Farm Credit Administra-

---

7. John M. Gaus and Leon O. Wolcott, *Public Administration and the United States Department of Agriculture* (Chicago: Public Administration Service, 1940), Foreword, pp. vii–viii; Paul H. Appleby, *Big Democracy* (New York: Knopf, 1945), pp. 11–12; author's interview with Alexander.
8. John B. Hutson, COHC, pp. 258–59; Samuel B. Bledsoe, COHC, Vol. I, pp. 82–83, 106.

Hutson, who was Assistant AAA Administrator, has interpreted these cleavages as clearly a struggle between a "left wing," concerned about consumer impacts of farm policies, and a "right wing," interested primarily in the farmer and his prices. Bledsoe, who served for several years as Assistant Information Director of the USDA before becoming Secretary Claude R. Wickard's assistant in 1941, has described the conflicts in the USDA as a "civil war" between the liberals and conservatives.

tion (FCA), and the Commodity Credit Corporation (CCC). All of these semiautonomous agencies originated in response to special problems—the Extension Service to promote improved farm and home practices through training and demonstration; the Forest Service to conserve the forest resources of the nation and to promote a more rational use of them; the AAA to regulate farm production and to help stabilize the prices of farm products; the SCS to preserve the fertility of the land; the REA to promote the electrification of rural America; the FCA to serve as a unified banker to the commercial farmer in need of credit; and the CCC to manage the surpluses in farm commodities. The uniqueness of the FSA—the essence of its challenge to the established agencies of the USDA—lay in its ostensible devotion to the chronically impoverished farm families who had been virtually ignored by the Department.[9]

The coordination of policy and the rationalization of administrative relations among these agencies, bureaus, and offices defied the most ingenious draftsmen of organizational charts. The problem was compounded by the particularistic tendencies among them to go their separate ways and to jealously guard their institutional boundaries. The SCS, for instance, was zealous in evangelizing its gospel of conservation, sometimes in conflict with the educational and extension activities of the Extension Service and the soil conservation financing services of the AAA. The Extension Service, on the other hand, had long claimed the right to be *the* medium of contact for the entire USDA in reaching out to the farmer on his farm, and resisted and resented the field activities of its competitors. The boundary between the FSA and the FCA was continuously an uneasy no-man's-land. For the Forest Service, the adoption of green uniforms was more than an expression of sartorial preference.

Furthermore, natural competition between the ideologies, technical specialties, claims for funds and prestige, and agency-clientele partnerships was intensified at times by conflicts among the cliental groups with which the agencies and bureaus were linked. The struggle between the American Farm Bureau Federation (AFBF) and the National Association of Soil Conservation Districts, for instance, was reflected in the relations between the Extension Service and the AAA. Therefore, there was little doubt in the minds of most people about what effect the developing rapport between the FSA and the National Farmers Union (NFU)—a major competitor of the

9. Gaus and Wolcott, *Public Administration and the USDA*, pp. 3–87, 262–71, 317–77; Appleby, *Big Democracy*, pp. 11–27.

AFBF—would have on the relations between the FSA and the Extension Service. The USDA, concluded Samuel B. Bledsoe, Assistant USDA Director of Information, "had schizophrenia in the very worst way."[10]

The situation would have been serious enough in a more quiescent government, but with the coming of the New Deal in the 1930's and with the consequent politicization of agricultural policy, the tasks of the USDA increased; many new action agencies were created; non-agriculturalists with different backgrounds, training, and value commitments flocked into the Department; and contacts with the farmer, once focused through the extension system, multiplied rapidly and became diffused. The need for coordination, not only within the USDA in Washington but also in the field, was therefore heightened, especially in land-use planning and development, conservation, extension and research, public information, and managerial housekeeping services. In the earlier years, necessary coordination had been secured, not by secretarial fiat from above, but rather in a form reminiscent of pre-World War II peace treaties among nations—occasional conferences of agency chieftains and the signing of memoranda of understanding. By the late 1930's, such passive methods of securing cooperation and coordination were not much more effective than international diplomacy in preserving world peace.

The difficulties of achieving unity were further compounded by the pattern of the Department's field involvement. In 1939, for instance, 53,638 USDA employees—82 per cent—were located outside of Washington, D.C. Ninety-four per cent of the employees in both the FSA and the SCS worked in the field. In organizing these competing armies, there was little territorial correspondence between the regional boundaries of major USDA agencies. Gaus and Wolcott found that even within individual agencies there was a "failure to formulate clearly any general conception lying behind the establishment of the regional offices," and that there was too much dependence on the peculiarities of individual agency programs, triviality, and excessive deference to provincial pride in the delineation of boundaries and designation of regional headquarters offices. The conflicts and cleavages of the USDA in Washington were thus multiplied erratically in thirty-eight cities in the United States. Leaders of the so-called "Agricultural Establishment"—the extension services, land grant colleges, county agents, and Farm Bureaus—frequently criti-

10. Bledsoe, COHC, Vol. I, p. 82.

cized the USDA for its duplication of effort and lack of consistency, but the absence of a departmental policy governing the organization and functions of regional offices, and the related lack of a unified departmental front on the regional level did not displease them. As a matter of fact, they looked upon regional offices as potential administrative "fifth columns" through which the USDA might supercede or circumvent state and local officials in the administration of agricultural policy.[11]

In response to general dissatisfaction with the situation, but more especially in an effort to clarify relations between the USDA on the one hand and the extension services and land grant colleges on the other, representatives of the Secretary's office in the USDA and a committee of the Association of Land Grant Colleges conferred in July, 1938, at Mt. Weather, Virginia. M. L. Wilson, Under Secretary of Agriculture, saw the conference as an opportunity to achieve greater "grass roots democracy" in the administration of agricultural programs.

Under the so-called "Mt. Weather Agreement," there was to be a division of labor, with the state colleges to be responsible for agricultural education and research, and the USDA to administer the various agricultural "action programs." In each agricultural county, the state extension service was to create an agricultural land-use planning committee composed of local farmers, with a subcommittee consisting of county representatives of the SCS, the AAA, and the FSA. A state committee composed largely of ex officio members, under the chairmanship of the state extension director, was to coordinate planning for each state, followed by coordination nationally with the USDA. The Extension Service would play the central coordinating role within the USDA, assisted by the BAE as the planning and research agency. This, in brief, was not so much a "peace treaty" as a "shotgun wedding" between the USDA and the extension services and land grant colleges.

Although the major action agencies were represented at the conference, there was virtually no sign in the final agreement that the voices of any but the extension representatives had been heard or heeded. In retrospect, M. L. Wilson, who went to Mt. Weather with

---

11. Gaus and Wolcott, *Public Administration and the USDA*, pp. 388–91, 493, 519–22.

By 1941, there were twenty-three bureaus, agencies, and offices in the USDA, with field operations in the United States. See USDA, *Directory of Organization and Field Activities of the Department of Agriculture*, Misc. Pub. No. 431 (Washington, D.C.: GPO, 1941), p. 144.

idealism and optimism the way another Wilson had gone to Versailles, has acknowledged that virtually everyone was left out of the agreement but the Extension Service and the state colleges. Like most political truces and shotgun marriages, the "Mt. Weather Agreement" turned out to be little more than a piece of paper.

The land grant colleges, which were not overly enthusiastic about a coordinated government in which their influence might be reduced, did little to save the system when it was challenged. Also, for obvious reasons, the leaders of the SCS, the AAA, and the FSA were fearful of being coordinated out of existence, and therefore did not exert themselves to make the arrangement work. The leaders of the AFBF, who preferred to deal with an uncoordinated USDA on the basis of a policy of divide and conquer, opposed the system as a potential threat to their own strategic position of power. With the coming of war, attended by a struggle between the committee system of the AAA and the network of land-use planning committees concerning which would serve as the organizational basis for wartime field coordination in agriculture, and with the Secretary of Agriculture's final decision to create a separate system of agricultural defense—later war —boards, the "peace" of Mt. Weather passed into history.[12]

There was an additional facet of bureaucratic life in the USDA with which the leaders of the FSA had to cope—William A. Jump, Director of Finance and Budget Officer of the Department. In every way, Jump was the dean of departmental budget officers in Washington. For more than a dozen years, he had served with the budget staff of the USDA where, in the words of Robert A. Walker, he "Consciously and skillfully . . . participated in, and often led, the movement to transform the federal budget from an accountant's workbook to a policy-oriented allocation of financial resources among public programs." Jump was also one of the few men whom Appleby found to have a departmental grasp of the USDA. The budget of the Department was large and complex, adequate budgetary review machinery was lacking, and, according to modern standards, Jump's staff was undermanned. However, his concept of his role and his skill in filling that role strengthened the USDA on Capitol Hill. He firmly believed in the importance of the executive function in the federal budget process, but at the same time he had a pre-New Deal reverence for the separation of powers, and believed in careful defer-

12. Gaus and Wolcott, *Public Administration and the USDA*, pp. 157–59, 463–75; Charles M. Hardin, *The Politics of Agriculture* (Glencoe, Ill.: The Free Press, 1952), pp. 87, 134–36; M. L. Wilson, COHC, Vol. 10, pp. 1805–32.

ence to congressional intent. Although he harbored no special sympathy for the FSA, he was consistently fair and was one of the agency's sources of strength in the Department, especially while Appleby retained his position in the Secretary's office.[13]

The leaders of the FSA were fully aware of the conflictual climate of the USDA, but they believed that they enjoyed a special advantage—considerable sympathy and support at the secretarial level. They knew that Wallace tended to be fickle and to lose interest in certain causes, and that he was often bored and impatient with administrative details, but he had proven his commitment to the FSA and its cause during the long struggle for passage of the Bankhead-Jones Farm Tenant Act. They also knew that Under Secretary Wilson, despite the limited powers of his office and his personal preoccupation with the problems of the northern Great Plains, had remained concerned about rural poverty, even after his divorce from the Subsistence Homesteads Division, and that he could be depended on as a friend at court.[14]

The locus of effective departmental strength for the FSA was the so-called "secretariat" in the office of the Secretary of Agriculture. Appleby was officially designated as the Special Assistant to the Secretary, but he actually exercised considerably more power and influence than his official title implied. An enormously industrious worker with a razor-sharp mind, he was assigned special responsibility for problems of administrative organization and the more politically sensitive issues reaching the Secretary's office. Given wide latitude by Wallace, Appleby made the most of his opportunities. Drawing on his own personal observation of the Appleby system in operation, Charles McKinley has recalled, for instance, that it "was a staff organization which in quality of membership, outlook, and identification with the managerial purposes of a top departmental career service resembled the permanent under-secretaries of the British ministerial system." Appleby became not only the leader of this "secretariat," but also the second most powerful man in the USDA, and therefore Alexander and Baldwin of the FSA believed that his support was as important to them as that of Wallace himself.[15]

---

13. Robert A. Walker, "William A. Jump: The Staff Officer as a Personality," *Public Administration Review*, Vol. XIV (Autumn, 1954), pp. 233–46; Inter-University Case Program, "Jump's Case," Processed (n.d.); author's interview with Baldwin.

14. Author's interviews with Alexander, Baldwin.

15. Charles McKinley, "Federal Administrative Pathology and the Separation of Powers," *Public Administration Review*, Vol. XI (Winter, 1951), p. 21.

Not only did Appleby believe that a strong FSA would help to achieve greater control by the Secretary of Agriculture over the special interests within the Department, but he also was personally sympathetic toward the FSA and its assault on poverty. He considered himself to be the agency's friend at court, but not its apologist. In retrospect, he explained his strategy as follows:[16]

> I was the friend and sharpest critic of the FSA. I was anxious to help underprivileged farm families, but I was also defensive of the FSA because I knew that it needed defense. I felt that it was my responsibility to keep the agency in line, but at the same time I also tried to improve its capacity to withstand attack. My goal was to push the FSA and to integrate it into the structure of the Department, not only to strengthen it as an operating agency, but also to help create a power complex, and in that way to enable the Secretary to throw his weight more freely.

There was also a personal dimension to Appleby's relations with the FSA. Baldwin, Assistant Administrator of the agency until 1940, and then Alexander's successor, had long been a close personal friend of Appleby, as we have already seen. During the first two years of the New Deal, he had worked as Appleby's assistant in the Secretary's office. Throughout their years in Washington, they lived three streets apart in Chevy Chase, Maryland, and each day they drove to work together. They saw each other socially, and their sons were close friends. When Appleby had special administrative tasks to be performed, involving matters above and beyond the FSA, he often turned to "Beanie" Baldwin. "Paul was thoroughly familiar with all of our trials and tribulations," Baldwin has recalled, "and while there were times when he slapped us down, we always had his strong personal support."[17]

The leaders of the FSA enjoyed yet another personal link to the leadership of the USDA in Milo R. Perkins. When Baldwin moved to the Resettlement Administration in 1935, his place in Wallace's office was filled by Perkins, who had grown up in Texas, and who had been successful in the burlap bag business. Sharing some of Wallace's intellectual and mystical interests, Perkins became one of the Secretary's few close personal friends. In 1937, he joined the staff of the FSA as an Assistant Administrator, reportedly to help keep the Secretary informed and, conversely, to help keep the agency out of trouble.[18]

16. Author's interview with Appleby.
17. Author's interview with Baldwin.
18. Author's interviews with Alexander, John Fischer, Henry A. Wallace.

This, then, was the institutional framework within which the leaders of the FSA were compelled to operate. From the very beginning, the agency was viewed by its competitors as potentially a very formidable contender for power within the Department.

The FSA: Structure and Function

As Alexander, Baldwin, and their assistants launched the FSA during the fall of 1937, they believed that the logic of the situation called for a continuation of the centralized organizational structure and unified chain of command which Tugwell had bestowed upon the Resettlement Administration. The importance of speed in processing the mounting applications for assistance and in creating the necessary administrative system for the new tenant purchase program; the fact that at its birth, the FSA was already a going concern, and that as far as practicable, continuity in policy and administration should prevail; Appleby's belief that there should be no decentralization until proper centralization had been achieved; the legacy of Tugwell's belief in centralized direction; and the knowledge that the FSA would be compelled to operate in a hostile climate—these were some of the influences and arguments which persuaded the leaders of the FSA to defy the hallowed principle of "grass roots democracy."

They had little faith in the panacea of local administration through committees of farmers, and they viewed the form of federal-state collaboration employed by the Extension Service as an invitation to political irresponsibility. To wage the battles that surely lay ahead, a military-type line organization seemed necessary. If they had sought a theoretic justification, they would have found it not in M. L. Wilson's democratic sermons, but in the positivist lectures of Chester I. Barnard, who, during the fall of 1937, was telling his audience at Boston's Lowell Institute that, "It is the deliberate adoption of means to ends which is the essence of formal organization."[19]

Alexander, Baldwin, and their assistants therefore created an administrative structure which embraced six operating levels—the Washington (D.C.) office, twelve regional offices, a state office in most states, district offices within the states, a county office in most of the counties in which they operated, and at the base of the

---

19. Chester I. Barnard, *The Functions of the Executive* (Cambridge: Harvard Univ. Press, 1948), p. 186.

pyramid, an office for each project, resettlement community, and migratory labor camp.

The structure and function of the Washington office, inherited from the Resettlement Administration, continued largely unchanged under the FSA. Over the years, changes were made in the division of labor, titles were revised, and functions were recombined and tasks reassigned, but in general the office consisted of the Administrator, from two to four Assistant Administrators who usually had functional responsibility for the coordination of related programs, and a variety of special assistants, coordinators, and consultants. Functional divisions—these were the major program units—varied in number from twelve to fourteen, and were headed by directors who reported in most cases to one of the Assistant Administrators. The primary operating divisions were the Rural Rehabilitation Division, the Tenant Purchase Division, and the Resettlement Division. In 1942, the Resettlement Division was dissolved and a Management Division and a Cooperative Division were created in its place. Major divisions, of course, were subdivided into specialized sections. Division directors maintained close communication with their functional field staffs, but had no authority to exercise a command role over them except through the FSA Administrator, to each regional director. Thus, the line of command ran directly from the FSA Administrator in the Washington office to his regional directors.

By 1939, the organization and staffing of the Washington office had been largely stabilized. Although there were important personnel shifts during the years that followed, such as Baldwin's replacement of Alexander as Administrator in 1940, and the transfer of approximately 600 of the 1,033 members of the Washington staff in 1942, under Assistant Administrator George S. Mitchell, to Cincinnati, Ohio, to help relieve wartime congestion in the nation's capitol, the pattern prevailed.

Most of the men at the top were not trained agriculturalists. FSA Administrator Alexander, it will be recalled, possessed a liberal arts degree from Scarritt-Morrisville College in Missouri and a divinity degree from Vanderbilt University. Assistant Administrator Baldwin had studied business administration at Virginia Polytechnic Institute. Assistant Administrator Hudgens was a graduate of The Citadel, a military academy in Charleston, South Carolina. Assistant Administrator Mitchell was a graduate in economics at the University of Delaware, a Rhodes Scholar at Oxford University, and the holder of a Ph.D. degree in economics from Johns Hopkins University.

The leadership of the FSA was not entirely lacking in agricultural orientation, however. Tenant Purchase Director Maris, as we have already seen, was a graduate in agriculture at the University of Missouri and a veteran of the Oregon State Extension Service. His counterpart, Rural Rehabilitation Director Maddox, had a baccalaureate in agriculture and economics and a master's degree in agricultural economics from the University of Arkansas, and later went on to earn a doctorate in economics at Harvard University, where he wrote a dissertation on the FSA under the direction of his mentor, John D. Black.[20]

There was a strong southern orientation among the leaders of the FSA, and most of them brought to their tasks a set of beliefs, background, experience, and values which distinguished them from the more conventional agriculturalists and farm politicians of the USDA. Most of these FSA leaders had been working together since the early days of the Resettlement Administration, and a large measure of consensus and solidarity had developed among them—their critics charged that they had been "injected with the Tugwell virus."

Transfers between the regional offices and Washington helped to leaven the leadership. Mitchell and Hudgens, for instance, had served as key regional directors before moving up to become Assistant Administrators, while Laurence I. Hewes, Jr., left Washington in 1940 to become director of the important FSA Region 9, headquartered in San Francisco, California.

There was considerable operational flexibility in the relations among the divisions and other staff units of the Washington office which continued throughout the life of the agency. For instance, despite organizational separation between the three substantive program divisions—Tenant Purchase, Rural Rehabilitation, and Re-

---

20. Baldwin to Appleby, Jan. 10, 1939; Harold D. Smith to Wickard, Feb. 3, 1942; Milton Siegel to George S. Mitchell, July 10, 1942; NA, RG 96. Transcript of telephone conversation between Baldwin and J. L. Buckley, Oct. 7, 1940, CBBP.

The move to Cincinnati, Ohio, was part of a general effort to create more office space in the buildings of the USDA. Approximately 600 of the 1,033 FSA employees in the Washington, D.C., office were affected.

The more important personnel changes included the following: Milo R. Perkins left in 1939 to become Associate Administrator of the AAA, President of the Federal Surplus Commodities Corporation, and, in 1942, Executive Director of the Board of Economic Warfare; in 1940, Baldwin replaced Alexander as FSA Administrator; in 1941, Major John O. Walker, and in 1942, James G. Maddox became Assistant Administrators of the FSA; and in 1942, Fischer, Director of Information of the FSA, left to join Perkins in the Board of Economic Warfare.

settlement—the farm and home planning section of the Rural Rehabilitation Division served all three. Similarly, the office of the chief engineer was primarily responsible for construction of housing for both the tenant purchase and rural rehabilitation programs, while the medical care staff, which was equivalent to a regular division, served the migratory, rural rehabilitation, and resettlement programs. The central unifying principle in the Washington office, especially after Baldwin replaced Alexander, was the concentration of effective policy-making and control powers in the hands of the Administrator. There was also an activist bent which caused the Washington office to resemble a military command under combat conditions.

From the Washington office, the formal line of command ran to twelve regional directors, each of whom was appointed by the FSA Administrator to whom each regional director was personally responsible for all programs of the FSA in his region. While the major divisions in the Washington office had no direct command over their functional staffs in the regions, the programs were unified at the regional level through the regional director. Most of the regional directors were aided by assistant directors, one of whom was responsible for resettlement and migratory labor activities, while the other was in charge of both the rural rehabilitation and tenant purchase programs. Regional staffs, which were particularly elaborate in major regions, included legal and financial managers, and technical advisers on farm and home planning, business procedures, labor relations, personnel management, information services, and engineering.

By 1939, the regional organization and its staff of directors had achieved a large measure of stability, despite some key changes during the years that followed. In general, Alexander and Baldwin appointed regional directors who possessed the necessary regional coloration and connections. T. Roy Reid, for instance, director of FSA Region 6 in Little Rock, Arkansas, embracing the states of Mississippi, Louisiana, and Arkansas, was a southern agriculturalist from South Carolina who had risen through the established state agricultural institutions and who enjoyed the trust of the Extension Service and the state colleges and extension services. Raymond C. Smith, director of FSA Region 3 in Indianapolis, Indiana, covering the states of Ohio, Indiana, Illinois, Iowa, and Missouri, was an agriculturalist with an extension background in Ohio. Howard H. Gordon, director of FSA Region 4 in Raleigh, North Carolina, embracing the states of Virginia, West Virginia, North Carolina, Tennessee, and Kentucky, had been raised on a farm in North Carolina and had been a professional agriculturalist and an official of the North Carolina Extension Service.[21]

FSA regional directorships also served as testing grounds for personal achievement. Hudgens and Mitchell, as we have seen, both served as regional directors before their promotions to Assistant FSA Administrator. Smith left Indianapolis in 1940 to become a chief agriculturalist in the BAE. Reid left Little Rock in 1941 to serve as an assistant to Secretary of Agriculture Claude R. Wickard, and a few months later became director of personnel for the USDA. Charles F. Brannan, director of FSA Region 10 in Denver, Colorado, went on to become President Harry S. Truman's Secretary of Agriculture.

Below the regional level and within each state, there was established a skeletal state FSA office, headed by a state director who was appointed by the FSA Administrator, upon the recommendation of the regional director. The state director was responsible to the regional director for the entire repertory of FSA programs in his state. In practice, the major program concern of the state office was with rural rehabilitation, although it included the subordinate tenant purchase program. The administration of resettlement projects and migratory labor camps by-passed the state office, which was primarily a staff unit rather than an operating level comparable to the regional office. When authority was delegated to district and county offices to approve and process loans in 1940, the state director was left with responsibility for personnel management, public relations, and coordination of FSA programs in his state. In thirty-five states in 1939, there were regular state offices, and in the remainder of the states, a regional supervisor or assistant regional director was responsible for a combination of states.[22]

Below the state level, there were district offices directed by district supervisors who were appointed by and responsible to the state director. The district generally included approximately seven county

21. In 1940, the headquarters office of FSA Region 9 was moved from Berkeley, California, to San Francisco; in 1941, the office of FSA Region 1 was shifted from Washington, D.C., to Upper Darby, Pennsylvania; and in 1942, FSA Region 13 was created in Puerto Rico.

22. For instance, Connecticut, New Hampshire, Massachusetts, and Vermont were grouped under an assistant to the regional supervisor, with an office in Boston. Delaware, Maryland, and New Jersey were combined under an assistant to the regional supervisor, with an office in New Brunswick, New Jersey. Oregon was under an official who served both as assistant regional director and state director.

offices, and the district supervisor was responsible for all FSA activities in his district except resettlement projects and migratory labor camps. The primary activity of the district office was the supervision of subordinate county supervisors through review of county procedures and decisions.

At the base of the organizational pyramid was the FSA county office, directed by the county rural rehabilitation supervisor and his assistants, usually including one or more county home management supervisors who were women with home economics training and who worked with the farmer's wife while the rural rehabilitation supervisor concentrated on the farm. County supervisors often assisted tenant purchase borrowers, but, in view of the narrower scope of the tenant purchase program, they spent most of their time with rural rehabilitation client families. During World War II, they assumed additional responsibilities connected with the relocation of farm families uprooted by defense construction, with the recruitment of farm labor, and with wartime production and conservation programs.

The distribution of supervisory field personnel in FSA Region 4—Virginia, West Virginia, Kentucky, Tennessee, and North Carolina—in 1938, to administer a total regional case load of approximately 55,000 client families, was illustrative:[23]

	Number
District Offices:	23
County Offices:	226
District Rural Rehabilitation Supervisors:	23
District Home Management Supervisors:	14
County Rural Rehabilitation Supervisors:	315
County Home Management Supervisors:	218
Average Case Load per County Supervisor:	135
Average Case Load per County Office:	184

One of the most distinctive features of FSA field staffing, especially between 1939 and 1942, was the heavy reliance on home economists, most of whom were professionally trained women. Until this time, the major action agencies of the USDA had been concerned with virtually every aspect of the *farm*—soil, crops, livestock, machinery and equipment, and farm buildings. Everything received attention but the farmer, his family, and his home. For some years prior to the depression, home economists had worked on the staffs of some state and county extension services, but they dealt with farm families

23. Mitchell to Alexander, Dec. 16, 1938, NA, RG 96.

who were higher on the agricultural ladder. The experience of the FSA during these years represented a major innovation: on a very large scale, professionally trained technicians were providing assistance not only to the low-income farmer's chickens and cows, but also to him and his family.

By 1941, there were 2,270 county offices in the field organization of the FSA, staffed by 4,178 rural rehabilitation supervisors and 2,586 home management supervisors throughout the forty-eight states, Puerto Rico, and Hawaii, with responsibility for approximately 800,000 rural rehabilitation client families. The concentration of activity, of course, was in the South. Altogether, fourteen states, most of which were in the South, accounted for 51 per cent of the county offices, 61 per cent of the rural rehabilitation supervisors, and 66 per cent of the home management supervisors.[24]

Responsibility for the county office was assigned to a county rural rehabilitation supervisor who was concerned with all aspects of the program in his county, although personally involved only in the farm management aspects, and to a county home management supervisor who was responsible for planning and supervising in matters affecting the farm family's home. Frequently, the supervisors traveled together to the client's farm. In each county, there were one or more assistant farm and home supervisors, depending on the size of the case load. In the South, one of the *assistant* farm and home supervisors was occasionally a Negro—it was reportedly one of Alexander's greatest disappointments that he was unable to persuade his regional and state directors to break the color barrier and to appoint Negro supervisors. "Not even the FSA was foolhardy enough to try to force that down the throats of the field organization," Baldwin has apologetically explained. However, there is no evidence to suggest that the leaders of the FSA in the Washington office were particularly strenuous in their efforts to promote such an appointment policy. As far as pigmentation of the skin was concerned, the personnel of the FSA did not vary greatly from those in other agencies of the USDA.[25]

County supervisors were appointed by regional directors, on the basis of nominations by state directors, and hopefully in accordance with standards prescribed by the Washington office. Clerical employees in the field organization were appointed through the clearance procedures of the office of Julian N. Friant, Special Assistant to the Secretary of Agriculture, but appointment of supervisory

---

24. *Byrd Committee Hearings*, Pt. 2, p. 407.
25. Author's interview with Baldwin.

personnel was not covered by the agreement. Personnel directors and appointing officers of the FSA attempted to enforce high recruitment standards, including a minimum qualification of a college degree or its equivalent in experience, but for a number of reasons, to be discussed below, the leaders of the FSA continued to wrestle with the problem of technical incompetence among county supervisory personnel.

The county FSA office was the administrative spearhead of the entire organization—the locus of direct encounter between the agency and its clientele. As already seen in the discussion of the Resettlement Administration, the acceptance of loan and grant applicants was the basic discretionary act. It had been transformed from a state responsibility, subject to ratification or veto by the Federal Emergency Relief Administration (FERA), to a clear-cut federal responsibility under Tugwell's agency, with delegation of operational responsibility to regional directors, in conformity with standards prescribed by the Washington office. This was the pattern that prevailed during Alexander's tenure as FSA Administrator, although during the first year or two, the backlog of pending applications forced many regional directors, with the support of the Washington office, to delegate the power of selecting clients to district supervisors. Officially, however, loan approval responsibility was centered in the regional office.

The initial decision on an application for a rehabilitation loan was made by the county rural rehabilitation and home management supervisors, who usually consulted with an *advisory* committee of farmers in the county. If the committee decided that the applicant should not be accepted on the program, the county supervisors usually rejected the applicant, although there was no requirement that they do so. If the committee approved the applicant, the loan docket, consisting of farm and home plans, the lease agreement (if the applicant was a tenant), any debt adjustment agreement that may have been arranged, the loan agreement, the application, and other supporting documents were inspected by district farm and home supervisors for soundness and conformity to standards. If any corrections were required, the docket was referred back to the county supervisor for revision. Following district approval, the docket was referred to the regional loan adviser, where it was reviewed by farm and home plan examiners, the security unit, and the finance and control unit in the regional office. If approved by the regional office, a voucher was forwarded to the U.S. Treasury disbursing officer for payment. If the loan was not approved by the regional office, the docket was returned to the county office for rejection or revision.

Ideally, the county supervisor played the role of teacher, banker, farm and home expert, family case worker, and community organizer. His or her purpose was not to think or do for the client family, but rather to encourage self-help. The key instrument—the farm and home plan—according to Maddox, was "a process of getting the responsible members of the family to 'think through' or analyze what their situation is, what realizable alternative courses of action they have, and finally what course of action they intend to follow in the future." There was always the danger, however, that impatient supervisors might substitute their own thinking and choices for those of their clients, and thus impose solutions and plans upon a confused and resistant family.[26]

In fulfilling this diverse and difficult role, the county supervisor was responsible for directing many varied activities in the assigned territory—(1) receiving applications for loans, grants, and services; (2) investigating the eligibility of applicants, and consulting with advisory farmers' committees and others in the community; (3) seeking debt and tenure adjustments with creditors and landlords; (4) guiding families in farm and home planning; (5) participating in the granting of approval for loans and grants; (6) cultivating leadership among client families through meetings, discussions, and demonstrations among client families, and encouragement of neighborhood and community activity; (7) frequent visits to client families on their farms; (8) making collections of loan payments and issuing of receipts; and (9) recommending action on defaulted cases and foreclosure when necessary. The FSA county supervisor was frequently called the "county agricultural agent with a checkbook."

The success of the program rested heavily on the delicate personal relationships between supervisor and client family. The supervisor spent hours on the client's farm during frequent visits, investigating seasonal programs, giving advice, furnishing technical information, and reviewing cash income progress and the client family's plans for spending their money. He attended approximately half of the neighborhood action group meetings and about three-fourths of the community and cooperative service group meetings. The home management supervisor, meanwhile, spent considerable time in intimate conversation with the client farm wife in her kitchen, discuss-

---

26. Maddox, "The FSA," pp. 184–85.

ing food preparation, raising children, and problems with her farmer husband. The success of this admittedly paternalistic relationship depended on many situational factors—competing social values, different training and experience, the personalities of supervisor and client, the severity of farm and home problems, and the customs and attitudes of the particular community.

Especially in the South, with its problem of race relations, the leaders of the FSA hoped that county supervisors might become the instruments through which the client family and the community could be interpreted to each other and thus the client's alienation reduced. To exploit the resources of the community, and thus to serve their role more effectively, supervisors often consulted with community leaders, local institutions, and representatives of other agencies of government in the community—the county or community extension service, county agricultural and home demonstration agents, and the 4-H Club leader; local officials of the SCS, FCA, AAA, and the National Youth Administration; the county or community governing board, the superintendent of schools, the health officer, and the leader of the welfare agency; leaders of local farm organizations, civic agencies, and churches; and others.[27]

In working with the dominant individuals and institutions in the community and in perhaps becoming identified with them, there was danger, however, that client families' trust in the supervisor might be undermined, and thus the delicate cliental relationship, on which effective rural rehabilitation presumably rested, would be destroyed. On the other hand, it was through community-wide consultation and involvement of the county supervisor that the client family might be linked to the community more closely, and thus socialized. Especially in areas where political alienation was strong among client families, such as in the South, the county supervisor helped to render government more meaningful to people for whom it had hitherto been represented by the sheriff, truant officer, and tax collector. Nevertheless, the leaders of the FSA constantly had to fight against the seduction of their county supervisors by extension officials and county agricultural agents, for as Alexander Leighton has suggested, "An administrative body is always part of the patterns of

---

27. Perkins to all FSA regional directors, Mar. 26, 1937, NA, RG 96; Perkins to Alexander, Aug. 22, 1937, CBBP; H. C. Holmes and J. A. Elliott, "Tennessee Farm Tenure Activities," *The Journal of Land and Public Utility Economics*, Vol. XIV (Nov., 1938), pp. 462–65; Joseph Gaer, *Toward Farm Security* (Washington, D.C.: GPO, 1941), p. 163; author's interviews with Ralph W. Hollenberg, Raymond C. Smith, Robert W. Hudgens, E. B. Whittaker, T. Roy Reid.

leadership and authority in the social organization of the community in which it operates."[28]

In 1940, as we have already seen, the leaders of the FSA made a calculated gamble in deciding to permit greater decentralization. Although they were still unhappy about the tendencies of county and district supervisors to "skim the cream" in their selection of clients and to discriminate against Negro applicants, Alexander, Baldwin, Hudgens, and others believed that sufficient internal unity of purpose, program coherence, and loyalty to institutional values had been accomplished generally in the FSA to delegate responsibility for selection of clients to district supervisors for all loans except the largest, which remained regional responsibilities, as we have already seen. Furthermore, they provided that the district supervisor should actually make his determinations within the county office, in close proximity to the client, presumably in order to permit the county supervisor a greater voice in the final decision. It was intended that supervisors in the county offices should be brought more actively into the formulation of agency policies respecting program building, budgeting and allocation of funds, adjustment of eligibility criteria, and the management of field personnel. They also justified their decision to decentralize by reasoning that instead of imposing rules from Washington, there might be more effective infusion of agency values through greater field participation in policy formulation.

In order for this arrangement to work effectively, however, there would have to be more positive effort toward preparatory indoctrination of field personnel. Prior to 1940, the primary means through which national standards were enforced and national controllability maintained was the conventional system of formal policy pronouncements, written regulations and instructions, and other official issuances, coupled with a system of field reports. With the delegation of loan approval responsibility to the district supervisor, the leaders in the Washington office launched an elaborate program of joint conferences, training institutes, and on-the-job training for field supervisory personnel. Policy *recommendations* from the Washington office were subjected to county, district, and regional review, criticism, and adjustment. Field personnel at all levels were provided with opportunities to influence more directly the policy decisions of

---

28. Alexander H. Leighton, *The Governing of Men* (Princeton, N.J.: Princeton Univ. Press, 1946), p. 343.

the men at the top. There was also more frequent and intimate personal interaction between the leaders in the Washington office, regional officials, and the men and women on the firing line in the states, districts, and counties. This, the FSA leaders believed, was a form of "grass roots democracy" which would not violate the principle of administrative responsibility.

These administrative changes contributed to an improvement of technical expertise and general morale in the field, but there is no evidence that the tendencies toward "skimming the cream" and discrimination against Negroes in the selection of client families were halted or reversed. Had the leaders of the FSA been more willing to pay the political price and to risk destruction, there is no doubt that they could have combatted the trends more effectively.

By 1942, when the FSA reached the high-water mark, its roster of personnel included more than 19,000 specialists of bewildering variety—administrative generalists, lawyers, accountants, statisticians, investigators, clerks, medical doctors, nurses, soil engineers, conservationists, welfare workers and family counselors, home economists, teachers, sociologists, political scientists, economists, and specialists in farm management, farm debt adjustment, environmental sanitation, preventive medicine, public health, and cooperative and community organization. Furthermore, to a greater extent than in the older established agencies and bureaus of the USDA, the field personnel of the FSA—this fact should not be exaggerated—had broader education and training in non-agricultural fields. In 1941, for instance, Theodore W. Schultz reported that the FSA led all other federal agencies in the number of its personnel who had had some education or training in the social sciences.[29]

As the leaders of the FSA struggled to maintain their control over this large and unwieldy organization, as they contemplated its increasing number and diversity of personnel, the growing initiative and influence of regional directors, the expanding role of district and county supervisors, the widening divergence between thinking in the Washington office and that in the field, and the frustrating resistances of field personnel to national policies, they felt like the dying Czar Nicholas in St. Petersburg who apocryphally declared that, "I do not rule Russia—ten thousand clerks rule my people."

29. Theodore W. Schultz, *Training and Recruiting of Personnel in the Rural Social Studies* (Washington, D.C.: American Council on Education, 1941), p. 186.

The Quest for Unity in Diversity

Among the leaders of the FSA, there was an ambivalence—a readiness or even an eagerness to exploit national political power and the presumed managerial advantages of large-scale organization, and, on the other hand, an aversion to the rarefied political atmosphere of Washington and the formalism, impersonality, routinity, and rigidity implicit in the bureaucratic form of human endeavor. To Alexander, for instance, the desire to travel frequently in the field was as much an escape from Washington as it was an interest in the grass roots.

In their quest for balance between national unity and field diversity, the leaders of the FSA restlessly searched for new administrative forms and procedures. Experimentation with the creation of "special administrative areas," continual recombining of functions, shifting of personnel between Washington and the field, receptivity to the theories and notions of the social sciences, dissatisfaction with the conventional pattern of regional organization, experimentation in training and indoctrination of field personnel—these were some of the manifestations of the agency's refusal to grow old and brittle.

In a sense, this quest reflected a reaction to the nationalizing trends of the 1930's. Following the pre-New Deal years of state and local primacy in public affairs, the depression years were marked by emphasis on *national* problems, *national* responsibility, *national* planning, and *national* administration. In 1936, for instance, President Roosevelt declared that he had to "think of agriculture from the point of view of forty-eight States, not separately, but as part of a Nation. In other words, there is no question as to what my duty as President is, and that is to view agriculture as a national problem . . . [not] a local problem."

Yet, America was in many ways a nation divisible. Had Roosevelt been compelled to do so, he would have confessed that in reality there were as many agricultures in the United States as there were rural regions, states, and localities. In 1938, viewing American agriculture from Emporia, Kansas, rather than from Washington, D.C., William Allen White declared:

From a standpoint of farm background and farm technique this isn't one nation. It's a whole flock of nations. There isn't hardly a Western state with a climate that's anyways near uniform from one boundary to the next. In fact, it's not easy to locate one county where weather and soils are uniform enough to accomodate any great number of cropping policies or programs. So far as farm counsel and supervision is concerned, the rural community is the best working unit.

Similarly, Sir Wilmot Lewis, correspondent for the *London Times*, reported that he had sat for more than thirty years in the press galleries of Congress watching the legislators make national policy, and that the process had always seemed to him to resemble a series of treaties among regions rather than a nation at work.[30]

Anyone who has even glanced at the mosaics of agricultural soil and crop maps cannot have escaped the enormous diversity of American agriculture. The South, for instance, the most populous of the nation's agricultural regions in the 1930's and containing 23 per cent of the American farm people, was a region of small land holdings where slightly over half of the farms were under fifty acres in size, where over 53 per cent of the nation's farm tenants were located. With its widespread chronic poverty, its general economic insecurity, its concentration on cotton and tobacco, its racial problem, and its political quiescence, the South had found virtually all of the national farm policies prior to the New Deal irrelevant.

On the other hand, there was the region of the Great Plains, with its rich land and semi-arid and capricious climate, with its interest in wheat and livestock, and where farms under 350 acres were insufficient for dry-land farming. There was California, with its extremes of desert and moisture belts, its one-crop ranches of 2,000 acres or more and its miniature Japanese vegetable gardens, and its heavy dependence on seasonal hired labor. In northern Georgia, the necessary initial investment for successful farming operations was approximately $1,500, while in Iowa it was $15,000. A six-day work week was possible for the farmer or hired worker in the Cotton South or Wheat West, but dairy operations in the North sometimes required an *eight-day* week. A farmer in Alabama might build an adequate barn for $400, while it required at least twice that amount to erect an adequate dairy barn in Wisconsin. Modern indoor plumbing was generally taken for granted in the Middle West and on the Pacific Coast, but in the Southeast it was often regarded as "coddling" when provided for farm tenants or low-income farmers. A wheat farmer in Kansas, cultivating several hundred acres of rich land with expen-

---

30. F.D.R., *Public Papers* (1936), Vol. 5, p. 45; William Allen White, quoted in Charles M. Wilson, "Accent on Community," *Commonweal*, Vol. 28 (Oct. 7, 1938), p. 605; Alexander, COHC, pp. 512–13.

sive machinery and an army of hired hands, was very different, indeed, from the southern tenant farmer or sharecropper who, it was often said, could move with his family simply by "spitting in the fire and calling the dog."

The southern cotton planter and plantation owner worried about the falling price of cotton and the loss of his docile tenants and sharecroppers. The New England dairy farmer and the Iowa corn farmer watched the price of dairy feeds from opposite directions. The southern white farmer worried about the Negro, the Texan anxiously watched the Mexican, while the Californian kept his eye on his Japanese-American neighbor. With all of this as background, regional treaties were often negotiated in the Capitol cloakroom and in the privacy of committees, and were ratified on the floor of the House and Senate, but out of this maelstrom of competing interests and anxieties one could hardly expect a balance between national unity of purpose; regional, state, and local needs; and, for those caught in the vise between these forces, something which, for lack of a better term, we might call social justice.

From the beginning of his tenure as director of the Rural Rehabilitation Division of the FSA in 1939, Maddox wrestled with the problem of adapting national program goals and standards to the special circumstances of local, district, state, and regional situations. Alexander understood the problem, but never made any serious effort to resolve it. Finally, in 1942, Farm Security Administrator Baldwin and his assistants concluded that existing political and administrative jurisdictions and levels of operation were inadequate for meaningful analysis of their problems and for effective program administration. Some FSA regions were too large; districts were not much more than arbitrary subdivisions of the states, with little reference to the problems and needs of the people embraced; and county-by-county planning and operation would have been entirely unfeasible. An administrative unit was needed, they believed, that would be related to uniformities with respect to natural resources, climate, soil use, size and composition of population, social and political institutions, and acceptable standards of living. They therefore created ninety-seven so-called "agricultural operating areas," based on the concept of "cultural region"—land use or type of farming, patterns of beliefs and behavior among farming people, and the responses of low-income farm families.

Their intention was to inject an "area specialist" between state and district levels of administration, with responsibility for developing an integrated FSA program for each area so defined and which would not violate any of the important characteristics in the area. These areas should serve eventually as the geographic unit for program planning, reporting, and analysis. However, before the innovation was fully operative, the leaders of the FSA reluctantly abandoned it. They had found, for instance, that district boundaries, which had been administratively important in the structure, could not be adapted to the new areas. Furthermore, many of the field personnel on whom the burden for coordinated activity would heavily fall had seemed utterly incapable of understanding what these areas were supposed to be, and had persisted in thinking and operating in county-state-regional terms. Finally, reductions in the budget and personnel of the FSA forced abandonment of the experiment.[31]

In the fall of 1939, a study committee consisting of six regional FSA officials representing all phases of the rural rehabilitation program reported to a regional conference in Washington and offered the following catalogue of what they believed were administrative failures: (1) general lack of understanding, farm background, and technical training among field personnel, especially during the early days; (2) insufficiently strict eligibility requirements, permitting too many "bad loans;" (3) too many loans to borrowers located on farming land that was inadequate for purposes being pursued; (4) too much pressure from supervisors to service all applicants in need of help; (5) insufficiently "businesslike" farm planning which failed to provide for orderly repayment of loans; (6) too much "red tape" and routine office work, which prevented supervisors from spending enough time with client families on their farms; (7) faulty record-keeping in county offices and inadequate financial statements of client families' situations; (8) one-man opinions on foreclosure recommendations; (9) uncertain land tenure which prevented long-range planning; and (10) inadequate correlation between field personnel planning and seasonal work load, making proper farm and home supervision impossible.[32]

---

31. A less ambitious innovation was the so-called "problem area" approach. Instead of attempting to build new administrative areas throughout the country on the basis of cultural, sociological, economic, political, and geological uniformities, there was coordination of FSA programs and cooperation with other federal agencies on the basis of the incidence of special emergency conditions. See Arthur F. Raper, *Tenants of the Almighty* (New York: Macmillan, 1943), for the experience in Greene County, Georgia.

32. FSA, Report of Committee No. 4, regional rural rehabilitation conference, Washington, D.C., Sept. 20, 1939, pp. 57–58, CBBP.

The committee explicitly acknowledged that these alleged administrative failures were probably related to the beliefs, values, and habits of client families—lack of understanding of the program, interest in farming only as a temporary haven until improvements in the economy might provide opportunities for other employment outside of agriculture, lack of initiative, personal dishonesty, domestic discord, and chronic sickness and ill health. However, these regional officials revealed, in their professed "businesslike and practical" approach and in their objections to what they believed were "utopian FSA policies," that they themselves were on the far side of the gulf that separated Washington and the field. Will Durant was probably right when he declared that, "Reform begins at home and Utopia is nowhere except in the understanding mind."

Despite the large measure of central control exercised by the Farm Security Administrator, the military type line organization, and the continuing efforts to improve procedures, a metamorphosis inevitably seemed to take place in the programs and policies of the FSA as they moved from the Washington office to the regional director, the county supervisor, and the project director. Alexander, for instance, was deeply and personally committed to more than statistical equity for the Negro, but in most of the southern counties his aspirations turned to dust. Hudgens and Maddox advocated a policy of "digging deeper," but many county and district supervisors "skimmed the cream." Baldwin sought a direct confrontation with hostile forces in the local community, but many of the county supervisors tended to mirror the established pattern of community leadership. Walker sowed what he believed were cooperation and social solidarity among resettlement project families, but usually reaped competition and conflict.

The experience of the FSA suggests that reconciliation between national unity of purpose—if such unity there can be—and field diversity involves considerably more than structural and procedural innovation and manipulation of organization charts. Coordination of government policy, Norton E. Long has written, "moves beyond the range of government charts and the habitat of the bureaucrats to the market place and to where people live and work."[33]

In resolving the issues of organizational structure, administrative procedure, allocation of funds, delegation of responsibility, and exercise of executive discretion, the leaders of the FSA were "in-

---

33. Norton E. Long, "Power and Administration," *Public Administration Review*, Vol. IX (Autumn, 1949), p. 261.

tendedly rational." However, as Herbert A. Simon has pointed out, "Human rationality operates . . . within the limits of a psychological environment [which] imposes on the individual as 'givens' a selection of factors upon which he must base his decisions." The psychological environment of the Washington office of the FSA was very different indeed from that of the county FSA office, in close proximity to the firing line. As we shall see in the following chapter, the "givens" imposed upon Alexander, Baldwin, Hudgens, and others in their offices along the Washington Mall differed considerably from those imposed on the field supervisors compelled to work, often alone and isolated, in a hostile rural environment. The achievements and failures, the unity and division, the strengths and weaknesses of the FSA were due not only to intendedly rational choices among alternative administrative and political means, but also to different and sometimes conflicting pictures in people's minds. Although the agency projected different images to different people, there was one common picture that was perceived by all—the FSA was a challenge to the *status quo*. It is to the nature and the implications of that challenge that we now turn.[34]

34. Herbert A. Simon, *Administrative Behavior* (New York: Macmillan, 1947), p. 108.

CHAPTER IX

THE FSA:
DISTURBER OF THE PEACE

Every reform is only a mask under which a more terrible reform, which dares not yet name itself, advances.

RALPH WALDO EMERSON[1]
Journals

In the minds of men, things are what they seem. Although the agrarian reforms pursued by the Farm Security Administration (FSA) did not amount to a revolution, and the leaders of the FSA were not revolutionaries, wherever the agency challenged the *status quo*, it was perceived with some terror as a disturber of the peace. And it mattered little whether the challenge was real or imaginary, actual or potential. The growing power of the FSA within the U.S. Department of Agriculture (USDA); the development of a special clientele possessing considerable political potential; deepening contact between the FSA and its client families; fears and resentments of people in hundreds of rural communities who believed that their own social status, prestige, political power, and profits were being threatened by uplifting those who were beneath them—these were some of the anxieties which conferred upon the FSA, like the Resettlement Administration before it, a subversive image.

During the first few years, while the depression continued and the

---

1. Ralph Waldo Emerson, *Journals*, E. W. Emerson and W. E. Forbes, eds., Vol. VII (New York: Houghton Mifflin, 1909–1914), p. 205.

popular disenchantment with the old order prevailed, these anxieties were manifested by occasional skirmishes in Congress, petitions of protest, periodic attacks in the press, and criticism from local groups and institutions, but the antagonisms did not coalesce and there was no concerted reaction. It was in this climate of fear, however, that the image of the FSA as a disturber of the peace was established and the seeds of future reaction were sown.

Challenge to the Pocketbook

From a macro-economic point of view, as we have seen, the impact of the FSA was negligible, except perhaps for a period during World War II when the agency emphasized production over social welfare goals and made a significant contribution to the nation's food and fiber needs. It was unpalatable for the leaders of the FSA and their friends to acknowledge this, perhaps, but as long as the agency's programs were concerned primarily with subsistence agriculture, their essential significance lay in their impact on the human condition of the people served and on the lives of the rural communities in which they operated. Paradoxically, the FSA was dismissed by its critics at the national level as economically irrelevant, while locally it was condemned as a threat to the economic *status quo*.

In virtually every rural community in which the programs of the FSA operated, they evoked economic fears among individuals and groups whose interests or security seemed threatened by the actions of the agency. By the end of the first year, for instance, John Fischer, Director of Information for the FSA, reported that, "within the last few months . . . powerful opposition has been encountered in areas where the work of the FSA runs counter to the established economy." One source of antagonism, out of proportion to the minor part that the activity played in the overall FSA program, was the practice of granting loans for completing small factories on resettlement projects, inherited from the Resettlement Administration, to manufacture hosiery as a means of balancing and supplementing the seasonal farm income of project families. Had the loans not been granted, FSA leaders argued, the government's investment already poured into the construction of the factories would be lost, and, furthermore, some other source of project income would have had to be found.[2]

2. John Fischer to Milo R. Perkins, Nov. 16, 1938, FHAF.

By the fall of 1938, after the FSA had loaned a total of $3,050,000 to four such resettlement projects for this purpose, a flood of protests from northern state governors and legislatures, from spokesmen for interested associations of manufacturers, and from members of Congress descended on the White House, the Secretary of Agriculture's office, and the office of Farm Security Administrator Will W. Alexander. Permeating these protests was the charge that the FSA was helping to subsidize unfair competition in the hosiery industry, and the not-so-subtle warning that in the impending congressional election, northern voters would retaliate against the Democratic party "for sacrificing northern business interests to the South." Franklin D. Roosevelt and Henry A. Wallace dismissed the rash of protests as an inspiration of the organized hosiery manufacturers of the North, and as campaign oratory motivated by the congressional campaign. However, the dispute blossomed into a noisy political skirmish with opponents of the administration in Congress. While it ended in a standoff, with the FSA continuing to complete the factories already started and Congress attaching restrictions to future appropriations, the overall result for the FSA was a residue of resentment which foes of the agency invoked from time to time.[3]

More relevant economic anxieties flowed from the resettlement and migratory farm labor programs. Wherever the operators of larger-scale farms and plantations depended on small farmers and farm workers as a source of cheap labor for part-time or seasonal work, there was opposition to anything that might upset the stability of the labor supply. Moving low-income farm families out of overpopulated areas meant the loss or reduction of this supply. In the migratory farm labor program, the FSA was damned if it did and damned if it did not. Florida citrus fruit growers, for instance, criticized the agency for moving too slowly in recruiting and transporting workers for them, while cotton planters in Mississippi, Georgia, and Alabama protested that their labor supply was being pirated from them. The Secretary of Agriculture was praised by the Imperial Valley Farmers Association of California for importation by the FSA of farm workers from Mexico, and then was condemned when the same FSA officials sought strictly to enforce the terms of the agreement with the Mexican Government covering the workers' wage rates, working conditions, and housing and sanitary facilities.[4]

3. A. Harry Moore to Franklin D. Roosevelt, Sept. 8, 1938, FDRL, OF 1568–Misc.; author's interviews with Mrs. Eleanor Roosevelt, Henry A. Wallace.
4. *House Hearings*, Farm Labor Program, p. 41; M. C. Wahl and B. A. Harri-

One of the particularly provocative programs, involving ideological anxieties as well as pocketbook issues, was the promotion of cooperative enterprises among the clientele of the agency. The growing number of local medical care groups for low-income farm families, for instance, provoked uneasiness among defenders of organized medicine and some rural practitioners. In the northern Great Plains, established cooperatives and commercial firms selling farm equipment and supplies feared competition from FSA-sponsored cooperative associations. Grain dealers and grain elevator cooperatives feared the FSA program of refinancing bankrupt grain elevators in Minnesota and Wisconsin.

The most controversial phase of the cooperative program was the promotion of cooperative land-leasing and farming associations, especially in the South. Plantation owners, local credit merchants, and rural bankers viewed them not only as direct economic threats to their interests, but also as steps toward subversion of the principle of private property and the entire southern plantation system. In February, 1939, for instance, President Roosevelt received a typical protest in the form of a petition signed by thirty-six members of the Arkansas General Assembly, declaring that the "people of any cotton-growing community resent the government's intrusion into their business and especially when it is a direct competition." They charged that "the leasing and operating of such competing farms is causing widespread unrest and panic and might even create a riot," that the FSA cooperative program "strikes viciously at the heart of the great system upon which economic security and the very life of the South depends," and that "in the interests of Americanism such practice [should] be discontinued."[5]

Secretary Wallace promptly reminded the President that he, the Chief Executive, had discussed the program several months earlier with Farm Security Administrator Alexander at Warm Springs, Georgia, and that he had given the program his blessing. In a reply to the Arkansas petitioners, drafted for the President's signature, Wallace rebutted each of the complaints. The cooperative farms were neither leased nor operated by the FSA, but by low-income farm families, most of whom had been farming in the area for years, and they were operating in accordance with prevailing local farming practices. "The Government," Wallace wrote, "is merely giving them

gan to Claude R. Wickard, Dec. 10, 1942, NA, RG 16.
 5. Petition of thirty-six members of Arkansas General Assembly to Roosevelt (through John E. Miller), Feb. 3, 1939, FDRL, OF 1568–Misc.

assistance similar to that given to many other low-income farmers in this and other areas." No coercion whatever was used on land owners who entered into leases with the cooperative associations, nor did the FSA promulgate any rules or regulations governing working hours or wages of the association members, contrary to the false charges of the petitioners. Rather than disrupting the farm labor supply, Wallace contended, the program was helping to stabilize the farming people in the community and also was helping them to assume their responsibilities as citizens. He ended by suggesting that the Arkansas petitioners "are under some misapprehensions as to the purposes of the program of the [FSA]," and informed them that Regional FSA Director T. Roy Reid would soon arrange to meet with them and clarify their understanding. Meanwhile, the program would continue.[6]

Wherever the FSA operated, economic fears were aroused. Opportunities for FSA loans and grants tended to weaken the dependence of the southern tenant and sharecropper on his landlord and credit-merchant. Promotion of improved leasing and tenure agreements educated ignorant tenants about their legal rights. Cooperative purchasing and marketing associations strengthened the economic bargaining power of low-income farm families in their communities. Encouragement of farm ownership among tenants did endanger the surplus of cheap farm labor available to southern planters, as did the migratory labor and resettlement programs.

Instead of welcoming the FSA as a moderating force or a safety valve, instead of viewing the agency as an instrument through which the harshness of depression, drought, and chronic insecurity of the economic system might be softened, instead of enjoying the beneficial "spilling-over effects" on the community, local leaders tended to see only the challenge to the established order. Some landlords ignored the fact that they received higher rents from FSA client families, and that such families were generally more productive and took better care of the land than before they went on the program. Local bankers tended to see only the competition from the FSA credit facilities and to forget the bank deposits of FSA clients. Local merchants and tradesmen tended to fear the competition from FSA-sponsored cooperatives more than they welcomed the increase in volume of business which FSA client families brought to rural business centers.

The President of the United States and the Secretary of Agricul-

6. Wallace to Marvin H. McIntyre, Mar. 2, 1939, with enclosures, FDRL, OF 1568–Misc.

ture might send long conciliatory letters to petitioners, regional FSA directors might conduct meetings to enlighten and pacify objectors, and Fischer's Information Division might generate mountains of press releases proclaiming the virtues of the FSA and its programs, but as long as the agency persisted in programs and policies that disturbed the economic peace, or even seemed to do so, it was likely that the climate of fear would prevail.

Conflict of Ideology

In no sense was the FSA more clearly and consistently a disturber of the peace than in the realm of ideas and attitudes. Despite its pragmatism and, at the same time, its attempt to fly the banner of agrarian idealism, the agency represented an ideological challenge to the *status quo*—an invitation to combat. In their official issuances, in their testimony before Congress, in their value statements, in their policy choices, in the pattern of their rewards and penalties, in their appointments of personnel, in their spontaneous behavior, in the inferences that could be drawn from their verbal expressions—in virtually everything that they did, the leaders of the FSA revealed an ideological strain. And in propagating that ideology, they were evangelists.

As we have already seen, chronic rural poverty was perceived as an unwelcome repudiation of the comforting system of ideas embodied in the Jeffersonian agrarian myth. Like myths generally, the agrarian orthodoxy died hard. Under the hammer blows of the economic depression and the resultant dislocation in agriculture, many rural people happily sought or tacitly accepted innovations which, in quieter times, would have been anathema. As long as the physical manifestations of general rural poverty were clearly visible and widely felt, the iconoclasm of the more militant New Dealers was tolerated. But as the pendulum began to swing back toward greater economic stability, poverty again retreated toward the dark side of the crescent moon, and the challenge to the *status quo*, implicit in the attempt to combat the hard core of that poverty, reawakened old fears. The ideology of the FSA was thus a double-edged sword: it sustained and unified the agency in a time of crisis, and, as the tide shifted, it helped to cleave the rock on which the agency was built.

"The present has hitherto been the willing victim of the past," James Harvey Robinson wrote in 1920, and he suggested that "the time has now come when it should turn on the past and exploit it in the interests of advance." Half a generation later, doctrines of the past were harnessed to the needs of the present in the development of an ideology—a system of ideas, beliefs, sentiments, and values—around which the leaders of the FSA organized their perceptions of the world, made their value commitments, and explained and justified their purposes and performance. As politicians, they often acted on the grounds of expediency and necessity, invoking their ideology to explain and justify existential requirements, but these leaders were themselves sensitive products of their times, reflecting both their contemporary climate and their heritage from the past.[7]

To the Jeffersonian tradition they owed much—a commitment to the pursuit of happiness, the paramountcy of humanity over institutions, the social utilitarian purposes of the state, pragmatic administration of the law, the sanctity of liberty and equality, the perils of bigness in human enterprise, the values of education, the moral superiority of the agricultural way of life, and, like the gentleman from Monticello after Shays' Rebellion, the belief that "a little rebellion, now and then, is a good thing, and as necessary in the political world as storms in the physical." The leaders of the FSA did not accept human progress as inevitable; they approached Jefferson from the social rather than the individual side; and they were closer to Hamilton and the Federalists in their ideas about the uses of power; but they were Jeffersonians at heart.

From Jefferson's nineteenth-century heirs, from the worshippers of the religion of humanity, from the utopian socialists, and from the Farmers Alliances and the Populists, the ideology of the FSA derived a sense of disadvantage, an optimistic reformist zeal, a nostalgic yearning for restoration of traditional institutions, such as subsistence agriculture and the family farm. They were neither Marxists nor Socialists, but democrats who tried to bridge the future and the past, and who searched for some workable balance between individual freedom of action and collective social security.

To many of its critics, the FSA was a radical institution seeking to promote dangerous innovations and "alien ways" on the American land, but to its leaders it represented a healthy exploitation of the past. Raymond C. Smith, for instance, who was one of the more articulate FSA regional directors, declared as follows in 1939:[8]

7. James Harvey Robinson, *The New History* (New York: Macmillan, 1920), p. 252.
8. Raymond C. Smith, address to FSA regional conference, Washington, D.C., Sept. 18–23, 1939, conference report, p. 16, FHAF.

The FSA is a conservative organization; in fact, it is an ultra-conservative organization. It is attempting to revive certain cultural forms from which farm people have been separated in time and place from an older, and, in some respects, better rural culture. . . . The FSA is encouraging the production of feed and food for home use on the farm; making the family more dependent upon the land and less on the marketplace. It is encouraging longer tenure in land, a relationship between land and people that makes for soil conservation and development of a richer community life. It encourages ownership of land by persons who farm it. It encourages farm families to look on land as a home as well as a business opportunity . . . as a place to live and die. While encouraging the farm families to aspire to a reasonably high standard of living, it also encourages the family to become security-minded.

The belief that man is gregarious, endowed with sufficient moral sense to distinguish between right and wrong; that human existence is organic rather than static and compartmentalized; that poverty is relative and social in character, that it is amenable to governmental remedies, and that immorality lies not in being poor but in society's complacent acceptance of poverty; that the perils in governmental inaction may be as great as those in governmental intervention; and that inequality is basically immoral—these were the tenets to which the FSA was ostensibly dedicated.

"Ideologies must be seen in the context of the needs they serve," Philip Selznick has suggested, and "it is a reliable assumption that something more urgent than patterns of belief will lie behind the strong advocacy of doctrine by an organizational leadership." Behind the doctrine of the FSA lay a concern about institutional survival. Despite the transfer of the Resettlement Administration to the USDA and passage of the Bankhead-Jones Farm Tenant Act, the claim of the FSA to legitimacy was tenuous and had to be continually reinforced. Wherever they looked—in the USDA, in the Roosevelt administration generally, in Congress, among the established farm organizations, in the press, among the state governments, in the local rural communities—the leaders of the FSA found large and dangerous residues of hostility.[9]

Partly as a result of its pre-natal struggles, and in part as a defense mechanism in its quest for equilibrium, the FSA was characterized by a seige mentality in which its ideology, despite logical inconsistencies and contradictions between ideas and actions, helped to preserve the agency against its enemies, as the faith of world

---

9. Philip Selznick, *TVA and the Grass Roots* (Berkeley and Los Angeles: Univ. of California Press, 1949), p. 264.

Jewry has preserved it in the Diaspora. The leaders of the FSA became preoccupied with the maintenance of loyalty to a set of beliefs which captured the reformist spirit of the New Deal and set the agency apart from other governmental institutions in the field of agriculture and in the government generally. In their staffing of the agency, their policy choices, their administrative methods, their indoctrination of personnel, their exhortation of clientele, and in their public justifications, they consistently sought to infuse the doctrine into the fiber of the organization.

The ideology of the FSA was operationalized in many themes and variations, with emphasis depending on situational needs and with care to minimize the affront to local sensitivities. "We want you to do your public relations work entirely devoid of fear," one regional official instructed his field staff. "Intelligently consider the public relations needs of the FSA in your locality and then, with your directions charted and your course set, go about doing the public relations job without fear that we might not approve." Despite strategic and tactical orchestration, the rhetoric *de rigueur* of the FSA was fairly consistent—the imagery and symbolism were rustic, an implicit faith in the virtues of poverty was pervasive, and the democratic mold of American society was invoked on every possible occasion.

As we have seen in our discussion of the separatism between the tenant purchase and rural rehabilitation programs, the lexicon of the FSA awarded an honored place to especially evocative language —"humanity, equality, opportunity, social justice, decency, democracy, potentiality, security." The essence of this ideology was eventually embodied in the following credo:[10]

We believe and know there is poverty on the land.
We believe and know that most of the poor on the land are poor through no fault of their own or any lack in them.
We believe that if the causes of rural poverty are abolished, rural poverty will disappear.
We believe that it is the Government's duty to help handicapped farm families.
We believe the Farm Security Administration program to be a sound approach to the problem of rural poverty.
We believe that sound farm and home management can do as much (and more) for the poor families as loans and grants.
We believe that the poorer the families, the greater our obligation to them.
We believe the Farm Security Administration was created for the poorest

10. Joseph Gaer, *Toward Farm Security* (Washington, D.C.: GPO, 1941), pp. 66–67.

farmers and farm workers, and not for those whose credit is good and who can rehabilitate themselves without government aid.

We believe rehabilitation can be attained only after the families are taught better farm and home practices.

We believe our program to be so sound that the people who understand it will accept it.

We believe that the success of the Farm Security Administration program depends on the intelligence and eagerness to serve on the part of all Farm Security Administration employees, and particularly on the part of the county staffs.

We believe that our faith in the low-income farmers is fully justified by the progress we have made so far.

We believe that the Farm Security Administration program will succeed.

The ideological character of the FSA was reflected in a conscious effort to link the agency to larger social and political issues and situations, to find greater meaning in the FSA than its own work, to encourage employees to develop a world view and to visualize themselves on the larger stage. Critics called this "professional liberalism," "doctrinary stubbornness," "the influence of Rexford G. Tugwell," and "enslavement to ideas," while it was defended on the grounds that program performance and institutional survival depended on all personnel being educated and informed about the larger world in which they were compelled to operate.

One of the manifestations of this tendency was in the agency's personnel training programs. Not content to limit training to immediate and technical tasks, sessions were invariably converted into academic exercises. In 1939, for instance, a week's conference of regional FSA officials was held at the Wardman Park Hotel in Washington. Raymond C. Smith addressed the gathering on the evolution of southern tenancy from slavery, and on the development of a laboring class in twentieth-century American agriculture. Carl C. Taylor talked about the sociology of poverty and inefficiency in agriculture, the relationships between economic and social equity and justice, and the causes of poverty and ignorance. Frank Lorimer, of the American University, discussed rural population trends, migration, and the economic and social position of the farmer in the national economy. Theodore J. Kreps, of the Temporary National Economic Committee, lectured on the failures of the capitalist system in the United States to provide for equitable gain among different social and economic classes in the country. James G. Maddox spoke on the importance of the individual, on the dignity of work, on the need for establishment of minima in levels of living, and on the importance of social cooperation. In the performance of every task, however minute and specialized it might be, Maddox declared, every employee of the FSA should remember that he was "doing something which is an integral part of a process . . . to capture for this country in a changed material setting some of the ideals of freedom and justice, opportunity, security, and equality, which we did capture many years ago and which we wish to hold." Maddox was followed by Secretary Wallace, who spoke more like the future Vice President of the United States than as Secretary of Agriculture, and by Gunnar Myrdal, the Swedish economist who was about to launch his monumental study of the Negro and the American dilemma. And as the regional officials departed for home, they were supplied with copies of a recent Wallace address on the subject, "What the Scientist Can Do to Combat Racism."[11]

C. B. Baldwin was not particularly adept in the manipulation of abstractions, nor was he as eloquent as some of his fellow leaders in the Washington office, but he was an evangelist in his ardent sense of identification with larger causes. The "givens" under which he made his choices in strategy and tactics came not only from the internal institutional needs of the FSA, but also from the external political environment. His friend, Paul H. Appleby, called him "a chameleon who absorbed loyalties from his situation." Invariably, in his public statements, in his correspondence, in his telephoning (which occupied much of his time), and in his travels, he was as concerned about the larger national issues as the more limited affairs of his agency. In 1936, for instance, he was enthusiastically swept up in the presidential and congressional election campaign. The transcripts of his telephone conversations in 1938 and the carbon copies of his correspondence during that year reflected his sense of personal involvement in President Roosevelt's attempt to "purge" hostile southern Democrats. In 1939, his mind was already occupied with the war against Fascism. In 1940, he was involved, with Appleby, in Wallace's campaign for the Vice Presidency.

Throughout the years, Baldwin, like the agency of which he was an important part, seemed to be in a constant state of combat—against "southern reactionaries," against "native American Fascism," against "southern racism," against the "agricultural establishment," against Roosevelt's political enemies, and against the foes of the New Deal.[12]

---

11. FSA, report of regional conference, Sept. 18–23, 1938, pp. 18–23, 42; CBBP.

12. Transcripts of C. B. Baldwin's telephone conversations, 1936–40; Baldwin to Will W. Alexander, June 20, Aug. 17, 1938, and to Jonathan Garst, July 27, 1940; CBBP.

This, then, was the militant ideology which the FSA carried into hundreds of rural communities, challenging many dogmas of the conventional wisdom. Several years later, in reminiscing with the author about the experience of the FSA, Alexander expressed a sense of puzzlement about the mixed reception which the system of ideas, beliefs, sentiments, and values of the agency received in many rural communities:

> A lot of the folks understood what we were trying to do, and they cooperated as best they could, but a lot of them, especially in the South, just couldn't seem to understand that what we were doing and telling them would help them to escape the prison of their traditions. I don't know—maybe they did understand and they were afraid.

Had the leaders of the FSA enjoyed the benefits of insights that have been developed in the past few years by social scientists studying the process of modernization, they probably would have realized that what they were attempting to achieve was, in essence, the change of an entire ethos of a people.[13]

Recent social science literature seems to agree that if modernization is to take place effectively, there must be not only technological innovation, but also fundamental changes in traditional attitudes toward social, economic, and political life. The new order of things that was implicit in much of what the leaders of the FSA said and did collided with many of the resistances which have been suggested by recent studies of the modernization process. The catalogue

---

13. An adequate inventory of recent social science literature on the resistances to social change would be a formidable task, and well beyond the scope of our study, but the following representative works, listed according to the year of publication, emphasize the continuities at work in society: Talcott Parsons, *The Structure of Social Action* (Glencoe, Ill.: The Free Press, 1949); Marion J. Levy, Jr., *The Structure of Society* (Princeton, N.J.: Princeton Univ. Press, 1952); Homer G. Barnett, *Innovation: The Basis of Cultural Change* (New York: McGraw-Hill, 1953); Robert K. Merton, *Social Theory and Social Structure*, rev. ed. (Glencoe, Ill.: The Free Press, 1957); Edward C. Banfield and Laura Fasano Banfield, *The Moral Basis of a Backward Society* (New York: The Free Press, 1958); Ralph Braibanti and Joseph J. Spengler, *Tradition, Values, and Socio-Economic Development* (Durham, N.C.: Duke Univ. Press, 1961); Oscar Lewis, *The Children of Sanchez* (New York: Random House, 1961); Max F. Millikan and Donald L. M. Blackmer, *The Emerging Nations* (Boston: Little, Brown, 1961), esp. pp. 18–42; Everett E. Hagen, *On the Theory of Social Change* (Homewood, Ill.: Dorsey, 1962); Fred W. Riggs, *Administration in Developing Countries* (Boston: Houghton Mifflin, 1964); David E. Apter, *The Politics of Modernization* (Chicago: The Univ. of Chicago Press, 1965); John C. McKinney and Edgar T. Thompson, eds., *The South in Continuity and Change* (Durham, N.C.: Duke Univ. Press, 1965); Myron Weiner, ed., *Modernization* (New York: Basic Books, 1966), esp. pp. 28–39, 258–69, 307–20.

of relevant impediments to induced social or cultural change might be summarized as follows:

1. The functionally and structurally interrelated character of the parts of a social or cultural system, involving what Max Millikan has called the "complex systems problem;"
2. Incompatibilities between traditional and modern attitudes toward change and continuity, time, work, material things, supernatural phenomena, authority, the state, the community, the family, and oneself;
3. The tendency for established ways of thinking to have lives of their own which persist beyond the circumstances which produced them:
4. The persistence of vested interests in established social, economic, and political relationships;
5. The individual's quest for certainty and his fear of the unknown;
6. The set of traditional attitudes toward subsistence agriculture, and, on the other hand, the modernizers' fallacies regarding the nature and efficiency of that type of agriculture; and
7. The particularly sensitive regional fears in the American South toward social and political instability.

"The modernization process," Millikan and Blackmer have concluded, "requires fundamental human attitudes to change in such ways as to make the efficient operation of a modern society not only possible but also psychologically congenial."[14]

The leaders of the FSA were not surprised to meet such resistances from their foes and from those who found moral and material security in the traditional order, but it seemed paradoxical to them that low-income farm families themselves—white and black—tended also to reflect traditional attitudes and to resist the efforts of the agency. For instance, the leaders of the FSA were unable to free their programs entirely from the ideological taint of charity and relief. Traditional attitudes in many of the rural communities tended to discourage potential FSA clients from acknowledging their poverty and coming forward for assistance. One study by the Bureau of Agricultural Economics (BAE) suggested that the FSA was perceived by many low-income farm families as a last resort rather than as a welcome opportunity. "To have to resort to the FSA," it was reported, was widely felt to be an "undesirable solution to problems that [needy farm families] are unable to meet otherwise."[15]

14. Millikan and Blackmer, *The Emerging Nations*, p. 26.
15. Earl H. Bell, "Culture of a Contemporary Rural Community," BAE, Rural Life Studies II (Sept., 1942), p. 67.

Similarly, conservative Democratic Representative Hampton P. Fulmer of South Carolina, who succeeded Marvin Jones as chairman of the House Committee on Agriculture, expressed a viewpoint that was widely held among his colleagues on Capitol Hill and among many of their constituents, when he declared that, "The only way to get relief under the Farm Security Administration is . . . to sign that you are not worth anything; in other words, almost make the statement that you are a pauper." To receive an allotment check from the Agricultural Adjustment Administration (AAA) was "good," while there was shame in "going on the FSA."[16]

Many of the rural rehabilitation techniques, such as crop diversification, contour plowing, farm and home planning and supervision, joint bank accounts, and proper timing of planting and harvesting collided with traditional beliefs and attitudes. Since the Soil Conservation Service (SCS) and the Extension Service tended to work with client families who were generally better educated, higher on the social and economic scale, and more experienced technologically—more modernized—these two agencies escaped some of the resistances encountered by county FSA supervisors. Client farmers of the FSA, for instance, frequently resisted crop diversification because they believed that it would "tie them down." They believed that milking cows and feeding chickens was "woman's work," that the ability to plow a straight furrow, despite the utility of contour plowing in combatting soil erosion, was a mark of distinction, or that the only proper time to plant potatoes was on Good Friday, irrespective of weather and soil conditions.

Particularly in the South, the rural rehabilitation program collided with traditional attitudes held by low-income farm families. Tenants and sharecroppers, for instance, usually celebrated "settlement time" at the end of the crop year by purchasing a few new articles of clothing for the family, something unusual to eat, or a desired item of furniture that was probably more decorative than useful. Under the terms of the carefully designed farm and home plan, enforced through a joint bank account with the county supervisor, there was perhaps no place for such "frivolity." Arthur F. Raper has described the conflict of values in Greene County, Georgia, as follows:[17]

---

16. U.S., Congress, House, Committee on Agriculture, Hearings, 77th Cong., 1st Sess., *Bills Relating to Relief for Certain Agricultural Producers in Stricken Areas Who Suffered Crop Failure in 1941* (Washington, D.C.: GPO, 1941), p. 8.

17. Arthur F. Raper, *Tenants of the Almighty* (New York: Macmillan, 1943), pp. 261–62.

It was sometimes difficult for them [client families] to understand that although they had received the checks in the mail, and their name was on the check, and had to be cashed by them, the check was granted for the purpose of buying seed, but the mother prevailed on the husband to spend it for clothes for the children. Shortly thereafter, with his money spent, the client appeared at the FSA office, requesting money to buy feed for the animals. From the point of view of the farm family, the money had been spent wisely, but the FSA supervisor tended to feel that the client had not cooperated, that he had violated the agreement. If the client refused to play by the rules, he could quit the game.

Receptivity of low-income farm families to the FSA varied from one cultural region to another, of course, and while accomodations were made to such diversity, there were collisions. One county FSA supervisor, for instance, reported the case of an Ozark Mountain family who had been resettled by the FSA in northern Missouri. Having started with nothing, the family was progressing satisfactorily on the rural rehabilitation program for the second year when they suddenly decided to return to the Ozarks. Amazed, the county supervisor discovered that their decision to leave, despite the material advantages in remaining and the certainty that renewed poverty awaited them in their Ozark homeland, was due primarily to the client wife's inability to secure emotional and spiritual satisfaction in the more formalized church that she had been attending in Missouri. The family therefore decided to return to fundamentalist joy and freedom in the Ozarks, at whatever material cost. Such existential dilemmas remained a source of conflict for the FSA and frustration for its officials.

The ideological challenge which the FSA presented was particularly apparent in the collision of the agency with deeply held beliefs and sentiments concerning governmental land purchasing and ownership. Many of the congressional objections to the granting of ninety-nine-year leases, the purchase of land for resale or lease to client families, and purchase of land for cooperative farming associations and wartime relocation corporations were rooted in an emotional fear that such activities were "un-American" and represented a "conspiracy to nationalize or socialize the land." FSA Administrator Baldwin's ill-concealed ambition to enlarge the land holdings of the FSA was not conducive to allaying these fears.

The FSA also challenged the aspiration for fee simple land ownership among low-income farm families themselves. While the tenant purchase program ostensibly was designed to satisfy that aspiration, the rural rehabilitation program was built on the assumption that ownership of land was not the ultimate purpose in life. The leaders of the FSA often invoked the symbolic power of the family farm, but a central tenet of the ideology of the FSA was the belief that a farm family might earn its livelihood from the land without becoming a slave to it. One of the major obstacles in the cooperative program was the persistence of land ownership as a symbol of social prestige. FSA Administrator Alexander and Under Secretary of Agriculture M. L. Wilson, for instance, journeyed to the Lake Dick cooperative farm in Arkansas on one of their periodic pilgrimages to the field, when they stopped a farmer to inquire about his progress. To the pain of the visitors from Washington, the farmer responded as follows:[18]

> We're getting along just fine. We got the best house to live in we ever had. We got some good land to plow. We got plenty to eat. I'm working harder than I used to, but the kids are better off, and the wife don't have to work in the fields any more. A few more years on this project and we can buy us a piece of land.

As the years passed and understanding of the FSA grew, many of the resistant attitudes accomodated to the innovative ideology of the FSA, and to a considerable degree the agency succeeded in reducing despair among low-income farm people. For hundreds of thousands of chronically impoverished farm families, who had known only failure and debt and who had felt only fear, suspicion, and a sense of inferiority, the source of salvation lay neither in the stars nor in Providence, but in Washington, D.C.—and in the FSA county supervisor's office. In 1939, for instance, Hortense Powdermaker reported that among many southern Negroes of the 1930's, Franklin D. Roosevelt became a symbol of hope. She recorded, as follows, a couplet composed by a Negro school child who had just enjoyed a meal through the school lunch program: "Say, my Lord just knows we've been fed / If it weren't for the President, we'd all be dead."[19]

Morton Rubin, in his study of a typical "black belt" plantation county, found that the monthly receipt of a government check was sufficient proof to Negro recipients that "somebody way off yonder" cared for them. And Representative Brooks Hays of Little Rock, Arkansas, found a modern parallel between the FSA and the biblical Absalom who alienated the hearts of the men of Israel from David, their king: A teacher in a small rural school in the foothills

---

18. Author's interview with Alexander.
19. Hortense Powdermaker, *After Freedom* (New York: Viking, 1939), pp. 138–39.

of the Ozarks early in the 1940's asked her class whether anyone could name the President of the United States. No one could do so, but after a while one boy raised his hand and said, "I don't know who is President, but I know that Mr. Hannah is the Farm Security supervisor."[20]

Similarly, in his study of the FSA program in Greene County, Georgia, Raper, with literary grace and sociological insight, discovered that the linkage of government and salvation was a persistent theme among FSA client families. The spirit was eloquently reflected by Louisiana Dunn Thomas, a Negro tenant mother of Siloam, in Greene County. Born the child of a tenant farmer, she grew up on a plantation where she worked with her brothers and sisters in the cotton fields. With only a fifth grade education, she developed a love of books, and often wrote poetry. She married a tenant farmer and over the years gave birth to thirteen children. Later in the 1930's, she and her husband were granted an FSA rural rehabilitation loan, and thus became "government farmers." In the following psalm of praise, she expressed the linkage of God and Government:[21]

> *Uncle Sam is my shepherd*
> *And I shall not want*
> *He help me to care for my children*
> *And raise all my food if I don't.*
>
> *He don't make me lie down in green pastures*
> *He lead me down to the tin warehouse*
> *And give me a cotton mattress.*
>
> *He restoreth my cow and pigs*
> *And chickens and some eggs*
> *He leadeth me in the path of sleeping*
> *When he gave me the cotton beds.*
>
> *Yea though I walk through the valley*
> *And shadow of death to stay here*
> *But as long as Uncle Sam hold everything*
> *No evil will I fear.*

20. Morton Rubin, *Plantation County* (Chapel Hill: Univ. of North Carolina Press, 1951), p. 185; *House Hearings*, Agr. Approp. (1944), 78th Cong., 1st Sess., p. 1466; author's interview with Brooks Hays.

21. Raper, *Tenants of the Almighty*, pp. 270–71.

Disturber of the Peace / [279]

> *Thou help me to prepare my table*
> *It's a wonderful thing to tell,*
> *Surely the next few days of my life*
> *On a government farm I will dwell.*

Such sentiments were greeted by leaders of the FSA as a welcome manifestation of the agency's success in winning the minds and hearts of the people they were seeking to serve. However, ideas often lead to action, and this did not go entirely unnoticed by the "banker-merchant-farmer-lawyer-doctor-governing class" in the South.

Challenge to the Southern Way of Life

In no region of the United States was the FSA perceived more distinctly as a disturber of the peace than in the South. Since it was there that peace and tranquillity were particularly prized, virtually every FSA program and policy seemed to touch a nerve. Most of the leaders of the FSA, as we have seen—Alexander, Baldwin, Robert W. Hudgens, Mitchell, Maddox—were southerners who knew their region. They waved no bloody flags, they conformed fairly consistently to southern protocol, and in most matters they avoided open violation of the rules of southern life. However, there could be no denying the fact that the agrarian reforms they pursued, modest though they were in scope and content, were subverting the southern *status quo*.

Especially in matters of race, the leaders of the FSA were careful. In their allocation of loan and grant funds, in their personnel appointments, in their cooperative and group enterprises, in their resettlement projects, and in their public information activities they adhered fairly consistently to southern attitudes and practices regarding race. However, despite their precautions, it was inevitable, perhaps, that the FSA would arouse southern anxieties. One of the first instances of this—it was illustrative of countless others over the years—occurred shortly after the creation of the FSA in the fall of 1937. The agency purchased a tract of land for subdivision into individual family farms and for settlement of Negro families on a segregated basis near Orangeburg, South Carolina. Careful measures were taken to isolate these Negro farms from the surrounding white farming community, but the very existence of the project aroused white concern.

Almost immediately, Secretary Wallace's office received a letter of protest from an Orangeburg attorney representing the alarmed white citizens. R. M. "Spike" Evans, an assistant to Wallace, sent a reply that was conciliatory, but conveyed the determination of the FSA and the USDA to proceed:[22]

> Your letter was brought to the attention of Mr. R. W. Hudgens, Regional Director of the FSA in Montgomery, Alabama . . . . He has under consideration a protecting belt along the highway across from land tenanted by white families on which no Negro families would live. Some such arrangement can be worked out so that this project, which of course will continue to be under Government supervision, will not encroach upon neighboring farms.
> You are assured that careful consideration will be given complaints of local people. However, we feel that this project can be operated so that it will not interfere with the rights of other citizens and that it will eventually be accepted as a real asset to the neighborhood.

Through such careful deference, the leaders of the FSA avoided both complete defiance or acquiescence, but they harbored no illusions regarding their submission to the southern pattern of legalized segregation and discrimination against the Negro. For Alexander, the pioneer of the interracial movement in Atlanta, this was a particularly bitter pill.

Perhaps the most potentially dangerous FSA threat to the southern way of life was the demonstration and dramatization of the relationship between chronic rural poverty, ignorance, social isolation, racial discrimination, and political impotence. "The Federal Government came not as a tax collector but as an alms giver," wrote W. E. B. DuBois in 1941. "A new and direct connection between the Federal Government and the individual citizen arose such as the South had never experienced before . . . a direct connection between politics and industry, between voting and wages, such as the South was born believing was absolutely impossible and fundamentally wrong."[23]

While southern low-income farm families had had little voice in the affairs of their government and little security through its legal institutions, there began to dawn among them in the 1930's an awareness of the connection between their own welfare and some of the new action programs of the New Deal. Examine, for instance, the

22. R. M. Evans to J. Leroy Dukes, Nov. 16, 1937, NA, RG 16.
23. W. E. B. DuBois, "Federal Action Programs and Community Action in the South," *Social Forces*, Vol. XIX (Mar., 1941), p. 377.

comparative voter participation among five southern states in the presidential election of 1936 and the special cotton referendum of the AAA two years later:[24]

State	Per cent of Potential Electorate Voting	
	1936 Presidential Election	1938 Cotton Referendum
Alabama	17.7	80.0
Arkansas	16.3	65.0
Georgia	16.5	65.3
Mississippi	13.5	74.8
South Carolina	11.7	85.9

It mattered little whether the differential participation was due to disparities in voter eligibility or variations in understanding and interest in the issues at stake; the fact remained that some of the action agencies of the New Deal were helping to crack the foundations of the established political order. No one has expressed this more eloquently than V. O. Key, in his landmark study of southern politics:[25]

About once a generation a great wave of political sentiment sweeps the United States, sentiment that stirs deeply the masses of the people and gives hope that the promise of American democracy can be fulfilled. These great groundswells do not leave the South untouched. The New Deal affected the masses of the South as had no political movement since the Populist uprising. Its program reached down to the grass roots and actually had some bearing on the course of human events. The southern voter had long been accustomed to a politics that consisted mainly of oratorical fulmination steeped with cadence and pompous promise but with little effect on the world of reality. In the New Deal, oratory came to life, something to cause even the most cloddish poor white to blink, perhaps langorously, in amazement. Here was a politics that was more than speakings, more than barbecues, more than hillbilly bands.

The FSA was in the vanguard of this "subversive" movement. While other agencies, such as the AAA, the SCS, and the Rural Electrification Administration (REA), distributed their benefits more broadly, with farmers in middle and upper classes receiving the lion's share, the FSA served those at or near the bottom. Furthermore, not limiting itself to technical problems of price, production, conserva-

---

24. Robert E. Martin, "Negro-White Participation in the AAA Cotton and Tobacco Referenda in North and South Carolina" (unpublished doctoral dissertation, Division of Social Studies, Univ. of Chicago, 1947), p. 103; author's interview with Martin.

25. V. O. Key, *Southern Politics in State and Nation* (New York: Knopf, 1949), p. 645.

tion, or electric power, the FSA promoted education, social interaction, and political awareness—even more dangerously, it preached a philosophy of life. It was thus more intimately and visibly involved in the changes that the New Deal was bringing to the South. If a scapegoat were needed, on whose head to hang the political sins of the New Deal, the FSA would do. John Fischer, in retrospect, found the southern fears understandable:[26]

> Those southerners who were bitterly opposed to us were opposed for understandable reasons. We were in many ways subversive of the *status quo*. Our efforts to improve farming techniques were not the ends, but rather the means by which poor farmers of the South—many whites but especially Negroes—might be made more effective politically and socially. The programs of the FSA represented a serious threat to the dependence of the farm tenant and sharecropper on his landlord, the storekeeper, and the court-house gang. The FSA moved into a county, and although the total expenditure may have been comparatively small, it nevertheless represented a symbol of hope to the poor farmer—more than a symbol, a living proof. It didn't take many FSA clients in a southern county to prove the fact that the FSA was real, that it was there, that the poor farmer need not be so entirely dependent on the rulers of his community.

"Everything can be said in the South if it is said 'in the right way' ... [and] reforms in interracial relations should be introduced with as little discussion about them as possible," wrote Gunnar Myrdal. The leaders of the FSA tried to observe this etiquette. They did not march about the South agitating or stump speaking on racial equality. Southern regional and state directors, who themselves were products of the South, were discreet. Public information issuances directed to the South were drafted with consideration for southern sensitivities. Great care was taken by those in the office of the Secretary of Agriculture and in the Washington office of the FSA to placate the fears of southern congressmen and others who protested against particular FSA activities which seemed "to promote class conflict" and "to stir up the races."[27]

Nevertheless, the leaders of the FSA developed a national image as champions of equality. There was no secret about Alexander's long involvement in the interracial movement in Atlanta, where he had defied some of the rules of segregation. Nor was there any need for FSA officials to shout "Black-Power" to arouse the fears of those who opposed any changes in the established relationships between

---

26. Author's interview with John Fischer.
27. Gunnar Myrdal, *An American Dilemma* (New York: Harper, 1944) pp. 36–37.

the races. Here, for instance, is an official statement of the agency's long-range objectives, which was distributed to a training conference for county supervisors and other field personnel, held in Little Rock, Arkansas, in 1942:[28]

In the long run the most fundamental approach to a solution of the problems of low income families is through the educational system and the breaking down of traditional social and political barriers which have been established. These barriers have usurped the rights of low income farm families. In fact, they have been disfranchised through actual practice.

In the educational approach it will be necessary to break away from traditional procedures even though the present system of local and state institutions can be utilized, thence remains a job of liberalizing these institutions to get them to do the job. *The educational approach will necessarily have to be reinforced with reform measures which will act as a buffer against short run reactionary tendencies* [italics not in the original].

Or consider the following statement of purpose by a rural rehabilitation official, which was part of the blueprint for the special Negro community program designed for eleven southern states:[29]

We are surely interested in the kind of farm a man has—his crops, his livestock, his house, and his barns. A well chosen, comfortable and efficiently operated farm is a basic requirement to good living in rural areas. But, after all, the reason for desiring good corn, cotton, peas, vegetables, cattle and milk is that we are basically interested in there being good people . . . . If out of all our work there does not come a sort of group solidarity supported by a bond of loyalties, and if out of it all there does not arise a leadership which can take over and carry on where our "management" leaves off, our new white houses are destined to become tombstones for a great idea that somebody had and a grand humanitarian effort that somebody made.

State legislators, officials of state administrative institutions, county politicians, and the more militantly conservative newspaper editors read such rhetoric with something less than enthusiasm.

Especially in a time of national economic dislocation, it was acceptable to promote the family farm, attack the "evils of tenancy" and encourage greater farm productivity and land conservation, even in the South. But to go beyond all this, to experiment with cooperative enterprises, to challenge established institutions, and to preach a doctrine of racial equality, social justice, and mass political action was viewed as an unforgivable sin. Critics avoided an open

---

28. FSA, "Problems of Low Income Farmers," memorandum prepared for Region 6 conference (n.d.), 1942; JABP.

29. Giles A. Hubert, memorandum from BAE to FSA, July (n.d.), 1939, CBBP.

attack on the more traditional features of FSA programs, but were unrestrained in their condemnation of the agency's more provocative challenges to traditional attitudes and practices. The FSA "has been vaccinated with the Tugwellian virus," editorialized the *Memphis* (Tennessee) *Commercial Appeal,* and "has fallen into the hands and under the blight of social gainers, do-gooders, bleeding-hearts and long-hairs who make a career of helping others for a price and according to their own peculiar, screwball ideas." And from the *Birmingham* (Alabama) *Age-Herald* came the charge that while promotion of the family farm and reduction of farm tenancy were in harmony with the American Creed, the FSA "has gone beyond the two things it was created to do and in directions of a collectivism exactly contradictory to the ideal of its creation." Instead of working for the achievement of the "American Dream," the critic went on, the FSA was promoting "socialistic dreams, dreams of things nearer revolution than reform, dreams of a governmental paternalism that goes beyond good sense or good policy."[30]

Those who cherished the *status quo* tended to see not the material and social progress being achieved among the clientele of the FSA, and the consequent benefits for the community and region, but the economic, social, and political changes that were impending, and they were afraid. It was into this climate, described so well by Wilbur J. Cash, in his book, *The Mind of the South,* that the leaders of the FSA rode:[31]

And so they were afraid, these Southerners, like all Americans and like all Western men. Afraid cloudily and, as always, without analysis, even subconsciously and blindly, but none the less really for all that. Afraid of all that stood without them, and perhaps even afraid of themselves. And because of their fears, desperately determined to hold fast, even in spite of themselves, to their own old certainties—somehow to island themselves from the threatening flood. . . . Because of their fears and their will, they were filled with hate for whatever differed from themselves and their ancient pattern. For hate, of course, is always and everywhere the correlative of fear: the mechanism through which men most often fortify themselves against their terrors.

Alexander, Baldwin, Hudgens, Maddox, Reid, and other southern leaders of the FSA were not heroes to these fearful southerners, but scalawags.

The political anxieties generated by the FSA in the South were

30. *Memphis* (Tenn.) *Commercial Appeal,* May 25, 1943; *Birmingham* (Ala.) *Age-Herald,* Mar. 11, 1943.
31. Wilbur J. Cash, *The Mind of the South* (New York: Knopf, 1941), p. 294.

part of a fear that was felt elsewhere in the country as well—that the Roosevelt administration was "Tamanyizing" agriculture, that it was building a political machine to perpetuate itself in power. Frequent charges were made that the FSA was attempting to influence elections in certain states, and these charges were not entirely without foundation. In August, 1938, for instance, the Washington office of the FSA received a report that FSA personnel in Georgia were supporting conservative Democratic Senator Walter F. George for re-election, and after consultation with southern regional FSA officials, it was decided that "we can at least pass word down the line that our employees in Georgia should follow the lead of the President and give [George's opponent] any assistance that may be possible without getting our program enmeshed too much in politics."[32]

As 1940 approached, rumors grew that Wallace was being groomed to succeed Roosevelt, and that the machinery and clientele of the USDA were going to be exploited to strengthen his claim to the Vice Presidency. Representative Guy L. Moser of Pennsylvania, for instance, complained that FSA officials were "roaming around" his district trying to build up a constituency, and Senator Kenneth D. McKellar of Tennessee charged that the AAA had already built a powerful political organization in the country and that the FSA was trying to do likewise. And to former President Herbert Hoover, the FSA "contained large lumps of pure socialism," and was nothing more than "vote fly paper."

Anti-Roosevelt southern politicians who had a vested interest in the maintenance of the *status quo* kept a wary eye on any New Deal programs that might upset the established order on which their power and privilege were based. They saw much to fear, not only in the policy impacts of the agency, but also in the possibility that the several thousand FSA field personnel and the hundreds of thousands of FSA client families might serve as a basis for what they

---

32. Baldwin to Alexander, Aug. 17, 1938, CBBP; H. J. Res. 83, Mar. 2, 1938; S. Res. 290, June 16, 1938.

During the spring of 1938, with talk growing of a presidential attempt to "purge" recalcitrant Democrats from Congress and with Republican warnings that Roosevelt intended to exploit the machinery and clientele of action agencies in agriculture, in the congressional election campaign, Congress enacted a joint resolution prohibiting the use of emergency relief funds in any way that might influence elections. To press the issue further, the Senate approved a resolution directing a special committee to investigate the alleged use of federal funds "in such a manner as to influence votes cast or to be cast in any primary, convention, or election in 1938, at which a candidate for Senator was to be nominated or elected."

believed would be the "corruption of the electorate." The programs and paraphernalia of other New Deal agencies were not entirely immune to these southern fears, but the ideological militancy and the reformative orientation of the FSA strengthened its image as a disturber of the southern way of life.[33]

Challenge to the Cliental Bloc

Like King David of Israel, who never forgot the humble shepherd boy's conquest of the giant Philistine warrior and who later was quick to perceive the threat implicit in his son Absalom's appeal to the hearts of the men of Israel, the leaders of the power structure in agriculture saw in the FSA a threat to themselves. Composed of the Extension Service in the USDA, state land grant colleges of agriculture and state extension services, county agricultural agents, the Association of Land Grant Colleges, county and state Farm Bureaus, and the American Farm Bureau Federation (AFBF), the so-called "cliental bloc" was not monolithic. In the long run, however, it represented an important source of danger to the life of the FSA. The roots of the fear of the FSA lay in the historical evolution of the cliental bloc itself, just as David's fear was rooted in his knowledge of the fickleness of people.[34]

33. Russell Lord, *The Agrarian Revival* (New York: American Association for Adult Education, 1939), pp. 216–18, and *The Wallaces of Iowa* (Boston: Houghton Mifflin, 1947), pp. 466–68; *Senate Hearings*, Agr. Approp. (1940), 76th Cong., 1st Sess., pp. 819–20; *Byrd Committee Hearings*, Pt. 1, p. 727; Herbert Hoover, *The Memoirs of Herbert Hoover: The Cabinet and the Presidency, 1920–1933*, Vol. II (New York: Macmillan, 1952), p. 412; Lewis Meriam, *Relief and Social Security* (Washington, D.C.: The Brookings Institution, 1946), p. 323; author's interview with Paul H. Appleby.

34. Gladys L. Baker, *The County Agent* (Chicago: Univ. of Chicago Press, 1939), pp. 1–45; Edmund de S. Brunner and E. Hsin Pao Yang, *Rural America and the Extension Service* (New York: Bureau of Publications, Teachers College, Columbia Univ., 1949), pp. 148–59; Charles M. Hardin, *The Politics of Agriculture* (Glencoe, Ill.: The Free Press, 1952), pp. 1–53; Orville M. Kile, *The Farm Bureau Movement* (New York: Macmillan, 1921), and *The Farm Bureau Through Three Decades* (Baltimore: Waverly Press, 1948); Grant McConnell, *The Decline of Agrarian Democracy* (Berkeley: Univ. of California Press, 1953), pp. 44–54; Wesley McCune, *The Farm Bloc* (New York: Doubleday, Doran, 1943).

The keystone in this structure was the formal tie between the Farm Bureaus and the state extension systems, conferring upon the Farm Bureaus a quasi-public status. In 1954, the long movement against this arrangement culminated with the formal tie being legally cut, although close informal relationships have endured. See the following: USDA, Office of the Secretary, Memorandum 1368, Nov. 24, 1954; William J. Block, *The Separation of the Farm Bureau and the Extension Service* (Urbana: Univ. of Illinois Press, 1960).

Starting shortly after the establishment of the USDA in 1862 and continuing over the decades coevally with the growth of both agriculture and the Department, there developed a complex arrangement for the administration of agricultural education and research. The system was based on three major congressional measures—the Morrill Act of 1862, which had provided public lands for establishment and endowment of state land-grant colleges of agriculture; the Hatch Act of 1887, which had laid the foundation for federal-state cooperation in agricultural research, through federal assistance in the establishment and operation of state agricultural experiment stations; and the Smith-Lever Extension Act of 1914, which had furnished a formal basis for cooperative federal-state educational and training programs of extension. Before the advent of the New Deal, federal aid to agriculture was in the form of grants-in-aid for agricultural education and research, rather than direct action programs, and it was through the following institutional machinery that the system operated.

In the USDA, the chief federal instrument was the Extension Service, while the Office of Experiment Stations administered funds for research in agriculture and rural life. State land-grant colleges of agriculture, experiment stations, and extension services were the channels through which most federal action programs, prior to the New Deal, were carried to the states. At the local level, the county agricultural agent was the chief line operator, on whose shoulders the entire system rested. Linked to this structure of official power was a parallel structure of private power based on organized farmers—the AFBF, the Association of Land Grant Colleges, and the network of state and county Farm Bureaus. Champions of the system called it a model of "grass roots democracy" and of "creative federalism." The more vehement critics viewed the system as a "cozy monopoly" over the machinery of agricultural policy making and administration and over the channels of access to farmers, a dangerous prostitution of federal power and responsibility, and an arrangement whereby large scale commercial farmers were enabled to dominate American agriculture.

The cutting edge of the system was the county agricultural agent, who in many ways served a role parallel, but superior, to that of the FSA county supervisor. A combination of technical expert, teacher, adviser, and evangelist, the county agent assisted the farmer, who presumably was a member of the quasi-public county Farm Bureau, in a variety of ways. He helped in designing farm management plans, taught the farmer how to improve his methods, instructed the farm family on how to set up and maintain farm and home records, assisted in the establishment of farm cooperatives and other joint enterprises, promoted 4-H Clubs among farm youths, served as an information and advisory center on all farm and home problems, and encouraged participation and leadership among client families. As the new action agencies of the New Deal entered the scene, he served their officials and clienteles. Through the county agent's role in the local administration of federal action programs, the symbiotic relationship between the AFBF and the extension system was strengthened during the 1930's.

The county agent played a particularly important role in helping to administer the acreage restriction programs of the AAA, especially in the South and the Middle West where it was estimated that approximately 94 per cent of farmers having contracts with the AAA were located. The strategic position of the county agent in the local administration of AAA programs encouraged the leaders of the AFBF to exploit the opportunity to use him in their membership drive in the South during the 1930's. William J. Block, for instance, has reported on the so-called "Alabama incident," in which one of the county agents in that state distributed letters to farmers in his area informing them that their AAA allotment checks were available in his office and invited them to enroll in the Farm Bureau.[35]

Alongside this official structure of federal, state, and local institutions stood the private system of county and state Farm Bureaus, organized nationally as the AFBF. During the New Deal years, the national organization was shrewdly led by Edward A. O'Neal, as president, and Earl C. Smith, vice president and also the president of the powerful Illinois Agricultural Association, which was actually the Farm Bureau in that state. With a claimed membership of 163,246 members in 1933, 65 per cent of whom were in the Midwest, the AFBF grew to a claimed membership of 828,486 farm families in 1944, largely through its drive in the South. By the late 1930's, the AFBF emerged as the most powerful general farm organization in the United States.

One of the keys to the growth of the AFBF, which we have already seen in our discussion of the passage of the Bankhead-Jones Farm Tenant Act, was the sectional alliance, between the Midwest and the South, on which the organization's national power rested. The alliance was reflected in the special AFBF interest in anything af-

---

35. Block, *The Separation of the Farm Bureau*, p. 25.

fecting corn and cotton. The Midwest-South alliance was also reflected in the rapport between Democrat O'Neal of Alabama and Republican Smith of Illinois. To preserve the alliance, the leaders of the AFBF consistently opposed anything that would subject agricultural policy to greater subordination to the political parties or that would undermine the blurring of partisan differences within their national organization. At the state level, ostensibly in the name of professionalism, they sought to protect the colleges of agriculture, experiment stations, and extension services from state political control and patronage.

Another key to the power of the AFBF—it also illuminates the nature of the FSA's challenge to the *status quo*—was the American federal system. The separation of powers, a bicameral Congress, the congressional committee system with its diffusion of legislative leadership, the over-representation of rural interests in Congress and state legislatures, and the diffusion of executive power and responsibility—these were the features that contributed to the organization's strategic position of pre-eminence in agricultural politics.

Having won their power, the leaders of the AFBF adhered to a strategy designed to serve two objectives: (1) maintain the diffused character of the government, and (2) prevent any other farm organization from following their example. Over the years, O'Neal, Smith, and most of their state lieutenants opposed anything that would challenge their organization's position. For instance, they fought measures to strengthen the hand of the Secretary of Agriculture. They watched over the powers and prerogatives of the Extension Service and other constituent agencies in their system. They frequently advocated greater federal appropriations for extension work, while urging decreases in funds for programs which they opposed or over which they exercised no influence or control. They advocated that all educational, information, and advisory services for farmers be concentrated in the hands of the Extension Service in the USDA, and that new action programs be administered through state institutions and county agents.

There was also a class character to this system—a tendency to work primarily with higher-income, more experienced commercial farmers who understood the value of the extension process. Resting on the presumption that the most effective approach to improvement of farming methods was through a "trickle-down" process in which the backward farmer might learn from his more progressive neighbor, extension leaders expected that the poor and ignorant farmer would be eager to come and learn, and county agents did little to stimulate a desire for improvement among those who needed it most. In 1939, for instance, Gladys L. Baker reported that among marginal and sub-marginal farm families in the South there was an impression that the county agent was a "symbol of domination [by] the rich and landowning class of farmers." In the work of the county agents, extension services, state land grant colleges of agriculture, county and state Farm Bureaus, and the AFBF, there was also careful deference to the pattern of racial segregation and inequality. While claiming to represent "the American farmer," the AFBF, in the words of its unofficial historian, was "a well-organized, well-financed body ... of the leading and most influential families in every state."[36]

In contrast to the FSA and the BAE, the extension services and county agents during the 1930's tended to concentrate on isolated physical problems of farming, and to neglect the human dimension. In 1941, Theodore W. Schultz asserted that the colleges of agriculture in the South and other areas where there were deeply rooted social and economic problems "have the least means to support research, extension, and teaching in the rural social sciences." In other words, the established leaders of agriculture played safe—they retreated into technology and they conformed to local and regional attitudes, avoiding wherever possible anything that might be construed as subversive of the social, political, or ideological *status quo*.[37]

It was against this impressive system that the FSA, like the Resettlement Administration before it, collided. Within the USDA, the FSA competed for power and position with the Extension Service. At the state level, some of the colleges of agriculture resented or feared the independence and separatism of the FSA. In 1937, for instance, Dean Dan T. Gray of the Arkansas State College of Agriculture wrote to Alexander that he was interested in seeing all agencies succeed in helping to serve the rural people of his state, but that "full counsel has not been secured by anybody, about any rural problem, until a discussion has been had with the officials of the College of Agriculture." And a year later, his argument was reiterated when the president of the University of Arkansas charged that the

---

36. Baker, *The County Agent*, p. 212; Christiana M. Campbell, *The Farm Bureau and the New Deal* (Urbana: Univ. of Illinois Press, 1962), pp. 24, 26; Kile, *The Farm Bureau Through Three Decades*, p. 1.

37. M. L. Wilson, "The Democratic Processes and the Formulation of Agricultural Policy," *Social Forces*, Vol. XIX (Oct., 1940), pp. 1–11; Theodore W. Schultz, *Training and Recruiting of Personnel in the Rural Social Studies* (Washington, D.C.: American Council on Education, 1941), pp. 27, 40.

FSA "has branched out on its own initiative and the land grant colleges have nothing to do with the matter except such things as may be brought about through personal and unofficial contacts with those representatives of the FSA who are stationed in the various states."[38]

Locally, of course, the FSA county supervisor was frequently perceived as an interloper on the preserve of the county agricultural agent, and FSA cooperative enterprises were sometimes feared as an opening wedge into the monopoly position of the county Farm Bureau in organizing farmers. Generally throughout the country, relationships between the supervisor and the agent were conditioned by local attitudes toward the FSA and by the general climate of relationships between the officials of the FSA and local leaders. In some counties, such as those in Alabama, the challenge was softened by the development of rapport between the supervisor and the agent. Since FSA county supervisors were usually younger and less experienced than county agents, assistance from the agents was often welcomed in those counties where the climate was congenial. However, some of the more ardent leaders of the FSA feared the cooperation between the two field officials as leading to the "brainwashing" of the FSA supervisor and subversion of FSA goals.

At the national level the posture of the AFBF toward the FSA, following passage of the Bankhead-Jones Farm Tenant Act, was characterized for a time by an attitude of tacit but suspicious acquiescence. As the years passed, however, the mood changed to open hostility, reflecting not a reaction to the FSA but the cooling of relations between the AFBF and the Roosevelt administration generally. Precipitated in 1936, the enmity became open warfare in 1940, and the FSA provided one of the battlegrounds.[39]

38. Dan T. Gray to Alexander, June 10, 1937; J. C. Futrall to R. A. Pearson, Apr. 5, 1938; NA, RG 96; Campbell, *The Farm Bureau and the New Deal*, pp. 158–65; Charles M. Hardin, "The Bureau of Agricultural Economics Under Fire: A Study in Valuation Conflicts," *Journal of Farm Economics*, Vol. 28 (Aug., 1946).

The FSA was not the only action agency of the USDA that challenged the cliental partnership between the Extension Service, the state colleges and extension services, and the Farm Bureaus. The AAA and the BAE were also under fire over the years.

39. Christiana Campbell, *The Farm Bureau and the New Deal*, pp. 156–78, has suggested that the outbreak of hostilities between the AFBF leaders and the New Deal was rooted in a variety of causes: (1) growing responsiveness of the leaders of the USDA to the interests of consumers and processors of farm products; (2) the rise of new action agencies during the 1930's as competitors of the Extension Service, and the efforts of USDA leaders, presumably inspired by Appleby, to achieve more effective centralized administration; (3) the so-called

Although the national leaders of the AFBF did not unleash their assault on the FSA until 1940, individual state Farm Bureau leaders openly attacked or attempted to obstruct the agency. H. L. Wingate of Georgia, Romeo E. Short of Arkansas, Hassil E. Schenk of Indiana, and Oscar Johnston of Mississippi (he later organized and led the Cotton Council) were among the more vigorous opponents. There was also the anomaly of Murray D. Lincoln of the Ohio Farm Bureau Federation, who was a liberal in politics, an advocate of the voluntary consumer cooperative movement, and a critic of the AFBF's self-conception as primarily a producers' organization. He was a consistent defender of the FSA, even after the leaders of the AFBF declared war.

There was paradox in the fact that those who had worked most vigorously during the 1920's and 1930's to secure a more equitable distribution of income between agriculture and the rest of the economy were the very ones who resisted most bitterly the attempts by the FSA to secure a more equitable distribution within agriculture. As Hudgens later saw it, "Solving problems by correcting causes involves changing a system, and a change in the system is an implied threat to vested interests and an implied criticism of current leaders."[40]

Conflict, Cooperation, and Institutional Equilibrium

It was within this frame of external fear and anxiety, provoked in part by the challenges of the FSA to the established order

---

"subversive" character of the FSA in threatening to upset the *status quo*; (4) proliferation of USDA field organizations and farmers committees, in competition with the federal-state-county extension system and county agricultural agents; (5) growing rapport between the Roosevelt administration and the NFU; (6) personal conflicts between the leaders of the AFBF and the leaders of the FSA, AAA, BAE, and other agencies in the USDA; and (7) partisan political pressures involved in the election campaign of 1940, producing a sectional split in agriculture between the farmers in the Middle West and those in the South, thus threatening to split the alliance between these two areas on which the strength of the AFBF had been built and maintained during the 1930's.

Appleby (in interview with author), on the other hand, has contended that, "Without any intention of making invidious comparisons, to say that the war between the Farm Bureau people and us in Agriculture was caused by our alleged attempts to 'freeze them out' or to make alliances with their enemies is equivalent to laying blame for the start of World War II at the door of the British and French for their attempts to freeze Hitler out of Europe."

40. Robert W. Hudgens, COHC, p. 215.

and in part by the more encompassing winds of political and social change, that the leaders of the agency maintained a balance between the forces of conflict and cooperation. As long as the problem of chronic rural poverty remained a reasonably well recognized issue of public concern, as long as there was a preponderance of support over opposition, and as long as the FSA avoided gratuitous provocations, the image of the agency as a disturber of the peace was softened and its institutional equilibrium maintained. While it is true that the FSA was used at times as a scapegoat for the political "sins" of the New Deal, and that it provoked fears not fully justified by the facts, it is equally true that as long as the agency remained reasonably loyal to its controversial purposes, there was little that could be done to avoid disturbance to the peace.

On only one occasion—the crisis of national union in the 1860's—have economic, social, political, and ideological cleavages converged to produce a complete fissure in American society. Generally, conflicts do not always follow the pattern of partisan allegiance or the convenient and exaggerated liberal-conservative dichotomy. All southern conservatives did not oppose the FSA, nor did all northern liberals support it. Some people, whose sensitivities about the *status quo* were aroused by the FSA, were more concerned about the predicament of chronically impoverished farm families than they were about preserving the established order. In the South, the programs and the rhetoric of the FSA may have alarmed many conservatives, but at the same time, the agency helped to sustain the hands of those political people who sought what they believed would be a more enlightened and equitable society.

The provocative character of the FSA during the so-called "golden years," from 1937 to 1942, was a source of both strength and weakness, but its full significance for the rise and decline of the agency can be understood only in terms of the changes that were occurring in the internal and external environment. Within the agency there was an ebb and flow in the quality of leadership and motivation, in the relations between Washington and the field, in the morale of personnel, in the coherence of programs and policies, and in the magnitude and composition of the budget and of the clientele. And in the world around there were also pendulums of change—in the relations between the President and Congress, in the political strength and vitality of the New Deal and the Roosevelt administration, in the posture of Congress toward the FSA, in the quality of leadership within the USDA, and in the shift of the country from peace to war, from economic depression to prosperity, from political reform to reaction. These were some of the pulls and propulsions, stemming in part from existential dilemmas, in part from clashing interests and ideological commitments, and in part from the larger historical context within which the leaders of the FSA pursued their organizational purposes.

Goal oriented though they were, the leaders of the FSA were not unmindful of what Bertram M. Gross has called "the iron law of survival"—the impulse among administrators toward institutional maintenance, including, if necessary, a readiness to engage in political and administrative opportunism. "We did not have as many tigers at the top of the FSA as we were said to have had," one official of the agency has declared in retrospect. The quest for equilibrium, as we shall see in the following chapter, occupied much of the energy and attention of the agency, especially as the war clouds gathered.[41]

41. Bertram M. Gross, *The Managing of Organizations* Vol. II (New York: The Free Press, 1964), p. 658; Philip S. Brown, Director of Information, FHA, to author, June 7, 1967.

CHAPTER X

THE QUEST FOR EQUILIBRIUM

The nature of finite things as such is to have the seed of passing away as their essential being: the hour of their birth is the hour of their death.

WILHELM FRIEDRICH HEGEL[1]
Science of Logic

In striving to preserve not mere existence but rather the essence of their agency's institutional life, the leaders of the Farm Security Administration (FSA) were not passive victims of circumstance, nor was their quest for a condition of institutional equilibrium simply adjustment to the events of life. Will W. Alexander, C. B. Baldwin, Robert W. Hudgens, and others were, rather, brokers who, in a highly creative manner, strove to build agreement between the social purposes of the agency and the values, beliefs, interests, and sentiments of those people who possessed effective political power. Their freedom of action in serving that brokership role was not unlimited, however, and they were constrained as well as facilitated by the internal structure and external environment of the FSA.

The FSA and its Constituency

According to the *Realpolitik* of the 1930's, the capacity of an administrative agency of government to perform its mission and to survive institutionally depended heavily on the kind of symbiotic

---

1. Wilhelm Friedrich Hegel (*Science of Logic*, Vol. I), as quoted by Norman O. Brown, *Life Against Death* (New York: Random House, 1961), p. 104.

relationship that existed between the Extension Service and the American Farm Bureau Federation (AFBF)—what John Kenneth Galbraith has called the development of "countervailing power." None of the leaders of the FSA in 1937 had read the mounting body of literature on what eventually became known as the "group thesis of politics," but they did see ample evidence around them in the U.S. Department of Agriculture (USDA) of its practice. The Soil Conservation Service (SCS), the Agricultural Adjustment Administration (AAA), the Extension Service, and other agencies that enjoyed greater political legitimacy than the FSA had found it desirable to develop an organized clientele.

During the years that followed, opportunities and incentives to build a cliental foundation were afforded in the resolution of major policy issues—definition of eligibility standards, use of emergency grants, "digging deeper," spreading benefits broadly rather than intensively, promotion of cooperative associations, and the encouragement of social and political solidarity among client families. Anything that might increase the number of clients, deepen the agency's contacts with them, and strengthen client families' sense of solidarity, the leaders hoped, would enhance the power of the FSA. By 1942, out of a potential clientele of almost seven million farm families earning less than $250 a year, the FSA had developed contractual, supervisory, and other relationships with approximately 800,000 low-income farm families. In terms of sheer numbers, this represented considerable political potential. Let us examine their capacity to serve as a source of political power for the FSA.[2]

First of all, the magnitude and composition of the agency's clientele were in constant flux. Variations in the degree of client attachment to the FSA, due to differences in contractual and supervisory relationships and in subjective attitudes of client families; the temporary nature of some forms of FSA assistance, and budgetary changes which imposed revisions in the number of client families accepted in each program; and the inadequacy of permanent case records, permitting many client families to be lost to the FSA, due to their mobility in the country—these were some of the reasons why the clientele of the FSA involved what Roy C. Macridis has called "a specious concreteness."[3]

A more profound obstacle to mobilization of the clientele was the

2. FSA, Rural Rehabilitation Division, *Program and Analysis Report No. 1*, rev., Apr. 29, 1940, CBBP.
3. Roy C. Macridis, "Interest Groups in Comparative Analysis," *Journal of Politics*, Vol. 23 (Feb., 1961), pp. 25–45.

chronic social and political impotence and quiescence among these low-income farm families. They were, in the words of Gerald W. Johnson, "all the dispossessed and disinherited, incapable of battling for their own way through a fiercely competitive world." By every conceivable measure, they were at or close to the bottom of the scale—a higher incidence of domestic discord, personality maladjustments, fear, suspicion, and discouragement; more children and older dependent family members; less education, poorer health, lower net income, smaller and less fertile farms, less adequate homes and farm buildings, less equipment and livestock, and lower productivity; and lower level of social and political participation and contact. The problem was further complicated by the fact that approximately 20 per cent of the client families were Negro. In view of the caste system of the South and the racial attitudes of *white* client families, it was particularly unlikely that an effective cliental group, based on a sense of social and political solidarity, might be built among them. The clientele of the FSA were neither a bold peasantry nor their country's pride, but if a cliental bridge were to be built between them and the FSA, these were the people with whom it would have to be fabricated.[4]

Baldwin and some of the other militant leaders of the FSA talked vaguely about "promoting local mass action" among client families. Alexander and Hudgens exhorted field personnel to try more vigorously to infuse a sense of solidarity among the clientele. Client families were encouraged to join existing local farm organizations in their communities. From time to time, the leaders of the agency discussed the need for some kind of mass organization, but their rhetoric never became a call to arms. In retrospect, when queried as to why a more vigorous effort was not made to organize and mobilize the clientele, Alexander offered the following explanation:

We were not really utopian idealists, although we often dreamed and talked as if we were; we were realists enough to know that if we had tried, we would probably have been destroyed; and to have depended on our county supervisors for such a task would have been futile.

4. Gerald W. Johnson, *Incredible Tale* (New York: Harper, 1950), pp. 202–3; FSA, "Rich Land—Poor People," *Research Report No. 1*, Processed (Jan., 1938), and "Farm Housing Needs," Processed (July, 1939); V. O. Key, *Southern Politics in State and Nation* (New York: Knopf, 1949), pp. 504–27; FSA and BAE, "Analysis of 70,000 Rural Rehabilitation Families," Processed (Aug., 1938); Larson, *Ten Years*, pp. 97–129; Hortense Powdermaker, *After Freedom* (New York: Viking, 1939), pp. 138–39; Morton Rubin, *Plantation County* (Chapel Hill: Univ. of North Carolina Press, 1951), pp. 108–32; Rachel R. Swiger and Conrad Taeuber, *Ill Fed, Ill Clothed, Ill Housed—Five Hundred Families in Need of Help*, BAE and FSA, Processed (Apr., 1942).

Although Galbraith has overstated his case, the experience of the FSA lends some support to his assertion that the agency "largely petered out because those aided lacked the organization to defend in Congress and before the public the efforts being made on their behalf." In other words, "countervailing power" is rooted in the determination of those groups in society who make their demands upon government; "it must be sought."[5]

Instead of waiting for the organizational impulse to emerge among their client families, the leaders of the FSA searched for natural allies among established interest groups and institutions. In the absence of any concerted assault against the FSA, however, they felt no sense of urgency in this quest. Many of the naturally sympathetic interest groups and institutions had already joined the cause, with varying degrees of attachment and political usefulness, during the campaign for passage of the Bankhead-Jones Farm Tenant Act, and during the years that followed, they remained shadowy constituents of the FSA, to be used only in case of emergency.

As the years passed, there accumulated a bewilderingly diverse assemblage of friends representing labor, ethnic groups, church organizations, academic interests, liberal reform groups, and the fringes of organized farmers—more or less the same coalition that had supported the drive for passage of the Bankhead-Jones bills in 1935 and 1937. Some of these groups, such as the National Farmers Union (NFU), the Southern Tenant Farmers Union (STFU), and the National Association for the Advancement of Colored People (NAACP), believed that their interests were directly affected by the work of the FSA, and tried to keep in close communication with the agency. Others, such as the church-affiliated groups, were only peripherally touched, but saw a community of interest with the FSA or felt a moral obligation to support it. Still other groups were simply part of the Roosevelt coalition and supported the FSA because they saw in it the essence of the New Deal. Some groups were actively seduced by the leaders of the FSA, while others were self-invited. "Sometimes, looking at our pack of friends, I felt schizophrenic," Alexander later reminisced, "and the more numerous and diverse they became, the more remote I felt from the real world of the needy sharecropper and tenant living in some shack along Tobacco Road."[6]

5. John Kenneth Galbraith, *American Capitalism*, p. 155; author's interview with Will W. Alexander.
6. John Fischer to all FSA Information Advisers, Dec. 10, 1940, NA, RG 96; author's interview with Alexander.

Some of these constituency relations offered real political strength to the FSA, while others promised nothing but the kiss of death. Support from the NFU, Murray D. Lincoln's Ohio Farm Bureau Federation, the American Federation of Labor (AFL), the Congress of Industrial Organizations (CIO), the Urban League, and the NAACP contributed strength to the FSA. Support from some of the others, however, seemed to substantiate the frequent charge made by critics that "the FSA and its crowd of friends are wooly-headed, pie-in-the-sky do-gooders and bleeding hearts."

The efforts of some groups and movements to identify with the FSA became positively dangerous for the agency. On one occasion, for instance, Margaret Sanger and her birth control group saw an opportunity in the rural rehabilitation program of the FSA to promote family planning methods among over-populated low-income farm families, and she sought Alexander's consent to promote her cause among the clientele. Personally sympathetic toward her objectives, but terrified at the thought of the likely reaction that her proposal would bring from the Catholic Church, he stood firm against the indefatigable lady's overtures. "If Will had played ball with Margaret Sanger," the Rev. John O'Grady later commented, "we'd have come down on him like a ton of bricks."[7]

One of the more natural allies of the FSA was the STFU, whose organizational efforts in 1934, remember, had contributed to the pressure for remedial action among farm tenants and sharecroppers in the South. Oganized during the summer of 1934 under the leadership of Harry L. Mitchell, with headquarters in Memphis, Tennessee, the STFU claimed a membership of 15,000 low-income farm tenants, sharecroppers, and farm laborers by 1942, organized in 130 local farming communities in six southern states. While conservative agriculturalists among the field organization of the FSA studiously kept their distance from the STFU, Mitchell and his group consistently supported the FSA locally and in Washington, D. C., and Mitchell himself became a fixture at congressional hearings.

A potentially more fruitful constituency relationship was that which developed between the FSA and the NFU. Viewed at one time as the "Little David" of agricultural politics, the NFU was destined to become one of the major competitors of the AFBF. Founded in 1902 by Isaac Newton Gresham, an uneducated itinerant farm laborer from Alabama who became a Populist organizer in the 1890's, the

---

7. Author's interview with Rev. John O'Grady.

NFU was in some ways an ideological heir to the nineteenth-century agrarian protest movement. Originally built on class lines, with membership concentrated in the low-income South, the NFU gradually became an organization of middle-income family farm owner-operators centered in the Great Plains. Long before the FSA arrived on the scene, the leaders of the NFU had discovered the difficulties of promoting organization among low-income, apathetic, illiterate southern farmers. During the 1930's, the NFU attacked the tendency of the AAA to discriminate against farm tenants and sharecroppers, defended the work of the Federal Emergency Relief Administration (FERA) and the Resettlement Administration, and supported passage of the Bankhead-Jones Farm Tenant Act.

Yet, even while lobbying in the political arena, its leaders remained loyal to the traditional NFU principle of political non-partisanship, and skeptical of politics and politicians. While it supported measures on behalf of low-income farmers, attention was concentrated on middle-status family farmers. In the South, there was less congruity between NFU membership and the FSA clientele than in the Great Plains.

During the 1930's, there was some ideological cleavage within the NFU, between radicals who favored militant political action and moderates who adhered to the organization's traditionally gradualist emphasis on education and promotion of cooperative associations. By 1940, the breach was healed, and under the more astute leadership of its new president, James G. Patton of Colorado, the NFU went on to become a major contender for influence and power in agricultural politics. Two years later, it claimed a membership of over half a million, concentrated in Kansas, Minnesota, North Dakota, Oklahoma, and South Dakota. The NFU was less conservative than the AFBF, but it was by no means an organization of low-income farm families.[8]

In a variety of ways, the FSA made a modest contribution to the growth of the NFU—encouraging client families to join local farm organizations affiliated with the NFU, lending funds and providing grants to families who in turn joined cooperatives affiliated with the NFU or bought life insurance from it, furnishing official information

---

8. John D. Hicks, *The Populist Revolt* (Minneapolis: Univ. of Minnesota Press, 1931), pp. 430–31; Roscoe C. Martin, *The People's Party in Texas* (Austin: Univ. of Texas Press, 1933), pp. 38–45; Wesley McCune, *The Farm Bloc* (New York: Doubleday, Doran, 1943), pp. 193–221; John A. Crampton, *The National Farmers Union* (Lincoln: Univ. of Nebraska Press, 1965), pp. 3–22, 34–52.

and technical assistance to NFU officers, and, outside of the South, serving a clientele that partially coincided with the membership of the NFU in certain localities. The efforts of some NFU state organizations to exploit their relationships with the FSA created some sharp antagonisms in certain states. William J. Block, for instance, has documented the controversy in Arkansas in 1942 and 1943, where the Dean of the Arkansas College of Agriculture militantly rebuffed efforts by the leaders of the Farmers Union in that state to secure equal treatment by the extension officials.[9]

The closest relationships between the FSA and the NFU were probably in Minnesota. FSA Administrator Baldwin was not exaggerating when he told his audience of NFU cooperative association leaders in St. Paul in December, 1940, that, "The program of the Farm Security Administration has had no better or more vigorous supporter than this group of farmers."[10]

Although more positive formal ties with the NFU were discussed from time to time, FSA leaders stopped short of the kind of bond that developed between the Extension Service and the AFBF. In view of the Great Plains orientation of the NFU and its middle-income membership, it is doubtful whether there could have been any enduring structural tie.

In 1941, at the time that the leaders of the FSA were belatedly beginning to think more seriously about either strengthening their ties to the NFU or building a cliental group of their own, Secretary of Agriculture Claude R. Wickard issued a memorandum which provided that no officer or employee of the USDA should participate in establishing any general farm organization, act as organizer for such a group, hold office or serve as financial or business agent, or participate in any way in membership campaigns or other activities designed to recruit members. Participation in the creation of groups to help administer federal programs, such as the cooperatives of the Rural Electrification Administration (REA) and FSA farmers committees, was permissible so long as the groups did not become general farm organizations or unite into state, regional, and national federations.

One explanation of Wickard's decision to issue the ruling was that

9. Crampton, *The National Farmers Union*, pp. 19, 156, 173; William J. Block, *The Separation of the Farm Bureau and the Extension Service* (Urbana: Univ. of Illinois Press, 1960), pp. 67, 69; author's telephone conversation with James G. Patton; author's interviews with Alexander, John A. Baker, C. B. Baldwin, Benton J. Stong.

10. C. B. Baldwin, "The Farmer's Job in Strengthening Democracy," address at St. Paul, Minn., Dec. 14, 1940.

the leaders of the USDA feared that competition between the AFBF and the NFU might entangle the USDA too deeply in farm organization politics. Others believed that it was in reaction to the growing trend toward the county agricultural agent becoming a "John the Baptist" for the AFBF. Some of the leaders of the FSA saw the decision as a reflection of Wickard's desire to protect the *status quo* in the constituency relationships of the Extension Service and other agencies of the USDA. The burden of the ruling fell most heavily on the FSA, which still operated largely without a formalized constituency relationship with any major interest group in the country.

Virtually all of the other general farm organizations and special commodity groups, which were also part of the structure of power in agriculture, were hostile to the FSA. Occasionally, an individual state affiliate of the National Grange, which was ideologically between the AFBF and the NFU, would defend the tenant purchase program, but on the whole the National Grange was perceived by the leaders of the FSA as hostile. The Associated Farmers of California, the Arizona Cotton Growers Association, the National Council of Farmer Cooperatives, and virtually all of the other commodity groups displayed attitudes toward the FSA during these years ranging from quiet suspicion to open hostility. The programs most frequently attacked were those involving resettlement projects, cooperative associations, transportation and housing for migratory farm laborers, and medical care groups. The leaders of the FSA viewed these conservative farm groups as enemies, and saw no basis for a *rapprochement*. The price of peace, they believed, would have been surrender.

One source of potential constituency support was the Roosevelt administration itself. As far as relations with the President were concerned, there was much less direct personal contact than there had been under Rexford G. Tugwell's Resettlement Administration, although Franklin D. Roosevelt himself never lost his interest and delight in some of the FSA innovations. On more than one occasion, according to the former First Lady, "he enjoyed chuckling over the discomfiture that the FSA people were giving our good friend Ed O'Neal of the Farm Bureau." After 1938, however, the White House became preoccupied with Europe and with the growing resistance of Congress generally, and thus the President became less accessible. Until 1940, when necessary, Henry A. Wallace, M. L. Wilson, and Paul H. Appleby served as the intermediaries for the agency at the White House, although Eleanor Roosevelt maintained her friendship with Alexander and her special interest in the resettlement and migratory labor programs. While there has been a tendency to explain the rise and decline of the FSA in terms of the President's active support and intervention on its behalf, it should be understood that, as Norton E. Long has suggested, "A picture of the Presidency as a reservoir of authority from which lower echelons of administration draw life and vigor is an idealized distortion of reality."[11]

From the national administration generally, the FSA received little active support. With William A. Jump intervening with the Budget Bureau, there was less basis for the kind of constituency relationships that had existed when the Resettlement Administration operated independently under Tugwell. The Budget Bureau, under Daniel W. Bell and Harold D. Smith, did not distinguish itself as particularly sympathetic to the programs of the FSA, and as congressional pressures against the FSA began to mount, the Bureau became more hostile. Since the majority of the employees of the FSA were not covered by the civil service laws, and the FSA conformed to civil service regulations strictly on a voluntary basis, relationships with the U.S. Civil Service Commission were tenuous. The separatism of the FSA also applied generally to relationships with most of the agencies and bureaus of the USDA and other federal departments. The closest relationships were probably with the leaders of the Bureau of Agricultural Economics (BAE), with whom the FSA shared a community of interest regarding the larger social purposes of the USDA. Both Alexander and Baldwin regarded Howard R. Tolley, Chief of the BAE during these years, as their friend and supporter. As the tenant purchase and rural rehabilitation programs evolved, with greater emphasis on field studies and measurement of achievements, collaboration between the FSA and the BAE ripened.

The only other agency in the USDA with which the FSA developed at least an approximation of a cordial constituency relationship was the SCS, under Hugh H. Bennett. There were a variety of reasons for the leaders of the SCS to perceive at least a limited community of interest between their agency and the FSA—Tugwell's influence in the creation of the Soil Erosion Service in 1933 (predecessor of the SCS); Bennett's religious commitment to soil conservation, which more than matched Tugwell's zeal for reform of man-land relations; the rapid growth of the SCS in the USDA and its competition with the Extension Service for power, therefore forcing Bennett to search for allies; and especially Bennett's passionate dis-

11. Author's interview with Mrs. Eleanor Roosevelt; Norton E. Long, "Power and Administration," *Public Administration Review*, Vol. IX (Autumn, 1949), p. 258.

like of the Extension Service because of the latter agency's involvement in efforts to freeze the SCS (and also the FSA) out of the territory covered by the Tennessee Valley Authority (TVA).

In December, 1937, under a memorandum of understanding signed by FSA Administrator Alexander and Bennett of the SCS, a modest program of technical cooperation between the two agencies in FSA Region 12 was launched in New Mexico and parts of Texas, Colorado, Kansas, and Oklahoma. Although the actual technical accomplishments of the program were very limited, the experience did encourage the leaders of the FSA, at least in the politics of the USDA and in their personal relationships, to consider Bennett and his assistants as their friends.

There was one potential constituency relationship that never developed—that with the TVA. In examining the process of "coöptation" between the leaders of the TVA and the state colleges of agriculture, extension services, and Farm Bureaus in the region, Philip Selznick has shown how the TVA joined the conservative agricultural establishment in treating the FSA like a pariah. For Selznick there was surprise and paradox in the lack of a *rapprochement* between the TVA and the FSA, despite the fact that they both represented "the more experimental phase of the New Deal, and both derived support from the liberal-labor movement in the United States."[12]

The absence of cooperation between the TVA and the FSA becomes less paradoxical when it is examined within the larger context of the inter-agency rivalry and separatism that existed in agriculture generally. The measure of policy coordination and national controllability achieved under Wallace and Appleby in the USDA was more personal than institutional, and with the departure of the men who established the system, the older pattern of decentralization and competition was reasserted. Lacking institutional mechanisms for inter-agency and inter-program cooperation, whatever was achieved depended largely on personal and *ad hoc* factors.

Furthermore, as we have seen, the leaders of the FSA were sepa-

---

12. Philip Selznick, *TVA and the Grass Roots* (Berkeley and Los Angeles: Univ. of California Press, 1949), pp. 166, 169–79; Arthur M. Schlesinger, Jr., *The Coming of the New Deal* (Boston: Houghton Mifflin, 1959), pp. 341–43; Paul V. Maris, *"the land is mine"* (Washington, D.C.: GPO, 1950), pp. 195–97; FSA and SCS, "Memorandum of Understanding for Technical Cooperation Between Soil Conservation Service, Region VI, and Farm Security Administration, Region XII," quoted in Larson, *Ten Years*, pp. 431–33; author's interview with Dillon S. Myer.

ratists themselves, cherishing their self-sufficiency and freedom of action, not fully trusting other agencies, not actively seeking their cooperation, and themselves not ready to make the necessary compromises and commitments on which effective and enduring interagency cooperation would have had to be built. The limited cooperation with the SCS, and the inability of the FSA to work effectively with the U.S. Employment Service in the migratory labor program were illustrative. There is nothing in the record to suggest that the leaders of the FSA really sought a *rapprochement* with the TVA, although it is true that they welcomed opportunities to work with it on an *ad hoc* basis, such as the relocation of farm families displaced by the construction of TVA reservoirs.

Farmers Committees: Political Strength or Administrative Quicksand?

By the late 1930's, the "grass roots democracy" of local farmers committees in planning and administration of farm programs had become a panacea. For M. L. Wilson (Under Secretary of Agriculture until 1940, and then Director of the Extension Service) and other priests of the faith, farmers committees were the most exciting political innovation of the twentieth century. Such committees were believed to be superior to political parties and interest groups in bridging the gulf between the state and the citizen; they supposedly enhanced popular understanding, promoted local initiative, and "humanized" public administration; and they were believed to strengthen an administrative agency's political basis by rendering the agency more acceptable to established local institutions. By 1939, according to the count of Carleton R. Ball, more than 892,000 people, over whom agency leaders exercised no formal power of command, were participating in the administration of action programs of the USDA, the Department of the Interior, and the TVA.[13]

---

13. Carleton R. Ball, "Citizens Help Plan and Operate Action Programs," *Land Policy Review*, Vol. 3 (Mar.–Apr., 1940), pp. 19–27; Donald C. Blaisdell, *Government and Agriculture* (New York: Farrar and Rinehart, 1940), pp. 166–82; Dale Clark, "The Farmer as a Co-Administrator," *Public Opinion Quarterly*, Vol. 3 (July, 1939), pp. 482–90; John D. Lewis, "Democratic Planning in Agriculture," *American Political Science Review*, Vol. XXXV (Apr.–June, 1941), pp. 232–49; F.D.R., *Public Papers* (1936), Vol. 5, p. 420; M. L. Wilson, "The Democratic Processes and the Formulation of Agricultural Policy," *Social Forces*, Vol. XIX (Oct., 1940), pp. 1–11, and "Farmers in a Democracy," *State Government*, Vol. XIV (July, 1941), pp. 155–56, 168–71.

In this respect, at least, the leaders of the FSA were heretics. Local farmers committees, they believed, represented not "grass roots democracy" but provincial irresponsibility. The delegation of official power to local citizens whom the government could not hire and fire would not "humanize" administration, but would prostitute it. In view of the hostile attitudes toward poverty and the poor that were held by the farmers who normally served on such committees, the rural rehabilitation program, it was believed, would sink into the quicksand of provincial pride and prejudice and administrative indecision. They decided, therefore, that while they had no choice in the tenant purchase program—operational farmers committees were mandatory under the terms of the Bankhead-Jones Farm Tenant Act —the rural rehabilitation committees inherited from the Resettlement Administration would continue on an advisory basis only. The state and county farm debt adjustment committees, which they had also inherited and which operated in a specialized way, could continue without blunting the thrust of the FSA.

At the state level, advisory committees, representing different geographical areas, commodities and types of farming, major farm organizations, state colleges and extension services, the farm press, and landlord and creditor interests, were established, ostensibly to give state officials an opportunity to advise the FSA on allocation of funds within their states—a specious function which ill concealed the lack of any serious intention among the leaders of the FSA to share power with such state committees. The functions of the state committees were defined vaguely, and in practice neither the FSA field officials nor the state agricultural leaders treated them seriously. They therefore degenerated into advisory committees to the tenant purchase program, with Paul V. Maris becoming their enthusiastic champion. Eventually, Maris was highly gratified with the role played by the state committees in such tasks as the designation of counties in which loans were to be granted, giving advice on the establishment of upper and lower tenant purchase loan limits, determining the value of farms to be purchased, and participating in inspection visitations to borrowers' farms—Alexander looked upon all of this merely as "busy work."[14]

14. FSA, Administrative Order, Aug. 5, 1937; Henry A. Wallace to State FSA Committeemen, Nov. 3, 1937, NA, RG 96; U.S., Congress, House, Committee on Agriculture, Hearings, 76th Cong., 3d Sess., *Amending the Bankhead-Jones Farm Tenant Act,* S.1826 (Washington, D.C.: GPO, 1940), pp. 15–28; Maris, *"the land is mine,"* pp. 41–48; author's interview with Alexander; Alexander, COHC, p. 605.

With the creation of state committees, Alexander saw an opportunity to promote the cause of racial equality. Since there were separate Negro and white state colleges of agriculture and extension staffs in the South—separate but not equal—he appointed Negroes to some of the southern state committees. Within a few days, he received a sarcastic letter from Senator James F. Byrnes of South Carolina, suggesting the following:

If it is believed that information as to the status of negro [sic] farmers ... can be secured only from negroes, your agent in the State can certainly be instructed to confer whenever necessary with such negroes as he believes are able to be of assistance.

Byrnes went on to warn that if the FSA persisted in its plan to include Negroes on the committees, "the negro will be the one to suffer." The future U.S. Supreme Court Justice and Secretary of State concluded with an admonition that was destined to become a familiar refrain: "Do not disturb the friendly relations now existing between the races." When Alexander refused to acquiesce, the Senator from South Carolina took the issue to the Secretary of Agriculture, and Wallace, who had originally supported the plan for Negroes on the committees, retreated. Thus ended Alexander's stillborn hope that the state committees in the South might at least have the semblance of the democracy they were supposed to serve.[15]

At the county level there were three types of FSA farmers committees—those devoted to tenant purchase loans, rural rehabilitation loans, and to debt adjustment. Most active were the tenant purchase committees, composed of three resident farmers appointed by the Secretary of Agriculture through the FSA Administrator, on nomination by the county agricultural agent and the FSA county supervisor. In practice, tenant purchase county committeemen were invariably acceptable to the local agricultural establishment. Under rules and regulations prescribed by Maris and the Tenant Purchase Division, county tenant purchase committees were empowered to carry out several day-to-day tasks, including review of loan applications—no tenant purchase loan could be granted without committee approval —and several advisory functions, involving disputes between client and supervisor, refinancing of clients, transfer of titles of property, and foreclosure proceedings.

15. James F. Byrnes to Alexander, Oct. 9, 1937; Alexander to Byrnes, Oct. 23, 1937; Byrnes to Alexander, Oct. 27, 1937; CBBP. Author's interview with Alexander.

More numerous, but with less operational power, were the *advisory* county rural rehabilitation committees, composed of three resident farmers appointed by the FSA county supervisor, subject to state committee approval. The rural rehabilitation committees were empowered to exercise several vaguely defined advisory functions regarding the eligibility of applicants, assistance to county supervisors in promoting understanding among the clientele, and in encouraging cooperation among them.

The division of labor and the relationships among the three types of county committees varied from county to county, and by 1941, the pattern had become a crazy quilt. During these years, virtually the only leader of the FSA in the Washington office who took the county committees seriously was Maris, who defended them not as instruments for the mobilization of the clientele, but rather "as a safeguard against the potential dangers of overcentralized administrative control." The majority of the leaders of the FSA, on the other hand, were more concerned about the tyranny of provincial hostility and tradition than the perils of authoritarian rule from Washington. While Maris was calling for more power to the committees, some leaders of the FSA were declaring that low-income farm families could not receive sympathetic treatment from farmers committees unless low-income farmers served on them.

In the spring of 1941, presumably to confer some order on the system, it was decided to establish advisory councils above the committees, as instruments of coordination. However, before the councils could become fully operative, the entire system of local farmer participation was overwhelmed by the urgencies of wartime mobilization during the winter and spring of 1942. Thus, the FSA council-committee system languished. For Maris, the most distressing wartime casualties were his annual schools for county committeemen, through which, in his words, "The rough edges of our ideas were smoothed off by our contacts with level-headed, straight-thinking, down-to-earth committeemen."[16]

Meanwhile, as will be brought out below, the political climate had been changing for the FSA. In Congress, the tide had begun

---

16. Larson, *Ten Years*, p. 77; Maris, *"the land is mine,"* pp. 39–68. FSA, Administrative Order, Oct. 5, 1937; Walter A. Duffy, address, Sept. (n.d.), 1941; FSA, Instruction 403.1, May 1, 1941; Baldwin to members of state advisory committees, May 14, 1941; FSA, agenda papers, annual tenant purchase conference, Washington, D.C., May 10–15, 1941; CBBP. Also, FSA, minutes of administrative staff meeting, May 4, 1943, PVMP.

The Quest for Equilibrium / [309]

to turn, and one of the indictments against the FSA was its "failure" to have utilized local farmers committees more actively. Finally, with the leaders of the FSA under mounting pressure from several directions and for additional reasons to be discussed below, Baldwin issued an order on July 23, 1943, abolishing the FSA county councils and committees, and setting up in their place in each county a single committee, composed of three members appointed for three years by the FSA regional director on nomination by the county supervisor. The new unified county committee was to have responsibility for all FSA programs in the county and there were important innovations respecting the rural rehabilitation program—no loans were to be granted without committee approval, and once a year there was to be a review of the client's achievements to determine whether sufficient progress had been made to warrant his continuation on the program. Thus, in the sixth year of its operation under the FSA, the essential social welfare character of the program was abandoned.[17]

Several years later, in retrospect, Maris asserted that, "If Baldwin and his crowd had paid more attention to the state and county farmers committees and less attention to the political party committees, they wouldn't have gotten into so much trouble." For Alexander, there was a similar lesson: "I don't think we worked hard enough to make the committee system work for us, and if we had they would have protected us from some of our enemies and brought us strength."[18]

The most vehement opponent of the committee system, as we have seen, was Appleby. He took his lesson from Wilson—Woodrow, not M. L.—who wrote in 1887 that "to fear the creation of a domineering, illiberal officialdom . . . is to miss altogether the principle . . . that administration in the United States must be at all points sensitive to public opinion." To this, Appleby added the suggestion that sensitive public administration will be achieved "not through sentimental efforts to incorporate small numbers of private citizens into the administrative process through advisory committees or the delegation of governmental authorities to citizens not governmentally responsible." Such limited and special citizen participation, Appleby believed, "could not be nearly as responsible as the governmental totality." In retrospect, he concluded that, "If the FSA had delegated substantial administrative power over the rural rehabilitation pro-

---

17. FSA, Instruction 403.1, Aug. 25, 1943; Larson, *Ten Years*, pp. 76–77; *House Hearings*, Agr. Approp. (calendar year 1943), p. 143.
18. Author's interviews with Alexander, Paul V. Maris.

gram to local farmers committees, it would have amounted to an act of suicide."[19]

Virtually absent from the dialogue over the uses and abuses of farmers committees was candid consideration of the extent to which such committees might be utilized for the frankly political purpose of protecting an administrative agency from conscious and premeditated obstruction or sabotage by hostile special interests in the local community. Nor is there any evidence in the record to suggest that the leaders of the FSA ever seriously considered the use of committees as the basis for a consciously constructed constituency relation comparable to the AFBF or the system of associated Soil Conservation Districts.[20]

The Quest for Internal Equilibrium

As we have already seen in the tendencies toward goal displacement and succession and in the incongruities between organizational expectations and individual field performance, the FSA was not immune to internal tensions which threatened to subvert organizational purposes and to upset the agency's institutional viability. In part, the problem was rooted in the psychological distance between people operating in different settings and at different levels of organization, bearing different responsibilities, and applying different "givens" to their choices and decisions involving knowledge and assumptions about future events, alternative courses of action, likely consequences of these alternatives, and their values and goals. In part, the problem was due to difficulties implicit in rapid bureaucratic growth—heavy workload, budgetary limitations, organizational imperfections, inadequate assignment and training of personnel, and faulty communications. The internal tensions were also due to the problem of competing definitions of organizational purpose that

---

19. Woodrow Wilson, "The Study of Public Administration," in Dwight Waldo, ed., *Ideas and Issues in Public Administration* (New York: McGraw-Hill, 1953), p. 75. Wilson's essay was originally published in *Political Science Quarterly*, Vol. 2 (June, 1887), pp. 197–222. See also Appleby, *Morality and Administration in Democratic Government* (Baton Rouge: Louisiana State Univ. Press, 1952), pp. 172–73. Author's interview with Appleby.

20. For an exception to this pattern, see the statement by E. C. McArthur, president of the South Carolina Association of Soil Conservation District Supervisors, in 1945, quoted in W. Robert Parks, *Soil Conservation Districts in Action* (Ames: Iowa State College Press, 1952), p. 214.

was implicit in the unorthodox character of some programs and practices.

A major source of difficulty was the quality of the field personnel. Many had been appointed originally by the FERA and the Subsistence Homesteads Division, without sufficient attention to their technical competence and their allegiance to the cause. In 1935, they were hurriedly transferred to the Resettlement Administration, and then were absorbed by the FSA two years later. Under the pressure of crisis and the mounting backlog of applications for assistance, there was never a thorough screening of the field personnel, and therefore the FSA inherited many county and district supervisors and project and labor camp directors whose competence and allegiance were questionable. Furthermore, even under the more systematic personnel policies of the FSA, some field people were appointed more on the basis of local politics than on merit.

Despite the fact that many of the FSA county and district supervisors and project and labor camp directors were recent graduates of the state colleges of agriculture, where they presumably had been exposed to the social sciences, they were, nevertheless, still products of orthodox agricultural training in which there was greater emphasis on handling cows, tractors and soil, than people. Such a technical orientation was appropriate, perhaps, in programs dealing with higher-income farmers who were more readily prepared to respond to technical assistance, but for success in working with hard-core poverty cases at the bottom of the pyramid, something more than a passing college grade in rural sociology was necessary. The traditionally trained professional agriculturalist tended to see the problems of low-income farm families in terms of prices and cost of production. Problems of social organization, labor relations, social status, economic opportunity, and welfare administration were alien to him.

Among the FSA regional directors, there was some disagreement over the relative merits between conventional agricultural training and a more sociological orientation. One director, who was of a conservative persuasion, suggested that the divergence between Washington's expectations and performance in the field was due to some of the supervisors and project and labor camp directors who worked from textbooks and were prisoners of their own jargon and expertise. In a letter to Baldwin in 1941, for instance, he suggested that the "sociologists" in the field were "like the lawyer who is annoyed because the layman cannot understand a complicated legal instrument that seems so simple and elementary to the legal mind." From the other side of the issue, Laurence I. Hewes, Jr., who himself had had a broad liberal education and who had been a disciple of Tugwell in the Resettlement Administration, saw the fault in the agriculturalists, as follows:[21]

> The County and District supervisors . . . are much more readily swayed by the general farming sentiment in their communities than they are with the sentiment and views held by more academic and enlightened people at the regional and national level. . . . I don't know of anything more hopeless than the feeling one has when one tries to discuss basic problems with them, and, believe me, I have tried. They just don't get it, and if they do get it, they will get it wiped out the next time they talk to the County Agent.

The problem was also rooted in differences in administrative habitat. The atmosphere of the Washington office was heavily charged with national points of view, and with influences flowing from the USDA, the White House, Congress, the liberal political climate of the New Deal, nationally organized interest groups, the national press, and other institutions to which the leaders of the FSA in Washington and in some of the regional offices were sensitive. In the field, on the other hand, especially in the small rural communities, supervisors and project and labor camp directors were compelled to maintain face-to-face relationships with client families, with clients' neighbors, with the local representatives of competing federal and state agencies, and with community leaders, many of whom were hostile. These field people also had to maintain their own personal positions in their communities. Promotion of group or cooperative action, "digging deeper," minimum farm labor wages, an "adequate" level of living, racial equity, and a "stake in democracy" had different meanings for those who were closer to the firing line than those in offices on the Washington Mall.

An example of this problem of transvaluation occurred in California during Hewes' regime as regional director. Edward C. Banfield, in his post-mortem study of the Casa Grande resettlement project in Arizona, has described Hewes' efforts to combat factionalism and feuding among the families of the project by sending Myer Cohen, his "specialist on social organization," to Casa Grande "to encourage the spirit of cooperation." Cohen was a young urban liberal with a degree in political science and with experience in

---

21. Fischer to Baldwin, July 30, 1941; Wilson Cowen to Baldwin, Aug. 20, 1941; Laurence I. Hewes, Jr., to Baldwin, Aug. 18, 1941; NA, RG 96.

The Quest for Equilibrium / [313]

relief administration. Upon his arrival at the project, he called all project members to the community hall for a discussion of "democracy and the desirability of a democratic community life." The "Arkies" from the hills of Arkansas and the "Dust Bowlers" from Oklahoma, Banfield reported, were "puzzled that Cohen should see a relationship between pie dinners and democracy." Himself chagrined, Cohen returned to San Francisco, his mission not accomplished, and a short time later he was promoted to assistant regional director in charge of project management.[22]

One of the major causes of internal tension within the FSA was the divergence in attitude regarding the capacity and human worth of client farm families. A comparative study by the BAE, for instance, of clients and supervisors in the South and Middle West was suggestive. Forty-two per cent of the supervisors surveyed in the South and 16 per cent in the Middle West gave evidence of what were called "disparaging attitudes" toward their client families. According to the study, these attitudes were reflected in the prevalence of such references to client families as "low-types, riff-raff, the poorer classes, illiterates, and ne'er do-wells." Evidence of autocratic attitudes among supervisors, it was reported, was found in such comments as, "You've got to keep a tight rein on some of these old hard-headed cotton farmers," or "You've got to keep close after these low-type families or they'll get out of hand." The survey reported that 64 per cent of the supervisors who were interviewed believed that client families would not follow farm and home management plans without close supervision. Such field attitudes were a rude challenge to official FSA doctrine regarding the "virtuous poor," and some southern members of Congress, literally outraged by the survey, attempted to have it suppressed.[23]

In 1939, this divergence between Washington and the field led to some remedial efforts. In the spring, James L. McCamy, professor of government and chairman of social studies at Bennington College, who became an assistant to Secretary Wallace in 1939, accompanied the Secretary, Resettlement Director John O. Walker of the FSA, and others on a visit to several rural resettlement projects in Arkansas and Mississippi. Throughout the journey, McCamy observed signs of what he believed was "disrespect for human dignity"

---

22. Edward C. Banfield, *Government Project* (Glencoe, Ill.: The Free Press, 1951), pp. 160–65.

23. BAE, "Attitudes Toward FSA Tenant Purchase Program," Study 122, Processed (Jan., 1946), pp. v, 1, 90–93, Appendix, p. 47; CBBP.

—FSA field officials addressed Negro farmers in an impolite manner, lines of black limousines filled with officious men would converge unexpectedly on some poor farm family and subject them to awkward interviews, or the visitors would brazenly walk with muddy feet across freshly washed farm house floors. In discussions following their journey, Wallace, McCamy, Alexander, and Walker decided to invite Harold D. Lasswell of Yale University to conduct a study of the "emotional consequences" of FSA practices and to propose remedies.

Lasswell and his assistants conducted their study and reported to Wallace that the response of FSA client families to the programs was conditioned by subjective attitudes held by both the clientele and their supervisors and project and camp directors. The report recommended that field administration might be made more effective through a variety of devices, including more frequent and intimate conferences between officials and clients, measurement of clients' attitudes, and improvement of field training and communication through experimentation with techniques of group dynamics.[24]

For the leaders of the FSA, the solution lay not in psychoanalysis or group dynamics, but in more conventional remedies—improved training and communication. In the fall of 1939, they conducted a two-week training course for supervisors and project directors at Tuskegee Institute in Alabama, and during the next two years many other courses, schools, and institutes, were held in various parts of the country. Alexander, Hudgens, James G. Maddox, Maris, and others traveled in the field, talked to FSA field officials, inspected projects and FSA offices, and addressed conferences and training sessions. Throughout all this activity, the emphasis was placed not on narrow administrative techniques, but on some of the FSA leaders' favorite topics, such as the causes and cures of poverty, national economic trends, the principles of democratic administration, and the philosophy of the FSA. "What we were trying to do," Alexander later explained, "was to give our supervisory people the education they should have had at the colleges of agriculture." This task, of infusing the ideology of the FSA into the fabric of the field staff, remained a central problem throughout the life of the agency.[25]

Major obstacles to success in this endeavor were the comparatively

24. James L. McCamy, "Humanizing Public Administration," in Felix A. Nigro, ed., *Public Administration Readings and Documents* (New York: Rinehart, 1951), pp. 461–78.
25. Author's interview with Alexander.

low salary schedule and the denial of civil service status to most of the FSA personnel. Throughout the life of the agency, the leaders struggled in vain with the personnel and budget offices of the USDA and with congressional appropriations committees to equalize FSA salaries, especially in the field, with their counterparts in other agencies. At work here was a vicious circle—lower salaries were justified by staff offices of the USDA and by Congress on the grounds that many of the FSA field personnel were younger and less experienced than those performing similar work in other agencies, and the lower salaries, in turn, assured that older, more experienced and perhaps more competent personnel would not be recruited. FSA state directors, for instance, averaged $500 less per year than their counterparts in the SCS and the AAA, while the differential between county agricultural agents and FSA county supervisors averaged from $500 to $1,000 per year. This amounted to differences of from 10 to 15 per cent of the annual salaries.[26]

The denial of civil service status affected the morale of FSA personnel and the stability of the agency even more directly. In the early days of the Resettlement Administration, it will be recalled, Tugwell had followed a policy of voluntarily subjecting the agency's personnel to standards formulated by the U.S. Civil Service Commission. Under the FSA, Alexander and Baldwin continued the policy, in the belief that when civil service coverage finally arrived, the agency would be ready. In 1940, with congressional consideration of Representative Robert Ramspeck's bill authorizing the President to extend civil service coverage to approximately 200,000 previously exempted positions, the leaders of the FSA believed that "covering-in" was imminent. Baldwin, his hopes high, submitted a statement to the Senate Committee on Civil Service in which he pointed out that most of the 16,175 employees of the FSA had been appointed on the basis of examinations designed by the U.S. Civil Service Commission, that the FSA was having great difficulty in recruiting and retaining its personnel because of the insecure character of employment without civil service protection, and that extension of the civil

---

26. U.S., Civil Service Commission, *Official Register of the United States, 1939* (Washington, D.C.: GPO, 1939), pp. 79–80, 108–09, 116–23. Milo R. Perkins to Appleby, Aug. 14, 1937; Appleby to Baldwin, Aug. 19, 1937; Warner W. Stockberger to Appleby, Aug. 18, 1937; CBBP.

The salaries of FSA labor camp managers were particularly low. Jonathan Garst, regional director of the FSA in California for a time, defended the disparity on the grounds that "too much prosperity would make camp employees less sensitive to the problems of migrant families." Author's interview with Garst.

service system to the FSA would help to reduce the costs of recruitment. Without civil service protection, the FSA would remain a happy hunting ground for pirating by competing governmental agencies.

Passage and promulgation of the Ramspeck Act proved bitterly disappointing to the leaders of the FSA. Despite the eligibility of FSA personnel for civil service protection under the Act's provisions, a rider attached to the Second Deficiency Appropriation Act of 1941 prohibited the use of funds in the Department of Agriculture Appropriation Act for fiscal year 1942, designated for "Loans, Grants, and Rural Rehabilitation," for compensating any persons covered by the civil service laws. The effect of the rider was a denial of civil service coverage to 90 per cent of the employees of the FSA—compared with 25 per cent for the USDA as a whole.

Finally, in July, 1942, over the desperate protests of FSA Administrator Baldwin, Congress included a provision in the regular Department of Agriculture Appropriation Act for fiscal year 1943, which continued the civil service restriction on FSA employees. As a result, approximately 90 per cent of the agency's employees were eliminated from the civil service laws. For Baldwin and his assistants, this was the writing on the wall.[27]

Relations with Congress

As long as legislative appropriations remain the lifeblood of public administration, Congress will continue to have the power of life and death over federal administrative agencies. Furthermore, to complicate executive life, an agency's relations with Congress are greatly affected by forces over which the leaders of the agency may have no influence or control.

From 1937 to the end of fiscal year 1942, relations between the FSA and Congress were governed as much by the executive-legislative pendulum as by the actions of the FSA. From the high noon of presidential influence in 1936, through the Supreme Court reform debacle

---

27. Second Deficiency Appropriation Act of 1941, 55 Stat. 541; Ramspeck Act of 1940, 54 Stat. 1211; Department of Agriculture Appropriation Act, fiscal year 1942, 55 Stat. 408. Claude R. Wickard to Franklin D. Roosevelt, Oct. 11, 1941; Marvin H. McIntyre to Wickard, Nov. 14, 1941; FDRL, OF 1568. *Senate Hearings*, Agr. Approp. (1943), pp. 460–61; Executive Order 8939, Nov. 13, 1941.

of 1937 and the ill-fated effort to purge anti-New Dealers from the Democratic party in 1938, to the conservative coalitions of 1939 to 1941, there was a growing political stalemate, which eventually turned to a rout of the New Deal. It was within this larger struggle that congressional resistance to the FSA grew, that the area of executive discretion narrowed, and that appropriations for the FSA, as summarized in the following table, reached a plateau and then plummeted:

Fiscal Year	Tenant Purchase Program (million $)	Rural Rehabilitation Program (million $)	Resettlement Program (million $)	Total (million $)
1937–38	10.0	118.3[1]		128.3
1938–39	25.0	175.0[1]		200.0
1939–40	40.0	143.0[1]		183.0
1940–41	52.5[2]	185.0[2]	1.5	239.0
1941–42	52.5[2]	183.9[2]	.7	237.1
1942–43	34.1[2]	140.3[2]	.5	174.9
1943–44	31.3[2]	80.0[2]	.4	111.7
Total	245.4	1,025.5	3.1	1,274.0

1. Includes funds for liquidation and management of resettlement projects.
2. Includes authorized FSA loans from Reconstruction Finance Corporation (RFC) for tenant purchase and rural rehabilitation loans to FSA clients.

During these years, as we have seen, the FSA enjoyed considerable freedom from congressional constraints, but there was always the possibility that occasional skirmishes with a few strategically situated members of the House or Senate might escalate into open warfare. Some of the opposition was highly personal, such as that of Democratic Senator Kenneth D. McKellar of Tennessee, who resented the decision of the leaders of the FSA to discontinue their practice of buying mules from one of his friends in Memphis, but who relented for a time when the FSA bought insurance from a company in which his political ally, "Boss" E. H. Crump, had an interest. Some of the skirmishes were covert designs to obstruct or wreck the FSA at a time when a frontal attack might have become a boomerang, while others were caused by fears, as we have seen, that relief and rehabilitation funds might be used for partisan political advantage. Other opposition was motivated by political feedback from rural communities in which the FSA was disturbing the peace of some congressional districts. Finally, like the Resettlement Administration before it, the FSA was simply a convenient and vulnerable target for anti-New Dealers, Roosevelt-haters, and bureaucrat-baiters in Congress.[28]

The particular programs and practices of the FSA that were singled out for attack were often merely targets of convenience—cooperative enterprises, resettlement projects, migratory labor camps, and special supervisory techniques designed for particularly needy and helpless low-income farm families. Had these attacks succeeded in eliminating funds for the FSA and imposing tight restrictions on administrative action, their effects on the FSA as a whole, however, would have been indiscriminate. In 1938 and 1939, for instance, the protracted dispute in the House Appropriations Committee over FSA loans to resettlement projects for completing and operating hosiery mills started under the Resettlement Administration was a skirmish that generated much heat and smoke, although it was concerned with an activity that was peripheral to the main thrust of the agency.

One of the first attacks after the FSA was established in 1937 was aimed at the jugular. As we have already seen, the supervisory techniques employed in the rural rehabilitation program, especially under the policy of "digging deeper," were reflected in administrative expenses averaging about 10 per cent of the appropriations—higher than for more conventional credit programs. Shortly before passage of the Bankhead-Jones Farm Tenant Act in 1937, Appleby anticipated the danger of any arbitrary restriction on administrative expenses in the rural rehabilitation program—a mandatory limit of 5 per cent was imposed on the tenant purchase program—and he offered the following admonition:[29]

... reduction in administrative expenses ... will inevitably result in the organization paying attention to the higher income group clients and less attention to the lower group clients, simply because it is easier to work with the former and under the increased work load the easier path will have to be chosen.

28. The members of the House Appropriations Committee who were particularly hostile to the FSA were the following: Republicans John Taber of New York, Richard B. Wigglesworth of Massachusetts, and Everett M. Dirksen of Illinois; and Democrats Clarence Cannon of Missouri, Clifton A. Woodrum of Virginia, and Malcolm C. Tarver of Georgia.

In the Senate the leaders of the FSA received the most intense scrutiny from the following: Republicans Styles Bridges of New Hampshire, and Henry Cabot Lodge, of Massachusetts; and Democrats Carter Glass and Harry F. Byrd of Virginia, Kenneth D. McKellar of Tennessee, and Ellison D. "Cotton Ed" Smith of South Carolina.

29. Appleby to Perkins, Aug. 5, 1937, NA, RG 16.

One Senator who clearly understood all this was Southern Democrat Harry F. Byrd of Virginia. Avoiding a frontal attack, he chose the easier route through the appropriations process. In 1938, during congressional consideration of funds for rural rehabilitation, in the Emergency Relief Appropriation Bill for fiscal year 1939, he introduced an amendment that would limit administrative expenses for the rural rehabilitation program to 5 per cent. As far as the leaders were concerned at the time, the restriction "would have wrecked our entire program for next year." "Beanie" Baldwin, serving as Acting Administrator in the absence of "Dr. Will" Alexander who was traveling in Europe, persuaded Appleby to impress the Secretary of Agriculture with the gravity of the situation, and Wallace, in turn, secured the personal support of the President in persuading the congressional conferees on the bill to eliminate Byrd's amendment.[30]

In the spring of 1939, conservative Democratic Representative Guy L. Moser of Pennsylvania launched an attack that was pregnant with meaning for the future. Objecting to FSA loans for hosiery mills connected with a few of the resettlement projects inherited from the Resettlement Administration, Moser charged that such enterprises threatened the entire hosiery industry of the United States. During House consideration of the agricultural appropriation for fiscal year 1940, he succeeded in having the funds for the tenant purchase program eliminated, even though loans to hosiery mills were financed separately under emergency relief appropriation acts. In heated testimony before the Senate Appropriations Committee, the congressman from Pennsylvania revealed a sentiment that he and some of his conservative House colleagues had harbored for two years:[31]

---

30. Baldwin to Alexander, June 30, 1938, CBBP.
31. Testimony of Rep. Moser in *House Hearings*, Agr. Approp. (1940), 76th Cong., 1st Sess., pp. 819–20, 823–24. R. N. Elliott to Wallace, Dec. 6, 1938; Wallace to Stephen Early, Dec. 19, 1938; FDRL, OF 1568. Also, Wallace's testimony in *House Hearings*, Agr. Approp. (1940), pp. 20–21.

On December 6, 1938, the Acting Comptroller General had informed Wallace that loans for industrial purposes on resettlement projects were a clearcut violation of the Emergency Relief Appropriation Act of 1938, and that the practice should be discontinued. Roosevelt and Wallace, on the contrary, insisted that while such loans might be politically unpopular in some areas, they were fully within the law. The President and Secretary of Agriculture also contended that efficient management of the resettlement projects, until they were liquidated, required that appropriate measures be taken to assure their success, and especially to protect the government's investment. The charge that these factories were a threat to private industry, they argued, was absurd.

On February 4, 1939, during House hearings on funds for the tenant purchase program and for management and liquidation of the resettlement projects, Repre-

When the Bankhead-Jones Farm Rehabilitation Act [sic] was before the House of Representatives in 1937, I was for it. . . . But with that legislative enactment, the Resettlement Administration . . . pounced upon the . . . Act as a nesting place and called themselves the Farm Security Administration. . . . [FSA field officials] have been roaming around over my district and other districts undertaking to build up a clientele where it did not exist. They have spoken of the case loads and one thing after another in order to bring about a condition justifying their continuation. . . . This octopus has reached out and taken this $175,000,000 relief fund and undertaken to use $3,500,000 of that money to build hosiery factories in the homestead areas.

Despite the passage of the Bankhead-Jones Farm Tenant Act, the FSA, at least in the minds of some members of Congress, was thus not a legitimate instrument of government.

Over the protests of Democrat Richard B. Russell of Georgia, who insisted that the issue over the hosiery mills had been settled—no additional factories were to be built—and that Moser's victim would not be the hosiery factories but the tenant purchase program, Moser contended that "the end justifies the means." He warned that he would continue his efforts, and that he would do everything possible to prevent the FSA from "roaming around getting people to accept service, soliciting."

These happenings in Congress were only sporadic attacks on the FSA, but they were potentially dangerous, with the shotgun employed more frequently than the rifle. Meanwhile, the southern stalwarts in Congress—Richard B. Russell, John H. Bankhead, Lister Hill, Tom Connally, and others in the Senate; and Marvin Jones, William B. Bankhead, John J. Sparkman, Sam Rayburn, and others in the House—unfailingly stood up for the FSA. However, as the years passed, as the strength of the conservative coalition against the New Deal grew, as charges against the FSA accumulated, as Harry F. Byrd in the Senate, and Clarence Cannon and Everett M. Dirksen in the House won converts to their assault on the FSA and the New Deal, it became increasingly more uncomfortable for the southerners to defend the FSA for practices which they themselves were beginning to believe were questionable or undesirable.

---

sentative Dirksen raised the issue again with Wallace. The Secretary attempted to make it clear to the committee that while he did not personally favor the creation of additional resettlement projects or the establishment of new industrial plants, he did intend to complete those already started and likely to prove successful, in order to provide needed revenue for resettlement projects where there was insufficient land to support agriculture. Wallace declared that he saw no reason to tie the hands of the FSA in this matter and that he intended to pursue his efforts to make the existing plants profitable.

Until 1940, the most consistent defense of the FSA came from forty-one Senators, all but three of whom were Democrats (fifteen were from the South, nine were from the Middle West, and ten were from the Western and Mountain States), and ninety-eight members of the House, all but five of whom were Democrats (fifty-seven were from the South, fifteen were from the Middle West, and fourteen were from the Western and Mountain States). Throughout these years, the pattern of support and opposition in Congress closely resembled that which had prevailed during the struggle for passage of tenancy legislation—a bi-partisan coalition of members from the South, the Middle West, and the Mountain and Western States. As long as their defense lines held, the leaders of the FSA, with some overconfidence, persisted in the belief that their congressional foes—Byrd, McKellar, Cannon, Dirksen and others—were not the Congress of the United States.[32]

There was a tendency for most of the leaders of the FSA to feel suspicious of Congress as a body—this was presumably a manifestation of their seige mentality—and they found little joy in the political give-and-take on Capitol Hill that is an important part of the "iron law of survival." As FSA Administrator, Alexander was reasonably effective in dealing with certain members of Congress on a person-to-person basis, but he suffered a torment in each encounter with the Senate and House appropriations committees. Similarly, Baldwin, who consistently maintained his Virginian courtesy, despite occasional provocations by the agency's harsher critics, preferred to avoid formal confrontations with congressional committees, and sought instead to deal on a personal basis with individual legislators. Consequently, Baldwin spent an enormous amount of time on the telephone and in confidential sessions with individual friends "on the Hill." For this, he was sometimes accused of "private politicking" and a "conspiratorial approach" in his dealings.[33]

32. Baldwin to Stanley P. Williams, Jan. 11, 1941; tabular materials on voting records of Senate and House pertaining to FSA legislation, 1937–41, prepared by FSA Information Division; CBBP.
   The most vigorous defenders of the FSA in the Senate included the following: Republicans Capper and Reed of Kansas, Norris of Nebraska, and Austin of Vermont. In the House, where the bipartisan spirit was more subdued, Republicans Burdick of North Dakota, Case of South Dakota, and Hope of Kansas; and Farmer-Laborites Buckler of Minnesota, and Gehrman and Hull of Wisconsin were particularly vigorous champions of the agency.

33. Alexander, COHC, pp. 660–64; transcripts of Baldwin's telephone conversations, CBBP; author's interviews with Alexander, Maris, Baldwin, Fischer, Robert W. Hudgens.

During the so-called "golden years" of the FSA, from 1937 to 1942, the leaders of the agency maintained their posture of isolation and suspicion toward Congress, most of the organized farm groups, state and local agricultural institutions, and other federal agencies. In part this was forced upon them by the hostility—latent and overt—which they encountered on virtually all sides, but it was also a manifestation of the agency's legacy of militancy inherited from Tugwell and the Resettlement Administration. Long before the automatic data processing revolution, the pattern of administrative behavior in the FSA demonstrated that institutions, like organisms generally, do have memories.

Equilibrium, Time, and Political Change

From 1937 to 1942, the FSA remained something of an anomaly—an agricultural agency of government pursuing reform goals but finding its justification and defensive symbolism in the past, led by men most of whom were not agriculturalists, exercising considerable political power but operating outside of the mainstream of political power in agriculture, structurally a part of the USDA but operating as an island within it, dedicated to the interests of a clientele but from whom little effective political support could be derived, and supported by basic legislation but not enjoying a clearcut congressional mandate. Like the honeybee, the FSA defied the laws of flight.

In some ways, the task of the astronaut is probably simpler and less hazardous than that of the public bureaucrat. For the space capsule in orbit, there is a condition of dynamic equilibrium which is built upon a system of multiple relations among variables that are known and measurable. Disturbance of one or more of these variables—gravity's pull, engine thrust, altitude, speed, temperature, pressure, azimuth—influences the system in a predictable way, and the necessary equilibrating adjustments can be made. In other words, the equation of space flight, at least in the neighborhood of earth, is no longer a mystery.

For the administrative agency of government, on the other hand, the equation of successful political and administrative navigation is still obscure. The variables have not been adequately conceptualized, the likelihood of quantification remains in the future, and there is not much conceptual consensus regarding the nature of political and administrative equilibrium—if, indeed, such a state ever really does or can exist.

The factors that were probably responsible for the "golden years" of the FSA were numerous and diverse—the urgency of depression; the influence of the President and the New Deal movement; the loyal support of a nucleus of congressional members; indifference or acquiescence among some of those people in Congress, the administration, and the farm organizations whose hostility during these years was latent rather than overt; the ideological commitment of the agency's leaders and their posture of institutional self-containment; the successful balancing of different and sometime competing organizational purposes within the FSA; and the innovative and expansionist impulses of the agency during the stage of institutional growth.

Although it is virtually impossible, at least in the present state of our knowledge and understanding, to convert this inventory of contributing factors or variables into a formula for political and administrative equilibrium, or to apply ordinal and cardinal measures to their ranking, there is, as David Easton has emphasized, at least some heuristic virtue in the use of the equilibrium model. Its value lies, he suggests, not in its use as a description of the empirical world, but rather as a device for analyzing and understanding that world. It perpetuates the idea of coherence in the political process and focuses on the problem of political change. Application of the equilibrium concept to the rise and decline of the FSA, for instance, focuses attention on the relationships among such variables as national partisan competition, presidential influence, congressional-executive relationships, interest group aggregation and articulation, economic and technological feasibility, and internal organizational solidarity. For students of poverty and politics, significance lies not so much in the state of equilibrium as in the quest for it.[34]

A particularly fruitful application of the equilibrium model, in which internal "adaptive adjustments" were related to external social change, is Peter M. Blau's study of a federal agency of government responsible for enforcing legal standards of employment. Approaching his subject from a functional direction, in which he distinguished between "functional" consequences that contribute to an organization's attainment of socially valued objectives, and "dysfunctional" consequences that interfere with the attainment of such objectives, Blau found that employees' commitment to the ideology of the New

---

34. David Easton, *The Political System* (New York: Knopf, 1953), pp. 266–306, and his "Limits of the Equilibrium Model in Social Research," in Heinz Eulau, Samuel J. Eldersveld, and Morris Janowitz, eds., *Political Behavior* (Glencoe, Ill.: The Free Press, 1956).

Deal was a factor in their behavior. However, he focused his view entirely on the internal "adaptive adjustments" within one district office of the federal agency, leaving the nature, intensity, direction, and variations of that New Deal commitment to others. Blau was methodologically justified, of course, in narrowing his frame, but as a result, his portrait was incomplete. Competition with other organizations, shifting public expectations, changes in the agency's claims to legitimacy, and alterations in the social, economic, and political climate generally were some of the environmental factors that were probably as important in the agency's quest for equilibrium as anything that happened within one district office.

Even those agency studies that have examined the impact of the external environment have generalized on the rules of institutional survival, but without sufficient attention to political change and the temporal dimension. Philip Selznick's examination of institutional commitments and the process of "coöptation" in the TVA, for instance, treats the New Deal and the larger political climate as fixed quantities, and for him, time seems to stand still. Similarly, Grant McConnell had a thoroughly historical perspective in his analysis of the "decline of agrarian democracy," but he treated the relationships between the FSA and the AFBF as though they existed in a temporal vacuum.[35]

The experience of the FSA cannot be fully understood unless it is viewed within the context of time and political change. The relative importance of such internal factors as innovation, routine, stability of employment, material rewards, ideological commitment, and operational flexibility, and such external factors as cliental support, amicable relations with Congress, presidential intervention, and political legitimacy changes over time as the pendulum of politics swings. Having examined the manner in which the leaders of the FSA sought to maintain their organization during the "golden years," it is now our task to focus on the configuration of forces and events which brought the agency to the great crisis of its life.

35. Peter M. Blau, *The Dynamics of Bureaucracy*, rev. ed. (Chicago: Univ. of Chicago Press, 1955), pp. 165, 200–1, 231, 241–42, 246; Selznick, *TVA and the Grass Roots*; Grant McConnell, *The Decline of Agrarian Democracy* (Berkeley: Univ. of California Press, 1953).

CHAPTER XI

THE FSA GOES TO WAR

War emphasizes regard for the general welfare, encourages unselfishness, stimulates co-operation, works for unity, and creates a certain exaltation of spirit.

ARTHUR C. MILLSPAUGH[1]
Democracy, Efficiency, Stability

"The tangled strands of history allow for little neatness," James MacGregor Burns has written of the shift from the New Deal to World War II. Although there was no precise time or place when the Farm Security Administration (FSA) lost its balance, there was a turning of the tide during the period from the convening of Congress in January, 1940, to the appropriations hearings in the House in January, two years later. With the mounting partisanship of the election year, with the growing preoccupation of Roosevelt with foreign affairs and the war in Europe, with the increasing resistance of Congress to the President, with the crescendo of demands for curtailment of non-defense governmental spending and for an end to "sociological experimentation," and with the coalescence of opposition to the New Deal, the foundations on which the strength of the FSA had rested during the 1930's began to crumble.[2]

1. Arthur C. Millspaugh, *Democracy, Efficiency, Stability* (Washington, D.C.: The Brookings Institution, 1942), p. 428.
2. James MacGregor Burns, *Roosevelt: The Lion and the Fox* (New York: Harcourt, Brace & World, 1956), p. 383; F.D.R., *Public Papers* (1940), Vol. 9, p. 16.

Strange as it now may seem—with wisdom of hindsight, perhaps—the momentum of the depression years persisted in the thinking and behavior of agricultural leaders for almost two years after Europe had plunged into war, despite the mounting fury of battle and the growing realization in the United States that American agriculture would probably have to feed the free world. Following the attack on Pearl Harbor, however, as programs and policies of the U.S. Department of Agriculture (USDA) were painfully reviewed and adjusted, as wartime production became the paramount goal, and as the reaction against the New Deal unfolded, the leaders of the FSA were compelled to fight for their lives.

Orientation to War

Three weeks after Adolph Hitler's panzer forces smashed into Poland in September, 1939, departmental personnel received a message from Secretary of Agriculture Henry A. Wallace that set the tone for the USDA: "I urge American farmers to proceed with their production plans as if the outbreak in Europe had not occurred." Pointing to the existing surpluses of cotton, wheat, corn, meat animals, and other major farm commodities, he confidently predicted that "the need for increases in supplies can be anticipated in ample time to make any necessary increases in acreages."

This was the spirit of "business-as-usual" that prevailed in American agriculture for eighteen months, despite the deepening involvement of the United States in assisting the Allied nations. Most of the leaders of the USDA, especially those whose agency programs and personal careers had been linked to conservation, acreage reduction, price enhancement, and the problem of surpluses, were more fearful of hasty expansion of production and repetition of other mistakes of World War I than they were about meeting the new demands being imposed by the so-called defense program. As late as December, 1940, Secretary Claude R. Wickard, who had replaced Wallace only a few months earlier, still believed that despite the changed world conditions, established policies were still called for—price assurance to producers of export commodities, incentive payments to encourage conservation practices, programs to increase food consumption at home, an improved land purchase and resettlement program, and greater technical cooperation among agencies of the USDA. There seemed to be no sense of official concern about the need for expansion of farm production.[3]

For the leaders of the FSA, the defense program represented a potential threat to the viability of their agency. Writing in January, 1940, a staff committee reported portentously to Will W. Alexander as follows:

> ... the continuation of activities connected with National Defense will absorb legislation and popular attention for some time in the future and ... there will be a tendency to economize on national programs connected with public welfare.

Meanwhile, it was suggested, the leaders of the FSA should try to justify the agency and its mission in terms of its contribution to the national defense. Writing in September, 1940, with France already gone and London reeling under the German Luftwaffe's fire bombs, Raymond C. Smith, an economist with the Bureau of Agricultural Economics (BAE) and a former FSA regional director, was declaring that the major purpose of the FSA was to make "a contribution to national defense ... through creating new opportunities for disadvantaged farm families [and] strengthening and improving democracy itself."[4]

Following the President's declaration of intention, at the end of 1940, that America would become "the great arsenal of democracy," and his signing of the Lend-Lease Act three months later, Secretary Wickard, defying considerable opposition within the USDA, announced his "Food for Defense" program as the beginning of the painful process of agricultural mobilization. During the months that followed, as the tempo of war increased, Wickard created the Office of Agricultural Defense Relations in the Office of the Secretary, and a system of USDA Defense Boards (later called War Boards) for coordination of action agencies in the field. In each state and county a Defense Board was established, composed of field representatives of the Agricultural Adjustment Administration (AAA), the Soil Con-

---

3. Will W. Alexander to Fellow-Workers, Sept. 26, 1939; "vaf" to C. B. Baldwin, Dec. 21, 1940; FSA, confidential memorandum, "Some Proposals for Meeting the New World Situation Confronting Agriculture" (n.d., n.n.), 1940; CBBP.

4. FSA, "Report of the Administrator's Committee on Cooperatives in Resettlement Communities," Jan. 2, 1940, Processed (n.d.), PVMP, p 33; James G. Maddox, address at regional FSA conference, Denver, Colo., Jan. (n.d.), 1940; Milo R. Perkins, address at Des Moines, Ia., Feb. 24, 1940; Raymond C. Smith, address at regional FSA conference in Indiana, Sept. 13, 1940; CBBP.

servation Service (SCS), the Farm Credit Administration (FCA), the BAE, the FSA, and other agencies.

To the chagrin of the Extension Service, the SCS, and the FSA, the whole system was organized around the structure of the AAA. The leaders of the FSA were particularly fearful that such an arrangement would destroy their agency's independence of the influence and control of commercial farming interests in the USDA. Laurence I. Hewes, Jr., the FSA regional director in California, described his experience as follows:

> Farm Security's long course of resistance to accepted channels of official agricultural institutions made this belated, unwilling surrender to their suzerainty most painful. I was in the position of an out-voted minority from the start. It was truly a humiliating experience.

This was the beginning of a struggle, over administrative coordination in the USDA, that was destined to continue throughout the war years.[5]

Another manifestation of the growing preoccupation with problems of farm production was the establishment in the summer of 1941, at the suggestion of the President, of an Agricultural Advisory Committee—Franklin D. Roosevelt called it the "food group"—to serve his administration and the USDA as a focus for discussion of food production problems. Although the membership of the group changed over time, it generally included the leaders of the major farm organizations, especially Edward A. O'Neal of the American Farm Bureau Federation (AFBF), James G. Patton of the National Farmers Union (NFU), Louis J. Taber of the National Grange, and John D. Miller of the National Cooperative Council. In practice, the committee served less as a serious policy body and more as a platform for debate over conflicting points of view. Eventually, Patton of the NFU was offended by the behavior of O'Neal of the AFBF, and he refused to participate in the committee as long as O'Neal remained.[6]

---

5. F.D.R., *Public Papers* (1940), Vol. 9, pp. 633-44; Claude R. Wickard, address at Charleston, S.C., press release, Apr. 19, 1941, CBBP; *New York Times*, Apr. 14, 1941; Bela Gold, *Wartime Economic Planning in Agriculture* (New York: Columbia Univ. Press, 1949), pp. 19-30; Dean Albertson, *Roosevelt's Farmer* (New York: Columbia Univ. Press, 1961), pp. 180-248; Laurence I. Hewes, Jr., *Boxcar in the Sand* (New York: Knopf, 1957), p. 155; USDA, Secretary's Memorandum 921, July 7, 1941, NA, RG 16.

It was believed at the time that Wickard's choice of the AAA field organization, as the basis for the boards, was influenced by the fact that his own previous experience in the USDA had been with the AAA—he understood the agency and trusted it.

6. Wickard to Edwin M. Watson, Aug. 29, 1941, NA, RG 16; Watson to

The FSA Goes to War / [329]

"There are wild horses loose in the world," wrote John D. Black, the Harvard University economist, in November, 1941, "and the first task is to bring them to leash." It was now over two years since the outbreak of the war and on the very eve of Japan's attack on the United States. Finally, at virtually the eleventh hour, Wickard committed the USDA unequivocally to the mobilization of agriculture when he launched his "Food for Freedom" campaign, and a few weeks later, against the backdrop of the calamity in the Pacific, he proceeded to centralize responsibility for program execution in the office of the Secretary. The USDA was now at war.[7]

Meanwhile, for the leaders of the FSA, the frustrating "national defense" period had been a time of opportunity and peril. The opportunity lay in the assignment of emergency defense tasks, as we have seen, such as transportation of farm laborers to areas of labor shortage, relocation of farm families dislocated by defense construction, and the defense housing program. There was peril, however, in the problem of adjusting the agency's rationale to the new circumstances of wartime America.

In the spring of 1940, Secretary Wallace had asserted before Senator Richard B. Russell's appropriations subcommittee that the rural rehabilitation program of the FSA "constitutes a first line of defense for hundreds of needy farm families which are suffering most severely from the economic dislocations of the war," and this was the theme that the leaders of the FSA invoked during the months that followed. To buttress their argument, they later pointed to the Census of 1940 which revealed that in 1939 nearly 57 per cent of all farmers in the United States had had gross annual incomes of less than $800. Low-income farmers, they asserted, still constituted the majority of the country's farm operators, despite returning prosperity for many of the larger-scale commercial farmers. Few crumbs were falling from the table.[8]

By 1942, Wallace's argument, as a justification for the FSA, was losing its appeal. For an increasing number of Americans, the de-

---

Edward A. O'Neal, Albert S. Goss, James G. Patton, and Ezra Taft Benson, Sept. 1, 1943, FDRL, OF 227–Misc.; Samuel B. Bledsoe, COHC, Vol. 2, pp. 250, 280, 369–70.

7. John D. Black, "Fundamental Elements in the Current Agricultural Situation," *Journal of Farm Economics*, Vol. 23 (Nov., 1941), pp. 712–25; USDA, Secretary's Memorandum 960, Dec. 13, 1941, NA, RG 16; Wickard to Harold D. Smith, Jan. 10, 1942, FDRL, OF 1; Albertson, *Roosevelt's Farmer*, pp. 250–51.

8. U.S., Congress, Senate, Appropriations Committee, Hearings, 76th Cong., 3d Sess., *Emergency Relief Appropriation Bill for 1941* (Washington, D.C.: GPO, 1940), p. 29.

pression was over or ending. With the attention of Congress, the White House, and the USDA now turning to the problems of farm production, the leaders of the FSA faced two problems of strategy: (1) how to prevent wartime dislocations from undermining the gains already made in the condition of chronically impoverished farm families, and (2) finding a more tenable and war-related *raison d'être* for the agency as a whole.

A clue to what their new strategy should be was suggested in a study conducted by John D. Black, assisted by Charles M. Hardin, at the request of Chester C. Davis, then director of the National Defense Advisory Commission. Black's conclusions, in part as follows, were music to C. B. Baldwin:

> Per dollar of public money paid to farm families or spent upon them, our studies indicate that the [FSA] produces much higher returns in increased productivity and permanent benefit to the families. It would therefore be a very unwise course of action to cut down on this particular type of expenditure at this time.... *It is difficult to overestimate the importance of carefully planned supervision to the success of the war food production program* [italics not in the original].

In reinforcement of Black's unequivocal support of the FSA, the staffs of the BAE and the FSA estimated that of almost six million farms in the United States at the time, approximately three million could expand their output within a year—over one million of them very substantially.[9]

FSA Administrator Baldwin and his assistants therefore decided to exploit what came to be known as the "small farmer issue." Partly because they sincerely believed that the mass of low-income or marginal farm families could make a significant contribution to wartime food needs, and partly in response to the requirements of organizational maintenance, they proceeded, at a regional conference in April, to prepare their plans for a shift of the agency's emphasis from social welfare goals to maximization of farm production. The larger commercial farms, they reasoned, were already suffering from labor, machinery, and other shortages, and were operating at or near peak efficiency, while the production of smaller or marginal farms could be greatly expanded through fuller employment of resident labor and provision of credit and supervision. And it could and should be done without sacrificing social welfare goals. Unless the small-scale farmer were given an opportunity to increase his production, he would not share in rising agricultural prosperity and would be forced

---

9. *Senate Hearings*, Agr. Approp. (1943), 77th Cong., 2d Sess., pp. 86–87; Gold, *Wartime Economic Planning in Agriculture*, pp. 181–82, 276–77.

down to the status of laborer, or out of agriculture entirely. Expansion of the rural rehabilitation program would help to retard the headlong wartime exodus of low-income rural families to the cities of the nation. Finally, they reasoned candidly, such a reformulation of organizational purpose would probably save the FSA from the doom that was awaiting other New Deal agencies.

On the other hand, critics of the FSA and those who had little faith in the productive capacities of small-scale farmers contended that before the war, 50 per cent of the farmers in the United States had produced 89 per cent of the country's commercial farm production, and therefore the increased production from small farms would be comparatively negligible. Instead of wasting public funds on the low-income farmer, whose ignorance and inefficiency unfitted him for modern farming altogether, it would be prudent during the emergency to invest in assisting the large-scale commercial farmer to increase his production. Now that a labor shortage was developing on such farms, the small-scale farmer and his family should be encouraged to seek work as farm hands or as industrial workers.

During the hectic days following the attack on Pearl Harbor, the leaders of the FSA and of the USDA agreed to promote the small farmer issue. At a special conference in Washington in January, they announced that the FSA and the small farmer would be harnessed to war. The major innovation would be the granting of small loans and provision of technical assistance to a large number of families not participating in FSA programs, in order to increase their production for home consumption, thereby relieving demands on the market. In working with the regular client families, every effort would be exerted to maximize production without sacrificing rehabilitation goals.

In June, 1942, Donald M. Nelson, head of the War Production Board, created a Foods Requirements Committee and appointed Secretary Wickard its chairman. Although the committee was far from the authoritative top level instrument that Wickard believed was necessary for directing war food production, he proceeded to perform the rituals of coordination. On August 21, still unhappy about his lack of effective power, he issued a directive to the FSA, specifying a wartime food program in which all phases of the agency's work would be mobilized for the food production needs of the nation.[10]

10. Wickard to Baldwin, Aug. 21, 1942, NA, RG 96; FSA, proceedings of Administrator's staff conference, Nov. 25–29, 1942; author's interviews with Baldwin, Robert W. Hudgens.

While this process of orientation to war was occurring, important changes were taking place in the leadership of the USDA and the FSA. Let us, therefore, return to 1940 and briefly trace the shift which produced a changing of the guard.

Changing of the Guard

In no other manner are the changing fortunes of an organization more readily revealed than in the pattern of top leadership. The departure of Alexander in June, 1940, was one of the clues to the future.

"Dr. Will" was at this time only fifty-six years old, but he was weary of his political and administrative tasks as Administrator. Having delegated much responsibility to his assistants—to C. B. Baldwin in particular—he had spent as much time as possible traveling in the field, evangelizing the doctrine of the FSA. A sensitive man, he was more effective in dealing with individuals than with groups, and with individual congressmen than with appropriations committees. The painful annual expedition to Capitol Hill to plead for his budget, increasing hostility against the FSA, the unsettlement of his personal domestic life caused by his frequent travels and his personal involvements in Washington, and his growing realization that the times called for a more tough-skinned Farm Security Administrator persuaded him to accept a vice presidency of the Rosenwald Fund. Just before his departure in June, he went to say farewell to Secretary Wallace. "As I turned to leave," Alexander later reported, "Wallace looked up and said, 'Will, don't you think the New Deal is undertaking to do too much for the Negroes?'" With this, the former Methodist minister departed, to march once again to the distant trumpet of racial equality.[11]

On July 1, at the suggestion of Alexander, which was heartily endorsed by Paul H. Appleby in the Secretary's office, the FSA found its combat commander in a very different man—C. B. "Beanie"

11. Alexander, COHC, pp. 658–65; Wilma Dykeman and James Stokely, *Seeds of Southern Change: The Life of Will Alexander* (Chicago: Univ. of Chicago Press, 1962), pp. 245–49; author's interviews with Alexander, Baldwin, Mrs. Eleanor Roosevelt.

Mrs. Roosevelt confided to the author that she had long felt that Henry A. Wallace neither fully understood nor adequately sympathized with the problems of the American Negro, and that Wallace was sometimes resentful, while he was Secretary of Agriculture, of her efforts to prod the USDA toward a more positive approach to the colored farmer's needs.

Baldwin. In the thirty-eighth year of his life, this son of a flour miller in Radford, Virginia, disciple of Rexford G. Tugwell, friend and admirer of Appleby, veteran of seven years in the USDA, and highly competent administrator whose managerial skills were curiously blended with ideological zeal took command of an agency over which the storm clouds were gathering.

Profound changes in command were also taking place in the USDA itself. In January, 1940, to achieve greater economic security, in preparation for the expected departure of Wallace as Secretary, and to provide stronger leadership for the Extension Service, M. L. Wilson returned to that agency, which he had left in 1926, to become its director. Appleby, who could have replaced Wilson as Under Secretary but who looked upon that position as a sinecure, preferred to remain where he was. Instead, he proposed to Wallace that the appropriate man for the position was Wickard—until 1933 a dirt farmer in Indiana and a fairly influential Democrat in midwestern farm circles. For the past few years, he had been director of the North Central Division of the AAA. Appleby believed that Wickard's agrarian and midwestern orientation would strengthen the President in the farm belt and he presumed that Wickard, like Wilson, would collaborate with his carefully built system of secretarial management in the Department. Through a process of elimination, and to the surprise of many people in the USDA, including the Indiana farmer himself, Wickard, on February 29, 1940, was promoted over the ranks to become Under Secretary of Agriculture.

During the following six months, ill-feeling developed between Wickard, who chafed in the honorific but relatively powerless second-ranking position, and Appleby, who became disappointed when Wickard refused to serve as a figurehead. Finally, in August, 1940, to virtually everyone's consternation in the USDA, Roosevelt and Wallace agreed that Wickard should replace Wallace, who had been nominated as the Democratic candidate for Vice President. Their decision was presumably based on a desire to maintain continuity in the Department.

At the same time, with some reluctance, Appleby consented to serve as Under Secretary. Two more mismatched men could not have been harnessed together. In background, intellect, experience, working habits, and personal relations, Wickard and Appleby were poles apart. However, Appleby viewed the arrangement as temporary, because for some time there had been talk in the Department about creating a British-type career assistant secretaryship in charge of departmental administration. Appleby hoped that during the next session of Congress appropriate legislation would be enacted and that he would be appointed to the new position. Meanwhile, he proceeded to operate as he had for so many years under Wallace.[12]

After the President's inauguration in January, 1941, all hope for a reorganization withered, and within a few weeks Wickard grasped the power of the Secretaryship and proceeded to dismantle Appleby's directorate. "I witnessed the complete disintegration within a few months of the gifted managerial group . . . which had grown up in the Wallace period under the leadership of Paul Appleby," Charles McKinley wrote in retrospect. In Wickard's nervous eagerness to assert himself and to bring in his own staff, he completely misunderstood that Appleby's system had been designed and employed as a staff instrument to strengthen the Secretary's control of the Department. Part of the problem was Appleby's habitual impatience with small talk and slow thinking, and part was Wickard's inability to work with a strong person and his mistrust of Appleby's motives.[13]

For the FSA, these changes meant the loss of crucial sources of institutional strength. Appleby was effectively isolated from major departmental decisions, and was left to languish in the office of Under Secretary. Samuel B. Bledsoe, who had served for many years under Milton S. Eisenhower in the Office of Information of the USDA, and who had become a bitter anti-New Dealer, Roosevelt-hater, and isolationist, replaced Appleby's friend, James D. LeCron, as assistant to the Secretary. T. Roy Reid, for many years an FSA regional director, came in to replace James L. McCamy as manager in the Secretary's office, but lasted only a few months before being appointed director of personnel for the USDA. Bledsoe, who by now was openly an enemy of Baldwin and the FSA, within a few months became executive assistant to the Secretary, to serve in a capacity somewhat comparable to that which Appleby had filled for Wallace.

---

12. Albertson, *Roosevelt's Farmer*, pp. 129–34, 150–59, 183–84; author's interviews with Paul H. Appleby, T. Roy Reid, Baldwin.

13. Charles McKinley, "Federal Administrative Pathology, and the Separation of Powers," *Public Administration Review*, Vol. XI (Winter, 1951), pp. 17–25; Gladys Baker to author, Mar. 22, 1967.

Baker has reported as follows on the relations between Wickard and Appleby: "Paul didn't waste time with small talk. He always wanted to get to the point in a hurry. A person with so much sensitivity and feeling of inferiority [as Wickard] would be prone to misinterpret Appleby's attitude. Furthermore, from my observation of Wickard and the people around him, I concluded that he was incapable of working with a strong person . . . . Paul told me that recommending the appointment of Wickard for Secretary was his biggest mistake."

The FSA Goes to War / [335]

Finally, the FSA lost Wallace. Wickard was personally sympathetic toward the agency—he probably understood the problems of the low-income marginal farmer more thoroughly than did Wallace—but he did not have the political stature in the administration or his predecessor's sophistication, nor did he have the close rapport with the President which Wallace had developed over the years. Also, by his own act, Wickard lost Appleby as an asset in helping to keep the Secretary of Agriculture out of trouble. In many ways, Wickard personally symbolized all of the rusticity for which some of the leaders of the FSA had contempt. Furthermore, Wickard felt personally insecure in navigating the shoals of farm politics, and therefore was more prone than Wallace toward appeasement of demands from such powerful quarters as the "economy bloc" in Congress, the AFBF, and the state agricultural institutions. Presumably with Bledsoe to help influence him, Wickard eventually grew distrustful of the FSA and its leaders, and therefore the gulf between the FSA and the leaders of the USDA widened.

The Tide Turns in Congress

Although the "golden years" for the FSA continued until 1942, the year 1940 marked a turning of the tide in relations with Congress. Problems of national defense, partisan conflict related to the election campaign of 1940, growth of the economy drive, and the accumulation of complaints and grievances generally against the FSA were some of the factors which contributed to a change in the political climate.

One of the FSA programs which attracted much political lightning, despite its very minor part in the overall repertory of the agency, was the resettlement project program. Prior to 1940, the program received energetic criticism, but it also enjoyed a large measure of sympathetic support, especially while the urgencies of the depression continued and the New Deal remained strong. Once prosperity began to return, however, and the nation's attention shifted to the greater anxieties of World War II, the vulnerability of the program provided a highly accessible target for those who were aiming not only at the FSA, but also at larger prey—the New Deal and the Roosevelt administration. In view of the special attention that the program attracted from congressional critics during the turning of the tide, it seems appropriate here to stop the clock of our chronology briefly, to return to the early days of the FSA, and to trace the political conflict over the resettlement projects and related activities.

In 1937, as we have already seen in chapter seven of this narrative, there was agreement in the FSA and in the USDA that no new resettlement projects would be established. During the first year, in the absence of a clear congressional or executive policy governing the schedule according to which projects would be sold to participating families and liquidated, the leaders of the FSA operated on the basis of Title IV of the Bankhead-Jones Farm Tenant Act, which provided simply for "completion and management" of the projects inherited from the Resettlement Administration. In some of these projects, additional land was purchased to make them more economical units of operation, and cooperative loans were granted, as we have seen, for industrial and other enterprises.

In 1938, when Congress started the practice of appropriating funds directly to the Secretary of Agriculture for rural rehabilitation purposes, it provided that the use of the funds in the resettlement project program should be limited to "liquidation and management of resettlement projects," and in subsequent years continued the restriction. Meanwhile, the leaders of the FSA, in the absence of anything more specific than the vague appropriation language, proceeded to complete and operate the inherited projects. They also went ahead with their plans for expansion of the program of cooperative leasing associations (based on individual family-type of farming) and cooperative farms, whose collective character made them easy to be confused with the inherited collective farms and cooperative farming communities inherited from the Resettlement Administration.

All of this—completion and management of the resettlement projects, development of land leasing associations and cooperative farming associations, and purchase of land for relocation corporations employed in the resettlement of families displaced by the defense program—was done openly and with the full knowledge and support of the Secretary of Agriculture, and, presumably, of the President. On June 30, 1938, for instance, Assistant FSA Administrator Baldwin reported to Alexander, who was in London, on progress being made in the resettlement project program:[14]

On Wednesday the Secretary approved cooperative loans for the construc-

---

14. Baldwin to Alexander, June 30, 1938, CBBP.

tion of Terrebonne [a cooperative plantation or "collective farm" for approximately seventy families, initiated by the Resettlement Administration in Louisiana].... Transylvania [a cooperative farming community for approximately 160 families, initiated by the Resettlement Administration in Louisiana], Scuppernong [a cooperative farming community for approximately 125 families, initiated by the Federal Emergency Relief Administration (FERA) in North Carolina], and the extension of Ferda [a cooperative plantation near Plum Bayou in Arkansas]. The Secretary also approved the use of $5,000,000 of Corporation [Reconstruction Finance Corporation] funds for land purchase. I have just received a letter from Roy Reid [T. Roy Reid, FSA Regional Director in Arkansas] in which he said that they expect to locate a large plantation for a Negro project in Mississippi within a short while. If this is done, I feel reasonably sure that the Secretary will approve a cooperative loan for the construction of the necessary facilities. I have also had a letter from Roy indicating that he is going ahead with plans for the development of the three plantations in Madison County, Louisiana, for Negroes.

By 1940, as we shall see in the pages that follow, congressional criticism had begun to increase against a number of FSA practices—alleged "slowness" in liquidating resettlement projects, continued promotion of land leasing and cooperative farming associations, the granting of ninety-nine year leases to some of the associations, and land purchasing generally. As James G. Maddox later observed, it was easy for critical members of Congress to connect all of these activities in their minds and to become suspicious—almost paranoiac—that the FSA "was promoting large-scale land nationalization schemes."

However, these activities were not being conducted secretly. None of them had been carried on without the clear approval of President Roosevelt and Secretary Wallace. And during the late 1930's, these enterprises had enjoyed more favorable press treatment than critics in later years would recall. Had there been clear congressional or executive policy governing the liquidation of the resettlement projects, Alexander, Baldwin, and their assistants would have complied, although regretfully. Until such a clarification of policy, they refused to be stampeded.

Their resistance was partly due to their fundamental opposition to anything that might contribute to the dissolution of the agency's scope of operations—a common bureaucratic posture. They believed that hasty liquidation would jeopardize the welfare of the families and the security of the government's investment. It was not until the summer of 1942 that the leaders of the FSA were given a clearcut directive in the matter, in the form of a letter from William A. Jump, Director of Budget and Finance in the USDA. In view of the insistent demands by congressional appropriations committees for liquidation of the resettlement projects, Jump wrote, it would be advantageous to both the FSA and USDA for the agency to prepare a timetable for liquidation of the projects over the next two or three years. The continued refusal of the leaders of the FSA to be stampeded into hasty abandonment was at least partially vindicated a year later when War Food Administrator Chester C. Davis—he was certainly no apologist for the FSA—felt compelled to remind Representative Harold D. Cooley, chairman of a special congressional committee to investigate the FSA, that the projects should be sold "only as rapidly as is consistent with the financial interest of the Government and with protecting the low-income farm families for whom they are developed." With this as background, let us now return to the shift in the tide for the FSA generally in its relations with Congress.[15]

Congressional consideration of the budget for FSA, during the spring of 1940, provided the focus for resentment against some of the agency's controversial practices. In the House, for instance, a provision was attached to the Emergency Relief Appropriation Act, for fiscal year 1941, prohibiting the use of rural rehabilitation funds to finance industrial, processing, and purchasing activities by cooperative associations, and forbidding the use of the funds for loans to enable FSA clients to join any cooperative associations not already in existence. At the same time, Democratic Representative Clarence Cannon of Missouri, chairman of the agricultural subcommittee of the House Appropriations Committee and one of the congressmen who had long objected to some of the practices of the FSA, succeeded in having funds for the tenant purchase program eliminated from the Department of Agriculture Appropriation Bill, for fiscal year 1941. Although Cannon's ire was directed more against the controversial rural rehabilitation, resettlement project, and cooperative association activities, his stroke against the tenant purchase program was viewed by leaders of the FSA as a reckless attempt to coerce the agency. A major effort was required, including the personal intervention of Senators John H. Bankhead and Richard B. Russell, House

---

15. Maddox, "The FSA," p. 493; William A. Jump to Baldwin, June 23, 1942, NA, RG 16; Chester C. Davis to Harold D. Cooley, June 17, 1943, CBBP; testimony of Baldwin, *House Hearings*, Agr. Approp. (1943), 77th Cong., 1st Sess. pp. 207, 223, 744; author's interviews with Appleby, Baldwin, Hudgens.

The favorable press treatment of the resettlement project program during the late 1930's was reflected in the following: *Memphis* (Tenn.) *Press-Scimitar*,

Speaker William B. Bankhead, Budget Director Harold D. Smith, and President Roosevelt to have the tenant purchase item restored in the final appropriation act.[16]

A less dramatic, but considerably more successful, effort to restrict the operations of the FSA was led by Democratic Representative Malcolm C. Tarver of Georgia. A conservative southerner and veteran of seven consecutive terms in the House, he had spent many of those years as a member of the agricultural subcommittee of the House Appropriations Committee. "Judge Tarver," as he preferred to be addressed (before coming to Washington, he had been a judge in the Georgia Superior Court), conceived his role to be that of an advocate of the interests of small-scale farmers, operating fifty or sixty acres, and to protect them against what he believed were "dangerous" trends in the country—concentration of land ownership, "selfish" efforts by large-scale commercial farmers attempting to monopolize the wealth in agriculture, executive "encroachments" on Congress, the rise of the organized labor movement which threatened the labor peace in the South, and the specter of Communism.

While Democrat Clarence Cannon of Missouri and Republican Everett M. Dirksen of Illinois were openly and consistently sympathetic to the AFBF and the cause of commercial farming, Tarver was a strong advocate of credit, price, and other farm policies that would aid, or at least not penalize, the small-farm operators of his district. He was moved, not by moral indignation about chronic rural poverty or social inequities, but rather by an orthodox agrarian reverence for land ownership, the family farm, and the stability of the southern rural way of life. Over the years, he had become well-informed and skillful in overseeing funds for the USDA, and thus became influential in the appropriations subcommittee, where he

---

Mar. 29, 1938; *Kansas City* (Mo.) *Weekly Star*, Apr. 6, 1938; *Greensboro* (N.C.) *News*, Apr. 10, 1938; *Marshall* (Tex.) *News-Messenger*, Apr. 20, 1938; *Birmingham* (Ala.) *Post*, Apr. 22, 1938; *Clarksburg* (W. Va.) *Exponent*, May 27, 1938; *Washington* (D.C.) *Daily News*, July 21, 1938; *Richmond* (Va.) *News-Leader*, Feb. 25, 1939.

16. Emergency Relief Appropriation Act, fiscal year 1941, 54 Stat. 611. John H. Bankhead to Franklin D. Roosevelt, Apr. 27, 1940; Harold D. Smith to Roosevelt, Mar. 16, 1940, FDRL, OF 1. The following newspaper editorials: "On With It," *Birmingham* (Ala.) *Age-Herald*, Feb. 7, 1940; "Restore This Appropriation," *Atlanta* (Ga.) *Journal*, Feb. 19, 1940; "Shall the Farm Tenancy Program be Stopped?" *Greenville* (S.C.) *News*, Feb. 20, 1940; "Foolish Economy," *Miami* (Fla.) *News*, Mar. 3, 1940; "Save the Farm Tenant Plan," *Birmingham* (Ala.) *News*, Apr. 28, 1940.

frequently served as a countervailing force against the influence of Cannon and Dirksen.[17]

During the 1930's, Tarver's ambivalence toward the FSA—some of his liberal critics called it confusion or blind stubbornness—became pronounced. He opposed many of the rural rehabilitation activities on the grounds that they tended to raise the level of needy farm families "too rapidly," which was "morally bad for them." He viewed the purchase and subdivision of bankrupt and abandoned southern plantations and the resettlement projects as "colonization and un-American." Provision of costly supervisory services for client families, he believed, tended to destroy their sense of self-reliance. And he considered the migratory farm labor program as a subversive attempt to "steal" the labor supply from the South, for the benefit of large-scale farm operators in the West. By 1940, Judge Tarver also had become suspicious of the political bonds that seemed to be growing between the FSA and some of the "dangerous" liberal and labor groups in the North.

During these years, he had supported the tenant purchase program, in the belief that government loans to farm tenants for promotion of farm ownership were legitimate, but as the trend toward larger loans for purchase of larger farms developed, he protested that the program was discriminating against the smaller-scale farmers of his district. Unable or unwilling to understand the differences between successful farming on small acreages in the South and efficient commercial farming in the Middle West, the Great Plains, or the ranching areas of the West, he began, in 1940, to demand restrictions on the tenant purchase program. During the subcommittee hearings on the appropriation for fiscal year 1941, he argued as follows:[18]

We are dealing here with the very poorest class of agricultural people. I think around two-thirds of the farmers in my district are tenant farmers. I do not see the point in buying one of those men a farm worth $7,500,

---

17. William J. Block, *The Separation of the Farm Bureau and the Extension Service* (Urbana: Univ. of Illinois Press, 1960), pp. 40, 264, has shown the enduring allegiance of Democrat Cannon of Missouri and Republican Dirksen of Illinois to the AFBF.

Judge Tarver was destined to be defeated in the Democratic congressional primary in 1946, largely, we are told, because of the campaign against him which was sparked by the Political Action Committee of the Congress of Industrial Organizations (CIO). See V. O. Key, *Southern Politics in State and Nation* (New York: Knopf, 1949), p. 657.

18. *House Hearings*, Agr. Approp. (1941), 76th Cong., 3d Sess., p. 952; Paul V. Maris, *"the land is mine"* (Washington, D.C.: GPO, 1950), pp. 168-70.

The FSA Goes to War / [341]

when you could buy four farms, for four tenants, at one-quarter of the price, which would buy a fairly good farm in my district for a tenant and one with which 99 percent of the tenants in my district would be satisfied. In other words, I do not think the purpose of this program is to buy expensive farms for a few who are selected but to buy farms of moderate value for as many tenants as you can. And I cannot understand why you buy expensive farms for some of those tenants, thereby depriving other tenants of a chance to get any farm at all.

The leaders of the FSA countered with the argument that they were attempting to preserve equity within each region, that an arbitrary restriction on size of loan, based on the needs of marginal cotton farmers in Georgia, would automatically eliminate farmers in the Middle West and the Great Plains, and, furthermore, that to grant tenant purchase loans for farms that were not economical farming units would amount to a subsidy to inefficiency.

Tarver prevailed, however, and he succeeded in having the so-called "Tarver Amendment" attached to the Department of Agriculture Appropriation Act for fiscal year 1941. It provided that no tenant purchase loans should be granted for purchase of farms of greater value than the average farm unit of thirty acres and more in the county, parish, or locality in which the purchase was to be made. The restriction was continued in subsequent appropriations for the program. As a result, the tenant purchase program was seriously impeded in finding adequate-sized farms for purchase, and in many parts of the country, tenant purchase borrowers were compelled to purchase farms in the more isolated and less desirable farming areas. The rising land prices that accompanied defense mobilization helped to aggravate the situation. Although the "Tarver Amendment" directly affected only the tenant purchase program, which was, it should be recalled, only a minor part of the agency's repertory, the whole affair was symptomatic of the increasing difficulties for the FSA in Congress.[19]

The turning of the tide in Congress in 1940 coincided with another development—the declaration of war by the leaders of the AFBF. During the presidential campaign of 1940, they grew increasingly more alarmed as partisan competition seemed to threaten their

---

19. Department of Agriculture Appropriation Act, fiscal year 1941, 54 Stat. 532; John D. Black, "Notes on 'Poor Land' and 'Submarginal Land'," *Journal of Farm Economics*, Vol. 27 (May, 1945), pp. 345–74; Charles M. Hardin, "The Bureau of Agricultural Economics Under Fire," *Journal of Farm Economics*, Vol. 28 (Aug., 1946), p. 649; BAE, "Attitudes Toward the Tenant Purchase Program," Study 122, Processed (Jan., 1946), p. 60.

bi-partisan coalition of the South and the Middle West—remember, AFBF president Edward A. O'Neal was an Alabama Democrat and vice president Earl C. Smith was an Illinois Republican. Two weeks before election day, O'Neal sent a telegram to Roosevelt, urging that in a forthcoming campaign address he stress "the importance of preserving the present farm program with continued effort to improve and decentralize administration." The suggestion was aimed, of course, not only at the FSA, but at the AAA, the SCS, and the field organizations and farmers committees of the action agencies in the USDA generally. Appleby advised the President against biting O'Neal's hook because, in Appleby's words, O'Neal "wants administration turned over to the State Extension Service and County Agents."[20]

Shortly after the votes were counted in November, when it became apparent that Roosevelt and Wallace had lost support among midwestern farmers, O'Neal again wrote to Roosevelt. He pointed to the split in agriculture and the loss of support in the Midwest, and, implying that the midwestern farm vote was a reaction to the policies of the USDA, he suggested that the only way to heal the breach was to appoint a new Secretary of Agriculture who could win the confidence of farmers—Roosevelt should replace Wickard with the Farm Bureau's friend, Chester C. Davis.

To punctuate their new mood of militant hostility, the leaders of the AFBF assembled in December at their annual conference in Baltimore, where they proposed a major reorganization of the USDA. In other words, if they could not dictate the selection of the Secretary of Agriculture, they would attempt to strip the office of its powers. In essence, they proposed that administration of all action programs of the USDA be centralized in the hands of a five-man "non-partisan board," composed of the "nation's agricultural leaders," with the Extension Service responsible for administration of all action programs in the states. Regarding the FSA specifically, they proposed that a thorough investigation be conducted of all of its activities, with special emphasis on the resettlement projects, the cooperative program, the purchase of land, and "the tendency [of the FSA] to expand its services to farmers who are not in need of relief." Following such an investigation, necessary steps should be taken to curtail the agency's programs.

Early in January, 1941, O'Neal, Smith, and some of the state Farm Bureau leaders personally carried their proposals to the President.

20. O'Neal to Roosevelt, Oct. 23, 1940; Appleby to Roosevelt, Oct. 27, 1940; FDRL, OF 1350.

"Here it is!" Roosevelt wrote in a note to Wickard, with the AFBF proposals attached, "What do I do next?" O'Neal and Smith were shrewd politicians, and they were realists. They had no serious expectation of success at the White House, and in the Congress they knew that the New Deal still enjoyed considerable Senate support. They therefore pressed their attack in the agricultural subcommittee of the House Appropriations Committee where they knew they would receive a welcome.[21]

On January 30, 1941, FSA Administrator Baldwin was called to testify, and under the hostile prodding of Tarver, Cannon, and Dirksen, he was interrogated in cat-and-mouse fashion and compelled to answer to a long bill of grievances against the FSA. Twelve days later, O'Neal and Smith, accompanied by eleven of their state Farm Bureau leaders, testified, and for the next three days were cordially encouraged to delineate their proposals.[22]

"In this grave hour of international crisis it is imperative that we have domestic unity," O'Neal declared, and to secure that unity, the AFBF proposed two goals: parity prices for farmers, and reorganization of the USDA. To eliminate duplication, jurisdictional conflicts, excessive administrative expenses, and confusion and inconvenience for the farmer, the Department should follow the "gratifying" example of the Tennessee Valley Authority (TVA) and work more closely through the state colleges of agriculture and extension services. Responsibility for national coordination of farm policy and administration should be placed in the hands of an "independent, five-man, nonpartisan board, appointed by the President and confirmed by the Senate," which should report periodically to Congress and to the President or the Secretary of Agriculture. All action agencies should be coordinated under the board. The FSA should be transferred to the FCA—its lending activities to be administered by the latter agency, and the farm and home planning function to be absorbed by the Extension Service. Throughout their testimony, the leaders of the AFBF stressed the charge that the FSA had corrupted the government's assault on rural poverty and that in the hands of the FCA and the Extension Service, the low-income farmer would be served more effectively and economically.

21. O'Neal to Roosevelt, Nov. 30, 1940, FDRL, OF 1350; Roosevelt to Wickard, with enclosures, Jan. 9, 1941, FDRL, OF 1; AFBF, *Nation's Agriculture*, Vol. XVI (Jan., 1941), pp. 18–20; Christiana Campbell, *The Farm Bureau and the New Deal* (Urbana: Univ. of Illinois Press, 1962), pp. 183–85.

22. House Hearings, Agr. Approp. (1942), 77th Cong., 1st Sess., Pt. 2, pp. 57–163.

Judge Tarver was from Georgia, but by nature he was a Missourian. Reorganization of the USDA, he insisted, was an executive affair. If there were a need for congressional consideration of the matter, discussion should be in the House Committee on Agriculture, not a subcommittee of the Committee on Appropriations. Subcommittee Chairman Cannon of Missouri, however, was effusive in his praise as he thanked O'Neal and Smith for "the most valuable contribution which has been made by anybody who has appeared before the committee this year." All other witnesses came for favors to beg or axes to grind, Cannon declared, and therefore, "It is a novelty to find someone asking economy, simplification, coordination . . . we hope that you will continue these studies, and that you will be in a position to elaborate on it next [congressional] session."[23]

In a written rebuttal to the AFBF, submitted to the subcommittee for the record, Secretary Wickard accused them of playing the game of divide and conquer. The "crux of the matter," he asserted, lay in the following issues:[24]

  (a) Shall the unified national farm program be broken down into 48 State programs?
  (b) Shall any of these separate State programs be dominated in any State by a farm organization?
  (c) Shall a State official have sole authority to nominate the members of any Federal board?
  (d) Shall we experiment with a discredited form of board administration now of all times in a period calling for sensitive reactions to world forces?
  (e) Shall we sacrifice the specialized zeal of the Farm Security Administration? Of the AAA? Of the SCS?
  (f) Does the Congress wish to establish a new principle in Federal-State relations under which States, though not required to match or even furnish any of the funds, are given responsibility for the execution of federally financed programs?

The subcommittee submitted a report to the House, which generally echoed the testimony of the AFBF. Specifically, they cited the work of the FSA as "exactly the character of work being done by the Extension Service agents and [it] undoubtedly constitutes a serious duplication." The House sustained the report and for fiscal year 1942 they went on to approve reduction of the rural rehabilitation loan fund authorization from $125 million to $100 million, and

---

23. *Ibid.*, pp. 396–522.
24. *Ibid.*, pp. 522–46, "Statement of the Secretary of Agriculture on American Farm Bureau Federation Suggestions," Feb. 25, 1941.

a cut of $7.3 million from the funds for rural rehabilitation administrative expenses. NFU president Patton was provoked to write a plea to the President:[25]

> I write to you in the anxious hope that you may find it possible and advisable to give by word, plan and action reassurances to the lower income groups that the advances which have been made during your administration will not be lost ... those who speak for agriculture while representing only the interests of the top one-fourth of American farmers are not entitled to be taken seriously.

Through the insistence of the Senate, and with the help of the President at a White House conference of Senate and House leaders, $20 million of the cut in rural rehabilitation loan authorizations and $6 million of the reduction in rural rehabilitation administrative expenses were finally restored. The prohibition against loans for membership in cooperatives was eliminated. There were no restrictions on the tenant purchase program, other than a continuation of the "Tarver Amendment."[26]

Through much of the remainder of 1941, the leaders of the FSA, caught between rising war fever, departmental indecision, mounting congressional hostility, and open opposition from the AFBF, lived with their anxieties. One of the brighter spots for them was the work of the House Select Committee to Investigate National Defense Migration, under the chairmanship of a loyal supporter of the FSA, Democratic Representative John H. Tolan of California, and composed of four other sympathetic members of the House. Ostensibly created to investigate the impact of the national defense program on migratory farm labor, the Tolan Committee became a thinly disguised champion of the FSA and of its handling of the migratory farm labor program. During 1941, they held public hearings throughout the United States, and Tolan, in his capacity as chairman of the committee, testified in support of the FSA at appropriation committee hearings.[27]

25. U.S., Congress, House, Appropriations Committee, House Report 176, Mar. 3, 1941, 77th Cong., 1st Sess. (Washington, D.C.: GPO, 1941), p. 4; Patton to Roosevelt, Apr. 7, 1941, NA, RG 16.
26. Harold D. Smith to Roosevelt, May 10, 1941, FDRL, OF 227; Department of Agriculture Appropriation Act, fiscal year 1942, 55 Stat. 408.
27. House Res. 63, Apr. 22, 1940.
In addition to Democratic Representative John H. Tolan of California, the House Select Committee to Investigate National Defense Migration (the Tolan Committee) included four additional House members who were sympathetic to the FSA—Democrats John J. Sparkman of Alabama and Laurence F. Arnold of Illinois, and Republicans Carl T. Curtis of Nebraska and Frank C. Osmers of New Jersey.

In November, with rumors circulating that Budget Director Smith and the "economy bloc" in Congress had agreed to cut drastically the FSA budget for fiscal year 1943, Tolan and some of his committee members paid a call on the Budget Bureau—they were briefed beforehand by members of Baldwin's staff. In their discussion at the Bureau they emphasized the wartime role that the FSA might play in the migratory labor program, in contributing to the nation's production needs, in serving low-income farm families not benefited by returning prosperity, and in helping to plan for the post-war slump that virtually everyone expected.

Assistant Director John B. Blandford and Chief Budget Examiner James E. Scott, representing the Bureau, were generally negative, and echoed much of the anti-FSA sentiment in Congress—(1) defense prosperity was helping all farmers, and therefore funds for the FSA should be reduced, and funds for the tenant purchase program should be entirely eliminated; (2) the migratory labor camp program should be made self-supporting; (3) the budget of the USDA should be unified, and the FSA, SCS, and Extension Service should be consolidated; and (4) the small marginal farm was an anachronism, large-scale commercial farming was the wave of the future, and the FSA should not try to resist the inevitable. Representative Tolan took the lead in rebutting these arguments, and reported that the Catholic Bishops had threatened to "come down on the Bureau of the Budget if they monkeyed with Farm Security."[28]

Finally, a few days later, a post-mortem on the meeting at the Budget Bureau was held with Assistant FSA Administrator George S. Mitchell. According to a member of the staff of the Tolan Committee who had participated in the meeting at the Bureau, Blandford had given the impression that his proposal for consolidation of the FSA, SCS, and Extension Service had already been discussed with Secretary Wickard, and that Wickard at least had not vetoed it. There was also the impression that Budget Director Smith "was very much down on the TP [tenant purchase] program and thought it could simply be abolished." In a memorandum to Baldwin, summarizing the meeting at the Bureau, one of Mitchell's assistants wrote that "if we lie down, we are licked; if we fight, and our friends with us, we may come through, but if you take what the Secretary's Office says and are a 'good boy' we will be cut and unmercifully—and be consolidated."[29]

28. F. P. Weber to Robert K. Lamb, Nov. 19, 1941, CBBP.
29. Memorandum (n.d., n.n.) to Baldwin, Nov. 22, 1941, CBBP.

The Byrd Committee

The turning of the tide for the FSA was also reflected in the launching of the offensive by the "economy bloc" in Congress. Through 1940 and 1941, they hammered away at the need for curtailment of non-defense federal spending and for elimination of New Deal experimentation. On September 20, 1941, a rider was attached to the Revenue Act of 1941 which created the Joint Committee on Reduction of Nonessential Federal Expenditures—the Byrd Committee—under the chairmanship of the Senator from Virginia. The leaders of the FSA greeted the creation of this committee, which was composed of some of the most indefatigable foes of the FSA and the New Deal, with something less than glee. Except for Senator Robert M. La Follette, Jr., Wisconsin Progressive, there was not a single dependable friend of the FSA among them.[30]

Although the Byrd Committee, as an investigative body, had no power comparable to that of the appropriations committees, it represented a formidable concentration of bipartisan congressional influence. In contrast to the Special Committee to Investigate the National Defense Program, under the chairmanship of New Deal back-bencher Senator Harry S. Truman of Missouri, the Byrd Committee promptly converted its "investigation" into an inquisition of the New Deal. The FSA was destined to serve as a main target.

30. Revenue Act of 1941, Pub. Law 250, Sec. 601; *Byrd Committee Hearings*, Pt. 2, pp. 366–414.

Senate members of the Joint Committee on Reduction of Nonessential Federal Expenditures (the Byrd Committee) were the following: Carter Glass, Democrat of Virginia, chairman of the Senate Appropriations Committee; Walter F. George, Democrat of Georgia, chairman of the Senate Finance Committee; Kenneth D. McKellar, Democrat of Tennessee, ranking Democratic member of the Senate Appropriations Committee; Gerald P. Nye, Republican of North Dakota, ranking Republican member of the Senate Appropriations Committee; and Robert M. La Follette, Jr., Progressive of Wisconsin.

House members were the following: Robert L. Doughton, Democrat of North Carolina, chairman of the House Ways and Means Committee; Thomas H. Cullen, Democrat of North Carolina, ranking Democratic member of the House Ways and Means Committee; Allen H. Treadway, Republican of Massachusetts, ranking Republican member of the House Ways and Means Committee; Clarence Cannon, Democrat of Missouri, chairman of the House Appropriations Committee; Clifton A. Woodrum, Democrat of Virginia, ranking Democratic member of the House Appropriations Committee; and John Taber, Republican of New York, ranking Republican member of the House Appropriations Committee.

Representing the executive branch of government were Treasury Secretary Henry Morgenthau, Jr., and Budget Director Harold D. Smith.

With this new arena available, the leaders of the AFBF, during the remainder of 1941, continued to promote their proposals and prepared for the next opportunity. At their annual conference, in Chicago in December, they were faced not with the awkward period of "national defense," but with all-out world war. In their formal resolutions they contented themselves with a reiteration of the demand for curtailment of non-defense spending, with no mention of the FSA, but their delegates approved a statement calling again for the board of directors to investigate the agency and its more controversial activities.

With the creation of the Byrd Committee, the congressional demands for economy and for an end to "New Deal socialism" converged with the AFBF assault against the New Deal. Byrd's investigative body would provide the platform and the AFBF the ammunition for a concerted drive against the FSA. On Friday morning, December 5, 1941, with only a day's notice, Baldwin was summoned before the committee, and two days later, on that grim Sunday afternoon of December 7, all pretenses of peace would vanish also for the American people.

The interrogation of Baldwin, on December 5, was an exploratory affair as Senators Byrd and McKellar led in probing for the clefts in the armor of the FSA. Administrative expenses, duplication between the FSA and the Works Progress Administration (WPA), the repayment records of loan borrowers, financial operations of the resettlement projects (McKellar was still upset about Cumberland Homesteads in Tennessee, and Byrd about Shenandoah Homesteads in Virginia), the mixture of loans and grants, and the growth of the FSA field organization—these were the issues they focused upon. And on the day before Christmas, Byrd submitted a preliminary report to the Senate. It included a series of recommendations which, if implemented, would have amounted to a death sentence for the New Deal. Included was the proposal that the FSA be abolished and all of its war-related activities "transferred to some more suitable agency."[31]

---

31. AFBF, *Nation's Agriculture*, Vol. 17 (Jan., 1942), pp. 12–14; Orville M. Kile, *The Farm Bureau Through Three Decades* (Baltimore: Waverly Press, 1948), pp. 267–68; O'Neal to G. F. Holsinger, Feb. 15, 1937, quoted in Campbell, *The Farm Bureau and the New Deal*, p. 186.

In its earlier years, especially during the 1920's, the AFBF had been viewed as a radical force in agricultural politics, and during the high tide of the New Deal in the 1930's, the leaders of the AFBF had found a useful ally in urban labor against their mutual foes—the "economy bloc" in Congress, of whom

For FSA Administrator Baldwin and his assistants, more burdensome than the necessity of having to testify before the committee were the demands that he and his staff prepare and submit to the investigators a number of elaborate statistical reports which, according to an estimate made later by Robert W. Hudgens, would require 300 man years of labor. "Senator Byrd deliberately tried to keep us off balance," Hudgens has recalled, and "almost every day we would get another call from him that required something that we could only get by telegram from the counties."

Treasury Secretary Henry Morgenthau, Jr., who was a member of the Byrd Committee but who did not actively participate in it, signed the report, but with the proviso that he did not support the recommendations involving agriculture. Budget Director Smith, who was also a member of the committee, declared that he could not sign because, in view of his position and his official participation in the preparation of the budget for fiscal year 1942–43, he could not "join in a report which may contain recommendations at variance" with the President's budget recommendations. Senator La Follette submitted a separate minority statement in which he opposed virtually every one of the committee's recommendations. The Wisconsin Progressive's statement included the following:

> To me the conclusion is inescapable that almost the full impact of the recommendations of the majority of the committee would, if enacted, fall almost entirely on the very lowest income groups among our population. This action would be unwise in time of peace; confronted with total war which may be of long duration, I regard it as a grave error in policy.

The leaders of the AFBF set to work in January on the "investigation" called for at their Chicago convention. O'Neal directed

---

Senator Harry F. Byrd of Virginia was an outspoken leader. By the early 1940's, however, a realignment had developed. As prosperity began to return, as the leaders of the AFBF identified themselves more openly with the interests of large-scale commercial farming, and as dependence of the AFBF on labor support lessened, AFBF leaders found new allies in organized business and among the very congressional economizers who were now fighting against "nonessential federal expenditures" and the New Deal.

In addition to their recommendations regarding the FSA, the Byrd Committee offered the following: The Civilian Conservation Corps and the National Youth Administration should be promptly liquidated; the WPA should be phased out as rapidly as possible; federal expenditures for highways, flood control, reclamation, and public buildings should be discontinued for the duration of the war; expansion of rural electrification should be postponed; and the administrative costs of the AAA system of farmers committees should be eliminated. The Byrd Committee did *not* recommend any curtailment of expenditures for the extension system.

general counsel Donald Kirkpatrick to dispatch six sleuths to eight states, with special instructions to look for incriminating evidence bearing on certain alleged malpractices of the FSA—cooperative associations, "socialized farming projects," the use of grants to "bail out" delinquent borrowers, "solicitation" of client families, excessive administrative and overhead costs, purchases of unnecessary equipment, and conflicts with the programs of the AAA and the Extension Service.

O'Neal and Smith were shrewd showmen and knew how to capture national attention. When the testimony of the AFBF opened before the Byrd Committee, on February 6, 1942, they persuaded the committee to hear Robert K. Greene, a probate judge from Greensboro, Alabama, who charged that the FSA had been paying the poll taxes of its clients, presumably in an attempt to build a political machine in the South. The truth of the matter was that in working out the farm and home plan with a prospective client family, the FSA county supervisor took into consideration all of the family's debts, including any delinquent taxes. As "proof" of his charge, Greene offered a letter from Ernest S. Morgan, FSA regional director in Montgomery, Alabama, which declared as follows:

... it is our conviction that a citizen is not complete and his rehabilitation is not to be completely accomplished, unless he is a voter, with a voice to be heard and a hand to be felt in shaping and directing his Government—in every definition and intention of the founding fathers, it is his Government.

This, presumably, was "subversive talk," and, according to the leaders of the AFBF, it was proof positive of the attempts by the FSA to overthrow the established order in the South.

A few days later, in his own testimony, FSA Administrator Baldwin vainly sought to calm the committee by explaining that poll taxes were normally included as a regular expense in the accounts of client families and were therefore a factor in the loans granted. He denied that his agency had ever made any attempts to actually pay the poll taxes of clients, and he challenged the AFBF to produce a single piece of admissible evidence to support their accusations.[32]

32. *Byrd Committee Hearings*, Pt. 2, pp. 355–414, and Pt. 3, pp. 699–920; U. S., Congress, Joint Committee on Reduction of Nonessential Federal Expenditures, *Preliminary Report*, Sen. Doc. 152, Dec. 24, 1941, 77th Cong., 1st Sess. (Washington, D. C.: GPO, 1941); author's interviews with Baldwin, Hudgens; Hudgens, COHC, pp. 200–01.

The character of the AFBF investigation of the FSA was partially revealed in a letter discovered by Senator La Follette and which he succeeded in having

The "poll tax plot" immediately became a front-page story in the newspapers across the United States, just as O'Neal and Smith had shrewdly anticipated. President Roosevelt, taken by surprise with a leading question from Phelps Adams of the *New York Sun* during a press conference on February 10, conceded that if the FSA were paying the poll taxes of its clients, that would be improper, but he emphasized that the agency was "extremely essential" for the war effort and hoped it would not fall victim to the economizers. The following morning, the *New York Times* reported that, "Mr. Roosevelt said he did not think that this [paying clients' poll taxes] should be done," and on the next day, Secretary Wickard, in his testimony before the appropriations subcommittee of the House, unequivocally refuted the poll tax charge.

Gardner "Pat" Jackson, self-appointed defender of the FSA, read in the newspapers what he believed were damaging stories about the President's reply to Phelps Adams, and immediately telephoned and wrote to the White House. He warned that the poll tax issue was going to be raised again at the President's next press conference, explained the truth of the matter, and enclosed some pro-FSA editorials and newspaper clippings for Roosevelt's information. At his press conference on February 13, Roosevelt defended the FSA against the accusations and declared that the whole controversy reminded him of earlier attempts by the same hostile people to deny the vote to recipients of the WPA. From Chicago, the *Sun-Times* editorialized that, "If the farmer pays his poll tax he can vote [and threaten] the Southern political oligarchy headed by Senator Byrd, hence the Byrd-O'Neal alliance against the FSA." And from Montgomery, Alabama, the *Alabama Journal* headlined the war on two fronts: "BRITISH STOP JAP ADVANCE," and "FDR DEFENDS POLL TAX LOANS."[33]

---

included in the record, over the protests of AFBF Legal Counsel Donald Kirkpatrick. The letter, written by one of the AFBF sleuths to his superior, read in part as follows: "Enclosed you will find detailed report of observations in Shelby County and evidence secured for some criticism made. Also what we were able to locate and find out in Clark County. If this is in line with what you had hoped to receive, or if there are other suggestions you might have after looking over these notes, I hope you will do so and notify me."

33. F.D.R., *Public Papers* (1942), Vol. 11, pp. 94–96; *New York Times*, Feb. 11, 1942; testimony of Wickard, *House Hearings, Agr. Approp.* (1943), 77th Cong., 2d Sess., Pt. 2, pp. 737–38; *Chicago Sun-Times*, Feb. 15, 1942; Montgomery, Ala., *Alabama Journal*, Jan. 24, Feb. 13, 1942; *Montgomery* (Ala.) *Advertiser*, Jan. 5, 1942; Gardner Jackson to Stephen Early, Feb. 12, 1942, FDRL, OF 1568.

With the ground thus well-prepared, O'Neal and Kirkpatrick proceeded with their case. Summing up, they indicted the FSA for the following alleged offenses: (1) "soliciting" clients, in order to build up the FSA and to "exaggerate" the real need for their programs; (2) using emergency grants for the purpose of "bailing out" delinquent loans and concealing the record of failure; (3) exaggerating the collection record on loans "for the purpose of deceiving Congress;" (4) encouraging borrowers to assume credit burdens beyond their financial capacities; (5) promoting "socialistic and impractical farming projects;" (6) duplicating the activities of the AAA and the Extension Service; (7) seeking to promote pressure groups in the country for the purpose of influencing congressional action; (8) operating with excessively high administrative expenses; and (9) seeking "to regiment" client families and to destroy their individualism, initiative, and self-respect.[34]

Point by point, Baldwin, assisted by Murray D. Lincoln of the Ohio Farm Bureau Federation, Harry L. Mitchell of the Southern Tenant Farmers Union (STFU), Patton of the NFU, and Howard R. Tolley of the BAE, attempted to refute the charges. The only member of the Byrd Committee present at the hearings who showed any interest in a more objective inquiry was—not surprisingly—Senator La Follete, the Wisconsin Progressive.

1942: The Battle of the Budget

In the perspective of time, the attacks upon the FSA in 1940 and 1941 were essentially a reconnaissance by the agency's foes, and they were a preview of larger things to come in 1942. With entry of the United States into the war in December and acceleration of national mobilization, a struggle over farm production and distribution, wages, prices, reorganization of the USDA, and other issues engulfed the FSA. The battle over the budget for agriculture—especially funds for the FSA—became a major focus in the struggle.

As the new year opened, the lines were drawn. Economizers and anti-New Dealers were determined to put an end to Roosevelt's "sociological experimentation." Both Republicans and Democrats sought partisan advantage in the changes that were impending. Farm organizations were anxious about preserving their competitive

---

34. *Byrd Committee Hearings*, Pt. 3, p. 745.

advantages. Representatives of large-scale commercial farmers saw an opportunity to exploit wartime prosperity and were opposed to any governmental policies that might hamstring them. Spokesmen for consumers' interests were determined that prices should be controlled, while critics of governmental planning warned against the growth of regimentation under the guise of wartime mobilization.

In this whirlpool of competing self interests and special definitions of the general welfare, the White House and the USDA were guided by a set of assumptions and objectives which were generally intended to achieve the following: (1) preservation of the Secretary of Agriculture's powers, especially over the planning and implementation of agricultural mobilization; (2) expansion and restructuring of farm production without contributing to excessive inflation; (3) provision of incentives to farmers through government subsidies rather than through parity in the marketplace; (4) Secretarial power to encourage farmers to raise certain crops through his control over surplus stocks held by the Commodity Credit Corporation (CCC); and (5) an *increase* in the budget for the FSA as a means of maximizing the production of small-scale and marginal farmers, instead of relying entirely on the production of larger commercial farms.

O'Neal and other leaders of the AFBF, characteristically claiming to speak for "the farmers of America," were particularly determined to resist the efforts of the Roosevelt administration to hold prices down. They also sought to free agriculture from governmental restraints, now that prosperity was returning and there was an unlimited demand for American farm production. There was no longer any need for governmental subsidies to farmers, O'Neal reportedly thundered at Secretary Wickard, "I want parity in the marketplace."

This was the situation as the legislators in the second session of the Seventy-seventh Congress began work on the appropriation for agriculture. Meanwhile, in preparation for the impending struggle over the FSA, Baldwin and his assistants mobilized their scattered army of liberal and labor friends. Since the hunter usually has the initiative, however, the FSA was placed on the defensive, and there it remained.

From January 12 through February 17, the House appropriations subcommittee, under Tarver's chairmanship, served as one of the main arenas within which the contending forces clashed. The leaders of the AFBF recited their familiar litany of charges against the FSA, while Baldwin and his supporters—members of the Tolan Committee, Rev. John O'Grady of the National Conference of Catholic Charities,

Robert Handschin of the NFU, Elizabeth Herring of the Young Women's Christian Association's governing board, and others—rallied to the defense of the FSA. There was virtually no questioning by the subcommittee about the subject which Baldwin would have welcomed an opportunity to discuss—the capacity and readiness of small-farm operators to contribute to the nation's food needs.

There was, however, persistent prodding on the alleged offenses of the FSA, especially its "violation of the principal of fee simple ownership of land," its "undermining of client families' self-reliance," and its promotion of "un-American social experiments." On January 20, for instance, Judge Tarver pressed Baldwin rigorously. The tenant purchase program, Tarver conceded, was "very valuable" as a means of promoting land ownership, but the resettlement projects and cooperative farming associations—he insisted on calling them "collective farms"—were converting farm families into "cogs in a machine." These enterprises were "very suspiciously related" to "sovietism" and should be discontinued. Baldwin's reply, that the FSA was committed, in theory and practice, to the family farm, that the agency was compelled to deal with many different types of low-income farm families, that some of these families required closer supervision than others, and that the cooperative type of farming "serves also as a very good training ground for farmers' families who are later to take their place on family-type farming operations," satisfied neither Tarver nor his fellow members of the subcommittee.[35]

As the hearings progressed, friends of the FSA rallied to the defense. The Tolan Committee in the House, for instance, issued a summary of Professor Black's report to Davis on the potential value of small farmers' production to the war effort. Edward J. Flynn of the Democratic National Committee solicited the opinions of state party leaders on the FSA, and finding that most of his state leaders were favorable, he personally urged Democratic members of Congress to support the President's budget recommendations for the agency. Gardner Jackson, who had persuaded Roosevelt to "suggest" to Wickard that a place be found for him in the Department, had gone to work in February, 1942, as an assistant to Under Secretary Appleby. By-passing his superiors, he wrote and telephoned directly to the White House, imploring the President to intervene to save

---

35. Wickard, Diary, May 15–16, 1942, quoted in Albertson, *Roosevelt's Farmer*, p. 279; *House Hearings*, Agr. Approp. (1943), 77th Cong., 2d Sess., Pt. 1, pp. 195–98, and Pt. 2, pp. 255–56, 348–78, 530–99, 607–74, 674–814.

the FSA budget. Wickard also continued to apply pressure on the President. Finally, at Roosevelt's direction, Marvin H. McIntyre called House Speaker Sam Rayburn and House majority whip Patrick J. Boland, urging them to rally the forces in the House.[36]

In the opinion of Michael Straight of the *New Republic*, however, these frenetic efforts were too little and too late. "Two years ago," he wrote, "the President paid the price that was demanded—control of the Defense Program and the sacrifice of the most militant of the men who had advanced the New Deal." Now, in the battle of the budget for 1943, the President's Faustian bargain was being consummated.[37]

Falling short of the demands by the leaders of the AFBF and by Cannon and Dirksen, that the FSA be put to death, the subcommittee sent a report to the House that was highly critical of the FSA but which sustained the President's budget request for the agency. This request, however, represented a reduction of 27 per cent below the current appropriation. The President had submitted it to the Congress before the decision was made to expand low-income farmers' production, and a supplemental budget request was in preparation at the time.

The foreboding of the *New Republic* seemed to materialize when the House approved the subcommittee's report in March. With respect to funds for the FSA, the House bill differed from the President's January budget request as follows:

Program	President's Budget	House Bill
Tenant Purchase		
Administration	$ 2,500,000	$ 1,250,000
RFC Loan Funds[1]	40,000,000	25,000,000
Rural Rehabilitation		
Administration	55,319,557	25,000,000
RFC Loan Funds[1]	75,000,000	70,000,000
Total	$ 172,819,557	$ 121,250,000

1. Authorized FSA loans from the Reconstruction Finance Corporation.

This represented an additional cut of 30 per cent in the funds requested by the President in January. Privately, Cannon was pre-

---

36. *Tolan Committee Hearings*, Pt. 28, pp. 10875–77. Charles H. Leach to Edward J. Flynn, Feb. 21, 1942; James T. Mathews to E. B. German, Mar. 9, 1942; Mathews to Marvin H. McIntyre, Aug. 13, 1942; FDRL, OF 1568. Jackson to McIntyre, Mar. 11, 1942, FDRL, OF 3453. "MDP" to McIntyre, Mar. 13, 1942; Wickard to Roosevelt, Mar. 13, 1942; FDRL, OF 1.

37. Michael Straight, "The Scabbard and the Sword," *New Republic*, Vol. 106 (Feb. 16, 1942), pp. 225–27.

sumably disappointed that the House had not gone further in reducing the funds and powers of the FSA, but publicly he was highly gratified. This bill, he declared, was an "exceptional accomplishment" because, "It is the first bill ever reported by the Committee on Appropriations on which the beneficiaries—the farmers—speaking through their farm organizations, have requested a reduction in appropriations."[38]

For two weeks, in late April and early May, hearings were held in Senator Russell's appropriations subcommittee. Despite the chairman's sympathetic handling of affairs and the efforts of Senators Bankhead, Chavez, and other administration stalwarts, the hearings became even more bitter than those in the House. Once again, the familiar parade of witnesses for and against the FSA appeared. O'Neal, Smith, and AFBF research director W. R. Ogg, accompanied by state Farm Bureau leaders from Georgia, Arkansas, Alabama, and Texas, reiterated their charges against the FSA. Senator Byrd of Virginia came and called the FSA the "most wasteful" and the "most disregardful of the true interest of the people and of . . . low income farmers" of all the agencies in the federal government. In what was probably the most bitter attack, Senator McKellar of Tennessee thundered against the alleged FSA practices of paying clients' poll taxes, promoting "socialized medicine," excessive spending on travel and publicity, wasting funds on "no-account people," and refusing to liquidate "useless and dangerous resettlement projects." Becoming personal, he charged that Baldwin was "not far removed from being a Communist—he may not be a Communist outright, but his sympathies appear that way, and we ought to be very careful as to how we spend this money."[39]

On the side of the defense, Secretary Wickard generally defended the administration's positions on the various issues at stake in the appropriation bill and ended with a plea for the life of the FSA:

It seems to me this is not only a very poor time to decrease the activities of the [FSA] but it is a time when consideration ought to be given to ex-

38. U. S., Congress, House, Appropriations Committee, House Report 1848, Mar. 2, 1942, 77th Cong., 2d Sess. (Washington, D. C.: GPO, 1942), p. 21; *Congressional Record*, Vol. 88, pp. 2412–54.

The House bill prohibited, with minor exceptions, the sale of CCC stocks of grain below full parity prices, and provided for full parity prices to farmers for normal yields of these grains from allotted acreages, but it did not include in the computation of the price returns the acreage adjustment payments as proposed by the President.

39. *Senate Hearings*, Agr. Approp. (1943), 77th Cong., 2d Sess., pp. 686–706, 716–26, 734–853.

The FSA Goes to War / [357]

tending and expanding [such] activities, not only for the family-sized farm of the small farmer but the migratory labor camp, so that we can more fully utilize the agricultural labor we have.

Meanwhile, Baldwin had mobilized his Gideon's army, and during the last week of April some of them converged on the hearing room— half a dozen members of Congress, Patton of the NFU and some of his state leaders, Rev. L. G. Ligutti of the Catholic Rural Life Conference, Rev. John O'Grady of the National Conference of Catholics Charities, Courtney Dinwiddie of the National Child Labor Committee, and Perry L. Green of the Ohio Farm Bureau Federation. M. L. Wilson of the Extension Service also came and expressed his opposition to the proposals of the AFBF that some of the functions of the FSA be transferred to his agency.[40]

Finally, in his own testimony, Baldwin once again defended the FSA. Not only was it not "un-American," he contended, but it was attempting to make the American dream a reality for hundreds of thousands of neglected low-income farm families. With characteristic candor, he pointed to what he believed was the crux of the matter:[41]

> Both our rural rehabilitation and our tenant purchase programs have been formulated with a view to assisting the family-type farmer in his struggle with those who would make farm hands out of farmers.
> It is in this context and only in this context that the current fight to weaken the [FSA] can be understood. The choice before the committee is whether the small independent farmer should be given an opportunity to maintain and improve his status or whether these large interests should be permitted to take advantage of the war situation to accumulate large land holdings and to make laborers out of farmers.

During the Senate hearings, in response to the belief that small-sized family-type farms could significantly contribute to overall farm production if given adequate assistance, the President had submitted to Congress a supplemental budget estimate for the rural rehabilitation program which represented a 90 per cent increase over the original estimate in his budget for 1943. Discussion in the Senate hearings and debate on the Senate floor were on the basis of the revised figures. In view of House resistance to even the original estimate, there was therefore an unrealistic quality in the Senate approach.

Final debate on funds for the FSA began in the Senate on May 18

---

40. *Ibid.*, pp. 86, 386–93, 460–65, 519–36, 588–96, 617–20, 640–42, 650–69, 861–66, 1014.
41. *Ibid.*, p. 1016.

with a discussion of "Beanie" Baldwin's loyalty to America. Baldwin had been outraged by McKellar's accusation that he was "not far removed from being a Communist," during the Senate hearings, and he privately told Senator Bankhead that he was going to sue the Senator from Tennessee unless he issued a retraction. Bankhead urged Baldwin to be calm, and then went to McKellar, his old friend and classmate from the University of Alabama, and gently suggested that if the Senator would desist from attacking the FSA during debate on the bill, Baldwin would forgive and forget. The irascible Senator from Tennessee would make no bargains, and on May 18, with the galleries crowded, he repeated his charges on the Senate floor: "I think Mr. Baldwin is a Communist. Let him sue me if he wants to. I'll waive the fact I'm a Senator."

Mild-mannered John Bankhead of Alabama, still popularly considered the "father of the FSA," rose to his feet and delivered a testimonial to the FSA Administrator, as follows:

> The Senator from Tennessee has boldly expressed the opinion . . . that Mr. Baldwin is a Communist, and he doubts the propriety and the wisdom of vesting any judgment, or discretion, or administrative power in Mr. Baldwin. . . . I have never seen any indication, nor have I ever heard any statement made by Mr. Baldwin which indicated in any way that he was a Communist, or that he was not in full accord with American institutions and the American form of government. I have at all times found him to be a gentleman, a Virginia gentleman, and if any criticism could be made of him it is because of his generosity, possibly his tender heart toward relieving the sufferings of the poor farmers who could not obtain credit, who had no standing, who had no means to enable them to stay upon the farm.

And Richard Russell of Georgia joined his colleague from Alabama, declaring that despite their differences of philosophy and method, he believed that Baldwin was "as far from being a Communist as any man could possibly be . . . . [He is] an honest, sincere, patriotic American."[42]

---

42. *Congressional Record*, Vol. 88, p. 4286; *Washington* (D.C.) *Times-Herald*, May 19, 1942; Styles Bridges, address on Sept. 7, 1950, "Communist Invasion of Agriculture" (Washington, D. C.: GPO, 1951); Whittaker Chambers, *Witness* (London: Andre Deutsch, 1953), pp. 240–41; Murray Kempton, *Part of Our Time* (New York: Simon and Schuster, 1955), pp. 57–58; Arthur M. Schlesinger, Jr., *The Coming of the New Deal* (Boston: Houghton Mifflin, 1959), pp. 52–54, and *The Politics of Upheaval* (Boston: Houghton Mifflin, 1960), pp. 181–207; U. S., Congress, Senate, Committee on the Judiciary, Hearings, 83d Cong., 1st Sess., *Interlocking Subversion in Government Departments* (Washington, D. C.: GPO, 1953), pp. 841–927; U.S., Congress, House, Un-

On May 20, after repeated efforts by Senators Byrd, Taft, and others to reduce funds for the FSA and to dilute the Secretary's powers over CCC stocks, the appropriation bill finally passed a series of last-minute test votes, and the funds for the FSA were approved by the lopsided vote of forty-eight to sixteen. The bill included a provision, as requested by the President, which empowered the Secretary to sell limited CCC stocks of grain for feed purposes at 85 per cent of parity, in contrast with the House provision for full parity, and it provided for inclusion of acreage adjustment payments in the computation of parity price, which was opposed by the House. In comparison with the House bill and the President's *revised* budget request, the Senate bill provided funds for the FSA as follows:

Program	Revised Request	Senate Bill	House Bill
Tenant Purchase Administration	$ 2,500,000	$ 2,000,000	$ 1,250,000
RFC Loan Funds[1]	40,000,000	40,000,000	25,000,000
Rural Rehabilitation Administration	65,000,000	50,000,000	25,000,000
RFC Loan Funds[1]	180,000,000	125,000,000	70,000,000
Total	$ 287,500,000	$ 217,000,000	$ 121,250,000

1. Authorized FSA loans from the Reconstruction Finance Corporation.

FSA funds in the Senate bill were 25 per cent below the President's

---

American Activities Committee, Hearings, 78th Cong., 2d Sess., *Hearings on H. Res. 282* (Washington, D. C.: GPO, 1945), Vol. 17, pp. 10212–17; author's interview with Baldwin.

For a number of reasons, a shadow has been cast on the FSA and on the names of some of its leaders. The lacerations of the "McCarthy years" of the 1950's; "Beanie" Baldwin's post-FSA activity on behalf of Wallace's Progressive party campaign for the Presidency in 1948, and Baldwin's other political involvements on the left after leaving the agency; the naming of individuals who were associated with the FSA or other agencies in the USDA during the 1930's, before various congressional investigating committees; and the exaggerated or untrue charges of Communism against individuals connected with the FSA, such as that by Senator McKellar—these are some of the contributing causes of an atmosphere of suspicion that has grown around the image of the FSA during the past decade and a half.

However, as Schlesinger has concluded, the American Communists opposed the New Deal fairly consistently. They also had little love for the FSA and for what it was attempting to do. There is nothing in the record to suggest that the FSA ever served the cause of Communism, wittingly or otherwise, although some of the agency's programs and people were convenient targets for zealous anti-Communists.

revised request, compared with a proposed cut of 58 per cent of that request in the House bill.[43]

The House and Senate bills were promptly deadlocked in conference, while a rash of pressure and polemics broke out over the issues involved in the appropriation bills. Ralph McGill, for instance, writing in the *Atlanta Constitution*, charged that the efforts of "organizations of large owners and producers" to cut FSA funds was a "damnable action," while other newspapers throughout the country drew up sides. On the morning of June 9, at the suggestion of Secretary Wickard and House Speaker Sam Rayburn, the President held a private meeting with Wickard, Cannon, and Tarver, who were leading the House resistance, in his White House bedroom, but the normally persuasive presidential efforts were in vain, and the deadlock continued. Later in June, the leaders of the NFU, the Congress of Industrial Organizations (CIO), the Ohio Farm Bureau Federation, and others joined in an urgent appeal to the President to stand fast, and provoked a counter appeal from the AFBF. Without waiting for the denouement, Secretary Wickard went to Mexico City, ostensibly to address an inter-American conference on agriculture but actually to initiate negotiations with the Mexican Government on importation of Mexican farm workers. Appleby remained at the USDA as Acting Secretary of Agriculture.

On July 7, with still no agreement in conference, Appleby wrote to the President. He emphasized that parity prices were not an issue in the controversy and reiterated that the FSA provisions in the House bill would cripple the war program for agriculture. Two days later, a bill was passed and signed, to provide for continuation of USDA funds for July, and still the deadlock went on.[44]

43. *Congressional Record*, Vol. 88, pp. 4263–4396.
44. Richard B. Russell to Roosevelt, May 21, 1942; Roosevelt to Russell, May 29, 1942; Wickard to Roosevelt, June 2, 9, 1942; Wayne Coy to Roosevelt, June 29, 1942; Appleby to Roosevelt, July 7, 1942; White House press release, July 9, 1942; FDRL, OF 1. Wickard to John W. McCormack, June 9, 1942, NA, RG 16. *Atlanta* (Ga.) *Constitution*, May 17, 1942; Albertson, *Roosevelt's Farmer*, pp. 283–89.

For the angry exchange of protests to the President and Congress, see the following: letter to Roosevelt, June 20, 1942, from Patton of the NFU, Murray D. Lincoln of the Ohio Farm Bureau Federation, William Green of the American Federation of Labor, Phillip Murray of the Congress of Industrial Organizations, J. G. Luhrsen of the American Railway Labor Executives Association, Rev. L. G. Ligutti of the Catholic Rural Life Conference, and Benson Y. Landis of the Federal Council of Churches of Christ in America; Roosevelt to Wickard, June 24, 1942; Appleby to Roosevelt, July 2, 1942; Jackson to Early, July 2, 1942; O'Neal to all members of Congress, June 23, 1942; Roosevelt to signers of letter of June 20, responding to their protests, July 3, 1942; FDRL, OF 1568.

On July 14, with the President now publicly prepared to accept no less than the Senate bill, and with the House nearing a showdown on a compromise, Acting Secretary Appleby again wrote to the President and offered what he called a "political judgment" about the struggle over the bill:[45]

> The country does not yet understand the issue. The farmers are generally pretty happy and are not pushing the members of the House to act as they have acted. The fight is an organizational fight. If you should take the issue to the country, farm people will support you.

The implication was that if the House refused to compromise or if the Senate surrendered, a presidential veto would be supported by the country.

Twenty-four hours later, the budget battle of 1942 ended in compromise. The Secretary of Agriculture won the power to sell limited quantities of CCC grain stocks for feed purposes at not less than 85 per cent of parity, computed on a cost plus payments basis. The price paid for House approval was a cut in FSA funds of 20 per cent below the amounts approved by the Senate. Since the battle had been fought on the basis of the President's *revised* budget request, rather than his original estimate, the final appropriation for the FSA represented a serious blow to plans for expanding the production of small-scale farms. The burden fell most heavily on rural rehabilitation, farm debt adjustment, water facilities projects, and migratory labor camps. The total appropriation for the FSA represented a decrease of approximately 43 per cent of the money the President requested. Furthermore, restrictions on the spending of funds, as demanded by the House, were also included in the measure. To Appleby and Baldwin, the compromise of 1942 "gave the howling wolves their first real taste of blood."[46]

During the next few months, the leaders of the FSA continued to search for a strategy of survival. At least for a while, there seemed little likelihood of promoting their "small farmer issue." The tenant purchase program, obviously enjoying considerable congressional support, could continue without having to be related to the war. Hope of expanding the rural rehabilitation program, for whatever reason, was dimmed for the current fiscal year. The cooperative program, land purchasing and leasing activities, war relocation corporations, and resettlement projects were definitely doomed.

---

45. Appleby to Roosevelt, July 14, 1942, FDRL, OF 1.
46. Department of Agriculture Appropriation Act, fiscal year 1943, 56 Stat. 664; author's interviews with Appleby, Baldwin, Hudgens.

The one war-related purpose remaining on which the FSA might pin its hopes for continued institutional viability was the migratory labor program, but now even that was meeting strong criticism from many directions, reputedly because of the agency's zealous attempts to enforce contract agreements protecting the rights of Mexican and other workers. Furthermore, for several months the House Agriculture Committee, now under the chairmanship of Hampton P. Fulmer of South Carolina, a conservative southern Democrat (Marvin Jones was now a judge of the U.S. Court of Claims), had been discussing its intention of conducting a full-scale investigation of the FSA, and criticism of the migratory labor program was one of the causes contributing to the Agriculture Committee's dissatisfaction. On the day before Thanksgiving, Baldwin convened a conference of regional directors in Cincinnati, Ohio, where part of the Washington office had been relocated, with the somber introduction that, "This is the most important conference in the history of [FSA] ... a crisis on top of an emergency." The "golden years" were now over.[47]

Institutional Viability: A Not-So-Delicate Balance

As in the life of organisms and individuals, so in the life of governmental organizations and institutions, the hour of crisis reveals the fundamental vitality of a system under strain. The hour of final crisis for the FSA would demonstrate that its vitality—its essential principle of life and its capacity for socially meaningful endurance—was rooted, however, not in a governing genetic code, but rather in a variety of institutional characteristics and in a set of internal and external relationships which tended to reinforce or complement each other. The lack of "countervailing power" among the clientele of the FSA, for instance, was at least partially compensated for, during the first few years, by the large measure of congressional permissiveness and the absence of concerted opposition from hostile special interests. The close rapport between the leaders of the FSA and some of the men around the Secretary of Agriculture complemented the lack of cooperation between the FSA and other action agencies of the USDA. Where the institutional viability of the FSA was endangered by the inadequacy of funds, it was reinforced by the high degree of flexibility and creativity exercised by the leaders of the agency. And the depression-related character of the organizational purposes of the FSA was partially balanced by the readiness with which the

47. FSA, proceedings of Administrator's staff conference, Nov. 25–29, 1942.

leaders exploited opportunities for goal succession, as peace and depression gave way to war and prosperity. The balance between the forces of integration and disintegration in the life of the FSA was not a precarious thing.

Marshall E. Dimock has suggested that, "Vitality in institutions, as well as in physical organisms, depends on how well the mechanism responds to the aging process and to environmental change." The experience of the FSA, especially between 1940 and 1942, demonstrates that the mechanistic and organismic analogies are considerably less applicable to human institutions than they are to insects and engines. The record does not suggest that there was an "aging process" at work in the life of the FSA or anything mechanical in the responses of the agency to its external environment. As a matter of fact, the vigor of the FSA seemed to increase as time passed, and the direction and rate of change in its adaptation to the external environment were not in accordance with the automatism and predictability which are implicit in the laws of mechanics. For instance, the significance of the attacks on the FSA by Cannon, Dirksen, Byrd, or O'Neal lay not in some intrinsic quality in their acts, but rather in the larger external environment and in the changing impacts which their attacks had upon the FSA over time. Where their hostility helped to strengthen the agency in the 1930's by reinforcing its internal resolve and external image as the vanguard of the New Deal, the same hostility provided the ammunition for a destructive political assault under changed circumstances in later years.

Administrative agencies of government do not simply grow old and die, and, furthermore, it is quite misleading to discuss the rise and decline of an agency in terms of life and death. Agencies may be legislated into oblivion by statutory action, or "reorganized" and "consolidated" out of existence by executive action. They may be starved of funds and power, and languish in impotence and despair— in what Bertram M. Gross has described as a form of institutional "hibernation." They may be dismembered and their parts used to enrich the soil from which other institutions may spring. They may rise and decline, and, like the fabled phoenix, rise once again, transformed and transfigured, from their own ashes. The idea of institutional survival, however, implies more than mere organizational persistence.[48]

48. Marshall E. Dimock, *Administrative Vitality* (New York: Harper, 1959), p. 9; Karl W. Deutsch, *The Nerves of Government* (New York: The Free Press, 1963), pp. 78–80; Bertram M. Gross, *The Managing of Organizations*, Vol. II (New York: The Free Press, 1964), pp. 665–66.

From the very beginning, the FSA was perceived, especially by its leaders and defenders, as the "social conscience of the New Deal." Far more than other New Deal agencies, the FSA drew its ideological nourishment and its external political support from the loose alliance of liberal, labor, and social welfare groups upon which the New Deal itself rested heavily. By the end of 1942, with the New Deal on the brink of oblivion and with the vectors of opposition to the FSA converging, the agency arrived at Armageddon. It is to that confrontation and its aftermath that we now turn.

CHAPTER XII

ARMAGEDDON AND AFTERMATH

There is no more forlorn spectacle in the administrative world than an agency and a program possessed of statutory life, armed with executive orders, sustained in the courts, yet stricken with paralysis and deprived of power. An object of contempt to its enemies and of despair to its friends.

NORTON E. LONG[1]
"Power and Administration"

As the difficult year 1942 came to a close, the leaders of the Farm Security Administration (FSA) were faced with a very portentous situation. Gone were the days of congressional acquiescence, the easy appeal to depression-based concern about poverty, the protective leadership of Henry A. Wallace and Paul H. Appleby of the U.S. Department of Agriculture (USDA), and the open door at the White House. As C. B. "Beanie" Baldwin and his assistants contemplated the forces massed against them, as they saw the budget cut of 1942 work its destructive effects upon their programs and performance, and as they witnessed the larger institutional foundation of the FSA dissolve, their inherently optimistic mood gave way

---

1. Norton E. Long, "Power and Administration," *Public Administration Review*, Vol. IX (Autumn, 1949), p. 257.

to great apprehension, and then to despair. The Works Projects Administration, the National Youth Administration, the Civilian Conservation Corps, the National Resources Planning Board—all were on the brink or had already gone over.

By the end of May, 1943, the press was reporting that the New Deal was in its death throes and that the FSA was fighting the climactic battle of its life. The casualty list of agencies and leaders was already long and growing, and before the year was over, the President himself pronounced the benediction when he confessed that "Win the War" was a more appropriate appellation for his administration than "New Deal." In exultation, Senator Kenneth D. McKeller offered his congratulations to Franklin D. Roosevelt:[2]

> I think this is excellent. "Win the War" is the supreme question before the people and the Democratic Party could not have a better slogan. It is the combined essence of patriotism, statesmanship, government, and politics at this time and the slogan could not be better. . . . I think that the dropping of the "New Deal" as a slogan is a good omen and I congratulate you.

For some champions of the New Deal at the time, it appeared that the President had lost interest in the FSA and that he was prepared to abandon the agency to its fate. In retrospect, however, Eleanor Roosevelt sought to place the situation in perspective:[3]

> My husband repeatedly emphasized that he could not afford to alienate crucial political support needed for the vital wartime programs that meant our country's very survival, by promoting issues that would have provoked unnecessary political conflict. Those who have suggested that he turned his back on all that the New Deal represented would not have felt that way if they had heard him talk, as I heard, about his plans for after the war. By 1943, he was forced to devote most of his personal attention and energies to the urgencies of war. From time to time, I tried to impress on him the need for his personal intervention on behalf of some program or agency in trouble, but as time went on he became more inaccessible.

For the FSA, the significance of Roosevelt's proclaimed shift from "Dr. New Deal" to "Dr. Win-the-War" lay not in his personal reorientation, for he had not been the major source of actual operational power for the agency—Presidents seldom are. More significantly, his shift represented the culmination of a change in the administration's

---

2. Malcolm Cowley, "The End of the New Deal," *New Republic*, Vol. 108 (May 31, 1943), pp. 729–32. Transcripts of President Franklin D. Roosevelt's press and radio conference, Dec. 28, 1943; Kenneth D. McKellar to Roosevelt, Dec. 24, 1943; Roosevelt to McKellar, Dec. 29, 1943; FDRL, PPF 2910.

3. Author's interview with Mrs. Eleanor Roosevelt.

overall political strategy, in deference to the wartime need for national solidarity and to the impending political campaign of 1944, a change that had been in the making at least since the entry of the United States into the war in December, 1941. The shift of the President's posture toward the New Deal also signaled the arrival of the master politicians, the grand coordinators, and the "czars" of mobilization in whose hands the fate of the FSA and other agencies would rest. This, then, was the larger stage on which the climactic struggle for the survival of the FSA was fought.

The Parisius Affair

Following the compromise in the appropriation for agriculture during the summer of 1942, problems of agricultural mobilization continued to plague the USDA and the White House. In an effort to coordinate the competing agencies and offices involved in mobilization, Roosevelt created, early in October, the Office of Economic Stabilization, and took former Senator James F. Byrnes from the Supreme Court as its first director. As anxieties over the dangers of food shortages and pressures for appointment of a "food czar" rose to a crescendo, the President issued an executive order on December 5, not creating a "food czar" but centralizing responsibility for the food program in the hands of Agriculture Secretary Claude R. Wickard. Federal agencies and offices involved in food production—the Agricultural Adjustment Administration (AAA), the Soil Conservation Service (SCS), the Farm Credit Administration (FCA), the Office of Agricultural War Relations (OAWR), food production functions of the War Production Board (WPB), parts of the Bureau of Agricultural Economics (BAE), and the FSA—were to be coordinated in a new agency called the Food Production Administration (FPA) under a Director of Food Production, to be appointed by the Secretary of Agriculture.

Federal agencies and offices concerned with food distribution were to be combined in a parallel agency to be called the Food Distribution Administration (FDA). The functions of the OAWR were to be divided between the FPA and the FDA. Economic Stabilization Director Byrnes was designated as the President's agent in resolving any disputes between the USDA and agencies involved in food administration. Roy F. Hendrickson, Agricultural Marketing Administrator, had been working for some time to win the position of Director of Food Distribution, and he was ready with a blueprint for organizing and staffing the FDA. His appointment by Wickard on December 10 was a natural and expected decision.[4]

The appointment of a Director of Food Production and the launching of the FPA, however, proved to be considerably more difficult, and involved a struggle that lasted for several weeks. The outcome proved to be another defeat for the FSA. Since the FPA chief would have considerable power, including especially the resolution of rivalries among agencies of the USDA seeking a role in the wartime food production program, there was much speculation about potential candidates for the job—OAWR Director M. Clifford Townsend, former Governor of Indiana, friend of Wickard, and at one time the director of organization for the Indiana Farm Bureau Federation; Commodity Credit Corporation (CCC) President John B. Hutson, former extension official from Kentucky, agricultural economist, close friend of Chester C. Davis, and former head of the tobacco section of the AAA; USDA Solicitor Robert H. Shields; and Samuel B. Bledsoe, Wickard's assistant. The appointment of any one of these men would have been interpreted as a serious threat to the FSA in the politics of the Department.[5]

To appreciate the denouement of this drama, it is necessary to understand Wickard's strategy at the time—or perhaps his lack of it. Laboring under a sense of personal insecurity, in his efforts to fill Wallace's shoes as Secretary, unsure of himself in his relationships with the President and with others in the White House, lacking personal rapport with the leaders of both the American Farm Bureau Federation (AFBF) and the National Farmers Union (NFU), suspicious of the militant New Dealers with whom the leaders of the FSA were congenial, and somewhat confused by the complexities of the problems facing him, Wickard was a highly nervous Secretary of Agriculture. Furthermore, rumors that Roosevelt was going to

---

4. *New York Times*, Sept. 22, 24, 1942; Executive Order 9280, Dec. 5, 1942; F.D.R., *Public Papers* (1942), Vol. 11, pp. 517–29; USDA, Secretary's Memorandum 1054, Dec. 10, 1942, CBBP; Gladys L. Baker's interviews, Jan. 14, 16, 1943, USDAHF.

5. Author's interviews with Robert W. Hudgens, C. B. Baldwin, Gardner Jackson, Dillon S. Myer. See the following: Samuel B. Bledsoe, COHC, Vol. 3, pp. 523–31, Vol. 4, pp. 540–628; U. S., Bureau of the Budget, War Records Section, *The United States at War* (Washington, D.C.: GPO, 1946), pp. 342–46; Dean Albertson, *Roosevelt's Farmer* (New York: Columbia Univ. Press, 1961), pp. 333–57; Committee on Public Administration Cases (sponsored by the Social Science Research Council), "The Story of Parisius," Mimeographed (n.d., n.n.).

appoint either Davis, who was head of the Federal Reserve Bank in St. Louis, or Marvin Jones, a judge of the U. S. Court of Claims, as a "food czar" were giving Wickard many sleepless nights. Confusing neutrality for strength, and chronically suspicious of others' motives, he attempted to carry water on both shoulders, and tended to react to situations rather than to anticipate them. Rather than build alliances on which his strength might be enhanced, he accumulated enmities and isolated himself so that when the final test came he found himself alone and helpless.

On December 10, to the great surprise of many of the leaders of the USDA, Wickard selected, as his Director of Food Production, a very dark horse candidate for the position—Herbert W. Parisius. A former Lutheran minister in Minnesota and instructor of languages and history at a small college in Wisconsin, a former FSA regional director in the latter state, and, for a short time in 1940, an assistant to the newly-appointed Secretary Wickard, Parisius was not well known in the USDA and had never held a major line position in the FSA or in any other agency. Those who knew him personally saw him as an ardent New Dealer, a humanitarian and "social welfare type," and a firm advocate of the "small farmer issue" as promoted by the FSA and the BAE. Passing over other candidates for the position of Food Production Director as too deeply involved in factional rivalries within the USDA, too ambitious, too lacking in ability, or not of dependable allegiance to him, Wickard unwittingly selected the man whom "Beanie" Baldwin, Gardner "Pat" Jackson, Judge Samuel I. Rosenman, and other ardent New Dealers had been quietly promoting for the job. With the announcement of Parisius' appointment, Baldwin and his assistants rejoiced.[6]

During his first weeks as Director of Food Production, the former history instructor was given an unforgettable education in the "politics of organization," nicely summarized as follows by Wallace S. Sayre:[7]

> Organization theory in public administration is a problem in political strategy; a choice of organization structure is a choice of which interest or which value will have preferred access or greater emphasis.

Parisius' first task was to prepare a reorganization plan in which the agencies involved were to be "consolidated" or "integrated."

---

6. Albertson, *Roosevelt's Farmer*, p. 335; author's interviews with Jackson and Baldwin.

7. Wallace S. Sayre, "Premises of Public Administration: Past and Emerging," *Public Administration Review*, Vol. XVIII (Spring, 1958), p. 104.

Wickard presumably conceived the task as primarily one of draftsmanship rather than politics, and instead of appointing a representative and influential group of agency leaders to assist Parisius, he designated a committee of three men who did not enjoy much influence among the competing agencies of the USDA—Solicitor Shields, Personnel Director T. Roy Reid, and Cameron G. Garman, one of Budget Director William A. Jump's subordinates. Without any prior plan of action, and with little time for preparation, Parisius set out to attempt what neither Appleby nor the Mt. Weather Agreement of 1938 had achieved—the unification of the USDA.

He generally ignored the committee of three appointed by Wickard, and while he consulted with a group of specialists from the Administrative Management Division of the Budget Bureau, to assure that his plan of organization would be sound from an administrative management point of view, he turned for greatest guidance to the agency that he believed possessed the most relevant skills and experience—the FSA. This was not surprising, in view of his belief that application of supervised credit and other rural rehabilitation methods to small-scale or marginal farmers would greatly help to achieve the planned increase of 20 per cent in food production goals for 1943.[8]

The remainder of the month of December was an exceedingly frenetic and unsettled period, as the Parisius plan unfolded in an atmosphere of growing fears, suspicions, and rumors. Among the chroniclers of these events and in the various reminiscences by observers and participants, there is considerable disagreement about who proposed what, who spoke to whom, and who agreed with whom about what. On one point, however, there is justifiable agreement—the Parisius plan that finally emerged was greatly influenced by the leaders, the thinking, the experience, and the institutional self-interest of the FSA.

All personal and institutional ambitions aside, the plan represented a logical and technically sound blueprint for rational unification of the food production agencies of the USDA and for expansion and restructuring of food production. Most of the features of the plan had been discussed within the USDA for years by those who had deplored the dysfunctional competition among constituent agencies and the lack of departmental control. Emphasizing the need for unity of command, with responsibility delegated to regional and county levels, Parisius proposed that the separate field organizations of the

---

8. USDA, Secretary's Memorandum 1054, Dec. 10, 1942; author's interviews with Baldwin, T. Roy Reid; Baker's interviews, Jan. 14, 16, 1943.

various agencies be integrated into a single unified field force, based on nine production regions generally conforming to the pattern of FSA regional organization. The influence of the FSA was also discernible in the heavy reliance of the plan on the functions of credit and supervision.[9]

In proposing a staff for the FPA, Parisius attempted to be scrupulously fair in allocating positions among the various agencies involved. As Associate Directors, but with nominal powers and presumably for public relations purposes, he naïvely recommended two influential and ambitious departmental politicians—FCA Governor Albert G. Black and OAWR Director Townsend. For the key operational position, with which would be placed responsibility for supervision of the field organization, Parisius overruled some of his advisers, who feared the likely repercussions, and decided on the one man whose experience and skill seemed to fit him best for the tasks that lay ahead—his friend "Beanie" Baldwin. In the remainder of his staffing recommendations, the AAA, SCS, FCA, and FSA were well represented.[10]

Parisius extracted promises from his advisers and consultants to divulge none of the details of the proposed reorganization until he might have an opportunity to secure some agreement or commitment from Wickard, but within a week, many of the features of his plan were either known or rumored throughout the USDA. On December 18, in a discussion with Parisius about the plan, Wickard expressed some reservations about the heavy emphasis on credit and supervision, but he approved the organizational scheme in principle, including especially the proposed integration of the field services. On most of the subordinate staffing recommendations, Parisius was not yet decided, and therefore did not report them to Wickard at the

9. FSA, preliminary organization chart and working documents, CBBP.

10. Parisius' staffing recommendations for the FPA included the following: James E. Wells, Deputy Governor of the FCA, to be Assistant Director of the FPA, for credit affairs; Ivy W. Duggan, Norris E. Dodd, and Harry N. Schooler, AAA directors for southern, western, and north-central problems respectively, to be Assistant Directors of the FPA, for their respective areas; John B. Wilson, Special Assistant to the Administrator of the Agricultural Conservation and Adjustment Administration, to be Special Assistant to the Deputy Director of the FPA; James G. Maddox, Director of Rural Rehabilitation in the FSA, to be Executive Assistant to the Food Production Administrator (Parisius); John T. Whalen, Personnel Director of the AAA, to be Personnel Director of the FPA; and Milton P. Siegel, Special Assistant to FSA Administrator Baldwin, to be Fiscal Officer of the FPA. To fill the nine regional positions, Parisius and his advisers agreed to name men from the AAA, SCS, FCA, and the Forest Service.

time, but in response to the proposal that Baldwin be appointed Deputy Director of the FPA, Wickard was positively adamant—under no circumstances could Parisius have the FSA Administrator for the position. Parisius acquiesced. Wickard gave Parisius the definite impression at the time that the evolving organization plan was generally satisfactory and that he should proceed to elaborate it. Suffering from a very heavy cold, the Secretary went home to bed, where he remained for the next week. It would prove to be one of the most unpleasant Christmas holidays of his life.

With Wickard ill at home, the pot continued to boil in the buildings along the Washington Mall. Although Baldwin was now disenchanted with Parisius' handling of the situation and was less than enthusiastic about the prospect of serving as Deputy Director, he was highly angered by what he believed was Wickard's summary and unfair rejection of his nomination for the position. "Pat" Jackson, in characteristic fashion, immediately complained to Vice President Wallace that Wickard was sabotaging Parisius, Baldwin, and the FSA. The leaders of the AAA, SCS, FCA, and other agencies involved in the reorganization became apprehensive and did some politicking of their own. With Baldwin and Jackson interpreting the resistance to Parisius' plan as an attack on the FSA, and with Shields, Bledsoe, and others suggesting darkly that the Parisius plan was a conspiracy by Baldwin and "the FSA crowd" to capture the FPA, the merits of the Parisius plan were largely lost in the commotion.

Just before Christmas, Shields and Bledsoe visited Wickard at home to warn him that Parisius' proposed plan of organization was really a Baldwin plot. After fretting for two days, Wickard decided that his two visitors had probably been right, and that Baldwin was at the root of all his difficulties in the Department and was probably responsible for his cool relations with the White House. On Christmas night, a highly agitated Secretary of Agriculture paid a call at the home of a surprised FSA Administrator to try to persuade Baldwin to resign his position with the FSA and to accept a vaguely described job with Hendrickson's FDA. Wickard, of course, possessed the power to dismiss Baldwin, but not the courage to provoke what he believed would be a dangerous political reaction from the friends of the FSA. The Secretary's extraordinary Christmas visitation accomplished nothing but a bitter exchange of recriminations and further laceration of their wounded relationship.

Following the year-end holidays, Parisius met one rebuff after another from Wickard. The Secretary had already vetoed his plan for the integration of the field forces and his selection of Baldwin as

Deputy Director. An alternative plan, to consolidate the credit services of the FSA and FCA, Wickard believed, might be satisfactory, so long as the unified programs were placed in the "safe" hands of FCA Governor Black. Wickard ridiculed Parisius' proposal for nonrecourse loans to low-income farmers for purchase of livestock. His proposal for the reorganization of the field forces and elimination of the USDA War Boards and AAA committees, which were obstructing many of the food mobilization measures, was also judged to be unsatisfactory. Parisius could proceed with his plan to reorganize the food agencies at the Washington level, but he had better eliminate any FSA influences.

Meanwhile, Wickard was becoming increasingly angered by the embarrassing press coverage of the dispute and by what he believed were attempts by "Beanie" Baldwin and "Pat" Jackson to undermine him as Secretary. By mid-January, Economic Stabilizer Byrnes was urging Judge Marvin Jones to assume responsibility for agricultural mobilization, as an assistant in the Office of Economic Stabilization. Wickard was attempting to persuade either FCA Governor Black or CCC President Hutson to replace Parisius—Hutson was not interested, unless he could retain his present position, and therefore recommended OAWR Director Townsend. Parisius was at home drafting his resignation.

Strengthened in his resolve to resign with a flourish by a visit from "Pat" Jackson, accompanied by Paul Sifton of the NFU, Parisius submitted his resignation on January 15, 1943. Wickard immediately announced that Townsend would replace Parisius as Director of Food Production, that Hutson would serve as Executive Officer and would also remain as CCC President, and that FCA Governor Black would serve as a titular Associate Director of the FPA. In a bitter parting blast, Parisius declared that if "an all-purpose agency of credit, procurement, and supervision" were established, and if Townsend "will exclude from his organization those money lenders who look with two glass eyes at the working farmer needing help to do his full share in this war," the projected 20 per cent increase in food output in 1943 could be achieved. The fallen Director of Food Production then went overseas to work for Governor Herbert H. Lehman's Office of Foreign Relief and Rehabilitation Operations. A few days later, Wickard, presumably convinced that Jackson was guilty of treachery, agreed that he should be fired, and Bledsoe promptly arranged for Jackson's position as an assistant to the Under Secretary of Agriculture to be abolished "for reasons of economy."

The resignation of Parisius and the firing of Jackson were widely reported in the press as grave defeats for the FSA by the AAA, FCA, and the AFBF. "FOOD PRODUCTION AGENCY PUT UNDER DIRECTION OF AAA," declared the *Denver Post*. "SURRENDER TO FARM LOBBY LAID TO WICKARD," headlined the New York *PM*. "F.D.R. MAY OUST WICKARD OVER SMALL-FARM AID," predicted Drew Pearson. *Time Magazine* reported that Wickard had surrendered to the "big farmers' lobbyists" who "insist production increases can come only through higher prices," and that Townsend was "acceptable to the farm bloc."[11]

Wickard was now an object of contempt to both the victors and the vanquished in the affair. Through his own vacillation and through the agitation by extremists on all sides of the issues involved, he had allowed the dispute to become excessively personalized and the issues oversimplified. Consequently, the alleged policy differences between himself and the leaders of the FSA were greatly exaggerated. His true positions on expansion and conversion of farm production, parity prices and subsidies, the small farm issue, the role of the FSA, and reorganization of the USDA were closer to the FSA than to the AAA, FCA, or the AFBF. Bledsoe, having contributed as much as any man to Wickard's predicament, decided to scurry for cover, and went off to work for Oscar Johnston's National Cotton Council, one of O'Neal's allies, and then for the National Association of Manufacturers.

For Wickard personally, Drew Pearson's prediction of his imminent downfall proved partly correct. By the time the dust of the Parisius affair settled, President Roosevelt had lost confidence in the leadership capacity of his Secretary of Agriculture, and instead of requesting his resignation, he decided to transfer the war food responsibility to stronger hands. In March, Roosevelt created the Administration of Food Production and Distribution, embracing the FPA (including the FSA) and the FDA. In April, the name of the new consolidated agency was changed to the War Food Administration (WFA). Structurally within the USDA but headed by Davis as War Food Administrator, who would report directly to the White House, the change had the effect of removing the Secretary of Agriculture, at

---

11. Albertson, *Roosevelt's Farmer*, pp. 338–40, 354; *Washington* (D.C.) *Post*, Dec. 23, 1942, and Jan. 8, 1943; *Baltimore* (Md.) *Sun*, Jan. 4, 16, 1943; New York *PM*, Jan. 10, 17, 1943; *New York Times*, Jan. 13, 1943; *Washington* (D.C.) *Times-Herald*, Jan. 16, 1943; *Denver* (Colo.) *Post*, Jan. 16, 1943; Drew Pearson, in *Philadelphia* (Pa.) *Record*, Jan. 24, 1943; *Time*, Jan. 25, 1943; author's interviews with Baldwin, Jackson.

least in war food matters, one step away from the President. Hendrickson retained his job as Director of Food Distribution, while Townsend and Hutson continued in charge of food production. FSA Administrator Baldwin would be responsible to Davis, through Townsend and Hutson.

O'Neal of the AFBF and his allies were jubilant, while speculation circulated that Baldwin's days were numbered. Townsend and Hutson, ostensibly in an effort to forgive and forget, held the olive branch to Baldwin, but the FSA Administrator looked upon their professions of peace as the graciousness of the victor to the vanquished and he remained watchful and wary. Wickard, in the knowledge that the President had not requested his resignation, decided to swallow his pride and remain as an emasculated Secretary of Agriculture. He was soon being described as "Washington's outstanding forgotten man." The Parisius affair, in effect, thus contributed to the achievement of some of the AFBF goals—removal of effective power from Wickard, assignment of responsibility for agricultural mobilization to a "safe" man, and the isolation, if not liquidation, of the FSA.[12]

Within three months, War Food Administrator Davis was himself a casualty. Like Wickard and Parisius before him, he had failed to survive the treacherous jungle of wartime mobilization politics. Ostensibly over a dispute with Economic Stabilization Director Byrnes, Price Administrator Prentiss Brown, and the President concerning

12. Executive Order 9322, Mar. 26, 1943, and Executive Order 9334, Apr. 19, 1943, in F.D.R., *Public Papers* (1943), Vol. 12, pp. 528–29; Albertson, *Roosevelt's Farmer*, pp. 358–83; John B. Hutson, COHC, pp. 353–55, 377; Claude R. Wickard to Roosevelt, Apr. 12, 1943, NA, RG 16; author's interview with Baldwin.

In April, 1943, there was irony for Wickard in an exchange with Chester C. Davis. Wickard had sent a draft of a letter to the White House for the President's signature, as a reply to an inquiry from Representative John H. Folger of North Carolina regarding the FSA budget. In his draft, Wickard emphasized the contribution that low-income farmers had already made to the nation's food needs, and he justified continued financial support for them. "The program of the [FSA] has been a most effective means of mobilizing the full strength of our small farm producers in the war effort," Wickard wrote, and added that, "I hope the Congress will provide for the continuation of that job and will provide funds for that purpose . . . . I regard the work of the [FSA] important from the standpoint of the war as well as from the standpoint of the future of our economy."

Davis returned the carbon copy of the draft letter to Wickard with an admonition that the letter was "rather more extravagant than I would ask the President to be on behalf of any agency in the Department," and he warned the Secretary of Agriculture that, unless the President specifically requested, individual agency heads in the USDA should not communicate directly with the White House.

food prices and subsidies, he submitted his resignation to the President on June 16, and before the month was over he returned to his bank in St. Louis. The leaders of the FSA were briefly cheered by Davis' departure and by the appointment of Judge Marvin Jones to succeed him as War Food Administrator, but the heat of battle from other quarters denied them the pleasure of relaxation.

Until Wickard's surrender in the Parisius affair, the FSA, despite its harassment, had remained a highly viable agency, with substantial support in Congress, in the White House, from the press, and from major interest groups. Its internal unity and coherence had largely persisted, and its experience and specialized zeal had fitted it to play an important role in the wartime food program. Despite the polemics generated over the issue, the argument on behalf of the productive capacity of small-scale farmers had found considerable support among objective economists. Just as there was much political appeal in the argument on behalf of small business, so might Wickard have exploited substantial latent support for a more vigorous defense of the small farmer.

Furthermore, despite the President's preoccupation with the war, he had given no indication that he intended to throw the FSA to the wolves, along with other New Deal agencies. Wickard's performance in handling the proposed reorganization of the USDA field organizations, coming only a short time after his readiness to compromise on the appropriation bill in 1942, reinforced the impression among some members of the administration that the FSA was no longer politically tenable, and weakened Wickard's stature within the USDA, in Congress, and in the eyes of the President. He had thus created a situation in which, from his own point of view, further retreat might mean his own survival.

In retrospect, it is tempting to seek scapegoats for the confounding of the Parisius plan for reorganization of the USDA. The political naïvete of Parisius; the insecurity, indecision, and suspicions of Wickard; the scheming and vindictiveness of Baldwin; the talebearing, agitation, and treachery of Jackson; the jealous resistance of the leaders of the AAA, SCS, FCA, and other agencies; the obstructive tactics and economic self-interest of O'Neal and the AFBF—these are some of the alleged explanations of the affair. However, as long as administrative organization in government is rooted in competing personal and political interests and values, the process of administrative reorganization can take place strictly in accordance with purely technical criteria of rationality only in some future beatific vision.

Armageddon and Aftermath / [377]

The final showdown in the life of the FSA came in 1943 with three crucial congressional tests—disposition of the farm labor program, the FSA appropriation for 1944, and the question of whether the House Agriculture Committee would launch a special investigation of the agency. Although there was no inevitability in the course of events, by 1943 Baldwin and his assistants had little cause to be optimistic, for, as the frontier philosopher, Josh Billings, appropriately observed, "When a man gets going downhill, it seems that everything was greased for the occasion."[13]

House Joint Resolution 96: The "Peonage Law"

The test on the farm labor program had been brewing for months. During the summer and fall of 1942, as we have seen, the FSA and the U.S. Employment Service shared responsibility for the *domestic* program, while importation of Mexican and other foreign farm workers was entirely an FSA enterprise. Meanwhile, leaders of the AFBF, the National Grange, the National Cotton Council, the Associated Farmers of California, and others began to complain about the growing farm labor shortage and about FSA enforcement of wage, housing, and working standards. In the fall, the House Agriculture Committee conducted special hearings on the labor problem, and in their report they expressed some dissatisfaction with existing administrative arrangements.[14]

With the creation of the FDA and FPA in the USDA in December, responsibility for the farm labor program was divided between them. After the appointment of Townsend as Director of the FPA in January, 1943, an Agricultural Labor Branch (originally called the Agricultural Manpower Branch) was created in the FPA, and Major John O. Walker of the FSA was assigned to direct it. All FSA personnel involved in farm labor planning were transferred with Walker, while responsibility for management of migratory labor camps, transportation of domestic workers, and importation of workers from Mexico and other foreign countries remained in the FSA under Baldwin.

Later in January, responsibility for recruitment and placement of

---

13. Donald Day, *Uncle Sam's Uncle Josh* (Boston: Little, Brown, 1953), p. 178.
14. R. M. Duncan to Roosevelt, Oct. 10, 1942, FDRL, OF 227; U.S., Congress, House, Agriculture Committee, Hearings, 77th Cong., 2d Sess., *Farm Labor and Production* (Washington, D.C.: GPO, 1942).

domestic workers was transferred from the U. S. Employment Service to the USDA by a directive of Paul V. McNutt's War Manpower Commission. Responsibility was delegated to the Extension Service, with the FSA retaining the labor camps, transportation of domestic workers, and the foreign program. Wickard proceeded to make additional efforts to coordinate the farm labor program within the USDA, and then requested Congress to appropriate more than $65 million for support of the program during calendar year 1943, with funds assigned directly to the Secretary of Agriculture.[15]

Congress, however, had other plans. The House began its hearings on Wickard's budget request on February 17, and met a united front among the conservative farm organizations. At the invitation of Clarence Cannon, the leaders of the AFBF, the National Grange, and the National Council of Farmers Cooperatives proposed a plan which would provide that the entire farm labor program and funds should be assigned to the Extension Service. The program, furthermore, should be decentralized to each state where the state extension service would be responsible for administration. Their plan also called for a prohibition against the use of any funds for the purpose of prescribing or enforcing any standards or regulations governing farm workers' wages, housing, working conditions, bargaining requirements, or union memberships. Finally, they proposed that Congress specifically

---

15. Wayne D. Rasmussen, *History of the Emergency Farm Labor Supply Program 1943–1947*, BAE Monograph XIII (Sept., 1951) pp. 35–42; Baker's interviews, Nov. 20, 1942, Dec. 29, 1942, Feb. 19, 1943, and Mar. 3, 1943, USDAHF; U.S., War Manpower Commission, Directive 17, Jan. 23, 1943, *Federal Register*, Vol. 8, p. 1426; USDA, Secretary's Memorandum 1075, Mar. 1, 1943, CBBP; author's interview with Baldwin.

Within two months after the creation of the Agricultural Labor Branch in the FPA under Major John O. Walker, Wickard performed what amounted to a ritual of coordination when he created an Agricultural Labor Administration in the USDA, and appointed Wayne H. Darrow, Director of Information for the AAA, to direct the new agency. Darrow was believed to be acceptable to both the FSA and the AFBF, but his role as manager of the anti-AFBF publication, *Spade*, should have left no doubt in anyone's mind as to his position. Darrow presented a plan for the administration of the farm labor program, which would have permitted a continued active role for the FSA. However, Wickard realized that by this time his efforts were irrelevant, in view of the impending creation of the War Food Administration and the expected shift of the farm labor program to "safe" hands. He therefore decided to carry on without major reorganization, with the Extension Service responsible for recruitment and placement of domestic labor, and the FSA continuing largely as in the past. See William J. Block, *The Separation of the Farm Bureau and the Extension Service* (Urbana: Univ. of Illinois Press, 1960), p. 47, for discussion of the publication, *Spade*.

prohibit any participation whatever by the FSA in the farm labor program.

In their report to the House on March 12, the Appropriations Committee ratified this plan. All responsibility for the farm labor program—domestic and foreign workers alike—should be transferred to the federal and state extension system, and the only provision for participation by the FSA was temporary responsibility for the Mexican program, until a new agreement could be reached with the Mexican Government. During consideration of the bill on the House floor, an amendment introduced by Judge Malcolm C. Tarver's friend, Representative Stephen Pace of Georgia, was approved. It provided that no farm labor should be transported out of a county without prior approval of the resident county agricultural agent, or out of a state without prior approval of the state commissioner of agriculture. On March 17, the bill, entitled House Joint Resolution 96, passed the House.[16]

While it was being considered by the Senate, Davis became War Food Administrator, and promptly appointed Lt. Col. Jay L. Taylor as a deputy administrator of the WFA, with the intention that he would be responsible for the farm labor program. Taylor was a former governor of the Federal Reserve Bank in Texas, a director of the National Livestock Marketing Association, and the owner of ranches in Texas and Mexico. According to a letter to Governor Earl Warren of California, from Charles C. Teague of the California Fruit Growers Exchange, reporting on Teague's efforts to promote passage of the House bill, California fruit growers were highly gratified with Taylor's appointment:[17]

> He seems to be a fine man and I believe he will make a fine Administrator, one that we will have no difficulty working with. I presented to him our plan for a new setup for recruitment, transportation, and housing of Mexican labor, together with the personnel records of the men that we have suggested to administer it. He indicated to me that he thought that he would take our recommendations.

One of Taylor's first official acts was to appoint Thomas Robertson, a rancher from Simi, California, to go to Mexico City and to conduct a comprehensive study of Mexican labor recruitment. Robertson, a friend of Teague, had previously prepared a plan for the California

---

16. *House Hearings*, Farm Labor Program, pp. 133–37, 151, 162, 204–5; U.S., Congress, House, Appropriations Committee, House Report 246, Mar. 12, 1943, 78th Cong., 1st Sess. (Washington, D.C.: GPO, 1943).

17. C. C. Teague to Earl Warren, Apr. 1, 1943, CBBP.

Fruit Growers Exchange, covering the recruitment of Mexican workers. According to Teague, one of the praiseworthy features of Robertson's plan was that it would be administered, under Davis and the WFA, by men "who have had Mexican experience [and] who are acquainted with Mexican customs and ways of doing business."[18]

Western farmers and ranchers naturally approved of the resolution, as passed by the House, except for the provisions designed to protect southern planters from what Tarver and Pace regarded as "western raiding" of southern farm workers. On April 1, Teague reported further to Governor Warren, as follows, on his efforts to secure support from the AFBF for revision of the resolution before the Senate:[19]

> The first man that I saw after coming to Washington was Ed O'Neal, President of the National Farm Bureau [sic].
> This was imperative in the interest of harmony in the national farm organizations . . . . I pointed out these fatal provisions in the bill and asked him to consent to amendments. At first he was adamant in refusing to do so. I then told him of our plan for a new setup for importation of Mexican labor. *He begged me not to present it to Secretary Wickard. When I asked him why, he said because it would work. His anxiety to get rid of Farm Security (with respect to the latter I was in complete sympathy),* [led him] *to insist on passage of Joint Resolution 96 without amendment* [italics not in the original].

During the Senate hearings on the bill, the familiar parade of witnesses appeared—representatives of the AFBF, National Grange, California Fruit Growers Exchange, and their allies—and, except for some minor objections, such as the language in the "Pace Amendment," they all favored the measure. The spokesmen for the NFU, Catholic Rural Life Conference, Southern Tenant Farmers Union (STFU), and the Congress of Industrial Organizations (CIO) and other labor groups, on the other hand, were not surprisingly opposed. Davis, the newly-appointed War Food Administrator, testified in support of the provisions for organizing the farm labor program around the extension system at state and county levels, but he urged that Congress not tie his hands by requiring that he employ the Extension Service at the national level. He made it explicitly clear, however, that "he certainly wouldn't want to turn the program over to the F.S.A. to administer."[20]

18. Teague to Warren, Mar. 30, 1943, CBBP.
19. Teague to Warren, Apr. 1, 1943.
20. U.S., Congress, Senate, Appropriations Committee, Hearings, 78th Cong., 1st Sess., *Farm Labor Program* (Washington, D.C.: GPO, 1943), pp. 59–201, 245–48, 257–61, 271–75; U.S., Congress, Senate, Appropriations Committee, Senate Report 157, Apr. 6, 1943, 78th Cong., 1st Sess. (Washington, D.C.: GPO, 1943).

On April 8, the Senate easily approved the bill by voice vote. It increased the House-approved sum of $26.1 million to $40 million; it relaxed the prohibition against participation by the FSA; and it reworded the prohibition against wage and other working conditions and against transportation of workers out of counties—the prohibition against transportation of farm workers out of states was entirely eliminated.

In the conference committee, the original House appropriation of $26.1 million was restored, the War Food Administrator was granted discretion in the assignment of a role to the FSA, the "Pace Amendment" was reworded to prohibit transportation of farm workers out of counties without prior approval of resident county agricultural agents, and restrictions on prescription and enforcement of wage and other standards were reworded so as not to automatically prevent the inclusion of prevailing wage rates in working agreements with employers of farm workers. The conference committee's compromise version passed the Senate on April 16 with a vote of thirty-nine to eighteen. Seventeen anti-administration Republicans, joined by Texas Democrat W. Lee "Pappy" O'Daniel, held out to the bitter end against any farm labor program whatever.[21]

Meanwhile, a storm of protest had developed among the measure's opponents on the left flank, who condemned it as a "peonage law." On April 7, for instance, the President received a telegram from "Eleanor" in California, where she had gone, at his request, "to look things over:" "Hope you will not sign bill taking away supervision of employment from Farm Security and putting it in hands of extension service. Sending you some important facts today airmail special much love." Gardner Jackson, still unemployed and "pawing over in my mind the fate that was handed out to me over at Agriculture," spoke to Marvin H. McIntyre at the White House on the telephone, and in a letter to the President on April 19, he urged Roosevelt to veto the bill. The provision that no farm workers should be moved out of a county without approval from the county agricultural agent, he contended, "virtually immobilizes the current supply of labor." The suggestion that a farm worker could step across the county line and escape the provision was hypocrisy, Jackson argued, because "most farm workers will not know their legal rights under the legislation [and] in areas where serious exploitation has long existed they will be subject to a kind of peonage." With respect to the transfer of the migratory labor camps to the Extension Service, Jackson declared,

21. *Congressional Record*, Vol. 89, pp. 3122–23, 3467.

"The only forces supporting this transfer are represented by Ed O'Neal, Oscar Johnston of the Cotton Council and Charlie Teague of the California citrus and walnut growers whose operations are under anti-trust laws indictment."[22]

During the next week, the White House was inundated by telegrams and letters of protest, some of which were inspired by FSA Administrator Baldwin. However, Roosevelt had already promised Senate and House leaders that he would support whatever bill emerged from conference, and on April 29, he signed House Joint Resolution 96 into law. Two weeks later, War Food Administrator Davis assigned responsibility for the farm labor program to his deputy, Lt. Col. Taylor. Baldwin was allowed to continue, under Taylor, to exercise the responsibilities of the FSA until Davis could decide on permanent administrative arrangements.[23]

On June 16, Baldwin, having just learned of Davis' decision to relieve the FSA of any participation in the farm labor program, drafted a bitter letter to the War Food Administrator. He deplored the fact that no one from the FSA had been consulted by the administration or Congress during consideration of the bill. He then went on to urge Davis to fire Robertson, the California rancher and friend of the organized fruit growers, on the grounds that Robertson allegedly had "made every effort to discredit the work of the FSA in California and Arizona," that he had "openly encouraged groups of farmers and public officials in California to protest our handling of any phase of the agricultural labor program," and that while he was on the federal payroll he had "attempted to use his position to secure workers for his own farm." Baldwin saw no justifiable reason for the unnecessary administrative delay and confusion that would result from a transfer of FSA functions at that time, when haste was so important, and urged that Davis reconsider his decision, especially with respect to the migratory labor camps.

However, the die was cast, and although Davis himself was to resign as War Food Administrator within two weeks, all FSA participation in the program was scheduled to cease on July 1. To ease the process of transition, many of the experienced subordinate FSA personnel who had worked on transportation of farm laborers and in the migratory labor camp progam were transferred to the Office

---

22. "Eleanor" to Roosevelt, Apr. 7, 1943, FDRL, OF 1568; Jackson (Apr. 19, 1943), Donald Henderson (Apr. 19, 1943), Phillip Murray (Apr. 29, 1943), Richard T. Frankensteen (Apr. 29, 1943) to Roosevelt, FDRL, OF 227.
23. 57 Stat. 70; WFA, Administrator's Memorandum 2, Apr. 30, 1943, CBBP.

of Labor in the WFA. Thus ended one of the most distinctive and provocative programs of the FSA, and a major opportunity for the agency to play a role in the war food program dissolved.[24]

Public Law 129: The "Death Appropriation"

The struggle of the FSA for survival did not take place on separate and compartmentalized battlegrounds. Simultaneously with the test over the farm labor program, there unfolded the larger and more crucial battle over the general budget for the FSA for the next fiscal year. The witnesses, the ammunition, the passion, and the litany of accusation and defense employed in one engagement spilled over into the other.

The major issue facing American agriculture in the spring of 1943 was farm production, and Baldwin, despite his defeats in the battle of the budget in 1942 and in the Parisius affair a few months later, decided to pursue again the "small farmer issue." This time, however, he was armed with what he believed was irrefutable evidence to vindicate his position. A survey by the BAE and the FSA, for instance, based on a 6 per cent sample of 463,941 actively supervised FSA client families, had revealed that FSA clients had increased their production proportionately more than did the average farmer in 1942, and that these small-scale and marginal farmers had contributed more than their share to the increases in seven of the nine vital farm commodities.[25]

The leaders of the FSA realized—but they did not advertise it— that these reported production increases by FSA client families were not wholly destined for the market, but included production for home consumption, and therefore the aggregate *economic* impact

---

24. Baldwin to Davis, June 16, 1943, CBBP.
25. FSA, *Annual Report* (1943), p. 11. FSA, "The Farm Security Administration Goes to War," 1942 Family Progress Report, Processed (May 15, 1943); FSA, "1943 Food Production of Active Standard Rural Rehabilitation Borrowers," Processed (Mar. 31, 1944), pp. 4, 10; CBBP. *Senate Hearings*, Agr. Approp. (1944), 78th Cong., 1st Sess., p. 618; *Senate Hearings*, Agr. Approp. (1945), 78th Cong., 2d Sess., p. 358; P. G. Peck and James C. Jensen, "Contributions of Farm Security Administration Borrowers to Agricultural Production Goals," *Journal of Farm Economics*, Vol. XXV (Feb., 1943), pp. 101–4.

In the midwestern region, according to the FSA-BAE study, the increased production by FSA client families represented 14 per cent of the war production goals for the region in 1942. For the country as a whole, 11 per cent of the total value of increases in production by all farmers in the 1942 crop year was contributed by FSA client families.

was less than the data suggested. Baldwin and his assistants argued, however, that by reducing the demand by FSA client families on available stocks of food and by raising the level of living and the health of hundreds of thousands of low-income rural Americans, the national interest was also being served. Furthermore, they contended, with the President calling for the mobilization of every possible food production resource, with the Extension Service sponsoring "victory gardens," with a "women's land army" being promoted to supplement the farm labor supply, then surely there was justification for the expenditure of government funds by the FSA for the mobilization of the small farmer.

House hearings on the appropriation for the FSA began before Judge Tarver's subcommittee (he had replaced Clarence Cannon as chairman), and for two days in March the FSA Administrator was compelled to listen to the indictment of his agency—borrowers under the tenant purchase program were selling their farms, in order to take advantage of rising land prices and thus to make a profit; the leaders of the FSA were "defying" the will of Congress in their "refusal" to hasten the liquidation of resettlement projects and cooperative farms; the FSA administrators of the farm labor program were "involuntarily" transporting farm workers and were "reshuffling" the agricultural population of the country; the medical care program of the FSA represented special treatment for the rural poor and discrimination against the needy families of the urban slums (for whom the members of the subcommittee had hitherto not been champions); and the provision of special diets for farm workers enroute from Mexico represented a wasteful extravagance. Baldwin vainly attempted to rebut each charge, and during the next few days he once again sent his Gideon's army of liberal congressmen, social action leaders of the churches, and representatives of liberal and labor organizations into battle.[26]

The forces of opposition to the FSA were thrown into the fray on March 8, and for several days the members of the subcommittee

---

26. *House Hearings*, Agr. Approp. (1944), 78th Cong., 1st Sess., pp. 974–94, 995–1107, 1411–12, 1426–32, 1436–81, 1530–34, 1447–49.

The witnesses who appeared for the defense of the FSA included the following: Democratic Representatives Voorhis of California, Hobbs and Sparkman of Alabama, Murdock of Arizona, Hays of Arkansas, White of Idaho, Kefauver of Tennessee, Patman of Texas, and Granger of Utah; Rev. John O'Grady of the National Conference of Catholic Charities; Benson Y. Landis of the Federal Council of Churches of Christ in America; Edith E. Lowry of the Home Missions Council of North America; Robert Hanschin of the NFU; and Elizabeth Herring of the National Board of the Young Women's Christian Association.

listened with great attention and sympathy to hostile representatives of the AFBF, the Irrigated Cotton Growers, and the National Cotton Council. H. S. Casey Abbott of the Irrigated Cotton Growers declared that the cotton growers of Arizona and California "want no more of Farm Security [and] we want to get back to the old basis of dealing with our old agencies." One of the most vehement witnesses was Oscar Johnston of the National Cotton Council who criticized the FSA for its "continuous expansion of bureaucratic regulation seriously jeopardizing the democratic system of government." He condemned the "socialistic efforts" of the agency, recommended that it be abolished and its "worthy programs" transferred to other agencies, and then went on to charge that the FSA was simply a scheme to undermine the principle of fee simple land ownership in the United States and to perpetuate the "un-American ideas" of Rexford G. Tugwell. Similarly, Edward A. O'Neal and W. R. Ogg of the AFBF took advantage of the opportunity to reiterate their demands that the FSA be abolished, the tenant purchase program transferred to the FCA, and other "needed functions" shifted to "appropriate existing State and Federal agencies."[27]

During the last two days of hearings, Baldwin was allowed to respond to the charges against him and his agency. The quotations by Johnston from the writings of Tugwell on the problems of agriculture in Puerto Rico, with the implication that those views governed FSA policy, were "cheap demagoguery and another example of the smear technique," Baldwin asserted. Charges of Communism against the FSA and himself were absurd. The accusation that he and his assistants were failing to liquidate resettlement projects and cooperative farms, as rapidly as was consistent with the government's investment and the welfare of the people involved, was patently untrue. The charge that the FSA was undermining the principle of fee simple land ownership was ridiculous, in view of the agency's contribution to the strengthening of the family farm. Finally, Baldwin reported that he did not believe that provisions for medical examinations of Mexican workers and special food for those suffering gastric disturbances en route to their assigned farms were costly pampering.[28]

The report of the House Appropriations Committee, on April 13, represented a resounding victory for the opponents of the FSA. The committee recommended that the FSA be abolished, with the tenant

27. Ibid., pp. 1389–92, 1482–1520, 1541–77, 1616–42.
28. Ibid., pp. 1642–1717.

purchase program transferred to the FCA, to be administered through the Federal Farm Mortgage Corporation, the federal land banks, and the national farm loan associations. Management and liquidation of resettlement projects and other enterprises should be transferred to the FCA. The farm and home management assistance activities of the FSA should be assigned to the Extension Service. The committee approved the President's budget request for the tenant purchase program, but recommended a reduction of more than 60 per cent in the rural rehabilitation program.

When the bill arrived on the House floor for debate, it was caught in a jurisdictional dispute between the members of the Appropriations Committee, who sought a rule prohibiting any amendments, and the House Agriculture Committee, whose chairman, Hampton P. Fulmer, charged that the Appropriations Committee was "usurping the legislative functions of the Agriculture Committee," and seeking "to completely revolutionize the programs of the Department of Agriculture." He further asserted that Tarver's subcommittee had been influenced by "big farmer" lobbying organizations seeking "to use the war emergency to destroy anything that does something for the small individual farmers." William P. Lambertson of Kansas, ranking Republican member of Tarver's subcommittee, was stung to a bitter response, but confessed that the dispute had nothing to do with competition between the committees: "abolition of the Farm Security Administration is the fighting point." Finally, after five days of caustic debate, the bill passed the House by voice vote on April 20, with funds for the FSA virtually eliminated—a sum of $500,000 for the administration of the tenant purchase program was included through a floor amendment.[29]

Before proceeding to the denouement of the appropriation battle, let us stop the clock at this point and examine briefly some of the additional facets of a very complex situation. First of all, the House Agriculture Committee, partly because of the defensive position into which it had been maneuvered by the House Appropriations Committee and also in response to anti-FSA sentiments held by some of its own members, decided that the time was ripe to launch its planned special investigation of the FSA. On March 18, the House passed a resolution creating the Select Committee to Investigate the Activities of the Farm Security Administration. Harold D. Cooley of North Carolina, one of the persistent critics of the FSA, was desig-

29. U.S., Congress, House, Appropriations Committee, House Report 354, Apr. 13, 1943, 78th Cong., 1st Sess. (Washington, D.C.: GPO, 1943), pp. 17–19; *Congressional Record*, Vol. 89, pp. 3592–3610.

nated as chairman. Not a single dependable friend of the agency was included among its additional six members.[30]

There was at this time an enormous public record of charges against the FSA, which had accumulated during the hearings of the Byrd Committee, the Tolan Committee, and the House and Senate appropriations subcommittees, but the Cooley Committee chose to dig for themselves, and they knew precisely where to strike political pay dirt. For ten days in May and nine days in June, thirty-four witnesses appeared for and against the FSA, including many of the familiar participants in previous committee hearings. The Cooley Committee hearing room became a platform for the airing and rebuttal of virtually every charge, complaint, grievance, and rumor against the agency—resettlement projects, cooperative farming associations, the emergency grant program, and the writings of Tugwell, whom the committee considered to be a continuing and sinister influence in the agency, despite the fact that for the previous several years he had been the Governor of Puerto Rico and out of communication with the FSA.[31]

The results of a very different kind of investigation, carried out during the spring of 1943, would have cheered the leaders of the FSA, if they had known about them. In April, War Food Administrator Davis decided to attempt to resolve the question about what to do with the FSA, and appointed a committee of consultants to conduct "a quiet examination into the objectives of the Farm Security Administration and the degree of success it has attained." He took care to assure that the consultants' findings and recommendations should not become known to FSA Administrator Baldwin or Assistant Administrator Robert W. Hudgens, for he realized the compulsion they would be under to exploit, in the defense of their embattled agency, any favorable findings. Davis desired a candid evaluation of the FSA, but it was generally understood that he would probably use the consultants' report as a prelude to removal of Baldwin and reorganization of the agency. The committee was composed of the following men: John D. Black of Harvard University, who served as chairman; Clarence Poe of the *Progressive Farmer*, a friend of

---

30. *Congressional Record*, Vol. 89, p. 2194.
The members of the Cooley Committee, in addition to the chairman, were the following: Democrats John W. Flannagan of Virginia, Orville Zimmerman of Missouri, and Stephen Pace of Georgia; and Republicans Clifford R. Hope of Kansas, Anton J. Johnson of Illinois, and Ross Rizley of Oklahoma.
31. *Cooley Committee Hearings*, Pts. 1, 2.
By the time the committee reported on the remainder of its hearings (Pts. 3, 4) in 1944, a total of 1,969 pages had accumulated.

O'Neal and the AFBF, but a loyal champion of the FSA; and Paul D. Sanders of Poe's publication, the *Southern Planter*. These consultants, in turn, sought the advice of others who represented a fairly wide spectrum of opinion in agriculture.[32]

Although the consultants never prepared a formal joint report to Davis, Black submitted a carefully detailed analysis of most of the charges and criticisms of the FSA, in the form of a personal and confidential report to Davis. His objectives, he wrote, were as follows:

> The need for this report arises from the circumstance that all needed facts about FSA activities are not now known. On one hand a campaign of attack has been organized against it that includes a considerable amount of misrepresentation and overstatement. Friends of FSA, however, are also guilty of sins of omission of pertinent facts and some commission of at least part untruths. Official testimony presented before committees of Congress falls short of developing full truths; and financial and statistical reports are inadequate to this end. This report . . . does represent at least the beginning of an attempt to state facts as they are.

In the rural rehabilitation loan program, which represented the bulk of the agency's activities and expenditures, Black found the following: (1) there were cases where loans were made to families unable to meet their repayment schedules; (2) some FSA county supervisors probably made dubious loans in order to meet their assigned quotas; (3) some farm and home plans were unduly optimistic in their estimates of anticipated receipts; (4) in the earlier years especially, many borrowers were burdened with too ambitious a program and too large a loan debt; (5) efforts were made, especially in the beginning of the program, to "rehabilitate" families living on too small or too poor farms; and (6) many of the FSA county supervisors were not sufficiently competent in farm management themselves. He concluded his analysis of the rural rehabilitation program with the following judgment:

> All of the foregoing are legitimate criticisms of the conduct of the FSA rehabilitation loan program. But they can be very easily overstated, and

32. Baker's interview with John D. Black, Feb. 1, 1946; Baker's "Organization and Leadership of the FSA" (unpublished MS); USDAHF. Author's interview with Marvin Jones.

Davis' consultants, in turn, sought the advice of the following: Roy Green of the Colorado State College; Extension Directors H. C. Ramsower of Ohio and David Watkins of South Carolina; President Roy Thompson of the New Orleans Land Bank; and O. B. Jesness of the University of Minnesota. William Allen White of the *Emporia* (Kan.) *Gazette* was invited to serve on the consulting committee but was unable to do so because of ill health.

Only two copies of Black's report to Davis in May, 1943, were prepared, and both were reportedly lost. The discussion here is based on Black's rough first draft.

commonly are; and the degree of fault has lessened much since 1935–37. At present, these mistakes have for the most part been brought within reasonable bounds, and further improvement is in prospect. It must be remembered that these loans are a new device, without any close precedent. Many county bankers had made some loans roughly of this type, and had given some of the same sort of guidance. But these had been on a highly individual and personalized basis. Here was a public agency doing it on a large scale . . . . [The rehabilitation program] *begins to look like one of the most significant social inventions developed in the field of agriculture in recent decades. Properly administered, such loans can be used both more extensively and more intensively to great advantage during the war and afterwards* [italics not in the original].

Black made similar judgments of the tenant purchase program, cooperative activities, and resettlement projects. He also saw the need, and made recommendations for, closer collaboration with the Extension Service, the FCA, and local private credit facilities. Regarding the political predicament of the FSA, he reported that "it is the bad manners of the FSA that has got it into its present difficulties," and that the leaders of the agency should "desist from [their] general habit of attacking and condemning almost everybody and everything that differs with [them]."

Black did not believe that the FSA should be abolished and its functions curtailed or transferred to other agencies. Rather, he recommended that the FSA be continued as a separate agency under the following conditions: (1) there should be greater collaboration and "dovetailing" with the FCA, Extension Service, and local private credit facilities; (2) greater use should be made of local farmers committees; (3) special programs for the lower-income farm families at the very bottom of the pyramid should be developed; (4) the rural rehabilitation program and the tenant purchase program should be continued "in full vigor;" (5) resettlement projects should be liquidated, but in an orderly manner; (6) the programs of the FSA "should be largely restricted to the three types of activity above named, and . . . activities not closely related to, and essential to, the success of these [should] be dropped;" and (7) Congress should "draw up a bill giving definite legislative status to the FSA and clearly defining its functions."

Although Black's report to Davis was primarily concerned with the economic and technical dimensions of the agency, and tended to lay all of the blame for its current political adversities on the alleged chauvinism of the leaders, the report nevertheless was the first candid and objective evaluation of the FSA since its creation. Davis resigned before he had an opportunity to act on the recommendations, but the report did exert an influence on the events that followed. Let us now, therefore, return to the battle over the appropriation bill for fiscal year 1944.

During House consideration of the bill and in preparation for action in the Senate, the leaders of the FSA and their allies prepared their last ditch defenses. Baldwin went to New York City on the day following House passage to mobilize some of his supporters there, and in an address at the Park Central Hotel he defended his agency against what he believed was the most damaging and unjustified accusation—that the FSA had been guilty of Communism. "The FSA has adhered to the Jeffersonian concept of agriculture," he told his audience. The helping of low-income farmers to become more secure, productive, and independent small farm operators was not Communism, but Capitalism, and the inspiration for the cooperative projects of the FSA lay not in the collective farms of Soviet Russia, but rather in the traditional sharing of grain mills, threshing facilities, and other community enterprises in colonial America.

Meanwhile, in Washington, the FSA had found welcome support from M. L. Wilson, Director of the Extension Service, who wrote to Representative John J. Sparkman of Alabama that as far as he was concerned, there was no duplication of effort between the FSA and the extension system, that programs for low-income farm families required the specialized zeal possessed by the FSA, and therefore the agency should be continued in full vigor. Also, James G. Patton of the NFU once again wired the President, urging him to exert the greatest possible pressure on Congress to restore the funds for the FSA.[33]

Reminiscent of the campaign for passage of the Bankhead-Jones Farm Tenant Act eight years earlier, Courtney Dinwiddie of the National Child Labor Committee, Patton of the NFU, William Allen White of the *Emporia Gazette*, Rev. L. G. Ligutti of the Catholic Rural Life Conference, and Benson Y. Landis of the Federal Council of Churches of Christ in America organized the Emergency Committee for Food Production, to defend the FSA. The "sponsors" of the committee, many of whom knew very little about the work of the FSA and had had virtually no intercourse with the agency, included a constellation of labor, church, social welfare, and press leaders.

Meanwhile, as will be discussed more fully below, it became com-

33. Baldwin address, New York City, Apr. 21, 1943, CBBP; *New York Times*, Apr. 22, 1943; M. L. Wilson to John J. Sparkman, Apr. 17, 1943, quoted in *Congressional Record*, Vol. 89, p. 3591.

mon knowledge that many members of the House had supported the elimination of funds for the FSA, not to kill the programs, but rather as a tactical maneuver to force the resignation or firing of Baldwin and some of his assistants, and thus to "cleanse" the FSA of its sins. From Memphis, Tennessee, for instance, the *Commercial Appeal* praised the "idea" of the FSA, but lamented that it had been "impregnated with ideologies and causes," and that if the agency were to continue, it "must have its top leadership overhauled [and] the Tugwells and Baldwins must be removed from positions of influence, and sound, practical men with a knowledge of what is needed for the small farmer given the reins." John Temple Graves, writing in the *Asheville Citizen*, declared that, "If the Farm Security Administration is to be saved I believe it will need to make a burnt offering." Only Baldwin's resignation, Graves concluded, "would convince Congress of a new policy, and unless Congress is so convinced, there is not going to be any Farm Security Administration."

On May 3, a few days before the beginning of Senate hearings on the appropriation bill, Senator Claude Pepper of Florida called McIntyre on the telephone and left a message for the President:[34]

> Senator Pepper 'phoned me this morning to say that he thought there was a chance for action by the Senate to rescue the Farm Security Administration situation.
> He told me that the fight was being made on Baldwin and that certain "powerful interests" were trying to induce Davis to fire him. Claude wanted me to pass this on to you because he things [sic] that would be calamitous.

Some years ago, Harry Golden of the *Carolina Israelite* reputedly made the following observation before a congressional committee:

> Anytime a bill is presented to the Congress, I can close my eyes and visualize who will appear. They will be about the same people who usually testify for or against a bill. You never have any new blood.

For six days in May, 1943, the hearings before Senator Richard B. Russell's appropriations subcommittee presented such a familiar scene. Many of the witnesses who had appeared before Tarver's subcommittee in the House made a return trip to Capitol Hill. O'Neal and Ogg of the AFBF, for instance, once again called for abolition of the FSA, and reiterated their charges of "inexcusable waste, extravagance, and incompetence, and the misuse of farm

---

34. *Memphis* (Tenn.) *Commercial Appeal*, Apr. 18, 1943; *Birmingham* (Ala.) *Age-Herald*, Mar. 11, 1943; *Asheville* (N.C.) *Citizen*, Apr. 30, 1943. Marvin H. McIntyre to Roosevelt, May 3, 1943, FDRL, OF 1568.

relief funds for the pursuit of socialistic objectives inimical to the American way of agriculture." As evidence to support some of their allegations, they cited "field investigators for the House Appropriations Committee," but when some of the Senators present sought to secure the identity of the "investigators," O'Neal could cite only Representative Everett M. Dirksen of Illinois as the source of information. Dirksen, in turn, had based his accusations on nameless "Budget officials," and when Senator Clyde M. Reed of Kansas sought access to the alleged report, the House Committee refused to cooperate. "Now, certainly if we are expected to be influenced by such reports," Reed declared, "those reports ought to be available for our examination." In further questioning by the Senators, it became apparent that many of the AFBF charges against the FSA were a repetition of their testimony in the House, where Dirksen had been cited as the source of information, but the Illinois congressman had refused to name his alleged informants.[35]

For the unqualified defense of the FSA, chairman Dinwiddie of the Emergency Committee for Food Production, Patton of the NFU, Representative William Lemke of North Dakota, M. W. Thatcher of the Farmers Union Grain Terminal Association of St. Paul, and others pleaded for the agency. Albert J. Goss of the National Grange abandoned the shotgun of the AFBF and offered his qualified support. The FSA, he declared, should abandon the "junk" inherited from the Resettlement Administration, and eliminate its "visionary and impractical projects [and its] wild schemes." The agency should not be abolished, but should be harnessed and kept on a more legitimate path: "the remedy is for Congress to map out the road it wants F.S.A. to follow, then put up the fences to keep them in the road. Give them a specific job and prohibit them from doing anything not expressly provided in the law." War Food Administrator Davis urged that the tenant purchase and rural rehabilitation programs be continued, although not necessarily by the FSA, and he implied that if the matter were left to him, he would probably either abolish the FSA or drastically reorganize it.[36]

During the hearings, Senator John H. Bankhead acknowledged the need for new basic legislation, and Senator Russell, conceding that errors of judgment had been committed by the leaders of the

---

35. *Senate Hearings*, Agr. Approp. (1944), 78th Cong., 1st Sess., pp. 725–54, 954.

36. *Ibid.*, pp. 264–68, 790–940, 975–80, 1045–88, 1101–47.

FSA, saw no need for the extreme action proposed by the House. Despite "these various social experiments that have been foisted upon some phases" of the agency, he declared, too many people "pay lip service" to the problem of rural poverty. "For my part," the Senator from Georgia concluded, "I am bitterly opposed to burning down the barn to get out a few rats."

In their report to the Senate, Russell's subcommittee refrained from advocating outright abolition. They agreed, however, that the time had come for major surgery—"legislation should be considered by the Congress at an early date looking to the consolidation and coordination of the various loan activities of the Department of Agriculture." Meanwhile, the FSA should be continued, and toward that end, the report recommended an appropriation that was only 5 per cent less than the amount requested by the President. On June 10, after four days of sharp debate, the Senate overrode last-minute attempts by Harry F. Byrd and others to eliminate all funds for the FSA, and sustained the report of the Appropriations Committee by a vote of sixty-six to twelve.[37]

While House and Senate conferees sparred over a compromise, a new surge of rumors began to circulate, suggesting that Davis was about to fire "Beanie" Baldwin. On June 24, President Roosevelt wrote to Davis, in response to pleadings from Patton of the NFU and other members of the Dinwiddie Committee, as follows: "I sincerely hope that you will not remove Baldwin as head of the Farm Security Administration. This is a matter which should be carefully looked into." Four days later, Davis' own resignation was accepted, and one of the first items on the agenda of his successor, Judge Marvin Jones, was the fate of Baldwin.

Jones believed that the final hour had struck for the FSA, at least in the form in which it had operated for almost six years. He also came to the reluctant conclusion that he could secure House consent to a reasonable compromise on the FSA only by reassuring the resistant congressmen that Baldwin would be replaced. "I called 'Beanie' in and told him that if he were sincere in his interest in the poor farmer—and I knew he was—he would accede to demands and leave, in order to salvage the remnants of the FSA."

Baldwin was not surprised by the turn of events, for he well knew that, like Tugwell before him, he had become one of the lightning

---

37. *Ibid.*, pp. 266, 736; U.S., Congress, Senate, Appropriations Committee, Senate Report 287, June 5, 1943, 78th Cong., 1st Sess. (Washington, D.C.: GPO, 1943), pp. 11–14; *Congressional Record*, Vol. 89, p. 5641.

arresters for the Roosevelt administration. He also had known for some time that Economic Stabilizer Byrnes and War Food Administrator Davis had been discussing his replacement as FSA Administrator. Furthermore, Baldwin knew that for several months, Harry L. Hopkins, a special assistant to the President, had been promoting a new position for him in the field of international rehabilitation. Early in 1943, for instance, Lend-Lease Administrator Edward R. Stettinius, Jr., had offered him a place, but Baldwin had decided to remain at the helm of the FSA, at least until the 1943 appropriation battle was concluded. More recently, he had been offered positions with Governor Herbert H. Lehman's Office of Foreign Relief and Rehabilitation Operations, and Assistant Secretary of State Dean Acheson was then considering him for a position with the organization being planned to coordinate the rehabilitation of post-war Italy. Baldwin promised Jones that he would make a decision very soon, and then went off on a western tour and a vacation at a dude ranch in New Mexico, to make up his mind. Meanwhile, Jones went ahead and informed the leaders of the House that they could count on Baldwin's departure in the near future.[38]

The appropriation bill that finally emerged from conference and won approval of the Congress was a mortal blow to the FSA and its leaders. Funds for the tenant purchase program were reduced by only 8 per cent of the amount in the current appropriation and were exactly what the President had requested. The rural rehabilitation program, however, was cut to 43 per cent of the amount for the current year. Land purchasing and leasing, all cooperative activities, and civil service status for the great majority of FSA employees were strictly prohibited. There were additional restrictions on the size of loans, the amounts that might be loaned in any one county, the use of State Rural Rehabilitation Corporation funds, and transfers of FSA funds from one county to another. On July 12, a reluctant President signed the "death appropriation bill" into law, while the leaders of the FSA began the personal business of exploring new job opportunities in other agencies, re-examining their home mortgages and apartment leases, and performing the other tasks preparatory to their expected exodus from the crippled agency.[39]

38. *Birmingham* (Ala.) *Age-Herald*, May 11, 1943; *Little Rock* (Ark.) *Gazette*, May 23, 1943; *Memphis* (Tenn.) *Commercial Appeal*, May 25, 1943. Roosevelt to Davis, June 23, 1943, FDRL, OF 1568. Author's interviews with Jones, Baldwin.

39. Public Law 129, July 12, 1943, 57 Stat. 392.

From Dissolution to Consolidation

The remainder of the drama is anti-climactic. Baldwin returned from his western vacation determined to resign and to accept the position with the U.S. State Department's planned organization for liberated Italy. At the end of August, he left the FSA in the hands of Robert W. "Pete" Hudgens, as Acting Administrator. On September 3, Italy surrendered and Baldwin was promptly pursued by reporters in Washington, seeking to interview the man expected to be the first American proconsul in liberated Europe. The following day, President Roosevelt sent the former FSA Administrator a letter, drafted by Jonathan Daniels, administrative assistant to the President, at the suggestion of Patton of the NFU, which read in part as follows:[40]

> I learn with regret of your leaving the Farm Security Administration, even though this carries you abroad on another vital war assignment. The eight years you have given to the rebuilding of the family farm as the keystone in our national agricultural structure have strengthened this Nation immeasurably....
>
> Criticism and resistance you have expected and received, but we know that the extension of democratic opportunity to those who do not have it inevitably faces the bitter opposition of selfish and short-sighted persons who fear the people. We see today in the work of the Farm Security Administration new principles of faith, once condemned, that are now demonstrated and established. We know that most of the rural poverty and hardships we have allowed to exist in this Nation are unnecessary, and that given the chance, the small farmer has the character and capacity to overcome his handicaps and assume his full share of responsibility for the Nation's welfare.
>
> The significant fact in the work of the Farm Security Administration lies not in the emergency measures which it employed to stave off total collapse, but in the bold and constructive program it developed in the face of high skepticism toward restoring the independence of the family farm and reestablishing it on a sound and lasting foundation. I hope there will never be a time when the people of this country will fear to seek new answers to old and unsolved problems.

The President's letter was a solace to Baldwin, but looking ahead to the challenges before him rather than backward to regrets about the past, he spent the next two months submerged in the work of planning his organization for Italy, in interviewing candidates for his staff, and in completing the personal tasks preparatory to going over-

---

40. Roosevelt to Baldwin, Sept. 4, 1943, CBBP.

seas. *Newsweek* magazine predicted at the time that "Beanie" Baldwin could be counted on to transfer his evangelism and specialized zeal to the larger challenge abroad. However, as the weeks passed he became discouraged by the failure of the American and British Governments to resolve issues concerning the relationships between the representatives of the two victorious nations, the role of the military, and the question of civilian control in liberated Italy. By Thanksgiving, Baldwin's hope for the job in Italy was gone; and he therefore accepted a position as director of Sidney Hillman's CIO Political Action Committee, in preparation for organized labor's drive to help win the vice-presidential nomination again for Wallace in the coming election campaign. Baldwin later went on to become the campaign manager of Wallace's presidential race in 1948, and then the national secretary of the Progressive party during the early 1950's.[41]

Meanwhile, to return to the FSA, Baldwin had urged that Hudgens should be appointed as his successor. War Food Administrator Jones and others agreed that although Hudgens would likely be a highly competent FSA Administrator and that he had personally escaped much of the criticism that had been heaped upon Baldwin, he was, nevertheless, too closely identified with the old order. The times called for an outsider with impeccable credentials, they believed, especially someone who could win the confidence of Congress.

On November 10, Jones announced the name of the man on whom the future of the FSA presumably would hinge—Franklin W. Hancock, a veteran of four terms as a Democratic Representative from North Carolina, during which time he had served on the conservative House Committee on Banking and Currency. He also had had administrative experience as a member of the Federal Home Loan Bank Board, director of the Home Owners' Loan Corporation, trustee of the Federal Savings and Loan Insurance Corporation, and director of the Defense Plant Corporation.[42]

Hancock had no intention of serving as the undertaker of the FSA. While in Congress, he had supported the passage of the Bankhead-Jones Farm Tenant Act, and had voted for FSA appropriations through the years. As a southern moderate, he firmly believed in the need for governmental credit programs to supplement those of com-

41. *Newsweek*, Sept. 20, 1943; *Washington* (D.C.) *Daily News*, Dec. 6, 1943. Baldwin to Harry S. Muir, Sept. 21, 1943, CBBP; author's interview with Baldwin.

42. Hudgens to Donald R. Murphy, Nov. 11, 1943, NA, RG 16; biographical file on Franklin W. Hancock, FHAF; author's interview with Hudgens.

mercial banking institutions and of the more conservative lending program of the FCA. He tended to agree, however, with those who charged that the FSA had sacrificed its claim to legitimacy by promoting socially undesirable and politically costly experiments. In other words, as some of the foes of the FSA had charged, the leaders of the agency had exploited the Bankhead-Jones Farm Tenant Act as a haven for the perpetuation of the programs and ideology of the Resettlement Administration. He hoped that Congress would soon enact new basic legislation for the FSA, but in the meantime, he would operate strictly within the intent of the Bankhead-Jones Farm Tenant Act and the appropriation acts. There would be no mass firing of personnel, but the agency would adhere to a more "sound and business-like" basis. In granting loans, careful attention would be given to the capacity of applicants to respond to assistance, and those who were not qualified for the rural rehabilitation program should be eliminated from the clientele. "Sympathy," Hancock declared, "should not supplant judgment."[43]

Although there was no mass "purge" of the FSA, there was an exodus of those personnel who were involved in and closely identified with the proscribed programs. By the end of the year, many of those leaders who had been personally close to Baldwin were gone. Hudgens, urged by Hancock not to resign, agreed to remain, and for consolation was awarded the more honorific title of "Associate Director." He continued in the agency, a lonely monument to past grandeur, until 1946 when passage of new legislation and major changes in program and organization persuaded him to resign and to take a position as director of field organization for the American Cancer Society. He later became director of the American International Association for Economic and Social Development, Nelson A. Rockefeller's private technical assistance organization, which was devoted to agricultural reform in Latin America. For several years, Hudgens, with a number of other veterans of the FSA, found great satisfaction in applying the methods of the FSA in Venezuela and other Latin American countries.

Most of the other leaders of the FSA were less sanguine than Hudgens about the prospects of the agency following Baldwin's departure. By the end of 1943, George S. Mitchell, James G. Maddox, Carl N. Gibboney, Raub Snyder, Mason Barr, Laurence I. Hewes, Jr.,

---

43. Hancock to FSA County Committeemen, Dec. 14, 1943; Hancock to FSA regional conference, Jan. 10, 1944; Hudgens to Hancock, Mar. 20, 1944; FHAF. *House Hearings*, Agr. Approp. (1945), 78th Cong., 2d Sess., p. 965.

N. Gregory Silvermaster, and others who had been close to Baldwin and influential in the agency had left. Within a few more months, most of the remaining senior staff members in the Washington office and most of the regional directors followed them.

The process of dissolution was reflected in the following downward curve of full-time FSA employees:

1942	19,045
1943	14,862
1944	11,176
1945	8,742

This represented an elimination of 54 per cent of the agency's personnel during the four-year period. A large proportion of those who left the FSA, and in many cases who had left the government entirely, had been in policy-making, supervisory, and professional positions. Since the essence of the FSA was the evangelism and specialized zeal of its leaders and personnel, the agency that emerged from this process of dissolution and consolidation was a very different organization, although it continued to bear the name.[44]

The change was also reflected, of course, in the budgets and policies of the FSA. The following data are indicative of what occurred under the careful and "businesslike" leadership of Hancock:[45]

Fiscal Year	Initial TP Loans[1]	Original Standard RR Loans[2]	Total TP Obligations[1]	Total RR Obligations[2]
1942	7,844	78,832	$47,772,615	$179,539,399
1943	4,794	52,392	30,756,554	135,060,391
1944	3,255	23,597	23,569,253	95,660,772
1945	1,853	30,000	13,125,494	91,843,816

1. Tenant Purchase Program
2. Rural Rehabilitation Program

In the spring of 1945, Hancock reported to Tarver's appropriations subcommittee in the House on his stewardship. The FSA no longer had responsibility for any duties in the farm labor program. Sixty

---

44. *New York Times*, Oct. 27, 1943; FSA, "Monthly Activity Report," Jan., 1944, Table 7-B, FHAF; *House Hearings*, Agr. Approp. (1945), 78th Cong., 2d Sess., p. 962; *Senate Hearings*, Agr. Approp. (1945), 78th Cong., 2d Sess., p. 369; author's interviews with Hudgens, Maddox, Raub Snyder; Laurence I. Hewes, Jr., to author, Jan. 23, 1961.

45. *House Hearings*, Agr. Approp. (1945), 78th Cong., 2d Sess., p. 962; *Senate Hearings*, Agr. Approp. (1947), 79th Cong., 2d Sess., p. 21; FSA, Form FSA-323 (1942-45).

of the 152 resettlement projects had been completely liquidated, and most of the remainder would soon be gone. Fourteen of the fifteen cooperative farming associations had been discontinued, and loans to cooperative associations were no longer being made. Of the 940,726 acres of land owned by the government, only 32.4 per cent—304,859 acres—remained to be sold. All long-term leases of government land had been cancelled. In the rural rehabilitation program, Hancock had complied with the congressional directive that no individual applicant should be loaned more than $2,500 in any fiscal year, and to further reduce the possibility of client "malingering" on the program, Hancock explained, he had established a maximum repayment period of five years. Furthermore, grant funds were now being used only where absolutely necessary to relieve human suffering. "We are conducting no program," Hancock assured the subcommittee, "carrying on no activity, that is not definitely within the authority given us."[46]

Many formerly hostile members of Congress were now visibly pleased. Shortly before Baldwin's resignation, for instance, Republican Representative Charles A. Plumley of Vermont had described the FSA and some of the other agencies of the USDA as "the largest group of bloodsucking barnacles on the ship of state," but in response to Hancock's report of progress, in the spring of 1945, Plumley was delighted: "It is a great satisfaction to have here before us somebody who can make such a presentation."[47]

Despite his careful deference to the desires of Congress, not even Hancock was entirely free from some of the criticism that Baldwin had received. For two years following Baldwin's departure, the leaders of the AFBF and their allies in Congress and among the farm organizations continued to demand the outright abolition of the FSA. And congressional appropriation hearings continued to ring with the familiar charges—FSA field personnel were still "soliciting" clients; the agency's administrative expenses were still excessive; the rate of liquidation of resettlement projects and cooperative enterprises and the sale of government-owned land were still too slow; there were still too many personnel in the field organization and in the public information staff; and the repayment record of borrowers was still faulty.

46. *House Hearings*, Agr. Approp. (1946), 79th Cong., 1st Sess., pp. 508–20.
47. Charles L. Plumley, quoted in *Sacramento* (Calif.) *Bee*, Apr. 13, 1943; *House Hearings*, Agr. Approp. (1946), 79th Cong., 1st Sess., pp. 561–62.

Like his predecessor, Hancock was driven to complain from time to time about the inadequacy of funds, the inability to accept more than half of the applicants for loans, the difficulties in providing more loans to returning war veterans, the hampering effects of restrictions on the size of loans and the effects of the county loan limitations, and the tendency for members of the congressional appropriations committees to persist in applying banking standards to the programs of the FSA. The growing disenchantment of FSA Administrator Hancock was reflected in an exchange in 1945 with Representative Lambertson of Kansas, one of Baldwin's erstwhile tormentors, over the charge that the medical care program of the FSA was "socialized medicine"—Hancock stoutly maintained that it was not. Lambertson was moved to express a thought that many of the FSA Administrator's former congressional colleagues had privately harbored: "I do not see how you fit into this program. I am surprised that you ever took this place." Hancock's response was brief and to the point: "I still have some humanity left in my soul."[48]

By the fall of 1945, Hancock had had enough and he submitted his resignation. Immediately there was speculation that at long last, "St. Pete" Hudgens would become Administrator. Once again, the ghostly army of FSA advocates among the labor unions, social welfare agencies, social action groups in the churches, and the NFU mobilized their forces. They attempted to persuade Secretary of Agriculture Clinton P. Anderson to appoint Hudgens as FSA Administrator, but Anderson selected an even more conservative man —Dillard P. Lasseter of Georgia. A veteran of the U.S. Foreign Service, former cotton textile manufacturer, member of the Georgia bar, former staff director of the House Civil Service Investigating Committee (the Ramspeck Committee), and at the time of his appointment as FSA Administrator, the southeastern regional director of the War Manpower Commission, Lasseter possessed none of the idealism and sense of commitment to the assault on chronic rural poverty that had characterized, in varying degrees, his predecessors. Under Lasseter's leadership, which endured until the advent of the Eisenhower administration, when a still more conservative administrator was appointed, the process of dissolution and consolidation was completed. In 1946, as we have seen, Hudgens finally lost his will to

48. *House Hearings,* Agr. Approp. (1945), 78th Cong., 2d Sess., pp. 967, 1101; *House Hearings,* Agr. Approp. (1946), 79th Cong., 1st Sess., pp. 507–607; *Senate Hearings,* Agr. Approp. (1946), 79th Cong., 1st Sess., pp. 272–356.

fight—by now he was regarded as the "last of the liberals" among the leaders of the agency—and when the regional organization was abolished and other changes were made in policy and administration, he decided to leave.[49]

There remains one piece of unfinished business before we allow the FSA to pass into history. Let us, therefore, return to 1943 and briefly trace the Cooley Committee's investigation of the FSA and the legislation that flowed from it. Responding to pressures from Bankhead, Russell, and others in the Senate who were growing impatient with the Cooley Committee's redundant and dilatory hearings on complaints against the long-criticized and, after 1943, proscribed activities of the FSA, Cooley introduced a hastily drafted bill in the House in March, 1944, even before his committee's report was submitted. His bill, which he claimed was based on the committee's forthcoming report, would abolish the FSA, and in its place would reconstitute the Farmers Home Corporation which had been provided for in the Bankhead-Jones Farm Tenant Act in 1937 but had been allowed to become dormant. In May, Cooley submitted his committee's report, which was little more than a recitation of charges and complaints that had been aired during the hearings in his committee and in many appropriation hearings.[50]

With the Congress in haste to adjourn for the presidential nominating conventions, and with the FSA now in the "safe hands" of former congressman Hancock, there was no sense of urgency about new legislation, and Cooley's bill was stillborn. In February, 1945, he introduced a second bill, essentially the same as the first, but the Congress was still not interested and the Cooley bill was ignored. Another year passed and in April, 1946, he introduced a third measure entitled the "Farmers Home Administration Act of 1946."

The latest bill provided that the FSA should be abolished and a new agency, to be called the Farmers Home Administration, created in its place. The Bankhead-Jones Farm Tenant Act should be amended, the rural rehabilitation program liquidated, and the tenant purchase program (hereafter to be called the farm ownership program) transferred to the new agency. Provisions were also made in

49. *Charlotte* (N.C.) *Observer*, Nov. 24, 1945; New York *PM*, Nov. 29, 1945; *Washington* (D.C.) *Evening Star*, Dec. 6, 1945. Biographical file on Dillard B. Lasseter, FHAF; author's interviews with Lasseter, Hudgens.

50. U.S., Congress, House, Select Committee of the House Committee on Agriculture, To Investigate the Activities of the Farm Security Administration, House Report 1430, May 9, 1944, 78th Cong., 1st Sess. (Washington, D.C.: GPO, 1944).

the bill for the transfer of the Emergency Crop and Feed Loan Division of the FCA to the new agency, for a modest program of loans to help returning veterans of World War II to become farm owner-operators, and for short-term loans for such purposes as the development of water facilities, farm housing, and emergencies such as flood and drought.

The bill was debated briefly in the House and Senate, and after passage by voice vote, President Harry S. Truman signed it into law on August 14. What had been the tenant purchase program in the FSA became the core of the new agency, with Paul V. Maris in charge of the program. Some of the more acceptable methods and techniques of the rural rehabilitation program, such as supervised credit, were continued in the new agency, but anything that suggested "sociological experimentation" was vigorously avoided. In the new world of 1946, with "Pete" Hudgens gone, Maris became the "liberal evangelist" of the Farmers Home Administration (FHA).[51]

During the first year of operations, 40 per cent of FHA loan funds went to loans for returning war veterans, and by 1950, veterans received 93 per cent of the farm ownership loans and 50 per cent of the loans for operating purposes. During these years, the leaders of the agency administered their programs carefully, avoided the "errors" of their predecessors, and became preoccupied with maintaining cordial relations with key members of Congress. In 1951—fifth anniversary of the establishment of the FHA—Representative Cooley, by this time considered to be the "father of the agency," offered proprietary praise:

> I take greater pride in this organization . . . than any other agency connected with agriculture . . . . I don't know of a single administrator who has kept in closer touch with Congress than has [FHA Administrator] Dillard Lasseter. And I know he was smart enough to know that by doing that very thing, he would achieve the confidence which he has enjoyed.

Three years later, with the FHA languishing under President Eisenhower's more conservative FHA Administrator, Robert B. Mc-Leaish, the pendulum seemed to have swung full stroke in the decline of the government's assault on chronic rural poverty. During a congressional appropriation hearing on the budget for the FHA, for instance, Representative Jamie L. Whitten of Mississippi, an erstwhile foe of the FSA when it was under attack, seemed to express the low

---

51. *Congressional Record*, Vol. 91, p. 1207; Vol. 92, pp. 3069, 3388. Pub. Law 731, 60 Stat. 1062. Author's interviews with Hudgens, Lasseter, and Howard Bertsch.

state of affairs for the FHA when he admonished Secretary of Agriculture Ezra Taft Benson for "starving the agency of funds" and for attempting "to consolidate it" out of existence: "you are fixing to say grace over the expiration of this very fine agency."[52]

In 1961, after more than fifteen years of hibernation, the FHA emerged from the relatively dormant years of Truman and Eisenhower. As part of the so-called "war on poverty," conceived by President John F. Kennedy and promulgated and envigorated by President Lyndon B. Johnson, the FHA, during the 1960's, has literally flooded the rural economy with credit. Farm ownership and operating loans, for instance, have increased from 3,938 loans amounting to $56.7 million in fiscal year 1961 to 14,500 loans amounting to $233.2 million in fiscal year 1966. From January, 1965, through June 30, 1966, the FHA, in cooperation with the Office of Economic Opportunity, assisted 35,000 low-income farm families by granting economic opportunity loans to individuals and cooperatives amounting to more than $50 million—individual loans averaged $1,640 per family, and most of the families receiving these loans were earning less than $1,500 per year for family living expenses. Individual and community recreation loans, from fiscal year 1963 to fiscal year 1966, totaled over $33 million, and went for development of outdoor recreational areas —swimming pools, golf courses, tennis courts, and similar installations not hitherto part of the American rural landscape. Altogether, from January 1, 1961, to June 30, 1966, the FHA, through these and other programs, injected more than $4.2 *billion* into the rural economy.

Reflected in these expenditures, and especially in the projections for the next few years, is the fact that the FHA, unlike its predecessor, is directed not toward case poverty, in which the causes of that poverty lie within the poor themselves, but rather toward insular poverty, due to the complex set of economic circumstances affecting the area or region of poverty as a whole. The thrust of the FHA, therefore, is less toward the individual chronically impoverished families at the very bottom, and more toward the rural community and toward non-farmer borrowers. In July, 1966, a writer in one

---

52. FHA, Administrative Letter 1 (010), Oct. 18, 1946; FHA, "Strengthening the Family Farm," Processed (Nov. 15, 1947), p. 4; Harold D. Cooley, address to FHA staff, Aug. 14, 1951; FHAF. FHA, *Report of the Administrator, 1949* (Washington, D.C.: GPO, 1949), p. 1; FHA, *Report of the Administrator, 1950* (Washington, D.C.: GPO, 1950), p. 1; *House Hearings*, Agr. Approp. (1955), 83rd Cong., 2d Sess., p. 66.

commercial banking journal wrote that "the growth plans [of the FHA] for the near future will make many a private lender green with envy."[53]

As far as comparisons between the FSA and the FHA are concerned, dollars may be deceiving, just as the intensity of battle in wartime is not necessarily commensurate with the number of bombing raids flown or the number of bullets fired. The essential difference between the FSA and its successor lies not in comparative expenditure statistics, but in mood, method, and subjective attitudes. Admittedly, as we have seen, the FSA was neither created, organized, nor funded to eradicate or substantially alleviate the kind of hard core rural poverty that has persisted in the United States during the past two decades, despite unprecedented national prosperity. However, in a variety of ways—in fact and in the minds of men—the FSA presented a challenge to the *status quo*. If it failed to eradicate or greatly ameliorate chronic rural poverty, it at least attempted to cope with it. The FHA, on the other hand, despite its much greater expenditures, its highly efficient administration, and its congenial relationships with Congress and with the agricultural establishment, has remained a docile agency, attracting none of the enmities of the FSA, but also evoking much less of the excitement and hope that characterized its embattled predecessor.

Administrative agencies of government may be analyzed, compared, and judged not only on the basis of their legislative foundations, organizational structures and administrative methods, budgets, and managerial and technological skills, but also on the basis of the foes they keep. The experience of the FSA—its rise and its decline—suggests that there is still some political virtue in Niccolò Machiavelli's advice to the Magnificent Lorenzo Di Piero Dè Medici:[54]

And let it be noted that there is no more delicate matter to take in hand, nor more dangerous to conduct, nor more doubtful in its success, than to set up as a leader in the introduction of changes. For he who innovates will have for his enemies all those who are well off under the existing order of things, and only lukewarm supporters in those who might be better off under the new.

53. FHA, "A Record of Accomplishment," Processed (Sept., 1966); FHA, "Contribution of Farmers Home Administration to Rural Areas Development Since 1961," Processed (n.d.) 1966; USDA, press release, July 22, 1966; Howard Bertsch, address at program review meetings, June, 1966, "Ours is a Sacred Trust;" author's telephone conversation with Philip S. Brown, Nov. 22, 1966; Fred Bailey, Jr., "USDA Turning Back Borrowers," *Banking*, July, 1966, p. 83.

54. Niccolò Machiavelli, *The Prince*, Ninian Hill Thompson, trans. (Oxford: Clarendon Press, 1898), p. 35.

CHAPTER XIII

RETROSPECT AND PROSPECT

Not the quarry, but the chase,
Not the laurel, but the race,
Not the hazard, but the play,
Make me Lord enjoy alway.

GELETT BURGESS[1]
"A Prayer"

Since Joseph in Egypt, the mere dreaming of dreams does not in itself achieve salvation for society from the scourge of want. In coping with massive social maladjustments, which may be beyond the control and comprehension of individual men, the power of government, whether embodied in Pharaohs, Parliaments, or Presidents, must be harnessed to appropriate administrative institutions. In turn, these institutions, if they are to perform effectively over time, must be built upon the rock of political legitimacy, linked to the sources of social power, and zealously maintained against the devouring jaws of time and change. Institutional survival, especially where governmental functions enjoying only marginal acceptability are concerned, involves a continual weighing of enormously complex forces in flux. The felt social needs, which agencies of government are presumably created to serve, may dissolve—or may seem to do so. The political sufferance of individuals and groups, whose vested interests in the

---

1. Gelett Burgess, "A Prayer," quoted in John Bartlett, *Familiar Quotations*, 13th ed. (Boston: Little, Brown, 1955), p. 829.

status quo may be challenged by remedial public action, may wither and turn to open hostility. Great political tides may turn; the sources of institutional strength may become the roots of institutional disaster; and dreams may turn to nightmares.

In post-mortem critiques of Farm Security Administration (FSA) experience, the search for causal meaning has led to considerable oversimplification. One of the persistent themes has been that during the "golden years," the leaders of the FSA preserved their institutional viability, but that they did so by winning small Pyrrhic victories that were destined to cost them the war. By excessive zeal in refusing to compromise on "minor administrative issues," it has been argued, and in failing to maintain a sufficiently broad basis of understanding and support in Congress, they allegedly stockpiled future adversity and squandered their political capital.[2]

Marvin Jones, for instance, was long a defender of his offspring, but in 1952 he charged that "the leaders of the FSA were impatient evangelists who attempted to circumvent obstacles by ignoring them [and] had they done more to cultivate Congress, the final chapter would have been different." Similarly, Will W. Alexander, who personally saw wisdom in the rural Negro preacher's formula—"avoid the impossible and cooperate with the inevitable"—concluded in 1951 that, "Some FSA leaders were too stubbornly ideological in their refusal to compromise with key members of Congress and in their refusal to abandon what was untenable and dispensable in order to preserve what was acceptable and crucial." Finally, James G. Maddox, in 1951, saw the following as one of the lessons for the future:[3]

Although there are dangers in bowing to the will of a few in Congress, there was poor handling of congressional relations and there was stubborn

---

2. David B. Truman, *The Governmental Process* (New York: Knopf, 1951), pp. 475–76; A. Whitney Griswold, *Farming and Democracy* (New York: Harcourt, Brace, 1948), pp. 163–74, 194–96; Grant McConnell, *The Decline of Agrarian Democracy* (Berkeley: Univ. of California Press, 1953), pp. 84–126, 177–79; Paul K. Conkin, *Tomorrow a New World* (Ithaca, N.Y.: Cornell Univ. Press, 1959), pp. 214–33; Dean Albertson, *Roosevelt's Farmer* (New York: Columbia Univ. Press, 1961), pp. 271–89, 315–57, 386; John Kenneth Galbraith, *American Capitalism* (Boston: Houghton, Mifflin, 1956), pp. 154–55; Murray R. Benedict, *Farm Policies of the United States, 1790–1950* (New York: Twentieth Century Fund, 1953), pp. 492–93.

Of the books cited above, the more satisfactory view of the decline of the FSA is that by Conkin, discussed in a chapter appropriately entitled, "The Old Society Reasserts Its Claims."

3. Maddox, "The FSA," pp. 505–08; author's interviews with Will W. Alexander, Marvin Jones, James G. Maddox.

refusal to recognize the wishes of a congressional handful. There should have been greater attention to keeping Congress informed about day-to-day operations. Had the FSA done so, it would have resulted in a much more orthodox program and less positive assistance to low-income farm families. It would have been a very difficult formula to follow.

In retrospect, the temptation is great to reconstruct the past in accordance with the wisdom of hindsight, or to reinterpret it for purposes of self-vindication. Our judgment of the FSA, however, should be based on the political realities that then prevailed, on the knowledge that was then available to the leaders of the agency, and on the contingencies that they faced—the "givens" which they applied to their choices.

The Roosevelt years were a time of intense conflict and contention in American politics and government—in contrast to the relative quietude of Dwight D. Eisenhower's administration and the "politics of consensus" pursued by Lyndon B. Johnson. During the New Deal years, the leaders of the FSA knew that the agency enjoyed a large measure of support in both houses of Congress and in the country, and they also knew that their most militant congressional foes—Harry F. Byrd, Kenneth D. McKellar, Clarence Cannon, Everett M. Dirksen, and their allies—were also foes of the New Deal and of the Roosevelt administration generally.

FSA resistance to these men was part of the larger struggle between the New Deal and the old order. The transfer of the Resettlement Administration to the U. S. Department of Agriculture (USDA), the passage of the Bankhead-Jones Farm Tenant Act, the abandonment of Rexford G. Tugwell's "resettlement idea," the moderation of the FSA in its approach to the Negro in the South, deference to demands by individual congressmen for their share of benefits, the avoidance of greater efforts toward militant mobilization of the clientele—all of these were acts of compromise and concession. Had the FSA readily granted more, under the circumstances that prevailed during the "golden years," it would have amounted to gratuitous surrender.

Climates, however, are fickle, and with new political winds blowing in wartime America, the formulas of the depression years lost some of their relevance. Roosevelt was a wise and wily navigator, and seeing the shift in the wind, he wasted little time in trimming his sails. Similarly, astute members of Congress—John and William Bankhead, Marvin Jones, Richard Russell, Lister Hill, Alben Barkley, and others—retreated to safer waters. "In the 1930's," confessed

Rev. John O'Grady of the National Conference of Catholic Charities, "I did things and said things on Capitol Hill—and got away with it—that I would not even have dreamed of during the years that followed."[4]

For the leaders of the FSA, however, strategic retreat was more difficult. The past association of the agency with Tugwell and the Resettlement Administration, the conscious cultivation of the FSA as the instrumentality and essence of the New Deal, the liability to the FSA for decisions and practices of predecessor agencies, and its general political posture—what John D. Black called its "bad manners"—were some of the sources of political vulnerability that were difficult or impossible to overcome or escape.

The question of whether the leaders of the FSA were "guilty" of "stubborn refusal to compromise" with Congress and with the structure of power in agriculture involves a problem of definition. If compromise is conceived as surrender, if the handful of hostile critics on Capitol Hill were not the embodiment of Congress, and if Edward A. O'Neal and his allies were not the voice of the American farmer, then the leaders of the FSA were politically and morally justified in their zealous allegiance to institutional commitments. However, if compromise is understood as a *mutuality of concession and adjustment*, then their failure, if any, lay in not having sufficiently encouraged the interaction and communication through which understanding might have been enhanced, and, presumably, mutual concessions and adjustments secured.

In terms of the environment in which they operated, the leaders of the FSA were faced with a dilemma in their relationships with Congress. On the one hand, from 1937 to 1942, there seemed to be no compelling reason for acquiescence to the demands of their foes on Capitol Hill. Under the whiplash of depression and drought, experimental action was demanded and expected. In the absence of clear congressional and executive policy concerning such practices as the mixing of loans and grants, land purchasing, ninety-nine year leases, and cooperative farming, there was no pressure at either end of Pennsylvania Avenue to seek clear congressional sanction for these practices. Neither President Franklin D. Roosevelt, nor Secretary Henry A. Wallace, nor administration leaders in the House and Senate showed much concern about hostility from the handful in Congress. There seemed to be no reason, therefore, to gratuitously

---

4. Author's interview with Rev. John O'Grady.

seek legislative sanction for practices that already seemed to enjoy congressional approval or acquiescence. In other words, "better let sleeping dogs lie."

On the other hand, "congressional intent" is neither clearly manifest nor static, and the prudent executive will continually re-explore and re-gauge it. Paul H. Appleby, for instance, with his battles in agricultural politics still fresh in mind, has described, as follows, the executive preoccupation with fathoming the mystery of congressional intent:

> In the national government, the administrative concern with "the intent of Congress" is never ending. The concern is not limited to the intent of a single enactment or to actual enactments altogether. It is a concern with the power to act, the possibility of enactment. Even more, it is a concern with the limiting opinions and attitudes of particular congressional committees, particular committee chairmen, and individual members of Congress rather generally. Any particular member of Congress can make life dreadful for anyone with respect to almost anything done administratively. No such pervasively penetrating concern on the part of individual administrators with respect to individual legislators is to be found in any other democratic government.

Had the leaders of the FSA been less goal-oriented and more sensitive to the political changes that were surrounding them, they probably would have paid closer attention to minority expressions of congressional intent and they might have been successful in appeasing their foes, but it would have been a Faustian compact. What was demanded of the FSA was not compromise—mutual concession and adjustment—but surrender.[5]

It is tantalizing to speculate about whether the more rational course of action for the leaders of the FSA would have been to adjust to the environment, as did the leaders of the Tennessee Valley Authority (TVA) and some other agencies, or to pursue their quest regardless of the glorious defeat toward which they were headed. Had they paid closer attention to their relationships with individual hostile congressmen and farm leaders, had they minded their manners, had they more readily abandoned some of the more controversial programs and practices, and had they, like the TVA, "coöpted" hostile forces and institutions in their environment, they might have escaped some of the harshness of the attack upon them and they might have gained some time, but these are exceedingly difficult

---

5. Paul H. Appleby, *Morality and Administration in Democratic Government* (Baton Rouge: Louisiana State Univ. Presss, 1952), p. 110.

questions to answer and they border on fruitless speculation. The heart of the matter is that the leaders of the FSA were constrained in their approach to the question of compromise, by their assessment of the likelihood of successful resistance, by the depth of their attachment to organizational goals, and by their ethical attitudes toward compromise itself.

Turning from the question of the rationality of the leaders of the FSA, there is an additional question remaining: who or what caused the decline of the FSA? A widely accepted explanation has been that the agency was "killed" by the American Farm Bureau Federation (AFBF), which saw in the field organization of the FSA and in the agency's role in the USDA a potential threat to itself and to its cliental partner, the Extension Service. Theoretic support for this explanation has been derived from the economic interpretation of politics, dramatized by a generation of muckrakers, and intellectually reinforced by the "group approach to politics." During the heat of battle in the early 1940's, it will be recalled, a popular explanation of the attack on the FSA was that the struggle represented a contest for power between the FSA and the AFBF. In 1948, Orville M. Kile, a former lobbyist for the AFBF and its unofficial historian, staked his organization's claim as follows:[6]

> The AFBF received much credit for stepping out boldly and scotching this bureaucratic machine which in its post-depression years was apparently doing its best to give a government-controlled socialistic, if not collectivistic, trend to American agriculture. At its peak FSA *had a nation-wide organization of over 18,000 employees, with approximately 2,000 offices,* and an annual payroll and expense account totaling at least $44,500,000. As of January 1, 1941, *737,204 farm families were in debt to FSA and operating under the direction and virtual control of its county supervisors* [italics not in the original].

The claim of the AFBF to the central role in the downfall of the FSA has been echoed by virtually every commentator on these events. The most positive statement of this interpretation has been provided by Grant McConnell, who saw the fate of the FSA as a chapter in the longer-range "decline of agrarian democracy" during the first decades of the twentieth century:

> There is nothing for which the Farm Bureau will fight with more determination than to secure for county agents a monopoly of local administration in agriculture. Not only does this maintain Farm Bureau influence

---

6. Orville M. Kile, *The Farm Bureau Through Three Decades* (Baltimore: Waverly Press, 1948), p. 264.

over the county agents, but, more significantly, it ensures that the agents will be able to make a maximum return to the Farm Bureau. Any rival administrative organization of the Department of Agriculture, or other department for that matter, is, therefore, a threat to the structure of power, and its destruction must be sought. *This, more than a direct threat to the agricultural labor supply, white supremacy in the South, or anything else, was the cause of the downfall of the Farm Security Administration* [italics not in the original].

This may largely explain the AFBF attack upon the FSA, although it is more likely that relationships with the Roosevelt administration generally and basic disagreements over farm policies were equally important factors, but the AFBF attack does not entirely explain the fate of the FSA.[7]

The coinage of group politics is exaggeration, and there has been a tendency to take group claims at face value. The unorthodox genesis of the FSA, flaws in its claims to legitimacy, ideological anxieties over FSA experimentation in social organization, southern fears of New Deal reforms generally, the decline of the New Deal, rising congressional resistance to the President, partisan exploitation of FSA vulnerability, policy changes by the leaders of the FSA in the early 1940's, shifts in public opinion, and dislocations flowing from World War II—none of these basic contributing factors to the decline of the FSA were the work of the AFBF.

Edward A. O'Neal, Earl C. Smith, and their allies exploited the situation, but they did not create it. With the possible exceptions of Cannon and Dirksen, the leaders in the congressional attack on the FSA were not the agents of the AFBF. The highly visible role played by the AFBF and allied farm organizations in the events immediately leading to Armageddon has strengthened the "group explanation" of the fall of the FSA, but the advice offered more than a century ago by George Cornewall Lewis remains relevant:

> Much practical error in assessing the comparative value of the different items of a composite cause, arises from the habit of over-estimating the importance of those events which immediately precede the effect in question. Where an effect depends on a long-prepared series of events, the chief merit is often attributed to those who gather in the harvest, rather than to those who ploughed and sowed the field. . . .

If students of group politics had more adequate concepts, categories, and measures of group influence—this is essentially the dif-

---

7. McConnell, *The Decline of Agrarian Democracy*, p. 177.

ficulty cited by David Easton, in any efforts to apply the equilibrium model to political life—a more precise division of credit might be made between those who sowed the seeds of decline for the FSA and those who reaped the harvest.[8]

There is yet another dimension to the alleged causes of the agency's decline—the contributory effects of particular policy decisions. The determination by C. B. Baldwin and his assistants in 1940 and 1941, for instance, to liberalize grant policy, to expand land purchasing, and to establish relocation corporations certainly contributed to the political vulnerability of the FSA. Similarly, the forthright position taken by the leaders of the agency on such issues as the role of the small farmer in wartime production, farm commodity prices, the organization and staffing of the Food Production Administration, coordination of USDA field organizations, and the expansion and restructuring of farm production during the war helped to range the FSA against powerful forces within the USDA and in agriculture generally, and further undermined the agency's capacity to survive. It would be difficult or impossible to isolate any particular decision, however, as a central cause of the decline.[9]

In retrospect, there is a temptation to perceive inevitability in the trend of events from 1937 to 1943. Although the leaders of the FSA were constrained by forces over which they had no control, faced problems they could not solve, and made commitments from which there was no retreat, they were not compelled simply to respond to the flux of circumstances. It was within their power—in many ways they exercised that power—to alter their environment, for as Abraham Kaplan has observed, "The historical situation sets limits to the conditions which can obtain, and therefore the eventualities that

---

8. George Cornewall Lewis, *A Treatise on the Methods of Observation and Reasoning in Politics*, Vol. 2 (London: John W. Parker and Son, 1852), p. 352.

9. Paul H. Appleby has ascribed considerable weight to Secretary Claude R. Wickard's decision to retreat, during the winter of 1942–43, on the issue of the small farmer's role in war food production, and on the questions of the role of the FSA in the USDA and the coordination of the Department's field organization. From a different point of view, Albertson has overemphasized the importance of the Parisius affair in the long-range decline of the FSA. This has led him to the shaky conclusion that the agency's downfall in 1943 was largely due to the decision by C. B. Baldwin, Robert W. Hudgens, and Gardner Jackson "to ruin the only man [Wickard] who stood between them and the Farm Bureau." The record suggests, however, that Wickard's ruination was largely self-inflicted, and that regardless of the behavior of FSA leaders in the affair, he was incapable of buffering the agency from its enemies.

Author's interviews with Hudgens, Jones, Appleby, Baldwin; Albertson, *Roosevelt's Farmer*, p. 386.

might ensue. That choice is limited surely does not imply that there is no choice at all." In their design of strategy, in their choice of weapons, in the pictures they carried in their heads, in their will to believe, and in their choice of battleground, the leaders of the FSA helped to determine the time, the place, the circumstances, and the outcome of their Armageddon. The generation of the FSA may have had a rendezvous with destiny, but in many ways it was a destiny partly of their own making.[10]

The experience of the FSA also suggests a lesson for today regarding the functions of conflict in politics and government. American pragmatism, Freudian psychology, management science, the alleged end of ideology, and the resurrection of Machiavelli have all conspired to emphasize the importance of adjustment, adaptation, reconciliation, and peace. Sociologist Jesse Bernard has distinguished between two kinds of conflict—illusory conflicts, based on personal interactions and largely unrelated to issues of the real world; and conflicts *about* something, which she has called *issue conflicts*. The conflicts with which we have been concerned in this study were primarily *about* something, although some critics of the FSA have condemned the leaders of the agency for struggling over issues of "minor administrative details." Administrative discretion, allocation of funds, definition of eligibility standards, recruitment and compensation of personnel, civil service protection, the role of farmers committees, experimentation in cooperative enterprises, the organization and function of regional offices, equity for the Negro—these were some of the so-called "details" over which conflicts were fought because in them the leaders of the FSA correctly perceived the linkages between organizational purpose, administrative method, and institutional survival.[11]

"Administrative efficiency demands the elimination of all possible friction between the ruler and the ruled," wrote Pendleton Herring in 1936, and the whole edifice of modern administrative management has been dedicated to that principle. Seymour M. Lipset has similarly argued for moderation of conflict, as follows:

... inherent in all democratic systems is the constant threat that the group

---

10. Abraham Kaplan, *The Conduct of Inquiry* (San Francisco: Chandler, 1964), p. 122.
11. Jessie Bernard, "Where is the Modern Sociology of Conflict?" *American Journal of Sociology*, Vol. LVI (1950), pp. 11–16; "Overview of Conflict, 1956: Variables," Working Paper, Northwestern University, Evanston, Ill., May 10, 1956; and her essay, "The Sociological Study of Conflict," in *The Nature of Conflict* (Paris: UNESCO, 1957).

conflicts that are democracy's life blood may solidify to the point where they threaten to disintegrate the society. Hence conditions which serve to moderate the intensity of partisan battle are among the key requisites of democratic government.

However, in the absence of genuine commitment among participants to the values of moderation and compromise, and in view of the persistent relevance of what E. E. Schattschneider has called the "law of imperfect mobilization of interests," the straining for consensus in a contest in which some participants are more equal than others may not lead to mutual concession and adjustment, but rather to the victory of the strong over the weak. Social conflict, Lewis Coser tells us, may not necessarily be dysfunctional. Like the battle-hardening of the soldier in combat, political conflict may strengthen an agency's capacity to survive—if it does not kill it.[12]

Turning from the tantalizing questions of institutional survival, there is yet another facet of the post-mortem examination that merits attention—chronic poverty itself. The persistence of a hard core of stagnant rural poverty in the United States, despite widespread national prosperity and after twenty-one years of effort by the Farmers Home Administration (FHA), suggests that the issue of "digging deeper" with which the FSA wrestled remains unfinished business on the American agenda. During the past few years, especially since the growth of the civil rights movement and, more recently, the "long hot summers" of violence in the black ghettos of the cities, concern about chronic poverty has become fashionable. However, since hopelessly poor farmers normally do not riot—nor do they vote—the poverty of the very low-income farm tenant, sharecropper, and migratory farm worker remains on the dark side of the crescent moon.

Between 1950 and 1959, farms with annual production of less than $2,500 declined more than 50 per cent, but they still represented during the early 1960's more than 40 per cent of all farms in the United States, and accounted for only 5 per cent of all farm products sold. The South lost approximately half of its non-white farm operators during the decade of the 1950's, but about 22 per cent of the farms in the South during the early 1960's were still operated by tenants and sharecroppers, and many Negro tenant families con-

---

12. Pendleton Herring, *Public Administration and the Public Interest* (New York: McGraw-Hill, 1936), p. 26; Seymour M. Lipset, *Political Man* (Garden City, N.Y.: Doubleday, 1960), p. 83; Lewis A. Coser, *The Functions of Social Conflict* (New York: The Free Press, 1956), p. 118.

tinued to live at a level relatively unchanged from the days of the Great Depression.

Despite the definitional and statistical intricacies and debates involved in measuring the magnitude, composition, and incidence of this chronic poverty, the fact remains that approximately one-third of the rural farm people in the United States live below the floor of acceptable American standards—many of them far below. Approximately 1.5 million rural and farm families earn less than $3,000 a year for living expenses. Included are a sizeable number of families in subsistence agriculture who contribute little or nothing to the agricultural economy and are therefore relatively untouched by rising prices. Also included are more than 1.5 million hired seasonal farm workers who are employed for less than 150 days of the year and earn a daily wage of approximately $5.25. These are the pariahs living in what Michael Harrington has bitterly described as the "Other America." For them, credit policies are almost a mockery.[13]

In 1935, Charles S. Johnson, Edwin R. Embree, and Will W. Alexander asked, in their book, *The Collapse of Cotton Tenancy*, "What is to become of the half million to million farm families—the two million to five million individuals—who are no longer needed as cotton tenants?" During the years since that time, the problem of surplus farm labor has haunted the American farm and city alike.

---

13. Michael Harrington, *The Other America* (New York: Macmillan, 1962), pp. 39–60; U.S., Bureau of the Census, *U.S. Census of Agriculture: 1959*, Vol. II, General Report (Washington, D. C.: GPO, 1962), pp. 12, 230, 232, 1004, 1013, 1014, 1203, 1204, 1205.

On September 27, 1966, President Lyndon B. Johnson issued Executive Order 11306, creating the National Advisory Commission on Rural Poverty, which he directed to conduct a comprehensive study of current Americal rural poverty, and to recommend remedial measures by local, state, and federal governments. Under the chairmanship of Governor Edward T. Breathitt of Kentucky, the Commission conducted hearings early in 1967 in various locations throughout the country. Assisted by a professional staff, headed by C. E. Bishop, vice-president of The University of North Carolina, the Commission issued a report, released in December, 1967, that was a severe indictment of federal programs to combat rural poverty. The fourteen million farm people living in stagnant rural poverty, the report declared, represented a "national disgrace," and the commissioners went on to contend that, "The urban riots during 1967 had their roots, in considerable part, in rural poverty." Specific recommendations were proposed that led the *Washington* (D.C.) *Post* to editorialize that, "In total, its recommendations would involve Federal commitment to rural change on a scale unprecedented as to both expenditure and intervention in local and state affairs."

President's National Advisory Commission on Rural Poverty, *The People Left Behind* (Washington, D.C.: GPO, 1967); *Washington* (D.C.) *Post*, Dec. 11, 1967.

Official policy statements invariably refer delicately to the need for development of opportunities for low-income farmers "outside of agriculture," but the question has, until very recently, been largely ignored in the formulation of federal policy.

In 1962, the influential Committee for Economic Development (CED) offered what it called an "adaptive program" for the final solution of agriculture's problems. A basic feature of this plan was the proposal that the farm labor force be reduced by one-third during a period of not more than five years. This was a polite way of declaring that permanent security for agriculture as a whole lies in a form of natural selection through which the most inefficient and unproductive farmers and their families should be encouraged to join the exodus to the cities. The CED offered little light on what was to become of the 1.8 million farm workers who were to be cast off the land.

One answer has come from the ghettos of Watts, Newark, Detroit, and virtually every urban center that has served as a magnet for the hundreds of thousands of rural people who have fled the countryside. In 1949, Edward C. Banfield offered a prophetic warning that, "The problem of rural poverty and insecurity, it now seems clear, must be solved in the cities," and he predicted that this conclusion "will be resisted by many valiant people who have struggled with great skill and tenacity ... to reform ... a segment of American life which was, and still is, abysmally in need of reform."[14]

In recent years, especially since the outbreak of violence in the black urban ghettos, the enduring Jeffersonian dream, reinforced by stubborn resistance to an effective assault on *urban* poverty, has led some of these valiant people to believe that, after all, solution to the problem of chronic rural poverty lies not in the cities but in the countryside. In 1966, for instance, FHA Administrator Howard Bertsch declared, as follows:

> Rural people are being pushed off the land by the brute forces of power and pressure, enticed off the land by the false promise of the cities. All this would not be so bad if we could believe that the cities ... could provide a haven for the farmers [who] are squeezed out by the sweeping trends toward bigness and concentration of power. But the cities are piling

---

14. Charles S. Johnson, Edwin R. Embree, and Will Alexander, *The Collapse of Cotton Tenancy* (Chapel Hill: Univ. of North Carolina Press, 1935), p. 46; Committee for Economic Development, *An Adaptive Program for Agriculture* (New York: CED, 1962), pp. 57–60; *Washington* (D.C.) *Post*, July 16, 1962; Edward C. Banfield, "Ten Years of the Farm Tenant Purchase Program," *Journal of Farm Economics*, Vol. 31 (Aug., 1949), p. 486.

up horror upon horror. The current shocker, "Crisis in our Cities," has enough scare stories in it to make a country boy like myself run from the very sight of a skyscraper, yes, even from the sight of a suburban shopping center.

And in August, 1967, Secretary of Agriculture Orville L. Freeman, at the convention of the National League of Cities, announced that a joint departmental symposium would be held to examine "one of the most urgent and important questions of our time: Should we try to check the accelerating movement of people from country to city?"[15]

In his opening address of welcome to the symposium, Secretary Freeman echoed the prophecy of Rexford G. Tugwell who dreamed a similar dream in an earlier time of national crisis:

... an American landscape dotted with communities that include a blend of small cities, new towns, and growing villages—each of these a cluster with its own jobs and industries, its own college or university, its own medical center, its own cultural, entertainment, and recreational centers, and with an agriculture fully sharing in national prosperity.

Richly punctuated with words of exhortation and of the need for adherence to the economic, political, and technological "facts of life," the dialogue, with only a few exceptions, was strangely lacking in a real sense of urgency. The disappointment of many lay participants in the symposium was eloquently expressed by Mrs. Maggie May Horton, a Negro anti-poverty volunteer from Fayette County, Ten-

---

15. Howard Bertsch, address at FHA review meetings, June, 1966, entitled, "Ours is a Sacred Trust"; Secretary of Agriculture Orville L. Freeman, address at convention of the National League of Cities, Boston, Mass., Aug. 1, 1967.

The dialogue proposed by Freeman, entitled, "Symposium on Communities of Tomorrow—National Growth and its Distribution," was held in Washington, D.C., on December 11–12, 1967. The sessions were attended by a constellation of men and women representing government, agriculture, business, industry, the press, colleges and universities, churches, and civic action organizations. The roster included the following: Vice-President Hubert H. Humphrey; Secretary of Agriculture Freeman; Secretary of Housing and Urban Development Robert C. Weaver; Secretary of Commerce Alexander B. Trowbridge; Secretary of Health, Education and Welfare John B. Gardner; Secretary of Labor W. Willard Wirtz; Secretary of Transportation Alan S. Boyd; Governor Harold E. Hughes of Iowa; Mayor Arthur F. Naftalin of Minneapolis, Minnesota; Paul N. Ylvisaker, Commissioner of the New Jersey Department of Community Affairs; Arthur S. Flemming, president of the University of Oregon; Barbara Ward (Lady Jackson); Wilbur R. Thompson, professor of economics at Wayne State University; Scott Greer, professor of sociology at Northwestern University; C. E. Bishop, vice-president of The University of North Carolina; William J. Baumol, professor of economics at Princeton University; Roy L. Ash, president of Litton Industries, Inc.; Vivian W. Henderson, president of Clark College, Atlanta, Georgia; James W. Rouse, president of The Rouse Company; and Philip M. Hauser, professor of sociology at the University of Chicago.

nessee. Standing in the elegant diplomatic reception room of the State Department on the last day of the symposium, before the attending members of the President's Cabinet, she conceded the need for long-range planning, but went on to declare as follows:[16]

> There have been many plans and now the question is: What will it do for Fayette County tomorrow? All of this planning that we have done, what will it do for the people in Fayette County as of today—not tomorrow? I'm just wondering can we survive until tomorrow?

Twenty-four years ago, in 1943, Professor John D. Black of Harvard University suggested that at some time in the future it might be necessary and desirable to re-examine the resettlement idea and to explore its applicability to the persistent problem of chronic rural poverty. Until now, however, the allure of the cities, persistent fears and prejudices among members of Congress, the power of hostile farm organizations, lack of public understanding and concern, and the docility of the USDA and the FHA have discouraged serious men from traveling again down the perilous path of sociological experimentation which was pioneered by the leaders of the FSA and their predecessors.

In the current dialogue about the need for a "new cities" policy in the United States, and in the growing interest in revival of the countryside as a way of combatting poverty on the farm and in the city, there is the germ of hope that the experience of the FSA will finally win the attention it has for so long awaited. If there is going to be a renewed assault on chronic poverty—a war in fact as well as in polemics—it will probably require some of the daring that characterized the agency with which we have been centrally concerned in this study.

During a post-mortem discussion in 1958, Tugwell conceded the importance of judicious administration and political prudence, but he also urged his younger successors in public service, who may feel compelled to combat social ills, to exercise some of the daring that characterized the Resettlement Administration and the FSA:[17]

> My final advice to those who are thus moved by injustices and human needs, and who think they perceive better possibilities through social organization, is to go ahead. Fail as gloriously as some of your predecessors

---

16. Notes of the author, who attended the symposium; *New York Times*, Dec. 12, 13, 1967; *Washington* (D.C.) *Post*, Dec. 11, 12, 13, 1967; USDA, Communities of Tomorrow: Agriculture/2000 (Washington, D.C.: GPO, 1967).

17. Rexford G. Tugwell, "The Resettlement Idea," *Agricultural History*, Vol. 33 (Oct., 1959), pp. 159–64.

have. If you do not succeed in bringing about a permanent change, you may at least have stirred some slow consciences so that in time they will give support to action. And you will have the satisfaction, which is not to be discounted, of having annoyed a good many miscreants who had it coming to them.

The alleged gratifications of glorious defeat, however, are unlikely to capture the hearts of this modern "cool" generation of public administrators and poverty warriors. Paradoxically, just when the technological means, the dampening of ideological fires, and the greater public recognition of poverty and social injustices have converged in time, there seems to be a loss of faith in the capacity of governments to *solve* problems. Now that *Homo economicus*, according to the administrative theorist, has been replaced by "satisficing man," and grand designs have presumably given way to successive limited advances, the goal of government seems to be merely to cope with problems, whether they involve poverty on the farm, destitution in the city, crime on the street, smog in the air, pollution in the water, or slaughter on the highway.[18]

The visionary optimism of Tugwell and his disciples was a defiant and blasphemous faith which is generally viewed today as naïve or quaint by many presumably sophisticated poverty warriors. Lacking such a faith, the social and political innovator is tempted to flee from conflict and to find refuge in feasibility and in a preoccupation with administrative minutiae and, perhaps, personal careerism. There is a tendency, perhaps, for concern about institutional equilibrium, maintenance, and survival to lead to conservatism. The leaders of the FSA, on the other hand, were risk-takers. In the eyes of some of its critics, the agency pursued a quixotic quest for the unattainable. However, even if the maladjustments of society are to be merely "managed" and not "solved," both a will and a way are necessary—political power, administrative means, and some of the optimism of the Man of La Mancha.

18. Charles E. Lindblom, "The Science of Muddling Through," *Public Administration Review*, Vol. 19 (Spring, 1959), pp. 79–88; Herbert A. Simon, *Models of Man* (New York: Wiley, 1957).

INDEX

A

Abt, John, joins staff of General Counsel in Agricultural Adjustment Administration, 54
Administration of Food Production and Distribution, established, 374
Agee, James, on use of term sharecropper, 155; on dangers of official acceptance, 157
Agger, Eugene E., appointed Assistant Administrator of Resettlement Administration, 97
Agrarian myth, described, 22–24; challenged, 30
Agricultural Adjustment Administration, established, 50–58; relations with Federal Emergency Relief Administration, 63–64; impact of programs on farm tenants, 130–31, 158; invalidation by Supreme Court, 160–61; role of county agricultural agent in, 288; influence of upon Claude R. Wickard, 328n
Agricultural Labor Administration, established, 378n

Agriculture, commercialization of, 27–28, 30, 32, 34; national diversity of, 257–58
Alexander, Will W., personal background of, 95–96; role of in Resettlement Administration, 95–96, 109, 122; role of in passage of Bankhead-Jones Farm Tenant Act, 95–96, 127–32, 145, 149–50, 154, 161, 162, 181–82, 190; accompanies Henry A. Wallace on tour of South, 122; on rural poverty, 127, 160; participates in President's Committee on Farm Tenancy, 167, 168; on achievements of standard rural rehabilitation loan program, 201; on policy of digging deeper, 218–19; on rise and decline of Farm Security Administration, 230, 406; on scope and complexity of Department of Agriculture, 235; on ideology of Farm Security Administration, 273; on cliental relationships of Farm Security Administration, 297, 298; on farmers committees, 306, 307, 309; on training of field personnel, 314; relationships

of with Congress, 321; resignation of from Farm Security Administration, 332

American Farm Bureau Federation, opposition of to Resettlement Administration, 115; role in passage of Bankhead-Jones Farm Tenant Act, 141; political structure and power of, 172, 288–89; relationships of with Franklin D. Roosevelt and New Deal, 172–73, 291, 291n, 349n; attack of on Farm Security Administration, 341–44, 348, 349–50, 352, 356, 378, 385; role of in decline of Farm Security Administration, 410, 411; mentioned, 12, 15. *See also* Edward A. O'Neal

American Federation of Labor, role of in passage of Bankhead-Jones Farm Tenant Act, 149; supports Farm Security Administration, 299. *See also* William Green

American Friends Service Committee, supports back-to-land movement, 68n

Appalachia, incidence in of rural poverty, 40. *See also* Rural poverty

Appleby, Paul H., personal background of, 55–56; on rural poverty, 80, 86, 87; role of in and ideas about Department of Agriculture, 87, 235, 242–43, 304, 334; role of in Resettlement Administration, 98, 102–3, 115, 232; on politics and administration, 103, 110n, 191, 231, 244; on Rexford G. Tugwell, 110n; role of in passage of Bankhead-Jones Farm Tenant Act, 129, 133, 167; relationships of with C.B. Baldwin, 243; on American Farm Bureau Federation and New Deal, 292n; role of in relationships of Farm Security Administration and President, 302; on farmers committees, 309; relationships of with Claude R. Wickard, 333–34; role of in budget battle of 1942, 360, 361

Aristotle, on political power, *viii-ix*

Arizona Cotton Growers Association, hostility of to Farm Security Administration, 302

Arnold, Thurman, joins staff of General Counsel in Agricultural Adjustment Administration, 54

Arthurdale, West Virginia, support of from Eleanor Roosevelt, 111

Associated Farmers of California, hostility of to Farm Security Administration, 302

B

Back-to-land movement, influence of upon development of Subsistence Homesteads, 68, 68n, 69

Bailey, Senator Josiah, role of in passage of Bankhead-Jones Farm Tenant Act, 151

Bailey, Liberty Hyde, on agrarian ideals, 28

Baker, Gladys L., on county agricultural agent, 290

Baldwin, C.B., personal background of, 56, 96; role of in purge of 1935 in Agricultural Adjustment Administration, 82, 83; relationships of with Paul H. Appleby, 96, 243; role of in Resettlement Administration, 96, 98, 109, 232; accompanies Henry A. Wallace on tour of South in 1936, 122; on policy of digging deeper, 218; on expansionist character of Farm Security Administration, 230; replaces Will W. Alexander as Farm Security Administrator, 246n, 332–33; ideological commitments of, 272; on relationships of Farm Security Administration with National Farmers Union, 301; on civil service status of employees of Farm Security Administration, 316; relationships of with Congress, 321; relationships of with Samuel B. Bledsoe, 334; interrogation of by Joint Committee on Reduction of Nonessential Federal Expenditures, 348; role of in battle of budget, 357, 385; convenes conference of regional directors in Cincinnati, Ohio, 362; role of in Parisius affair, 369, 371; on passage of House Joint Resolution 96, 382; resignation of from Farm Security Administration, 391, 394, 395; works for Political Action Committee of Congress of Industrial Organizations, 396. *See also* Farm Security Administration

Ball, Carleton R., on farmers committees, 305

Banfield, Edward C., on political influence, 144; on Casa Grande, Arizona, cooperative farming project, 216, 312–13; on rural poverty, 416

Bankhead, Senator John H., role of in Subsistence Homesteads, 69, 70, 71, 71n, 75; personal background of, 132–33; supports passage of Bankhead-Jones Farm Tenant Act, 132–40, 146, 160, 162, 166, 186–87; compared with Marvin Jones; supports Farm Security Administration, 320, 338; defends C.B. Baldwin against charges of Communist sympathies, 358; role of in battle of budget of 1943, 392. See also Bankhead-Jones Farm Tenant Act

Bankhead, Speaker William B., supports passage of Bankhead-Jones Farm Tenant Act, 181–82; on farm tenancy, 184; supports Farm Security Administration, 320, 339

Bankhead-Jones Farm Tenant Act, goals of sponsors of, 126–27; analysis of provisions of bills leading to, 133–34, 138–39, 177–78, 182, 185, 186–87; analysis of pattern of congressional support and opposition to, 151–52, 178–79; approved by Congress and signed by President, 187; evaluation of process involved in passage of, 187, 189–90; executive promulgation of, 188–89; provisions of governing programs of Farm Security Administration, 195, 200, 214, 217

Barbour, Senator W. Warren, introduces congressional resolution to investigate Resettlement Administration, 114

Barnard, Chester I., on functions of executives, 85; on rational cooperative action, 144

Baruch, Bernard, sponsors George N. Peek as Secretary of Agriculture, 57; criticizes rural resettlement projects, 111

Bean, Louis H., serves as statistical analyst in Department of Agriculture, 56

Bell, Daniel W., relationships of with Farm Security Administration, 303

Benedict, Murray R., on report of President's Committee on Farm Tenancy, 175–76

Bennett, Hugh H., relationships of with Farm Security Administration, 303–4

Bernstein, Marver H., on institutional evolution, 10

Bertsch, Howard, on crisis of cities, 417–18

Billings, Josh, on poverty, 22–23; on historical inevitability, 377

Black, Albert G., participates in President's Committee on Farm Tenancy, 168; resigns from Farmers Home Corporation, 189n; role of in Parisius affair, 371, 373

Black, Senator Hugo L., role of in patronage problems of Resettlement Administration, 101-2

Black, John D., on production economics, 33n, 38–39; as member of National Advisory Committee on Subsistence Homesteads, 71n; participates in President's Committee on Farm Tenancy, 168; on resettlement project program, 216; on World War II, 329; conducts study of Farm Security Administration for Chester C. Davis, 387–90; on political vulnerability of Farm Security Administration, 408; on relevance of resettlement idea, 418

Black power, as expression of political discontent, 27; mentioned, 282–83

Blaisdell, Thomas C., appointed as economic adviser to Rexford G. Tugwell, 98

Blandford, John B., hostility of to Farm Security Administration, 346

Blau, Peter M., on administrative goals, 13–14, 15, 107, 323–24. See also Goal formulation

Bledsoe, Samuel B., replaces James D. LeCron in office of Secretary Henry A. Wallace, 334; role of in Parisius affair, 368, 372, 373; resigns from Department of Agriculture and goes to work for National Cotton Council, 374

Block, William J., on county agricultural agents, 288; on relationships between National Farmers Union and Extension Service, 301

Borah, Senator William E., opposes passage of Bankhead-Jones Farm Tenant Act, 151

Brand, Charles J., role of in Agricul-

tural Adjustment Administration, 54, 57
Brownlow, Louis, as Member of National Advisory Committee on Subsistence Homesteads, 71n
Bureau of Agricultural Economics, inherits land program from Resettlement Administration, 188; study by on client attitudes toward Farm Security Administration, 274; relationships of with Farm Security Administration, 303; study by of small-farm production, 383, 383n; mentioned, 8, 56
Bureau of the Budget. See Harold D. Smith; Daniel W. Bell
Burns, James MacGregor, on political style of Franklin D. Roosevelt, 49; on historical analysis, 324
Byrd, Senator Harry F., attacks Resettlement Administration, 111; role of in passage of Bankhead-Jones Farm Tenant Act, 151; attacks Farm Security Administration, 319, 320, 321, 356, 359; relationships of with American Farm Bureau Federation, 348n. See also Congressional relationships
Byrnes, Senator James F., on Negroes in farmers committees, 307; appointed Economic Stabilization Director, 367; role of in resignation of C.B. Baldwin as Farm Security Administrator, 394

C

Caldwell, Erskine, on rural poverty, vii
Cannon, Representative Clarence, attacks Farm Security Administration, 318n, 320, 321, 338, 344. See also House Appropriations Committee
Capper, Senator Arthur, appealed to for support of tenancy legislation, 150
Carter, John Franklin, as Director of Information Division in Resettlement Administration, 98, 117
Carver, Thomas Nixon, and production economics, 33
Case study method, value of, 5n
Catholic Rural Life Conference, influence of in promotion of back-to-land movement, 68n. See also Bankhead-Jones Farm Tenant Act
Catholic bishops, support Farm Security Administration, 346
Christgau, Victor, role of in purge of 1935 in Agricultural Adjustment Administration, 81
Civil rights, as issue in President's Committee on Farm Tenancy, 171–72
Civil Service Commission, relationships of with Resettlement Administration, 99; relationships of with Farm Security Administration, 303, 315
Civil service, status of personnel of Farm Security Administration, 315–16
Civil Works Administration, rural programs of replaced by rural rehabilitation program of Federal Emergency Relief Administration, 62
Cliental bloc, structure of, 286–89; challenged by Farm Security Administration, 286–92, 286n; class character of, 289–90. See also American Farm Bureau Federation; Extension system
Collapse of Cotton Tenancy, The, and passage of Bankhead-Jones Farm Tenant Act, 130–31, 146n, 415
Committee for Economic Development, on farm policy, 416
Committee on Extension Organization and Policy, and Resettlement Administration, 115–16
Committee on Negroes in the Economic Recovery, role of in passage of Bankhead-Jones Farm Tenant Act, 127
Communism, Farm Security Administration accused of, 359n; C.B. Baldwin defended against charges of, 390
Compromise, nature of, 408; practice of by leaders of Farm Security Administration, 409
Comptroller General, on funds for relief and rural rehabilitation, 91–92; on legality of transfers of funds to state rural rehabilitation corporations, 94; on resettlement project program, 215; dispute of with Attorney General over defense reloca-

Index / [425]

tion corporations, 227; opposes Farm Security Administration, 319n
Conflict, in administrative institutions, 57–58, 86–87, 413–14; in Agricultural Adjustment Administration, 76–83; in Resettlement Administration, 110, 110n
Congress of Industrial Organizations, appeals to President in support of Farm Security Administration, 360
Congressional relationships, of Farm Security Administration, 276–77, 316–22, 317, 335–47, 407–9. *See also* Equilibrium
Conkin, Paul K., on resettlement project program, 216
Connally, Senator Tom, supports passage of Bankhead-Jones Farm Tenant Act, 151, 179; supports Farm Security Administration, 320
Constituency relationships, of Farm Security Administration, 295–305
Cooley, Charles H., influence of in community analysis, 39
Cooley, Representative Harold D., personal background of, 178; designated as chairman of House committee to investigate Farm Security Administration, 386–87; introduces remedial legislation, 401; on gratification with performance of Farmers Home Administration, 402. *See also* Select Committee to Investigate the Activities of the Farm Security Administration
Coolidge, President Calvin, vetoes McNary-Haugen bill, 35; on poverty, 37
Cooperative associations, general discussion of, 204–7; promotion of in Kansas, Minnesota, Montana, Nebraska, and North and South Dakota, 205; lack of statutory provisions for in Bankhead-Jones Farm Tenant Act, 205; achievements of evaluated, 207
Cooperative program, political opposition to, 265–66; prohibitions on in Emergency Relief Appropriation Act for fiscal year 1941, 338
Coöptation, refusal of Farm Security Administration to employ, 12; as employed by Tennessee Valley Authority, 304; as conceived by Philip Selznick, 324. *See also* Tennessee Valley Authority
Coser, Lewis A., on social conflict, 414
Countervailing power, conceived by John Kenneth Galbraith, 296; as condition to be sought, 298; lack of in Farm Security Administration, 362
Country Life Commission, appointed by President Theodore Roosevelt, 28; followed by country life movement, 39; compared with President's Committee on Farm Tenancy, 170
County agricultural agent, role of, 287–88. *See also* American Farm Bureau Federation; Extension Service; Gladys L. Baker
County supervisor, racial biases of, 201; role of in administration of Farm Security Administration, 249–54; relations of with county agricultural agents, 291. *See also* Farm Security Administration
Cummings, Homer, and violation of civil rights of farm tenants, 159

D

Dahl, Robert A., on administrative goal formulation, 13; on administrative rationality, 15–16; on political power and influence, 144; on democratic ritualism, 144; mentioned, 154
Dailey, Joseph L., appointed to direct rural rehabilitation program of Resettlement Administration, 97
Darrow, Wayne H., appointed to direct Agricultural Labor Administration in Department of Agriculture, 378n
Davis, Chester C., role of as Agricultural Adjustment Administrator, 54, 58, 67–68, 76, 81–82; role of in passage of Bankhead-Jones Farm Tenant Act, 129, 133, 154; on wartime relocation program, 226; on liquidation of resettlement projects, 338; resigns as War Food Administrator, 375–76; relationships of with Secretary Claude R. Wickard, 375n; on migratory farm labor program, 380; mentioned 52, 342; *See also* Agricultural Adjustment Administration
Debt adjustment program, general discussion, 209–10; compared with ten-

ant purchase program, 210; achievements of evaluated, 210
Defense housing program, described, 228
Democratic party, in election campaign of 1932, 45, 48; significance for in passage of Agricultural Adjustment Act, 53; role of in patronage problems of Resettlement Administration, 99–100; and national convention of 1936, 164; supports Farm Security Administration, 354. *See also* James A. Farley
Department of Agriculture, and extension work, 31; institutional conflict in, 54, 83, 86–87, 235–44; scope and complexity of, 235–36; cliental relationships in, 237–39; impact of New Deal on, 239; field organization in, 239–41; role of William A. Jump in, 241–42; role of Paul H. Appleby in, 242–43. *See also* Paul H. Appleby; Bankhead-Jones Farm Tenant Act; Henry A. Wallace; Claude R. Wickard
Digging deeper, as goal displacement, 218–21; and dysfunctional consequences, 312
Dimock, Marshall E., on institutional vitality, 10, 13, 363
Dinwiddie, Courtney, supports Farm Security Administration, 357, 390
Dirksen, Representative Everett M., opposes Farm Security Administration, 319n, 320, 321, 355, 363, 392
DuBois, W. E. B., supports passage of Bankhead-Jones Farm Tenant Act, 150; on impact of New Deal on South, 280

E

Easton, David, on equilibrium analysis, 8–9, 12, 12n, 323
Elections, campaign of 1928, 36, 37–38; campaign of 1932, 47–49; campaign of 1936, 164–66
Ely, Richard T., influence of on agricultural economics, 33, 33n, 35, 39, 96
Embree, Edwin R., supports passage of Bankhead-Jones Farm Tenant Act, 127, 128, 130, 133
Emergency Committee for Food Production, supports Farm Security Administration, 390
Emergency Relief Appropriation Act of 1935, funds from for rural rehabilitation and relief, 92, 94, 104, 112
Emergency Relief Appropriation Act of 1938, funds from for rural rehabilitation, 234, 319, 319n
Emergency Relief Appropriation Act for Fiscal Year 1940, provisions of governing Farm Security Administration, 234
Emerson, Ralph Waldo, on leadership, 94; on reform, 262
Equilibrium, in analysis of administrative institutions, 8–12 *passim*, 16, 17, 322, 323, 405–6, 413; in rise and decline of Farm Security Administration, 282–94, 310–16, 323–24, 325, 362–64; concern about and political conservatism, 419
Evans, R. M., role of in Department of Agriculture, 189n, 280
Extension system, development of, 30–31, 286–87; neglect of rural poverty by, 31; opposes Resettlement Administration, 115, 116–17; relationships of with American Farm Bureau Federation, 172; mentioned, 8, 275, 286, 286n, 303, 304. *See also* Cliental bloc
Ezekiel, Mordecai, role of in Department of Agriculture, 52, 56, 57, 115

F

Fairway Farms, influence of on Subsistence Homesteads, 35, 61. *See also* M. L. Wilson
Falke, Grace E., role of in Resettlement Administration, 98, 109, 121. *See also* Rexford G. Tugwell
Family farm, defined, 29; decline of, 30; as policy goal, 165, 166, 184, 268. *See also* Ideology
Farley, James A., role of in patronage problems of Resettlement Administration, 98, 113
Farm bloc, influence of on farm policy, 34, 52. *See also* Congressional relationships
Farm Bureau, development of, 286n, 287. *See also* American Farm Bureau Federation

Index / [427]

Farm Credit Administration, role of in development of farm debt adjustment program, 92, 99, 209; compared with Farm Security Administration, 181; relationships of with Farm Security Administration, 253, 343, 371–76 *passim*, 385, 389, 397; mentioned, 138, 237, 238, 328, 367
Farm debt adjustment program, described, 209–10. *See also* Farm Credit Administration
Farm Foundation, role of in Fairway Farms, 35. *See also* Henry C. Taylor
Farm Holiday Association, role of in farm politics, 45, 49–50, 85, 99
Farm Security Act of 1937, approved by House of Representatives, 184–85
Farm Security Administration, general characteristics of, 4, 220–21, 245–46, 275, 279; political equilibrium of, 12, 256–61, 262, 279–86, 293, 295, 324, 335, 361, 362, 397–98, 409–10, 412; role of in New Deal, 18–19, 293–94, 298, 364; administrative features of, 231–35, 244–55, 258–59, 304–5, 311–12, 398; funding of, 233–34, 352–62, 383–94, 398; impact of World War II upon, 325–35, 353; replaced by Farmers Home Administration, 402. *See also* C.B. Baldwin; Congressional relationships; Equilibrium
Farm Tenancy, as social problem, 24–26, 42, 155, 160; impact of crop restriction programs upon, 76–79. *See also* Agricultural Adjustment Administration; Rural poverty
Farmers committees, as issue in passage of Bankhead-Jones Farm Tenant Act, 183; general analysis of, 305–10. *See also* Grass roots democracy; Rural rehabilitation program; Tenant purchase program
Farmers Home Administration, Farm Security Administration compared with, 403–4
Farmers Home Administration Act of 1946, enacted, 401–2
Farmers Home Corporation, established, 177, 189, 232
Farmers Union Grain Terminal Association, relationships of with Farm Security Administration, 205. *See also* National Farmers Union
Federal Council of Churches of Christ in America, supports back-to-land movement, 68n; supports passage of Bankhead-Jones Farm Tenant Act, 149
Federal Emergency Relief Administration, established, 58–68; programs of analyzed, 201, 203, 221. *See also* Harry L. Hopkins
Federal Subsistence Homesteads Corporation. *See* Subsistence Homesteads
Fischer, John, appointed to direct Information Division of Resettlement Administration, 122–23; resigns from agency, 246n; on political opposition to agency, 263; on southern fears of agency, 282
Flynn, Edward J., supports Farm Security Administration, 354
Food Distribution Administration, established, 367
Food for freedom program, role of in wartime adjustments of Department of Agriculture, 228–29, 327, 329
Food Production Administration, established, 367
Food Requirements Committee, established, 331
Frank, Jerome N., role of in Agricultural Adjustment Administration, 54, 57, 58, 76, 82
Freeman, Orville L., on rural-urban balance, 417
Friant, Julian N., role of in patronage problems of Resettlement Administration, 99, 250
Fulmer, Representative Hampton P., role of in passage of Bankhead-Jones Farm Tenant Act, 178, 180; on relief stigma of Farm Security Administration, 275

G

Galbraith, John Kenneth, on poverty, 21; on economic analysis, 176
Garner, John Nance, influence of on Marvin Jones, 137
Gaus, John M., on historical analysis, 8; on Department of Agriculture, 235
General Accounting Office, role of in auditing of accounts of Subsistence Homesteads, 73. *See also* Comptroller General

George, Henry, on poverty, 26
Giddings, Franklin H., influence of in country life movement, 39
Glick, Philip M., recommends creation of state rural rehabilitation corporations, 63
Goal formulation, and public administration, 13, 48n, 57; as goal displacement, 13–14, 194–95, 217–21, 310; as goal succession, 14, 194–95, 200, 221–29, 310, 362–63; in Resettlement Administration, 103–8. *See also* Peter M. Blau; Bertram M. Gross
Goodnow, Frank J., on politics and public administration, 9
Grant program, general description and analysis of, 201–3
Grapes of Wrath, The, quoted, viii
Grass roots democracy, in administration of Subsistence Homesteads, 73; in administration of Department of Agriculture, 305, 306. *See also* Farmers committees; M. L. Wilson
Gray, Dean Dan T., and relationships with land grant colleges, 116, 116n, 290
Gray, Lewis C., and land program of Agricultural Adjustment Administration, 65; appointed Assistant Administrator of Resettlement Administration, 96–97; supports passage of Bankhead-Jones Farm Tenant Act, 133, 140, 141, 145; participates in President's Committee on Farm Tenancy, 167, 168; transferred to Bureau of Agricultural Economics, 188
Great Plains, agricultural maladjustments in, 34, 50
Green, William, participates in National Advisory Committee on Subsistence Homesteads, 71n; supports passage of Bankhead-Jones Farm Tenant Act, 130n, 149
Greenbelt communities, political resistances to, 105–6, 111–12
Gross, Bertram M., on goal formulation, 14–15, 93; on institutional equilibrium, 83, 191, 294, 363; on legislative process, 123–24, 192
Group politics, and micro-institutional analysis, 6; role of in rise and decline of Farm Security Administration, 296, 410–12. *See also* Constituency relationships

Group services program, described, 203–4. *See also* Cooperative associations; Cooperative program
Gulick, Luther, on politics and public administration, 9

H

Hancock, Franklin W., appointed Farm Security Administrator, 396; personal background, 396; performance of as Farm Security Administrator, 396–400
Handschin, Robert, supports Farm Security Administration budget, 354
Hardin, Charles M., assists John D. Black in study of Farm Security Administration, 330
Harding, Warren G., on normalcy, 37
Harriman, Henry I., supports establishment of Agricultural Adjustment Administration, 51; supports establishment of Subsistence Homesteads, 71, 71n
Harrington, Michael, on rural poverty, 415
Harrison, Senator Pat, role of in establishment of Subsistence Homesteads, 70
Hays, Brooks, supports passage of Bankhead-Jones Farm Tenant Act, 98, 146, 161; on Farm Security Administration as threat to *status quo*, 277–78
Hegel, Wilhelm Friedrich, on life versus death, 295
Hendrickson, Roy F., appointed public information officer of Subsistence Homesteads Division, 71; appointed Director of Food Distribution, 367–68
Herring, Pendleton, on politics and public administration, 9, 413
Hewes, Laurence I., Jr., on Resettlement Administration, 102; on passage of Bankhead-Jones Farm Tenant Act, 161; directs evacuation of Japanese-Americans from West Coast, 227; on training and competence of field personnel, 312; on relationships with defense boards, 328
Hibbard, Benjamin H., role of in development of agricultural economics, 33, 33n

Hill, Representative Lister, supports Farm Security Administration, 320
Hiss, Alger, mentioned, 54
Historical analysis, and public administration, 5n, 9
Hoover, Herbert, and poverty, 37–38, 39, 61; and Research Committee on Social Trends, 43–44; political style of, 49; on Farm Security Administration, 285
Hope, Representative Clifford R., on tenancy legislation, 180
Hopkins, Harry L., and Franklin D. Roosevelt, 48; personal background of, 59–60; role of in development of Federal Emergency Relief Administration, 60–64; and reorganization of Federal Emergency Relief Administration, 89
Horton, Maggie Mae, on poverty, 417–18
House Agriculture Committee, role of in passage of Bankhead-Jones Farm Tenant Act, 139–40, 141, 161–62, 184; plans to investigate Farm Security Administration, 362; accuses House Appropriations Committee of usurping powers, 386. See also Congressional relationships; Select Committee to Investigate the Activities of the Farm Security Administration
House Appropriations Committee, role of in attack on Farm Security Administration, 318, 318n, 343, 353–56, 379, 384–86
House Joint Resolution 96, and migratory farm labor program, 377–83
House Select Committee to Investigate National Defense Migration, supports Farm Security Administration, 345. See also John H. Tolan
Howe, Frederic C., role of in Agricultural Adjustment Administration, 54–55, 76, 82
Howe, Louis McHenry, intervenes in details of Subsistence Homesteads, 72
Hudgens, Robert W., personal background of, 61; joins staff of Subsistence Homesteads, 71; role of in Resettlement Administration, 100 101; on passage of Bankhead-Jones Farm Tenant Act, 191; on medical care program, 208; on expansionist character of Farm Security Administration, 230; as Associate Director of Farm Security Administration, 397; resigns from agency, 397, 400–401; on effects of Joint Committee on Reduction of Nonessential Federal Expenditures, 349
Hutson, John B., role of in Food Production Administration, 368, 373

I

Ickes, Harold L., role of in development of land program, 65; role of in Subsistence Homesteads, 70, 71, 71n, 72
Ideology, of Farm Security Administration, 267–79. See also Thomas Jefferson, Family farm
Imperial Valley Farmers Association of California, opposes Farm Security Administration, 264
Institute for Research in Social Science. See Howard W. Odum
Institutional analysis, in study of politics and public administration, 7–8. See also Equilibrium
Irrigated Cotton Growers, opposes Farm Security Administration, 385

J

Jackson, Gardner, role of in Agricultural Adjustment Administration, 55, 76, 79, 82; on impact of crop restriction programs on farm tenants, 158–59; and Democratic platform of 1936, 165; testifies before House Agriculture Committee on tenancy legislation, 179; on American Farm Bureau Federation, 351; becomes assistant to Under Secretary of Agriculture, 354; role of in Parisius affair, 369, 372; on House Joint Resolution, 96, 381–82
Jefferson, Thomas, agrarian ideals of, 22, 23, 28, 65, 267, 416
Johnson, Charles S., supports passage of Bankhead-Jones Farm Tenant Act, 127–32, 150, 168, 174–75
Johnson, Gerald W., on clientele of New Deal, 297
Johnston, Oscar, attacks Farm Security Administration, 292, 374, 382, 385
Joint Committee on Reduction of Nonessential Federal Expenditures, at-

tacks Farm Security Administration, 347–52. *See also* Harry F. Byrd

Jones, Marvin, role of in passage of Bankhead-Jones Farm Tenant Act, 132–40, 153, 160–61, 162, 166, 178, 180–84 *passim*; personal background, 136–37, 138; role of as chairman of House Agriculture Committee, 153; influence of on Democratic platform of 1936, 165; supports Farm Security Administration, 320; on resignation of C.B. Baldwin, 393; on rise and decline of Farm Security Administration, 406

Jump, William A., role of in Department of Agriculture, 241–42; relationships of with Farm Security Administration, 303

K

Kaplan, Abraham, on conceptualization, 11; on inevitability in history, 412–13

Kennedy, President John F., mentioned, 40

Key, V. O., on impact of New Deal on South, 281

Kile, Orville M., on role of American Farm Bureau Federation in decline of Farm Security Administration, 410

Kleberg, Representative Richard M., opposes passage of Bankhead-Jones Farm Tenant Act, 178, 184

Knapp, Seaman A., role of in development of extension system, 30–31

L

La Follette, Senator Robert M., supports Farm Security Administration, 347, 349, 350n, 352

Lambertson, Representative William P., on abolition of Farm Security Administration, 386

Land-grant colleges, relationships of with Resettlement Administration, 115–17. *See also* American Farm Bureau Federation; Cliental bloc

Land ownership, worship of, 23

Land program, of Resettlement Administration, 92, 104–7

Landon, Governor Alf, attacks Democrats for failure to enact tenancy legislation, 165

Lansill, John S., role of in land program of Federal Emergency Relief Administration and Resettlement Administration, 65, 97

Larson, Olaf F., on achievements of rural rehabilitation program, 212–13

Lasseter, Dillard P., appointed Farm Security Administrator, 400

Lasswell, Harold D., on study of politics, 144; conducts study of Farm Security Administration, 314

Laura Spelman Rockefeller Foundation, assists Fairway Farms, 35; mentioned, 51

Lee, Frederick P., role of in drafting of Agricultural Adjustment Act, 52

Legislative process, evaluation of in passage of Bankhead-Jones Farm Tenant Act, 155–56. *See also* Bankhead-Jones Farm Tenant Act

Legitimacy, of Agricultural Adjustment Administration, 57, 58; of Federal Emergency Relief Administration, 67, 68; of Subsistence Homesteads Division, 75–76; of Resettlement Administration, 112, 119–20, 123–25; nature of, 123–25, 192; and passage of Bankhead-Jones Farm Tenant Act, 155–56, 191; of Farm Security Administration, 234, 269

Leighton, Alexander H., on community power, 253–54

Lemke, Representative William, on passage of Bankhead-Jones Farm Tenant Act, 189

Lerner, Max, on poverty, 19

Lewis, Representative David J., introduces relief bill in House, 59

Lewis, George Cornewall, on theory of causation, 411

Ligutti, Reverend L.G., supports Farm Security Administration, 357, 390. *See also* Catholic Rural Life Conference

Lincoln, Murray D., supports Farm Security Administration, 299, 352. *See also* Ohio Farm Bureau Federation

Lindblom, Charles E., on goal formulation, 13; on rationality in public administration, 15–16

Index / [431]

Lippmann, Walter, on Hoover administration, 38
Lipset, Seymour M., on conflict, 413–14
Long, Senator Huey, relationships of with New Deal, 85, 89; relationships of with Resettlement Administration, 100–101
Long, Norton E., on politics and public administration, 260, 303, 365
Lumsden, Edith, supports establishment of Subsistence Homesteads, 69, 70

M

McCamy, James L., on dysfunctional consequences in Farm Security Administration, 313
McConnell, Grant, on relationships of Farm Security Administration and American Farm Bureau Federation, 324, 410–11
Macfadden, Bernarr, promotes back-to-land movement, 68n; appointed to National Advisory Committee on Subsistence Homesteads, 71n
McGill, Ralph, on congressional opposition to Farm Security Administration, 360
Machiavelli, Niccolò, statecraft of, 9; on hazards of reform, 404
McIntyre, Marvin H., and attacks on Resettlement Administration, 113; role of in passage of Bankhead-Jones Farm Tenant Act, 131, 160–61
McKellar, Senator Kenneth D., demands share of patronage from Resettlement Administration, 102; attacks resettlement projects of Resettlement Administration, 111; attacks Farm Security Administration, 285, 317; accuses C.B. Baldwin of Communist sympathies, 356, 358, on decline of New Deal, 366
McNary, Senator Charles L., supports passage of McNary-Haugen bills, 35–36, 51, 52, 54; introduces resettlement bill in Senate, 68
Macridis, Roy C., on group politics, 296
Macro-analysis, uses of, 5, 6n, 176, 263
Maddox, James G., role of in passage of Bankhead-Jones Farm Tenant Act, 140–41, 189; and policy of digging deeper, 197, 218, 219, 220; on cooperative associations, 207; becomes Assistant Administrator of Farm Security Administration, 246n; on social meaning of Farm Security Administration, 271–72; on congressional relationships, 337; recommended for position in Food Production Administration, 371n; on rise and decline of Farm Security Administration, 406–7
March, James G., on rationality, 15
Maris, Paul V., personal background of, 97–98, 109–10; role of in Resettlement Administration, 97–98, 109–10, 116; role of as director of tenant purchase program, 195–99; on expansionist character of Farm Security Administration, 229–30; on farmers committees, 306, 308, 309; on political strategy of Farm Security Administration, 309; assigned responsibility for farm ownership program of Farmers Home Administration, 402. See also Tenant purchase program
Marshall, Alfred, on poverty, 19–20, 39
Matthews, Donald R., on lobbying in Congress, 147
Medical care program, described and evaluated, 208–9
Merriam, Charles E., participates in President's Research Committee on Social Trends, 43–44; on tasks of government in depression, 46
Merton, Robert K., mentioned, 13
Micro-institutional analysis, utility of in study of politics and public administration, 5, 6, 6n, 7, 176
Migratory farm labor program, described, 221–25, 264; politics of, 362, 377–78, 382–83
Miller, Francis Pickens, supports passage of Bankhead-Jones Farm Tenant Act, 146–47
Miller, Herman P., on poverty, 20
Millspaugh, Arthur C., on political consequences of war, 325
Mitchell, George S., appointed to direct Labor Relations Division of Resettlement Administration, 97; conducts post-mortem on battle for budget in 1941, 346
Mitchell, Harry L., leads in unionization of farm tenants, 79; advocates

tenancy legislation at Democratic national convention of 1936, 165; defends Farm Security Administration, 352. *See also* Southern Tenant Farmers Union

Mitchell, Wesley C., participates in President's Research Committee on Social Trends, 43

Morgan, Arthur E., seeks to direct Subsistence Homesteads, 70

Morgenthau, Henry, Jr., as disciple of George F. Warren, 33n; advises Franklin D. Roosevelt during campaign of 1932, 48; participates in planning for establishment of Agricultural Adjustment Administration, 51; participates in planning for establishment of land program, 65; participates in Joint Committee on Reduction of Nonessential Federal Expenditures, 349

Morley, John, 31, on statesmanship and social change, 31

Moser, Representative Guy L., attacks Farm Security Administration, 285, 319–20

Mount Weather Agreement, 240–41

Myrdal, Gunnar, on interracial relationships in South, 282

N

Nashville Policy Group, supports passage of Bankhead-Jones Farm Tenant Act, 147n

National Advisory Commission on Rural Poverty, reports to President Lyndon B. Johnson, 415n

National Advisory Committee on Subsistence Homesteads, advises M.L. Wilson and Harold L. Ickes, 71, 71n

National Association for the Advancement of Colored People, protests against crop restriction programs of Agricultural Adjustment Administration, 80; supports passage of Bankhead-Jones Farm Tenant Act, 150; supports Farm Security Administration, 298, 299

National Association of Manufacturers, attacks Federal Emergency Relief Administration, 67

National Catholic Welfare Conference, supports back-to-land movement, 68; supports passage of Bankhead-Jones Farm Tenant Act, 148. *See also* John A. Ryan

National Committee on Rural Social Planning, protests against crop restriction programs of Agricultural Adjustment Administration, 158–59; petitions Democratic national convention in 1936, 165. *See also* Gardner Jackson; Harry L. Mitchell

National Committee on Small Farm Ownership, supports passage of Bankhead-Jones Farm Tenant Act, 145, 146

National Cotton Council, attacks Farm Security Administration, 385. *See also* Oscar Johnston

National Council of Farmers Cooperatives, attacks Farm Security Administration, 302, 378

National Farmers Union, supports Farm Security Administration, 205, 298, 299–301, 360. *See also* James G. Patton

National Grange, attacks Farm Security Administration, 141, 302, 378

National Urban League, supports passage of Bankhead-Jones Farm Tenant Act, 150

Negroes, as farm tenants and sharecroppers, 25; discrimination against by extension system, 31; philanthropy to, 43; discrimination against by Farm Security Administration, 196–97, 200–201, 202, 211, 254, 260, 279–80, 307, 314; Farm Security Administration programs for, 283; as clients of Farm Security Administration, 297

Neighborhood action groups, as instruments of rural rehabilitation, 207–8

Nelson, Lowry, participates in work of President's Committee on Farm Tenancy, 168

New Deal, development of, 18, 47–49; conservative attitudes toward, 53; role of Farm Security Administration in, 66, 312; exploitation of history by, 68; role of Agricultural Adjustment Administration in, 79; and crisis of 1935, 85–86; in dissolution, 225, 325, 352, 364, 365–67; impact of on South, 280–82, 285–86. *See also* C.B. Baldwin; Franklin D. Roosevelt

Nixon, H.C., on southern farm ten-

Index / [433]

ancy, 25; supports passage of Bankhead-Jones Farm Tenant Act, 146
Norris, Senator George W., persuaded by Franklin D. Roosevelt to support Subsistence Homesteads appropriation, 69–70; mentioned, 27
Nourse, Edwin G., participates in President's Committee on Farm Tenancy, 168

O

Odum, Howard W., personal background of, 40–41; participates in President's Research Committee on Social Trends, 44; supports passage of Bankhead-Jones Farm Tenant Act, 128n, 130n
Office of Agricultural Defense Relations, established, 327
O'Grady, Reverend John, supports Farm Security Administration, 299, 353, 357; on congressional relationships, 408
Ohio Farm Bureau Federation, supports Farm Security Administration, 357, 360
O'Neal, Edward A., supports establishment of Agricultural Adjustment Administration, 50, 52; participates in National Advisory Committee on Subsistence Homesteads, 71n; participates in President's Committee on Farm Tenancy, 171–72, 173; personal background of, 173–74; on rural poverty and tenancy, 174; on passage of Bankhead-Jones Farm Tenant Act, 179; role of as leader of American Farm Bureau Federation, 288; relationships of with Franklin D. Roosevelt and New Deal, 342–43; on assignment of wartime food production responsibility to Chester C. Davis, 375. *See also* American Farm Bureau Federation

P

Parisius, Herbert W., personal background of, 369; appointed Director of Food Production, 369; role of in Parisius affair, 369–76 *passim*, resigns as Director of Food Production, 373

Parisius affairs, and reorganization of Department of Agriculture, 367–77
Parity, as solution to problems of agriculture, 32–33; as issue in battle of budget in 1942, 353
Party patronage, as problem in Resettlement Administration, 100–102
Patten, Simon N., influence of in agricultural economics, 33, 33n
Patton, James G., supports Farm Security Administration, 300, 352, 357, 390, 393; relationships of with Edward A. O'Neal, 328. *See also* National Farmers Union
Peabody, John Foster, supports passage of Bankhead-Jones Farm Tenant Act, 131, 145
Pearson, Drew, on Parisius affair, 374
Peek, George N., role of in Agricultural Adjustment Administration, 51, 54, 57–58, 76
Pepper, Senator Claude, supports Farm Security Administration, 391
Perkins, Milo, role of in Department of Agriculture, 189n, 243, 246n
Pickett, Clarence E., role of in Subsistence Homesteads Division, 71, 72
Pierce, Representative Walter M., opposes passage of Bankhead-Jones Farm Tenant Act, 161–62, 178
Plumley, Representative Charles A., on performance of Franklin W. Hancock as Farm Security Administrator, 399
Poe, Clarence, on rural poverty, 44–45; on impact of crop restriction programs on farm tenants, 78–79; supports passage of Bankhead-Jones Farm Tenant Act, 141; participates in study of Farm Security Administration by John D. Black, 387–88
Political science, tasks facing, 16–17
Poverty. *See* Rural poverty
President's Committee on Farm Tenancy, role of in passage of Bankhead-Jones Farm Tenant Act, 167–77; on migratory farm laborers, 221–22. *See also* Bankhead-Jones Farm Tenant Act
President's Research Committee on Social Trends, and Hoover administration, 43–46 *passim*
Pressman, Lee, role of in Agricultural Adjustment Administration, 54, 82;

role of in Resettlement Administration, 97
Production economics, and problems of agriculture, 33–34
Public administration, as subject of inquiry, 7, 9, 10
Public Law 129, and decline of Farm Security Administration, 383–94
Purge of 1935, and conflict in Agricultural Adjustment Administration, 77n, 81–83

R

Ramspeck Act, promulgation of disappoints leaders of Farm Security Administration, 316
Raper, Arthur F., on cliental responses to Farm Security Administration, 275–76; quotes Louisiana Dunn Thomas, 278–79
Rationality, and public administration, 14–16, 194–95, 230, 419
Rayburn, Representative Sam, relationships of with Marvin Jones, 136; supports Farm Security Administration, 320
Realpolitik, in politics and public administration, 9, 295; practiced by leaders of Farm Security Administration, 198
Reconstruction Finance Corporation, funds from for Farm Security Administration, 226, 233, 317, 359
Reedsville, West Virginia, Eleanor Roosevelt participates in planning of, 72; criticized by Bernard M. Baruch, 111
Reid, T. Roy, plans cooperative associations, 206; and political opposition to cooperative associations, 266; replaces James L. McCamy in Secretary of Agriculture's office, 334
Reno, Milo. See Farm Holiday Association
Republican party, in election campaign of 1932, 45; opposition of to Resettlement Administration, 115; in election campaign of 1936, 164–65
Resettlement Administration, establishment of, 90–94; organizational structure of, 93–94; staffing of, 94–103; programs and performance of, 103–8, 203, 209, 221, 222; political opposition to, 106, 110–15, 120; work of public information by, 117–19; legitimacy of, 119–20, 163; transfer of to Department of Agriculture, 121–22
Resettlement program, of Resettlement Administration, 92, 111–13; of Farm Security Administration, 214–17; as object of political hostility, 263–64, 319–20; liquidation of, 336–39
Robertson, Thomas, appointed to review Mexican farm labor program, 379–80
Robinson, James Harvey, on uses of past, 267–68
Robinson, Senator Joseph T., dependence of Franklin D. Roosevelt on, 81; supports passage of Bankhead-Jones Farm Tenant Act, 136, 151, 162, 187
Robson, William A., on political semantics, 117
Rockefeller Foundation, supports passage of Bankhead-Jones Farm Tenant Act, 127
Rockefeller, John D., contributes to financing of Fairway Farms, 35
Rogow, Arnold A., on social obligations of political science, 16–17
Roosevelt, Eleanor, supports resettlement projects, 70, 72, 111; on President's relationships with American Farm Bureau Federation, 302; on decline of New Deal, 366; on House Joint Resolution 96, 381
Roosevelt, Franklin D., and New Deal, 12, 18–19, 85–86, 89–90, 324, 366–67; political and administrative style of, 44n, 49, 90, 159; in campaign of 1932, 46, 47–49, 69; and Federal Emergency Relief Administration, 58–68 *passim*; and land program, 65, 66n; and Subsistence Homesteads, 69–70; on impact of crop restriction program on farm tenants, 81; and Resettlement Administration, 82, 87–94 *passim*, 100–101, 113, 123; role of in passage of Bankhead-Jones Farm Tenant Act, 131, 156, 160–61, 162, 166–67, 168, 179–80, 181–82, 185, 189; devotion of to Jeffersonian agrarian ideals, 167; relationships of with Farm Security Administration, 226, 265, 302–3, 350–51, 355, 360; on national planning in agriculture, 256; relationships of with American

Index / [435]

Farm Bureau Federation, 291, 291n, 302, 342–43; on resignation of C.B. Baldwin, 395. See also New Deal
Roosevelt, Theodore, on rural poverty, 28, 29
Rosenman, Judge Samuel I., supports selection of Parisius as Director of Food Production Administration, 369
Rosenwald Fund, supports education for Negroes, 43; supports passage of Bankhead-Jones Farm Tenant Act, 127
Rural poverty, as political issue, 17–22 passim, 26–27, 30–31, 32, 37, 45–46, 158; development of, 29, 39–40, 41–43; persistence of in United States, 414–15
Rural rehabilitation program, of Federal Emergency Relief Administration, 61–64; of Resettlement Administration, 91–92, 103–8 passim; of Farm Security Administration, 199–214
Rural sociology, development of, 39–43
Russell, Senator Richard B., supports passage of Bankhead-Jones Farm Tenant Act, 151; supports Farm Security Administration, 320, 338, 356; defends C.B. Baldwin against charges of Communist sympathy, 358; concedes errors by Farm Security Administration, 392–93; responds to political change, 407
Ryan, Reverend John A., participates in National Advisory Committee on Subsistence Homesteads, 71n; supports passage of Bankhead-Jones Farm Tenant Act, 130n. See also National Catholic Welfare Conference

S

Sanger, Margaret, seeks to promote birth control in rural rehabilitation program, 299
Sayre, Wallace S., on dysfunctional consequences in public administration, 13; on politics of administrative organization, 369
Schattschneider, E. E., on group politics, 414
Schlesinger, Arthur M., Jr., on New Deal, 150; on decision-making habits of Franklin D. Roosevelt, 159; on Communism and New Deal, 359n
Schmiedeler, Reverend Edgar, supports passage of Bankhead-Jones Farm Tenant Act, 130n
Schultz, Theodore, on report of President's Committee on Farm Tenancy, 175; on economic policy, 177; on social science in training of field personnel of Farm Security Administration, 255; on extension system and county agricultural agents, 290
Select Committee to Investigate the Activities of the Farm Security Administration, established, 386–87; submits report and recommendations, 401–2
Selznick, Philip, on institutional analysis, 8; on relationships between Farm Security Administration and Tennessee Valley Authority, 304; on coöptation, 324
Senate Appropriations Committee, role of in establishment of Resettlement Administration, 91; and budgets of Farm Security Administration, 356–58, 391–93
Senate Committee on Agriculture and Forestry, role of in passage of Bankhead-Jones Farm Tenant Act, 69, 139, 142, 150–51, 178, 185. See also Ellison D. Smith
Separatism, between tenant purchase and rural rehabilitation programs, 270; between Farm Security Administration and agricultural agencies, 304–5
Shields, Robert H., role of in Parisius affair, 368, 372
Simon, Herbert A., on administrative rationality, 15, 194–95, 230, 260–61
Slichter, Sumner, on New Deal, 89–90
Small farmer issue, in strategy of Farm Security Administration, 330–31, 383–84
Smith, Earl C., on panaceas in farm policy, 179; role of in American Farm Bureau Federation, 288–89, 341–42; attacks Farm Security Administration, 342, 343, 344, 350, 356, 411. See also American Farm Bureau Federation
Smith, Senator Ellison D., opposition of to Subsistence Homesteads, 69; role of in passage of Bankhead-Jones

Farm Tenant Act, 142, 145, 152. See also Senate Committee on Agriculture and Forestry

Smith, Harold D., relationships of with Farm Security Administration, 303, 339, 346, 349

Smith, Raymond C., on conservative character of Farm Security Administration, 269; on adjustment of Farm Security Administration to World War II, 327

Social change, resistances to, 273, 273n, 274

Soil Conservation Service. See Hugh H. Bennett

Southern Policy Committee, supports passage of Bankhead-Jones Farm Tenant Act, 146–47

Southern Tenant Farmers Union, opposition of to crop restriction programs of Agricultural Adjustment Administration, 79–80, 158, 159; participates in President's Committee on Farm Tenancy, 174; supports Farm Security Administration, 298, 299

Sparkman, Representative John J., supports Farm Security Administration, 320

Spillman, William J., on agricultural economics, 33, 51

Steinbeck, John, on migratory farm workers, 221

Stern, Edgar, supports passage of Bankhead-Jones Farm Tenant Act, 130n

Stevenson, Adlai, appointed to staff of General Counsel in Agricultural Adjustment Administration, 54; mentioned, *viii*, *viiin*

Straight, Michael, on decline of New Deal, 355

Subsistence Homesteads, establishment of, 68–74; relationships of with Agricultural Adjustment Administration and Federal Emergency Relief Administration, 74–75; achievements of, 75

Supreme Court, as subject of microanalysis, 6; invalidates New Deal measures, 112, 160–61

Symposium on Communities of Tomorrow, discusses urban-rural balance and poverty, 417, 417n, 418

T

Taber, Louis J., participates in National Advisory Committee on Subsistence Homesteads, 71n. See also National Grange

Taft, Senator Robert A., opposes funds for Farm Security Administration, 359

Tannenbaum, Frank, on rural poverty, 42–43; role of in passage of Bankhead-Jones Farm Tenant Act, 127–61 *passim*, 190

Tarver, Representative Malcolm C., personal background of, 339–40; relationships of with Farm Security Administration, 318n, 340–60 *passim*, 379, 384

Taylor, Carl C., role of in Subsistence Homesteads, 71; role of in Agricultural Adjustment Administration, 73; role of in Resettlement Administration, 97, 110, 116n, 117; on sociology of poverty, 271

Taylor, Frederick W., and scientific management, 9

Taylor, Henry C., influence of in land program, 33, 33n, 96; participates in President's Committee on Farm Tenancy, 174

Taylor, Lt. Colonel Jay L., appointed Deputy War Food Administrator, 379

Teague, Charles C., on migratory farm labor program, 379, 380

Tenant purchase program, origins of in Resettlement Administration, 94; compared with rural rehabilitation program, 198; and relationships with Congress, 198, 198n; separatism of, 198–99; achievements of, 199; compared with debt adjustment program, 210; elimination of funds for, 338; transition of under Farmers Home Administration, 402. See also Paul V. Maris

Tennessee Valley Authority, relationships of with Farm Security Administration, 304; compared with Farm Security Administration, 343

Thatcher, M.W., participates in President's Committee on Farm Tenancy, 168; supports Farm Security Administration, 205, 392. See also National Farmers Union

Thomas, Louisiana Dunn, on faith in government, 278–79
Thomas, Norman, on impact of crop restriction programs of Agricultural Adjustment Administration on farm tenants, 158
Tobacco Road, quoted, vii–viii
Tolan, Representative John H., supports Farm Security Administration, 345, 353
Tolley, Howard R., supports Farm Security Administration, 303, 352
Townsend, M. Clifford, role of in Parisius affair, 368, 373
Truman, David B., on ordeal of executives, 16
Truman, Harry S., as chairman of Senate Special Committee to Investigate National Defense Program, 347; signs Farmers Home Administration Act of 1946, 3, 402
Tugwell, Rexford G., ideas of, 23, 36–37, 74, 76, 86, 87–88, 94–95, 98, 104–5, 163; relationships of with Franklin D. Roosevelt and New Deal, 48, 56, 58, 84–85, 88, 164; career of, 33n, 36, 120–21, 122, 163; role of in Department of Agriculture, 56, 57, 73, 91; participates in planning of land program, 65; participates in National Advisory Committee on Subsistence Homesteads, 71n; and purge of 1935 in Agricultural Adjustment Administration, 82, 83; and Resettlement Administration, 84, 88–89, 94, 100–101, 108, 109, 122, 145; supports passage of Bankhead-Jones Farm Tenant Act, 128, 140, 143, 154, 167; influence of on Farm Security Administration, 244, 271, 284; on experience of Resettlement Administration and Farm Security Administration, 418–19; mentioned, 52, 54

U

U.S. Employment Service, relationships of with Farm Security Administration, 223, 225, 305

V

Vance, Rupert B., on rural poverty, 41
Vandenberg, Senator Arthur H., opposes Bankhead-Jones Farm Tenant Act, 151

W

Wagner, Senator Robert F., introduces relief bill, 59
Waldo, Dwight, on hierarchy of purposes, 13
Walker, Major John O., role of in Farm Security Administration, 214, 223, 246n; appointed to direct Agricultural Labor Branch in Department of Agriculture, 377
Wallace, Henry A., personal background of, 35–36; relationships of with Agricultural Adjustment Administration, 50–55 *passim*, 80, 81–82; on Subsistence Homesteads, 74; on poverty, 86; on New Deal, 89, 332; role of in establishment of Resettlement Administration, 86–89 *passim*, 104; role of in passage of Bankhead-Jones Farm Tenant Act, 128–43 *passim*, 154, 164, 166, 180, 181–82; relationships of with Farm Security Administration, 215, 265–66, 302, 326, 329; elected Vice President, 335
War Manpower Commission, and migratory farm labor program, 223, 224
Warren, George F., influence of, 33, 33n, 48, 51
Westbrook, Colonel Lawrence, appointed to direct rural rehabilitation program of Federal Emergency Relief Administration, 62; supports passage of Bankhead-Jones Farm Tenant Act, 141; mentioned, 97
White, Walter, on impact of crop restriction program of Agricultural Adjustment Administration on farm tenants, 80
White, William Allen, supports passage of Bankhead-Jones Farm Tenant Act, 130n; on diversity in American agriculture, 256–57
Whitehead, Alfred North, on ideological conflict, 87
Wickard, Claude R., forbids promotion of general farm organizations by officers of Department of Agriculture, 301, 302; on impact of World War II on agriculture, 328; role of in Department of Agriculture, 326–35 *passim*; establishes Food for Freedom program, 327; influence of

Agricultural Adjustment Administration upon, 328; responds to attack by American Farm Bureau Federation, 344; defends budget of Farm Security Administration, 356–57; accused of retreating under fire, 360; role of in Parisius affair, 367–77 *passim*; wartime political strategy of, 368–69

Willoughby, W.F., on politics and public administration, 9

Wilson, M.L., career of, 35, 73, 333; role of in Agricultural Adjustment Administration, 51, 52, 57; and Subsistence Homesteads, 70, 71, 72, 73; on rural poverty, 86; supports passage of Bankhead-Jones Farm Tenant Act, 129, 145, 146, 167, 168, 179; on farmers committees, 183, 305; on Mt. Weather Agreement, 240–41; supports Farm Security Administration, 302, 357, 390

Wilson, Woodrow, on legislative process, 126; on politics and public administration, 309; mentioned, 29, 30

Witt, Nathan, appointed to staff of General Counsel in Agricultural Adjustment Administration, 54

Wolcott, Leon O., on Department of Agriculture, 8

World War II, impact of upon Department of Agriculture and Farm Security Administration, 209, 221, 222–23, 225–29, 249, 326–32, 353